Ius Gentium: Comparative Perspectives on Law and Justice

Volume 84

Ius Gentium is a book series which discusses the central questions of law and justice from a comparative perspective. The books in this series collect the contrasting and overlapping perspectives of lawyers, judges, philosophers and scholars of law from the world's many different jurisdictions for the purposes of comparison, harmonisation, and the progressive development of law and legal institutions. Each volume makes a new comparative study of an important area of law. This book series continues the work of the well-known journal of the same name and provides the basis for a better understanding of all areas of legal science.

The *Ius Gentium* series provides a valuable resource for lawyers, judges, legislators, scholars, and both graduate students and researchers in globalisation, comparative law, legal theory and legal practice. The series has a special focus on the development of international legal standards and transnational legal cooperation.

More information about this series at http://www.springer.com/series/7888

Aniceto Masferrer
Editor

Criminal Law and Morality in the Age of Consent

Interdisciplinary Perspectives

Springer

Editor
Aniceto Masferrer
Faculty of Law
University of Valencia
Valencia, Spain

ISSN 1534-6781 ISSN 2214-9902 (electronic)
Ius Gentium: Comparative Perspectives on Law and Justice
ISBN 978-3-030-64162-7 ISBN 978-3-030-64163-4 (eBook)
https://doi.org/10.1007/978-3-030-64163-4

This Springer imprint is published by the registered company Springer Nature Switzerland AG
The registered company address is: Gewerbestrasse 11, 6330 Cham, Switzerland

Contents

Criminal Law and Morality Revisited: Interdisciplinary Perspectives

Aniceto Masferrer

Abstract The relationship between morality and criminal law must constantly evolve to meet the needs of changing times and circumstances. Social changes and new situations require new answers. This chapter will take the famous 'Wolfenden Report' (1957) as a starting point for reviewing the interaction of criminal law and morality, in the context of the broader relationship between politics, law and morality. Moral laws and civil laws have different limits and practical purposes, as is made clear in the writings of Aristotle, Thomas Aquinas and Spanish scholastics such as Francisco de Vitoria, Domingo de Soto and Francisco Suárez. Modern philosophers such as Descartes, Hobbes, Rousseau, Kant, and Mill also raise important issues concerning the relation between law and morality. This chapter will draw the line between and explain the inescaple connections between criminal law and morality.

The controversial relationship between morality and politics, and morality and law has been studied for more than two thousand years. Yet, it has never been definitively solved and most likely will never be. Law belongs to human culture, which touches upon a dynamic reality: relating nature to freedom and to culture. If such relations are not clearly understood, as it is the case today, then the same is true of the relation between morality and law.

This issue was very much a subject for debate in the wake of the 'Wolfenden Report' (1957), published by the British Parliament's *Committee on Homosexual Offences and Prostitution* chaired by Sir John Wolfenden.[1] This well-known text called for decriminalising consenting homosexual relationship among adults, brought

This work was undertaken in the context of the research project entitled "Las influencias extranjeras en la Codificación penal española: su concreto alcance en la Parte Especial de los Códigos decimonónicos" (ref. DER2016-78388-P), financed by the Spanish 'Ministerio de Economía y Competitividad.'

A. Masferrer (✉)
Faculty of Law, University of Valencia, Valencia, Spain
e-mail: aniceto.masferrer@uv.es

[1]Committee on Homosexual Offences and Prostitution, *Report of the Committee on Homosexual Offences and Prostitution.* London: Her Majesty's Stationery Office, 1957; it was reprinted in the

A. Masferrer (ed.), *Criminal Law and Morality in the Age of Consent*, Ius Gentium: Comparative Perspectives on Law and Justice 84,
https://doi.org/10.1007/978-3-030-64163-4_1

a fierce debate in its wake. But beyond the specific recommendations of the 'Wolfenden Report', the discussion revolved more generally around the relation between criminal law and morality,[2] with Patrick Devlin and Herbert L.A. Hart as the main protagonists.[3]

The Report was notably ambiguous concerning this complex relation. On the one hand, it pointed out that "[u]nless a deliberate attempt is made by society, acting through the agency of the law, to equate the sphere of crime with that of sin, there must remain a realm of private morality and immorality which is, in brief and crude terms, not the law's business."[4] On the other hand, the Report recognised that the purpose of criminal law went beyond the mere protection of life, freedom and property: "Its function [...] is to preserve public order and decency, to protect the citizen from what is offensive or injurious, and to provide sufficient safeguards against exploitation and corruption of others...".[5]

The Report was right to recommend the decriminalization of homosexual behaviour between consenting adults in private,[6] but it did not provide a coherent, theoretical framework on the relation between criminal law and morals. There is no doubt that not all immoral behaviour—or sins—should be criminalized: sins and crimes are not the same, as the moral and legal orders differ. It follows that Human law should never attempt to forbid all vices.

The relation between criminal law and morality derives from the relation between politics, law and morality, whose provinces are different. Moral laws and civil laws have different limits and practical purposes. The sphere of moral law is much broader than civil law, which means, for example, civil laws should never concern themselves with the criminal thoughts a person may have inasmuch as they do not go beyond that, i.e. any kind of external act. As to practical purposes, civil laws have their own ethical-practical rationality, which affects not only the reasoning process but also the realm to which it applies.

Moral law—or natural law—is the light of the intellect, or practical reason—that directs the acts of everyone in accordance with the purpose—or *telos*—of human life, namely, happiness. Moral laws are supposed to distinguish good from evil and provide the principles that enlighten human behaviour and lead humans to their perfection and to a life of virtue. Moral laws or natural laws affects the whole moral order, as far as it is naturally knowable to unaided human reason.[7] Natural law is

---

US with the title *The Wolfenden Report: Report of the Committee on Homosexual Offences and Prostitution*. New York: Stein and Day (1963).

[2]Chesser (1958), Berg (1959).

[3]Devlin (1959, 1962, 1965) and Hart (1963, 1965).

[4]Wolfenden Report, § 62 (I am using the text quoted by Devlin (1989)).

[5]Wolfenden Report, § 13.

[6]In 2003 the US Supreme Court struck down the sodomy law in Texas and, by extension, invalidated sodomy laws in thirteen other states, making same-sex sexual activity legal in every U.S. state and territory (Lawrence *v.* Texas, 539 U.S. 558).

[7]Thomas Aquinas, *Summa theologiae*, 1–2, q. 19, a. 4, ad 3: "Although the eternal law is unknown to us according as it is in the Divine Mind: nevertheless, it becomes known to us somewhat, either

simply moral law as far as it is knowable by natural human reason and it refers to all moral virtues, regulating their rational structure, and also forbids all vices.

Civil law does not cover the same range as moral law since it only establishes what is politically necessary and opportune, and it punishes only what is necessary from a strictly political point of view (which Aquinas called the "common good of justice and peace"), and to which today we could add "liberty". It is clear that not everything natural moral law commands or prohibits must also be commanded or prohibited or even criminalised by civil or positive law.[8] Thus, while moral laws measure all human acts, civil laws just order the community with respect to the common good.

The legal-political domain is different but not opposed to, or at odds with, the practical reasoning of morality. The formal object, however, is different since it seeks to guarantee human life in a social community and this requires avoiding anything that, by threatening social peace, liberty and justice, could make coexistence unbearable. For that to be possible, the first requirement is security granted by the state to protect vulnerable people from violence exerted by either powerful individuals or the state itself. For that to be possible, the state has the "monopoly on violence", a Max Weber category whose origins can be traced back at least to Thomas Hobbes and Jean Bodin.[9] The state's use of legitimate force through passing and applying coercive laws is justified to guarantee the survival and security of individuals, and both goods (survival and security) constitute the first content of the aforementioned "common good".[10]

Hence, while moral laws regulate individual behaviour seeking the good in the acts themselves, civil laws regulate relations between individuals seeking the common good. Civil laws do not seek to promote the moral perfection of individuals, but rather to guarantee security and provide as much as possible the conditions for a peaceful, free and fair society, in which individuals could be happy and develop good lives making their own choices. If the purpose of moral and civil laws is different, the reasons why behaviour might be immoral (contrary to moral or natural law) or illegal (contrary to civil or especially criminal law) are also different. For example, while moral laws forbid any kind of lie, civil laws prohibit only those lies that could cause real damage to someone considered relevant enough for the whole of society, because they threaten social order as well as safe and peaceful coexistence.

Thus, civil laws should never sanction or even punish behaviours for the exclusive reason of being gravely immoral. In other words, constitutional states should never use their coercive power sanctioning civil laws to enforce a moral order or to force

---

by natural reason which is derived therefrom as its proper image; or by some sort of additional revelation."

[8]Rhonheimer (2013a, b), 282.

[9]Weber (1919); of the English translations available, I am using *Weber's Rationalism and Modern Society* (translated and edited by Tony Waters and Dagmar Waters), New York: Palgrave Books, 2015, pp. 129–198; Jean Bodin, *Les Six livres de la République* (1576); Thomas Hobbes, *Leviathan* (1651).

[10]Here I am following Martin Rhonheimer's line of reasoning (1995), 271–334; I am using the English version: Rhonheimer (2010), ch. 7.

individuals to lead their lives according to a particular morality. For example, if any state approves a law criminalising abortion, this should not be to avoid immoral actions or help individuals lead a virtuous life, but rather to protect those whose lives would be gravely threatened by this (abortion), and also to protect pregnant women from social pressure in general or from particular individuals (e.g. partner or relatives). Therefore, the reasons for criminalising this behaviour should not be moral, but legal-political (although this realm should not necessarily be seen as opposed to morality).[11] The protection of human life through civil law is a political and legal duty, and the reasons why some forms of violence or threats against life are criminalised should also be political and legal, although this would also entail the use of other kinds of arguments (e.g. biological, anthropological, ethical and sociological, etc.).

These ideas are in line with a vein of thought that generally runs from Aristotle to Thomas Aquinas, although they did not envisage civil laws in the same terms. Aristotle maintained that civil laws should be formative or educational, leading individuals towards a virtuous life.[12] He envisaged law as the best state tool for public control and education the best for the individual.[13] Thus, legislating was the best option for people willing to help others to be better as humans.[14]

Christian thought, however, made a distinction between divine and human laws, giving rise to a dualism whereby the purpose of morality and civil laws was different—albeit not necessarily opposed. In this vein, Irenaeus of Lyons, for example, defended security as the main goal of civil laws, so "men may not eat each other up like fishes."[15] Following this line of reasoning, Augustin, when distinguishing between the earthly and the heavenly city, clearly stated their different goals: how the former seeks, above all, "an earthly peace, and the end it proposes, in the well-ordered concord of civic obedience and rule, is the combination of men's

[11] See Rhonheimer (2013b), Why Is Political Philosophy Necessary, 1–35.

[12] Aristotle, *Nicomachean Ethics* X, 9, 3rd paragraph (I am using the version available at https://classics.mit.edu/Aristotle/nicomachaen.html): "But it is difficult to get from youth up a right training for virtue if one has not been brought up under right laws."

[13] Aristotle, *Nicomachean Ethics* X, 9, 7th paragraph: "For public control is plainly effected by laws, and good control by good laws; whether written or unwritten would seem to make no difference, nor whether they are laws providing for the education of individuals or of groups-any more than it does in the case of music or gymnastics and other such pursuits."

[14] Aristotle, *Nicomachean Ethics* X, 9, 9th paragraph: "And surely he who wants to make men, whether many or few, better by his care must try to become capable of legislating, if it is through laws that we can become good.".

[15] See, for example, Irenaeus of Lyons, *Adversus haereses* [Against Heresies] V, 24, 2 (I am using the version available at https://www.newadvent.org/fathers/0103.htm): "Earthly rule, therefore, has been appointed by God for the benefit of nations, and not by the devil, who is never at rest at all, nay, who does not love to see even nations conducting themselves after a quiet manner, *so that under the fear of human rule, men may not eat each other up like fishes*; but that, by means of the establishment of laws, they may keep down an excess of wickedness among the nations" (emphasis is mine).

wills to attain the things which are helpful to this life."[16] Consequently, Christians are called to live under, "diversities in the manners, laws, and institutions whereby earthly peace is secured and maintained, but recognizing that, however various these are, they all tend to one and the same end of earthly peace."[17]

Thomas Aquinas inherited this Christian legacy, and unlike Aristotle, maintained that civil laws should not primarily attempt to lead individuals towards virtue and moral good. According to him, peace was the main purpose of political communities and civil laws:

> "Now note that the end of human law is distinct from the end of divine law. For the end of human law is temporal peace within the political community (*temporalis tranquillitas civitatis*), and human law achieves this end by curbing exterior acts that involve evils capable of disturbing the peaceful state of the political community. By contrast, the end of divine law is to lead a man to the end of eternal happiness…".[18]

Thus, Thomas Aquinas' way of thinking, like the Committee that drafted the "Wolfenden Report", was that human law should never try to forbid all vices:

"Now human law is framed for a number of human beings, the majority of whom are not perfect in virtue. Wherefore human laws do not forbid all vices, from which the virtuous abstain, but only the more grievous vices, from which it is possible for the majority to abstain; and chiefly those that are to the hurt of others, without the prohibition of which human society could not be maintained: thus human law prohibits murder, theft and such like".[19]

This means that, according to Thomas Aquinas, the relation between divine and civil law was asymmetric, and the latter should not entirely follow the former. He even argued that this was not a defect of civil law but something proper to its own realm and disposed by divine law:

---

[16] Augustine, *De civitate Dei* [The City of God] XIX, 17 (I am using the version available at https://www.newadvent.org/fathers/1201.htm): "The earthly city, which does not live by faith, seeks an earthly peace, and the end it proposes, in the well-ordered concord of civic obedience and rule, is the combination of men's wills to attain the things which are helpful to this life. The heavenly city, or rather the part of it which sojourns on earth and lives by faith, makes use of this peace only because it must, until this mortal condition which necessitates it shall pass away. Consequently, so long as it lives like a captive and a stranger in the earthly city, though it has already received the promise of redemption, and the gift of the Spirit as the earnest of it, it makes no scruple to obey the laws of the earthly city, whereby the things necessary for the maintenance of this mortal life are administered; and thus, as this life is common to both cities, so there is a harmony between them in regard to what belongs to it.".

[17] Augustine, *De civitate Dei* [The City of God] XIX, 17: "This heavenly city, then, while it sojourns on earth, calls citizens out of all nations, and gathers together a society of pilgrims of all languages, not scrupling about diversities in the manners, laws, and institutions whereby earthly peace is secured and maintained, but recognizing that, however various these are, they all tend to one and the same end of earthly peace. It therefore is so far from rescinding and abolishing these diversities, that it even preserves and adopts them, so long only as no hindrance to the worship of the one supreme and true God is thus introduced.".

[18] Thomas Aquinas, *Summa theologiae*, 1–2, q. 98, a. 1 (I am using an English version available at https://www3.nd.edu/~afreddos/summa-translation/TOC-part1-2.htm).

[19] Thomas Aquinas, *Summa theologiae*, 1–2, q. 96, a. 2.

> "Human law is said to permit certain things not in the sense that it approves of them, but rather in the sense that it is incapable of directing them. However, there are many things directed by God's law that cannot be directed by human law, since there are more things subject to a higher cause than to a lower cause. Hence, the very fact that human law does not intrude into matters that it cannot direct flows from the order of the eternal law."[20]

However, he added that one thing is that civil law neither regulates nor forbids everything contained in divine law, but another to approve what is explicitly condemned by divine law (e.g. you shall not kill).[21] Furthermore, Aquinas explained that the asymmetry between divine law and civil law was not a sign of civil law's imperfection, but a manifestation of its own nature: that was different from divine law.[22] In this manner he distinguished between crime and sin.[23]

In fact, Western medieval and early modern legal traditions show that it was uncommon to criminalise behaviours merely because they were immoral acts or a sin, despite the fact that the distinction between crime and sin was not properly enforced in the context of some Christian territories governed by absolutist monarchs—who might have intently resorted to some medieval ideas.[24] However, this reality does not allow us to sustain, as some scholars apparently do, that until the Enlightenment there was no distinction between crime and sin.[25]

Aquinas' criterion to elucidate which immoral acts—or sins—should be regulated as a crime by civil law, was the common good. In his view, political power could approve laws to criminalize behaviours if they were—directly or indirectly—against the common good. After stating that "human law does not prohibit all the vices" and "does not command the acts of all the virtues," he states the following:

> "…human law does not issue commands concerning all the acts of all the virtues; instead, it commands only those acts which can be ordered toward the common good either (a) immediately, as when certain acts are done directly because of the common good, or (b) mediately,

---

[20]Thomas Aquinas, *Summa theologiae*, 1–2, q. 93, a. 3, ad 3.

[21]Thomas Aquinas, *Summa theologiae*, 1–2, q. 93, a. 3, ad 3: "It would be different if human law were to approve of things that the eternal law condemns." Note that this text is the response to argument 3 cited below. Thomas Aquinas only argues against the affirmation that, because the human law does not prohibit everything the divine law does, not every human law is derived from the eternal law. Aquinas argues that exactly the fact that human law is not able to prohibit everything that is prohibited by divine law, does not contradict its being part of the eternal law, but only that it cannot perfectly reach (*assequi*) it.

[22]Thomas Aquinas, *Summa theologiae*, 1–2, q. 93, a. 3, ad 3: "Thus, it does not follow from this that human law does not flow from the eternal law; rather, all that follows is that human law does not perfectly measure up to the eternal law." There is no need to be a believer to grasp the consistency of Aquinas' argument and understand it. Moreover, the concept of eternal law in fact is not theological, but philosophical. The concept of divine law (revealed, divinely posited law) is not "theological" either. The concept of revelation can be grasped philosophically. It is only the belief in divine law, that is, the believe in the factual existence of a revealed of divinely posited law, which seems to me to be on the theological level because it presupposes faith.

[23]See Gilby (1958).

[24]See Carlyle (1903–1936); Arqulliere (1955).

[25]See Masferrer (2017c), 299–321; Masferrer (2017b), 693–756.

> as when the lawmaker commands certain acts pertaining to good discipline through which citizens are formed in such a way that they might conserve the good of justice and peace."[26]

For Thomas Aquinas, states can pass laws commanding "certain acts pertaining to good discipline," only if such external behaviour is really needed for the preservation of justice and peace, and not because it would constitute a moral good for individuals. He defended the view that political communities and civil laws are not required to seek the moral good of individuals but the common good of the whole society, namely, preserving social peace and justice. It is not the task of civil law to make good men, but preserve the conditions to guarantee social peace and justice. That is the common good of the society and hence the main goal of civil law, unlike moral law that concerns itself with moral good and the perfection of each individual.

In this regard, Spanish scholasticism developed Aquinas' ideas on the relation between divine law, natural law and civil law.[27] Francisco de Vitoria,[28] Domingo de Soto[29] and Francisco Suárez,[30] among others, developed his distinction between natural law and human law (or civil law), particularly Soto and Suárez, who, in their

---

[26]Thomas Aquinas, *Summa theologiae*, 1–2, q. 93, a. 3.

[27]Thomas Aquinas, in his *Summa theologiae*, when tacklig the quaestiones of legal argument (Prima Secundae, Q. 90–114), distinguished and dealt with the four *leges* (*aeterna*, q. 93; *naturalis*, q. 94; *humana*, q. 95–97; *divina*, q. 98–114).

[28]Francisco de Vitoria, *Comentarios a la Secunda Secundae de Santo Tomás*, Salamanca, 1952, t. VI, *Quaestio nonagesimasexta* ('De potestate legis humanae'), *Articulus secundus* ('Utrum ad legem humanam pertineat omnia vitia cohibere') (in I, 2 *De lege*, *Quaest*. XCVI, art. II), p. 430: "Utrum ad legem humanam pertineat omnia vitia cohibere. Respondet quod non, et est notanda ratio. Non enim est quam multi putant. Quia enim leges ponuntur imperfectis oportet quod possint ferre. *Ratio quam dant aliqui est quia ea non turbant pacem reipublicae.* Non curant leges ut fornicatio, etc." (emphasis is mine); on I, 2 *De lege*, *Quaest*. XCVI, art. III ('Utrum lex humana praecipiat actus omnium virtutum'), p. 430, Vitoria made no comment at all; "Ut autem lex humana sit iusta et possit obligare, non sufficit voluntas legislatoris, sed oportet quod sit utilis reipublicae et moderata cum ceteris" (*Obras de Francisco de Vitoria. Relecciones*, ed. por T. Urdánoz, Madrid: Teológicas, BAC, 1960, n. 16, p. 183).

[29]Domingo de Soto, *De iustitia et iure*, Salamanca, 1553 (1st ed.), t. I ('De legibus'), Liber I, Quaest. VI, Art. II; I use the following edition: *Tratado de la Justicia y del Derecho* (trans. by Jaime Torrubiano Ripoll), Madrid: Editorial Reus, 1922, Vol. I, Lib. I, Ques. VI: 'Del poder de la ley humana', art. 2: 'Si es propio de la ley humana refrenar todos los vicios', pp. 139–143; see also Lib. I, Ques. VI: 'Del poder de la ley humana', art. 3: 'Si la ley humana manda los actos de todas las virtudes', pp. 143–146.

[30]Francisco Suárez, *Tractatus de legibus ac deo legislatore*: in decem libros distributus…, Conimbricae: Apud Didacum Gomez de Loureyro, 1612, Liber III ('De lege positiva humana secundúm se, et prout in pura hominis natura expectari potest, quae lex etiam civilis dicitur'), cap. I-XXXV, pp. 116–213); Liber V ('De varietate legum humanarum, et praesertim de penalibus, et odiosis'), cap. I-XXXIV, pp. 270–367; I use the edition (both in Latin and Spanish) entitled *Tratado de las Leyes y de Dios legislador*, Madrid: Instituto de Estudios Políticos, 1967, vols. I–III; see, for example, Lib. I ('De natura legis in communi'), cap. 3 ('De necessitate, et varietate legum'), n. 18: "…necessitas manat ex eo, quod lex naturalis vel divina generalis est, et solum complectitur quaedam principia morum per se nota, et ad summum exteoditur ad ea, quae necessaria et evidenti illatione ex illis principiis consequuntur; praeter illa vero multa alia *sunt necessaria in republica humana ad eius rectam gubernationem et conservationem*; ideo necessarium fuit, ut per humanam rationem aliqua magis in particulari determinarentur circa ea, quae per solam rationem naturalem

famous *De Iustitia et Iure* and *Tractatus de legibus ac deo legislatore*, respectively, dealt with the matter quite extensively. Following in Aquinas' footsteps, they maintained that the purpose of civil law was the common good, and the first was social peace and justice.[31]

Aquinas' category of "common good" for a political community was based upon an idea of nature—and human nature—that came from Aristotle and was both universal and teleological.[32] Both traits of nature were not admitted by nominalists, the mainstream scholastics from fourteenth century onwards.[33] For them, universals—or concepts—were not real, only individual; hence, human nature does not exist, only individual persons do. William Ockham and Joannes Buridanus stated that not all nature had a purpose, only that with self-awareness or a conscience. In other words, only God had ends, not nature itself. This idea gave rise to the emergence of mechanicism.[34] Descartes—like Leibniz and Wolff—developed this idea and, under Platoon's influence, rejected the Aristotelian unity of human nature by distinguishing between *res cogitans* and *res extensa*. The dualism between nature and reason, in which nature was commonly understood from a mere physicist perspective, permeated the whole modern thought.

All modern state theories worked from a non-teleological interpretation of nature. For example, in the case of Thomas Hobbes and Jean-Jacques Rousseau the original

---

definiri non possunt, et hoc sit per legem humanam, et ideo fuit valde necessaria"; Lib. I ('De natural egis in communi'), cap. 3 ('De necessitate, et varietate legum'), n. 20: "Tandem vero haec positiva lex in civilem et ecclesiasticam distinguitur: quam divisionefti philosophi non agnoverunt, quia supernaturalem finem et specialem potestatem ignorarunt. Et ideo apud illos idem est lex humana, quae civilis, quam temporalem solet Augustinus appellare. *Est enim illa, quae ad civitatis politicam gubernationem, et ad temporalia iura tuenda, et in pace ac iustitia rempublicam conservandam ordinatur. Unde leges civiles circa haec temporalia bona seu corporalia versantur*"; Liber II ('De lege aeterna, at naturali, ac iure gentium'), cap. I-XX, pp. 98–194; Liber III ('De lege positiva humana secundúm se, et prout in pura hominis natura expectari potest, quae lex etiam civilis dicitur'), cap. I-XXXV, pp. 195 ff. (emphasis is mine).

[31]Domingo de Soto, *Tratado de la Justicia y del Derecho*, Lib. I, Ques. VI: 'Del poder de la ley humana', art. 3: 'Si la ley humana manda los actos de todas las virtudes', pp. 143–146, p. 145: "En suma, *la ley humana sólo prescribe aquellos deberes que atañen al bien común*, o de suyo y próximamente, como tomar las armas para la guerra pública: o indirectamente (como dicen), como lo que toca a la buena enseñanza, por la cual se *preparan los ciudadanos al bien de la justicia y de la paz*"; Francisco Suárez, *Tratado de las Leyes y de Dios legislador*, Lib. I ('De natura legis in communi'), cap. 3 ('De necessitate, et varietate legum'), n. 19: "Et ex utroque licet amplius rationem explicare. Nam in hoc fundatur, quod *homo est animal sociabile, natura sua postulans vitam civilem et communicationem cum aliis hominibus, et ideo necesse est ut recte vivat, non solum ut privata persona est, sed etiam ut est pars communitatis*, quod ex legibus uniuscuiusque communitatis maxime pendet. Deinde oportet, ut unusquisque non tantum sibi, sed etiam aliis consulat, *pacem et iustitiam servando, quod sine convenientibus legibus fieri non potest. Item necesse est, ut ea, quae ad commune bonum hominum seu reipublicae spectant, praecipue custodiantur, et observentur*: singuli autem homines et difficile cognoscunt id, quod expedit ad commune bonum, et raro illud per se intendunt; et ideo necessariae fuerunt leges humanae, quae communi bono consulerent, ostendedo quid agendum sit propter tale bonum, et cogendo, ut fiat" (emphasis is mine).

[32]On this matter, see González (1996), 85–125.

[33]See the works by Carpintero (2004, 2006, 2013).

[34]See González (1996), 127 ff., particularly 131–132.

"state of nature" was conceived as something opposed to the social dimension of man, and as a temporal reality, something that existed just in the beginning, being fortunately overcome through the social contract.[35] For Hobbes, as opposed to Aristotle—who defined man by nature for his political character—, the legitimacy of the state comes from its duty to preserve the survival and security of individuals. Isolated individuals living in an unbearable environment of violence, the state of nature (*homo homini lupus*), decide out of fear to enter into a contract whereby they renounce their right to self-defence and transfer their whole power and rights to a sovereign.[36] In short, men become free and secure by abandoning their original nature or state of nature.

Unlike Aristotle, Rousseau thought that individuals—or human beings—could be either men or citizens, and presented the notions of nature and reason (or freedom or history) as incompatible. As Spaemann pointed out, the root of this incompatibility lies in the non-teleological notion of nature.[37] For Rousseau, man is by nature an individual without language and society, so their socialization implies leaving nature behind.[38]

Although Immanuel Kant sought to overcome the reductionisms of mechanicism and empiricism, he neither prevailed over dualism nor brought back the teleological notion of nature. In his treatise on anthropology, he made a distinction between the physiological and pragmatic perspective: while physiological knowledge revolves around what nature did with man, pragmatic knowledge focuses on what man can or should do through his free will.[39] As can be seen, nature is presented as disconnected to human freedom, almost as much as it was in Hume's thought when he rejected the connection between what things are and what things ought to be, or, in other words, when claiming the impossibility of coherently moving from descriptive statements (what things are) to prescriptive ones (what things ought to be).[40]

This thought paved the way to historicism, so relevant in the nineteenth century. In this vein of thought, Wilhelm Dilthey, for example, stated that "what is man, only

[35] See Spaemann (1992), 102.

[36] Masferrer, Talavera (forthcoming, 2021).

[37] Spaemann (1989), 34–37; González (1996), 148.

[38] Spaemann (1989), 35–36.

[39] Kant (1798; cited by Spaemann, 1989, 23).

[40] David Hume, *A Treatise of Human Nature* (1739), III, part I, section I: "In every system of morality, which I have hitherto met with, I have always remarked, that the author proceeds for some time in the ordinary way of reasoning, and establishes the being of a God, or makes observations concerning human affairs; when of a sudden I am surprised to find, that instead of the usual copulations of propositions, *is*, and *is not*, I meet with no proposition that is not connected with an *ought*, or an *ought not*. This change is imperceptible; but is, however, of the last consequence. For as this *ought*, o *ought not*, expresses some new relation or affirmation, 'tis necessary that it should be observed and explained; and at the same time that a reason should be given, for what seems altogether inconceivable, how this new relation can be a deduction from others, which are entirely different from it. But as authors do not commonly use this precaution, I shall presume to recommend it to the readers; and am persuaded, that this small attention would subvert all the vulgar systems of morality, and let us see, that the distinction of vice and virtue is not founded merely on the relations of objects, nor is perceived by reason."

history tells him."[41] The dichotomy between *res cogitans* and *res extensa* contributed to the emergence of thinkers who focus on the former—like Sartre for whom man has an unrestricted freedom—,[42] or others who focus on the latter, like Charles Darwin or Richard Dawkins who mainly define and characterize man for his physical or biological dimension.[43] It goes without saying that there were other philosophers or thinkers who brought human dualism to its extreme consequences: Friedrich Nietzsche and Sigmund Freud are probably the most representative figures whose influence is still undeniable today.

The Aristotelian, and particularly Thomist, categories that distinguish moral law from civil law collapse if considered from three perspectives: (1) human nature does not really exist or, if it does, it only refers to *res extensa*, being somehow an obstacle for man to grow as a person and develop his own free choices; (2) human freedom is not the product of human nature but just its mere physical substratum, being unconceivable that man might act freely thanks to his nature; and (3) human nature has no teleological dimension that enables human reason to grasp the purpose and the limits of his life and his free choices.

If human nature refers, above all, to the physical or biological aspect of man, then it is more than reasonable that, as Moore argued, animal behaviour cannot serve as a model of human behaviour.[44] Without a teleological conception of human nature, the meaning of the common good becomes impossible. The idea that there cannot be a common good at all because men do not share anything else other than a *res extensa* that restricts *res cogitans* which is supposed to be unrestricted freedom not subject to previous natural instances, have important consequences not only in the legal realm, but also in the social sciences in general, and particularly in moral theology, moral philosophy, political philosophy and social ethics. These ideas, for example, contributed to the emergence of wrong interpretations of Thomas Aquinas' moral philosophy.[45]

In law this philosophical doctrine has had consequences, both in the spheres of public law and private law. To begin with, two different notions have replaced the 'common good', namely, "public interest" and "public utility".[46] In addition, the meaning of some interdisciplinary legal notions such as "good morals" or "public

---

[41] Wilhelm Dilthey, *Gesammente Werke*, B. VIII, p. 224 (cited by Spaemann, 1989, 25).

[42] Franz Adler argues that the influence of phenomenologist epistemology led Sartre to think that "[m]an chooses and makes himself by acting. Any action implies the judgment that he is right under circumstances not only for the actor, but also for everybody else in similar circumstances" ("The Social Thought of Jean-Paul Sartre", *American Journal of Sociology* 55, 3).

[43] Richard Dawkins (1978), 145 and VIII—cited by Spaemann, 1989, 27–28—, affirms, for example, that "a mother is a machine for the optimal propagation of her genes", and that "we are machines for survival, robots blindly prepared for the conservation of those selfish molecules that we call genes".

[44] Moore (1983), § 28 (cited by González, 1996, 190–191).

[45] On this matter, see Rhonheimer (1987, 2006).

[46] Douglass (1980), 103–117; MacIntyre (1990), 344–361; Simm (2011), 554–562; Strang (2005), 48–74.

morality",[47] that were so relevant for centuries, have become notably devoid of meaning because they are not compatible with a legal system lacking a good that is common to all individuals who share the same nature.

If there is no common good, freedom becomes an absolute value,[48] and the purpose of civil law changes radically, turning into a tool of the state to mediate different and even antagonist individual choices, sometimes regardless of its negative impact on the whole social community. In addition, in order to protect such absolute individual freedom, states adopted Mill's "harm principle", whereby political power only can exercise its power over individuals, "against his will, (…) to prevent harm to others."[49] As Mill pointed out, the only reason for interfering with liberty was self-protection.[50] Without harm, the state should not interfere with individual choices. Sexuality becomes a paradigmatic area of individual choices in which state should not interfere.[51] If sexuality has no human purpose and moral value beyond to what is given to it by individuals, states should not interfere with it and furthermore confer legal protection under the umbrella of the right to privacy or even financially benefit some options, regardless of the social consequences of some sexual models. This new sexual paradigm adopted by states and legally implemented has radically changed some areas of law.

Many private law institutions have gone through radical transformations. Marriage is, most probably, one of the most important ones. The reason is easily understandable: if *res extensa* (or nature) is inferior to *res cogitans* (reason), and reason means moral autonomy not subjected to any previous instance, personal choices should not be restricted by physical conditions (masculinity, femininity), possible natural consequences of physical unions (children), and even less so by moral duties of loyalty or faithfulness. This explains why civil laws have admitted, and even facilitate, divorce, same-sex marriage,[52] in vitro fertilization. Only cultural circumstances explain why other forms of personal union are not yet admitted, such as incestuous marriages, polygamy (including both polygyny and polyandry). In fact, polyamory has been spreading notably in the last decade. The worst consequences of this change affect the most vulnerable part of families, namely, the children.

In the sphere of public law, relevant transformations have affected constitutional law and criminal law. Touching on both legal fields, the notion of human dignity,

---

[47] Legarre (2001), 268–277.

[48] John S. Mill, *On Liberty* (1859; I'm using the online version available at https://www.bartleby.com/130/), Introduction, n. 13: "The only freedom which deserves the name, is that of pursuing our own good in our own way, so long as we do not attempt to deprive others of theirs, or impede their efforts to obtain it."

[49] Mill, *On Liberty*, Introduction, n. 9: "That principle is, that the sole end for which mankind are warranted, individually or collectively, in interfering with the liberty of action of any of their number, is self-protection. That the only purpose for which power can be rightfully exercised over any member of a civilized community, against his will, is to prevent harm to others. His own good, either physical or moral, is not a sufficient warrant."

[50] Ibid.

[51] Kuby (2012, 2017) and Stanton (1992).

[52] From a historical perspective, see Dahan (2012), 75–108.

which appeared in the legal realm after the Second World War and whose origins and historical development were connected to human nature,[53] collapsed, becoming a useless concept.[54] As has been noted, Kant's attempt to affirm a "secular" dignity, based on autonomous freedom and on the ability to autonomously compose one's life, was a failure.[55]

The permanent creation of new "human rights" has gravely affected the substance and credibility of the current human rights system,[56] particularly when some of the new rights have become the most important ones, having primacy over the traditional fundamental rights such as freedom of conscience, freedom of speech, religious freedom and freedom of association, among others, and leaving vulnerable people unprotected.[57] In this vein, the right to privacy has gradually become the bulwark to protect the new so-called "sexual and reproductive rights".[58] Some states grant financial benefits to those who are willing to go through surgery to change their sex, but do not provide any support for those who would like to change from homosexuality. Furthermore, some laws prescribe sanctions for those who, unsatisfied with their sexual orientation, dare to seek help from a doctor.[59] Sex became a civil liberty paradigm.[60]

In the realm of criminal law, the replacement of the "common good" with the "public interest" or "public utility" affects an important legal category, namely, the legally protected good which is linked to human dignity and constitutes the cornerstone of criminal law. Both human dignity and legally protected goods are the most relevant notions of criminal law and have moral implications. *Velis nolis*, criminal law cannot be fully separated from morality. Most criminal policies and reforms generally entail moral options and by necessity have moral implications. For example, the Western tendency to replace the category (generally reflected in a rubric in criminal codes) 'Crimes against honesty' by another "Crimes against sexual freedom" has moral implications and shows a moral option: what is criminalised is not a conception of moral honesty that might be considered relevant for a peaceful society, but violence to someone in order to have a sexual relation against his/her real will, or

---

[53] Masferrer (2016), 221–256 and Masferrer (2019b), 203–213.

[54] Macklin (2003), 1419–1420.

[55] Carpintero (2016), 97–116, particularly 102; see also Carpintero (2012, 2013a).

[56] Masferrer (2017a), 331–358.

[57] Masferrer, García-Sánchez (eds.) (2016).

[58] On how the meaning and the purpose of the right to privacy radically changed to cover individual autonomy, see Sandel (1989), 521–538; Sandel (1996); Sandel (2005), 122–144, particularly 124–133; see also Wheeler (2015), ch. 4; Masferrer (2018), 813–841.

[59] LGBTI laws approved in many jurisdictions forbidding individuals who seek medical treatment concerning his/her sexual orientation follow the 18th Principle of "Yogyakarta Principles", that is a 2006 document drafted to be used as "a universal guide to human rights which affirm binding international legal standards with which all States must comply" (available at https://yogyakartaprinciples.org/); on this document, see Kuby (2017), ch. V, 127–155.

[60] Wheeler (2015) and Masferrer (2020).

without violence but through some kind of abuse (age, parenthood, educator, tutor, etc.).[61]

The decriminalization of abortion is the logical outcome of UN, EU and national states' policies promoting "sexual and reproductive rights".[62] If "safe sex" is considered a right, it would be illogical to criminalize the natural consequence of some kinds of sexual behaviour when contraceptive means fail or for whatever other reasons. In addition, sexual behaviour belongs to the individual's privacy and this realm is legally or constitutionally protected (right to privacy), thus its criminalisation would be incoherent. Thus states should guarantee the so-called "right to consequence-free sexual intimacy".[63] Despite all this, it is undeniable that the decriminalization of abortion is a moral decision with relevant moral, sociological, legal and political consequences.[64] And again, the most vulnerable party of an abortion (e.g. the unborn child) is hardly protected.[65] Note that the primacy of hedonism and amusement might easily lead to different kinds of violence.[66] Abortion is probably the gravest case, but there are more: pornography is another one in which violence is most patent.

Laws regulating pornography have also undergone notable changes, today generally permitted. In the context of an increasingly erotic society, it is easy for millions of minors to be exposed to degrading images promoted by companies that run multimillion businesses online and disseminate indecent images that are contrary to a minimum standard of humanity and public morality.[67] While "public indecency" in general terms is forbidden in many jurisdictions,[68] it is not always clear what constitutes illegal public nudity and not infrequently laws are not effectively enforced.

Today nobody denies the relevance of "public ethics" or "public philosophy",[69] as the basis of moral behaviour in open societies. In other words, that which defines what is good and what is evil for multicultural communities. Public ethics is a basic moral pattern, universal and generalizable, constituted by values and prescriptions of conduct, which affects individuals as citizens. Thus, this public ethics includes those principles and rules which are necessarily so that the coexistence of individuals in a society can be described as fair. The basic normative content of this public ethics is

[61]On the role of violence to crimes related to sexuality in the early modern age, see Juhel (2012), 111–146.

[62]Wheeler (2015), ch. 5; see also, for example, Fathalla (1992), 3–29; see also Kuby (2017), 103 ff. (on the UN policy), 157 ff. (on the EU policy).

[63]On this matter, see Mulder (2014).

[64]In Sandel's view, for example, "[t]he justice (or injustice) of laws against abortion and homosexual conduct depends, at least in part, on the morality (or immorality) of those practices" (Sandel 1989, 122).

[65]Masferrer (2019a), 361–408.

[66]Ballesteros (1981), 265–315, particularly 280–293.

[67]Legarre, Gregory (2017).

[68]For the US, for example, the U.S. Supreme Court declared the right of states to outlaw public nudity, arguing that states have an interest in "protecting societal order and morality," and that public nudity is not "free expression" protected by the First Amendment (*Barnes v. Glen Theatre*, 501 U.S. 560, 568, 1991).

[69]On this matter, see Sandel (2005).

human dignity and human rights. In this sense, law and morals are united in "public ethics" as a basis of civil law and criminal law.

According to the liberal ideal whereby,"individuals find their good in different ways, and many things may be good for one person that would be no good for another",[70] there is "no *social entity* with a good that undergoes some sacrifice for its own good, (...) only individual people, different individual people, with their own individual lives,"[71] and "political decisions must be, so far as possible, independent of any particular conception of the good life, or of what gives value to life."[72] Such a liberal ideal do not provide any consistent point of departure to ascertain a sound "public ethics" for society and the supposed state neutrality excludes what might be really good for society, that is, what socially matters, the intrinsic value or social importance (beyond individual choices). As Sandel pointed out, "[i]f the self is prior to its ends, then the right must be prior to the good."[73] Note that some liberals changed their view, such as John Rawls concerning the notion of "public reason"[74] and Ronald Dworkin regarding the relation between law and morals.[75] In this vein, Dworkin, after admitting that "morality and law" name departments of thought that are in principle distinct, though perhaps interdependent in various ways," suggested changing the traditional understanding as follows:

> "I want now to suggest that this traditional understanding, which encourages us to chart relations between two different intellectual domains, is unsatisfactory. We might do better with a different intellectual topography: we might treat law not as a separate from but as a department of morality. We understand political theory that way: as part of morality more generally understood but distinguished, with its own distinct substance, because applicable to distinct institutional structures. We might treat legal theory as a special part of political morality distinguished by a further refinement of institutional structures."[76]

Treating "law not as a separate from but as a department of morality" implies recognizing that "[a]ll societies, whatever their virtue or lack thereof, must maintain some modicum of social order or they risk extinction,"[77] and that such order is necessarily moral. Morality implies duties, and rights as their consequence, and not the other way around, as liberals usually defend.[78]

The relationship between morality and criminal law must constantly evolve to meet the needs of changing times and circumstances. Humans cannot be detached from time and historical development. Social changes and new situations require

---

[70]Rawls (1971), 448.

[71]Nozick (1974), 32–33.

[72]Dworkin (1978), 127.

[73]Sandel (2005), 147–155, particularly 153 (see *The New Republic*, 7 May 1984).

[74]Rawls (1997), 765–807; Rawls (1999, 2002).

[75]Dworkin (2006); on 'Law and Morals', see his 'Introduction' entitled 'Law and Morals', 1–35.

[76]Dworkin (2006), 34–35.

[77]Etzioni (1997), 10.

[78]Etzioni (1997), 19: "Civil libertarians are concerned with rights and not with duties; with entitlements and not with national service, tithes, and taxes. Above all, they oppose guidance by the government, and more indirectly by others, as to one ought to do."

new answers. In doing so, since the relation touches at least upon criminal law, legal philosophy and legal history, interdisciplinary approaches are always needed. This constitutes the contents of this book, which contains fifteen original contributions written by legal scholars from different European and American universities. The authors do not attempt to solve the complexity of the relation between morality and criminal law, but at least to express their criticism, offer proposals and stimulate further thought. If "[t]he principle of morality" is "to think well,"[79] thinking constitutes the first requirement.

That was the conclusion of a seminar I organized at the University of Valencia in September 2017 to commemorate the 60th anniversary of the abovementioned "Wolfenden Report", and the starting point of this book, which was devised within the context of that seminar. Many articles and book chapters have tackled the relation between criminal law and morality, but there are no books dealing specifically with the topic,[80] as there are books on the relation between law and morality in general. So, this book attempts to fill in this gap. Moreover, it does so by tackling the topic from an interdisciplinary perspective (criminal law, constitutional law, legal philosophy and legal history, among others). It is divided into three essential parts, dealing with the relation between criminal law and morality: Part I "Historical Perspectives"; Part II "Philosophical Perspectives" and Part III which touches on "Controversial Issues" such as abortion, pornography and euthanasia.

The historical content of Chapter "Criminal Law and Morality Revisited: Interdisciplinary Perspectives" illustrates the pertinence of approaching the relation between criminal law and morality from a historical perspective. It would otherwise be impossible to comprehend the current situation (even more so to provide possible criteria), ideas and arguments that might contribute to make criminal law more humane and just. The purpose of the chapter and Part I ("Criminal and Morality: Historical Perspectives") is to unveil some key historical factors that have configured the current criminal law and its relation to morality. In doing so, the authors' analyses are interdisciplinary, dealing with criminal law, legal history, legal philosophy and political philosophy.

In Chapter "The Rise of Ethical Reproach in Spanish Late Scholasticism", Harald Maihold deals with "The Rise of Ethical Reproach in Spanish Late Scholasticism." He argues that, according to modern criminal law doctrine, punishment was defined as a strong evil imposed by a sovereign for a guilt that was bound by an ethical reproach to the perpetrator. Heavy actions imposed by a sovereign can be found since the states of ancient history. Sin punishment and ethical blame, however, were unknown in the criminal law of those times. Then, in the heresy trials of the High and Late Middle Ages, self-understanding of criminal justice in practice was analogous to God's last judgment, and criminal justice was strongly based on the sacrament of penance. The idea of punishment was pinpointed also in theory not before the

[79] Pascal (1658), 232 (extracted from "What is Morality? Pascal's Heartfelt Answer", *Nordicum-Mediterraneum* (available at https://nome.unak.is/wordpress/09-2/c64-conference-paper/what-is-morality-pascal-s-heartfelt-answer/#_edn13).

[80] See, for example, Duff, Green (2011), but it did not touch directly upon our topic.

emergence of a peculiar literature on criminal law. Nevertheless, in canon law the notion of penalty still covered a wide range, beginning with penalties in the modern sense up to so-called "penalties" that could be imposed without any guilt but for certain reasons, for example medical and restorative penalties. Maihold explains that it only was in the sixteenth century, when Franciscan theologian Alfonso de Castro (1495–1558), one of the authors of the School of Salamanca, narrowed down the concept of penalty to its proper notion, defining it as an evil (or disease) that is to be imposed because of an own past sin of the perpetrator. In parallel to this, De Castro emphasized that by committing the criminal offence, the transgressor was not only bound to pay the penalty, but also "bound to blame": the one who broke a criminal law was burdened with sin. An ascertainment of the guilt-obligation of criminal law was a significant course setting for the ethical reproach which is addressed to the perpetrator by the modern criminal law. Criminal law did not only aspire to objective compensation by punishment, but also to a subjective state of the perpetrator: comprehension of their guilt, which was intended to speak to them as a moral person. For Maihold, the fact that an obligation in conscience was partially accepted even without a judicial conviction clearly shows that the ethical stigma was implied not only by condemnation, but now by the criminal threat itself. In its time, this can be understood as a response to the stress of conscience by the Protestant theologians, as an attempt to lead the religious deviance of the heretics relying on individual conscience back to ecclesiastical obedience by the authority of the criminal law.

Chapter "Liberties, Rights and Punishments in Modern Natural Law Liberty, Rights and Punishments", is by Manuel Rodríguez Puerto (University of Cádiz, Spain). The author explains that the arrival of modern legal conceptions did not lead to the strict separation of law and morals, but the moral consideration was influenced by an individualist point of view. The key to the arguments defended by the so-called school of modern natural law was to identify natural law, subjective right and liberty. The aim of the school of modern natural law was to defend a radical alternative to the scholarship of *ius commune. Ius commune* conceived law as the right solution of a controversy; and the right answer was induced from the human interrelationship arisen in the midst of social issues. Law was justified by the human necessities and the principles of natural law. This connection implied a close relation between morality and law in the foundation of legal order. The purpose of criminal law was to defend the fundamental legal goods rooted in objective principles. Rodríguez-Puerto shows how the School of modern natural law refused that objective conception of legal science. And the modern iusnaturalists rejected the strict connection between law and morals (from Thomasius onwards). But, finally, the key of their view of criminal law had a moral foundation because the purpose of this branch of law was to protect a human good: the natural liberty of the individuals.

In Chapter "Roman Dutch Criminal Law and Calvinism Calvinist Morality in De Criminibus (1644) of Antonius Matthaeus II" Janwillem (Pim) Oosterhuis (University of Maastricht, The Netherlands) touches upon the relation between crime and morality in the Calvinist sphere. "Roman Dutch Criminal Law and Calvinism: Calvinist Morality in *De criminibus* (1644) of Antonius Matthaeus II," he not only shows the pervasiveness of Calvinism in criminal law in the early modern Dutch Republic, but also points out certain inherent ambiguities of Calvinism in Matthaeus' restatement of criminal law. Matthaeus' Calvinist conviction becomes particularly evident in the contested issues of criminal law. In discussion with Civil and Canon lawyers, but particularly also with other Reformed theologians and legal scholars, Matthaeus developed his own stance, on how to interpret and explain Roman criminal law and local customary criminal laws in light of the orthodox—Calvinist—religion. Matthaeus' consequent Calvinism can help to explain certain "modern" opinions, such as his rejection of torture as a means to extracting confessions. Due to the absolute primacy of divine will and law in *De criminibus*, the role of natural, practical reason remains quite limited. Indeed, although Matthaeus distinguished between moral and enduring laws with direct bearing on criminal law and religious prescripts without such direct consequence for the law, he failed to give any clear reason or criterion for such distinction. For criminal law, the enduring moral laws were to be found mainly in the Decalogue and the Mosaic Laws that explicated those commandments. According to Matthaeus, these enduring moral laws of the Decalogue corresponded with natural law. Basically, both Tables of the Decalogue, covering civil and spiritual morality respectively, should be upheld via criminal law. But in these commandments Matthaeus chose to strictly uphold some but was more lenient about others. Due to judicial discretion in the punishment of crimes, the teachings of Matthaeus could potentially have a far-reaching influence on such punishment. Importantly, Matthaeus did not equate all biblical teachings with enduring moral laws valid for the courts on earth. He notably refused to criminalize heresy. Indeed, for Matthaeus apparently many of the teachings of Jesus and the apostles concerned the conscience and what was right before the court of conscience. Matthaeus did not, however, provide a consistent reasoning for the underlying distinction between "private" and "public" morality. Despite a lack of theoretical clarity in distinguishing between divine and natural law, "public" and "private" morality, and enduring morals laws and religious prescripts, for Matthaeus in the end personal faith and dedication to God was distinct from law: the orthodox religion had to be taught, rather than imposed.

In Chapter "The Role of Nature in the Secularization of Criminal Law in Europe (17th–19th Centuries)" I analyse "The Secularization of Criminal Law in the Enlightenment" in order to ascertain and revise: Its Real Scope and Contribution." I show that some 17th-century contractualist legal philosophers such as Hobbes, Pufendorf and Locke, strove to separate criminal justice from religious, theological, or "moralist" arguments and founded it upon natural philosophy. In doing so, they resorted to nature, natural law and natural reason. Hence, they clearly distinguished between crime and sin. Enlightened authors adopted this legacy. In doing so, they did not defend a criminal law detached from morality, as if utilitarianism was the mainstream of the eighteenth-century criminal jurisprudence. Unlike Bentham, the majority of criminal law reformers such as Montesquieu, Beccaria, Rousseau, Voltaire and Kant, were not utilitarian, so most of them accepted both the social contract and laws of universal nature. This chapter also demonstrates that in Spain and France there was continuity on this matter with the nineteenth century. Some of the most important nineteenth-century criminal lawyers resorted to—in as did most of the enlightened authors—nature, natural law and natural reason. In doing so, they defended the relation between criminal law and morality, and distinguished between crime and sin, rather than confusing or identifying these categories. Although both utilitarianism and legal positivism notably grew in France and Spain during the nineteenth century, they did not become the mainstream of criminal law jurisprudence until the twentieth century. I argue that perhaps those who today share a utilitarian conception of criminal law (nowadays undeniably the mainstream) are looking at the past anchored in the present, so they come to a false conclusion after misunderstanding enlightened criminal law jurisprudence.

In Chapter "Habits of Intelligence. Liberty of Expression and the Criterion of Harm in John Stuart Mill", Ignacio Sánchez-Cámara (University of Rey Juan Carlos, Spain) touches a central issue regarding the relation between criminal law and morality, namely, the "Habits of Intelligence. Freedom and no harm principle in "On liberty" by J. S. Mill." It contains an analysis of Mill's defence of liberty of expression and his Criterion of Harm as a principle to delimit the scope in which society can limit the freedom of people. Its contribution to the solution of some legal problems is also discussed. The aristocratic liberalism of Mill, despite its insufficient foundation and the difficulty of specifying the consequences of the harm criterion, constitutes a vigorous defence of individual freedom and a critique of the claim by democratic government who claim they are the holders of "spiritual power". Neither the people nor their representatives can impose what is right or wrong in the moral order, or the correct interpretation of the facts of the past, or even scientific or religious truth. Mill´s theses are a successful criticism of the criminalization of opinion crimes, such as the so-called hate crimes, that can lead to the destruction of freedom. The word can commit a crime, for example through insult, slander, perjury or inducement to crime, but not through the expression of judgements, opinions, criticisms or evaluations. Ultimately, the text deals with the philosophical foundations of criminal law with as regards freedom of expression.

Part II ("Criminal Law and Morality: Philosophical Perspectives") starts with Chapter "The Fundamentals of Ethics" in which Francisco Carpintero (University of Cádiz, Spain) touches upon the "Fundamentals of Ethics" from a philosophical and historical perspective. Carpintero holds that those who have been trained during the twentieth century are heirs to several overlapping ethical traditions, without normally being aware of the fragmentary and frequently incoherent nature of their ideas. In his chapter, the author shows the origin of the two main schools of Western philosophical thought: Nominalism and Thomism. Concerning the former, it was represented by John Duns Scotus and fully developed by Francisco Suárez. They did not admit that all the precepts of the Decalogue had an actual metaphysical consistency, but were just "modes" established in our reason. This means, for example, that one has to obey them because, once their knowledge is assumed, God's *lex imperans* orders it so. Through this path the Decalogue and Morals become a forever constituted *corpus* with a supposedly metaphysical nature. In this way Ethics becomes mere normativism and the question that arises is why every man has to obey the Decalogue. Thomism is the other tradition of thought. In Carpintero's opinion, this school has been misunderstood from a historical perspective because there has been a tendency to interpret it through the light of Scholasticism left by Suárez. That was a serious mistake from which there was no going back. The author explains that Thomas Aquinas did not propose a rigid ethics which could be known axiomatically starting from some initial axioms. As Eisenhart explained at the beginning of the seventeenth century, the agility of Metaphysics clashes with the rigidity of Logics. But this explanation was liking preaching in the desert. In the chapter, Carpintero tries to expound once again what Thomas Aquinas explained in his time but it was unfortunately forgotten in History.

In Chapter "What is Perfectionism?", Francisco J. Contreras (University of Seville, Spain) analyses "What is perfectionism." In the relationship between morality and criminal law, there are two fundamental options, namely, perfectionism and libertarianism; here Contreras deals with the former. He explains that perfectionism is "the tenet whereby the state and the law may legitimately contribute to "making men good", that is, help them to choose what is morally right, to practise virtue, and thus to attain the good life. In contrast, antiperfectionism would be the philosophical approach which, as stated by Joseph Raz, "rejects the idea that the state has a right to impose a conception of the good on its inhabitants," meaning that political power "should be blind to the truth or falsity of moral ideals, or of conceptions of the good". Or, put another way, "governments must be neutral regarding different people's conceptions of the good." John S. Mill's famous "harm principle" typically reflects the antiperfectionist approach. After the introduction, Contreras' analysis works from Aristotle, Saint Augustin and Aquinas (1), and then tackles the Hart-Devlin debate (2), the discussion between liberals vs. communitarians (3), Joseph Raz's perfectionist liberalism (4), and finally the doctrine of Robert P. George and the role of government in the maintenance of moral ecology. Criticising the flaws' arguments of both Devlin and Hart, and rejecting the exclusionary disjunctive between antiperfectionist liberalism and anti-liberal communitarianism, Contreras praises Joseph Raz's perfectionist liberalism as an appropriate compromise approach. He concludes that "from Aristotle and Saint Augustin all the way to Joseph Raz and Robert P. George, an important tradition of thinking has upheld a claim which, however "bigot" it may sound in present times, is actually quite obvious: that law and state inevitably have a profound influence on a society's mores; and that, therefore, it is vital that such influence should be as healthy and positive as possible."

In Chapter "Build and Restore Good Human Relationships. Overcoming the Retributive Paradigm as a Key Issue for the Theory of Justice", Luciano Eusebi (Catholic University of Milan, Italy) submits to a moral and rational criticism the idea, so strongly rooted in our culture, that interprets justice in terms of correspondence between behaviours and, generally, between every plural reality (every *duality*) as implying, at least, a potential conflict. This is a perspective—icastically represented by the image of the scale—according to which, once a negative judgment has been made against a certain, individual or collective human reality, this would legitimize the mutually negative action towards that reality: for its damage, its defeat, its exclusion from the weft of solidarity bonds and many times, as happened in the course of history, for its very elimination. If the law, as the author observes, has worked to limit the consequences of such a vision, nevertheless it has not succeeded in getting rid of it. For instance, the essentially retributive modalities that have characterized, until today, the infliction of sanctions provided by the criminal justice systems respond to a pattern of human relationships with far more extensive repercussions than the limited field of the fight against crime. This has an impact on international relations, in the way of understanding political confrontation, in economic rapports and even in personal ties. It is the same scheme, after all, that has legitimized over the centuries the classic theories of a "just" war, which need to be overcome if, faced with weapons of possible total destruction, we want to guarantee a future for mankind. The alternative is found in a *project-oriented* justice, in accordance with the principles of restorative justice: so that the *negative for negative* logic will be overcome, pursuing, rather, the aim of returning to *make just and fair*, for everyone, relationships that have not been so. The retaliation of the evil does not reactivate, by itself, the good. Examples of such orientation are offered, in particular, with regard to conceiving crime prevention and the evolutionary perspectives of criminal sanctioning systems.

In Chapter "Paternalism and Moral Limits of Criminal Law" Luigi Cornacchia (University of Università degli Studi di Bergamo, Italy) analyses the notion of paternalism. "Paternalism and moral limits of criminal law" deals with criticisms of the libertarian foundation of anti-paternalism, as being unable to protect the person in weakness. The liberal approach is grounded on the principle of moral relativism, but at the same time states that laws forbidding or even criminalizing activities that do not harm others are (absolutely) immoral law. Furthermore, the "individual-oriented" harm Principle, with its main principle of the respect for the "sanctity" of individual autonomy, makes it hard to constrain the expansion of criminal law. Most important, the protection of vulnerable human beings is not guaranteed by a simple procedural control on the validity of consent. It is the moral duty of criminal law to focus on the need for true protection of vulnerable persons from other's unexpressed insidious pressure and to avoid exploitation of those who are weak, old, ill or disabled. If it is right, the principle of respect for autonomy and the principle of care, which forms the basis of tutorial paternalism, are linked rather than antagonistic. Such conclusions seem to comply with the Wolfenden Report, which stated that "the law's function is…to provide sufficient safeguards against exploitation… of others, particularly those who are especially vulnerable because they are young, weak in body or mind, inexperienced, or in a state of special physical, official or economic dependence". Cornacchia's chapter warns of the new despotic paternalism of the "best interest", established by experts in contempt of the principle of respect for autonomy, rooted in the technocratic "gold" standard of the quality of life.

In Chapter "Human Dignity and Legally Protected Goods in Criminal Law", Pedro Talavera (University of Valencia, Spain) deals with the relation between "Human Dignity and the Protected Legal Good." He argues that criminal law protects certain basic goods because they directly or indirectly are connected with the dignity of the person. However, in cases such as euthanasia, prostitution or surrogacy motherhood, the appeal to the dignity of the person is used, in the opposite sense, as the basis for decriminalization. In these cases, dignity is identified exclusively with the autonomy of the person and their capacity to dispose of all their goods, even if they are essential.

Thus, euthanasia is no longer conceived in terms of homicide or aiding suicide, but rather the discretionary disposal of life; prostitution as the discretional exercise of sexuality; surrogate motherhood, the discretional use of procreative capacity; experimenting with human embryos as discretional donations of biological material for science, etc. Dignity is no longer the basis for protecting basic goods and then becomes the basis for protecting the person's will. Dignity is something more than autonomy, therefore, the basic goods of the person are not absolutely discretional. There is within a person something that could be called an "ontological remnant of humanity", which can be attacked or harmed without necessarily harming a specific fundamental right (life, freedom, intimacy, honour, etc.). For Talavera, the "remnant of humanity", which refers to the ontological core of dignity (requirement of absolute respect), is covered and protected by the concept of "moral integrity". Moral integrity means the irrevocable requirement of all persons to be treated as such, and not degraded, debased or objectified; a requirement, which constitutes a fundamental legal good that merits protection under criminal law. And, this protection under criminal law, insofar as it is linked to the most intimate core of dignity, prevents certain conducts from being decriminalized regardless of changes in social morality or whether it includes the consent of those who perform them. For this author, there are actions, which can harm or undermine dignity, because they involve exploiting, objectifying, debasing, degrading or humiliating the person. For this reason, conducts such as prostitution (in which a person is exploited as a mere object of sexual pleasure) or surrogate motherhood (in which the woman's reproductive capacity is purchased) always constitute an attack on the moral integrity of the person, regardless of their consent, and in any case must be decriminalized.

In Chapter "From Eunomia to Paideia: The Educating Nature of Law", Vicente Bellver (University of Valencia, Spain), with the title "From *eunomia* to *paideia*: the educating nature of law," deals with the relationship between law and education from a philosophical-practical perspective. It begins by illustrating the notable similarities between both and then goes on to address two questions: (1) whether law should educate citizens in moral virtues; and (2) if the education of citizens should concern itself with reinforcing obedience to laws. As regards the first, it considers Aristotle's thinking on the educating role of law. For the second the author reflects on Rousseau's concept of "civil religion", as a kind of education that guarantees the submission of people to the laws of the state. According to professor Bellver both thinkers offer interesting, yet incomplete, proposals on these questions, so he attempts to compensate by recourse to two emblematic texts in the political and legal history of the world: The Universal Declaration of Human Rights and, more specifically, Pericles' Funeral Oration. Aristotle understood that law had to fulfil an educating function in moral, but failed to outline to what extent in order to avoid abuses. Rousseau understood that political society rests on pre-political bases, but his proposal for civil religion almost inevitably leads to an authoritarian regime. In Pericles' Funeral Oration one can find the limits so that law is able to correctly fulfil its educating role, as well as the religious pre-political bases which involve citizens in constructing a life in common. These pre-political bases generate a kind of civil religion which appeals to the emotions without cancelling out the exercise of reason, and promotes subjecting the citizen to the law without having to renounce criticism.

Part III ("Criminal Law and Morality: Controversial Issues") starts with Chapter "From Crime to Right", entitled "From crime to right. The crisis of the title as reason of law," by Marta Albert (University of Rey Juan Carlos, Spain). The author questions whether a crime can turn into a right and discusses the process by which a crime becomes a subjective right. Partial decriminalization of the relevant conduct is the first step on the path to be considered as a right. An analysis of this legal technique shows how it is almost impossible to avoid injury to the legal asset protected by penal law. The article then focuses on the conception of subjective right that allows an understanding of the implementation of conducts deserving ethical reproach as legally enforceable: that is, the defence of the "right to do wrong". The path from crime to right is explained by these two phenomena. They also show us the "price" that theory of law is supposed it dues: the complete unintelligibility of subjective right as legal concept, due to the impossibility of differentiating itself from what is conceived as lawful or as a liberty. The author not only reveals the evident risks of this conception of subjective rights but also contributes to a better understanding of the concept of rights by underlining five ideas: (1) the need to relocate personal autonomy in the legal arena. The logos of the Law do not have to do with autonomy but with justice: giving to everyone his due (what he deserves), that is the very essence of Law; and (2) from the perspective mentioned above, some suggestions are made: (i) the revision of partial decriminalization as a legal technique, so it does not become the first step to the complete lack of protection of relevant legal asset; (ii) the clear distinction between what is not prohibited or what is explicitly allowed and what is legally enforceable. To have a right means to have a power over a third party, who becomes a new duty holder; and (iii) the consideration of subjective right in the perspective of the legal relationship where it comes on to the scene. In this relationship we can find not only the third-party duties, but also the existence of a just title. It is the reason why the bearer of the right is able to bind others. The legal definition of abuse or fraud of Law should be applicable, especially when rights begin to be used to violate the above-mentioned logos of the Law: to give to each person what is truly owed to them.

Chapter "The Role of the Criminal Law in Regulating Pornography" touches upon pornography. With the title "The Role of Criminal Law in Combatting Pornography," Gerard V. Bradley (University of Notre Dame, USA) argues that anyone can now see how the affordability, accessibility, and anonymity of the Internet has produced an explosion of pornography in countries across the globe. In his view, it is no longer an exaggeration to say that most of us live in "pornified societies". And there is a growing body of peer-reviewed social scientific evidence, which shows that the fall-out of this explosion includes many malignant effects on valuable relationships (especially including marriage) and on overall psycho-sexual health. "Pornification" is, in other words, a serious threat to human well-being. Anyone can see, too, that traditional means of trying to stymie pornography will no longer do: criminal prosecutions could never address more than an infinitesimal fraction of cases; moving sex trades to a localized "combat-zone" cannot affect the Internet; interdicting the production and transport of pornography is impractical. Bradley thinks that new means of conceptualizing an organized social response, and of executing that response, are needed. Effective social control of obscenity in a porn-saturated society calls for a creative partnership among educators, pastors, and other culture-forming actors to *morally stigmatize* pornography as degrading and harmful. Public authority has an indispensable role to play in this partnership, for law powerfully shapes culture and thus shapes *us*—our actions, our attitudes, and our conception of right and wrong.

Chapter "Dignity at the End of Life and Decriminalization of Euthanasia" deals with other current controversial issue, namely, euthanasia. "Justice in the End of Life: Legal Issues around the Decriminalization of Euthanasia" by Jorge Nicolás Lafferriere (Catholic University of Argentine), affirms that human dignity is one of the central axes of the transformation carried out in criminal law. Lafferriere addresses the discussion around the proposals for the decriminalization of euthanasia in the light of dignity. The author argues that if dignity is identified with personal autonomy exclusively, the legal system faces important inconsistencies to be able to guarantee fundamental rights at the end of life. This is especially true in the case of unconscious people, who cannot make decisions. Neither does autonomy provide a strong reason to decide what is fair in the-end-of-life decisions. If dignity is approached from a utilitarian quality of life perspective, then problems arise in the legal consideration of euthanasia linked to determining the quality of life and when a life is "unworthy" of being lived. Applying a utilitarian criterion to legitimize euthanasia leads to the so-called slippery slope argument. There is an increase in the cases in which euthanasia is applied and a progressive trivialization of the causes legally admitted to put an end to life. For this reason, this article points out that only an ontological vision of dignity, as an inherent value of the person, can offer solid criteria to make legal decisions at the end of life.

References

Primary Literature

Aquinas T, Summa theologiae (I used an English version available at https://www3.nd.edu/~afreddos/summa-translation/TOC-part1-2.htm)
Aristotle, Nicomachean Ethics (available at https://classics.mit.edu/Aristotle/nicomachaen.html)
Arqulliere HX (1955) Augustinisme politique. Essai sur la formation des théories politiques du Moyen Age, J Vrin, Paris
Augustine, De civitate Dei [The City of God] (available at https://www.newadvent.org/fathers/1201.htm)
Bodin J (1576) Les Six livres de la République
de Vitoria F (1952) Comentarios a la Secunda Secundae de Santo Tomás, Salamanca
de Vitoria F (1960) Obras de Francisco de Vitoria. Relecciones, ed. por T. Urdánoz, BAC, Madrid
Hobbes T (1651) Leviathan
Hume D (1739) A Treatise of Human Nature

Irenaeus of Lyons, Adversus haereses [Against Heresies] (available at https://www.newadvent.org/fathers/0103.htm)
Kant I (1798) Anthropologie in pragmatischer Absicht, Königsberg
Mill JS (1859) On Liberty (available at https://www.bartleby.com/130/)
Pascal B (1658) Art of Persuasion (Harvard: Harvard Classics, 1993–2013 [1909–14]) (What is Morality? Pascal's Heartfelt Answer, Nordicum-Mediterraneum, available at https://nome.unak.is/wordpress/09-2/c64-conference-paper/what-is-morality-pascal-s-heartfelt-answer/#_edn13).
Soto D de (1553) De iustitia et iure, Salamanca (I use the following edition: Tratado de la Justicia y del Derecho, trans. by Jaime Torrubiano Ripoll, Editorial Reus, Madrid, 1922)
Suárez F (1612) Tractatus de legibus ac deo legislatore: in decem libros distributus..., Conimbricae (I use the edition (both in Latin and Spanish) entitled Tratado de las Leyes y de Dios legislador, Instituto de Estudios Políticos, Madrid, 1967, vols. I–III)

Secondary Literature

Ballesteros J (1981) La violencia hoy: sus tipos, sus orígenes. Ética y política en la sociedad democrática. Espasa-Calpe, Madrid, pp 265–315
Berg C (1959) Fear, punishment, anxiety and the Wolfenden report, George Allen & Unwin
Carlyle AJ (1903–1936) A history of medieval political theory in the west, William Blackwood, Edimburgh-London 6 vols. (reed. 1970)
Carpintero F (2004) Justicia y ley natural: Tomás de Aquino, y los otros escolásticos. Servicio de Publicaciones de la Facultad de Derecho, Universidad Complutense Madrid
Carpintero F (2006) El desarrollo de la idea de libertad personal en el pensamiento medieval. Universidad Panamericana-Porrúa, México
Carpintero F (2012) La crisis del Estado en la Edad Posmoderna. Thomson-Aranzadi, Cizur Menor
Carpintero F (2013a) Dogmas y escepticismo. Presupuestos de Filosofía del derecho, Escuela Libre de Derecho-Porrúa, México
Carpintero F (2013b) La ley natural. Historia de una realidad inacabada, UNAM, México
Carpintero F (2016) La dignidad humana en Tomás de Aquino. Persona Y Derecho 74(1):97–116
Chesser E (1958) Live and let live: the moral of the Wolfenden report, Taylor Garnett & Evans
Dahan JR (2012) La différenciation sexuelle au sein du couple, aproche de droit comparé: droit canonique, droit hébraïque, évolution de droit francais. In: Les sexualités: répression, tolérance, indifférence (Maryse Baudrez & Thierry Di Manno, dirs.), Bruylant, Bruxelles, pp 75–108
Dawkins R (1978) Das egoistische Gen, Berlin
Devlin P (1959) The enforcement of morals, Maccabaean lecture in jurisprudence of the British Academy, British Academy—Oxford University Press, London (it was also published with the title "Morals and the Criminal Law." Oxford University Press, The Enforcement of Morals (1965)
Devlin P (1962) Law, democracy and morality 110 University of Pennsylvania Law Review 635
Douglass B (1980) The common good and the common intest, political theory, vol. 8 No. I, February, 103–117
Duff RA, Green S (2011) Philosophical foundations of criminal law. Oxford University Press, Oxford
Dworkin R (1978) Liberalism. In: Private and Public Morality (ed. Stuart Hamphsire), Cambridge University Press, Cambridge
Dworkin R (2006) Justice in Robes. Belknap Press, Cambridge, MA
Etzioni A (1997) The new golden age: community and morality in a democratic society. Profile Books, London
Fathalla MF (1992) Reproductive health in the world: two decades of progress and the challenge ahead. In: Khanna J, Van Look PFA, Griffin PD (eds) Reproductive health: a key to a brighter future- Biennial Report 1990–1992. World Health organization, Geneva, pp 3–29

Gilby Th (1958) Principality and polity. Aquinas and the rise of state theory in the west, Longmans, Green and Co., London-New York-Toronto
González AM (1996) Naturaleza y dignidad. Un estudio desde Robert Spaemann, Eunsa, Pamplona
Hart HLA (1963) Law, liberty and morality. Oxford University Press, Oxford
Hart HLA (1965) The morality of the criminal law. Oxford University Press, Oxford
Juhel C (2012) Le maintien de l'ordre moral à la fin de l'ancien régime: l'example donné par le conseil souverain de Roussillon (1660–1790). In: Les sexualités: répression, tolérance, indifférence (Maryse Baudrez & Thierry Di Manno, dirs.), Bruylant, Bruxelles, pp 111–146
Kuby G (2012) Die Globale sexuelle Revolution: Zerstörung der Freiheit im Namen der Freiheit, Fe-Medienverlag, 2012 (I used its Spanish version, La revolución Sexual Global. La destrucción de la libertad en nombre de la libertad, Editorial Didaskalos, Madrid, 2017)
Legarre S (2001) The use of the term '(Public) Morality' in the European Convention on Human Rights: a brief history. In: Yee S, Tieya W (eds) International law in the post-cold war World. Essays in memory of Li Haopei, Routledge, London-New York, pp 268–277
Legarre S, Gregory M (2017) Secondary effects and public morality, 40 Harvard J Law Public Policy 320 (2017) (available also as Notre Dame Law School Legal Studies Research Paper No. 1716, at https://ssrn.com/abstract=2972229)
MacIntyre A (1990) The privatization of good. Rev Polit 52:344–361
Macklin R (2003) Dignity is a useless concept. BMJ 327:1419–1420
Masferrer A (2016) Taking human dignity more humanely: a historical contribution to the ethical foundations of the constitutional democracy. In: García-Sánchez E (ed) Human dignity of the vulnerable in the age of rights: interdisciplinary perspectives Masferrer A. Springer, Dordrecht-Heidelberg-London-New York, pp 221–256
Masferrer A (2017a) Derechos de nueva generación. In: Derechos humanos. Un análisis multidisciplinar de su teoría y praxis (Enríquez Sánchez JM, Masferrer A, Aguilera Portales RE, eds.), UNED Madrid, pp 331–358
Masferrer A (2017b) La distinción entre delito y pecado en la tradición penal bajomedieval y moderna. Una Propuesta Revisionista De La Historiografía Española, Europea Y Anglosajona, Anuario De Historia Del Derecho Español 87:693–756
Masferrer A (2017c) The need for a secularized criminal law: past, present and future. A proposal to unravel a complex issue in the western society. In: Trending topics of law and justice: legal English workshops 2015/16, Tirant lo Blanch, Valencia, pp 299–321
Masferrer A (2018) Libertad sexual y derecho a la privacidad en la tradición norteamericana (1965–2015). In: Pensar el tiempo presente. Homanaje al profesor Jesús Ballesteros Llompart, Tirant lo Blanch, Valencia, I, pp 813–841
Masferrer A (2019a) El derecho al aborto en la jurisprudencia mexicana. Contribución al estudio de la influencia norteamericana en el constitucionalismo mexicano. In: Garduño Domínguez G, Andreu Gálvez M (eds.) La Constitución mexicana de 1917: estudios jurídicos, históricos y de derecho comparado a cien años de su promulgación, Instituto de Investigaciones Jurídicas—Universidad Nacional Autónoma de México (UNAM), Ciudad de México, pp 361–408
Masferrer A (2019b) Human Dignity in the Early Sixteenth Century Spanish Scholasticism: Francisco de Vitoria and Fray Bartolomé de las Casas. In: Dondorp H, Schermaier M, Sirks B, (eds.) De rebus divinis et humanis. Essays in honour of Jan Hallebeek, Vandenhoeck & Ruprecht Verlage, Göttingen, pp 203–213
Masferrer A, García-Sánchez E (eds) (2016) Human dignity of the vulnerable in the age of rights: interdisciplinary perspectives. Springer, Dordrecht-Heidelberg-London-New York
Masferrer A (2020) De la honestidad a la integridad sexual. La formación del Derecho penal sexual español en el marco de la cultura occidental, Thomson Reuters-Aranzadi, Cizur Menor
Masferrer A, Talavera P (forthcoming) Law as reason vs law as will in the fight against terrorism: from a Hobbesian conception of law to an Orwellian society. In: Mariona Llobet, Manuel Cancio, Clive Walker (eds.) Precursor crimes of terrorism: the criminalisation of terrorism risk in comparative perspective, Edward Elgar Publishing
Moore GE (1983) Principia Ethica. Universidad Autónoma de México, México

Mulder C (2014) Sex, drugs, and religious liberty, Public Discourse, January 6th, 2014 (available at https://www.thepublicdiscourse.com/2014/01/11728/)
Nozick R (1974) Anarchy, state, and Utopia. Basic Books, London
Rawls J (1971) A theory of justice. Belknap Press, Cambridge, MA
Rawls J (1997) The idea of public reason revisited, The University of Chicago Law Review 64, no. 3 (Summer 1997), 765–807 (reedition in The Law of Peoples, Harvard University Press, Cambridge, MA, 1999, fourth printing, 2002)
Rhonheimer M (1987) Natur als Grundlage der Moral. Die personale Struktur des Naturgesetzes bei Thomas von Aquin: Eine Auseinandersetzung mit autonomer und teleologischer Ethik, Tyrolia-Verlag, Wien-Innsbruck (I used its Spanish version entitled Ley natural y razón práctica. Una vision tomista de la autonomía moral, Pamplona: Eunsa, 2006, 2nd ed)
Rhonheimer M (1995) Diritti fondamentali, legge morale e difesa legale della vita nello stato constituzionale democrático. Annales Theologici 9:271–334 (I used the English version Ethics of Procreation and the Defense of Human Life, Washington DC: Catholic University of America Press, 2010, ch. 7)
Rhonheimer M (2013a) The common good of constitutional democracy: essays in political philosophy and on catholic social teaching. The Catholic University of America Press, Washington DC
Rhonheimer M (2013b) Why is political philosophy necessary. The common good of constitutional democracy: essays in political philosophy and on catholic social teaching. The Catholic University of America Press, Washington DC, pp 1–35
Sandel MJ (1989) Moral argument and liberal toleration: abortion and homosexuality. California Law Rev 77:521–538 (later republished in Democracy's Discontent, Harvard University Press, 1996; and in Public Philosophy: Essays in morality in politics, Cambridge, MA: Harvard University Press, 2005, pp. 122–144)
Sandel MJ (2005) Public philosophy: essays in morality in politics. Harvard University Press, Cambridge, Mass
Simm KK (2011) The concepts of common good and public interest: from Plato to biobanking. Camb Q Healthc Ethics 20(4):554–562
Spaemann R (1989) Lo natural y lo raciona, Rialp Madrid
Spaemann R (1992) Rousseau: von der Polis zur Natur. In: Der Mensch –ein politisches Tier? Essays zur politischen Anthropologie, Reclam
Stanton DC (1992) Discourses of sexuality from Aristotle to AIDS. University of Michigan Press, Ann Arbor
Strang JL (2005) (2005) The role of the common good in legal and constitutional interpretation. University of St. Thomas Law J 3(1):48–74
Weber M (1919) Politik als Beruf (I used the English version entitled Weber's Rationalism and Modern Society, translated and edited by Tony Waters and Dagmar Waters), New York: Palgrave Books, 2015, pp. 129–198)
Wheeler LA (2015) How Sex became a civil liberty. Oxford University Press, Oxford

Other Sources

Barnes v. Glen Theatre, 501 U.S. 560, 568, 1991
Committee (1957) Committee on homosexual offences and prostitution, Report of the Committee on homosexual offences and prostitution, Her Majesty's stationery office, London (reprinted in the US with the title The Wolfenden Report: Report of the committee on homosexual offences and prostitution. New York: Stein and Day, 1963)

Lawrence v. Texas, 539 U.S. 558, 2003
Devlin P (1989) Morals and the criminal law. In: The enforcement of morals [1965], Oxford University Press, p 3

Criminal Law and Morality: Historical Perspectives

The Rise of Ethical Reproach in Spanish Late Scolasticism

Harald Maihold

Abstract According to the modern criminal law doctrine, punishment is defined as a strong evil imposed by a sovereign for a committed guilt that is bound with an ethical reproach to the perpetrator. Strong actions imposed by a sovereign have been found since the early states in antiquity. Sin punishment and ethical blame, however, still had been unknown in the criminal law of those times. Then, in the heresy trials of the High and Late Middle Ages, self-understanding of criminal justice in practice was analogous to God's last judgment, and criminal justice was strongly based on the sacrament of penance. Yet, not before the emergence of a peculiar literature on criminal law, the idea of punishment was pinpointed also in theory. Nevertheless, in canon law the notion of penalty still possessed a wide range, beginning from penalties in the modern sense up to so-called "penalties" that could be imposed without any guilt but for certain reasons, for example medical and restorative penalties. It only was in the sixteenth century, when Franciscan theologian Alfonso de Castro (1495–1558), one of the authors of the School of Salamanca, narrowed down the concept of penalty to its proper notion, defining it as a disease that is to be imposed because of an own past sin of the perpetrator. In parallel to this, he emphasized that by committing the criminal offence, the transgressor was not only bound to pay the penalty, but also "bound to blame": he who broke a criminal law was burdened with sin. An ascertainment of the guilt-obligation of criminal law was a significant course setting for the ethical reproach which is addressed to the perpetrator by the modern criminal law. Criminal law did not only aspire to an objective compensation by punishment, but also to a subjective state of the perpetrator, comprehension of his guilt, which was intended to communicate with him as a moral person. The fact that an obligation in conscience was partially accepted even without a judicial conviction, clearly shows that the ethical stigma was implied not only by condemnation, but already by the criminal threat itself. In its time, this can be understood as a response to the stress of conscience by the Protestant theologians, as an attempt to lead the religious deviance

This text is based on a Spanish Version: Maihold (2011), 125–136.

H. Maihold (✉)
Hamburg, Germany
e-mail: harald.maihold@yahoo.de

A. Masferrer (ed.), *Criminal Law and Morality in the Age of Consent*, Ius Gentium: Comparative Perspectives on Law and Justice 84,
https://doi.org/10.1007/978-3-030-64163-4_2

of the heretics relying on individual conscience back to ecclesiastical obedience by the authority of the criminal law.

1 Purpose of Penalty, Notion of Guilt and Ethical Blame in Today's Discussion

If a car driver on a highway exceeds the speed limit, cannot brake up in time and causes an accident involving collision with a pedestrian, according to our legal system, this case leads to various consequences. Private law will hold the motorist responsible for the damage: he or she has to pay for the hospitalization of the pedestrian. Administrative law will fine him or her for the speeding and, if necessary, withdraw his or her driving licence. Finally, criminal law will hold him or her accountable for (negligent or intentional) assault and either punish him with imprisonment or (s)he will have to pay a special amount as punishment for his infraction. The special nature of criminal punishment compared to other legal consequences is that punishment gives the offender an "ethical reproach", which accuses the offender of having chosen the wrongdoing, even though he or she[1] could have decided by himself to support the law. Two important principles are dominating the modern criminal law: The guilt principle (no punishment without guilt)[2] and the principle of punitive personality (punishment should only affect the author of the offense).[3]

Hardly any criminal lawyer in the German-speaking discussion would dare to deny the blaming character of criminal punishment. At first glance, this could be astonishing, because there is barely any question in German jurisprudence is as controversial as the legitimacy of the state's criminal claim. At second glance, then, the ideas that are associated with the concept of blame are not quite as uniform as one should assume facing the common term. This is evident in the attributes attached to the word "reproach". Some authors are speaking of a "moral reproach",[4] perceiving the blame as something highly personal, which charges the culprit because of his guilt and which appeals to him as a person capable of a moral action. Others on the other hand, are speaking of a "socio-ethical reproach",[5] perceiving reproach as something society uses to express its disapproval of a perpetrator.

Opinions as to what the "ethical reproach" of punishment precisely means, how it is to be legitimized and what purpose it may pursue, thus are quite different, depending on which of the different theories of criminal reasoning they are based on: Those who essentially consider punishment as an act of retribution or of negation of the crime will also assume the ethical blame associated with the punishment as an appropriate, and indeed necessary, response to the injustice committed by the

---

[1]The masculine form is also used below for female offenders or persons.

[2]Kaufmann (1961) passim; Frister (1988) passim; Erber-Schropp (2016) passim.

[3]To this principle and its philosophical problems cf. Erhardt (2014) passim.

[4]Schmidhäuser (1963), 36; Maurach/Zipf (1992) § 1 N. 9.

[5]Jeschek/Weigend (1996), 59; Roxin (2006) § 3 N. 46.

perpetrator.[6] Those, however, who don't consider punishment as an end in itself and assume that punishment should serve social purposes, will take ethical blaming above all as a communicatory act, an appeal society addresses to the offender to behave lawfully in future (so-called special prevention), an appeal addressed to other persons not to follow the bad example of the offender and to deter them from similar acts by the example of punishment (so-called negative general prevention), and an appeal addressed to society to adhere to the norm, the transgression of which is answered with punishment (so-called positive general prevention). Whereas the previous, so-called classical criminal doctrine, still prevailing in the post-war period, had essentially taken punishment as an act of retribution of the committed injustice, due to the criticism of guilt notion in the 1970s, inter alia questioning free will of man, retaliation and special prevention appeared as obsolete.[7] The younger doctrine, which largely was influenced by Niklas Luhmann's systemic theory, therefore grounds punishment basically on the aspect of confirmation of the norm, arguing for a more or less purely general preventive justification of punishment, that takes the guilt of the perpetrator only functionally as an occasion for social reaction.[8] Criminal law today less and less is talking about "guilt" and "imputation", but more and more about "responsibility" (in German terms "Verantwortung"[9] or "Zuständigkeit"[10]). This leads to a significant extension of the criminalization of social behaviour we, for example, can recognize in the extension of environmental criminal law or the re-establishment of corporate punishment in Swiss law.[11] However, since there is a lack of financial resources that would be necessary for full execution, criminal law is increasingly finding itself reduced to a symbol to declare what should be permitted or forbidden.

In all this, the representatives of the preventive-symbolic criminal law and of the functionalized notion of guilt not only continue to use the term "punishment", but also continue to assume that such punishment should be associated with socio-ethical blaming.[12] However, general preventive ethical blaming leads to inextricable contradictions: An appeal that is directed solely to the future, has no recipient and must be left unheard.[13] A blame, which is obviously pronounced solely for the purpose of systemic stabilization, also seems to carry a double standard and to be

---

[6]The Kantianian approach today is preferably carried out by Köhler (1997), 48 ff. More differentiated von Hirsch (2005), who in cap. 1 and 2 recurres on the blaming as an adequate reaction to man-made injustice, but justifies the infliction of evils by its preventive purposes.

[7]Kargl (1982), 195 ff., 375 ff.

[8]Jakobs (1976) passim; Jakobs (1991), 6 ff, 476 ff.

[9]Fundamentally from a philosophical point of view Jonas (1979) passim.

[10]Jakobs (1991), 469.

[11]Maihold (b), 380 ff. For a good introduction to the current discussion see von Freier (2009), 98 ff.; Krämer (2015) passim.

[12]Jakobs (1991), 9. Cf. also Roxin (2006) § 3 N. 46: „Aus dem Umstand, dass in der Bestrafung ein sozialer Tadel liegt, [folgt nicht], dass die Strafe wesensmäßig Vergeltung oder auch nur Übelszufügung ist. Denn man kann aus der Missbilligung eines Verhaltens ebenso gut die Folgerung ableiten, im Sinne resozialisierender Einwirkung auf seine künftige Vermeidung abzuzielen."

[13]Bayertz (1995), 63 ff.

dishonest because the accusation is made to the perpetrator not for his own sake, but only as an instrument of foreign state purposes.[14] In a punitive theory that punishment is only understood as a vehicle for systemic stabilization, the offender is no longer treated as an autonomous subject, but only as an object, thus contradicting the image of man and the understanding of the state shaping the democratic constitutional state of modern times.[15]

One should ask whether the theory of punishment could not deal without ethical blaming at all. A look through the history of criminal law may reveal the fact that punishment has not always been used to carry an attached ethical blame. Therefore, let us take a closer look at the historical roots of the ethical blame of punishment.

2 The Free-of-Blame Medieval Term of the "Punishment"

It is no longer a secret that the term "punishment" first emerged in the course of the church's heresy trials of the "legal" twelfth century. Previously, the law didn't know a special sanction that would be attached with ethical blaming.

According to this, the principle of guilt and the principle of punitive personality were still unknown to the elder law. Penal sanctions that we encounter in the Middle Ages were not of highly personal character, in fact, they were not limited to people with personal responsibility at all. Medieval law also had knowledge of "punishment" against underage children, insane people, animals and even inanimate things.[16] Punishment of people, in addition, was sometimes carried out not on the living person, but on their corpses or portraits.[17]

Finally, such punishments could also hit innocent third parties. Punishments for foreign guilt were generally accepted in the science of that time. The so-called confession-jurisprudence listed numerous case groups, in which even God himself "punished" one person for another, and summarized them in catalogues.[18] For the crime of majesty or heresy of the father, for example, the "father's punishment" was also extended to his posterity.[19] Or to give another example, entire communities or cities, whose leaders had refused obedience, were occupied with the church's interdict, a "collective punishment" that meant inter alia, that the clerical services could no longer be held within the city, so even newborn infants could not be baptized.[20] In order to justify such punishments, secular jurists were able to invoke provisions

[14]Bock (1991), 649 ff.

[15]Cf. Von Hirsch (2005), 27 ff.

[16]Maihold (2005), 123 ff.

[17]Maihold (2013), 78 ff; Maihold (2005a) passim. Paradoxically, such "punishments" of corpses and portraits seem to have occurred only since the sixteenth century, when at the same time the principle of public criminal law, that all crimes must also be punished, started to prevail.

[18]Maihold (2005), 121 ff.

[19]Maihold (2005), 140 ff.

[20]Maihold (2005), 116 ff.

of the Roman emperors, and church jurists could rely on numerous biblical passages in which God, as in the case of Sodom and Gomorrah, wiped out entire cities for the sin of some individual citizens.

In the German legal history of the early twentieth century, this sort of clan liability was commonly associated with an assumed pre-receptional Germanic law, but many cases of similar liability in Roman and canon law prove that by no means it was a typical Germanic legal phenomenon.[21]

3 Arising of the Idea of Sin Punishment

The "birth of punishment", we can observe in the practice of the heresy trials of the twelfth century. In the documents of these trials, namely in the south of France, in the Langedoc, and in northern Spain, in Catalonia and Aragon, punishment deliberately was attached for the first time with an ethical blame, and for this purpose, the concept of *puniri* has been introduced. The Greek loan word *poena*, originally also used for private penalties and fines, went through a metamorphosis, by now standing as *legitima poena* for the new penal sanction. Eventually, the German word "Strafe" has been detectable only since the fourteenth century.[22]

Yet, the guilt principle, had not been unknown before. With Aristotle and the Greek philosophers, it went without saying that only the author of a crime could be punished.[23] In the Christian Middle Ages, however, it was not Aristotle but the Bible that used to be the starting point of any scientific research. The Hebrew thought was far less individualistic than the Greek one, and so the Bible contains numerous reports of "punishments" of innocents claiming to be observed by theology and the related sciences. In theology, the guilt principle first has taken place in the idea of divine justice, that in eternal life everyone will be repaid according to his deeds. For temporal hardships, however, God imposed them on innocents to test them or prove his omnipotence.[24]

Since earthly courts, both of the church or the state, had to emulate the divine judgment whenever possible, these principles were taken up by canon and secular law. In canon law, the principle of guilt was extended to the spiritual punishment of excommunication, which was said to be capable of harming the soul.[25] In secular law, the guilt principle first called for irreversible corporal punishments. In other temporal punishments without permanent impact, however, the importance of the

[21] Maihold (2000) passim; Maihold (2005c), 117 ff.

[22] Achter (1951), 26 ff, 97 ff.

[23] Although Aristotle does not distinguish between culpa and causa, it is clear to him that only the author of an act can be punished, just as the knowledgeable action constitutes the injustice of the act, the premeditated the malice of man, see Aristotle (2002) book 5, cap. 10.

[24] Maihold (2005), 109 ff, 131 ff.

[25] Raymundus de Peniaforte (1603) lib. 3, tit. 32, § 6, 377; Dictum Gratiani ad C. 24, q. 3, c. 1, pars 1, § 4, cit. after Friedberg (1879).

guilt principle was limited. Next to the guilt of the offender, some more reasons for a punishment were in discussion: „Sine culpa, *nisi subsit causa*, non est aliquis puniendus."—"Without guilt, *if there is no reason*, nobody is to be punished.", this rule of the Liber Sextus, a collection of decretals by Bonifacius VIII. Issued 1298, summarized the situation quite well.[26] Even the term *puniri*, marking the new notion of punishment, did not only mean the new, blaming *culpa*-punishment, but even guilt-independent penalties for other reasons ("*causa*-punishments").

One reason for the dilatory reception of the new concept of punishment certainly lies in the fact that in the twelfth century there was still a lack of criminal jurisprudence that could have reflected the new notion. The development of punitive personality is very closely connected with the development of a professional literature of criminal jurisprudence. If one takes a look into Italian *maleficium*-tracts, which at the beginning of the fourteenth century depicted criminal law for the first time in context, one will realize immediately that these treatises hardly reflect the concept of punishment theoretically, but largely still remain in the broader notion of punishment coming from the medieval tradition. The reference to sin, both as a requirement and a consequence of the punishment, seems to be lacking in these treatises![27]

Summing up, it can be said that the modern concept of punishment has remained unknown to secular and church lawyers for a long time. As the following section will show, it was first formulated in theology, from where it slowly entered the canon and through this very slowly infiltrated the secular law. This development didn't come to an end until the late eighteenth century.

4 The Notion of Sin Penalty

The notion of sin penalty emerged with the modern criminal jurisprudence from theology not before the early modern period. The beginning of the development becomes apparent in the theory of punishment by Thomas Aquinas (1224/25–74), which was based on Aristotle, but tried to reconcile it with the broader concept of punishment of the medieval tradition. Along with penalty in proper meaning (*poena rationem poenae, poena simpliciter considerari*), the Thomasian notion of penalty included medical (*poena medicinalis*) and restorative penalties (*poena satisfactoria*). The principle of guilt applies only to the first one as well as to punishments in spiritual goods. Though Thomas in fact did not limit the concept of punishment entirely to the sin penalty—he also knew cases of a punishment for foreign guilt—his "punishment in its proper sense" indicates the clear tendency to become independent.[28]

---

[26]Liber Sextus 5, 13, 2, cit. after Friedberg (1881).

[27]Maihold (2005), 136 ff.

[28]Thomas Aquinas (1887–1894) Summa theologica 1 II, q. 87, a. 8; 2 II, q. 108, a. 4. Cf. Maihold (2005), 152 ff.

But it was not before the Thomasian Renaissance of the sixteenth century that the concept of punishment became more and more sharpened to sin penalty.[29] With Francisco de Vitoria (1486–1546), the founder of the Dominican theological school of Salamanca, we observe a shift in emphasis in the direction of sin penalty when he increases the "proper" penalty to a "most proper" (*poena propriissime*), in addition to which the correctional punishment as "punishment without punitive character" is turned out to be paradoxical.[30]

Finally, the work of Franciscan theologian Alfonso de Castro (1495–1558) was groundbreaking for the new notion of penalty. As a preacher in Flanders, a professor in Salamanca, a diplomat, and court chaplain of the Spanish kings, he spent his life defending the Roman Catholic position against the Lutheran doctrine and thereby earned the nickname "scourge of heretics". The study of heresy led Castro to criminal law. In his main work, *De potestate legis poenalis libri duo* (1550), Castro dealt, generally, with the concept of criminal law, with the nature and purposes of punishment and the relationship between crime and punishment. Punishment (*poena*) was defined by Castro as "a disease that causes damage to the subjected person and that is to be imposed because of his or her own past sin". Other "evils" (*afflictiones*), which are not imposed for one's own sin, according to Castro should be no longer denominated as "punishments". As a consequence, the tripartite division of punishment found by Thomas Aquinas and Vitoria was brought to an end.[31]

Castro's notion of punishment was of a significant impact on the theologians and canonists of his time. Among the theologians, especially Domingo de Soto (1494–1560), who also received a chair of theology in Salamanca in 1552, rigorously continued to apply Castro's concept of punishment.[32] The canonist Martín de Azpilcueta (1493–1586), who teached in Salamanca and Coimbra, also took up Castro's narrow concept of punishment and criticized the inaccurate use of many of the church's penal laws.[33]

Although the Salmantine canonist and legist Diego de Covarrubias y Leyva (1512–1577), who had been taught in canon law by Azpilcueta, nowhere explicitly dealt with the penal concept of Alfonso de Castro, and although he still seems to be widely within the canonical tradition, in his essay on punishments for foreign guilt one senses the influence of the new concept of punishment. Whereas the Liber Sextus, as we remember, had comprehended punishments without guilt as a part of the rule ("*sine culpa, nisi subsit causa*"), Covarrubias separated rule and exception, with the effect

[29]The great impact of Late Spanish Scolasticism on criminal law principles in general is portrayed by Maihold (2014), 149 ff. To the principle of proportionality of crime and punishment see also: Schnyder (2010) passim.

[30]Vitoria (1932–1952), Com. ad Summa theologica 2 II, q. 108, a. 4 (tom. V, 235 ff.). Cf. Maihold (2005), 174 ff.

[31]Castro (1550) lib. 1, cap. 3 (fol. 15r): „Poena est passio inferens nocumentum illam sustinenti, aut saltem apta ad inferendum, nisi aliunde impediatur, inflicta aut contracta propter proprium peccatum praeteritum ". Cf. Maihold (2005), 181 ff.

[32]Soto (1582) lib. 1, q. 6, a. 5 (fol. 19v–20v).

[33]Azpilcueta, Comm. De lege poenali fragmentum, in cap. Fraternitas 12. q. 2, namely num. 10–14, published posthumously, cit. after Azpilcueta (1616) tom. II, 234 ff. Cf. Maihold (2005), 206 ff.

that the principle of guilt, expressed in the rule, became self-reliant. The "*causa*-punishments", as exceptions to this rule, were then claiming for a special justification. While Covarrubias, as a result, allowed felonies without an own guilt, the justification he provided for them shifted these sanctions into areas outside the criminal law. According to Covarrubias, there were considerations of contractual theory about a general consensus among all subject of the law, justifying a deviation from the natural law guilt principle. Suitable for this, Covarrubias avoided the use of criminal language for these sanctions, using such a terminology instead that understands guilt not as sin but as an obligation and replaces "punishment" with "liability": Not of *peccatum* he is speaking, but of *debitum*, not of *puniri*, but of *tenere-solvere*. Although the change of the terminology is not strictly observed everywhere, a new vocabulary was developed that conceptually captured the distance between the non-debt-based sanctions and the proper punishment.[34]

Francisco Suárez, a jesuit and probably the most important author of the *late* Late Spanish Scolasticism, in his groundbreaking work *De legibus ac Deo legislatore,* recurred to punishment only incidentally by dealing with the variety of human law, especially with penal and other "odious" laws like tax laws. Nevertheless, we can observe a juxtaposition of theological legitimization and secular purposes of punishment. According to Suárez, punishment served the stabilization of the state community, but with the parallelization of crime and sin the state's punishment also supported the adjustment of religious guilt. In the end, the punishment of criminals came out as a duty both of the state officers as well as of the criminal himself, thus turning against the common view of his time that regularly granted the judge a wide discretion, and supporting the Castrensian view of the obligation of the human penal law in the conscience of each subjected person.[35]

Among the secular jurists, commonly denominated the legists, the Castrensian concept of punishment was not immediately taken up with all consequences. The largest group of lawyers were practitioners who did not question the legitimacy of punishment and were not interested in theological and metaphysical reflections on the meaning of punishment at all. A smaller group of these practically oriented lawyers got under the influence of the canon law, namely of Covarrubias. The radical solution of Castro and Azpilcueta didn't prevail among them, but at least the theoretical framework for the establishment of the guilt principle was taken, which was able to precede the discussion of exceptions. Only a very small group of lawyers, most notably the Salamanca-educated Fernando Vázquez de Menchaca (1512–1566), received their concept of punishment directly from Castro.[36] Through these teachers, the theological concept of penalty was communicated into the German doctrine of natural law and criminal law of the seventeenth century.[37]

---

[34] Covarrubias y Leyva, Variarum Resolutionum libri IV, lib. 2, cap. 8, cit. after Covarrubias y Leyva (1679) tom. II, 200 ff. Cf. Maihold (2005), 214 ff.

[35] Suárez (1612) lib. 5, 456 ff. Cf. Grunert (2013), 255 ff.

[36] Vázquez de Menchaca (1572) lib. 2, cap. 55, num. 17 ff (fol. 144r). Cf. Maihold (2005), 226 ff.

[37] Maihold (2015), 51 ff.

Finally, criminal law has gradually been freed from non-guilt elements, while the elder non-punitive sanctions have been retained under changed circumstances, such as civil or "policey" penalties resp. misdemeanours, as political, theological or educational measures.[38]

5 The Ethical Reproach of the Criminal Law

In parallel with the narrowing of the concept of criminal penalty to sin penalty, punishment, due to Alfonso de Castro and his successors, is equipped with an ethical reproach. In the theological texts, this is expressed in the conclusion that by committing the criminal offence, the transgressor is not only bound to pay the penalty (*obligatio ad poenam*), but also "bound to blame" (*obligatio ad culpam*).[39] Guilt is not only a requirement,[40] but also a consequence of the penal sentence: he who breaks a criminal law, is burdened with sin.[41] This means a subjective state, a sinner's feeling of guiltiness.

This obligation to blame in the opinion of the theologians not only results from a clear moral criminal law that explicitly orders that its transgressor is obligated to blame (e.g. the Law of excommunication), but also from so-called mixed penal laws (*leges mixtae*) that to the transgression of a norm attach a punitive threat without expressly ordering the obligation to blame. That is, according to the theologians, because the obligation to blame already results from the punitive threat that demands obedience from the subjects of law. Acts of criminal law obligate to blame, not because they are penal laws, but because they are moral laws.[42]

Yet, this is different from laws that Alfonso de Castro and his successors describe as more criminal laws (*leges pure poenales*), although this term actually contradicts the new technology of penalty. A mere criminal law does not prohibit, but it allows something under a condition; it doesn't threaten any "real" punishment, but merely determines a fee to be paid for the action named by the law, for example the

---

[38]For details cf. Maihold (2005), 265 ff.

[39]Castillo Hernández (1941), 60 ff.; Mañaricua Neure (1949), 35 ff.; Navarrete Urieta (1959), 1405 ff.; Savall (1935), 240 ff.; López Riocerezo (1949), 242 ff.

[40]The definition of the penal code, however, is broader than that of the penalty: „Lex poenalis est lex, quae statuit poenam alicui infligi propter culpam commissam." Castro (1550) lib. 1, cap. 3 (fol. 19v). Although the penal code requires a committed guilt, it does not necessarily require a guilt of the person beeing punished. So the law that punishes the children of the heretics for the crimes of their father may be called a penal code, because it contains a "real punishment" in Castro's sense, not for the children, but for the father.

[41]Vitoria (1932–1952) Com. ad Summa theologica 1 II, q. 90, a. 4 and q. 96, a. 4 (tom. VI, 414 ff., 430 ff.); Castro (1550) lib. 1, cap. 8 (fol. 62v); Soto (1582) lib. 1, q. 6, a. 5 (p. 19v). Cf. Maihold (2005), 192 ff.

[42]Azpilcueta, „Comm. De lege poenali fragmentum", num. 16 ff., 23 ff., cit. after Azpilcueta (1616) tom. II, 237f, 238c-e; Soto (1582) lib. 1, q. 6, a. 5 (fol. 20r); more exactly even Aragon (1597) Comm. ad Summa theologica 2 II, q. 62, a. 3 (162 ff.).

importation of grain.[43] Thus, the so-called *leges pure poenales* are strange foreign bodies within in the theologian's doctrine of criminal law, a relic from the days of the expansive notion of penalty.[44]

Hence, the guilt-involvement of the criminal law meant at first that along with the committing of the crime, the offender was burdened with sin. In addition, the question arose whether or not the perpetrator was bound to blame even without a sentence by his individual conscience *in foro conscientiae*. Alfonso de Castro obviously would accept this regarding the ecclesiastical laws that order a penalty occurring by law (*ipso iure*), particularly in case of the sentence of excommunication.[45] This can be understood as a response to the stress of conscience by the Protestants.[46] The prevailing view among theologians and canonists, however, was very critical towards a duty in conscience to self-serving the sentence. The perpetrator was indeed obliged in conscience to suffer the punishment. To require the offender to enforce the penalty actively in himself, however, is inconsistent with the character of punishment as a suffering and even "inhuman", because it would contradict the principle of natural law that no one would be obliged to blame or to judge himself.[47]

An ascertainment of the guilt obligation of criminal law was a significant course setting for the ethical reproach which is directed at the perpetrator by the modern criminal law. Criminal law does not only aspire to objective compensation by punishment, but also to a subjective state of the perpetrator, comprehension of his guilt, which is intended to communicate with him as a moral person. This subjective aspect of the penal code, which was beyond the performance of the legally determined "condition", the moral blemish, was missing in the earlier criminal law. It is only here that it was brought to bear, mediated by the Spanish theology of the sixteenth century, after the criminal concept based on guilt had created its conditions. The fact that an obligation in conscience partially was accepted even without a judicial conviction, clearly shows that the ethical stigma was implied not only by condemnation, but already by the criminal threat itself.

6 Is the Ethical Blame to be Abolished in Criminal Law?

The insight that an ethical reproach of punishment dates back to the time of the Spanish Inquisition raises doubts as to whether it is still appropriate in an enlightened, modern criminal law. This leads us back to the question posed at the outset, whether

---

[43]Castro (1550) lib. 1, cap 8 and 9 (fol. 64r, 67 ff.); Soto (1582) lib. 1, q. 6, a. 5 (fol. 20v); Aragon (1597) Comm. ad Summa theologica 2 II, q. 62, a. 3 (165).

[44]The notion of *leges pure poenales* goes back to Henry of Ghent (1219–1295), cf. Maihold (2005), 196.

[45]Castro (1550) lib. 1, cap. 3 (fol. 19v–20r), lib. 2, cap. 5 (fol. 131v-141v). Cf. Maihold (2005), 192 ff.; Lavenia (2004), 183 ff.

[46]Baylor (1977), 119 ff.

[47]Vitoria, „Relectio De temperantia", num. 7, cit. after Vitoria (1997) p. 348; Aragon (1597) Comm. ad Summa theologica 2 II, q. 62, a. 3 (163 ff.); Simancas (1569) tit. 9, num. 167 s (fol. 33r).

or not a theory of punishment could deal without any ethical reproach. If, in face of the crisis of guilt principle and free will, ethical blaming and, associated with this, the stigmatization of the perpetrator have lost their power of persuasion ("labeling approach"), then why shouldn't ethical blaming be abolished, replacing criminal law by an ethical neutral sanction in the traditional sense? Couldn't, perhaps, a neutral sanction contribute to conflict resolution even better than blaming and labelling? Ultimately, this consideration would mean abolishing of the criminal law in its present form by replacing it with something completely new.[48]

But how could this completely new form of punishment look like, this reaction of the state to deviant behaviour, which is considered to be necessary for the purpose of standardization? So far, criminal lawyers haven't found an adequate answer to this question. A sanction imposed for the purpose of standard confirmation, therefore, is externally very similar to punishment and could be easily confused with each other. The attempt to undress such a criminal sanction of its ethical blame, fails, though, with the so-called duck test: What quacks like a duck, waddles like a duck, swims like a duck, looks like a duck, that probably seems to be a duck.

In other words: As long as the external appearance of the punishment does not change, but only a new theory is imposed on it, the essence of the punishment remains as a blaming sanction. A criminal law without ethical reproach would hardly be comprehensible in the eyes of the criminal who is obliged to suffer a punishment.[49]

What is certainly even more important, is the objection that criminal law cannot dismiss its ethical censure without falling behind the modern age. Going back to the Middle Ages is not possible for the modern state holding the state's monopoly on force, it contradicts the developed legal culture, the image of man and the understanding of the role the state has to play in the modern age. A free-of-blame criminal law that no longer blames the offender for violating the law would deprive the victim of its claim to ascertain the unlawfulness of the offence, consequently leading to the victim's revenge and self-justice. By taking the offender's chance of responding to the ethical reproach, it would reduce him from a subject actively involved in the trial into a mere passive object of a state's action; it would not treat him as a person capable of a moral action, but as a predator.[50]

This does not mean that criminal law could not be abolished at all. The great philosopher Hegel, who, as it's generally known, posed the abstract idea of punishment as a balance to guilt, a "negation of the negation," mentioned that, in future times, possibly a state of society would be reached in which the norms are so strongly anchored in society that punishment no longer would be necessary.[51] However, as long as the prevailing view in society is that its norm system suffers from crime and a governmental response to the crime in purpose of standardization is required, one must unavoidably adhere to the punishment, imposing a sanction that expresses an

[48]Cf. Lüderssen (1995) passim.

[49]Cf. Edney/Bagaric (2007), 333.

[50]Cf. Von Hirsch (2005), 33 ff. To the whole subject cf. Maihold (2005), 12 ff.

[51]Cf. Seelmann (2001), 857 ff., 866 ff.

ethical reproach *and thereby* directing an appeal to the perpetrator taking him as a moral person able to act reasonably.

Primary Literature

Aragon P (1597) In secundam secundae Divi Thomae Doctoris Angelici Commentaria. De iustitia et iure, Landry, Lugduni
Aristotle (2002) In: Broadie S, Rowe C (eds) Nicomachean ethics, Oxford University Press, Oxford
Azpilcueta M (1616) Opera, Gymnich, Coloniae Agrippinae
Castro A (1550) De potestate legis poenalis, Andreas de Portonariis, Salamanca (reprint Madrid 1961)
Covarrubias y Leyva D (1679) Opera omnia, Tournes, Coloniae Allobrogum
Friedberg E (1879–1881) Corpus Iuris Canonici, tom. 1/2, Tauchnitz, Lipsiae
Raymundus de Peniaforte (1603) Summa de poenitentia et matrimonio, Tallinus, Roma (reprint Meisenheim/Glan 1967)
Simancas J (1569) De catholicis institutionibus, Angulo, Compluti
Soto D (1582) De iustitia et iure, Pesnot, Lugduni
Suárez F (1612) Tractatus de legisbus ac Deo legislatore, Gomez de Loureyro, Conimbricae
Thomas Aquinas (1887–1894) Summa theologica, Romae
Vázquez de Menchaca F (1572) Controversiarum Illustrium aliarumque usu frequentium libri III., Feyerabend, Frankfurt am Main
Vitoria F (1932–1952) Comentarios a la Secunda secundae de Santo Tómas, Beltrán de Heredía PV (ed), Biblioteca de Teólogos Españoles, Salamanca
Vitoria F (1997) Vorlesungen II (Relectiones): Völkerrecht, Politik, Kirche, ed. by Horst U, Justenhoven H-G, Stüben J, Kohlhammer, Stuttgart

Secondary Literature

Achter V (1951) Geburt der Strafe. Klostermann, Frankfurt am Main
Bayertz K (1995) Eine kurze Geschichte der Herkunft der Verantwortung. In: Bayertz K (ed) Verantwortung: Prinzip oder Problem? Wissenschaftliche Buchgesellschaft, Darmstadt
Baylor MG (1977) Action and person: conscience in late scholasticism and the Young Luther. Brill, Leiden
Bock M (1991) Ideen und Schimären im Strafrecht. Z Gesamte Strafrechtswissenschaft 103:636–656
Castillo Hernández S (1941) Alfonso de Castro y el problema de las leyes penales, o, la obligatoriedad moral de las leyes humanas. Universidad de Salamanca, Salamanca
Edney R, Bagaric M (2007) Australian sentencing: principles and practice. Cambridge University Press, Cambridge
Erber-Schropp JM (2016) Schuld und Strafe: eine strafrechtsphilosophische Untersuchung des Schuldprinzips. Mohr Siebeck, Tübingen
Erhardt J (2014) Strafrechtliche Verantwortung und personale Identität, Dissertation, Universität Biel (lulu.com, November 9, 2014)
Frister H (1988) Schuldprinzip, Verbot der Verdachtsstrafe und Unschuldsvermutung als materielle Grundprinzipien des Strafrechts. Duncker & Humblot, Berlin

Grunert F (2013) Strafe als Pflicht: Zur Strafrechtslehre von Francisco Suárez (DL V). In: Bach O, Brieskorn N, Stiening G (eds) 'Autctoricas omnium legum'. Francisco Suárez', De legibus' zwischen Theologie, Philosophie und Jurisprudenz, frommann-holzboog, Stuttgart-Bad Cannstatt, p. 255–266
Jakobs G (1976) Schuld und Prävention. Mohr Siebeck, Tübingen
Jakobs G (1991) Strafrecht Allgemeiner Teil. de Gruyter, Berlin
Jeschek HH, Weigend T (1996) Strafrecht Allgemeiner Teil, 5th edn. Duncker & Humblot, Berlin
Jonas H (1979) Das Prinzip Verantwortung: Versuch einer Ethik für die technologische Zivilisation. Insel-Verlag, Frankfurt am Main
Kargl W (1982) Kritik des Schuldprinzips: Eine rechtssoziologische Studie zum Strafrecht. Campus, Frankfurt am Main
Kaufmann A (1961) Das Schuldprinzip: Eine strafrechtlich-rechtsphilosophische Untersuchung. Winter, Heidelberg
Köhler M (1997) Strafrecht Allgemeiner Teil. Springer, Heidelberg
Krämer K (2015) Individuelle und kollektive Zurechnung im Strafrecht. Mohr Siebeck, Tübingen
Lavenia V (2004) L'infamia e il perdono. Tributi, pene e confessione nella teologia morale della prima età moderna, Il Mulino, Bologna
López Riocerezo JM (1949) Doctrina de Fray Pedro de Aragón acerca de la Ley humano-positiva y efectos obligatorios de la Ley penal, Anuario de Derecho Penal y Ciencia Penales 242–262
Lüderssen K (1995) Abschaffen des Strafens? Suhrkamp, Frankfurt am Main
Maihold H (2000) "Der Sohn antwortet für den Vater nicht." - Die deliktische Sippenhaftung: Ein deutschrechtlicher Grundsatz? In: forum historiae iuris (www.forhistiur.de), Article of October 9, 2000
Maihold H (2005) Strafe für fremde Schuld? Die Systematisierung des Strafbegriffs in der Spanischen Spätscholastik und Naturrechtslehre, Böhlau, Köln
Maihold H (2005a) „Ein Schauspiel für den Pöbel"—Zur Leichnamsstrafe und ihrer Überwindung in der Aufklärungsphilosophie, (Rechtsgeschichtliche Vorträge 29), Budapest
Maihold H (2005b) Zur Geschichte der Verbandsstrafe. Himeji Law Review 44:380–361
Maihold H (2005c) Die Sippenhaft: Begründete Zweifel an einem Grundsatz des "deutschen Rechts." Mediaevistik 18:117–144
Maihold H (2011) El Castigo del pecado y la reprobación ética: La evolución del derecho penal moderno en la doctrina española del derecho natural. In: Cruz Cruz J (ed) Razón Práctica y Derecho. Cuestiones filosófico-jurídicas en el Siglo de Oro español, Eunsa, Pamplona, pp 125–136
Maihold H (2013) Die Bildnis- und Leichnamsstrafen im Kontext der Lehre von den crimina excepta. Z Savigny-Stiftung Rechtsgeschichte, Germanistische Abteilung 130:78–102
Maihold H (2014) God's wrath and charity—criminal law in (counter-)reforming discourse of redemption and retribution. In: Decock W et al. (eds), Law and religion: the legal teachings of the Protestant and Catholic reformations, Vandenhoeck & Ruprecht, Göttingen, p 149–173
Maihold H (2015) "das aus grosser barmhertzickeyt mus unbarmhertzig seyn"—Legitimation und Grenzen der Gottesstrafe in der theokratischen Strafrechtslehre des 16. und 17. Jahrhunderts. In: Piltz E, Schwerhoff G (eds), Gottlosigkeit und Eigensinn: Religiöse Devianz im konfessionellen Zeitalter, Duncker & Humblot, Berlin, p 51–82
Mañaricua Neure A (1949) La obligatoriedad de la ley penal en Alfonso de Castro. Rev Esp Derecho Canónico 4:35–64
Maurach R, Zipf H (1992) Strafrecht Allgemeiner Teil vol. 1, 8 ed, C.F. Müller, Heidelberg
Navarrete Urieta JM (1959) Alfonso de Castro y la ley penal. Rev De La Escuela De Estudios Penitenciarios 141:1405–1414
Roxin C (2006) Strafrecht Allgemeiner Teil, vol. 1, 4 edn, C.H. Beck, München
Savall D (1935) Fray Alfonso de Castro (1495–1558): La orientación voluntarista de su Derecho Penal. Arch Ibero-Americano 38:240–255
Schmidhäuser E (1963) Vom Sinn der Strafe. Vandenhoeck & Ruprecht, Göttingen
Schnyder S (2010) Tötung und Diebstahl: Delikt und Strafe in der gelehrten Strafrechtsliteratur des 16. Jahrhunderts, Böhlau, Köln

Seelmann K (2001) Hegel und die Zurechnung von Verantwortung. In: Britz G (ed) Grundfragen staatlichen Strafens. Festschrift für Heinz Müller-Dietz, C.H. Beck, München

von Freier F (2009) Zurück hinter die Aufklärung: Zur Wiedereinführung von Verbandsstrafen, Goltdammer's Archiv für Strafrecht 98–116

von Hirsch A (2005) Fairness, Verbrechen und Strafe: Strafrechtstheoretische Abhandlungen. Berliner Wissenschaftsverlag, Berlin

Liberties, Rights and Punishments in Modern Natural Law

Manuel Rodríguez Puerto

Abstract The aim of this chapter is to show the intersection of law and moral in criminal law from the point of view of legal theory in early Modernity. To understand this question, the chapter treats succintly the concepts of law, crime and moral good in the legal science of ius commune; this conception was based on an objectivized notion of justice; consequently, criminal law was conceived as a protection of basic moral goods. Legal theory of early modernity (centered here in the Modern School of Natural Law) described the law as a natural bundle of individual liberties. The legal order is designed to protect that freedom and, specifically, the aim of criminal law was to protect basic individual freedoms. Modern thought distinguished theological goods from legal principles, but the intention was the protection of the most important moral good: the individual freedom.

1 Introduction

The Enlightenment brought about fundamental changes in European criminal law concerning notions characteristic of what was considered jurisdictional society, and was heavily influenced by Romanist juridical science. It was Francisco Tomás y Valiente who spotlighted differences between the notions of criminal law held by Romanist and Enlightened jurists. Enlightened jurists were concerned with defending individual rights or freedoms and had substituted crosslinking crime and sin for a focus on social damages, working from the basis of new notions about reason and secularization.[1] These new ideas also led enlightened jurists to reject Romanist casuistry, the indeterminacy of penalties and the closely dependent judicial discretion based on the detailed consideration of crimes. Furthermore, Enlightened thought not only defended a strict principle of legality built around the State's regulatory

[1] Tomás y Valiente (1969), 93 ff., 238 ff. See also Prieto Sanchís (2001), 158 ff. Along similar lines, see Ferrajoli (1989), 157 ff. 211–212; and for an alternative viewpoint, Masferrer (2017), 693–756.

M. Rodríguez Puerto (✉)
Departmente of Public Law, University of Cadiz, Jerez de la Frontera, Spain
e-mail: mjesus.rodriguez@uca.es

A. Masferrer (ed.), *Criminal Law and Morality in the Age of Consent*, Ius Gentium: Comparative Perspectives on Law and Justice 84,
https://doi.org/10.1007/978-3-030-64163-4_3

monopoly, but also advocated the reform of punishments—criticising the cruelty of some of these—and the use of torture as a means of procedural investigation.

However, the following pages are not devoted to studying such specific aspects, but rather a theoretical question: the different orientations illustrated by the concepts of law defended by Romanists and enlightened jurists as a point of reference for their equally diverse notions about criminal law. This comparison will shed some light on the resulting transformation in the mentality of society with the advent of juridical Modernity and, to some extent, the relationships between morals and law, because criminal law provides protection for what society deems most valuable.

2 The Changes in the Concept of Law

For law, the arrival of modernity meant a radical change that affected various spheres of the theory and practice of jurists, and one of the most relevant aspects of this development is the process of subjectivising law. This process evolved in stark opposition to the juridical culture of *ius commune,* which had been drawn up during the Late Middle Ages via glosses and commentaries based on Justinian's compilation of Roman Law. These foundations had a decisive influence on how jurists characterized law during the Late Middle Ages and continued through to a world which modernity had to confront.

The notion of subjective right did not play a dominant role within this medieval concept of law, which is quite understandable since Roman jurists did not set out a precise concept of law in a subjective sense. This has been the subject of some debate among scholars of Roman law, such as Álvaro D'Ors who, based on his analysis of classical sources, concluded that these jurists were not aware of the modern distinction between objective and subjective right: they used the term *ius* to name a "just position", that is, the juridical qualification of a given situation which could embrace powers or duties.[2] D'Ors tempered his explanation by adding that he was not attempting to give a fixed definition of the concept of law in classical jurisprudence, but rather to demonstrate there was no clear distinction between objective and subjective right.[3]

The medieval Romanists, who worked from Roman texts as drawn up by Justinian's compilers, likewise were not predisposed towards a "subjectivised" notion of law. Indeed, glossators and commentators conceived of law in terms of a group of precepts which give form to the requirements of justice in a more specific manner.[4]

---

[2]D'Ors (1980), 306 ff.

[3]D'Ors (1955), 825. Roman Law was not a compendium of laws or individual powers, but instead a group of doctrines elaborated by the prudent when resolving problems put before them. D'Ors (1975), 11 ff. In any event, this issue has been a subject of discussion among scholars of Roman law. On this question, see Megías (2003), 35–54.

[4]That was the sense that Acursius gave to the identification of Law with an *ars*. See Acursius (1628) gloss "i" in Digesto, I, I, I. Some time later, Baldus degli Ubaldi also sees *ius* as a concretization of the tenets of justice; see degli Ubaldi (1599) com. 9 to *De iustitia et iure*, I, I, fol. 7. Concerning

These precepts regulated different human behaviours and shaped powers and faculties, but they did not constitute law itself. Although these jurists accepted that in certain situations law could consist of the power to act derived from the rules and requirements of this problem (e.g. ownership, usufruct or servitude), law did not immediately ensue from the subject's very personality, as was later claimed by the modernists. The theologian Thomas Aquinas was probably the one who best expressed that "objectivised" concept of law when he explained the object of justice (*ius*) emerges from the interpersonal relationship itself (*medium rei*), and not from the person of the very same agent. This Thomist concept has been clarified by philosophers of law such as Michel Villey, Javier Hervada and Francisco Carpintero.[5]

The importance given to the inter-relations and problems shaped by society led these jurists to think that law emerged from the *interpretatio* of laws linked to the circumstances of the case. Alien to a systematic way of thinking, they developed a casuistic law which complied an enormous number of flexible solutions adapted to the variability of everyday life.[6] For them the primary goal was a just resolution of the case and not a person's power or freedom. Consequently, the idea of law as faculty or power did not emerge from within *ius commune,* but instead belongs to the theological speculation which followed the guidelines set out by John Duns Scotus and his alternative to the objectivised consideration of justice advocated by Thomas Aquinas. It is true that canonists had already used *ius* with the sense of a faculty or power and that this meaning was used by those involved in the debate about apostolic poverty.[7] However, the theoretical reflections which understand law as a power or faculty regulated by the law appears with the theology stemming from Scotus, as demonstrated in the studies by Alejandro Guzmán and Francisco Carpintero.[8] The sixteenth and seventeenth centuries Spanish Scholastics, such as Luis de Molina and Francisco Suárez, played a major role in this process, though they linked juridical faculties to the prior existence of legislation which respected the objective demands of the nature of the thing and social utilities. In any event, their work was fundamental to developing law as a faculty.[9]

Paradoxically, a way was open for subjectivizing law within the very same Romanist juridical science: one of the meanings Roman law attributed to natural law, namely, equal freedom of everyone in the state of nature.[10] Jurists in the Late

---

the process of establishing Law by the *interpretatio* of legislators and jurists, see Vallejo (1992), 40 ff., 302 ff. Paolo Grossi highlights the independence between political power and common law: Law is not a product of political will, but rather of discovery, interpretation and adaptation by the intelligence of jurists; see Grossi (1996), 40 ff., 153.

[5]Villey (1979), 87 ff. Along similar lines, see also Hervada (1978), 42 ff. Hervada (1987), 156. See also, Carpintero (2002), 26; Carpintero (2004), 50 ff.

[6]On the question of how common law jurists worked, see Carpintero (1982). See also Lombardi (1975), 104 ff.

[7]Tierney (1997) per totum. See also, Kriechbaum (1996), 29 ff.; Helmholz (2003), 301.

[8]Carpintero (2003), 71 ff; Guzmán (2009), 21 ff.; also Brett (1997), Folgado (1960), 13–330.

[9]Carpintero (2003) and Guzmán (2009), 197 ff.

[10]Roman texts offered different meanings of natural law: what always is good and equitable, what nature teaches to every living being, the freedom of the state of nature, the basic moral tenets

Middle Ages did not extrapolate the need to base juridical and social order on individual freedom from this doctrine, rather it was simply another consideration to take into account when redacting their complex system of juridical regulations. However, this view changed in the sixteenth century when suspicious minds began to question jurisdictional objectivization. It was the Spaniard, Fernando Vázquez de Menchaca, who pointed out this new way of understanding natural law, as demonstrated by Francisco Carpintero: Vázquez had situated individual *utilitas* as the starting point of his political theories by understanding agreement between naturally free individuals as the key element to constructing all social and juridical order.[11] In the end, as a result of all these speculations in the early decades of the seventeenth century, jurists and theologians seemed to be clear that law essentially consists of a collection of powers and faculties exercised over individuals themselves, things and other people.[12]

The School of Modern Natural Law emerged from this theoretical juncture, which represented the culmination of the subjectivization of law. Although this may have begun with the considerations mentioned earlier (notion of law as a faculty, state of nature), it gives these factors a new direction to situate the origin of all law in the natural freedom of the individual.[13] This School was to build a theory of law from a rationalist and secular base that would transform society.[14] In particular, it was developed in protestant Germany beginning in the final decades of the seventeenth century thanks to the work of Samuel Pufendorf,[15] nevertheless these Iusnaturalists considered the Dutch jurist Hugo Grotius to be their precursor,[16] a choice which reflected a vested interest. These jurists, protestants, although critical of the then dominant Lutheran orthodoxy in the universities of Reformation Germany, could not

obtained through reason, the juridical solutions created by natural reason and existing in every nation (that is to say, the *ius gentium* which is always half way between natural and positive law). I am indebted to Francisco Carpintero's accurate and detailed study of these iusnaturalist doctrines characteristic of *ius commune*; see Carpintero (2000), 20 ff.

[11]See Carpintero's monograph (1977a, b) per totum. More recently, Carpintero (2000), 159 ff.

[12]This idea was also widespread among Romanists; a particularly illustrative example is the work by Hughes Doneau.

[13]Actually, this individualism was quite relative because the basis upon which to build the State through a social contract in many modern iusnaturalists is not the individual considered in isolation, but rather society. See Böhme (1993), 14 ff. According to him, this attitude is amended to some degree at the end of the eighteenth century.

[14]See Hervada (1987), 249 ff.

[15]Hans Welzel stated that modernity had defended two notions of human nature: one empirical and "existentialist" like Hobbes, and another idealized like Grotius: Both lines of thought would be present in Pufendorf's writings. See Welzel (1971), 116 ff., 133. Recently, Ian Hunter has described two paths in German Modern Iusnaturalism: one "metaphysical", which includes Christian Wolff and Inmanuel Kant; and another followed by Samuel Pufendorf and Christian Thomasius, which was built on jurisprudence and more empirical knowledge, concerned with building a society from civic humanism and individualistic empiricism. See Hunter (2001) 127 ff., 148 ff., 217 ff. Regardless of these differences, as pointed out in the following pages, all of them would agree on describing the basis of law as a strictly individual power or freedom.

[16]A good example of this historiography that enthrones Grotius as the initiator of this School is Christian Thomasius' book (1719), 65. On these iusnaturalist modern attitudes, see Francisco Carpintero's study (1988), 383–412.

use Catholic writers as foundation stones for their proposals, despite the role these had clearly played in establishing the notion of law as faculty. Although Grotius was no innovator and often cited Catholic theologians and jurists, he was at least protestant and his name could be used without raising eyebrows.[17] His *De iure belli ac pacis libri tres* had enough theoretical substance to perform this role, and in addition, as an Arminian, he had significant problems with Dutch Calvinist orthodoxy, as did Pufendorf and his followers with the Orthodox Lutherans.[18]

In any event, when dealing with the concept of law, Grotius follows the path laid out by Spanish Scholastics. In his treatise *De iure belli ac pacis libri tres*, he explains that there are three meanings to the term law. First, that which is just (in the Thomist sense), though he mentions this in passing to then forget it later; second, the idea of faculty and third, enacted law or rule. Of these, the one that most interests him is the meaning of faculty, which he defines as a "moral quality", pointing out that it is a strictly personal reality: it belongs directly to the person, even if it is projected onto a thing. Because of this moral quality, a person can licitly act or have something and this quality can be "perfect" (also called faculty) or less "perfect" (*aptitudo).* He considers the notion of moral quality as the meaning of the word *ius,* which constitutes law in its real sense.[19]

Significantly, he adds that this faculty or quality is manifest from two perspectives: *potestas* or freedom which is used to decide one's own acts; and *dominium,* which concerns things and our debtors. This is nothing especially new compared to what was said by Scholastics at that time. Grotius adds that the aim of society is to protect "what belongs" to each citizen (*suum*), comprising life, body, freedom and those goods necessary to live.[20] The notion that society exists to protect its citizens' goods was not new either: since the Middle Ages many clearly viewed political power as serving the common good. However, society now appears to be in accordance with the private goods of the individual (what belongs to them). Incidentally, Vázquez de Menchaca—whom Grotius had read—had already supported these ideas in much stronger terms.

Samuel Pufendorf, unlike Grotius, was not a writer of the transition: he was the first jurist to hold a chair in Natural Law and wrote a treatise expressly devoted to

[17]Francisco Carpintero points out that Grotius is an epigone of juridical humanism, and Pufendorf to some extent also. See Carpintero (1977b) *in fine*. Cfr. Also Bergh (2002), 70, 84.

[18]It is worth recalling that Protestantism maintained (and still does) a problematic relationship with the idea of natural law. Luther's fallen nature cannot sustain the kind of reasonable justification typical of iusnaturalist thought. On this problem, see Bohn (2004) per totum. It seems that this modern iusnaturalism had to look for its doctrines elsewhere, as did Scholasticism, in spite of the disdain that it inspired. In the middle of the twentieth century, Hans Welzel highlighted the historiographic renewal that shed light on the scholastic influences in modern iusnaturalism; Welzel (1971), 110 ff. Of course, modern iusnaturalists gave a different meaning to those contributions, but leaves room to question whether this difference came from the protestant position. Nevertheless, some authors see Lutheran influence in Samuel Pufendorf, for example, in his individualistic view. This is what Malte Diesselhorst stated in (1981), 198. However, this is a complex matter which requires further research.

[19]Grotius (1651) book I, chap. I, § IV ff., 2 ff.

[20]Grotius (1651) book I, chap. II, § I, 15.

this subject. It is true that it reflects some influences from juridical Humanism—there are abundant references to authorities dating to classical Antiquity,—but he is a clearly modern author. When he expounds the concept of law, he accepts the notion of moral quality which already held sway in the seventeenth century. Although he mentions other meanings, such as a statute, a compendium of a country's laws or a legal judgement, he writes that the "most frequent" definition is that of a moral quality, by which we command the people righteously, have goods or we are owed something.[21] Being more a philosopher than Grotius, Pufendorf delves into the theoretical foundations of the definition of law. He divides reality into two entities, *entia physica* and *entia moralia*: the former belong to the sphere of physical science and are governed by the necessary and mechanical laws; the latter belong to intelligence and freedom, which are, accordingly, created by intelligent beings through their free action and comprise both the commandments God gave to human beings as well as regulations established by man about his own life. The importance of this reflection cannot be stressed enough. It indicates that moral life—which includes law—is based on different manifestations of will which cannot be rooted in anything other than its very quality of being a free will: any reality alien to the combination of wills, belongs to the sphere of physical beings, consequently, it remains alien to the world of moral freedom. Some Premodern thinkers, like Thomas Aquinas or Romanist jurists, thought that law consisted of adjusting the rules and tenets to the requirements of a problem. Of course, for them law only existed among men, beings endowed with intelligence and free will; it was not induced only by a person's will, but rather mainly from the problematic surroundings and contexts in which human life developed.

When Pufendorf reduces jurisprudence to manifestations of will unpolluted by any external adherence to will itself, law consists of a combination of powers.[22] In fact, he explains that *ius* is both an active and passive moral quality, which consists of a power to demand something from somebody, but also presupposes the passive capacity to be a holder of those powers.[23] Being a passive moral quality, Pufendorf feels obliged to detail its different qualities. First it implies the power to own goods, but not to demand them nor an obligation to provide them. Second, it does not empower one to demand them, but it does oblige the counterparty voluntarily, "due to some moral virtue", because imposition is not admissible unless there is a pressing need. Third, and finally, it concerns the kind of moral qualities which do oblige completely as they are regulated by a law.[24] Consequently, Pufendorf understands law as the power

[21] Pufendorf (1759) book I, chap. I, § XX, 20.

[22] In fact, Pufendorf was the last manifestation of a tendency which began centuries before. All scholasticism that had followed the line taken by Duns Scotus since the fourteenth century posed moral life as adjusting to a series of commandments which, in the end, came from God. Less distant in time, Francisco Suárez had specified that obligation born from law was a necessary moral effect of the legislator's will, and this effect was completely different from effects resulting from physical causes. See Suárez (1967) book III, chap. XX, 9, 284. Concerning moral entities in Pufendorf, see Welzel (1986), 20–22.

[23] Pufendorf (1759) book I, chap. I, § XX, 20.

[24] Ibidem.

to demand certain behaviours with all the ensuing consequences. As mentioned before, these proposals are not completely new because they follow the scholastic line[25] (something that neither Pufendorf nor his followers wanted to acknowledge). Nevertheless, individualism and the subsequent rejection of an objective nature of the thing do separate these Iusnaturalists from the Scholastics.

From then onwards, all modern Iusnaturalists began to adopt this concept of law, independently from other foundational philosophical aspects. Christian Thomasius started from a more traditional viewpoint of law in his *Instituciones de Jurisprudencia Divina*, but in his later *Fundamenta iuris naturae et gentium*, he criticized Pufendorf's radical difference between the physical and moral entities. Notwithstanding, at both stages Thomasius maintains that law is a manifestation of power: the law as a commandment—the product of an *imperium*—which grants powers and faculties.[26] His follower, Nicolaus Hyeronimus Gundling, explained that "law is a freedom, faculty or active power, which Grotius calls the attribute of a person",[27] although it should be noted that he begins speaking about law in general and the eternal law created by God, the last instance of Justice.[28] This law, understood as power, can be divided into innate and acquired: the first one has at birth and by divine concession (for example, freedom, which is a right everybody has by nature); while acquired rights ensue from a human act, for example *imperium* or private property.[29] Christian Wolff and those jurists who followed him, in spite of their differences with the line set out by Thomasius, also work from the basis of law as an individual power and freedom. In this case, it is divine creation which imposes the duty to perfect oneself and grants the power or moral faculty to achieve this. This power, Wolff explains, is the law.[30] A similar viewpoint is maintained by his followers Daniel Nettelbladt and Ioachim Georg Darjes, who understand law as a faculty or power that lies within the individual.[31] The same line is adopted by Gottfried Achenwall[32] who, like the authors just before him, begins by expounding natural law and the obligations derived from it. The perfect obligation is that which, when there is a breach, entails a moral faculty which empowers victims to defend themselves by force against their attacker. This moral faculty is the law that Achenwall defines as the moral faculty which entails the existence of a perfect obligation; put another way, it is a natural right to demand something from somebody, including by coercion. He specifies that it is a perfect natural right in a subjective sense.

---

[25]On this question see Guzmán (2009), 223–224.

[26]Thomasius (1718), book. 1, chap. 1, § 13–14, 19 ff.

[27]Gundling (1728) chap. I, § LVIII, 19.

[28]Gundling (1728) chap. I, § II ff, 3 ff.

[29]Gundling (1728) chap. I, § LXI–LXII. Concerning changes in the German University by Thomasius, a critic of the dogmatically Lutheran teachings and a defender of a concept of a secularized law based on a theory of affections with empirical basis, see Hammerstein (1972), 61 ff., 73 ff.

[30]Wolff (1754), I, tome 1, § 45–46, 29–30.

[31]Nettelbladt (1767) pars III. Sect. IV, membrum I, *De iure in se spectato*. Chap. I, tit. I. § 229, 90. Cfr. Darjes (1764) special part, sect. I, chap. II, § 278, 146.

[32]Achenwall (1774) tit III § 37, 22 § 23–24.

Leaving aside linking law to being able to employ coercion (which was already widespread within modern Iusnaturalism), what I would now like to highlight is the link between obligation and law. Achenwall stresses that individuals are naturally obliged to preserve their life, therefore, they have a natural right consisting of a moral faculty to remove obstacles to this self-preservation.[33] Also in the mid-eighteenth century, Alexander Gottlieb Baumgarten set out the characteristics of moral action in his *Natural Law*, which has to be free to set out the natural laws which link human beings and corresponding obligations (*officia*). Among those obligations are those that man has towards other men, such as conceding to each their rights.[34] The law coincides with what belongs to everyone (clearly scholastic terminology) and includes all external use which does not contravene the laws, the option to force another person to fulfil an obligation if it cannot be achieved by other means, or remove the impediment for the use of the law.[35] According to Baumgarten, law understood in these terms is a moral faculty.

All of these considerations culminate with the advent of the Kantian school of thought. It is interesting to note that the development of Kantian theories in Law did not initially originate from the philosopher himself, but rather from the jurists who adopted his theories and published treatises on this question before Kant's contribution appeared.[36] One of these was Theodor von Schmalz, who claimed to be the first to apply Kant's theory to the *Naturrecht*.[37] Being a defender of systematic thought, like a good modern thinker he explains natural law with remarkable clarity in terms of two basic categories: absolute and applied natural law. As regards absolute natural law, he breaks this down into two sub-categories: pure and hypothetical law, and applied law. Schmalz' explanation of absolute natural law begins with the difference between scientific natural reality and the plane of freedom and reason, to which the plane of morals and law belongs. This is based on the Kantian tenet which requires individuals to be an end in themselves and not a means.[38] Original rights derive from here, from personal freedom, which form the core of the law within pure absolute natural law, namely, the right over oneself, over one's own actions and the right which manifests itself in the use of things. With the unfolding of these liberties, other rights are acquired, such as private property, which are part of acquired absolute rights. Applied natural law, means putting these natural principles into practice in the empirical world: it takes shape in the form of the State, which emerges from a social contract (Schmalz is not very clear about whether it belongs to absolute or applied natural law) and draws up the laws that contain positive law. When Kant made statements on the matter, he would see law as an outward emanation of an

---

[33] Achenwall had taught in Göttingen, where the German Enlightenment influenced by Thomasius was widespread. See Hammerstein (1972), 311–312.

[34] Baumgarten (1763) chap. 2, § 124–125, 57–58.

[35] Baumgarten (1763) chap. 2, § 156, 70.

[36] Cattaneo (1981), 69. Carpintero (1989), 16 ff.

[37] Schmalz (1795), 17.

[38] Schmalz (1795) chap. 4, § 39 ff., 43 ff.

inner freedom which all people have and which requires a universal law to regulate the co-existence of liberties.[39]

3 Romanist Criminal Law

The relationships between the concept of law and the contributions of criminal law by the *ius commune* jurists are not easy to unravel, because they did not set out to establish them as such. It is important to take into account that the criminal laws they commented on did not always have their origins in Roman law, but rather had been established by the rulers of their age. We might easily think, however, that if they saw law as the fruitful outcome of interpreting the needs of justice, they must have also understood punishments as legal realities embedded in these needs. Theologians adopted the same view. For example, Saint Thomas Aquinas addressed this issue when he dealt with vices contrary to justice, both in their commutative as well as distributive dimensions: the former contained illicit facts such as homicide, and the latter partiality or unfair bias against people.[40] It is worth remembering that all manner of illicit facts are included in these questions, which nowadays we would include in the strict sense of criminal law, such as civil liability and tort law. What is clear, however, is that the foundation of criminal prohibition is the existence of an objective good protected by Justice. Centuries later, Domingo de Soto, follower of Thomas Aquinas, also analysed crimes (without referring directly to them) when studying injustice and he explained that there is offence when harm is done to the law (*ius*), and that harm can affect people or their goods. And as the first temporal good is life, it is necessary to begin with homicide when studying this question.[41] A little later the theologian Luis de Molina elaborated his treatment of law according to the different human faculties; an offence harms these faculties, that is, rights.[42] It seems clear that for theologians the key to criminal protection (using anachronistic terms) lies in there being human goods in the form of rights or faculties, and in the end based on the nature of the thing, rigorously objective and expressed in natural law.

The jurists (as was usually the case) did not enter into too many detailed theoretical discussions, nevertheless they were quite clear about the foundations of criminal laws. One of the most well-known books on this subject edited in the sixteenth century was Alfonso de Castro's *De potestate legis poenalis libri duo*, in which he holds that in every criminal precept the legislator's main intention does not take form in the punishment, but rather leans towards one or other virtuous act.[43] The main problem

[39]Kant (1982) § C, 337. See Carpintero (1989), 103 ff.

[40]Aquinas (1978) II-II, q. 61 ff.

[41]Soto (1968) book. I. q. 1, 382.

[42]Molina (1614) tome II, *dispositio* I, 1.

[43]Castro (1921), book I, 332–333.

that concerns him is precisely the enforceability of criminal law, and that this is based on law being just according to the typical criteria in scholastic thought.

Antonio Gómez offers a pertinent example of the penal doctrines in jurisdictional society in his *Variae resolutions iuris civilis*, published in the sixteenth century, a work which was still being republished in the eighteenth century. He classifies crimes as either public or private, depending on their gravity. The difference lies in that anyone can bring charges for public crimes, whilst only the person affected can do so in the case of private crimes. Gómez adds that a public crime is first and foremost an offence against God, and hence an offence against everybody. In contrast, in every crime, both public and private, there is an offence against the republic and a part of it, hence it is a public good which is at stake.[44] Gomez holds that in crime prohibition exists by divine and natural law, hence ignorance is not admissible: natural instinct dictates that nobody should harm others or do to others what you would not want for yourself.[45] Gómez offers jurists an analysis of penalties and punishments corresponding to each crime, which allows us to see how he assesses the different protected goods. He begins with the crime of lèse majesté, which can be against the divine majesty, in other words heresy, or against the human majesty (the prince or the republic), and goes on to discuss homicide, violence, theft, injury and finally the "stellionatus", a term used for various crimes committed through deceit.[46]

The relationship with the divine order, and accordingly with the notion of sin, was usual in Romanist penal treatises, but we must not forget that the function of this branch of law is to protect human goods as established by the needs of justice, which the jurist interprets as objectivised. So, we need to be careful not to give too much credence to their identifying sin with crime, because these jurists and theologians also understood that goods and interests were at stake which lay within the natural world of humans.[47] For *ius commune* and for the theologians within the Thomist lineage, law was not a mere emanation of God's creative will. Within this order, human beings enjoyed a degree of relative autonomy to govern their own reality interwoven with varying and unpredictable circumstances, which meant that the viability of an eternal natural and immutable law governing all human actions was impossible. It is true that the ultimate basis of justice was theological, but this did not imply that all contents of law (including criminal laws) were of this nature. For this reason, the protection of the common good as something essentially human was a central consideration in criminal law.[48]

This perception of the relative autonomy of humans also appears in one aspect which would be decisive in shaping modernity: the role of freedom, characteristic of the state of nature. Following an established tradition of Romanist and theological thinking, Vázquez de Menchaca believed that defending oneself belonged to

---

[44]Castro (1921), book I, 5–7 and 17.

[45]Gómez (1794), tome 3, chap. 1, 34.

[46]See Gómez (1794), tome 3, chaps. 2–7.

[47]On this question, see Masferrer (2017) per totum.

[48]This characteristic of the thomist theology and the *ius commune* has been revealed by Carpintero (1992), 21–200. Carpintero (1992), 351–394. Carpintero (2000), 13 ff., 95 ff.

natural law and addressed the tutelage of goods such as one's own body. Furthermore, Vázquez de Menchaca based criminal liability on the fact that laws, including sentences, are a product of consensus.[49] Domingo de Soto also expressed the same opinion and, as we will see, this idea would prove important for modern Iusnaturalists.[50]

In any event, the Romanist juridical concepts, bound to casuistry and the objectivization of legal requirements, were not so concerned with the protection of the most strictly speaking personal dimensions of humans, with the recognised consequences in the criminal sphere.[51] On the other hand, this concern with specific cases led jurists to complex and somewhat long-winded arguments and references to judicial arbitration dedicated to adapting the punishment to the case.[52]

4 The Criminal Law of Modern Iusnaturalism

As we have already seen, these jurists maintain a very close interrelationship between individual freedom and law, and so criminal protection should then be oriented towards the protection of this freedom.

In the beginnings of the School of Modern Natural Law, Hugo Grotius reveals traditional traits when he discusses whether punishments are the result of commutative or distributive justice. According to his understanding, the offender deserves the punishment and with that, commutative justice comes into play.[53] Like the Scholastics, Grotius links the reality of crime to offence, and he explains that delinquents are not injured when they are punished.[54] He warns that offence must not be done to others if there is no motivation to obtain any good. This good is utility, not only for who has sinned but also those who did not concern themselves with whether there was a sin or not, or both.[55] Grotius explains that the aim of punishment is to correct: to prevent re-offending and to set an example.[56] However, he does not set out a list of rights and goods protected by criminal laws.

Samuel Pufendorf, who copiously quotes Grotius, continues with his explanations. He also questions whether imposing punishment falls to commutative or distributive justice, concluding that neither is well-equipped for this: crime is a deviation from the law; those who govern impose punishment—a task which requires a combination of

[49]See Vázquez de Menchaca (1564) book I, chap. 18, 3, p. Book 2, chap. 45, 3, p. 15.

[50]Soto (1968) book 5, q. art. 8.

[51]María Paz Alonso offers some examples of these damages for the individual in (1982) per totum.

[52]According to Benjamín González Alonso, the judicial decision was not always a caprice and an irregularity, because it was limited by doctrine and judicial style. See González Alonso (2003) p. 228 ff. A similar nuance is expressed by Pedro Ortego (2004), 230–233.

[53]Grotius (1651) book. 2, chap. 20, 2, p. 291.

[54]Grotius (1651) book. 2, chap. 20, 4, pp. 292–293.

[55]Grotius (1651) book. 2, chap. 20, 4, p. 294.

[56]Grotius (1651) book. 2, chap. 20, 9, p. 297 and 13, p. 302.

prudence along with the office of government—and this belongs to universal justice. Pufendorf is quite keen to argue that punishments are not a product of the social contract, but of the authority of the political sovereign (prevailing civil authority).[57]

A particularly important aspect of these detailed treatises is the role of the state of nature. The starting point of all modern iusnaturalists is natural rights, which refer to certain goods built on individual freedom: powers ranging from one's own body to external goods. In effect, Samuel Pufendorf maintains that natural law establishes the duties of humans towards themselves and others, such as not causing harm, and along these lines he analyses different damages to different goods and rights, such as homicide.[58] However, this analysis refers to the state of nature and here there is no *ius puniendi* because all individuals are on an equal footing, whilst imposing a punishment entails someone from a higher level. Criminal law, consequently, only emerges after the creation of a political society by means of a social contract drawn up by the sovereign. However, her/his mission is the protection of those natural rights, as the sovereign is, after all, the one authorized to defend them.

As regards the aim of punishments, Pufendorf places them in the realm of utility. He explains that it does not seem iniquitous that the one who inflicts harm should suffer harm, but in human punishments we must not simply consider the harm done, but rather the utility of the punishment. The goal of human punishment is to prevent damages and offences, which happens when the one who sinned corrects her/himself, when others forsake the desire to sin because of this example or when coercion is used to prevent the one who sinned from doing any further harm.

Following Grotius (whom he does not cite in this topic), Pufendorf states that the utility of punishment concerns both the one who sinned, the one who did not want the sin to exist and finally, everyone, because punishments encourage abstaining from similar acts.[59] In order to underline this utilitarian consideration, he states that within the human forum there is no vindictive justice which demands given punishments for given crimes according to a measure decided by nature, but rather the measure is the utility of the republic which is determined by the sovereign's prudence.[60] On the other hand, quantifying punishments will depend on the nature of the damaged object, which leads Pufendorf to offer a progressive scale of goods protected by criminal law. The first place is occupied by God and the most detestable acts are those which try to offend Him; next is disturbing public order in the community and finally those crimes which affect only one person. The latter are described within their own progressive ranking: the most important is life, which is the foundation of all temporal goods (expressed in the same terms as Domingo de Soto who, naturally, is not cited); next is damage to non-vital parts of the body, but without which life would become miserable; followed by crimes against families which are founded on

---

[57]Pufendorf (1759) book 8, chap. 3, § 4–5, 314 ff.

[58]Pufendorf (1759) book. 3, chap. I, § 1, pp. 297–98, § 7, 306–308.

[59]Pufendorf (1731) book 2, chap. 13, § 6 ff., 350–351.

[60]Pufendorf (1759) book 8, chap. 3, § 14, 356 ff. The relevant role of utility in Pufendorf is highlighted by Krieger (1985), 92 ff. Fiorillo (1992), 44, 50–51.

marriage; then actions which harm those things necessary for life or for a comfortable life; and finally, acts against honour and civil estimation.[61] One can easily see that the catalogue of protected goods is very similar to that established by Spanish Scholastics, although references to them are conspicuous by their absence from these pages. Certainly, it is important not to be misled by Pufendorf's use of the word "sin": his criminal theory is not a transposition of theological categories.

The importance of utility also leads him to state that certain acts, vices in themselves, must not be punished in so far as it is pointless to do so within the human forum. This is the case with internal acts, such as thinking about sinning or a desire, which should not be punished. It is likewise the case for those sins which neither directly nor indirectly relate to another human or society as the punishment of these acts lies in God´s hands. Another exclusion is the frequent vices of the soul derived from corrupting mortals, whose punishment with punishments would destroy the political community, unless they were very serious.[62] These explanations made by Pufendorf may seem quite liberal, but we must remember that the scholastic tradition since Thomas Aquinas had maintained that not all vices had to be forbidden, as this could lead to greater harm. Similarly, Spanish Scholastics had stated that internal acts should not be punished by the courts.[63]

Referring punishment to social utility was a growing trend among Pufendorf´s followers, such as Christian Thomasius and Nikolaus Hyeronimus Gundling. In *Institutiones de jurisprudencia divina*, Thomasius explains that the origin of political society originates from an external motive: the fear of evil or bad people, as opposed to marriage or paternity which are "intrinsic institutions". Consequently, *ius puniendi* is one of the powers a sovereign has.[64] He stresses that the aim of punishment is neither compensation nor restitution, but rather atonement, security and correction. In fact, what Thomasius has in mind is protecting rights because he immediately clarifies that atonement is the objective of divine not human punishment, while correction also refers to others and not only the perpetrator of the crime, which presupposes that the crime is public and known.[65] In his later *Fundamenta iuris naturalis et gentium*, he underlines the difference between divine and human punishments and consigns atonement exclusively to divine punishments and a matter for theologians.[66] Thomasius clarifies that the law originating from the *imperium*, and designed to keep the

---

[61] Pufendorf (1759) book 8, chap. 3, § 18, 342–343.

[62] Pufendorf (1759) book 8, chap. 3, 14, 332–334.

[63] Carpintero (2013), 101–109.

[64] Thomasius (1702) book III, chap. 6, § 12, p. 555, § 26, p. 558.

[65] Thomasius (1702) book 3, chap. 7, § 32 ff, 590 ff. Concerning the aims of punishment in Thomasius, see Cattaneo (1976), 24 ff. Cattaneo places this jurist among the initiators of the German Enlightenment and highlights his disengaging criminal law from theological roots. He also points out that the *emendatio generalis* has nothing to do with the re-education of the criminal but rather concerns intimidating in general. Cattaneo (1976), 33, 47–48.

[66] Thomasius (1718) book 3, chap. 7, § 3 ff., 278–279. Here the *officia circa poenas* appear among the duties of the people who live in society.

peace, imposes fear on the wicked by different means, among them punishment: it is the *ius puniendi*, which lies with the State.[67]

Gundling coincides with these considerations. He discusses at great length the self-defence of rights in the state of nature, which would be protected by the *ius puniendi* of the State: in effect, punishments depend on the sovereign. Gundling adds nothing to what was expounded by Thomasius concerning the aim of punishment, namely, the utility of the republic, that is to say, correction and security, and not expiation: the future good is the aim of the penalty.[68]

When the School was already consolidated, Gottfried Achenwall now saw the role of criminal law clearly in terms of protecting natural rights. As we have already seen, he stated that natural law consists of faculties aimed at self-preservation, which is a natural duty. As a consequence, there is a strict natural right to not tolerate the attacks of others who oppose a person's self-preservation. This right called the right of preservation and also the right of resistance, namely the right to oppose by force those who put a barrier to prevent self-preservation.

This act of force against whoever impedes self-preservation is a punishment in the philosophical sense. From this right of self-preservation descends *ius puniendi*, which includes actions that do harm to whom attacks and also to prevent similar acts from the same subject, or from others by example.[69] Once the political society (the *respublica*) is established, Achenwall explains that when a subject attacks the right of another, s/he does not fulfil their duties and so this deed is unjust and a damage. If it is a deliberate or maleficent deed, it is classified as a crime and especially, so if it wilfully transgresses criminal law, namely, one which carries a sanction if not followed. In contrast a culpable deed is quasi-delict. Independent of this classification, *ius puniendi* is the domain of the sovereign, because for the sake of public safety along with the sovereign's executive power, the right to try and secure the rights of each subject falls to the sovereign. Therefore, it is a right to use force against the criminal subject to defend the subject who is the object of the harm and to keep them safe and free from harm. This right to punish crimes is the jurisdiction of the sovereign, that is to say, to try to prevent delinquent subjects from not committing further crimes.[70] The scheme of ideas is already clear: the individual, in the state of nature, has a natural right to procure her/his self-preservation; once power has been conferred to the State, it is endowed with this right with the sole aim of maintaining security in the exercise of rights.

Alexander Gottlieb Baumgartem sets out very similar ideas, that is offence derived from the concept of law as a moral faculty: the action which prevents someone from exercising a duty.[71] He is especially concerned with expounding the possible harmful acts against the rights that could take place in the state of nature. He clarifies that

---

[67] Thomasius (1718) book 3, chap. 7, § 47, 158.

[68] Gundling (1744) chap. 13, § 5 and 6, 270 ff. Id. (1747) chap. 35, § 16–17, 424 ff. § pp. 430–431. Id. (1728) chap. 36, § 29 ff., 441–442.

[69] Achenwall (1774) chap. 6, § 109, 99.

[70] Achenwall (1774), book 3, Sect. 6, § 191, 193–194, pp. 175–177.

[71] Baumgarten (1763), chap. 2, § 148, pp. 67–68.

in this situation nobody has the right to punish another because punishment implies linking the punishment to the law, which requires *imperium*, something the state of nature, characterized by equality, does not have.[72] However, in this situation the right of defence does exist in the face of harm to the right.[73] After these considerations, as is common in this School, Baumgarten goes on to the study the social contract.

Christian Wolff adopts the same position. He starts from the rights of the individual in the state of nature. The damage of a perfect right is an offence, which is forbidden and, of course, not allowed. As nobody is allowed (*dürfen*) to commit an unjust act, nobody must be harmed, hence everyone has a right to not suffer a harm committed by another. And this right, which everyone has whoever they are, is the right of security; security because they are free from the fear of suffering harm. Because of this right, one is allowed to resist those who try to cause harm and this defence is a right that everyone has by nature to defend themselves and includes all those acts necessary to do so. Among these are acts to defend themselves from attacks, which implies the option of force against who intend harm. And this possibility may consist of the other envisaging the possibility of harm. As a consequence, one is allowed to cause a natural harm to the one who has harmed the right, so that s/he does not want to repeat the same action; at the same time, the example will be useful to prevent similar behaviour by others. Nature is that which gives everyone the right to punish anyone who harms them. As long as the punishment is intended to modify the convictions of the offender, it is a corrective punishment, and if it is intended to make others refrain from carrying out the same harmful action, the punishment is exemplary. Wolff highlights that these rights to security, defence, and imposing a punishment are included among people's innate rights.[74] After the creation of a political society by a social contract, this power to punish passes to the sovereign. In effect, among the final objective of the State is internal peace and order, namely, being free from the fear of the unlawful and of damage to rights. For this reason, the imposition of punishments is part of the ruler's rights: the State ensures that everybody's rights shall be respected and that citizens can get what it is legally due to them, which includes punishing those who harm rights.[75]

In the final phase of the School, which is represented by the Kantians as stated earlier, the role of criminal law is the same. Theodor von Schmalz, whose pioneering spirit in Kantian Iusnaturalism mentioned earlier, clearly states that the right to apply punishment, namely, the coercive right to defend oneself from unlawful attacks belongs to natural law, more specifically to hypothetical right.[76] These harmful acts by others can be the object of our right (that is, of our power), because they are contrary to legal obligations and they affect the external freedom of another or the rights on which this freedom is founded (original or derived) and they bestow the right to act against the offenders. This proposition can be expressed in another

[72]Baumgarten (1763), chap. 1, § 24, p. 86.

[73]Baumgarten (1763), chap. 6 ff § 123 ff., pp. 116 ff.

[74]Wolff (1754) § 90–95, pp. 56–59.

[75]Wolff (1754) p. II, § 972, p. 697, § 1028, pp. 740–741, § 1043, pp. 754–755.

[76]Schmalz (1795) chap. 9, 93, p. 75.

way: no person shall harm another, which does not require any additional proof or argument.[77] In hypothetical natural law, Schmalz does not distinguish between what we nowadays would call civil liability and crimes, or between *dolus*—or criminal intent—and negligence—or culpability.[78] The perpetrator of the harm has the duty to indemnify and to cease said actions, and failure to do so means s/he no longer merits the respect which derives from the dignity of her/his rational nature. At this moment, the option of defending oneself from the acts of the aggressor arises. Although interfering in the acts of others (it is the original right) is generally prohibited, this prohibition disappears when dealing with impeding an act contrary to reason, as is the case with the party who harms someone else.[79] According to Schmalz, the right to self-preservation is not the justification for this intervention, because it is licit to impede harmful actions directed at other people. The key is that the perpetrator forfeits her/his right to not be harmed.[80] The punishment appears in the act of defence, which is returning the legal harm to the one who acted against the right of another. This nuance is important for Schmalz: there is only punishment when a right is affected, and in addition, it is licit in this case to interfere in the right of others against their will as they have forfeited this right because of the very unlawfulness of their first act.[81] Once the State has been established by a social contract, the individual's right to punish or impose punishment, passes to the State.[82] On this point, Schmalz distinguishes between the basis of the right to punish and the purpose behind applying the punishment: the former is the combination of rights and their limitations, which is founded on absolute natural law; and in the case of the latter, the reasons operate on a more empirical level. In effect, these aims can be to correct either the offender or others, though Schmalz clarifies that this correction refers only to improving the person as a citizen and not to their inner perfection. In contrast, prevention must be understood as an educating process from childhood onwards in which the punishment is associated with the crime and physical rejection is added to moral rejection.[83] Some years before, Schmalz had written that the aim of the right to punish was to safeguard rights by example.[84]

From this moment of reflection onwards, Schmalz abandons the fixed laws of reason, because he states that the limits, degrees and kinds of punishments do not come from the rules of the external right (understood as natural rights); instead they must be established by free political choice and the prudence of legislators. Among other things, it would be necessary to take into account the harmful effects of criminal action on the everyone; otherwise, there is no general and complete criminal law. There are crimes that are punished in all civilized countries, but many others which

---

[77] Schmalz (1807) book 4, chap. 3, 147–149, pp. 135–136.

[78] Schmalz (1807) book 4, chap. 3, 137.

[79] Schmalz (1807) book 4, chap. 3, 141.

[80] Schmalz (1807), 144.

[81] Schmalz (1807), 147.

[82] Schmalz (1795), chap. 11, 172, p. 113. Schmalz T von (1807) book 5, chap. 5, pp. 377 ff.

[83] Schmalz (1807), book 5, chap. 5, p. 380.

[84] Schmalz (1795), chap. 9, 93, p. 75.

depend on a range of circumstances: indemnity is impossible, the degree of danger the act involves or a particular interest by the State.[85]

Schmalz's scheme was to be the habitual one found among these Kantian iusnaturalists. Wilhelm Traugott Krug, for instance, states that criminal law has no other purpose than to ensure or protect the right (*Recht*), which is achieved by exercising coercion over the will and the forces of the one who causes damage to the right. This coercion is exercised in two ways. First, a threat which impedes the execution of the evil will by the subject who wants to harm a right. Second, removing the will to harm a right, that is, the means by which this is achieved. It is also possible to obstruct the power to cause said damage or to eliminate it.[86] We find a similar attitude in Anton Bauer who, like all his colleagues, states that right as a faculty derives from reason itself: an attribute of a person which includes arbitrary acts that co-exist with other similar attributes.[87] But once the State has been established, its power is aimed at safeguarding rights and the goal of sovereign rights is legal certainty. The State is immediately charged with this task and does so in two ways: defending the limits of every right and threatening harm to a right with the application of a punishment (the latter is the function of criminal law).[88] These are nothing more than state institutions in charge of dealing with damages to rights, and to this end they can use coercion. According to Bauer, a punishment is the legal outcome of damaging a right and a law which threatens with a perceptible harm based on the need to preserve everyone's rights.[89] Protected rights are those affected by public or state crimes that harm the rights of the State: they represent an attack on the State as a whole, endanger its very existence by attacking the dignity of state authorities, or they are an attack on the power of the State. Private crimes, in turn, refer to the rights of the State's subjects, both those of the individual as well as those of the citizen (such as life).

It is striking that Kant himself adopted a particular position towards punishment by defending a retributive concept of punishment based on the offender contravening universal law and on the person's defence as an end in itself: punishment cannot be used with utilitarian aims.[90] This posture was not shared by other authors who, like Schmalz, had applied practical criminal philosophy to criminal law.[91] As regards other matters, Kant writes about public and private crimes along somewhat traditional lines and, all said and done, the key to the Kantian proposal is also to protect natural

---

[85]Ibid.

[86]Krug (1811) § 25, pp. 123 ff.

[87]Bauer (1808) § 39, p. 44.

[88]Bauer (1808) § 224, pp. 255–256.

[89]Bauer (1808) § 248, p. 284.

[90]Kant (1982), 452 ff. One analysis of the polemics about the retributive concept of punishment expounded by Kant is given by Mario Cattaneo (1981) pp. 189 ff. Cattaneo thinks that Kant's greatest contribution to criminal law is supporting a person's dignity conceived as an end in itself. Cattaneo M (1981), 270.

[91]Naucke (1969), 30 ff.

rights (conceived as freedoms), as it corresponds to what he calls public law in which criminal law is embedded.[92]

5 Conclusions

When Cesare Beccaria sets out his reform of criminal law, he states that laws are agreements between free men, responding to the needs of men tired of the continuous state of war. Through this pact they sacrificed part of their freedom to enjoy the rest with assurances under the auspices of sovereign power. One of the attributes of this sovereign is the right to punish crimes in the defence of public safety, and the justification and level of punishments reflects the damage caused to society.[93] As we have seen, these were not original approaches, because Beccaria limited himself to following in the footsteps of the School of Modern Natural Law. We find a similar situation with Manuel de Lardizábal and his explanations about basing punishments on the protection of reserved freedom after establishing the social contract.[94] Both Beccaria and Lardizábal criticized Romanist juridical science and advocated clear laws which did not need to be interpreted and allowed legal certainty instead of casuistry and legal arbitration characteristic of the jurisdictional society, which still existed when their books were written. Therefore, the change that involved the transition from the juridical science of *ius commune* to the iusnaturalist is evident. Elevating the free individual as the keystone of all legal systems necessarily led to conceiving criminal law as a reality which originally lies in the natural right to self-defence of individual freedom and, after the social contract, resides in the State's protection of these very freedoms. In line with their assumptions, these iusnaturalists did not expound criminal law as the sum of punishments in the face of heterogeneous behaviours, but rather the defensive barrier that protects the spheres of freedom. Behind this essential difference it appears equally clear that the criminal law of Modern Natural Law was very dependent on its individualistic practical philosophy: an alliance between law and morals, despite the apparent separation claimed by writers like Thomasius. Furthermore, in the end this separation practiced by modern thinkers is a response to a moral reason. In effect, when clearly distinguishing theological and juridical questions, the intention is to achieve greater security in order to protect the spheres of freedom. The aim is not the evaluative asepsis of what is legal, but rather the defence of natural rights. That is precisely the mission of criminal law.

---

[92] Kant (1982), 452 ff.

[93] Beccaria (2008) § 1 ff, pp. 4 ff, § 7, p. 15. Beccaria bitterly criticises Romanist juridical science (cfr. Preface p. X ff.) and asks that it be removed from juridical interpretations of laws (§ 4, pp. 8–9).

[94] Lardizábal (2001), 111–112. On the other hand, Lardizábal criticises Rousseau's contractualism (pp. 117–118), because he believes it is contrary to Christianity.

References

Primary Literature

Accursio (1628) Digesto, Corpus Iuris Civilis iustinianei, cum commentariis Acursii, scholis Contis, et D, Gothofredi lucubrationis ad Acursium. Lyon (Reprint de Otto Zeller, Osnabrück, 1965)
Achenwall G (1774) Prolegomena iuris naturalis in usum auditorium. Gottingen
Bauer A (1808) Lehrbuch des Naturrechts. Marburg
Baumgartem AG (1763) Ins Nature. Halle
Beccaria C (2008) Tratado de los delitos y de las penas. Granada, Comares
Darjes GI (1764) *Institutiones Iurisprudentiae Univeralis in quibus omnia iuris naturae socialis et gentium capita in usum auditorii sui methodo scientifica explanantur*. Jena (6ª ed)
de Castro A (1921) De potestate legis poenalis libri duo. L. Sánchez Gallego´s edition, Publicaciones de la Universidad de Murcia, Murcia
de Lardizábal M (2001) Discurso sobre las penas. Servicio de Publicaciones de la Universidad de Cádiz, Cádiz
de Molina L (1614) De iustitia et iure opera omnia. Venetiis
de Soto D (1968) De iustitia et iure. Instituto de Estudios Políticos, Madrid
degli Ubaldi B (1599) In primam digesti veteris partem commentaria. Venetiis
Gómez A (1794) Variae resolutiones juris civilis, communis, et regii tomis tribus distinctae. Madrid
Grotius H (1651) De Jure belli ac pacis libri tres. Amsterdam
Gundling NH (1728) Ius naturae ac gentium connexa ratione novaque methodo elaboratum et a praesumtis opinionibus aliisque ineptiis vacuum. Halle
Gundling NH (1744) Erläuterung über Samuelis Pufendorfi zwey Bücher De Officio. Hamburgo
Gundling NH (1747) Ausführlicher Discours über das Natur- und Völcker-Recht. Frankfurt/Leipzig
Hammerstein N (1972) Jus und Historie. Vandenhoek & Ruprecht, Gottingen
Kant I (1982) Die Metaphysik der, Sitten. W. Weischeidel, Suhrkamp, Frankfurt/M
Krug WT (1811) Naturrechtliche Abhandlungen oder Beiträge zur natürlichen Rechtswissenschaft Leipzig
Nettelbladt D (1767) Systema elementare universae iurisprudentiae naturalis in usumpraelectionum academicarum adornatum. 3ª ed. Halle
Pufendorf S (1731) De officiis hominis et civis prout ipsi prascribuntur lege naturali libri duo. Giessen
Pufendorf S (1759) De Jure Naturae et Gentium libri octo. In: de Mascovius G (ed) Frankfurt und Leipzig (Reprint de Minerva GMBH, Frankfurt a. M, 1967)
Suárez F (1967) Tractatus de legibus ac Deo legislatore. Instituto de Estudios Políticos, Madrid
Thomasius C (1702) Institutiones Iurisprudentiae Divinae libri tres. Halle
Thomasius C (1718) Fundamenta juris naturae et Gentium. Halle/Leipzig
Thomasius C (1719) Paulo plenior Historia Juris Naturalis. Halle
Vázquez de Menchaca F (1564) Controversiarum Illustrium aliarumque usu frequentium libri tres. Venetiis
von Schmalz T (1795) Das reine Naturrecht. Königsberg. This is a reprint entitled *Das Recht der Natur* (Scientia, Aalen, 1969)
von Schmalz T (1807) Handbuch der Rechstphilosophie. Halle (Reprint Scientia, Aalen, 1970)
Wolff C (1754) Grundsätze des Natur- und Völkerrechts worin alle Verbindlichkeiten und alle Rechte aus der Natur des Menschen in einem beständigen Zusammenhange hergeleitet warden. Halle (Reprint de Scriptor, 1980)

Secondary Literature

Alonso MP (1982) El proceso penal en Castilla (siglos XIII-XVIII). Ediciones Universidad de Salamanca, Salamanca
Aquinas T (1978) Summa Theologiae. BAC, Madrid
Böhme H-J (1993) Politische Rechte des Einzelnen in der Naturrechtslehre des 18. Jahrhunderts und in der Staatstheorie des Frühkonstitutionalismus. Duncker & Humblot, Berlin
Bohn J (2004) Herrschaft ohne Naturrecht. Duncker & Humblot, Berlin
Brett AS (1997) Liberty, right and nature: individual rights in later scholastic thought. Cambridge University Press, Cambridge
Carpintero F (1977a) Del Derecho natural medieval al Derecho natural moderno: Fernando Vázquez de Menchaca. Servicio de Publicaciones de la Universidad de Salamanca, Salamanca
Carpintero F (1977b) <<Mos italicus>>, <<mos gallicus>> y Humanismo raconalista. Ius Commun 6:108–171
Carpintero F (1982) En torno al método de los juristas medievales. Anuario Hist Derecho Esp 52:617–647
Carpintero F (1988) La Modernidad Jurídica y los católicos. Anuario De Filosofía Del Derecho 5:383–412
Carpintero F (1989) La cabeza de Jano. Servicio de Publicaciones de la Universidad de Cádiz, Cádiz
Carpintero F (1992a) Nuestros prejuicios sobre el derecho natural. Persona y Derecho 20:21–200
Carpintero F (1992b) Historia y justicia según los juristas de formación prudencial. Anuario de Filosofía del Derecho 9:351–394
Carpintero F (2000) Historia breve del Derecho Natural. Colex, Madrid
Carpintero F (2002) Tomás de Aquino ante la ley natural. Dikaiosyne 8:11–60
Carpintero F (2003) El desarrollo de la facultad individual en la Escolástica, in VV.AA., El derecho subjetivo en su Historia. Servicio de Publicaciones de la Universidad de Cádiz, Cádiz: 35–288
Carpintero F (2004) Justicia y ley natural: Tomás de Aquino y los otros Escolásticos. Servicio de Publicaciones de la Facultad de Derecho de la Universidad Complutense, Madrid
Carpintero F (2013) Francisco Suárez defendió la libertad de conciencia, In: Estudios de Filosofía del Derecho y Filosofía política. Homenaje a Alberto Montoro Ballesteros. Servicio de Publicaciones de la Universidad de Murcia, Murcia
Cattaneo M (1976) Diritto e pena nel pensiero di Christian Thomasius. Giuffrè, Milano
Cattaneo M (1981) Dignità umana e pena nella filosofia di Kant. Giuffrè, Milano
Diesselhorst M (1981) Zur Zwei-Reiche-Lehre Martin Luthers, in Lombardi L/Dilcher G (eds.) Cristianesimo, secolarizzazione e diritto moderno. Nomos/Giuffrè, Baden-Baden/Milano, 141–197
D'Ors A (1955) Varia Romana. Anuario de Historia del Derecho Español: 825–835
D'Ors A (1980) Aspectos objetivos y subjetivos del concepto de <<ius>>. Nuevos papeles del oficio universitario. Rialp, Madrid, 280–311
D'Ors A (1975) Elementos de derecho Privado romano. EUNSA, Pamplona
Ferrajoli L (1989) Diritto e ragione. Laterza, Bari
Folgado A (1960) Evolución histórica del concepto del Derecho subjetivo. Estudio especial en los teólogo-juristas del siglo XVI. Biblioteca 'La Ciudad de Dios' Pax Iuris, San Lorenzo de El Escorial. It was also published in (1960) Anuario Jurídico Escurialense I: 13–330
Fiorillo V (1992) Tra egoismo e socialità. Il Giusnaturalismo di Samuel Pufendorf, Jovene, Napoli
González Alonso B (2003) Jueces, justicia y arbitrio judicial. Algunas reflexiones sobre la posición de los jueces ante el Derecho en la Castilla moderna. In: Vivir el Siglo de Oro. Poder, Cultura e Historia en la época moderna. Ediciones Universidad de Salamanca, Salamanca: 223–242
Grossi P (1996) L´ordine giuridico medieval. Laterza, Roma/Bari
Guzmán A (2009) El derecho como facultad en la Neoescolástica española del siglo XVI. Iustel, Madrid
Helmholz RH (2003) Natural human rights: the perspective of the Ius commune. Catholic Univ Law Rev 52:301–325

Hervada J (1978) Introducción crítica al derecho natural Pamplona. EUNSA, Pamplona
Hervada J (1987) Historia de la ciencia del derecho natural. EUNSA, Pamplona
Hunter I (2001) Radical enlightenments: civil and metaphysical philosophy on early modern Germany. Cambridge University Press, Cambridge
Kriechbaum M (1996) Actio, ius und dominium in den Rechtslehren des 13. und 14 Jahrhunderts. Aktiv, Ebelsbach
Krieger L (1985) The politics of discretion. Pufendorf and the acceptance of natural law. The University of Chicago Press, Chicago
Lombardi L (1975) Saggio sul diritto giurisprudenziale. Giuffrè, Milano
Masferrer A (2017) La distinción entre delito y pecado en la tradición penal bajomedieval y moderna una propuesta revisionista de la historiografía española, europea y Anglosajona. Anuario Hist Derecho Esp 87:693–756
Megías JJ (2003) El derecho subjetivo en los juristas romanos. Rev Estud Hist-Jurídicos Valparaiso 25:35–54
Naucke W (1969) Über den einfluss Kants auf theorie und praxis des strafrechts im 19 Jahrhundert. In: Blühdorn J, Ritter J (eds) Philosophie und Rechtswissenschaft. Vittorio Klostermann, Frankfurt a. M
Ortego P (2004) Notas sobre el arbitrio judicial *usque ad mortem* en el Antiguo régimen. Cuadernos de Historia de Derecho, 211–233
Sanchís LP (2001) La filosofía penal de la Ilustración. In: Barba PG, Fernández E, Asís R (eds.) Historia de los derechos fundamentales. Tomo II: S. XVIII. Vol. II: La filosofía de los derechos humanos. Dykinson, Madrid: 127–244
Tierney B (1997) Origins of natural rights language: texts and contexts, 1150–1250 and the beginning of the dispute. The idea of natural rights, natural law and church law. Scholar Press, Atlanta, pp 1150–1625
Tomás y Valiente F (1969) El derecho penal de la monarquía absoluta. Tecnos, Madrid
Vallejo J (1992) Ruda equidad, ley consumada. Concepción de la potestad normativa (1250–1350). Centro de Estudios Constitucionales, Madrid
van der Bergh GCJJ (2002) Die hollandische elegante Schule. Frankfurt a.M: Vittorio Klostermann
Villey M (1979) Compendio de filosofía del derecho. Trans. Diorki (revised by Valdés J, Valdés M), vol. I, EUNSA, Pamplona
Welzel H (1971) Introducción a la filosofía del derecho. Trans. by F. González Vicén, Aguilar, Madrid
Welzel H (1986) Die naturrechtslehre Samuel Pufendorf. De Gruyter, Berlin/New York

Roman Dutch Criminal Law and Calvinism: Calvinist Morality in *De Criminibus* (1644) of Antonius Matthaeus II

Janwillem Oosterhuis

Abstract The pervasiveness of Calvinism and Calvinist morality on criminal law in the early modern Dutch Republic, is shown through an analysis of the work of Antonius Matthaeus II, *De criminibus* (*On crimes*) of 1644. In Matthaeus's restatement of criminal law, certain inherent ambiguities of Calvinism become manifest. Matthaeus's Calvinist conviction becomes particularly evident in contested issues of criminal law. At these places, in discussion with Civil and Canon lawyers, but particularly also with other Reformed theologians and legal scholars, Matthaeus developed his own stance, on how to interpret and explain Roman criminal law and local customary criminal laws in light of the orthodox—Calvinist—religion. Matthaeus's consequent Calvinism can help to explain certain 'modern' opinions, such as his rejection of torture as a mean to achieve confessions. Due to the absolute primacy of divine will and law in *De criminibus*, the role of natural, practical reason remains quite limited. Indeed, although Matthaeus distinguished between moral and enduring laws with direct bearing on criminal law and religious prescripts without such direct consequence for the law, he failed to give any clear reason or criterion for such distinction. For criminal law, the enduring moral laws were to be found mainly in the Decalogue and the Mosaic Laws that explicated those commandments. According to Matthaeus, these enduring moral laws of the Decalogue corresponded with natural law. Importantly, Matthaeus did not equate all biblical teachings with enduring moral laws valid for the courts on earth. He notably refused to criminalize heresy. Indeed, for Matthaeus apparently many of the teachings of Jesus and the apostles concerned the conscience and what was right before the court of conscience. Matthaeus did not, however, provide a consistent reasoning for the underlying distinction between 'private' and 'public' morality. Despite a lack of theoretical clarity in distinguishing between divine and natural law, 'public' and 'private' morality, and enduring morals

A draft of this paper I presented at the American Society of Legal History, Houston, Texas, 9 November 2018: I am indebted to the detailed comments of Jacob Giltaij, Willem Geelhoed and particularly Aniceto Masferrer.

J. Oosterhuis (✉)
Maastricht University, Maastricht, Netherlands
e-mail: janwillem.oosterhuis@maastrichtuniversity.nl

A. Masferrer (ed.), *Criminal Law and Morality in the Age of Consent*, Ius Gentium: Comparative Perspectives on Law and Justice 84,
https://doi.org/10.1007/978-3-030-64163-4_4

laws and religious prescripts, for Matthaeus eventually personal faith and dedication to God was distinct from law: the orthodox religion had to be taught, rather than imposed.

1 Introduction

This chapter discusses the influence of Calvinism and Calvinist morality on criminal law in the early modern Dutch Republic, using the work of Antonius Matthaeus II, *De criminibus* (*On crimes*) of 1644 as a point of reference.[1] The Dutch Republic between 1600 and 1650 largely precedes the modern secularization of society.[2] In this period there still is a strong and intimate connection between state and church, or rather magistrate and church.[3] Religious belief and practice were still part of everyday life; people were basically all living inside various religious communities.[4] Apart from maybe a few exceptions, religious belief and practice as such were not challenged or problematized, unlike for instance in our own age.[5] Moreover, Calvinism was a dominant current within the Reformed religion in the early modern Dutch Republic. The conditions in this period seem ideal for Calvinism for exercising a strong influence on the Dutch legal environment, including criminal law—unlike for instance in the late nineteenth and twentieth centuries.[6] The question is how a Calvinist legal scholar like Matthaeus chose to restate criminal law in line with his Calvinist conviction. The possible consequences of the influence of Calvinism on the work of Matthaeus have not been systematically analyzed.[7] Such analysis of Matthaeus's work for his underlying religious convictions might help to explain why he defended certain positions,

[1]For translation and references the reprint of the fifth 1761 Antwerp edition is used, Matthaeus (1987–1996). Book, title, chapter and section references apply to any edition; the page references are to the 1761 edition unless indicated otherwise.

[2]See Taylor (2007), 1–22. Taylor distinguishes three types of secularization: (i) separation between state and church at an institutional level, i.e. the secularization of the public space; (ii) secularization as the decline of religious belief and practice in society; and, (iii) secularization of the conditions of religious belief and practice, i.e. challenging and problematizing religious belief and practice.

[3]On the deep interrelation between church and state in this period, Van Deursen (1991), 298–309; Van Deursen (2010), 1035–1078. For Early Modern Calvinist ideas and theories on the relation between church and state see e.g. Witte (2008), 62–76, 89–94, 122–134. Although since the beginning of the Dutch Revolt around 1568, the Reformed Church had developed relatively independent from the authorities, soon the various States started to take more and more control in Church matters. See e.g. E Rabbie, in: Grotius (1995), 11–16.

[4]See e.g. Van Deursen (1991), 1–5, 227; Israel (1998), 392.

[5]See e.g. Taylor (2007).

[6]For an analysis of the influence of Calvinism and Calvinist morality on criminal law in the late nineteenth and twentieth centuries, see e.g. Pompe (1956), 428–437; and on the relation between Calvinism and Calvinist morality and criminal law in this period fundamentally and in great detail, Stamhuis (1988).

[7]See e.g. Broers (2006), 14, 66. See in general e.g. Schlüter (1929); Van de Vrugt (1982, 1986), 23–35, here 24–25, 28–31; Van de Vrugt (1987), 166–170.

including quite 'modern' ones, such as the inadmissibility of torture in achieving confessions.[8]

To single out possible Calvinist elements in Matthaeus's work, first some general characteristics of Calvinism are discussed, also in contrast with Arminianism, a competing current within the Reformed religion in the early modern Dutch Republic. The Calvinist approach to law is characterized by the absolute authority of divine law, also over the state, and the importance of the Decalogue for the ordering of social life. Matthaeus's treatise on criminal law will be analyzed for these elements. Finally, a conclusion will be drawn about the pervasiveness of Calvinism and Calvinist morality in the work of Matthaeus.

2 Calvinism Versus Arminianism

Calvinists had strong ideals about the malleability of society, the idea that society could be reshaped and reformed—society as a whole and not just the church. In early Calvinism, no strict boundaries between religion, church and state were drawn yet: all were integral part of society.[9] Calvinist scholars unequivocally placed divine law above all other laws, including natural law. In this sense, Calvinists were more voluntarists than rationalists: they referred directly to the revealed will of God. God's will, also in matters of predestination and grace, was paramount. The correct interpretation of divine will was crucial: dogmas did matter. In Calvinist thinking—and also Lutheran for that matter—the Decalogue or Ten Commandments were dealt with as a central piece of legislation, as legal rules valid for contemporary society.[10] In religious matters, Calvinists made the state essentially subordinate to the church: magistrates had to rule and shape society in accordance with the correct biblical—Calvinist—teachings.[11] According to for example Jean Calvin (1509–1564) and Theodore Beza (1519–1605), a magistrate was the custodian of both tables of the Decalogue. Through the Decalogue, God outlawed all positive laws of the Christian state that were considered impious or unjust. Impious laws violated the First Table commandments against false gods, graven images, blasphemy, or Sabbath breaking.

---

[8]Less conclusive are e.g. Schlüter (1929), 2–3; De Monté VerLoren (1942), 1, 215; Van de Vrugt (1982), 37–38; Margaret Hewett, Biographical Notes, in: Matthaeus, *De criminibus* I, p. xx; Broers (2012), 78.

[9]See e.g. Taylor (2007), 126–128; Witte (2008), 89 ff. Contrary to clearer boundaries drawn between law, nature, morality and religion in eighteenth and nineteenth centuries criminal legal scholarship, see e.g. Masferrer (2021a, b), 1–27, 97–144; or the sharp distinction between law, morality and religion in Domingo (2016), 166–169.

[10]See e.g. Witte (2008), 127–129, 183. On Lutheranism, see e.g. Witte (2002), 113–115; Remmelink (1989), 4–5 (although Luther himself was against a direct application of Mosaic laws—other than the Decalogue—on contemporary society); Pihlajamäki (2006), 171–204, here 179–180.

[11]Witte (2008), 127. In Luther's two-kingdom theory, the equality between magistrate and church, and also family, was more absolute, Witte (2002), 5–8, 108–113.

Unjust laws violated the Second Table commandments against killing, stealing, adultery, perjury, and coveting.[12] Positive laws could thus be evaluated in light of the Decalogue and moreover brought in accordance with these commandments: for laws to be pious and just, they had to be in conformity with the Decalogue and the laws pertaining to it.

Calvinism and Calvinist morality gain more relief in comparison with Arminianism, of which Hugo Grotius (1583–1645) can serve as a prominent example.[13] Fundamental to Grotius's view on society seems a natural order, principally explained in *De iure belli ac pacis*. Contrary to previous natural law scholars, Grotius's natural law is one with normative implications. Rules that by reason could be deduced from nature, should also be imposed on society.[14] For Grotius, this natural order and the law to be derived from it, still find their origin in God. God is reasonable, rational, and he willed a nature that is rational, including humans created after his image.[15] Despite Grotius himself being a declared Christian, his theory placed God at a distance, it made God's influence an indirect one.[16] The normative element in Grotius's natural law is that such natural order does not just give information on how things are, but also about how they ought to be. Human beings are capable, rational, free and sociable and able to lead a life glorifying God. The prescripts that could be deduced from nature and thus valid for all human beings were, by nature, fairly limited: thus also the natural religion that could be demanded from everyone was rather limited. For Grotius not dogmas were central to a God pleasing life, but the ethical, practical part. Unsurprisingly, Grotius was an irenic, humanist Christian: he envisaged unity of all Christians—in his exile even with Catholics—regardless under which government they lived; and such unity could only be reached with a limited set of necessary dogmas.[17] This was not just an ideal: Grotius tried to implement such policy during his political life in Holland. When Grotius was in power, together with i.a. Johan van Oldenbarnevelt (1547–1619), the Staten of Holland indeed enforced tolerance in the Dutch Reformed Church for all teachings that were within a set of just necessary dogmas. According to Grotius, and many contemporaries, the Staten were above the church: the state had to guarantee peace in society including the church—for Grotius with the purpose of facilitating people in leading a life to the glorification of God.[18] This policy and its underlying values brought Grotius into direct conflict with the

[12] Witte (2008), 127; Witte (2002), 108–113.

[13] For many scholars, Grotius and his works somehow mark the transition towards a secular age. Admittedly, Grotius does not seriously challenge or problematize belief and practice as such. He does, however, include them in his discussion. See e.g. Tuck (1979), 67–75; Tierney (1997), 316–342; O'Donovan (2004), 167–203; Taylor (2007), 126–8.

[14] See Taylor (2007), 126–128.

[15] See e.g. Nijman (2017), 87–110.

[16] See e.g. Besselink (1989), 47–54.

[17] See e.g. Posthumus Meyjes (1984), 43–63; Grotius (1988).

[18] See e.g. Grotius (1995).

Calvinist faction within the Dutch Reformed church, leading to his political downfall in 1619 and later exile.[19]

So, despite similar ideas on the ability and necessity to reshape society, Grotius—but before him for example also Justus Lipsius (1547–1606)[20]—had fundamentally different ideas on the relation between natural law and divine law, and the relation between state and church. For Calvinists divine law held primacy over natural law, and religion and church over politics and state, clearly showing the Calvinistic affinity with the preceding age of faith.[21]

3 Calvinist Morality in Antonius Matthaeus II's *De Criminibus* (1644)[22]

Antonius Matthaeus II (1601–1654), the first professor of law at Utrecht University, was a Calvinist and his extraordinary *De criminibus* (1644) is devoted to criminal law. Because this contribution deals with the influence of Calvinist morality on criminal legal scholarship, Matthaeus's *De criminibus* will be taken as a point of reference. Hewett and Hallebeek have characterized Matthaeus as a 'staunch but balanced Protestant'[23] and others made similar characterizations.[24] Matthaeus was indeed born into a staunchly Reformed, more precisely Calvinist family: his father, Antonius Matthaeus I and also a professor of law, relocated several times, from Herborn to Marburg and ultimately to Groningen also—and importantly—for confessional reasons: in 1625 the Marburg University became Lutheran.[25] After Matthaeus II moved to Utrecht, he became a practicing member of the Reformed *Buerkerk*, where he thrice served as an elder. In this time, he moreover agitated against the practice of high interests by Lombards.[26]

His reputation of a balanced Protestant, he earned on various occasions, notably for defending the academic freedom of the Utrecht University against the authority of local churches[27] and for the tactical way he solved the potentially extremely disruptive dispute between Gijsbert Voet (1589–1676) and René Descartes (1596–1650). Voet, professor of Divinity in Utrecht, argued vehemently against the rationalist method of methodical doubt of Descartes, whereupon the latter replied with rather personal attacks as well, on the Utrecht Academy and Voet respectively. Precisely

[19]See e.g. Van Deursen (1991), 1–5, 227; Israel (1998), 392.

[20]See Taylor (2007), 126–127.

[21]See Taylor (2007), 119–122, 125.

[22]The following builds partly upon Oosterhuis (2019), 225–240.

[23]Hewett and Hallebeek (1998), 122.

[24]Schlüter (1929), 2; Van de Vrugt (1982), 27 and 35; Van de Vrugt (1986), 24–25, 28–31; Van de Vrugt (1987), 166–170.

[25]Schlüter (1929), 7–8; Van de Vrugt (1986), 24–25.

[26]Van de Vrugt (1986), 29–30.

[27]Van de Vrugt (1986), 28.

these personal attacks provided the City Council (*vroedschap*) assisted by Matthaeus as assessor and later as rector, the opportunity to just formally reproach Descartes, without having to deal with the matter substantively.[28]

In 1644, he published his treatise on criminal law, *De criminibus*. In line with the Roman Dutch legal tradition, Matthaeus used books 47 and 48 of Justinian's Digest, the *libri terribiles*, as his framework. Within this framework, in true humanist vein, Matthaeus dealt with criminal law, both Roman and local customary, in a systematic, even mathematic way—unlike many of his predecessors, who had given often rather unsystematic overviews of criminal law.[29] Matthaeus started with a novel introductory section, the prolegomena, in which he discussed: What is a crime? Who can commit crimes? Against whom crimes are committed? The classification of crimes.[30]

The sources referred to in *De criminibus* reveal Matthaeus's thorough training in Roman law, but also the humanist tradition in which he is standing.[31] Obviously—but in a contribution devoted to the influence of Calvinism perhaps appropriate to note—Matthaeus referred by far the most to Roman law sources: the Justinian Code, the Digest, the Institutes of Justinian, the Novels of Justinian, Leo and Theodosius respectively, and the Theodosian Code.[32] Almost six thousand references to over three thousand different texts throughout the *Corpus Iuris Civilis*, testify of his thorough training in Roman law.[33] As a Calvinist, his references to Canon Law are quite limited,[34] certainly compared to the classical writers, so revered by humanists: Cicero is the most cited individual writer in *De criminibus*.[35] A closer look at the index of the later writers—jurists, historians, theologians and others—cited by Matthaeus, contains the usual names—e.g. Accursius (±1182–1263), Bartolus de Saxoferrato

[28]Hewett and Hallebeek (1998), 121–122; Van de Vrugt (1986), 30–31; Van de Vrugt (1987), 167–168.

[29]Such as Jan Matthijssen († after 1419), Philips Wielant (1440–1520) and Joost de Damhoudere (1507–1581) and Melchior Winhoff (±1500–after 1576) on local criminal law, see De Monté VerLoren (1942), 100–129, but also Julius Clarus (1525–1575) and Benedikt Carpzov (1595–1666), see Schlüter (1929), 19–20.

[30]See e.g. Schlüter (1929), 19–21; Van Binsbergen (1986), 93; Van de Vrugt (1982), 42–5; Broers (2012), 111.

[31]The modern indices to the 1987–1996 reprint of the 1761 edition of Matthaeus, *De criminibus* IV, 760–797, give an unprecedented insight in the sources used by Matthaeus.

[32]See Matthaeus, *De criminibus* IV, 760–789, Indices I The Justinian Code, II Digest, III The Institutes of Justinian, The Novels of Justinian, V The Novels of Leo, VI The Theodosian Code, VII The Novels of Theodosius.

[33]See Matthaeus, *De criminibus* IV, 760–767, Index I The Justinian Code, contains 1,613 references to 840 different texts; Index II Digest, 768–786, contains 4,073 references to 2,174 different texts; Index III The Institutes of Justinian, 787, contains 165 references to 99 different texts.

[34]See Matthaeus, *De criminibus* IV, 790, Index VIII Canon Law, contains 74 references to 64 different texts.

[35]See Matthaeus, *De criminibus* IV, 793–794, Index X Classical Writers, contains 77 writers. Cicero is cited a 129 times, Tacitus (68 times) and Plato (64 times) take the second and third place among the classical writers.

(1313–1357)—including well-known Canonists and Moral theologians—e.g. Covarruvias (1512–1577), Antonius Gomez (1500–1572)—but also famous legal humanists, such as Cujacius (1522–1590), Franciscus Duarenus (1509–1559) and Hugo Donellus (1527–1591).[36] But this index also already betrays Matthaeus's Reformed or rather Calvinist conviction, as some Lutheran—Philip Melanchton (1497–1560), Martinus Chemnitius (1522–1586), Wolfgang Musculus (1497–1563)—and many prominent Calvinist theologians figure in it: Calvin, Beza, Petrus Martyrus Vermigli (1499–1562), William Perkins (1558–1602) to name but a few. In light of the Calvinist preference for referring directly to the Bible, Matthaeus's references to scriptural passages seem relatively modest in number—not even two hundred and fifty references—whereby references to the Old Testament vastly outnumber those to the New Testament.[37] Here, it has to be kept in mind that *De criminibus* was based on lecture series teaching Roman criminal law to students. Moreover, often Calvinists found the Civil law to be in harmony with divine law[38]: then there was less need to refer to the Bible. In contested issues, however, divine law, and more specifically the Decalogue and the teachings pertaining to it, should be decisive for a Calvinist like Matthaeus. Therefore, in the following sections Matthaeus's biblical references are discussed and used as a key to unlock the pervasiveness of his Calvinist conviction in his teachings on criminal law. These sections concern: the punishment of crimes; retributive justice in punishing crimes; the definition of crimes; the relation between states, divine law and religious freedom; and the relation between religion, morality and law. Finally, a conclusion will be drawn about the pervasiveness of Calvinism and Calvinist morality in the work of Matthaeus.

3.1 Punishing Crimes in Accordance with the Decalogue

As will be discussed further below, crimes should be defined in accordance with divine law, notably the Decalogue. But not only what constituted a crime fell within the remit of divine law, also the discretion how to punish a crime was determined by divine will, according to Matthaeus. Following divine law would sometimes result

[36]See Matthaeus, *De criminibus* IV, 791–792, Index IX Jurists, historians, theologians and other later writers. The index contains 134 entries, of which Cujacius is most cited (70 times).

[37]See Matthaeus, *De criminibus* IV, 795–797, Index XI Biblia Sacra. The index contains a total of 237 references to 193 different Scriptural passages: 202 references to 161 different passages in the Old Testament; 34 references to 31 different passages in the New Testament; 1 reference to an Apocryphal passage. Of the Old Testament references are by far the most to the Mosaic books: 143 references to 105 passages (21 references to 13 passages in Genesis; 48 references to 33 passages in Exodus; 23 references to 18 passages in Leviticus; 9 references to 7 passages in Numbers; 42 references to 34 passages in Deuteronomy), against 59 references to 56 passages of other books of the Old Testament (Joshua, Judges, I and II Samuel, I and II Kings, II Chronicles, Job, Psalms, Proverbs, Isaiah, Jeremiah, Ezekiel, and Hosea). The books of the New Testament referred to are: Matthew, Mark, Luke, John, Acts, Romans, I Corinthians, I Timothy, and Revelation.

[38]See e.g. Witte (2008), 164–165. This holds, for that matter, also for the Lutheran tradition, see e.g. Witte (2002), 126.

in the moderation of punishment compared to common opinion; sometimes Civil or local laws on punishment would be in conformity with divine will; sometimes divine law would require a more severe punishment than the Civil or local laws had laid down. In the following sections emphasis is given to occasions were Matthaeus choose to deviate from the Civil or local laws—concurring places have been dealt with far less.

3.1.1 On Theft, Damage and Attempt to Murder

In a passage on the punishment of theft, already quite at beginning of his treatise, Matthaeus explained why the Decalogue and the laws pertaining to it, played such a crucial role in determining crime and punishment. Matthaeus's explanation immediately and undeniable shows his Calvinist conviction. The key elements on the supremacy of divine law, the binding nature of the Decalogue, but also the meaning of proportionate justice, are dealt with.

The question was whether the legislator should punish simple theft with the death penalty,[39] more specifically what ought to be thought about the constitution of Emperor Frederick II (1194–1250) where he ordered a thief of 5 solidi or more to be hanged.[40] According to Matthaeus, this and other penalties, such as the gallows or cutting up, were much too harsh and not in accordance with proportionate justice, which required appropriate penalties to be imposed on offences. Matthaeus had a range of arguments, including that: capital punishment is contrary to proportionate justice which dictates that the penalty ought to correspond to the crime in just proportion; capital punishment is not inflicted upon someone who damages something, even if such damage is more than 5 solidi; *stuprum* (sexual abuse) is not a capital offence, although *stuprum* is a more serious offence than theft; the punishment for adultery had been made non-capital—although it should be made capital again for the Christian world, according to Julius Clarus (1525–1575): why then not convert the punishment for simple theft into a non-capital one? And finally, thieves are strangled, while assassins are struck by the sword, which is less painful.[41]

But Matthaeus's first, and probably most fundamental argument was that the death penalty for a simple theft was contrary to divine law (Exodus 22:1 et seqq). This law was holy and immutable (Deuteronomy 4:2; Revelations 22:18–19) and still standing despite the advent of Christ. According to Matthaeus, the Ten Commandments and the Mosaic rules explaining those Commandments were binding upon Christians, including magistrates:

---

[39] A simple theft is not violent and does not amount to sacrilege, embezzlement or manstealing, Matthaeus, *De criminibus* 47.I.II.6 (p. 58).

[40] Libri Feudorum 2.27.

[41] Matthaeus, *De criminibus* 47.I.II.6 (pp. 58–59).

> All Mosaic Laws, on the evidence of Duarenus[42] and Contius,[43] which pertain to the teaching of the Decalogue have their foundation in natural equity and bind Christians today. This law does not exclusively belong to the courts, but in part to morals: since our Saviour in different places confirms laws of this nature (for example John 8:3; I Corinthians 10:8; Matthew 15:3–4; Matthew 26:52; Job 12:8 juncto Deuteronomy 15:11; Matthew 5:8 et seqq.), it follows that they are not abolished and cannot be abolished by the decree of any human being, since every magistrate ought to be the servant and executor of the divine will (Romans 13:1–4).[44]

Subsequently Matthaeus argued that capital punishment for manstealers (Deuteronomy 24:7) and temple robbers (Joshua 7) were exceptions to this rule, only reinforcing it.

In the passage quoted above, Matthaeus argued that the rule that simple theft should be punished with a fine—and not a capital penalty—was not only juridical (*judicialis*), but partly moral (*moralis*). Here, Matthaeus employed terminology principally in use by theologians and moralists, both Catholic and Protestant. These theologians distinguished between three types of biblical laws: (i) moral laws (*lex moralis*), the enduring moral teachings of the Decalogue and the New Testament; (ii) juridical, forensic or civil laws (*lex juridicales, ius forensi*), the rules and procedures by which ancient Israelites and apostolic Christians governed their religious and civil communities; and (iii) ceremonial laws (*lex ceremonialis*), the Mosaic laws that governed the religious life of the ancient Israelites.[45] Certain Protestant theologians argued that only the *definition* of crimes was part of the moral and enduring law, but that the *punishment* of those crimes was part of the juridical or civil law, and thus at the discretion of magistrates.[46] As proponents of this view, Matthaeus listed some prominent first and second generation Reformers—French, Italian, German and English: Calvin, Vermigli, Melanchton, Chemnitius and Perkins. Matthaeus argued, however, that also the *punishment* of crimes was part of the moral law, at least partly, admittedly in the sense that magistrates were limited in their discretion insofar that they should not impose a capital penalty for theft. Indeed, several Protestant theologians defended that the kinds of punishment of the crimes in the Mosaic Laws pertaining to the Decalogue were also of a moral and enduring nature, not just the definition of the crimes. Of the Reformed theologians listed

---

[42] Duarenus (Omnia Opera, ad D.24.3, in the title de Nuptiis. n 3).

[43] Contius (Lectiones juris subcisivae.2.1).

[44] Matthaeus, *De criminibus* 47.I.II.6 (pp. 58–59): *Omnes leges Mosaicae, testibus Duareno & Contio, quae pertinent ad tuitionem decalogi, & fundamentum habent in naturali aequitate, hodieque Christianos obligant. Lex haec non est mere judicialis, sed ex parte moralis: cujus generis leges cum salvator noster passim confirmet, ut Joh. 8. 3. & I. Cor. 10. 8. Matth. 15. 3. & 4. Matth. 26. 52. Joh. 12. 8. junct. Deut. 15. 11. Matth. 5. 8. & seqq. consequens est, abolitas non esse, ac ne potuisse quidem aboleri cujusquam hominis constitutione, cum minister & executor divinae voluntatis omnis magistratus esse debeat Rom. 13. 1. 2. 3. 4.*

[45] Witte (2008), 156. See e.g. Vermigli, Loci communes in app. Lib. 4. in resl. 4. quaest. and class 2. Cap. II, n. 33 and 35; William Perkins, Armilla aurea, cap. 27, quoted by Matthaeus, *De criminibus* 47.I.II.6 (pp. 62–63). The distinction, used by jurists, whether in civil and canon law, would roughly be between natural law; law of nations; civil or positive law.

[46] See e.g. Witte (2008), 163–164. See on the Lutheran theory of punishment e.g. Witte (2002), 128–135; Pihlajamäki (2006), 180–183.

by Matthaeus to support his opinion, Vermigli and Musculus, had a quite nuanced opinion. The more strict opinion that simple theft should never be punished capitally was held by a number of Calvinist Divinity professors at Leiden—Franciscus Junius (1545–1602), Lambertus Daneau (1535–1590) and André Rivet (1572–1651)—, Strasbourg—Johannes Piscator (1546–1625)—and Franeker—Guilelmus Amesius (or William Ames, 1576–1633). For this opinion Matthaeus finally found support with some philosophical and legal authorities, ancient and recent: Plato, Thomas More (1478–1535), Theophilus, Andreas Alciatus (1492–1550) and last but not least Grotius.

> And recently still Hugo Grotius wrote that it is not right for someone to be condemned to death except for crimes which the law, given through Moses, punished by death, or which by sound reasoning, are equal to them. For in a matter as serious as this, a knowledge of the Divine Will, which alone calms the mind, cannot be obtained from anywhere other than from that law which certainly did not establish the penalty of death for a thief.[47]

Here, Matthaeus referred to Grotius with unqualified agreement, to underscore the importance of law's ultimate source, God's will. Typically, Matthaeus referred precisely to Grotius where the latter alluded to divine will; this nicely fits in with Matthaeus's admittedly more Calvinist, voluntarist approach.[48] For Matthaeus, divine will was decisive: divine law ranked highest, above natural law or civil law.[49] However, in justifying the non-capital punishment of theft, Matthaeus referred to divine law and nature in the same breath: 'All Mosaic Laws, (...), which pertain to the teaching of the Decalogue have their foundation in natural equity.'[50] The correspondence between the Decalogue and the Mosaic laws pertaining to it, and natural law and equity will be discussed more extensively below.[51]

Matthaeus applied essentially the same principle to the punishment of damage unlawfully inflicted (*lex Aquilia*):

> Furthermore, if in that question of the punishment for theft, reference had constantly to be made to Divine Law, why in the present dispute also should one not be able to abide by

[47]Matthaeus, *De criminibus* 47.I.II.6 (p. 65): *Et nuper admodum Hugo Grotius scripsit, fas non esse, quenquam ad mortem damnari, nisi ob delicta, quae lex per Mosen data morte punivit, aut quae his sunt paria recta aestimatione: Nec enim posse notitiam divinae voluntatis, quae sola animum tranquillat, aliaunde in hoc negotio tam gravi haberi, quam ex illa lege, quae certe mortis poenam in furem non constituit.* Reference to Grotius, De jure belli ac pacis 2.1.14. Matthaeus extended this principle also to thieves in public baths, Matthaeus, *De criminibus* 47.X.II.2 (p. 175).

[48]Matthaeus did not follow Grotius in his distinction between expletive and attributive justice, limiting the divine law or will to the realm of attributive justice. See e.g. Tuck (1979), 42–44; Van Deursen (1991), 227–228.

[49]See also e.g. Matthaeus, *De criminibus* 47.I.IV.4 (p. 81).

[50]Matthaeus, *De criminibus* 47.I.II.6 (58–59): *Omnes leges Mosaicae, (...), quae pertinent ad tuitionem decalogi, & fundamentum habent in naturali aequitate, hodieque Christianos obligant. Lex haec non est mere judicialis, sed ex parte moralis: cujus generis leges cum salvator noster passim confirmet, ut Joh. 8. 3. & I. Cor. 10. 8. Matth. 15. 3. & 4. Matth. 26. 52. Joh. 12. 8. junct. Deut. 15. 11. Matth. 5. 8. & seqq. consequens est, abolitas non esse, ac ne potuisse quidem aboleri cujusquam hominis constitutione, cum minister & executor divinae voluntatis omnis magistratus esse debeat Rom. 13. 1. 2. 3. 4.*

[51]See below, 3.5 Religion, Morals and Criminal Law: the Courts of Heaven and Earth.

> the sacred pronouncement that for damage a monetary and not capital penalty is inflicted (Exodus 21:32-4 et seqq and Exodus 22:5 et seqq). I reply: I not only admit but I even declare that there is almost the same principle involved in damage and theft. Neither crime is per se and by its nature capital, but each is aggravated only by its quality and by circumstances.[52]

Divine law took precedence, not just over local laws, but also over the Civil law. Attempt to murder someone knew for instance capital punishment under Roman law (e.g. D. 48.8.1; D. 48.8.7; D. 48.8.14; C. 9.16.6(7)). But the common school of thought and also judicial practice over the whole world departed from this rule: Matthaeus mentioned—marginally—a score of mostly Canonist, Catholic criminal lawyers (Covarruvias, Clarus, Gomez, Petrus Rebuffus (1487–1557), Prosperus Farinacius (1554–1618), Petrus Gudelinus (1550–1619)) but also editors of court decisions, such as Joachim Mynsinger von Frundeck (1514–1588) for the Reichskammergericht and Johan van den Sande (1568–1638) for the court of Friesland. And Matthaeus supported wholeheartedly this practice: decisive for him was, as always, divine law, where attempt to murder was not punished capitally (Exodus 21:12, 18 and 19; Numbers 35:16 et seqq.; Deuteronomy 19:4).[53]

3.1.2 On Unnatural Lust, False Testimonies and Soothsayers

Often, however, Roman law was in accordance with divine law,[54] for instance where the Civil law provided capital punishment for unnatural lust[55] and false testimonies,[56] but also in case of the punishment of diviners. The term 'diviners' included astrologers, augurs, haruspices, oracles, soothsayers, interpreters of dreams, fortunetellers, as well as magicians (and thus probably also witches, although Matthaeus did not mention witches explicitly): 'Magicians are sorcerers who bewitch others with incantations, curses and magic spells, and who make wax figures in order to kill a man'.[57] Diviners awaited capital punishment, both under Civil and divine law.[58] Also people who consulted diviners had to punished capitally, although an exception

---

[52]Matthaeus, *De criminibus* 47.II.II.3 (p. 96): *Adhaec si in illa quaestione de furti poena fuit omnino recurrendum ad divinam legem, cur non in praesenti quoque controversia sacro oraculo stetur, quod pro damno pecuniarias poenas non capitalem infligit? Exod. 21. v. 32. 33. 34. & seqq. nec non Exod. 22. v. 5. & seqq. Respondeo: Non solum confiteor, sed & profiteor, eandem fere esse damni atque furti rationem; neutrum crimen* per se*& sua natura capitale esse, sed qualitate duntaxat & rebus circumstantibus gravari.*

[53]Matthaeus, *De criminibus* 48.V.III.11 (p. 377).

[54]In this contribution only a few of the references in *De criminibus* where Civil law and Scripture concurred, have been dealt with.

[55]Matthaeus, *De criminibus* 48.III.VI.8 (p. 323).

[56]Matthaeus, *De criminibus* 48.VII.II.1 (p. 421).

[57]Matthaeus, *De criminibus* 48.V.V.2 (p. 387): *Magi sunt malefici, qui carminibus, diris, devotionibus defigunt alios, qui fingunt cereas imagines hominis necandi causa.*

[58]Matthaeus, *De criminibus* 48.V.V.2 and 4 (pp. 387–388). Contrary to Van der Vrugt (1982), 36–37, and particularly Schlüter (1929), 2–3, who both give the impression that Matthaeus dismisses witchcraft almost entirely. Theft was also aggravated when committed with magic spells, Matthaeus, *De criminibus* 47 I.III.8 (p. 72).

could be made for people who did so 'from extreme naivety and ignorance, since they think that to consult a soothsayer is not the same as invoking strange gods, it seems that they must be punished more leniently.'[59] Matthaeus admitted the—sporadic—possibility of magic and magic spells, although it was then eventually Satan who was behind these spells: 'It is not that there is any power in the spells and charms themselves, but it is because the enemy of the human race does not wish to help evildoers unless a dreadful incantation is pronounced'.[60] But generally Matthaeus appeared to consider magic as just an illusion: 'However, not all must be described to spells. Sometimes these things are done with such sleight of mind and hand that they deceive the eyes of bystanders and the ignorant mob consider such imposters as magicians.'[61]

3.1.3 On Adultery, Incest and Manstealing

About the punishment of adultery, Matthaeus was stricter than many of the preceding generations.[62] Particularly Pope Alexander III's classification of adultery as a minor crime (X. 2.1.4.2.), gave Matthaeus the opportunity to scorn the holy fathers and clerics: their indulgence of adultery was because they were inclined to it themselves. Christians should never consider adultery trivial.[63] Matthaeus therefore also disapproved of Novels 134.10, where Justinian abolished capital punishment for an adulterous woman in derogation of a Constitution of Constantine (C. 9.9.29(3)0.4) which ordered that violators of a marriage be punished with the sword.[64] Justinian's derogation and also the punishment of adultery in many other nations was way too lax, according to Matthaeus. Divine law stated that if someone committed adultery with another's wife, both had to be put to death (Leviticus 20:10 and Deuteronomy 22:22). Here, Matthaeus referred again back to his argument on the sometimes partly moral nature of the punishment of crimes:

> This law [i.e. on the capital punishment for adultery] does not belong exclusively to the courts nor was it written for the Jews alone, but is in accordance with natural reason and it has reference to the observation of the seventh commandment and it must be regarded as of a mixed nature, in part belonging to the courts and in part moral. Laws of that kind bind us even today, as I said in the preceding book in the Title on Theft.[65]

---

[59] Matthaeus, *De criminibus* 48.V.V.5 (p. 388): *nam si nimia simplicitate & imperitia id fecerint, dum putant diversa esse, ariolum consulere, & Deos alienos invocare, mitius castigandi videntur.*

[60] Matthaeus, *De criminibus* 47.XI.I.5 (p. 174). Again contrary to Van der Vrugt (1982), 36–37.

[61] Matthaeus, *De criminibus* 47.XI.I.5 (p. 174).

[62] See e.g. on the judicial practice in medieval Haarlem, Müller (2013), 4–31; Müller (2015), 92–100.

[63] Matthaeus, *De criminibus* Prolegomena.IV.4 (pp. 35–36).

[64] Matthaeus, *De criminibus* 48.III.II.2 (p. 290).

[65] Matthaeus, *De criminibus* 48.III.II.4 (p. 292): *Haec lex non mere forensis est, solisve Judaeis scripta, sed cum ratione naturali constet, & pertineat ad tuitionem septimi praecepti, mixti generis censenda est, partim forensis, partim moralis: cujus generis leges hodieque nos obligant, ut diximus lib. praeced. tit. de furt.*

Earlier, in his discussion of the punishment of theft, Matthaeus had argued that also the punishment of crimes was part of the moral law, at least partly, admittedly in the sense that magistrates were limited in their discretion how to punish certain crimes: for the punishment of theft a magistrate should remain below the threshold of capital punishment—but had discretion otherwise.[66] For adultery, on the other hand, a magistrate had apparently very little discretion, according to Matthaeus, as he in principle had to impose the death penalty: here, Matthaeus's adherence to divine law resulted in a more severe punishment than was—and would be—customary in the Low Countries.[67] It seems that for Matthaeus where the punishment of a crime was mentioned in the Decalogue or the Mosaic laws pertaining to it, such punishment was in part of a moral kind, in the sense that magistrates had to stay within the limits of the Biblical punishment—the punishment of certain crimes did not belong exclusively to the courts' discretion, i.e. positive criminal law. As in his argument about the punishment of theft, Matthaeus again pointed out the correspondence between natural reason and the Decalogue or the Mosaic laws pertaining to it ('reference to the observation of the seventh commandment').[68]

In similar fashion, Matthaeus wondered why Justinian had not maintained capital punishment for incest, because according to divine law incest, like adultery, was punished with death (Leviticus 18 and 20; Deuteronomy 27).[69]

And finally, for the punishment of manstealing, Matthaeus preferred the constitutions of Diocletian and Constantine over the Lex Cornelia and Lex Fabia: the latter knew monetary penalties and later the mines, whereas the first knew capital punishment. Also in this case, Matthaeus preferred the stricter constitutions of Diocletian and Constantine precisely because they were consonant with divine law in punishing manstealing with the death penalty (Deuteronomy 24:7; Exodus 21:16).[70]

3.1.4 On Adultery Again and Sacrilege

Sometimes Matthaeus would employ a rather extensive interpretation of what was acceptable according to divine law. In the title on adultery, Matthaeus as usual also discussed at length the customs of the States of Utrecht and neighboring customs. Matthaeus had quite some understanding for the custom of Holland to no longer follow divine law—making a violated girl respectable with marriage *and* dowry (Exodus 22:16)—but to separate marriage and dowry; which separation was admitted also by divine law itself, according to Matthaeus. Because poor and completely

---

[66]See above, Matthaeus, *De criminibus* 47.I.II.6 (pp. 58–65).

[67]See again Müller (2013), 4–31; Müller (2015), 92–100, and for later periods, e.g. Broers (2006), 63–66; Faber (1983), 79–80, 214, 255–256; Verhaar and Van den Brink (1989), 64–93.

[68]The correspondence between the Decalogue and the Mosaic laws pertaining to it, and natural equity or reason will be discussed more extensively below, 3.5 Religion, Morals and Criminal Law: the Courts of Heaven and Earth.

[69]Matthaeus, *De criminibus* 48.III.VI.5 (p. 322).

[70]Matthaeus, *De criminibus* 48.XII.II.1 (p. 457).

wanton girls schemed for marriage with rich youths by relying on the divine law, as Grotius narrated for Holland.[71]

When it came to sacrilege, Matthaeus had to interpret the punishment laid down in local laws quite broadly to be in accordance with the punishment foreseen in the laws pertaining to the Decalogue. The statutes of Utrecht punished blasphemy—which fell under the crime of sacrilege—less severely than the Civil law, where it was punished capitally (Novels 77.1.2). Under the statutes of Utrecht, the first blasphemy was punished with imprisonment, the second with flogging, and the third with flogging, perforation of the tongue and exile, 'at the discretion of the judge'. Matthaeus argued that on the basis of this judicial discretion, a judge could eventually inflict even capital punishment for gross blasphemy: according to Matthaeus this would 'satisfy at least partly the pious complaints of those who lament that the death penalty which was also laid down by divine law (Leviticus 24:16) has been abolished by our most irreligious ways.'[72] Here, Matthaeus seemed to accept with some equanimity the less severe punishment of blasphemy under the statutes of Utrecht, compared to the punishment for blasphemy under the Civil law and particularly divine law—contrary to for instance the punishment of adultery. Admittedly, what constituted blasphemy was connected with religious freedom, and for many Calvinist theologians, including Calvin himself, but particularly Beza, this freedom had become crucial.[73]

3.1.5 Discretion in Punishment

In the title on punishment in general, Matthaeus discussed what kinds of punishment could be imposed, for which he regularly referred to the Holy Writ. Certain punishments were out of the question. Matthaeus rejected branding and confiscation of property by the Pope because of heresy (*majestas*), with reference to Deuteronomy 14:1–2, where the Hebrews were totally forbidden to mark any part of the body,[74] and Luke 12:13 respectively, where 'our Saviour himself refused to meddle with such things to such an extent that he would not perform the duty of a judge and divide an inheritance between two brothers.'[75] Confiscation of property therefore had nothing to do with the Pope.

But, according to Matthaeus, often a judge's discretion depended very much on the circumstances. A judge could inflict corporeal punishment for gross negligence: not only Civil law gave several examples where gross negligence was capitally punished, but also divine law gave an example where gross negligence was capitally punished

[71] Matthaeus, *De criminibus* 48.III.VII.17 (p. 331). Reference to Grotius, Inleidinge 3.35.8.

[72] Matthaeus, *De criminibus* 48.X.VI.6 (p. 450): *Eaque sententia admissa satisfaciemus, si non ex asse, saltem pro parte piis eorum querelis, qui dolent capitalem poenam, quam lex divina quoque sanxerat Lev. 24. pessimis moribus sublatam.*

[73] See Witte (2008), 129, 140–141. See also below, 3.4 States, Divine Law and Religious Freedom.

[74] Matthaeus, *De criminibus* 48.XVIII.I.11 (p. 588).

[75] Matthaeus, *De criminibus* 48.XVIII.II.6 (p. 593): *quibus Salvator noster adeo se non immiscuit; ut ne arbitri quidem officio fungi, & dividere inter fratres hereditatem voluerit.*

(Exodus 21:29).[76] Attempt, however, should generally be punished less severely, according to Scripture.[77] Sometimes an entire group had to be punished for a crime it committed, sometimes only the leaders.[78] But punishment should always be proportionate: if a judge imposed capital punishment for a crime, it should not impose a non-capital punishment for the same crime. Indeed,

> whenever Natural Law and the provisions of Divine Providence lay down by what penalty a particular class of crime is to be punished, a judge or legislator should not readily allow himself to be led astray from these.[79]

At this point, Matthaeus again mentioned capital punishment for crimes such as murder or adultery, and non-capital punishment for a thief.[80]

In many cases, Matthaeus's rather strict Calvinist position would thus be in line with Civil law—as with the punishment of diviners—or local statutes or customs, or even result in a moderation of the punishment under these laws, such as for theft, damage unlawfully inflicted, or attempt to murder. His initial audience, his students, was naturally Protestant. His students had to be introduced into a Calvinist teaching of the law and thus reference to the supreme authority of divine law for criminal law was obvious, just as making his students and readers familiar with well-known Reformed theologians. Precisely because magistrates—to whom some of his students would also come to belong—had considerable discretion in deciding on a punishment,[81] Matthaeus's Calvinist teachings on how to punish could have considerable influence on actual judicial practice. Matthaeus stressed that divine law was in accordance with retributive and proportionate justice when it came to punishing.

3.2 *Punishment as Retributive Justice and the Rejection of Torture*

When Matthaeus discussed the punishment of *iniuria*, he emphasized the necessity of retributive, proportionate justice. He rejected *talio* (retaliation in kind) as a leading principle for the punishment of *iniuria*, with reference to divine law:

> As far as the law of God concerned, (...) it must not be understood as concerning simple *talio*, but proportionate justice, if I may say so. For that rule which the Almighty God gives [i.e. Exodus 21:24], is intended to explain that the punishment ought to fit the crime, (...).[82]

---

[76] Matthaeus, *De criminibus* 48.XVIII.IV.11 (p. 612).

[77] Matthaeus, *De criminibus* 48.XVIII.IV.13 (p. 613).

[78] Matthaeus, *De criminibus* 48.XVIII.IV.30 (p. 622).

[79] Matthaeus, *De criminibus* 48.XVIII.IV.31 (p. 625): *Inprimis quoties naturalia jura, & divina providentia constiuta docent, qua poena unumquodque admissi genus coërcendum sit; haut facile judex legislatorve ab eis se abduci patiatur.*

[80] Matthaeus, *De criminibus* 48.XVIII.IV.31 (p. 625).

[81] See e.g. Faber (1983), 213–227.

[82] Matthaeus, *De criminibus* 47.IV.II.2 (pp. 126–127): *Quod ad legem divinam attinet, ea non recte adducitur pro Pythagoreis: non enim de simplici talione accipi debet sed proportionate ut ita loquar.*

Retributive justice also had to be observed in the punishment of the crime of *laesio majestas* (high treason and sacrilege). In this context, Matthaeus extensively discussed the lex Julia and the Constitution of Arcadius and Honorius (C. 9.8.5).[83] The latter constitution laid down for the punishment that principally the sons should be put to death with their father who was guilty of *majestas*.[84] Matthaeus was adamantly against punishing sons for the crime of their father:

> Punishment of an offence is ἐχδίχησις (an avenging); therefore where there is no offence there ought to be no punishment (D. 48.19.20, C. 9.47.22) and the penal laws should be a terror to the guilty and a protection to the innocent. Finally, each one is subject to a lot fitting his own deeds, and he is not made a successor to another man's crime (D. 48.12.26). If someone cannot observe this equity from natural law, let him then at least observe Divine Law which forbids children to be punished for the crime of their parent (Deuteronomy 24:16).[85]

To be sure, Matthaeus was not against capital punishment of *majestas* per se. In his discussion of local customs concerning *majestas*, it appears that Matthaeus fundamentally agreed with the conviction of *majestas* of Oldenbarnevelt 'and those who conspired with him' by a court constituted by all provinces.[86] But regarding the punishment of *majestas*, Matthaeus also approved of local customs that were milder towards children and property.[87]

Ea enim formula, qua Deus Opt. Max. utitur, significare vult, poenas delictis aequas esse debere, (…).

[83]Matthaeus, *De criminibus* 48.II, see e.g. 48.II.II.2 (p. 220).

[84]Matthaeus, *De criminibus* 48.II.III.10 (p. 245).

[85]Matthaeus, *De criminibus* 48.II.III.10 (p. 245): *Poena peccati ἐχδίχησις est: ubicunque igitur peccatum nullum, ibi nec poena esse debet l. si poena 20. D. de poen. l.sancimus 22. C. eod. legesque poenariae nocentibus terrori, innocentibus praesidio esse debent. Denique unusquisque ex suo admisso forti subjicitur, nec alieni ciminis successor constituitur l. crimen 26. D. eod. Hanc ipsius naturae aequitatem si quis non advertit, advertat saltem ad legem divinam; quae vetat liberos ob delicta parentum puniri Deut. XXIV. vers. XVI.*

[86]Matthaeus, *De criminibus* 48.II.V.1 (p. 264). See also in detail Hewett and Hallebeek (1998), 122.

[87]Where Matthaeus discussed whether the legitimate portion must be left to children of a traitor, he explained that nowadays: 'Only the property of the father is confiscated. And there are indeed some towns that enjoy as a special privilege the concession that either the traitor's property is not confiscated at all, or the citizen whose possessions are to be confiscated can buy them back for a certain sum, usually not a large one. Such is the privilege of the city of Delft and by it a most learned man is said to have saved himself from confiscation of his property. The charter runs almost as follows: (…) 'Let no citizen of Delft be punished in any manner or way with a greater part of his possessions than 60 lb.' (Matthaeus, *De criminibus* 48.II.V.7 (p 267): *publicanturque sola patris bona. Quin etiam civitates nonnullae singulari privilegio gaudent, ut aut bona omnino non publicentur, aut civis cujus bona publicanda sunt, redimere ea certo pretio, & plerunque non magno possit. Tale est privilegium civitatis Delphensis, quo vir doctissimus publicationem bonorum a se defendisse dicitur, in hunc ferme modum conceptum: Ne quis civis Delphensis ullo modo casuve majore parte bonorum mulctetur, quam libris LX.* Here 'most learned' should be preferred over 'very clever' as a translation of *doctissimus*.) This concerned Grotius. Although Matthaeus thus agreed with Grotius' conviction of *majestas*, he also approved of the fact that this punishment should only affect Grotius, and not his children or property. Indeed, on 17 May 1630, the Court of Holland allowed Grotius to use this old privilege to buy his property back for sixty pounds. See Nellen (2015), 438; Moll (1902), 99–100.

Matthaeus thus considered punishment retribution for an offence. And therefore he was also a declared opponent of torture as method of obtaining the truth. For Matthaeus it was simply not sufficiently clear whether torture was indeed a lawful method of obtaining the truth. According to Matthaeus, the arguments against torture were stronger when balanced in the scale of reason.[88] He needed this scale of reason, as he could derive no clear argument from divine law, only an *a contrario* argument:

> although very many juridical laws are found in the Holy Bible, however no trace of interrogation under torture can be found. It is very unlikely that, if torture were necessary to obtain the truth, such a wonderful discovery would have been omitted by the Almighty God (to criticize his commandments is to commit a sin).[89]

Therefore Matthaeus's most important argument against torture rested on natural equity:

> First and foremost is that it is utterly abhorrent to natural equity for anyone to be tortured before it is established that he is guilty. For all physical pain is punishment even if it is inflicted before sentence. However, there ought to be no punishment, where there is no offence since punishment is retribution for an offence.[90]

Taken together, these arguments show that Matthaeus's 'modern' position on the inadmissibility of torture, was based on the idea that punishment is and has to be retribution for an offence; for Matthaeus, this idea was eventually grounded on Scripture, for example on the above passage that children should not be punished for the crimes of their fathers (Deuteronomy 24:16). Here, Matthaeus's modern opinion is thus directly based on his Calvinist conviction and the application of this conviction on criminal law.[91]

3.3 *Defining Crimes: Abortion and Adultery*

When it came to defining crimes, divine law served as the ultimate authority for Matthaeus as well. Sometimes his direct reliance on Scripture would lead to an

---

[88] Matthaeus, *De criminibus* 48.XVI.V.1 (p. 559). For instance, in proceedings against Cornelis de Witt, reference was made to Matthaeus' rejection of torture; see Binsbergen (1986), 106–107. About torture in the Low Countries, see also Müller (2015), 92–100; Van de Vrugt (1978), 145–146; Binsbergen (1986), 114; Faber (1983), 111–149. In general see e.g. Pihlajamäki (2006), 178–179 and the literature referred to.

[89] Matthaeus, *De criminibus* 48.XVI.V.1 (p. 561): *quod cum plurimae in sacro codice leges judiciariae inveniantur, nullum tamen quaestionis vestigium reperiri queat. Minime vero verisimile est, si ad veritatem indagandam quaestio necessaria esset, Deum Opt. Max. cujus leges sine scelere imperfectionis argui non possunt, tam praeclarum inventum praetermissurum fuisse.* For consistency '*judiciariae*' has been translated with 'juridical' instead of 'judicial'.

[90] Matthaeus, *De criminibus* 48.XVI.V.1 (p. 560): *Quorum primum & praecipuum est, quod a naturali aequitate prorsus abhorreat, cruciari quenquam, antequam constet nocentem esse. Omnis enim cruciatus corporis poena est, etiamsi ante sententiam inferatur. Poena autem esse non debet, ubi peccatum non est, cum peccati sit animadversio.*

[91] Less precise De Monté VerLoren (1942), 1, 215; Van de Vrugt (1982), 37–38.

extension of what constituted a crime. Matthaeus for instance considered any abortion murder because even the seed contained the whole fruit: the son of Judah was put to death because he spilled his seed, intended for the name of his brother (Genesis 38:9).[92] When divine law deviated from Roman Law in defining a crime, Matthaeus principally followed divine law. For murder, it makes no exception who you kill, freeman or slave (e.g. Exodus 21:12).[93] Indeed, masters don't have the right to kill their own slaves (Exodus 21:20–21).[94] Also for suicide no exception was made (Genesis 9:5).[95]

Sometimes Matthaeus however limited a crime to just that what was laid down in the Civil law, thereby reserving the most severe punishment for only a particular offence. Adultery is a case in point. As discussed above, Matthaeus argued that adultery should be capitally punished in accordance with the Decalogue. But unlike many Calvinist theologians, Matthaeus had a rather limited conception of what constituted adultery, primarily based on Roman law: adultery exclusively meant the intercourse of a man with another's wife (e.g. D. 48.5.6.1 and D. 50.16.101).[96] Importantly, Matthaeus did not extend adultery to an affair between a married man and an unmarried woman: this was *stuprum* (sexual abuse), but not adultery—and thus punished less severely, i.e. not capitally. Here, Matthaeus disagreed with eminent Reformed theologians—Vermigli, Musculus, Beza—but also the Italian legal scholar Jacobus Menochius (1532–1607). They argued the opposite with reference to the Bible, but on this point Matthaeus stuck to the Civil law, also because of policy reasons:

> For who does not know that the main reason for virtue must apply to women, because of respect for their sex, because of foul mixing of blood, and the substitution of offspring, and because of the disgrace to the family, and the whole state?.[97]

Although Matthaeus could understand that a married man having an affair with an unmarried woman was an adulterer in light of the first marriage, i.e. between Adam and Eve, this would never come to a court on earth, but only to the heavenly court: 'For the heavenly judge punished crimes in one way and the judge of this world in another.'[98] Even polygamy should not be considered adultery according to Matthaeus.[99] Here Matthaeus distinguished between the courts of heaven and earth, each with their own jurisdiction. Before discussing the consequences of such distinction for the relation between law and religion, first Matthaeus's view on the relation between states, divine law and religious freedom will be discussed.

---

[92] Matthaeus, *De criminibus* 47. V.I.3 (p. 143).

[93] Matthaeus, *De criminibus* 48.V.I.7 (p. 365).

[94] Matthaeus, *De criminibus* 48.V.I.8 (p. 366).

[95] Matthaeus, *De criminibus* 48.V.I.8 (p. 367).

[96] Matthaeus, *De criminibus* 48.III.I.3 (pp. 274–275).

[97] Matthaeus, *De criminibus* 48.III.I.12 (p. 283): *Quis enim nescit, majorem pudicitiae rationem uxoribus constare debere, quapropter sexus verecundiam, qua propter foedam feminum confusionem, & adulterinorum suppositionem, qua propter dedecus familiae, totiusque civitatis?*

[98] Matthaeus, *De criminibus* 48.III.I.12 (p. 283): *Etenim aliter coelestis judex, aliter judex hujus seculi exigit crimina.*

[99] Matthaeus, *De criminibus* 48.III.I.13 (p. 284).

3.4 States, Divine Law and Religious Freedom

At several instances, Matthaeus emphasized that a state or prince is subordinate to divine law. In the title concerning proof, Matthaeus for example stated that a single witness must not be heard, even if such single witness was the Emperor or the Pope himself: not even the Emperor, who is only above Civil law, can change this law, as it rests on the authority of divine law (Deuteronomy 17:6 and 19:15).[100] But two witnesses were sufficient (reference to St Paul, I Timothy 5:19) and not more or even many more, as Canon Law occasionally prescribed.[101]

In the title on theft, Matthaeus discussed whether the fisc (more or less equivalent to a public prosecutor) could claim stolen property for itself. Matthaeus appeared to be adamantly against such practice, because:

> not even the emperor, who has supreme power and is above the law, can take something away from private citizens without cause, …. For natural reason, the precepts of the law and also the eighth commandment state that no one must be harmed, that no one's property shall be taken away without cause. That which is ours cannot be transferred to another, without our own cooperation. Moreover, the emperor is not above Divine Law, nor the Law of Nature, and furthermore, he voluntarily submits his preeminence to the Civil Law, ….[102]

Matthaeus thus strongly disapproved of the law among the Batavi (i.e. the people of Holland), that property thrown into the sea to lighten a ship must be raised within one year and six weeks, and if that was not done, it awarded the property to the fisc.[103] Matthaeus's indignation about interference with individual property in the customs of Holland shows a certain preoccupation with the sovereignty of the state: not only magistrates, but even the emperor was subordinated to divine law.

Indeed, the most fundamental disagreement between Matthaeus and Grotius appears to be on a state's sovereignty. In the chapter on imperial pardon, Matthaeus stated that emperors had no right to pardon those crimes that had to be capitally punished according to divine law. More precisely:

> that the emperor may rightly grant pardon for those crimes which are punished in terms to the Civil Law rather than in terms of Divine Law, but that pardon for those crimes which Divine Law or right reason and the consent of the *Ius Gentium* wish to be punished capitally, can in no way be granted by the emperor. The basis for this view is firm and immovable, namely because the emperor is only above the Civil Law and not above Divine and Natural

---

[100] Matthaeus, *De criminibus* 48.XV.III.1-2 (p. 517).

[101] Matthaeus, *De criminibus* 48.XV.III.6-7 (pp. 519–20).

[102] Matthaeus, *De criminibus* 47.I.IV.4 (p. 81): *nam si ne princeps quidem, cujus potestas summa atque legibus soluta est, cuiquam privatorum suam sine causa auferre potest, …. Naturalis enim ratio, atq; secundum juris praeceptum, nec non praeceptum divinum octavum dictant, neminem esse laedendum; nemini rem suam sine causa auferendam: id quod nostrum est, sine facto nostro ad alium transferri non posse. Princeps autem neque divinis, neque naturalibus legibus solutus est: quin etiam civilibus ultro submittit principatum; ….*

[103] Matthaeus, *De criminibus* 47.I.IV.4 (p. 82). Marginal reference to Grotius, Inleidinge 2.4.36. However, at the place marginally referred to, Grotius actually only discussed how a res nullius, more specifically, goods cast up by the sea, could be appropriated. Grotius, Inleidinge 2.4 (Van't bekomen van ongeeigend goed), 36.

> Law to which, as a human being, he is also liable. Nor is he above the *Ius Gentium* to which he is bound as a member and part of the human society.[104]

Matthaeus then went on at some length giving mainly biblical references to argue his case.[105] He then introduced his opponents:

> Now let us see how we must satisfy those who in their zeal to show their dutifulness to their lords and masters grant them more than right reason and public utility demand. Of these a certain most learned gentleman has recently philosophized on the whole question as follows.[106]

Matthaeus then reproduced the three grounds for punishment, as elaborated by this 'most learned man': (i) the reformation of the offender; (ii) the interests of him in whose interest it was that the offence should not have taken place, so that he should not again suffer the like at the hands of the same man or at the hands of others; (iii) the interests of the other citizens so that they should not suffer anything at the hands of the same man and so that others be deterred from committing crimes.[107] According to Grotius, if either all these ends fell away or could for instance be reached in another way, a penalty—including capital punishment—could be remitted.[108] Matthaeus then went on to extensively refute these three arguments.[109] He was particularly offended by Grotius's argument that natural law did not order to punish offenders, but only permitted punishment, i.e. did not forbid it[110]—which illustrates Grotius's limited conception of natural law as expletive justice.[111] Moreover, Matthaeus added a fourth end to punishment:

---

[104] Matthaeus, *De criminibus* 48.XIX.V.2 (p. 647): *recte largiri principem indulgentiam eorum criminum, quae civili magis, quam divino jure vindicantur; quae autem divina lex, aut recta ratio, gentiumque consensus capitis supplicio puniri jubet, eorum indulgentiam a principe tribui nullo modo posse. Cujus sententiae fundamentum firmum & immotum est, quod princeps legibus duntaxat civilibus solutus sit, non divinis & naturalibus, quibus obligatur tanquam homo; non gentium legibus, quibus tanquam membrum & pars humanae societatis obnoxius est.*

[105] Matthaeus, *De criminibus* 48.XIX.V.2 (pp. 647–648). Including Genesis 9:5-6, which text would also be used by late 19th and early twentieth century Calvinist criminalists, such as Damnes Paulus Dirk Fabius (1851–1931) and Bernard Gewin (1873–1911), to defend capital punishment for murder, see Stamhuis (1988), 21, 33.

[106] Matthaeus, *De criminibus* 48.XIX.V.2 (p. 649): *Videamus quemadmodum satisfaciendum sit illis, qui dum dominantibus obsequium approbare student, plus iisdem largiuntur, quam aut recta ratio, aut publica utilitas postulat. Ex his vir quidam doctissimus de re tota novissime ita philosophatus est.*

[107] Matthaeus, *De criminibus* 48.XIX.V.2 (p. 649). See Grotius, De jure belli ac pacis 2.20.6–9.

[108] Matthaeus, *De criminibus* 48.XIX.V.2 (p. 649). See e.g. Grotius, De jure belli ac pacis 2.20.13–20. Probably he had the execution of Oldenbarnevelt in mind.

[109] Matthaeus, *De criminibus* 48.XIX.V.3 (pp. 649–652).

[110] Matthaeus, *De criminibus* 48.XIX.V.3 (p. 649). See Grotius, De jure belli ac pacis 2.20.21. Such wide-ranging judicial discretion in punishing was, for that matter, more or less in line with the positions of many early Protestant Reformers, such as Calvin, Vermigli, Melanchton, Chemnitius and Perkins; see e.g. Witte (2008), 163–164; Witte (2002), 128–135. See also above, 3.1.1 On Theft, Damage and Attempt to Murder.

[111] See e.g. Grotius, De jure belli ac pacis 2.20.10.

> Namely that the evildoer must be removed from our midst, that the earth be not polluted by crimes, and lest the Supreme Judge exact punishment from those who have neglected to vindicate crimes.[112]

These passages, admittedly, illustrate most clearly the difference between Matthaeus's and Grotius's approach of a state's sovereignty and of the central place of divine law in the punishment of crimes. Grotius, wary of the religious and political disputes causing endless conflicts and wars in his native Holland and the rest of Europe, attached far greater importance to a strong sovereign allowing him greater power—here exemplified by the imperial pardon—and consequently denied a broad right of resistance against a sovereign; only for instance in case of self-defense.[113] Grotius considered the sovereign to be only bound to natural law, which was understood by Grotius as expletive, strict justice. Principally a sovereign was not bound by his own laws and was above lower magistrates. A state was the highest community and thus ranked also above the individual: a contract between sovereign or state and people legitimized a people's duty to obey. Popular sovereignty was rejected.[114]

Matthaeus acutely singled out this more 'absolutist' approach of Grotius in *De jure belli ac pacis*, of which Grotius was indeed accused of by some of his Reformed contemporaries.[115] Matthaeus considered the sovereign to be subject to divine and natural law; he considered it inconceivable that a state would not set 'an example for the common herd'.[116] Matthaeus's approach resembles some of the ideas of certain Reformed scholars, such as François Hotman (1524–1590), Beza and Philippe du Plessis-Mornay (1549–1623), who had strong contractarian ideas about the relation between people and state or sovereign.[117] Building on earlier medieval ideas Hotman had argued that rulers ultimately were constituted by the people.[118] Beza subsequently argued that a three-way political covenant existed between God, the rulers, and the people. Political rulers had to abide by the law of God and the law of nature; the best source and summary of the law of God and nature was the Decalogue.[119] If a

---

[112]Matthaeus, *De criminibus* 48.XIX.V.3 (p. 650): *nempe, ut malus e medio tollatur; ut ne terra inquinetur flagitiis, neve vindictam ab iis, qui neglexere scelera vindicare, supremus judex sumat.* This idea was also familiar to the Lutheran theory of punishment; see e.g. Witte (2002), 130–132, 151–152; Pihlajamäki (2006), 181–182.

[113]Grotius appeared to have limited a people's right to resistance over the course of the years: in *De jure praedae* he had granted a more extensive right of resistance, whereas he mitigated this position in *De jure belli ac pacis* to a stronger role of the sovereign. See e.g. Tuck (1979); Vermeulen (1982/3), 55–57; AC Eyffinger and BP Vermeulen in: De Groot (1991), 15–16.

[114]See e.g. Tuck (1979), 78–80; Eyffinger/Vermeulen, in: De Groot (1991), 15.

[115]Such as Johannes Felden in 1653, on whose critique see e.g. Tuck (1979), 75, 79.

[116]Matthaeus, *De criminibus* 48.XIX.V.3 (p. 650): *exemplum in vulgus*. Setting an example for the common herd corresponds with an educational purpose in criminal law; according to Protestant theologians, such as Melanchton, law also had such educational function, see Witte (2002), 128–129, 135, 163, 170.

[117]Matthaeus was at least familiar with two of these authors, Beza and Hotman, as he referred to their work, see Matthaeus, *De criminibus* IV, p. 791, Index IX Jurists, historians, theologians and other later writers. See on Hotman and particularly Beza, Witte (2008), 81–141.

[118]See Witte (2008), 124–125.

[119]See Witte (2008), 126–127. Compare also Matthaeus, *De criminibus* 48.XIX.V.2 (pp. 647–648).

sovereign did not fulfil his duties but violated existing laws and privileges, foremost the First and Second Tables of the Decalogue, his people would be free to oppose him, according to Beza.[120] Ultimately, he could then be lawfully removed, although Matthaeus admittedly offered no opinion on this exact consequence.

On a few occasions, Matthaeus's arguments are admittedly indeed in line with the idea that a state is there for the people, and not the other way around. For instance in the title on Public and Private Violence, where Matthaeus explained that abduction fell under public violence, and had to be considered a most serious offence:

> Violence itself is an offence and indeed a public one and it ought to be eliminated as far as possible from well-established states, in particular in which liberty is equal for all.[121]

This somewhat sidelong observation ties in with the Calvinist idea that the state ought to protect citizens, including their religious liberty. For many Calvinist theologians, including Calvin himself, but particularly Beza, religious freedom had become crucial.[122] Importantly, Matthaeus refused to discuss heresy at all:

> I am adding nothing about heresy, although this is a most serious crime in the eyes of the Catholics, and although many unique features apply in interrogating and punishing heretics. However, after we obtained our liberty by force of arms, that fearful inquisition was banished from our Provinces, and since we believe that the orthodox religion must be taught rather than imposed, a description of this cruel form of trial will be superfluous.[123]

Although the state was thus subordinate to divine law, this did not mean that the orthodox—Calvinist—religion had to be imposed by the state. Rather, according to Matthaeus, law and religion were—to a large extent—separate, as will be discussed in the following section.

3.5 *Religion, Morals and Criminal Law: The Courts of Heaven and Earth*

The orthodox religion should thus not be imposed by the state, although the state was subservient to divine law. This becomes clear at the few instances where Matthaeus distinguished between the court of heaven and courts on earth.

---

[120] See Witte (2008), 133–134. See also e.g. Eyffinger/Vermeulen in: De Groot (1991), 15.

[121] Matthaeus, *De criminibus* 48.IV.II.5 (p. 346): *Vis ipsa crimen est, & quidem publicum, debetque exulare quantum potest e bene constitutis civitatibus: iis inprimis, in quibus libertas omnibus aequa est.*

[122] See e.g. Witte (2008), 128.

[123] Matthaeus, *De criminibus* 48.X.VI.7 (p. 450): *De haeresi nihil adjicio, tametsi enim Pontificiorum moribus gravissimum hoc crimen est, multaque in inquirendo & vindicando singularia observantur; tamen cum libertate armis parta horribilis illa inquisitio e nostris provinciis exulet, religionemque orthodoxam docendam non imperandam credamus, enarratio crudelis judicii supervacua futura est.*

As discussed above,[124] Matthaeus could understand that a married man having an affair with an unmarried woman was considered an adulterer in light of the first marriage. But according to Matthaeus, such affair would however never come to the court on earth, but only to the heavenly court: 'For the heavenly judge punished crimes in one way and the judge of this world in another.'[125] In this context Matthaeus remarked that 'in this matter Beza talks like a theologian, punishing crimes of the mind and not of the hands.'[126] So, Matthaeus did not consider everything that was wrong according to the orthodox religion also as legally wrong—although he called both 'crimes', without distinguishing between 'sin' and 'crime'.[127]

On the other hand, for Matthaeus not everything that was legally right was also right according to the teachings of the Gospel. Under the Civil law, sometimes a killing could take place with impunity: thieves, when they wrest your property from you with a drawn sword, become robbers and can be killed with impunity (e.g. D. 9.2.4.1; D. 47.2.55(54)0.2).[128] Although such behavior was considered legally right, it was not in agreement with the Gospel, according to Matthaeus:

> However, this verdict will be pronounced in the court of the land and not in the court of conscience, for in the writings of the apostles, there is absolutely no correlation between taking a cloak and taking the life of a man.[129]

In the above passages, Matthaeus distinguished between rules of criminal law and religious prescripts, expressing the divine will: the first were upheld via the law, but not the latter. However, as discussed extensively in the preceding sections, Matthaeus in numerous instances pointed out how criminal law, and particularly the punishment of crimes, could—and should—be brought into accordance with divine law, the moral and enduring teachings in the Bible. In *De criminibus*, Matthaeus thus made a distinction between Biblical moral teachings that had a direct bearing on criminal law—moral and enduring laws—and teachings that had no such direct consequence for the law—religious prescripts. The meaning of this distinction can be more fully understood in the context of contemporary Protestant theology.

For Protestant theologians, such as Luther, Melanchton, but also Calvin, Beza and Althusius, the Decalogue and the Mosaic laws explaining those, but also teachings of Jesus, such as the Beatitudes and the Golden Rule, were moral and enduring laws.[130]

---

[124] See above, 3.3 Defining Crimes: Abortion and Adultery.

[125] Matthaeus, *De criminibus* 48.III.I.12 (p. 283): *Etenim aliter coelestis judex, aliter judex hujus seculi exigit crimina.*

[126] Matthaeus, *De criminibus* 48.III.I.13 (p. 284): *Disserit enim Beza quidem hac de re ut Theologus, mente non manu exigens criminal: (…).*

[127] Unlike for instance Thomas Hobbes (1588–1679), see on this Masferrer (2021a, b), 1–27, 97–144, and in more detail, Masferrer (2017), 693–756.

[128] Matthaeus, *De criminibus* 48.V.II.7 (p. 371).

[129] Matthaeus, *De criminibus* 48.V.II.7 (p. 371): *Verum, haec quoque sententia in foro Caesaris, non in foro conscientiae pronunciabitur. Cum enim apostolica pagina auferenti pallium & vitam hominis proportio prorsus nulla sit.*

[130] See e.g. Witte (2008), 127–9, 160–163, 183. On Lutheranism and particular Melanchton, see e.g. Witte (2002), 113–115, 123, 125–132. Earlier, for instance Thomas Aquinas had also considered the Decalogue to correspond with natural law principles; see Witte (2002), 127.

These moral laws governed different aspects of life. Importantly, the commandments of the First Table—to acknowledge one God and make no graven image, to utter no blasphemy, and to keep the Sabbath day holy—were natural law principles that defined the spiritual relation between God and men; these rules entailed the spiritual morality. The commandments of the Second Table—to honor one's parents, not to kill, not to commit adultery, not to steal, not to give false testimonies, and not to covet—were the natural law principles that defined the relations between men; these rules concerned civil morality.[131]

Matthaeus firmly stood in this Protestant tradition—both Lutheran and Calvinist—because he indeed considered the Decalogue and the Mosaic rules explaining those commandments, as a central piece of legislation, as legal rules valid for contemporary society, and equated them with natural law: for Matthaeus the Decalogue and the Mosaic teachings pertaining to it indeed corresponded with 'natural equity', 'natural reason', natural law' or 'the law of nature'.[132] Although Matthaeus uses the terms divine law and natural law respectively, he appears to make no fundamental distinction between divine and natural law.[133] In *De criminibus*, the borderline between divine and natural law thus remains unclear. Natural reason seems necessary to know natural law; but many moral and enduring principles in divine law can also be grasped by natural reason.

For Matthaeus, the more fundamental distinction appears not to be between divine law, natural law and human law (that is, positive or civil law),[134] but between divine law (which appears to encompass natural law) and the positive, civil law. But even on this point, Matthaeus did not give any clear reason or criterion to distinguish between moral and enduring laws—which had to be enforced by criminal laws—and religious prescripts—with a sometimes undeniable moral character but which should not be enforced by secular law.

Indeed, for the purpose of criminal law, Matthaeus relied heavily on the commandments of the Second Table of the Decalogue governing civil morality: e.g. not to

[131] See e.g. Witte (2008), 59, 127–9, 160–163, 183; Witte (2002), 128–132, 169–173.

[132] See above, e.g. Matthaeus, *De criminibus* 47.I.II.6 (pp. 58–9), 48.II.III.10 (p. 245), 48.III.II.4 (p. 292), 48.XVIII.IV.31 (p. 625), 48.XIX.V.2 (p. 647).

[133] Protestant theologians such as Calvin, Beza and Althusius did not make a clear distinction between divine law and natural law either; see e.g. Witte (2008), 59, 127, 157–158. On the relation between divine and natural law in twentieth century Calvinist legal scholarship, see e.g. Stamhuis (1988), 39–42 (Willem Nieboer) and 55–56 (Herman Dooyeweerd), and on the persistent discomfort of Calvinist theology with natural law, see e.g. Douma (1978).

[134] For example, Thomas of Aquinas, in his *Summa Theologiae*, when tackling the legal issues (Prima Secundae, Q. 90–114), distinguished between four *leges* (*aeterna*, q. 93; *naturalis*, q. 94; *humana*, q. 95–97; *divina*, q. 98–114); see on this e.g. Masferrer (2021a, b), 1–27, 97–144.

kill,[135] not to commit adultery,[136] not to steal,[137] not to give false testimonies.[138] But also the commandments of the First Table governing spiritual morality—e.g. against idolatry[139] and blasphemy[140]—were to be upheld through criminal law. Unsurprisingly, Matthaeus's references to the Old Testament, and particularly to the Mosaic laws explaining the Decalogue, vastly outnumbered his references to the New Testament.[141]

Importantly, however, Matthaeus refused to criminalize heresy,[142] although for several Protestant theologians it too belonged to the realm of spiritual morality governed by the First Table of the Decalogue.[143] For Matthaeus, however, religious doctrine apparently fell outside 'public' or external morality—whether civil or spiritual—but belonged to internal or 'private' spiritual morality.[144] Moreover, religious prescripts based on the teachings of Jesus and the apostles seemed to concern primarily the conscience and what was right before the court of conscience: admittedly, these rules also corresponded with such internal spiritual morality. Doctrine and religious prescripts connected with the internal or 'private' spiritual morality were not to be imposed via criminal law and brought before courts on earth, but to be taught and brought before the heavenly courts.

The theory underlying *De criminibus* thus appears ambiguous: due to the absolute primacy of divine will and law, the role of natural, practical reason remains quite limited. Indeed, although Matthaeus distinguished between moral and enduring laws with direct bearing on criminal law and religious prescripts without such direct consequence for the law, he failed to give any clear reason or criterion for such

[135]On murder, see above 3.1.1 On Theft, Damage and Attempt to Murder; 3.3 Defining Crimes: Abortion and Adultery.

[136]On unnatural lust, adultery and incest, see above 3.1.2 On Unnatural Lust, False Testimonies and Soothsayers; 3.1.3 On Adultery, Incest and Manstealing; 3.1.4 On Adultery Again and Sacrilege; 3.3 Defining Crimes: Abortion and Adultery.

[137]On theft, see above 3.1.1 On Theft, Damage and Attempt to Murder; 3.4 States, Divine Law and Religious Freedom.

[138]On false testimonies, see above 3.1.2 On Unnatural Lust, False Testimonies and Soothsayers.

[139]On soothsayers, see above 3.1.2 On Unnatural Lust, False Testimonies and Soothsayers.

[140]On sacrilege, see above 3.1.4 On Adultery Again and Sacrilege.

[141]See Matthaeus, *De criminibus* IV, 795–797, Index XI Biblia Sacra. The index contains a total of 237 references to 193 different Scriptural passages: 202 references to 161 different passages in the Old Testament; 34 references to 31 different passages in the New Testament; 1 reference to an Apocryphal passage. Of the Old Testament references are by far the most to the Mosaic books: 143 references to 105 passages (21 references to 13 passages in Genesis; 48 references to 33 passages in Exodus; 23 references to 18 passages in Leviticus; 9 references to 7 passages in Numbers; 42 references to 34 passages in Deuteronomy), against 59 references to 56 passages of other books of the Old Testament (Joshua, Judges, I and II Samuel, I and II Kings, II Chronicles, Job, Psalms, Proverbs, Isaiah, Jeremiah, Ezekiel, and Hosea). The books of the New Testament referred to are: Matthew, Mark, Luke, John, Acts, Romans, I Corinthians, I Timothy, and Revelation.

[142]On heresy, see above 3.4 States, Divine Law and Religious Freedom.

[143]See Witte (2002), 131–132, 137, 153, 159–160.

[144]For a contemporary distinction between private and public morality, see Domingo (2016), 133–136.

distinction. Also where Matthaeus appears to distinguish between 'public' or external morality—whether civil or spiritual—and 'private' or internal spiritual morality, he fails to give any consistent reasoning,[145] unlike for instance Thomas Aquinas when distinguishing between individual morality and morality of political communities.[146] Nevertheless, Matthaeus stood clear of imposing the 'private' spiritual morality of the orthodox religion on society via criminal law. For Matthaeus the observance of orthodox doctrine and religious prescripts were distinct from ordering society via criminal law: the orthodox religion had to be taught, rather than imposed.

4 Conclusions

Matthaeus's Calvinist conviction is undeniable in *De criminibus*. This Calvinist conviction becomes particularly evident in contested issues of criminal law. At these places, in discussion with Civil and Canon lawyers, but particularly also with other Reformed theologians and legal scholars, Matthaeus developed his own stance, on how to interpret and explain Roman criminal law and local customary criminal laws in light of the orthodox—Calvinist—religion. For Matthaeus, as a true Calvinist, the ultimate source of law was divine law. Matthaeus's consequent Calvinism can help to explain certain 'modern' opinions, such as his rejection of torture as a mean to achieve confessions. The inadmissibility of torture was based on the idea that punishment was a retribution for an offence: for Matthaeus, this idea was eventually grounded on Scripture, i.e. the divine will, the ultimate source of law. Here, Matthaeus's modern opinion is thus directly based on his Calvinist conviction and the application of this conviction on criminal law.

Due to the absolute primacy of divine will and law in *De criminibus*, the role of natural, practical reason remains quite limited. Indeed, although Matthaeus distinguished between moral and enduring laws with direct bearing on criminal law and religious prescripts without such direct consequence for the law, he failed to give any clear reason or criterion for such distinction.

For criminal law, the enduring moral laws were to be found mainly in the Decalogue and the Mosaic Laws that explicated those commandments. Matthaeus referred to these enduring moral laws of the Decalogue as 'natural equity', 'natural reason', 'natural law', 'the law of nature'. Basically, both Tables of the Decalogue, covering civil and spiritual morality respectively, should be upheld via criminal law. But in these commandments Matthaeus chose to strictly uphold some and to be more lenient about others. In principle, adultery and murder had to be punished capitally, while theft should be punished non-capitally: here the biblical prescripts on punishment were of a partly moral nature and judges should not readily depart from those rules. But the punishment for blasphemy was less strict in the statutes of Utrecht compared

[145] Although Matthaeus occasionally referred to public utility, see e.g. Matthaeus, *De criminibus* 48.XIX.V.2 (p. 649).

[146] See on this e.g. Masferrer (2021a, b), 1–27, 97–144.

to the capital punishment foreseen in Scripture—with Matthaeus's apparent approval. Due to the judicial discretion in the punishment of crimes, the teachings of Matthaeus could potentially have far-reaching influence on such punishment.

Matthaeus did not, however, equate all biblical teachings with enduring moral laws valid for the courts on earth. Importantly, he refused to criminalize heresy. Indeed, for Matthaeus apparently many of the teachings of Jesus and the apostles concerned the conscience and what was right before the court of conscience. This internal or 'private' spiritual morality, i.e. doctrine and religious prescripts were not to be imposed via criminal law and brought before courts on earth, but to be taught and brought before the heavenly courts—although Matthaeus again did not provide a consistent reasoning for his underlying distinction between 'private' and 'public' morality. Despite a lack of theoretical clarity in distinguishing between divine and natural law, 'public' and 'private morality, and enduring morals laws and religious prescripts, for Matthaeus eventually personal faith and dedication to God was distinct from law: the orthodox religion had to be taught, rather than imposed.

References

Besselink L (1989) The Impious Hypothesis Revisited. Grotiana 9:3–63

Broers EJMFC (2006) Van plakkaat tot praktijk : strafrecht in Staats-Brabant in de zeventiende en achttiende eeuw. Ars Aequi Libri, Nijmegen

Broers EJMFC (2012) Geschiedenis van het straf- en schadevergoedingsrecht: een inleiding. Maklu, Apeldoorn

De Groot H (1991) Denken over oorlog en vrede. Uitgegeven, ingeleid en van aantekeningen voorzien door Eyffinger AC en Vermeulen BP. Ambo, Baarn

De Monté VerLoren JP (1942) Geschiedenis van de wetenschap van het strafrecht en strafprocesrecht in de noordelijke Nederlanden vóór de codificatie. Geschiedenis der Nederlandsche rechtswetenschap II.2. Noord-Hollandsche uitg.mij, Amsterdam

Domingo R (2016) God and the secular legal system. Cambridge University Press, Cambridge

Douma J (1978) Natuurrecht, een betrouwbare gids? Vuurbaak, Groningen

Faber S (1983) Strafrechtspleging en criminaliteit te Amsterdam, 1680–1811: de nieuwe menslievendheid. Gouda Quint, Arnhem

Grotius H (1988) Meletius, sive de iis quae inter Christianos conveniunt epistola. Critical Edition with Translation, Commentary and Introduction by Posthumus Meyjes GHM. Brill, Leiden

Grotius H (1995) Ordinum Hollandiae ac Westfrisiae pietas. Critical edition with English translation and commentary by Rabbie E, Brill, Leiden

Hewett M, Hallebeek J (1998) The prelate, the praetor and the Professor: Antonius Matthaeus II and the Crimen Laesae Majestatis, Utrecht 1639–1640. Legal History Rev 66:115–150

Israel JI (1998) The Dutch Republic: its rise, greatness, and fall, 1477–1806. Clarendon Press, Oxford

Masferrer A (2017) La distinción entre delito y pecado en la tradición penal bajomedieval y moderna. Una propuesta revisionista de la historiografía española, europea y anglosajona. Anuario De Historia Del Derecho Español 87:693–756

Masferrer A (2021a) Criminal law and morality revisited: interdisciplinary perspectives. In: Masferrer A (ed) Criminal law and morality in the age of consent. Springer, Heidelberg, pp 1–27

Masferrer A (2021b) The role of nature in the secularization of criminal law in Europe (17th–19th Centuries). The criminal law of the enlightenment revisited. In: Masferrer A (ed) Criminal law and morality in the age of consent. Springer, Heidelberg, pp 97–144
Matthaeus A (1987–1996) De criminibus. Introduction and English translation by Hewett ML, Stoop BC, vols I-IV. Juta, Cape Town
Moll G (1902) De confiscatie der goederen van Hugo de Groot. Oud-Holland. Nieuwe Bijdragen Voor De Geschiedenis Der Nederlandsche Kunst, Letterkunde, Nijverheid, Enz. 20:83–112
Müller M (2013) Het felle leven en het kalme gerecht. Misdaad en straf in vijftiende-eeuws Haarlem. Pro Memorie 15(2):4–31
Müller M (2015) De oudste vermeldingen van pijnlijke verhoren in Holland en de strengheid van de strafrechtspleging in middeleeuws Haarlem. Pro Memorie 17(1):92–100
Nellen H (2015) Hugo Grotius. Brill, Leiden
Nijman JE (2017) Grotius' Imago Dei Anthropology: Grounding Ius Naturae et Gentium. In: Koskenniemi M, García-Salmones Rovia M, Amorosa P (eds) International law and religion: historical and contemporary perspectives. Oxford University Press, Oxford, pp 87–110
O'Donovan O (2004) The justice of assignment and subjective rights in Grotius. In: O'Donovan O, Lockwood O'Donovan J (eds) Bonds of imperfection: Christian politics, past and present. Eerdmans, Grand Rapids, Michigan, pp 167–203
Oosterhuis J (2019) A staunch Protestant on an irenic Remonstrant: Matthaeus's references to Grotius in *De criminibus*. In: Dondorp H, Schermaier M, Sirks B (eds) De rebus divinis et humanis. Essays in honour of Jan Hallebeek. Vandenhoeck & Ruprecht, Göttingen, pp 225–240
Pihlajamäki H (2006) Executor divinarum et suarum legum: Criminal law and the Lutheran reformation. In: Mäkinen V (ed) Lutheran reformation and the law. Brill, Leiden, pp 171–204
Pompe WPJ (1956) Geschiedenis der Nederlandse strafrechtswetenschap sinds de codificatiebeweging. Geschiedenis der Nederlandsche rechtswetenschap II.3 Noord-Hollandsche Uitgevers Maatschappij, Amsterdam
Posthumus Meyjes GHM (1984) Grotius as an irenicist. In: Feenstra R (ed) The World of Hugo Grotius (1583–1645). APA—Holland University Press, Amsterdam & Maarssen, pp 43–63
Remmelink J (1989) Luther en het strafrecht : een kritische bespreking van uitspraken van Maarten Luther over het strafrecht. W.E.J, Tjeenk Willink, Zwolle
Schlüter F (1929) Antonius Matthaeus II. aus Herborn, der Kriminalist des 17. Jahrhunderts, der Rechtslehrer Utrechts. Schletter'sche Buchhandlung, Breslau
Stamhuis EF (1988) Protestantse bijdragen aan het Nederlandse strafrechtsdenken sinds 1880. VU Uitgeverij, Amsterdam
Taylor Ch (2007) A secular age. The Belknap Press of Harvard University Press, Cambridge, Massachusetts and London
Tierney B (1997) The idea of natural rights. Eerdmans, Grand Rapids, Michigan
Tuck R (1979) Natural rights theories. Cambridge University Press, Cambridge, Their origin and development
Van Binsbergen WC (1986) Poenaal panorama : strafrechtshistorische verkenningen. Tjeenk Willink, Zwolle
Van de Vrugt M (1978) De Criminele ordonnantiën van 1570: enkele beschouwingen over de eerste strafrechtcodificatie in de Nederlanden. De Walburg Pers, Zutphen
Van de Vrugt M (1982) Aengaende Criminele Saken. Kluwer, Deventer
Van de Vrugt M (1986) Antonius Matthaeus II 1601–1654, Utrechts eerste primarius iuris. In: Van den Bergh GCJJ, Spruit JE, Van de Vrugt M (eds) Rechtsgeleerd Utrecht, Levensschetsen van elf hoogleraren uit driehonderdvijftig jaar Faculteit der Rechtsgeleerdheid in Utrecht. De Walburg Pers, Zutphen, pp 23–35
Van de Vrugt M (1987) Antonius Matthaeus II (1601–1654). In: Veen TJ, Kop PC (eds) Zestig juristen, Bijdragen tot een beeld van de geschiedenis der Nederlandse rechtswetenschap. W.E.J, Tjeenk Willink, Zwolle, pp 166–170
Van Deursen ATh (1991) Bavianen en slijkgeuzen: kerk en kerkvolk ten tijde van Maurits en Oldebarnevelt. Van Wijnen, Franeker

Van Deursen ATh (2010) Maurits van Nassau, 1567–1625: De winnaar die faalde. In: Van Deursen ATh (ed) De Gouden Eeuw compleet. Bakker, Amsterdam, pp 1035–1078

Verhaar V, Van den Brink F (1989) De bemoeienissen van stad en kerk met overspel in het achttiende-eeuwse Amsterdam. In: Faber S (ed) Nieuw licht op oude justitie : misdaad en straf ten tijde van de Republiek. Coutinho, Muiderberg, pp 64–93

Vermeulen BP (1982/3) God, wil en rede in Hugo de Groots natuurecht. Wijsgerig Perspectief 23:54–58

Witte J Jr (2002) Law and protestantism: the legal teachings of the Lutheran reformation. Cambridge University Press, Cambridge

Witte J Jr (2008) The reformation of rights: law, religion and human rights in early modern calvinism. Cambridge University Press, Cambridge

The Role of Nature in the Secularization of Criminal Law in Europe (17th–19th Centuries)

The Criminal Law of the Enlightenment Revisited

Aniceto Masferrer

Abstract Some authors have argued that enlightenment authors endorsed a social contract that was not compatible with the existence of laws of nature or a moral foundation for criminal law, while nineteenth-century liberal criminal lawyers founded criminal law upon a natural law theory, based on divine commands. This chapter demonstrates on the contrary that enlightenment authors did not necessarily make a sharp distinction between morality and criminal law, nor did 19th-century criminal lawyers adopted a conception of criminal law that was too heavily dependent on morality, as it was defended by medieval and early-modern-age scholars. The traditional dichotomy between enlightened thinkers and traditional criminal lawyers does not apply well to nineteenth-century Spain and France.

1 Introduction: The Myth of an Enlightened Criminal Law Without Morality

It has been argued that in some European jurisdictions, such as in France and Spain, 19th-century criminal law scholarship betrayed some of the main criminal law principles defended by the Enlightenment. In this regard, Diego Silva Forné wrote as follows:

> The change of political circumstances that entails the progressive consolidation of the liberal state – and its drift towards conservatism – provoked in the legal culture a gradual withdrawal

This work was undertaken in the context of the research project entitled "Las influencias extranjeras en la Codificación penal española: su concreto alcance en la Parte Especial de los Códigos decimonónicos" (ref. DER2016-78,388-P), financed by the Spanish 'Ministerio de Economía y Competitividad.'

A. Masferrer (✉)
Faculty of Law, University of Valencia, Valencia, Spain
e-mail: aniceto.masferrer@uv.es

A. Masferrer (ed.), *Criminal Law and Morality in the Age of Consent*, Ius Gentium: Comparative Perspectives on Law and Justice 84,
https://doi.org/10.1007/978-3-030-64163-4_5

from Enlightenment thought, which was reflected in a new overlay between Law and Morals, so functional confusion to the established power.[1]

He argued that Kant's foundation of criminal law greatly influenced some authors such as Pellegrino Rossi (in France) and Joaquín Francisco Pacheco (in Spain), among others.[2] On Rossi, he stated:

Criminal law realizes the absolute justice but only against the violations of duty that notably threatens the social order. Anyway, Rossi is located in the then prevailing school of thought that re-linked morality and law, which equated crime to sin, leaving behind the patient work of the Enlightenment. In the same sense, it also rejected the social contract.[3]

Silva Forné's ideas were not original since they came from previous scholars. For example, Virto Larruscain argued that whereas some criminal lawyers who were particularly attached to Enlightenment thought held the view that criminal law derived from a social contract that was seen as a political necessity or a necessary measure for the wellness of all individuals (Filangieri, Romagnosi, Bexon or Carmignani), other liberal criminal lawyers founded criminal law upon a natural law (whereby God reveals his precepts to human beings) and endorsed the criminal laws with an absolute function in all its fundamental principles (Rossi, Carrara).[4]

I do not really understand how it can be argued that Gaetano Filangieri founded the idea of criminal law upon the social contract, as he was a firm believer of the laws of nature.[5] In his *Science of legislation*, he stated that human happiness depended precisely on following the laws of nature:

No man can ignore his laws, because they are not the ambiguous results of the maxims of the moralists, nor of the sterile meditations of the philosophers, but *the dictates of that principle of universal reason, of that moral sense of the heart, which the author of nature has recorded in all the individuals of our species, as a living measure of justice and honesty, which speaks to all men in the same language, and prescribes at all times the same laws.*[6]

Iñesta-Pastor more recently followed the same line of thought in his exhaustive work on the 1848 Spanish criminal code, by arguing that,

In opposition to the utilitarianism of Beccaria, and the enlightened philosophy, that denied the ideas of morality and justice, Rossi bases criminal law on the moral order and absolute justice, placing its limit in the need for conservation of social order. In doing so, Rossi's thought was in line with the then prevailing current that linked morality and law again, rejecting both the Enlightenment and contractual approaches.[7]

---

[1]Silva Forné (2001), 292; all translations are mine, unless otherwise indicated.

[2]Kant (1797); see also, Murphy (1952, 1979); for a comparative between Thomas of Aquinas and Kant's retributive theory of punishment, see Koritansky (2005), 319–338.

[3]Silva Forné (2001), 293.

[4]Virto Larruscain (1984), 67; see also Cardenal Murillo (1990), 46–47.

[5]On Gaetano Filangieri and his supposed influence in Spain, see Antón Oneca (1965a, b), 271; Sánchez Osés (1966), 413–438; Galindo Ayuda (1991), 388–395; other authors maintain the opposite view, namely, Sainz Cantero (1967), 512–513; Lalinde Abadía (1991), 453–506; Sanchez Blanco (1991); Baró Pazos (1991), 1–40, particularly 25–26; Sánchez González (2007), 70; Lorente Sariñena (2007); Astigarraga (2007).

[6]Filangieri (1822); Filangieri (1821), 65.

[7]Iñesta-Pastor (2011), 264.

And later on, describing some of Rossi's main ideas, she added:

> In this way, the penalty is justified by having a moral value correlative to the value of the crime committed, and, as the legal order represents the social order, to attempt against it implies doing so against the moral order, thereby confusing morals and law.[8]

Concerning the allegedly link between morals and law, and, more specifically, between sin and crime defended by some 19th-century criminal lawyers like Pellegrino Rossi, Luigi Ferrajoli argued that the resort to what he calls an "'external ontological reference' as sufficient for the theoretical-juridical definition of crime and justification ethical-policy for its punishment, does not fulfill any function of limitation of the positive law (and therefore, of the state authority, as Enlightenment thought did), so it endorses its contents and encourages its extension to any moral or natural deviation."[9]

I do not fully agree with this thesis. I think it is not entirely accurate to maintain that enlightened thought endorsed a social contract that was never compatible with the existence of both laws of nature and a moral foundation of criminal law. In my view, the truth is that neither enlightened authors necessarily called for a break between morality and criminal law nor 19th-century criminal lawyers adopted a conception of criminal law too attached to morality, as it was defended by medieval and early-modern-age scholars. For example, Filangieri rejected "the maxims of the moralists" and "the sterile meditations of the philosophers," but not "the dictates of that principle of universal reason, of that moral sense of the heart, which (...) prescribes at all times the same laws."[10]

My thesis is that there is a common ground in the process of systematization, humanization and secularization of the 18th- and 19th-century criminal law science,[11] a link that connects these three notions, giving birth to a new, modern criminal law in Europe. The mainstream—or common ground—is right reason and, more specifically, the role of nature. The notions of nature, reason and justice were still at the basis of the criminal codes of the eighteenth and nineteenth centuries, and can also be found in the criminal-law discourses of criminal lawyers from different European jurisdictions.

An analysis of legal doctrine from the seventeenth century shows how often lawyers used or resorted to the notion of nature, and more particularly of human nature, in striving to develop the criminal law in line with the ideals of humanization and secularization.[12] The role of nature also enables us to understand why it took

---

[8] Iñesta-Pastor (2011), 266.

[9] Ferrajoli (1997), 229; for the English version, Ferrajoli (2018).

[10] See Footnote 6.

[11] On the contribution of the codification movement towards the criminal law development that might be synthesized in three aspects—systematization, humanization and secularization—, see Masferrer (2009, 2010).

[12] On the use of 'human nature' as the foundation of 'human dignity', see Masferrer (2016).

such a long time to decriminalize some behaviours that, according to our current mentality, were required by the secularization process.[13]

I will divide this chapter in three parts. Part I will describe the role of nature in the legal-philosophy and political-philosophy discourse; more specifically, I will show how some 17th-century legal philosophers and political philosophers endorsing the social contract—like Hobbes Pufendorf and Locke—used the notion of nature when dealing with criminal law. In Part II, I will describe how 18th-century lawyers and legal philosophers resorted to the notion of 'nature' to justify the convenience to punish some behaviours that were, according to the understanding of some scholars such as Ferrajoli, Virto Larruscain, Silva Forné and Iñesta-Pastor, improper for an Enlightened criminal law and should have been condemned and decriminalized with determination, and Part III will show how 'nature' continued to play an important role in (i) explaining the relationship between criminal law and morality; (ii) defining the notion of crime; and (iii) justifying the criminalization or decriminalization of some behaviours in the nineteenth century.

2 The Role of Nature in the Secularization Process of Criminal Law

Enlightened thought did not come out of the blue. In this vein, "the ideas of Montesquieu, Beccaria, Rousseau, Voltaire, Kant, Bentham, and Blackstone, among others, concerning some of the sexual misbehaviors persecuted and punished in the early modern age, do not really show a clear break with the supposed 'Christian' or 'moralizing' criminal law."[14] The reason for this is the existence of a certain, scholarly line of continuity from the seventeenth century onwards. For Jean Domat and Samuel von Pufendorf, among others, criminal law revolved around nature, natural law and natural reason.[15] Even 17th-century English thinkers like Thomas Hobbes and John Locke clearly distinguished between crime and sin, and connected the criminal law with morality and natural order.

[13]Let me give an example. It is well known that Bentham was the first to argue for the decriminalization of the crime of sodomy at the end of the eighteenth century. However, such claim was not common in the end of the eighteenth century or in the first middle of the nineteenth century. In fact, many European criminal codes continued to persecute and punish this behaviour during the twentieth century. The reason for this was, mainly, the role of nature, since it was thought that such behaviour was somehow against nature and should be prevented for a variety of reasons (including medical, health or other reasons related to hygiene, the preservation of health, and the prevention of illness).

[14]Masferrer (2017), 735 ff.

[15]The notion of natural reason was already present in Stoicism which clearly influenced some Roman lawyers; on this matter, see Watson (1971); Vander Waerdt (1994); in Thomas of Aquinas' thought this notion was central and 16th-century Spanish Scholasticism followed the same path; as will be seen, non-Catholic lawyers and political philosophers used it as well, although its meaning and role varied.

The criminal law doctrine of the Enlightenment should not be lightly equated with utilitarianism. Montesquieu, Beccaria, Rousseau, Voltaire, Kant, Tomasius and Wolff, among others, were not utilitarians. In fact, Kantian thought was at odds with utilitarianism and legal positivism. Moreover, most of the 18th-century legal philosophers, when dealing with the need for criminal law reform, did not deny the role of nature, natural order and social order. Moreover, some contractual approaches to legal philosophy and political philosophy were not necessarily at odds with the recognition of nature.

That also explains why this was still the mainstream among the 19th-century criminal lawyers. In this regard, there is no doubt that the Kantian doctrine against utilitarianism notably succeeded and highly influenced the fate of the 19th-century criminal law science—not only in Germany but in other European jurisdictions—and for similar reasons it went through a revival after the Second World War.[16]

2.1 *Criminal Law, Nature and Morality in the 17th Century*

If enlightened authors developed what had been done by previous ones, whose contribution to the secularization of law was notable, and it would not be fair to maintain that the secularization of criminal law was due to the 18th-century Enlightenment, I need to show the legacy the enlightened authors received from the past and, more specifically, the criminal law ideas of some contractualist legal philosophers like Hobbes, Pufendorf and Locke. In doing so, I will emphasize the role of nature in criminal law and how contractualists clearly distinguished the notions of crime and sin.

2.1.1 Thomas Hobbes

Thomas Hobbes (5 April 1588–4 December 1679), for example, showed in his work *Dialogue* the clear distinction between crime and sin. After reproaching someone for not distinguishing between these categories,[17] he pointed out:

> All crimes are indeed sins, but not all sins crimes. A sin may be in the thought or secret purpose of a man, of which neither a judge, nor a witness, nor any man can take notice; but a crime is such a sin as consists in an action against the law, of which action he can be accused, and tried by a judge, and be convinced or cleared by witnesses.[18]

Hobbes insisted on the idea that a crime, unlike a sin, needed the commission of some deed or word forbidden by law:

---

[16] As it is well known, after the Second World War Kant's doctrine witnessed a revival and contributed to the "glorification of autonomy," as Fletcher (1984, 171) pointed out.

[17] Hobbes (1839–1845b).

[18] Hobbes 1839–1845c).

> A crime is a sin, consisting in the committing, by deed or word, of that which the law forbiddeth, or the omission of what it hath commanded. So that every crime is a sin but not every sin a crime. To intend to steal, or kill, is a sin, though it never appear in word, or fact: for God that seeth the thoughts of man, can lay it to his charge: but till it appear by something done, or said, by which the intention may be argued by a human judge, it hath not the name of crime.[19]

Hobbes differentiated between the sins against 'natural laws' and the crimes against 'civil laws':

> From this relation of sin to the law, and of crime to the civil law, may be inferred, first, that where law ceaseth, sin ceaseth. But because the law of nature is eternal, violation of covenants, ingratitude, arrogance, and all facts contrary to any moral virtue, can never cease to be sin. Secondly, that the civil law ceasing, crimes cease: for there being no other law remaining, but that of nature, there is no place for accusation; every man being his own judge, and accused only by his own conscience, and cleared by the uprightness of his own intention. When therefore his intention is right, his fact is no sin: if otherwise, his fact is sin; but not crime. Thirdly, that when the sovereign power ceaseth, crime also ceaseth; for where there is no such power, there is no protection to be had from the law; and therefore every one may protect himself by his own power: for no man in the institution of sovereign power can be supposed to give away the right of preserving his own body; for the safety whereof all sovereignty was ordained. But this is to be understood only of those that have not themselves contributed to the taking away of the power that protected them; for that was a crime from the beginning.[20]

As can be seen, no reference to God was needed to define 'crime' in the 17th Century. For Hobbes, as for all other early modern age authors, there was no crime unless the behavior produced damage to either an individual or the community. Many times the damage affected both individuals and society around them.[21] Hobbes, in the *Dialogue*, asked why heresy was made a crime.[22] In his answer, he did not seem to think that heresy was made a crime solely because it offended God; on the contrary, he explained the historical reasons as to why political power decided to make it a crime.[23] It was not only to use religion as a key factor to achieve political unity and social cohesion, but also to avoid social unrest and conflict. In other words, the ideas of 'social order' and 'social peace' were at the core of this political decision, instead of being the purpose of punishing a sin committed against God, as some authors have suggested.

No explicit reference to God was needed to define crime before the Enlightenment. However, there was no doubt about the existence of 'natural laws'. Any act against 'natural law' was a sin, but not a crime ("the civil law ceasing, crimes cease," as Hobbes stressed). Besides, lawyers thought that civil laws should reflect the 'natural order' because the 'social peace' or 'social order' could not be achieved without

---

[19]Hobbes (1839–1845d).

[20]Hobbes (1839–1845e).

[21]Hobbes (1839–1845f).

[22]Hobbes (1839–1845g): "Since you have told me how heresy came to be a name, tell me also how it came to be a crime; and what were the heresies that first were made crimes."

[23]Hobbes (1839–1845h).

complying with the 'natural order'. This did not necessarily imply criminalizing all acts that were against natural order, in particular those which did not produce any apparent social damage such as moral scandal, pathologies, and physical illnesses.

Authors may of course manipulate the natural order, extending it to matters whose natural character might be discussed, according to not only a current mentality but also to a particular historical period. Hobbes for example, insisted that there was no need to specify the particular behaviors, "enumeration of facts", constituting the crime of treason, because, being "high-treason [is] the highest *crime* at the common-law, (...), therefore not only the statute, but the reason itself, without statute makes it a crime." The question did not just concern the dichotomy between statutory law and common law, but also the idea that common law was supposed to deal with matters related to natural law and natural reason. This explains why Hobbes thought that "[t]reason is a crime of itself, *alum in se*, and therefore a crime at the common-law."[24]

In defending the principle of non-retroactivity of criminal law, Hobbes compared the 'civil laws' with the 'natural laws'. In other words, he drew this important criminal law principle from the 'natural law order':

> No law, made after a fact done, can make it a crime: because if the fact be against the law of nature, the law was before the fact; and a positive law cannot be taken notice of, before it be made; and therefore cannot be obligatory. But when the law that forbiddeth a fact is made before the fact is done; yet he that doth the fact, is liable to the penalty ordained after, in case no lesser penalty was made known before, neither by writing, nor by example, for the reason immediately before alleged.[25]

Legal science in general, and in particular criminal law, was immersed in the notions of nature, natural order and human nature. This enabled Hobbes to describe the motives and the driving forces behind why crimes were carried out, or, in other words, why men committed crimes. In his description, the notion of 'nature' appeared frequently,[26] although not always with the same meaning.

2.1.2 Samuel Von Puffendorf

As illustrated, some scholars think that the social contract and natural law are not compatible or, in other words, the criminal-law thought of contractualists cannot be attached to a morality based upon natural law. This is an over simplistic view of the issue. Puffendorf, for example, combined the social contract and human nature when dealing with criminal law.[27] In analyzing the duties "to be practised by one Man towards another," he argued that some of them "proceed[ed] from that *common Obligation* which it has pleased the Creator to lay upon all Men in general; others

---

[24]Hobbes (1839–1845i).

[25]Hobbes (1839–1845j).

[26]In this regard, it is revealing to read what he thought about the role of passions in committing a crime; see Hobbes (1839–1845k).

[27]For a complete account of the relation between natural law and social in Samuel von Pufendorf, see his De Jure naturæ et gentium (1672).

take their Original from some certain *Human Institutions,* or some *peculiar, adventitious* or accidental *State* of Men." The former may be called 'Absolute duties'—and "are *always* to be practised by *every* Man towards *all* Men"—while the latter 'Conditional duties.'[28]

Among the 'absolute duties' that derived from the moral order, Pufendorf pointed out that the first rule was "that *one do no Wrong to the other*; and this is the *amplest* Duty of all, comprehending *all Men* as such," "because without it *Human Society* cannot be preserved." And he added:

> For I can live *quietly* with him that does me *no Good,* or with whom I have no manner of correspondence, provided he does me *no Harm* (...). But I can by no means live *peaceably* with him that *wrongs* me.[29]

Pufendorf applied this doctrine to crimes, by arguing that citizens' duties came from both nature ("such as our Laws, Bodies, Limbs, Chastity, Liberty") and *Human Institution* or *Compact,* "Whence all those Actions are hereby made Crimes, by which any Wrong is done to others, as Murther, Wounding, Striking, Rapine, Theft, Fraud, Violence, whether practis'd directly or indirectly, mediately or immediately, and the like."[30]

He emphasized the link between moral duties, rights deriving from nature and human laws, and the damage. Moreover, for him damage meant "all Manner of *Harm, spoiling, diminishing,* or *taking away* what is already ours, or *intercepting* that which by an *absolute Right* we ought to have, whether it be bestowed upon us by Nature, or given us by Man and Human Laws; or lastly, the *Omission* or *Denial* of paying what by a *perfect Obligation* is due to us."[31]

Pufendorf thought that any damage required reparation and repentance from the evildoer and pardon from the victim. After affirming that "*[r]evenge* is by the *Law of Nature* condemned, as proposing no other End, than doing Mischief to those who have hurt us, and pleasing our selves in their Sufferings," he added that that "the *Publick* may inflict a *Punishment* on the Aggressor, though he have given satisfaction to the *Private* Man, if the Act was *Criminal,* and in its Nature *Evil.*"[32]

As Pufendorf stated, some acts are *Criminal* in its Nature *Evil.* He explained that for a behavior to be criminal, it is not enough to be a sin, even a serious one. It needs

---

[28] Pufendorf (2003), Chapter VI: Of the Duty of One Man to Another, and First of Doing No Injury to Any Man, I. Reciprocal Duties of two Sorts; available at https://oll.libertyfund.org/titles/888#lf0217_label_261.

[29] Pufendorf (2003), Chaps. IV, II. No wrong to be done. L.N.N.1.3.c.1; available at https://oll.libertyfund.org/titles/888#lf0217_label_262.

[30] Pufendorf (2003), Chaps. IV, III; available at https://oll.libertyfund.org/titles/888#lf0217_label_263.

[31] Pufendorf (2003), Chaps. IV, V. Damage how to be accounted. L. N. N. l. 3. c. 1. §3; available at https://oll.libertyfund.org/titles/888#lf0217_label_265.

[32] Pufendorf (2003), Chaps. IV, XIII. Recapitulation; available at https://oll.libertyfund.org/titles/888#lf0217_label_273.

to cause a real harm. This is why "[t]he *Acts of the Mind within it self*, which are merely internal (…), are all exempted from the Stroke of human Punishments."[33]

Pufendorf thought it was hard to believe that just hope or fear might usually make a sufficient impression to prevent evil thoughts leading to another's harm, because these motives alone never lead people to doing good. Commenting on this issue in Pufendorf's work, an anonymous writer highlighted the responsibility of those in charge of the education of others; they "are obliged, by natural law, to give them the taste for sound precepts and to orient them so as to acquire a habit of virtue which, like a second nature, will guide their wills toward the good." Citing another work by Pufendorf,[34] who followed Aristotle's doctrine, he added that "[t]his is the best method of effective teaching, for (…) manners are stronger than laws."[35] It was then unrealistic for Pufendorf to imagine a corrupt heart from whose external actions are entirely innocent.

If education consisted in acquiring "a habit of virtue which (…) guide the wills toward the good," behaving according to such good—and not just good will—contributed to increase and consolidate human reputation. On the contrary, Pufendorf stated that reputation perishes "either by Reason *of the Course of a Man's Life*, or in *Consequence of some* Crime."[36] Conviction for any crime was incompatible with human reputation.[37]

2.1.3 John Locke

John Locke distinguished three kinds of laws whereby men judge their actions: divine laws, civil laws, and philosophical law (or laws of reputation). The acts that fulfil or infringe these laws are considered duties or sins (divine law), criminal or innocent (civil law), and virtues or vices (philosophical law or law of reputation).[38]

For Locke, divine law—"the measure of sin and duty"—is the "law which God has set to the actions of men, whether promulgated to them by the light of nature, or the voice of revelation." He believed that "[t]his is the only true touchstone of

---

[33] Pufendorf (2003), Chap. XIII: Of the power of life and death, XI. Internal Acts of the Mind, not subject to them. L. N. N. l. 8. c. 3. §14; available at https://oll.libertyfund.org/titles/888#lf0217_label_734.

[34] Pufendorf (1672), Book VII, Chap. ix, §4.

[35] Pufendorf (2003), The Judgment of an Anonymous Writer on the Original of This Abridgment *With reflections of the translator, intended to clarify certain of the author's principles*: X. disposed man will sin not least by failing to do what he should do. So it is dangerous, or at best unrealistic, for our author to imagine a corrupt heart, the external actions of which are entirely innocent; available at https://oll.libertyfund.org/titles/888#Pufendorf_0217_654.

[36] Pufendorf (2003), Chap. XIV: Of Reputation, VIII. Lost by an ill Condition of Life, L. N. N. l. 8. c. 4. §7; available at https://oll.libertyfund.org/titles/888#lf0217_label_760.

[37] Pufendorf (2003), Chap. XIV: Of Reputation, IX. And his Crimes; available at https://oll.libertyfund.org/titles/888#lf0217_label_761.

[38] Locke (1824), vol. 1; available at https://oll.libertyfund.org/titles/761#Locke_0128-01_706), Chap. XXVIII: Of Other Relations, 'Laws', §7; available at https://oll.libertyfund.org/titles/761#Locke_0128-01_706.

moral rectitude; and by comparing them to this law it is, that men judge of the most considerable moral good or evil of their actions: that is, whether as duties or sins, they are like to procure them happiness or misery from the hands of the Almighty."[39]

Civil law—"the measure of crimes and innocence"—is the "the rule set by the commonwealth to the actions of those who belong to it, (…) rule to which men refer their actions, to judge whether they be criminal or no." The offences committed against this law are punished by "the force of the commonwealth, engaged to protect the lives, liberties, and possessions of those who live according to its law."[40]

Finally, Locke calls philosophical law—"the measure of virtue and vice"—as "the laws of opinion or reputation." Interestingly, he relates this law to the divine law:

> Virtue and vice are names pretended and supposed every-where to stand for actions in their own nature right and wrong; and as far as they really are so applied, they so far are co-incident with the divine law above-mentioned.[41]

Locke emphazises that although men render "to the public the disposing of all their force, so that they cannot employ it against any fellow-citizens", "they retain still the power of thinking well or ill, approving or disapproving of the actions of those whom they live amongst, and converse with: and by this approbation and dislike they establish amongst themselves what they will call virtue and vice."[42]

The content and extent of Locke's distinction between divine law, civil law and philosophical law is debatable, but at least he rightly put—in line with the most common 16th and 17th-century jurisprudence—criminal laws in the domain of civil or human laws, far away from divine laws and sins.

John Locke considered crime as a deviation of right reason and the principles of human nature. In his view, crime "consists in violating the law, and varying from the right rule of reason," whereby the evildoer "so far becomes degenerate, and declares himself to quit the principles of human nature." Like Pufendorf, he held that the one who had been damage had, "besides the right of punishment common to him with other men, a particular right to seek *reparation* from him that has done it."[43]

---

[39]Locke (1824), Chap. XXVIII: Of Other Relations, Laws, 'Divine law, the measure of sin and duty': §8; available at https://oll.libertyfund.org/titles/761#Locke_0128-01_707.

[40]Locke (1824), Chap. XXVIII: Of Other Relations, Laws, 'Civil law, the measure of crimes and innocence': §9; available at https://oll.libertyfund.org/titles/761#Locke_0128-01_708.

[41]Locke (1824), Chap. XXVIII: Of Other Relations, Laws, 'Philosophical law, the measure of virtue and vice': §10; available at https://oll.libertyfund.org/titles/761#Locke_0128-01_709.

[42]Locke (1824), Chap. XXVIII: Of Other Relations, Laws, 'Philosophical law, the measure of virtue and vice': §10; available at https://oll.libertyfund.org/titles/761#Locke_0128-01_709.

[43]Locke (1764).

2.2 *Criminal Law, Nature and Morality in the 18th Century*

In the eighteenth century the connection between criminal law, laws of nature and morality did not decline at all.[44] Most enlightened authors received that legacy and notably developed it. Jeremy Bentham and his utilitarianism was not part of the Enlightment mainstream. Now I will show briefly in general terms the role of nature in the new criminal law conception, and then I will explore the notion of crime and its distinction from sin, analyzing how 18th-century criminal lawyers justified the convenience not to decriminalize some behaviours particularly related to sexual and religious moral issues.

2.2.1 The Role of Nature in the New Criminal-Law Conception

Yves Cartuyvels, who has extensively worked on the 18th-century codification of criminal law,[45] emphasized 18th-century criminal codes derived from iusnaturalism. He shows that criminal codes were drafted taking into account the connection between law and science, law and nature, and law and anthropology.[46] Concerning the link between law and nature, he explained that the radical transformation of the criminal law was not just formal, but substantive, giving rise to a rational 'moral nature', a morality that could be found or discovered by the light of human reason.[47]

Natural reason was the necessary tool to carry out a kind of logical symbiosis between 'legal prescription' and 'moral order,' a moral order that was in line with the imperative laws of nature. In other words, law was the result of permanent—or *continuum*—deductive operations that derived from the natural law, whose knowledge was possible thanks to the natural reason, and the positive law. In this line of thought, the seventeenth century French lawyer Domat, referring to criminal law, made a clear distinction between natural laws—laws that were essentially or necessarily just—and positive laws—laws that were arbitrary and sought the individual utility—.[48]

For Jean Domat, Christian Tomasius and Christian Wolff, criminal law revolved around nature, natural law and natural reason. The influence of the school of natural law was, according to Cartuyvels, three-fold: (i) the state-legal monism, (ii) the scientific reason, and (iii) the morals of nature. Concerning the latter, criminal codes were

---

[44]As I defended in my paper "The Role of Nature in the 18th-century criminal law discourse: A Critical and Comparative Analysis", I delivered at the *British Legal History Conference* 2017, entitled 'Networks and Connections', held at the University College London (London), 5–8 July (5 July), 3:45 pm–5:15 pm.

[45]See, for example, Cartuyvels (1994, 1996, 1997).

[46]Cartuyvels (1994), 377 ff.

[47]Cartuyvels (1994), 377, Footnote 14, citing Christian Wolf, 1758, Chap. 1, XXIV.

[48]Cartuyvels (1994), 378, Footnote 16, citing Domat, 1777, t. I, Chap. XI, Art. 20, and t. II, preface.

regarded as tools that should contain a scientific truth in accordance with nature.[49] Let me briefly explain this point.

As Cartuyvels pointed out, the mind of the code's drafter thought that his task consisted in following a natural morality that, being just and true, might progressively replace religion in the criminal law domain.[50] In this regard, Joseph II wrote, in the political testament, that the four foundational principles of politics that were called to be linked to law were nature, reason, justice and truth.[51] This explains why lawyers connected the notion of crime to behaviours against nature and natural laws, and why the social order and social peace were supposed to be based upon a natural morality and a natural order. In this line of thought, Pufendorf thought that what distinguished human behavior from that of animals was moral liberty, and Christian Wolff regarded the 'moral man' as the subject of the law in general and criminal law in particular.

2.2.2 The Notion Crime and Its Distinction from Sin

There is no doubt that in the eighteenth century the criminal law was secularized. However, it would be wrong to state that the secularization of law in general and in particular of criminal law started in the Age of Enlightenment.[52] Secularization was a complex process which commenced much earlier in the sixteenth and seventeenth centuries, as this era already contained elements of secularization.[53]

As stated at the beginning of this paper, some scholars, such as Beccaria, Mostesquieu, Voltaire and Lardizábul and others believed that secularization of criminal law came into existence during the Age of Enlightenment. According to these scholars, during the era of enlightenment, not only did the intellectual or theoretical approach to crime change, and would eventually be detached from religion and sin, but also did the provisions of criminal law abolishing the crimes related to sexuality imposed by Christianity. This common belief does not fit with the historical reality, which was not that straightforward.

For some scholars, if the criminal law of the sixteenth and seventeenth centuries was characterized by the 'non distinction' ('*indistinctio*') between law and religion, law and morals as well as crime and sin, the eighteenth century heralded in the emergence of 'distinctions' which earlier minds, albeit with few exceptions, could not have even imagined.[54]

Other scholars have summarized the secularization of criminal law in theeighteenth century, and particularly the state's new approach to behaviors related to sexual morals, by stating that political powers took the option not to interfere into the domain of private sexuality. Unlike England which continued the legal regulation

[49] Cartuyvels (1994), 383–385.

[50] On this matter, see Hermann (1984).

[51] Cartuyvels (1994), 383, citing Joseph, II, 1791, t. I, 6.

[52] Masferrer (2009).

[53] Sellert (1983); Masferrer (2009), 136–138.

[54] Clavero (1990), 66–67.

of sexuality,[55] France was the first European jurisdiction to endorse this new policy of non-intrusion.[56] Scholars indicated that Germany[57] adopted a similar position to France. However, it should be noted that these scholars examined a long-term process and period which encompassed both the eighteenth and nineteenth centuries.

Referring to Germany, it has been argued by Rublack, the early modern process of state-formation, which made sexual morality a corner-stone of public morality, abandoned its determination to maintain such tension between officeholders and subjects, and decided to relax "the regulatory demands during the late Eighteenth century."[58] As Rublack indicated, "the relaxation of regulatory demands" occurred in the late Eighteenth Century, and not before.

From a legislative perspective, there is clear evidence that the criminalization of sexual misconduct did not cease.[59] Furthermore; it has been shown that particular behaviors like sodomy were persecuted and punished in a harsher way than ever before; however fortunately, these repressive laws were frequently not enforced.[60] There is evidence that at the time of the publication of the book, *Offences against One's Self*, by Jeremy Bentham, which defended the decriminalization of sodomy,[61] sodomy was still being as persecuted in the main European cities including London, Amsterdam, and Paris.[62] This severe persecution caused sodomy to move into secrecy.[63]

The harsh criminalization of sodomy was not an exception. Other sexual misbehaviors were also severely punished during the eighteenth century. In the late eighteenth century and beginning of the nineteenth century, sexual misconduct continued to be punished through criminal laws. The French criminal codes of 1791 and 1810, which did not punish but treated sexual behaviors as violations, constituted an exception all over Europe.[64] France is considered the first state in which sodomy was decriminalized. The Constituent Assembly of 1789–1791 dropped longstanding, although rarely enforced, laws against 'sodomy' and 'pederasty' in the course of its broad modernization of the Penal Code in 1791. However, it should not be forgotten that the revised Police Code continued to treat 'gross *public* indecency' as a misdemeanor alongside the corruption of minors 'of either sex.' These changes occurred without any recorded legislative debate.

---

[55]England maintained the death penalty for those convicted for committing the crime of sodomy until 1861, year in which this punishment—established by Henry VIII through the 'Buggery Act' (1533)—was replaced by prison and forced labor.

[56]Nye (1998), 107.

[57]Rublack (2002), 213–214.

[58]Rublack (2002), 200.

[59]Other conducts which had been tolerated in the early modern age continued to be so. A clear example of it is the prostitution, as scholars have shown; see, for example, Bullough (1985), 61.

[60]Bentham (2002), 19: "...estos crímenes parecen haber sido perseguidos en la Europa de las Luces con más saña y dedicación que nunca."

[61]Bentham (1785); I use the Spanish version, already cited in the Footnote 60.

[62]Bentham (2002), 20–22.

[63]Bentham (2002), 21–22.

[64]Gunther (2009), 10–11.

Despite this, legal historians continue to attribute this first decriminalization of sodomy to the wave of Enlightenment secularization of law and society. I have doubts as to whether the decriminalization of sodomy was mainly due to secularization, as the sodomy laws of the nineteenth century were not enacted for either 'religious' or 'confessional' reasons.

It is true that legislators of the nineteenth century recognized that, as a 'victimless crime,' sodomy could not be penalized without violating basic principles of the French legal system.[65] However, the ploy was to determine whether homosexuality could be shown to cause harm, and if the social damage could be proven, then the view that homosexuality was a purely private consensual practice would not be admitted at all, and this view continued until the twentieth century. It has been stressed that from the eighteenth century onwards sodomy was considered "not as a sin against God, but rather as a sin against society."[66]

I think that the consideration of it as a sin was not the principal reason why this conduct was punished either before or after the Enlightenment. In any case, it seems clear that legal sources do not support the aforementioned thesis whereby in the eighteenth century sexual misconduct was not criminalized because belonged to the domain of private sexuality.

Some may argue that the criminalization of sexual misbehaviors in the eighteenth century was due to the absolutist political system, which was reluctant to undertake the needed reforms to modernize criminal law. In my view, this is not entirely true. A careful examination of the ideas of some of the most remarkable thinkers of the Enlightenment era revealed that the secularization of criminal law did not necessarily imply the decriminalization of those behaviors which according to some scholars, perpetrators needed to have been punished for their sinful character.

As will be seen, the ideas of some authors such as Montesquieu, Beccaria, Rousseau, Voltaire, Kant, Bentham and Blackstone, regarding some of the sexual misbehaviors which were persecuted and punished in the early modern age, do not show a clear break with the supposed 'Christian' or 'moralizing' of criminal law.

Montesquieu

Charles-Louis de Secondat, Baron de La Brède et de Montesquieu (January 18, 1689–February 10, 1755) stated that "[t]hough all crimes be, in their own nature, public, yet there is a distinction between crimes really public and those that are private, which are so called, because they are more injurious to the individual than to the community."[67] He thought that "a good legislator is less bent upon punishing, than preventing, crimes," and that it was preferable "to inspire good morals than to inflict penalties."[68]

---

[65]Gunther (2009), 13–14.

[66]See *H-France Review* Vol. 12, January 2012, No. 5.

[67]Montesquieu (1777a).

[68]Montesquieu (1777b).

He distinguished four types of crime depending on whether they were prejudicial to religion, morals, public tranquility or the security of the subject.[69]

While Montesquieu found it very abnormal to punish crimes such as witchcraft, heresy and those against nature with the death penalty, he did not criticize their criminalization. He argued that witchcraft did not exist; that heresy was susceptible to an infinite number of distinctions, interpretations, and limitations; and that crime against nature were often obscure and uncertain. However, he did not call for the decriminalization of these behaviors.[70] His lack of criticism against 'crimes against nature', and particularly against sodomy, may be due to his rejection of this behavior. He thought this crime would never make "any great progress in society, unless people are prompted to it by some particular custom," so all "customs preparatory to this crime" should, "like every other violation of morals, be severely proscribed by the civil magistrate."[71]

The belief that laws should enhance modesty, discretion as well as good morals and customs, was particularly germane in order to be able to remain continent. According to Montesquieu, the incontinency was not a consequence of the laws of nature. "When, therefore, as he pointed out, the physical power of certain climates violates the natural law of the two sexes, and that of intelligent beings, it belongs to the legislature to make civil laws, with a view of opposing the nature of the climate and re-establishing the primitive laws."[72]

Therefore, while Montesquieu disregarded the crimes of witchcraft and heresy, he had no compulsion to request their abolition. Concerning the crimes against nature, he thought that they should not be punished with death, but laws should proscribe these practices because they were against nature; otherwise "nature will soon defend or resume her rights."[73]

No explicit references to 'Christianity' are found in Montesquieu's argumentation,[74] but he firmly believed in nature, which good laws should not ignore. He thought that laws were bound to nature and that if there were medical reasons arguing that there was evidence showing that the practice of sodomy produced physical weakness, as it was argued in the eighteenth and nineteenth centuries, Montesquieu, like other thinkers, was not in favor of decriminalizing this behavior.[75]

---

[69] Montesquieu (1777c).

[70] Montesquieu (1777d).

[71] Montesquieu (1777d).

[72] Montesquieu (1777e).

[73] See Footnote 158.

[74] Montesquieu (1777f).

[75] Montesquieu (1948), L. 12, cap. 6; on this matter, see also Vázquez García and Moreno Mengíbar (1997), 224–225.

Cesare Beccaria

After manifesting his will to avoid talking about "certain class of crimes, which has covered Europe with blood,"[76] Cesare Beccaria (March 15, 1738–November 28, 1794), stated that he prefers to "write only of crimes which violate the laws of nature and the social contract, and not of sins, even the temporal punishments of which must be determined from other principles than those of a limited human philosophy."[77]

He criticized the lack of proof with which crimes of adultery and sodomy were adjudicated; cases in which "presumptions, half-proofs, etc. are admitted,"[78] but he did not object the criminalization of these behaviors.

Concerning adultery, Beccaria argued, after considering the causes of this crime,[79] for which "the opportunities are so frequent, and the danger of discovery so easily avoided, that it were much easier for the laws to prevent this crime, than to punish it when committed."[80] According to him, whereas all crimes tended "to the destruction of society," adultery "proceeds from an abuse of that necessity which is constant and universal in human nature; a necessity anterior to the formation of society, and indeed the founder of society itself."[81]

Beccaria lamented that torture was employed to prove the crime of sodomy. Although he did not criticize its criminalization, he maintained that education was the principal determinant in preventing these cases in which, "in order to make men useful to others, (…) begins by making them useless to them."[82]

Concerning blasphemy, after describing the history of this crime and criticizing its lack of determinacy,[83] Beccaria seems to object to the criminalization of "[t]he words which are called oaths and blasphemy, (…) commonly vague terms that may be variously interpreted."[84]

Beccaria criticized those who 'imagine' that "the greatness of the sin should aggravate the crime." Whereas, according to him, "the relations between man and man are relations of equality," and "necessity alone hath produced (…) the idea of

---

[76]Beccaria (1872), *CHAPTER XXXIX: OF A PARTICULAR KIND OF CRIMES*; available at https://oll.libertyfund.org/title/2193/202770/3339536.

[77]*Ibid.*

[78]Beccaria (1872), *CHAPTER XXXI: OF CRIMES OF DIFFICULT PROOF*; available at https://oll.libertyfund.org/title/2193/202754/3339482.

[79]Beccaria (1872), *CHAPTER XXXI: OF CRIMES OF DIFFICULT PROOF*; available at https://oll.libertyfund.org/title/2193/202754/3339483.

[80]Beccaria (1872), *CHAPTER XXXI: OF CRIMES OF DIFFICULT PROOF*; available at https://oll.libertyfund.org/title/2193/202754/3339486.

[81]Beccaria (1872), *CHAPTER XXXI: OF CRIMES OF DIFFICULT PROOF*; available at https://oll.libertyfund.org/title/2193/202754/3339484.

[82]Beccaria (1872), *CHAPTER XXXI: OF CRIMES OF DIFFICULT PROOF*; available at https://oll.libertyfund.org/title/2193/202754/3339488.

[83]Beccaria (1872), *CHAPTER V: OF PROFANATION*; available at https://oll.libertyfund.org/title/2193/202797/3339611.

[84]Beccaria (1872), *CHAPTER V: OF PROFANATION*; available at https://oll.libertyfund.org/title/2193/202797/3339612.

public utility, which is the foundation of human justice". He argues that the relations between God and man are based upon dependence and if the degree of sin depends on the malignity of the heart, which is impenetrable to finite being, how then could the degree of sin serve as a standard to determine the degree of crimes? He believed that even "if that were admitted men may punish when God pardons, and pardon when God condemns; and thus act in opposition to the Supreme Being."[85]

Beccaria not only thought that those who imagine that "the greatness of the sin should aggravate the crime were wrong", but also those who imagine that "a crime is greater, or less, according to the intention of the person by whom it is committed." In his view, "[m]en, often with the best intention, do the greatest injury to society, and with the worst, do it the most essential services."[86]

Jean-Jacques Rousseau

Jean-Jacques Rousseau (June 28, 1712–July 2, 1778) did not seem to have contributed much to the discussion on the secularization of criminal law, but he posited two opinions. On the one hand, he criticized those who upheld that tempting "a married woman to adultery is no less severely punished than he that commits it; for they believe that a deliberate design to commit a crime is equal to the fact itself."[87] On the other, he argued that "[i]n a well-governed State, there are few punishments, not because there are many pardons, but because criminals are rare; it is when a State is in decay that the multitude of crimes is a guarantee of impunity."[88]

Voltaire

François-Marie Arouet (21 November 1694–30 May 1778), commonly referred to as Voltaire, similarly to Beccaria,[89] criticized the indeterminacy of the crime of blasphemy. He lamented that, considering "that what is blasphemy at Rome, at our Lady of Loretto, and within the walls of San Gennaro, is piety in London, Amsterdam, Stockholm, Berlin, Copenhagen, Berne, Basel, and Hamburg, (...) even in the same country, in the same town, in the same street, people treat one another as blasphemers."[90] Recognizing that "[p]unishments are almost always arbitrary, which is a

---

[85] Beccaria (1872), *CHAPTER VII: OF ESTIMATING THE DEGREE OF CRIMES*; available at https://oll.libertyfund.org/title/2193/202706/3339309.

[86] Beccaria (1872), *CHAPTER VII: OF ESTIMATING THE DEGREE OF CRIMES*; available at https://oll.libertyfund.org/title/2193/202706/3339307.

[87] Rousseau (1901), Chapter: *Of Their Slaves, and of Their Marriages*; available at https://oll.libertyfund.org/title/2039/145528/2721199.

[88] Rousseau (1901), *CHAPTER V: the right of life and death*; available at https://oll.libertyfund.org/title/638/71007/1686978.

[89] See Footnotes 170 and 171.

[90] Voltaire (1901), vol. III, Chapter: *BLASPHEMY*; available at https://oll.libertyfund.org/title/352/53884/633265.

great defect in jurisprudence," he added that "this defect opens the way for clemency and compassion, and this compassion is no other than the strictest justice, for it would be horrible to punish a youthful indiscretion as poisoners and parricides are punished. A sentence of death for an offence which deserves nothing more than correction is no other than an assassination committed with the sword of justice."[91]

Voltaire was not able to accept, unlike his contemporary thinkers, the criminalization of adultery. He could not understand the indissoluble character of marriage and thought that the Roman Catholic Church was wrong in defending this indissoluble bound as natural,[92] criticizing the payment of taxes for absolution, given at the tribunal of conscience, of this sin.[93]

Immanuel Kant

Immanuel Kant (April 22, 1724–February 12, 1804), after defending "the Right of the Sovereign as the Supreme Power to inflict pain upon a Subject on account of a Crime committed by him,"[94] distinguished between the crimes violating the 'security of property in the State' and the 'penal offences against Humanity.' According to him, rape, pæderasty,[95] and bestiality were among the latter.[96] And he added:

> …the perpetration of a penal offence against Humanity generally. Such, in particular, are the relations of rape, pæderasty, and bestiality. The former two would have to be punished by castration (after the manner of the white or black eunuchs in a seraglio), and the last by expulsion for ever from civil society, because the individual has made himself unworthy of human relations. Per quod quis peccat per idem punitur et idem. These crimes are called unnatural, because they are committed against all that is essential to Humanity. To punish them by arbitrary penalties is literally opposed to the conception of a penal Justice. But even then the criminal cannot complain that wrong is done to him, since his own evil deed draws

---

[91] *Ibid.*

[92] Voltaire (1901), vol. III. Chapter: *ADULTERY*; available at https://oll.libertyfund.org/title/352/53693/631586.

[93] Voltaire (1901), vol. VII. Chapter: *TAX—FEE*; available at https://oll.libertyfund.org/title/1660/202435/3331973.

[94] Kant (1887), Chapter: *Constitutional and Juridical Consequences arising from the Nature of the Civil Union*; available at https://oll.libertyfund.org/title/359/55842/641046; the passage cited stems from "explanatory remarks on the first principles of the doctrine of sex crimes," an appendix added to a new printing (also 1797) in response to a review. It stems from one of his last works, known in English as *The Metaphysics of Morals*. Published in 1797, when the philosopher's mental powers had ebbed, the book is generally regarded as a compilation of lecture notes. On this basis, the material would have been developed some years earlier.

[95] Note that for Kant, and for Germans today, the term pæderasty or *Päderastie* does not refer to pedophilia, but to anal penetration. As such, it could in principle refer to heterosexual behavior, but as this was little noticed at the time, the primary reference is to men having sex with men in this manner.

[96] Kant (1887), Chapter: *Objection as to the Faculty of Desire*; available at https://oll.libertyfund.org/title/359/55891/641172.

> the punishment upon himself; and he only experiences what is in accordance with the spirit, if not the letter, of the penal Law which he has broken in his relation to others.[97]

For Kant, the "unnatural use (and thereby abuse) of one's *sexual* organs is a violation, in the highest degree," which deserved to be punished by the sovereign. In fact, he thought that this conduct was morally worse than suicide (or self-murder).[98] This behavior was, according to him, a violation (even in the highest possible degree) of the duty owed by man to himself.

Kant, trying to "prove upon grounds of reason the inadmissibility of that unnatural excess," did not use theological or religious arguments. His view was "that man meanly abdicates his personality, when he attempts to employ himself as a bare means to satisfy a brutal lust." Following the comparison with self-murder, he argued that "the headlong obstinacy of the suicide, who casts away life as a burden, is no effeminate surrender to sensitive excitement, but shows valour, and so leaves ground for reverencing the humanity he represents; while this other resigns himself an abandoned outcast to brutality, enjoying his own self-abuse—that is, he makes himself an object of abomination, and stands bereft of all reverence of any kind."[99]

William Blackstone

William Blackstone (10 July 1723–14 February 1780) differentiated 'spiritual sins', adjudicated by ecclesiastical courts, from 'temporal crimes', adjudicated by secular criminal courts.[100] Dealing with the kinds of crimes, he stated that the fourth type comprised all offences, "more immediately against God and religion." After citing several forms of blasphemy, he added that "these are offences punishable at common law (…) for Christianity is part of the laws of England."[101] The Commentaries on the Laws of England contained, as in many Continental jurisdictions, the crimes of blasphemy, common swearing, cursing, witchcraft, conjuration, enchantment, or sorcery, simony and the misbehaviors of religious impostors.[102]

---

[97] Ibid.

[98] Kant (1886), Chapter: *PART I: OF THE DUTIES OF PERFECT AND DETERMINATE OBLIGATION*; available at https://oll.libertyfund.org/title/1443/56276/1351965.

[99] Kant (1886), Chapter: *PART I: OF THE DUTIES OF PERFECT AND DETERMINATE OBLIGATION*; available at https://oll.libertyfund.org/title/1443/56276/1351966; as can be seen, Kant did not adopt religious terminology.

[100] Blackstone (1893), *CHAPTER XIX: OF COURTS OF A CRIMINAL JURISDICTION*; available at https://oll.libertyfund.org/title/2142/198923/3154159.

[101] Blackstone (1893), *CHAPTER IV: OF OFFENCES AGAINST GOD AND RELIGION*; available at https://oll.libertyfund.org/title/2142/198893/3153824.

[102] Blackstone (1893), Chapter: *BARRON FIELD, AN ANALYSIS OF BLACKSTONE'S COMMENTARIES ON The Laws of England*; available at https://oll.libertyfund.org/title/2142/198964/3156831.

Jeremy Bentham

Jeremy Bentham (15 February 1748–6 June 1832), in Principles of Morals and Legislation (1780) pointed out that the offences against one's self were "too open to controversy" and constituted a "subject beyond dispute."[103] Five years later, in his work Offences against One's Self (1785),[104] he was the first scholar who clearly defended the decriminalization of sodomy.

He did not agree with the 'natural' or 'medical' arguments, which concluded that the practice of sodomy generated negative effects for both individuals (illnesses), and communities (demography). Bentham thought that was a prejudice because medical doctors had not provided supporting evidence. Besides, this practice was present in the Antiquity (Greece and Rome) and the aforementioned negative effects had not emerged.

Bentham's utilitarianism was not compatible with the natural foundation regarding morals and ethics. Nature and natural approach were replaced by the pragmatic and empirical study of particular cases. If the law should promote happiness to as many people as possible, and happiness was understood as the experience of pleasure (as an opposite to pain), a careful analysis should be conducted on the number of people who would benefit from pleasure and were prejudiced with pain, before deciding whether some behaviors ought to be punished.

Bentham thought that it was not enough to mitigate punishments imposed on those convicted of sodomy. He argued that sodomy should be fully decriminalized, unlike Beccaria and other enlightened thinkers. In his view, what mattered was not whether this behavior was natural or unnatural, but whether its practice and punishment contributed to citizens' happiness.

He did not attempt to consider those alleged pathological consequences of this practice. Even if those consequences did occur, criminalization would generate more pain as it was fairly difficult to prove this behavior before the judge, and this would subsequently produce false accusations and extortions. Nevertheless, even if one could accept that those who practice it were ill, the best strategy would be to help them through education and discipline rather than punishment.

One may think that Bentham was in favor of this practice or promoted it, however, that is not true. He characterized it as a 'perverted taste', an 'infection of taste', an 'act to the highest degree odious and disgusting' and a 'depraved taste.' Bentham's expressed views were more related to aesthetics ('nausea', 'repugnance') than theology ('peccadis nefandus', 'act against nature'), ethical ('vive', 'immorality') or therapeutic ('illness', 'anomaly').[105] Although he thought the action disgusting, he did not think that this constituted the reason to criminalize it; otherwise laws would be enacted out of caprice by governments. Besides, he thought that the disgusting effects, generated by witnessing the behaviors, was due more to prejudice than anything else,

---

[103] Bentham (1838–1843a).

[104] See Footnotes 147 and 148; on this matter, see Bentham (2002), 37–42.

[105] Bentham (2002), 40.

and this prejudice could disappear if the act were considered from the perspective of utilitarianism.

Concerning adultery, Bentham seemed to regard its criminalization as a consequence of the Christian tradition of European territories, as opposed to the Muslim tradition, for example. Unlike Voltaire, who could not understand both the indissoluble character of marriage and the damage caused by adultery, Bentham understood it as a consequence of the breach of a bond produced by the contract. Otherwise, "no contract, no breach: no marriage, no adultery."[106] Although he was, somehow, surprised by the number of offences punished by the law of Christian countries,[107] he recognized that, in these cases, both the legislator and tribunals were concerned with the "peace and honour of families."[108]

Manuel De Lardizábal

Manuel de Lardizábal y Uribe (San Juan del Molino, Spain, 22 December 1739–25 December 1820), in his famous work Discurso sobre las penas (1782),[109] incorrectly stated that during the Sixteenth and Seventeenth Centuries there had been complete confusion between crime and sin.[110] Most probably, he exaggerated the connection between crime and sin as a way to reinforce his idea of distinguishing these categories. He argued that criminal law purported to protect society from any harm and to promote social order. Consequently, he opined that criminal laws should only punish those behaviors which may disturb the public tranquility and security of individuals. He curiously argued that sin did not belong to the social order because its existence is not dependent on society but on men's dependence on God. However, he thought that behaviors against religion should be punished considering that religion constituted a strong bond of the society.[111]

2.2.3 Common Features of Enlightened Thought on Criminal Law

What are the common features of enlightened thought?

First, whereas the final outcome of enlightened thinkers was not always far from what the criminal law science of the Ancien Régime—under both the theological influence and the pressures of absolutist political power—defended, some of the

---

106 Bentham (1838–1843b).

107 Bentham (1907), Chapter: §3. *Genera of Class I*; available at https://oll.libertyfund.org/title/278/20765/941632.

108 Bentham (1838–1843c).

109 Lardizábal (1782).

110 See Footnote 28, and its main text.

111 Lardizábal (1782), 94–99; see also Tomás y Valiente (1969), 235.

arguments which were used changed notably. In this vein, no religious or theological references can be found in what authors explored when postulating why some behaviors should or should not be criminalized.

This did not imply the decriminalization of those behaviors which, according to some scholars, were punished because they were sins against religious faith or Christian morals. As was previously mentioned, Montesquieu disregarded the crimes of witchcraft and heresy, but he did not dare to ask for their abolition. All enlightened authors, except Bentham, thought that sodomy should be criminalized. What's more, from a legislative perspective, this crime was more severely criminalized in the eighteenth and nineteenth centuries than prior to that era.[112] All authors favoured the criminalization of religious crimes (blasphemy among them), and other behaviors related to moral sexuality in similar ways as argued in the past (adultery, bigamy, incest, rape—*stuprum*—, sodomy, bestiality, etc.). Aside from the crimes of witchcraft and heresy, which were generally disregarded, with consistency in the opinions for its decriminalization, no clear statements were made regarding the decriminalizing of the others.

However, enlightened scholars differed from the earlier criminal lawyers in two aspects: First, no theological or religious arguments were used, and second, they all advocated for less severe punishments. This was as a consequence of the principles of humanitarianism and proportionality between crime and punishment. They defended, for example, the imposition of life imprisonment or hard labour instead of the death penalty for those convicted of sodomy.[113] Nonetheless, this had already happened in many territories from the beginning of the Seventeenth Century.[114]

Can it be assumed that the enlightened thinkers were against Christian faith and morals? Some were, however, others were not, but they all believed that criminal law should not be based on religious or Christian-moral arguments such as the ideal of celibacy or chastity religious faithfulness.

Second, these intellectuals generally based their arguments upon natural philosophy. Once theology had been rejected, they tended to resort to philosophy, but philosophy was founded upon nature, therefore, for them, the main criteria to judge whether a specific behavior may cause damage either to society or particularly to individuals was human nature. Beccaria pointed out that he wrote "only of crimes which violate the laws of nature and the social contract, and not of sins."[115] This may explain why their final opinions were not that far from that of the earlier science of criminal law. It should be noted that nature, even much more that theology, had also been pervasive within the earlier criminal law system of the *ius commune*. This also explains why they thought that sexual "deviations" such as masturbation or sodomy

---

[112]On this matter, see Footnotes 147, 148, 149, 150, and their main texts.

[113]From a legislative perspective, Pietro Leopoldo of Tuscany was the first who abolished death penalty for all crimes (1786), becoming not only the first Western ruler to do so, but also the first ruler to abolish death penalty for sodomy (which was replaced by prison and hard labor).

[114]See, for example, the case of Valencia, in Tomás y Valiente (1990), 54.

[115]See Footnote 164 and its main text.

could be avoided with a proper education.[116] This would change later, particularly when the philosophy of utilitarianism replaced philosophy based on nature. In this regard, perhaps, it should not be a surprise that Bentham was the first scholar who reasoned for the decriminalization of sodomy.

Third, unlike Beccaria and Lardizábal, who both emphasized the distinction between crime and sin, and that "the greatness of the sin should not aggravate the crime", many enlightened authors did not pay much attention to the relationship between crime and sin. How can one explain this lack of interest towards a subject which, according to some scholars, constituted one of the main regressive and intolerable features of criminal law before the eighteenth century? There could be a multiplicity of reasons; perhaps because they realized that that was not the main problem; perhaps they knew of no author stating that behaviors were criminalized because they were sins; or perhaps they understood that they were not the pioneers of the secularization of the law.

Scrutiny of this era revealed that from the late Middle Ages behaviors had never been criminalized just because they were sins, although theological reasons, along with others which were always linked to social order, social peace and natural order, were adduced. Furthermore, they knew that criminal law of the Sixteenth and Seventeenth Centuries had made remarkable progress in many aspects, although its implementation had not always been possible due to absolutist political powers which were reluctant to or resisted change as much as possible.

Fourthly, the legacy of the Seventeenth-century criminal law jurisprudence explains why some of the most renowned Eighteenth-century criminal law reformers saw no problem with endorsing the social contract and recognizing the existence of nature—or natural order—that was both prior and preeminent to the social contract. However, the way they sometimes made compatible both foundations—'public utility' on the one hand and the 'human nature' or 'laws of nature' on the other—was not entirely coherent. In this regard, Beccaria, for example, after manifesting his will to avoid talking about a "certain class of crimes, which has covered Europe with blood,"[117] adds that he prefers to "write only of crimes which violate the *laws of nature* and the *social contract*, and not of sins, even the temporal punishments of which must be determined from other principles than those of a limited human philosophy."[118] Later on, he stated that whereas all crimes tended "to the destruction of society," adultery "proceeds from an abuse of that necessity which is *constant and universal in human nature*; a necessity anterior to the formation of society, and indeed the founder of society itself."[119]

And fifthly, unlike most of Enlightment criminal law reformers, Utilitarians like Bentham did not accept categories such as 'laws of nature', 'social orden' based

[116]Bentham (2002), 30.

[117]Cesare Bonesana di Beccaria (1872), *CHAPTER XXXIX: OF A PARTICULAR KIND OF CRIMES*; available at https://oll.libertyfund.org/title/2193/202770/3339536.

[118]*Ibid.*

[119]Beccaria (1872), *CHAPTER XXXI: OF CRIMES OF DIFFICULT PROOF*; available at https://oll.libertyfund.org/title/2193/202754/3339484.

upon a 'natural order', and 'natural reason', among others. However, utilitarianism was not the mainstream of the 18th-century criminal law jurisprudence. This idea is connected to the 19th-century criminal law jurisprudence.

2.3 *Criminal Law, Nature and Morality in the 19th Century*

If—as said—the criminal law doctrine of the Enlightenment should not be equated with utilitarianism, the 19th-century criminal-law discourses in Europe did not really constitute a break in comparison to those of the eighteenth century. They rather strove to develop some of the ideas of the Enlightenment and correct some shortcomings and inconsistencies. One inconsistency was precisely the combination of 'social contract' and 'laws of nature' as the foundation of criminal law in general and as the legitimation of the state to punish the offenders in particular. As the French scholar Faustin Hélie pointed out,

> This doctrine, which rests on a historical fiction, has been knocked down by the philosophy of the nineteenth century, and better than anyone, Mr. Rossi has demonstrated its inaccuracy. Man has been born in society and for society: it is there, as M. de Broglie said, his state of nature (…) His physical organization, his instincts, his needs, everything reveals his natural sociability (…) it is not but in the midst of his fellows that he can develop his intelligence and exercise the duties that the moral law imposes on him.[120]

The role of nature continued to be present in the 19th-century criminal law discourses, but its relevance varied depending on the specific chronological and geographical contexts.

In Spain, for example, the resort to nature and to natural laws particularly permeated criminal law. In fact, the main Spanish representatives of enlightened thought—e.g. Gregorio Mayans y Siscar and his pupil Joaquín Marín y Mendoza, who was the first to occupy a university chair of Natural Law in Spain—never admitted a natural law detached from Scolasticism or contrary to an objective ethics.[121] And that was the mainstream all over 19th-century Spain.[122] This explains why the deputy of the Spanish parliament Fernández Baeza lamented that another deputy—called Seijas—had not followed the principles of nature in drafting some parts of the 1848 Spanish criminal code.[123] Joaquín Francisco Pacheco, one of the drafters and the main commentator of the 1848 SCC, argued that society has the right to approve criminal laws, but these laws should be in accordance with nature and reason, since society has no right to decide what is just or unjust.[124] He added that the goodness

---

[120] Hélie (1863), LXVII and LXVIII; the text can also be found in Silva Forné (2001), 294, Footnote 260.

[121] See, for example, Marín y Mendoza (1776, 1999).

[122] See, for example, Mendizábal Martín (1897, 1897–1899).

[123] DSC, Congreso, 11 de marzo de 1848, p. 1734.

[124] Pacheco (1856), vol. I, 77, n. 35.

of human laws derives from divine laws and natural laws.[125] In his view, some criminal law institutions like self-defense found their origins in human nature and that explained why they were always in force and contained in all codes.[126] Tomás María de Vizmanos and Cirilo Álvarez Martínez, in their commentaries to the 1848 SCC, maintained the existence of older laws in society that were higher than human laws, referring to the laws of nature, and adding that it would be immoral to approve any human law against them.[127] In other words, the criminal legislator should not go against reason and nature.[128] A Valencian criminal lawyer stated that the development of the science of criminal legislation required a good knowledge of human nature and that political order and moral order depended on such science.[129]

2.3.1 The Influence of the Enlightenment on 19th-Century Criminal Law

Spain was not an exception. Lawyers from most of European jurisdictions resorted to nature to justify the convenience to criminalize or decriminalize some behaviour. This is the case of Ortolán, Faustin Hélie, Bérenger,[130] Rossi and Garraud[131] in France; Carrara—among others—in Italy[132]; somehow Röder in Germany[133]; Pacheco and Groizard y Gómez de la Serna—among others—in Spain; Tejedor and Obarrio in Argentina, etc. Most of them belonged to the eclectic,[134] neo-classical school of criminal law that, opposed to the positivist thesis of the social defence,[135] was the mainstream in the 19th-century Europe.

Thus there is a considerable degree of continuity between the 18th-century criminal law doctrine and the 19th-century criminal law discourses all over Europe. The cases of Italy, Germany, France and Spain are quite revealing.

Now I will give evidence of French and Spanish cases, focusing mainly on two authors, Pellegrino Rossi (for France) and Joaquín Francisco Pacheco (for Spain). Both Rossi and Pacheco, who highly influenced the 19th-century criminal law

125 Pacheco (1856), vol. I, 77, n. 38.

126 Pacheco (1856), vol. I, 149–150.

127 Vizmanos and Álvarez Martínez (1848), t. I, 181.

128 Vizmanos and Álvarez Martínez (1848), t. I, 160–161.

129 Vicente Almazán (1852), t. II, 169.

130 Bérenger (1855).

131 Garraud (1881, 1888–1894, 1898–1902, 1907–1929); on René Garraud, see Halpérin (2006).

132 Filangieri (1821).

133 Röder (1846, 1855, 1864, 1867, 1875, 1876).

134 On the eclecticism in the 19th-century Spain, see Iñesta-Pastor (2011), 262–290; in Spain, the eclecticism's doctrine dominated during the whole nineteenth century, and its influence can be also seen in the 1870 Spanish criminal code; on this issue, see Silvela (1903), 172; Castejón (1970), 63; Groizard (1870), 79–88, 254–255; Iñesta-Pastor (2016), 225–226.

135 Ancel (1965; reprinted 1998).

doctrine in France and Spain,[136] resorted to the notions of nature, human nature and natural reason when linking criminal law and morality.

I will also explore how these lawyers looked at the relationship between criminal law and morals, and whether their thought was in line with the ideal of secularization of law in general and of criminal law in particular. In doing so, I will analyze their discourses concerning criminal law, showing the importance of some categories like 'nature', 'natural order' and 'social order,' and how these categories explain the links between the criminal-law and the moral provinces. The moral foundation of criminal law might also explain the criminalization of certain behaviors, particularly of those which were considered as contrary to good customs and morals such as adultery, incest, dishonest abuses prostitution and bigamy.

2.3.2 Pellegrino Rossi and Other French Criminal Lawyers

Pellegrino Rossi

In France, Pellegrino Rossi asked himself the following question:

> Are not the moral and political orders connected through the most intimate and close links?

In his view, the criminal law was the legal branch most connected to morality:

> Now, the criminal is of all the parts of the legislation that most directly can influence the universal ideas of the moral order. The criminal law is the one in whose virtue the power exercises more particularly the charge of declaring in an imperative way the principles of the just and unjust, of good and evil in the sphere of public order. Is not this the duty and the right of legislator?[137]

For Rossi, the legislator was not allowed to create criminal laws at his whim or caprice, because…

> Without a doubt, it is not positive law that creates law, nor what we call criminal law, nor what we call civil law, nor any other law. Law is pre-existent to all things, and peoples manifest notions of it, before the legislator traces the written laws on his model.[138]

The moral order, that is pre-existent to the political or positive order, could be destroyed as the laws approved by legislator reflect a mere power—or violence—detached from reason and justice:

> Finally, this is destroyed, to the extent that this is within the reach of man, when in social laws openly usurps force the place of justice, and the criminal courts are no more, I dare say so, than tenebrous caverns where the innocent go to atone for the guilt of having their side of reason and justice.[139]

---

[136]On Rossi's influence upon Spanish criminal doctrine and criminal law, see Iñesta-Pastor (2016), 212–214; Iñesta-Pastor (2011), 262–290; Iñesta-Pastor (2018), 249–250.

[137]Rossi (1839), vol. I, 13.

[138]Rossi (1839), vol. I, 14.

[139]Rossi (1839), vol. I, 15.

Rossi maintained that criminal laws should comply with truth and justice; otherwise, the public morality would be gravely affected and people eventually would approve the error and the injustice:

> The error and the injustice exert particularly a pernicious influence on the morality of the people, when they come from above. What at first caused, and rightly so, censure and contempt, may eventually become a belief and merit general approval.[140]

For Rossi, "there is no civilization that is truly progressive without liberty,"[141] and "political liberty, that is an indispensable condition of the civilization, cannot exist without inmediate justice, and particularly without criminal justice." And he added:

> [H]ence the evidence of the intimate connection that links criminal law with moral order in civil societies.
>
> This also results in the crime of those who have turned criminal law into an obstacle against civilization, either by depriving individuals of the necessary freedom, or by denaturalizing in the law the notions of justice and truth.[142]

Rossi recognized that the advance of natural sciences contributed to the progress of moral and political sciences and the improvement of laws. However, the value of criminal laws does not depend much on the progress of natural sciences. They rather follow the fate of moral sciences, to which the legislator should be attached[143]; otherwise, citizens would be perverted:

> But if the legislator deceives himself with the moral relations of things, by altering them or willingly denaturalizing them, he should no longer be accused of a simple material and determinable evil: then he perverts the citizens, confuses the ideas of just and unjust, and does not protect, but he works to destroy the social order.[144]

Rossi mentioned the criminalization of different opinions on religion as an example of "an error, very manifest and discredited," that "denaturalized the notions of God and justice, and turned out a peaceful religion into a place for hatred and vengeance."[145] However, as Rossi stated, it would be very easy to add other examples contained in the past like the 'imaginary crimes', in which imaginary mind were indeed the relations of social order, and false moral connections were arbitrarily established by political power. Rossi argued that these crimes were still present in some criminal codes and their effects continued to be as deplorable as always.[146]

How to learn from the errors of the criminal law tradition? For Rossi, the criminal legislator should prevent from falling in any of the two extremes, namely, the confusion—or identification—between criminal provisions and moral precepts, and

[140]Rossi (1839), vol. I, 15.
[141]Rossi (1839), vol. I, 16.
[142]Rossi (1839), vol. I, 17.
[143]Rossi (1839), vol. I, 17–18.
[144]Rossi (1839), vol. I, 18.
[145]Rossi (1839), vol. I, 18–19.
[146]Rossi (1839), vol. I, 19.

the promulgation of criminal laws with complete disregard to moral principles.[147] In his view, "criminal law, in addition to always limiting its action to the preservation of society, should find its point of departure or source in the principles of absolute justice, and not allow anything that is contrary to the duties of humanity and the dignity of man."[148]

For those who, like Rossi, profess such 'principles of absolute justice', "the criminal system was inextrically linked not only to the material conservation of political order but also to the development of moral principles in civil societies."[149] This explains why criminal law was "unfortunately—according to Rossi—one of the most difficult political sciences to advance" or improve.[150]

Where did such difficulty come from? Because both "making laws and adjudicating them are two essential acts of social justice."[151] And he added:

> But to make the law is to recognize what are the unjust actions of man, and among these which are quite harmful for society to punish them; finally, what should be the punishment, to avoid equally that the term of human justice is passed or frustrated.[152]

Rossi did not defend a criminal law based just upon eternal principles, did he neither ignore such principles. He rather argued that criminal laws were composed of

> ...eternally immutable principles of the just and the unjust, and of application adapted to the moral sensibility of man, and to the particular state of each political body, namely, of truths of all times, of all places, that they exist independently of external events, and that they can not but exist; of local and temporal truths that exist with the facts to which they refer, that change, modify and disappear with them; and of general and local truths at the same time, that depend on the condition of man, but that modify the circumstances in which it is placed.[153]

In other words, Rossi stated that "the criminal law is composed of an absolute and a relative part, of a variable part and of an invariable part, of a part in which man can not influence anything, and of another that he can modify, modifying his own way of existing; in a word, of precepts of justice and utility rules."[154]

Such bidimensionality—permanent in its moral foundation and principles, dynamic according to its historical circumstances—made the development of criminal law particularly difficult. Moreover, "the making of the positive criminal law required the resort both to the truths of philosophy and psycology and to the historical origins. The most difficult part mainly consisted in combining in their fair proportion both elements."[155] In doing so, "the decisions of the universal reason and human

[147]Rossi (1839), vol. I, 19.
[148]Rossi (1839), vol. I, 20.
[149]Rossi (1839), vol. I, 20.
[150]Rossi (1839), vol. I, 20.
[151]Rossi (1839), vol. I, 20.
[152]Rossi (1839), vol. I, 20–21.
[153]Rossi (1839), vol. I, 21.
[154]Rossi (1839), vol. I, 21.
[155]Rossi (1839), vol. I, 21.

conscience—without confusing them with the suggestions of selfishness and the demands of the passions—should be kept."[156]

Rossi argued that the moral order encompassed all duties, including those towards God, towards oneself and towards others.[157] The moral order—with its duties—and the social order have different scopes. For Rossi, the social order only demands the fulfillment of the duties connected to rights whose protection justifies the use of violence and force, of the required duties."[158] Hence

> The civil power may not impose penal sanctions on an immoral act, if it is proven otherwise that public order is very little interested in repressing it by positive law, if it is proven to be a very rare crime and that does not cause any concern.[159]

In Rossi's view, the crime is "the infringement of a duty required in damage of society or of individuals."[160]

Rossi emphazised that althought "the right to punish derives from the moral order, it should neither go beyond the moral law nor follow it always in all rigour; it should rather stop at the point that no longer claims the general interest." And he added:

> It [The right to punish] can make us fall behind the moral law, never go beyond it. It can make us set subsidiary and more reduced rules than the moral law, but it can never make us establish them contrary to the nature of absolute justice, from which human justice is just a derivation.[161]

Rossi did not reject general utility. After clarifying that "the alteration of the laws of moral order goes beyond the human capacity," and that "man does not dispose of the nature of things,"[162] he defended that general utility may guide the legislator in the application—or adjudication—of the criminal law[163]:

> This is how to establish the balance of advantages and disadvantages: not to decide if an act is immoral, not to establish, in the abstract, the right to punish; but to recognize whether its exercise [the right to punish] would disturb, instead of maintaining social order, if it would do more harm than good.[164]

Rossi stated that human—or positive—law and, more specifically, criminal law was composed of the 'declarative part' and the 'criminal sanction'. Concerning the former, he pointed out as follows:

> The declarative part of the criminal law expresses two ideas. It proclaims that such a fact has the character of a moral crime and that society needs to punish it. Now, from whom can one expect a frank and sincere expression of these two truths? This is the question.[165]

---

[156] Rossi (1839), vol. I, 21.
[157] Rossi (1839), vol. I, 210.
[158] Rossi (1839), vol. I, 211.
[159] Rossi (1839), vol. I, 210.
[160] Rossi (1839), vol. I, 211.
[161] Rossi (1839), vol. I, 219.
[162] Rossi (1839), vol. I, 221.
[163] Rossi (1839), vol. I, 220–221.
[164] Rossi (1839), vol. I, 221.
[165] Rossi (1839), vol. I, 299.

Rossi's answer to that difficult question was clear: the conscience of man has the ability to discern whether behaviour constitutes a moral crime or not:

> The first of these truths lies in the conscience of man. It is necessary to look for it in this sanctuary in which good is kept separate from evil, the just from the unjust; in this court that sometimes errs, but at least never cheats.[166]

Since having human conscience is not a priviledge for few people, Rossi argued that the danger of a wrong moral judgment from human conscience was less probable when more people came to the same conclusion. In this vein, he affirmed that "[t]he lie is little to fear in numerous and unanimous witnesses."[167]

As said, each man is able to make a right judgment in his own conscience. However, declaring whether a 'moral crime' constitutes also a 'social crime', meaning that the behaviour deserves to be criminalized and persecuted by criminal justice, concerns the legislator. In other words, the legislator needs to declare what 'moral crimes' will be persecuted as 'legal crimes', because "[t]here is no legal crime, whatever the act itself might be, if the positive law has not put it in the catalog of crimes." In cases in which a 'moral crime' might be persecuted as a 'legal crime' only under certain circumstances, then the legislator needs to determine such circumstances.[168]

Claudio José Tissot

Claudio José Tissot argued that the knowledge of criminal law cannot be reduced to the study of its concrete application, as well as of foreign legislations, but must start from principles, which are, in short, rational ideas that constitute the basis of all criminal order. Consequently, "denying these principles" would make it impossible to "give a reason for criminal law."[169]

M. Ortolán

Ortolán also linked—or related—criminal law to morality. After defending the 'need for a general scientific communication',[170] he analyzed the method of legal science, and criticizes the tendency of some schools that presented separately the historical, philosophical and practical elements.[171] In addition, he added two other elements: the moral[172] and the religious.[173] Concerning the moral one, he stated:

---

[166]Rossi (1839), vol. I, 299.

[167]Rossi (1839), vol. I, 299.

[168]Rossi (1839), vol. I, 336–337.

[169]Tissot (1880), Introduction, VIII.

[170]Ortolán (1845), 14–18.

[171]Ortolán (1845), 18.

[172]Ortolán (1845), 21–22.

[173]Ortolán (1845), 22–24.

> The domain of morality does not begin only where the law ends.
>
> Morality is in the law and is beyond the law: it goes further than it; but wherever the law is, there must be morality because this is the general law, the supreme law.
>
> The law is no more than a means that society employs to sanction those precepts whose observance it is important to ensure. It cannot be extended to all, unless it degenerates into tyranny, into inquisition; but it is not allowed to leave its circle either, because I ask, gentlemen, what would be the law outside morals? The immoral law.[174]

Ortolán related law to morality, but neither can—nor should—the latter follow all the rules of morality "unless it degenerates into tyranny, into inquisition," nor can—or should—the former dispense with it, thus leading to an "immoral law." According to Ortolán, developing and improving this relationship is the object of legal science, upon which its progress depends:

> The progress of legal science consists in establishing in the best possible way the appropriate limitation, the fair reserve that has to be kept, either because the law sanctions principles of human morality that had been unknown or violated in the past, such as legal equality among men, which forbids any of them to be owned by another; or because it draws away from those principles on which morality had unduly extended his empire, as it occurred, for example, with the old and sometimes horrible punishment against crimes of conscience, intimate crimes, carnal crimes.[175]

Ortolán, unlike Rossi, is more explicit about the importance of nature and natural reason, which are at the foundation of morality. In this vein, he argues that "positive law must be enclosed in natural law, in the same way that natural law is contained in morality."[176]

Ortolán connected criminal law, nature and reason. When dealing with the 'legitimate foundation of the right to punish,'[177] he departs from the different theories (*revenge*, *social contract*, *reparation*, *conservation* or *social defense*, *utility*, *absolute justice*), because "[i]n our opinion, none of those systems is exact, and all of them lead to unacceptable consequences."[178] And then he defends the two ideas that are at the basis of his conception of the right to punish:

> 51. In order to demonstrate the social right to punish, it is essential to resort to two ideas. The one of the absolute justice, with the one of the need for the social utility.
>
> Deduced from the nature of man and society, complex nature (spirit and matter), that right can not have more than a complex base.
>
> 52. That goodness should be remunerated with goodness, and evil with evil, is a conception of human reason in every time and in every country: there is more, it is for us a feeling: we experience a moral joy if that relationship is observed, and we suffer morally if it is disregarded. Thus, the idea, the feeling of absolute justice, demonstrates incontestably, that the guilty of an offence deserves a punishment proportioned to it.[179]

---

[174] Ortolán (1845), 21.

[175] Ortolán (1845), 21.

[176] Ortolán (1845), 75–76; concerning the "distinción entre la moral, el derecho natural y el derecho positivo', see pp. 75–76.

[177] Ortolán (1878), vol. I, 23–25.

[178] Ortolán (1878), vol. I, 23.

[179] Ortolán (1878), vol. I, 23.

As can be seen, the right to punish—as well as any criminal provision—must be deduced "from the nature of man and society," from which comes the complexity of natural law and the moral rules that should govern human behavior. But the observation of that nature that is the key to absolute justice is not enough either, because it requires the complement of social utility.

These two ideas—absolute justice and social utility—that according to Ortolán are the basis of the right to punish, appear again when dealing with the definition of crime:

> 248. (…). Crime is any action or external omission, which violates absolute justice, whose repression matters for conservation or social welfare, which has been defined beforehand, and to which the law has imposed a penalty.
>
> 249. In positive law and practical jurisprudence, you can stick to this much simpler, but completely material, definition: 'crime is any infringement of criminal law.'.[180]

Ortolán, like Rossi, also understood crime as something more than the punishment of immoral conduct, because it should be proved that his "repression matters for conservation or social welfare," and must be previously established by the legislator. That is why, from a strictly positive and practical perspective, he defines the crime as "any infringement of the criminal law" as long as the arbitrariness of the criminal legislator is restrained.[181]

Louis Proal (1843–1900)

The work of the French jurist Louis Proal, Crime and punishment (1892), awarded by the Academy of Moral and Political Sciences of France, was quickly translated into Spanish and published in Spain.[182]

The author, magistrate of the Court of Appeals of Aix, pointed out that although the great thinkers of the 17th-century were spiritualists and great advocates of free will (Descartes, Bossuet), his followers in the 18th-century, by neglecting "the physical side of man," triggered "a reaction against spiritualism."[183] This explains why in the 18th-century, along with the great spiritualist authors (Buffon, Montesquieu, Voltaire, Rousseau), other authors (Holbach, La Mettrie, Helvetius, Naigeon) arose who "blatantly denied the existence of the soul and moral freedom, explaining virtue and vice, for the organism."[184]

According to the Darwinists, the evolutionists and the utilitarians, "to believe in a human kingdom, in a different nature between man and animals, is 'a dream of a

---

[180]Ortolán (1878), vol. I, 84.

[181]Ortolán (1878), vol. I, 85.

[182]Proal (1893); see Footnotes 12 and 55; his main work *La criminalité politique* (1895) was translated into English in 1898, becoming a well-known book in Anglo-American jurisdictions; on this matter, see Schafer (1971).

[183]Proal (1893), 6.

[184]Proal (1893), 6.

delusional metaphysician.'"[185] And it is a dream because, according to the Darwinian doctrine, "the so-called moral sense derives primitively from social instincts,"[186] "it is nothing but the result of education."[187] So much so that, according to Letourneau's opinion, "[t]he procedures used in the domestication of animals, and those that have been created by primitive morality, are essentially identical: the one and the other rest in the fundamental property of the nerve cell, the ability to impregnate oneself, to save impressions."[188]

From the Darwinian perspective, therefore, the moral law is no more than an imposition on the will, a duty based on "an absolute rule that compels by itself."[189] In short, it was a voluntarist morality lacking any basis or rational foundation. This is how Proal concludes his description of the prevailing culture at the end of the nineteenth century:

> As we can see from this rapid exposure, we are in a time of intellectual and moral breakdown: the evolutionists recognize it and congratulate it, in the confidence that a new utilitarian moralilty, stripped of all metaphysical and religious concern, will replace it very soon the old moral of our parents; 'because the new morals are born with preference in times of social breakdown.'[190] Theological morality is childish in the eyes of these novators; Spiritualist morality also seems contemptible: the idea of God, the belief in the soul, in free will, are chimeras, metaphysics is no more 'than a sweetened theology.' Kant, Jouffroy and the spiritualists are visionaries.[191]

With these terms, Proal summarizes the situation of the existing schools of thought in Europe at the end of the nineteenth century, which affected the notion of freedom and, consequently, also criminal law, "which is the one that suffers the attacks of the deterministic theories."[192] His conclusion is clear:

> If criminal law today goes through a crisis, such as morality, it must be attributed to the progress of determinism. Rejecting the spiritualist beliefs on which the positive laws were based, the novators are logically forced to seek the explanation of the crime in the organism, and to separate criminal responsibility from moral responsibility.[193]

---

[185]Proal (1893), 10.

[186]Darwin, *La descendencia del hombre*, 3rd ed., p. 128; cited by Proal (1893), 10.

[187]Proal (1893), 10.

[188]Letourneau, Charles, *La evolución de la moral*, p. 68, 174; cited by Proal (1893), 10.

[189]Proal (1893), 11.

[190]Donde cita a Letourneau, *La Evolución de la moral*, p. 460 (I use the following edition: Letourneau C (¿?) Génesis y evolución de la moral, Publicaciones de La Escuela Moderna, Barcelona.

[191]Proal (1893), 11.

[192]Proal (1893), 12.

[193]Proal (1893), 12.

2.3.3 Joaquín Francisco Pacheco

It is difficult to exaggerate the relevance of this figure as politician and lawyer in general[194] and, more particularly, as criminal lawyer.[195] Pacheco was one of the drafters and the main commentator of the 1848 SCC.

He argued that society has the right to enact criminal laws, but these laws should be in accordance with nature and reason, since society has no right to decide what is just or unjust.[196] He added that the goodness of human laws derives from divine laws and natural laws.[197] In his view, some criminal law institutions like self-defense found their origins in human nature and that explained why they were always in force and contained in all codes.[198]

It has been asserted that Pacheco's criminal thinking should be synthesized with the following principles: "the right to punish based upon natural law, free will as the foundation of human behaviour, crime as a disturbance of the legal order, and basically retributive punishment."[199] It is well known that the foundation of the penalty and the right to punish were not exclusively retributive.[200] What historiography has not done is to explain Pacheco's foundation and connection of some of these principles.

A careful reading of Pacheco's work reveals the importance of the concept of nature and reason in his legal thought in general and in criminal law field. In his view, human nature explains the lack of the foundation of contractual theories and, therefore, its rejection as the origin and legitimating basis of the penalties and the right to punish:

> We see, then, gentlemen, how the system of the social pact, considered as the source and legitimation of penalties, vanishes. It is false historically, and without any foundation of reality in itself; impossible of all points, considering our human nature.[201]

Pacheco did not reject public utility at all, which he describes as 'large,' 'extensive' and 'principal in matters of law.' What he does not admit is its consideration as "absolute principle and generator of all legitimacy," which constitutes, in his opinion, "a remarkable error, which falsifies and destroys the essence, upsetting the essential ideas of human nature."[202]

---

[194]Gómez de la Serna (1865); Díez del Corral (1956); Acedo Castilla (1996); Baró Pazos (2006), vol. 2, t. 1, n. 732, 256.

[195]Romero Girón (1886); Revuelta Benito (1945); Cuello Calón (1948); Jiménez de Asúa (1951); Antón Oneca (1965a, b); Calvo Rubio (1966); Tomás y Valiente (1994); Iñesta-Pastor (2016), 215–219.

[196]Pacheco (1856), vol. I, 77, n. 35.

[197]Pacheco (1856), vol. I, 77, n. 38.

[198]Pacheco (1856), vol. I, 149–150.

[199]Morillas Cueva (1978), 82–83; recogido por Iñesta-Pastor (2016), 217, nota el pie n. 50.

[200]See, for example, Iñesta-Pastor (2016), 217, Footnote 47 and 48 (where some references can be found, e.g. Antón Oneca (1965a), 480; Tomás y Valiente (1994), 39, 65.

[201]Pacheco (1842), vol. I, 42.

[202]Pacheco (1842), vol. I, 71–72.

The existence of human nature is precisely what leads Pacheco to reject a purely voluntarist conception of the law:

> The power to make laws is not then free in the bad sense, it is not arbitrary in its works, even less that of making criminal laws: the law is not the will of those who legislate. There is a common conscience, to which they must subject themselves, which they must declare and expose in their provisions, if they desire for them the intimate and true character, whose appearance is conferred by their sanction and promulgation. The formula 'because that is my will' is the greatest absurdity that has been committed against intelligence, the greater blasphemy that has been pronounced against Justice, the most scandalous insult against the dignity of the human race.[203]

For Pacheco, it is "the greatest absurdity (...) against intelligence" to conceive law as mere will, because "legislating is not an act of caprice," but "an act of intelligence" that requires knowledge of the "natural relations, which make up what we call Justice."[204] In his view, then, there is a close relationship between human nature, the rational conception of the law and justice, which is incompatible with a utilitarian foundation of Law:

> No [legal theory] that confesses a rational theory, none that has principles, none that has philosophical pretensions, none can consent to the idea that laws should only be mere and capricious wills. According to the utilitarian, the law will be the declaration of what is convenient, as according to us the declaration of the just; but always a declaration, but always recognizing something prior to it, not independent of it, but on the contrary, on which it depends, on which it has to be founded.[205]

While utilitarians look for what is convenience, Pacheco looks for what is just, and what is just cannot be found outside human nature. Hence, according to this criminal lawyer, "severely seeking the nature and origin of the 'social crime'" can be found "the 'moral crime', which is its necessary foundation. If there was no moral crime, the social crime would not exist."[206]

In his famous book *Código penal concordado y comentado*, the notions of nature, reason, conscience and justice appear frequently. When commenting on Art. 3 SCC 1848, dealing with committed crime, frustrated crime and the attempted crime, Pacheco praised the Two Sicilies criminal codes and modern criminal lawyers who defended these categories that "derive from nature, and that good sense and reason and practice approve them as both philosophical and useful."[207] In this vein, he pointed out that the 1848 SCC, then, "advanced our law, not only the old one, but most of the contemporary," and this is because it "followed better than them the teachings of philosophy."[208]

When examining Art. 8.4 SCC 1848, regarding the exemption from criminal liability, and in particular to self-defense, he pointed out that this institution is not

---

[203] Pacheco (1842), vol. I, 90.

[204] Pacheco (1842), vol. I, 90.

[205] Pacheco (1842), vol. I, 91.

[206] Pacheco (1842), vol. I, 92.

[207] Pacheco (1856), vol. I, 98.

[208] Pacheco (1856), vol. I, 99.

new, but "[i]nnate in our mind and in our conscience, deduced from the most intimate of human nature, it has been consigned in all times and by all codes, with more or less perfection, but always in an explicit and strict way."[209] And that is because of the nature that prescribes the "supreme moral law, which leads us to love our fellow men" does not demand, as a rule, that we should love them more than we love ourselves."[210]

However, where Pacheco most clearly stated—in his *Código penal concordado y comentado*—the relevance of nature and reason in his criminal law jurisprudence is undoubtedly in the 'Introduction' and, later, when dealing with the definition of crime.

Conceiving nature as the basis of criminal law led Pacheco to affirm that "crime, in its fundamental notions, has been and is always one (…), as long as our nature does not change." In other words, if "the offence is disobedience to the precepts of the law," "the damage of human rights" or "the violation of holy things," and "[a]ll this forms and performs evil," it is understandable that "all this has appeared and will appear as vituperable, as condemnable, as punishable, in the mind and conscience of men, as long as men have conscience and have reason."[211]

However, this natural and rational foundation of criminal law, which means that, in essence—or "in its fundamental notions"—is not altered or changed, does not mean that criminal law is a static reality. Not at all, because, according to Pacheco, criminal law, in "its forms, its extension, its application, what is transient and accidental in them, changes, is modified and becomes the eternal turn of the societies and human thoughts."[212] This double dimension of criminal law, partly permanent—or static—and partly changing—or dynamic—, is analogous to the field of morality, given that both fields regulate human behavior and, above all, share the same foundation, nature and laws. In this regard, Pacheco used a parallelism between the criminal law – regulating the crime—and the moral law:

> Evil is one, always one; but the evils vary, according to the times and the peoples, and the doctrines, and the customs. It happens here what also happens in other analogous and concordant phenomena of the moral world. Duty is one; but the duties are diverse, according to the ages and the nations. The law is one; but laws increased, diminished, exchanged and modified according to civilization. The holy is one; but not everywhere its idea of the same fate is conceived or applied, not everywhere he attains sanctity to its own objects. Thus, the supreme basis, as we said before, the rational origin, the primitive foundation of the crime more or less distinctly perceived and explained, are as immutable, as eternal, as the reason: the applicative part and the material fact of the crime itself are so little constant, so modifiable, so subject to variation and transit, as the immense accidents that characterize human societies.[213]

---

[209] Pacheco (1856), vol. I, 149.

[210] Pacheco (1856), vol. I, 149–150.

[211] Pacheco (1888), vol. I, Introduction, XI–XII.

[212] Pacheco (1888), vol. I, Introduction, XI–XIII.

[213] Pacheco (1888), vol. I, Introduction, XIII.

The same happens with the punishment, whose "primitive idea" in essence does not vary—nor can it vary—but it does vary "its application and its realization."[214] If the offence brings with it an evil, the punishment—or the penalty—is nothing other than "an evil to be imposed on the guilty, in atonement and as a consequence of that other, called crime, by which they disturbed society and damaged their fellowmen."[215] And he added:

> That reaction that instinct demands, that *approves the conscience, that justifies the dispassionate reason*, that is the one that has constituted, and constitutes, and has to constitute, while the world exists, the eternal, indestructible principle of punishment. In the evil for the offender consists the essence of punishment; as in the evil, known and voluntary, done to the innocent and to the whole society, consists the essence of the crime.[216]

That evil is, then, the permanent part of punishmnent. What varies is "the catalog of the evils available to the legislator," whose "list is not eternal and always its own: that catalog can not but be variable, to be rectifiable to infinity."[217] And he added:

> Each period of society, each step in the development of its civilization, each stop in progress, either retrograde or retrograde of ideas, supply a portion of different evils, or change and disrupt the already absolute, already relative, value of that until then they knew and appreciated. The arsenal, then, of the penalties is subject to that ebb and flow of needs and opinions. What once would have been a great evil, may be a small evil in the day: what in the past may have been considered the slightest punishment, may be a day of intolerable seriousness.[218]

As can be seen, Pacheco did not have a progressive conception of history, because ideas, in their evolution, can be "progressive or retrograde." He shows anyway "how the mobility of the form in the penalties is not less great or less noticeable than the mobility of the form in the crimes."[219]

Dealing with the definition of crime, Pacheco shows the role of nature and reason in its criminal law doctrine. Art. 1 SCC 1848 read as follows:

> Crime is any action or voluntary omission punishable by law. Actions or omissions punishable by law are always considered voluntary, unless otherwise stated. Whoever voluntarily executes the act, will be responsible for it, and will incur the penalty prescribed by law, even if the evil falls on a person other than the one to whom it was proposed to offend.[220]

Defining the offense as "any action or voluntary omission punishable by law" might seem to assume a purely voluntarist conception of law that Pacheco—like most 19th-century Spanish criminal lawyers—did not share at all. Perhaps this explains why precisely in this context he developed his doctrine on the foundation of criminal law. Although of the definition of crime—in Art. 1 SCC 1848—it could be inferred

---

[214]Pacheco (1888), vol. I, Introduction, XIII.

[215]Pacheco (1888), vol. I, Introduction, XIII.

[216]Pacheco (1888), vol. I, Introduction, XIII–XIV.

[217]Pacheco (1888), vol. I, Introduction, XIV.

[218]Pacheco (1888), vol. I, Introduction, XIV.

[219]Pacheco (1888), vol. I, Introduction, XIV.

[220]Art. 1 CP 1848; art. 1 CP 1850; art. 1 CP 1870; see Masferrer and Ramos Vázquez (2017), 193–201.

that Pacheco departed from a positivist or utilitarian legal theory, he made clear that this conclusion would be far removed from reality. For this reason, he declared as "necessary" that "the law should make the greatest effort to be right"—or reasonable—and that "that judgment be justified by itself in the eyes of universal reason," so that it is only a crime "what the entire conscience of human race may have irrevocably sealed with that seal of just reprobation."[221]

What did Pacheco understand by 'just reproach'? For him, the legitimacy of the criminal law does not come from the act of prohibition in the Austinian sense of the expression, because the supremacy of the law does not "dispense from obeying and fixing its precepts to the precepts of another more eminent sovereign, to the precepts of the reason."[222] And he added:

> Human law alone deserves this name, because it is a declaration of another higher and supreme law: it is only obeyed, because the world presumes that it fulfills its duties, and that it is in fact what it should be. When it evidently lacks its character, when it violates the rules that must inspire it, when it marches wildly, without another motive, without other direction than the individual whim, than the will of its authors, than the interest of a more or less numerous fraction, but fraction always, in such cases, the law loses its legitimacy, its works are not holy, its character and its name are denaturalized and exchanged.[223]

For Pacheco, nature, reason and justice are three closely related notions: there is no justice without conformity with nature, whose laws are understood as "precepts of reason." This conception is at odds with a voluntarist notion of criminal law, which means that "not any act can make a crime. Neither of what naturally is can stop doing it. It is reason who points out its work."[224] Hence the distinction between 'moral crime'—or sin—and 'social crime'—or crime—.[225] Pacheco recognizes that society has the right to enact criminal laws declaring punishable acts and imposing punishments, but can not—and should not—'create' justice or injustice since both predate human laws:

> The society, it is true, has the right to make criminal laws: it has the right to impose punishments declaring punishable actions. But in his works it is necessary that he adjust himself to nature and reason. It is not in his power to create justice or injustice: both have preceded the human precepts, which would never have been, if they did not inspire them. 'To say that there is nothing just or unjust – Montesquieu has rightly written – but what positive laws command or forbid, would be to say that before the first circle was drawn, all the radios were not equal.' *If there is a legal crime, if it could have been, it is because the moral crime, the natural crime existed previously.*[226]

The relationship between 'legal crime' and 'moral crime' proposed by Pacheco did not imply an identification or confusion between both categories. According to him, between the criminal law and the moral law there should not be an "absolute

[221] Pacheco (1888), vol. I, 76, n. 32.

[222] Pacheco (1888), vol. I, 76, n. 33.

[223] Pacheco (1888), vol. I, 76, n. 33.

[224] Pacheco (1888), vol. I, 76–77, n. 34.

[225] A este respecto, véase Pacheco (1888), vol. I, 77–79.

[226] Pacheco (1888), vol. I, 77, n. 35.

agreement in all points, but absolute harmony, and so to speak, full concentricity."[227] And he added:

> The spheres of nature and positive law are different, and it would be a mistake to pretend that their dispositions were perfectly adapted. The second can not follow all the steps of the first; it can not and must not sanction what it indicates, advises or declares. Its horizon is of less extension, its means are more limited. But it is necessary, yes, that they do not contradict each other, and that it does not condemn especially that one, whose circle is smaller, which approves, which perhaps prescribes the other, more expanded and more severe by its nature. In such a case there would be confusion, there would be disorder, the positive law would fail to its duty.[228]

The laws of nature and the positive laws could not be contradicted, so that the law established a 'social crime' that did not constitute a 'moral crime,' or vice versa, that is, that it might not be established as a 'social crime' a conduct that, in addition to constituting a 'moral crime,' might produce significant social damage. Pacheco, being aware of addressing a complex question, saw it necessary to "show the dependence that legal justice has on moral justice."[229]

Pacheco maintained that "there would be no good or bad in human laws, if previously there were no such categories in the laws of God and in the nature of man." And he added:

> Nature and supreme and primitive laws are the basis upon which reason can state human laws. Made for society, having no object but the order and welfare of it, have taken and must take from the others, general, complete, absolute, the part merely necessary for its purpose. Everything that did not lead to it, everything that did not fit the needs of society, all that has remained the subject of morality and reason, subject to its judgment, but exempt from social legislation. God and conscience will judge man in that immense space: society and its laws do without such extension, and are limited to what touches upon their interests, and what falls under their means. If they have ever gone beyond that sphere, they have committed a notorious usurpation.[230]

As Pacheco affirmed, criminal laws must take from moral laws—or from nature—only "the part that is merely necessary for its purpose," leaving everything else "exempt from social legislation." 'Legal justice' and 'criminal justice' have their parallelism with the 'social crime' and the 'moral crime'—or sin –, "identical in their origin," but distinguishable by the "different sphere to which they correspond, and because of the unequal extension of one and the other."[231]

Making clear that "not everything we recognize as bad must not even qualify as a crime in our precepts," Pacheco laid down some criteria in order to "determine imperiously the limits of our law and our particular justice."[232] What are those limits? Pacheco mentioned the following four:

---

[227] Pacheco (1888), vol. I, 77, n. 36.

[228] Pacheco (1888), vol. I, 77, n. 36.

[229] Pacheco (1888), vol. I, 77, n. 37.

[230] Pacheco (1888), vol. I, 77, n. 38.

[231] Pacheco (1888), vol. I, 77–78, n. 39.

[232] Pacheco (1888), vol. I, 78, n. 40.

> 1) "That society might have an interest in it, that is resented by its perpetration, that might produce effective, assignable damages, not only of the internal order, but also of the external order";
>
> 2) "That society itself has adequate means to punish those evils, whose declaration and condemnation must be made in its laws";
>
> 3) "That these evils [– or damages –] can not be repressed, impeded, avoided, by other means softer than penalties"; and
>
> 4) "That such means of penalty, necessary and possible, do not bring with them greater inconveniences than the good that is expected from their application".[233]

In this line of thought, Pacheco affirmed that the human—or social—law, being "a necessary companion of man, participant in his imperfection and in his misery (…), has to confess himself extremely inferior to the moral laws that govern the spirits." Thus human law should stick to the "limited object whose satisfaction is entrusted to it, the narrowness and imperfection of the means it uses; it is necessary that it should face itself, and that it should not have presumptions repugnant to its true character."[234] Otherwise, the world would revolt against a 'social law' that went beyond the sphere and extent that corresponds to it:

> The world revolts when the human law wants to reach thoughts, and punish them; because thoughts only belong to God, and society has no power at the bottom of souls. The world revolts, or at least laughs, when it sees the criminalization of suicide; because it is foolish to pretend to punish beyond death to whom through death put himself beyond our reach. The world would condemn the use of means of true penalty, as a sanction of civil obligations, however there is an evil in failing them; because that evil is more easily corrected by other means, and does not require the infliction of a punishment, cruel and condemnable as unnecessary.[235]

Pacheco explained that he wanted to make these "few and general reflections" to deal with the definition of crime in order to reject "any tendency of materialism and immorality."[236] He concluded his reflections with the following words:

> Here, then, is the necessary, indispensable relationship that exists between social evil and moral evil, between crime according to natural laws and crime according to positive laws. To understand the latter, it is necessary to understand the former, without which this certainly would not exist, with which it must be harmonious, to which it cannot be contrary, of which, however, it must be different. Concentric circles, as we have just said, but of varying size: material and limited application the one, of what is moral and without limits in the other: similar and diverse at the same time, as human intelligence and divine intelligence, of which are emanations and results, are similar and diverse.[237]

Pacheco was so aware of the idea that not all 'moral crimes'—or sins—must be classified as 'social crimes' that the beginning of volume II of his *Código penal concordado y comentado* reiterated that such part contain "all the actions that the law

---

[233] Pacheco (1888), vol. I, 78, n. 40.

[234] Pacheco (1888), vol. I, 78, n. 41.

[235] Pacheco (1888), vol. I, 78, n. 41.

[236] Pacheco (1888), vol. I, 79, n. 42.

[237] Pacheco (1888), vol. I, 78–79, n. 42.

has considered severely punishable." And he added that "those that are not included, those that the legislator has excluded, should not be considered as crimes, they are not subject to the justice of the world, and not subject to criminal sanction."[238] Later on, he added:

> Not all the actions that are today a crime, ought or should be at any time, even if it is, as they are now, must have or should be punished with identical penalties. These lists, these sanctions, are the variable part of criminal law (...). Society moves, man varies, civilization ordinarily progresses. Understanding that this portion of law could or should remain stationary would certainly be to conceive an absurdity.[239]

2.3.4 Contribution of the Enlightened Criminal Law to the 19th-Century Criminal Jurisprudence

Was there continuity between the 18th-century criminal law reformers and 19th-century criminal discourses in France and Spain?

First, the final outcome of both enlightened thinkers and 19th-century criminal lawyers was not always far from what the criminal law science of the Ancien Régime defended, but some of the arguments used changed notably. In this vein, no religious or theological references can be found in what authors explored when explaining why some behaviors should or should not be criminalized.

The 19th-century criminal law undertook reforms decriminalizing some crimes like witchcraft and heresy—remember that Montesquieu disregarded these crimes, but he did not dare to ask for their abolition—but others remained in force for a long time. For example, both 18th- and 19th-century authors favoured the criminalization of religious crimes (blasphemy among them), and other behaviors related to moral sexuality in a similar way in the past as adultery, bigamy, incest, and rape—*stuprum*—

.

However, from 17th the century onwards criminal lawyers differed from the earlier criminal lawyers in three aspects:

(1) No theological or religious arguments were used; criminal lawyers thought that criminal law should not be based anymore on religious or Christian-moral arguments such as the ideal of celibacy, chastity or religious faithfulness.
(2) They all defended that punishments should be less severe. It was a consequence of the principles of humanitarianism and proportionality between crime and punishment. They defended, for example, that the death penalty should not be imposed for those convicted sodomy, but life imprisonment or hard labor was instead appropriate.[240] Note that this already happened in many territories from the beginning of the seventeenth century.[241]

---

[238] Pacheco (1888), vol. II, 6, n. 4.

[239] Pacheco (1888), vol. II, 6, nn. 6–7.

[240] From a legislative perspective, Pietro Leopoldo of Tuscany was the first who abolished death penalty for all crimes (1786), becoming not only the first Western ruler to do so, but also the first ruler to abolish death penalty for sodomy (which was replaced by prison and hard labor).

[241] See, for example, the case of Valencia, in Tomás y Valiente (1990), 54.

(3) Lawyers strove to emphasize the distinction between crime and sin, and that "the greatness of the sin should not aggravate the crime". They defended such separation as a requirement of the modernization of criminal law and criticized the close relationship between crime and sin in the European criminal law tradition.

Second—and connected to the first—, they generally based their argumentation upon natural philosophy. Once the theology had been rejected, they tended to resort to philosophy, but a philosophy founded upon nature. According to them, the main criterion to judge whether a specific behavior may cause damage either to society or to particular individuals was human nature. Remember Beccaria pointing out that he wrote "only of crimes which violate the laws of nature and the social contract, and not of sins."[242]

3 Concluding Considerations

The secularization of criminal law was a long and complex process that goes beyond the contribution of the Enlightenment. From a jurisprudential perspective, it started much earlier. As seen, some 17th-century contractualist legal philosophers such as Hobbes, Pufendorf and Locke, strove to separate criminal justice from religious, theological, or 'moralist' arguments and founded it upon natural philosophy. In doing so, they resorted to nature, natural law and natural reason. Hence they clearly distinguished between crime and sin.

This 17th-century legacy was adopted and notably developed by enlightened authors who claimed for urgent criminal law reform. In doing so, they did not defend a criminal law detached from morality, as if utilitarianism was the mainstream of the 18th-century criminal jurisprudence. Unlike Bentham, the majority of criminal law reformers such as Montesquieu, Beccaria, Rousseau, Voltaire and Kant, were not utilitarians, so most of them accepted both the social contract and laws of universal nature.

Some scholars maintain that 19th-century criminal lawyers betrayed some of the main criminal law principles defended by the Enlightenment because enlightened thought endorsed a criminal law derived from a social contract and rejected another criminal law based upon natural law. This thesis is simply false and misleading. Some of the most important 19th-century criminal lawyers resorted—in conformity with most of the enlightened authors—to nature, natural law and natural reason. In doing so, they defended the relation between criminal law and morality, and distinguished between crime and sin, rather than confusing or identifying these categories. Those who defend the opposite thesis would need to prove that utilitarianism was the mainstream of the enlightened criminal law reformers. That would be a very difficult task, if not an impossible one. Both utilitarianism and legal positivism notably grew in France and Spain during the nineteenth century but did not become the mainstream of criminal law jurisprudence until the twentieth century.

---

[242] See Footnote 76 and its main text.

It might well be that those who today share a utilitarian conception of criminal law—that nowadays is undeniably the mainstream—are looking at the past with the mind and eyes anchored in the present, so they come to a false conclusion after misreading, misunderstanding or misrepresenting enlightened criminal law jurisprudence. They just create a myth. Evidence contradicts this Whiggish view of the Western criminal law tradition.

References

Primary Literature

Beccaria (1872) An essay on crimes and punishments. By the Marquis Beccaria of Milan. With a commentary by de Voltaire M. A New Edition Corrected, W.C. Little & Co., Albany

Bentham J (1785) Offences against one's self (I also use the Spanish version: De los delitos contra uno mismo, Clásicos de Pensamiento Biblioteca Nueva, Madrid, 2002)

Bentham (1838–1843c) Chapter: of publicity and privacy, as applied to judicature in general, and to the collection of the evidence in particular, vol 6, Chap X. Available at https://oll.libertyfund.org/title/1923/116124/2364369

Bentham J (2002) "Introducción" a Jeremy Bentham. De los delitos contra uno mismo, Clásicos de Pensamiento Biblioteca Nueva, Madrid

Bentham J (1838–1843) The works of Jeremy Bentham, published under the Superintendence of his Executor, John Bowring, William Tait, Edinburgh

Bentham J (1907) An introduction to the principles of morals and legislation. Clarendon Press, Oxford

Bérenger A-M-T (1855) De la répression pénale, de ses formes et de ses effets, Paris

Blackstone W (1893) Commentaries on the laws of England in Four Books. Notes selected from the editions of Archibold C, Coleridge C, Stewart K and others, Barron Field's analysis, and additional notes, and a life of the author by George Sharswood. In Two Volumes, J.B. Lippincott Co., Philadelphia

Filangieri C (1821) Ciencia de la legislación (translation by Juan Rivera), Imprenta de D. Fermín Villalpando, Madrid, 6 vols

Filangieri C (1822) Ciencia de la legislación (traducción de Jaime Rubio), Imprenta de Núñez, Madrid, 3rd ed, 3 vols (I also used the following edition: Ciencia de la legislación, traducción de Juan Rivera, Imprenta de D. Fermín Villalpando, Madrid, 1821, 6 volumes, vol I)

Garraud R (1881) Précis de droit criminel (I use the 11th ed, Paris, 1912; https://gallica.bnf.fr/ark:/12148/bpt6k4156089.texteImage)

Garraud R (1888–1894) Traité théorique et pratique de droit pénal français, vol. 5, 6, 2nd ed, pp 1898–1902

Garraud R (1907–1929) Traité théorique et pratique d'instruction criminelle et de procédure pénale (6 vol, with his son Pierre Garraud)

Gómez de la Serna P (1865) Obras Jurídicas de D. Joaquín Francisco Pacheco, Revista General De Legislación Y Jurisprudencia 27:228–240

Groizard A (1870) El Código penal de 1870, concordado y comentado. Esteban hermanos impresores, Burgos, II

Hélie F (1863) 'Introduction' to Pellegrino Rossi, Traité de Droit Pénal, 3rd ed. (rev. by F. Hélie), v 1, Librairie de Guillaumin et Cie., Paris

Hobbes T (1839–1845a) The English works of Thomas Hobbes of Malmesbury; now first collected and Edited by Sir William Molesworth, Bart. Bohn, London, 11 vols

Hobbes (1839–1845b) Chapter: a dialogue of the common law, vol 6. Available at https://oll.libertyfund.org/title/770/89920/2026935
Hobbes (1839–1845c) A dialogue of the common law, vol 6. Available at https://oll.libertyfund.org/title/770/89920/2026937
Hobbes (1839–1845d) Chapter XXVII: of crimes, excuses, and extenuations, vol 3. Available at https://oll.libertyfund.org/title/585/89872/2025966
Hobbes (1839–1845e) Chapter XXVII: of crimes, excuses, and extenuations, vol 3. Available at https://oll.libertyfund.org/title/585/89872/2025967
Hobbes (1839–1845f) Chapter XXVII: of crimes, excuses, and extenuations, vol 3. Available at https://oll.libertyfund.org/title/585/89872/2026018
Hobbes (1839–1845g) Chapter a dialogue of the common law, vol 6. Available at https://oll.libertyfund.org/title/770/89920/2027289
Hobbes (1839–1845h) Chapter a dialogue of the common law, vol 6. Available at https://oll.libertyfund.org/title/770/89920/2027291
Hobbes (1839–1845i) Chapter a dialogue of the common law, vol 6. Available at https://oll.libertyfund.org/title/770/89920/2027116
Hobbes (1839–1845j) CHAPTER XXVII: of crimes, excuses, and extenuations, vol 3. Available at https://oll.libertyfund.org/title/585/89872/2025973
Hobbes (1839–1845k) CHAPTER XXVII: of crimes, excuses, and extenuations, vol 3. Available at https://oll.libertyfund.org/title/585/89872/2025982
Kant I (1797) Metaphysische Anfangsgründe der Rechtslehre
Kant I (1886) The metaphysics of ethics by Immanuel Kant, trans. Semple JW ed with Introduction by Rev. Henry Calderwood, T. & T. Clark, Edinburgh
Kant I (1887) The philosophy of law: an exposition of the fundamental principles of jurisprudence as the science of right, by Immanuel Kant, trans. Hastie W, Clark, Edinburgh
Lardizábal M de (1782) Discurso sobre las penas contraído a las leyes criminales de España para facilitar su Reforma, Imp. Joaquín Ibarra, Madrid, 2nd ed. There are many editions: Imp. Repullés, Madrid, 1828; 3rd ed. Biblioteca Criminoldgica y Penitenciaria, vol 1, ed. La Lectura, Madrid, 1916; 4th ed: Revista de Estudios Penitenciarios, n 174, Madrid, 1966—I used this one—; 5th ed: Poda, Méjico, 1982, Prologue by J. Piña y Palacios
Locke (1764), ch. II: Of the State of Nature, § 10; available at https://oll.libertyfund.org/titles/222#Locke_0057_259
Locke J (1824) The works of john locke in nine volumes, Rivington, London, 12th ed. https://oll.libertyfund.org/titles/761#Locke_0128-01_706
Mendizábal Martín L (1897) Programa de Elementos de Derecho natural. Imprenta de Ramón Miedes, Zaragoza
Mendizábal Martín L (1897–1899) Elementos de Derecho natural, Zaragoza, 3 vols
Montesquieu (1948) On the spirit of the laws
Montesquieu (1777) The Complete Works of de Montesquieu M, Evans T, London, 4 vols
Montesquieu (1777a) Chapter: Chap. V: That virtue is not the principle of a monarchical government; available at https://oll.libertyfund.org/title/837/71126/1688041
Montesquieu (1777b) Chapter: CHAP. IX: Of the severity of punishments in different governments, vol 1. Available at https://oll.libertyfund.org/title/837/71216/1688454
Montesquieu (1777c) Chapter: Chap. IV: that liberty is favoured by the nature and proportion of punishments, vol 1. Available at https://oll.libertyfund.org/title/837/71430/1689202
Montesquieu (1777d) Chapter: Chap. VI: Of the crime against nature, vol 1. Available at https://oll.libertyfund.org/title/837/71434/1689226
Montesquieu (1777e) Chapter: Chap. XII: Of natural modesty, vol 1. Available at https://oll.libertyfund.org/title/837/71620/1689735
Montesquieu (1777f) Chapter: Chap. VI: of polygamy considered in itself, vol 1. Available at https://oll.libertyfund.org/title/837/71608/1689702
Ortolán M (1845) Curso de legislación penal comparada. Lecciones pronunciadas en la Facultad de Derecho de Paris, Imprenta de la Sociedad Literaria y Tipográfica, Madrid

Ortolán M (1878) Tratado de Derecho penal, según la ciencia racional, la legislación positiva y la jurisprudencia (traducido por Melquíades Pérez Rivas). Librería de Leocadio López, Madrid
Pacheco JF (1842) Estudios de Derecho penal. Lecciones pronunciadas en el Ateneo de Madrid en 1839 y 1840, Madrid: Boix, Editor, vol. I
Pacheco JF (1856) El Código penal concordado y comentado, Madrid, 2nd ed
Pacheco JF (1888) El Código penal concordado y comentado, Imprenta y fundición de Manuel Tello, Madrid, 6th ed
Proal L (1893) El delito y la pena (traducción y prólogo de Pedro Armengol y Cornet). Librería de Subirana Hermanos, Barcelona
Proal L (1895) La criminalité politique (1895) (English translation, 1898)
Pufendorf S von (1672), De Jure Naturæ et Gentium
Pufendorf S von (2003) The whole duty of man according to the law of nature (trans. Tooke A ed Hunter I, Saunders D, with two discourses and a commentary by Barbeyrac J, trans. Saunders D, Liberty Fund, Indianapolis)
Röder KDA (1846) Zur Rechtsbegrundung der Besserungsstrafe
Röder KDA (1855) Grundgedanken und Bedeutung des römischen und germanischen Rechts
Röder KDA (1863) Der Strafvollzug im Geist des Rechts
Röder KDA (1864) Besserungsstrafe und Besserungsstrafanstalten als Rechtsforderung
Röder KDA (1867) Die herrschenden Grundlehren von Verbrechen und Strafe in ihren inneren Wiedersprüchen
Röder KDA (1875) Estudios sobre derecho penal y sistemas penitenciarios
Röder KDA (1876) Las doctrinas fundamentales reinantes sobre el delito y la pena en sus interiores contradicciones. Ensayo crítico preparatorio para la renovación del Derecho penal, traducido del alemán por F. Giner, Librería de Victoriano Suárez, Madrid
Romero Girón V (1886) Pacheco y la legislación penal en España. In: La España del siglo XIX, Madrid
Rossi P (1839) Tratado de Derecho penal (traducción de Cayetano Cortés), Imprenta de D. José María Repullés, Madrid 2 vols
Rousseau J-J (1901) Ideal empires and republics. Rousseau's social contract, more's Utopia, Bacon's New Atlantis, Campanella's City of the Sun, with an Introduction by Andrews CM, Walter Dunne M, Washington DC
Silvela L (1903) El Derecho español estudiado en principios y en la legislación vigente en España, Establecimiento Tipográfico de Ricardo Fe, Madrid, 2nd ed
Tissot CJ (1880) El Derecho penal estudiado en sus principios, en sus aplicaciones y legislaciones de los diversos pueblos del mundo o Introducción filosófica é histórica al estudio del Derecho penal (versión castellana de la edición de 1880 por J. Ortega García, aumentada con notas y algunas indagaciones del autor por A. García Moreno), F. Góngora y Compañía Editores, Madrid
Vicente Almazán M (1852) Estudios filosóficos sobre la legislación, Imprenta de José Rius, Valencia. https://janetchapmansandrahill.info/pdf-links/descarga-pdf-libros-enlinea-97436.html
de Vizmanos TM, Álvarez Martínez C (1848) Comentarios al Código penal. Establecimiento tipográfico de J. González y A, Vicente, Madrid
Voltaire (1901) The works of voltaire. A contemporary version. A critique and biography by Morley J, notes by Smollett T, trans. Fleming WF, DuMont ER, New York

Secondary Literature

Acedo Castilla JF (1996) Ideas Jurídicas de Don Joaquín Francisco Pacheco (1808–1865). Discurso leído el 11 de febrero de 1996 en la Real Academia Sevillana de Legislación y Jurisprudencia, Madrid

Ancel M (1965) Social defence: a modern approach to criminal problems (translated by Wilson J), Routledge, reprinted 1998
Antón Oneca J (1965a) El Código penal de 1848 y D. Joaquín Francisco Pacheco, Anuario De Derecho Penal Y Ciencias Penales 18:473–495
Antón Oneca J (1965b) Historia del Código penal de 1822. ADPCP 17:262–278
Astigarraga J (2007) La ilustración napolitana imputada. Críticas y censuras a la Scienza della legislazione de G. Filangieri en la España de finales del siglo XVIII. In: Nuevo Mundo Mundos Nuevos (online), Colloques, 18.6.2007. https://nuevomundo.revues.org/6911
Baró Pazos J (1991) Historiografía sobre la Codificación del Derecho Penal en el siglo XIX. In: Rueda G (ed) Doce Estudios de Historiografía contemporánea. Universidad de Santander, Santander, pp 1–40
Baró Pazos J (2006) Joaquín Francisco Pacheco Gutiérrez (1808–1865). In: Diccionario crítico de juristas españoles, portugueses y latinoamericanos (hispánicos, brasileños, quebequenses y restantes francófonos). Zaragoza-Barcelona, vol 2, t. 1, n 732, 256
Bentham (1838–1843a) Classes of offences, Chap. XVIII. §1, vol 1. Available at https://oll.libertyfund.org/title/2009/139415/2639145
Bentham (1838–1843b) Chapter: letter IV: proposed trial by JURY, vol 5. Available https://oll.libertyfund.org/title/1996/130177/2570421
Bullough VL (1985) Prostitution and reform in eighteenth-century England. In: Maccubbin RP (ed) Tis nature's fault. Unauthorized sexuality during the enlightenment. Cambridge University Press, Cambridge
Calvo Rubio JA (1966) Pacheco, penalista. Revista De Derecho 26:28–54
Cardenal Murillo A (1990) La responsabilidad por el resultado en el Derecho penal (Estudio histórico-dogmático de sus manifestaciones en el Libro I del Código penal español). Edersa, Madrid
Cartuyvels Y (1994) Eléments pour une approche généalogique du code pénal. Déviance Et Société 18(4):373–396
Cartuyvels Y (1996) D'où vient le code pénal?: une approche généalogique des premiers codes pénaux absolutistes au XVIIIe siècle. Presses de l'Université de Montréal/Presses de l'Université d'Ottawa/De Boeck Université, Montréal et al
Cartuyvels Y (1997) Le droit pénal entre consolidation étatique et codification absolutiste au XVIIIe siècle. Le penal dans tous ses Etats. Justice, Etats et Sociétés en Europe (XIIe-Xxe siècles), Bruxelles, pp 252–278
Castejón F (1970) Las ideas penales en la época del Código penal de 1870. In: Conmemoración del centenario de la Ley provisional sobre organización del Poder Judicial y del Código penal de 1870, Real Academia de Legislación y jurisprudencia, Madrid
Clavero B (1990) Delito y pecado. Noción y escala de transgresiones. In: Tomás y Valiente F, Clavero B, Hespanha AM, Bermejo JL, Gacto E, Alvarez Alonso C (eds) Sexo barroco y otras transgresiones premodernas. Alianza Universidad, Madrid, pp 57–89
Cuello Calón E (1948) Centenario del Código penal de 1848. Pacheco penalista y Legislador. Su influjo en este cuerpo legal, Información Jurídica, pp 5–15
Díez del Corral L (1956) Pensamiento político de Joaquín Francisco Pacheco. I.E.P, Madrid, pp 277–302
Ferrajoli L (1997) Derecho y razón. Teoría del garantismo penal (trad. de Andrés Ibáñez P, Ruiz Miguel A, Bayón Mohino JC, Terradillos Basoco y R, Cantarero Bandrés J), 2nd ed, Trotta, Madrid (see the English version, Law and Reason. The Theory of Penal Guarantees, Editori Laterza, 2018)
Fletcher GP (1984) Human dignity as a constitutional value, 22 U. W Ontario L Rev 171:171–182
Galindo Ayuda F (1991) La Scienza della legislazione en España. Gaetano Filangieri e l'Illuminismo Europeo, Atti del Convengo "Gaetano Filangieri e l'Illuminismo Europeo." Guida, Nápoles, pp 375–401
Gunther S (2009) The elastic closet: a history of homosexuality in France, 1942–present. Palgrave Macmillan, New Yorkand Houndmills

Halpérin J-L (2006) "René Garraud (1849–1930)", Criminocorpus [En ligne], Histoire de la criminologie, 1. La revue et ses hommes, mis en ligne le 01 janvier 2006. https://journals.openedition.org/criminocorpus/117

Hermann S (1984) From philosophers to legislators, and legislators to gods: The French civil code as secular scripture, 1984 U. Ill L Rev 597:1984

Iñesta-Pastor E (2011) El Código Penal Español de 1848, tirant lo Blanch, Valencia

Iñesta-Pastor E (2016) La interpretación del eclecticismo en la doctrina y en la legislación penal de la España del siglo XIX. Ius Fugit 19:209–230

Iñesta-Pastor E (2018) The influence exerted by the 1819 criminal code of the two sicilies upon nineteenth-century spanish criminal law codification and its projection in Latin America. In: Masferrer A (ed) The western codification of criminal law: the myth of its predominant french influence revisited. Springer, Dordrecht-Heidelberg-London-New York, pp 243–278

Jiménez de Asúa L (1951) Don Joaquín Francisco Pacheco en el Centenario del Código Penal español. El Criminalista (Buenos Aires) 9:13–33

Koritansky P (2005) Two theories of retributive punishment. In: Kant I, Aquinas T (eds) History of Philosophy quarterly 22(4):319–338

Lalinde Abadía J (1991) El eco de Gaetano Filangieri en España. Gaetano Filangieri e l'Illuminismo Europeo, Atti del Convengo "Gaetano Filangieri e l'Illuminismo Europeo." Guida, Nápoles, pp 453–506

Letourneau C Génesis y evolución de la moral, Publicaciones de La Escuela Moderna, Barcelona

Lorente Sariñena M (2007) De la suerte normativa de la ciencia de la legislación: Filangieri y la codificación moderna en la España decimonónica. In: Nuevo Mundo Mundos Nuevos (online), Colloques, 28.1. 2007. https://nuevomundo.revues.org/3510

Marín y Mendoza J (1776) Historia del Derecho natural y de gentes, Madrid (I use the edition by Salvador Rus Rufino, Diputación de Valencia, Valencia, 1999)

Masferrer A (2009) Codification of Spanish criminal law in the nineteenth century. A comparative legal history approach. J Comparative Law 4(1):96–139

Masferrer A (2010) Liberal state and criminal law reform in Spain. In: Sellers M, Tomaszewski T (eds) The rule of law in comparative perspective. Springer, Dordrecht-Heidelberg-London-New York, pp 19–40

Masferrer A (2016) Taking human dignity more humanely: a historical contribution to the ethical foundations of the constitutional democracy. In: Masferrer A, García-Sánchez E (eds) Human dignity of the vulnerable in the age of rights: interdisciplinary perspectives. Springer, Dordrecht-Heidelberg-London-New York, pp 221–256

Masferrer A (2017) La distinción entre delito y pecado en la tradición penal bajomedieval y moderna. Una Propuesta Revisionista De La Historiografía Española, Europea Y Anglosajona, Anuario De Historia Del Derecho Español 87:693–756

Masferrer A, Ramos Vázquez I (2017) Noción y clasificación del delito en la Codificación española: una aproximación comparada con la Codificación francesa y alemana. In: Masferrer A (ed), La Codificación penal española. Contribución al estudio de sus influencias extranjeras, y de la francesa en particular, Aranzadi–Thomson Reuters, Pamplona, pp 167–218

Morillas Cueva L (1978) Derecho Penal e Ideología. In: Derecho y Economía en la sociedad española actual, Granada, pp 82–83

Murphy JG (1952) Philosophy of right (trans.by T. M. Knox), Oxford University Press, Oxford

Murphy JG (1979) Kant's theory of criminal punishment. In: Retribution, justice, and therapy. Philosophical studies series in philosophy, vol 16. Springer, Dordrecht

Nye RA (1998) Masculinity and male codes of honor in France. University of California Press, California

Revuelta Benito R (1945) El Código penal de 1848 y su gran comentarista don Joaquín Francisco Pacheco. Revista De La Escuela De Estudios Penitenciarios 6:31–33

Rublack U (2002) State-formation, gender and the experience of governance in early modern Württemberg. In: Rublack U (ed) Gender in early modern German history. Cambridge University Press, Cambridge

Sainz Cantero JA (1967) El informe de la Universidad de Granada sobre el Proyecto que dio lugar al Código penal de 1822. ADPCP 20:509–538
Sanchez Blanco F (1991) Europa y el pensamiento español del siglo XVIII. Alianza, Madrid
Sánchez González DM (2007) Historiografía penal española (1808–1870): La Escuela Clásica. In: Alvarado J, Serrano Maíllo (eds), Estudios de Historia de las Ciencias criminales, Dykinson, Madrid
Sánchez Osés J (1966) Gaetano Filangieri. ADPCP 19:413–438
Schafer S (1971) The concept of the political criminal, 62. J Crim L Criminol Police Sci 380
Sellert W (1983) Die Krise des Straf- und Strafprozeßrechts und ihre Überwindung im 16. Jahrhundert durch Rezeption und Säkularisation. In: Säkulare Aspekte der Reformationszeit. München-Wien, pp 27–48
Silva Forné D (2001) La codificación penal y el surgimiento del Estado Liberal en España, Revista de Derecho Penal y Criminología 7:233–312. https://e-spacio.uned.es/fez/eserv.php?pid=bibliuned:revistaDerechoPenalyCriminologia-2001-7-5070&dsID=Documento.pdf
Tomás y Valiente F (1994) Joaquín Francisco Pacheco y la Codificación Penal. In: Códigos y Constituciones (1808–1978). Madrid, pp 31–79
Tomás y Valiente F (1969) El Derecho penal de la Monarquía absoluta (siglos XVI-XVIII), Madrid
Tomás y Valiente F (1990) El crimen y pecado contra natura. In: Tomás y Valiente F, Clavero B, Hespanha AM, Bermejo JL, Gacto E, Alvarez Alonso C (eds) Sexo barroco y otras transgresiones premodernas, Alianza Universidad, Madrid, pp 33–55
Tomás y Valiente, El Derecho penal de la Monarquía absoluta
Vander Waerdt PA (1994) Philosophical influence on roman jurisprudence? the case of stoicism and natural law. In: Haase W (ed) Philosophie, Wissenschaften, Technik. De Gruyter, Philosophie, pp 4851–4901
Vázquez García F, Moreno Mengíbar A (1997) Sexo y razón. Una genealogía de la moral sexual en España (siglos XVI-XX), Akal, Madrid
Virto Larruscain MJ (1984) El caso fortuito y la construcción del sistema de culpabilidad en el Código Penal de 1848. Servicio Editorial de la Universidad del País Vasco, Bilbao
Watson G (1971) The natural law and stoicism. In: Long AA (ed) Problems in stoicism. London, pp 216–236

Habits of Intelligence. Liberty of Expression and the Criterion of Harm in John Stuart Mill

Ignacio Sánchez Cámara

Abstract The essay analyzes J. S. Mill's criteria to delimit the scope in which a person can be forced to act or refrain from acting by others or by society in general, and exposes and criticizes its consequences for freedom of expression and to determine the limits of Criminal Law intervention.

Isaiah Berlin considered the English thinker John Stuart Mill (1806–1873) to be the founder of modern liberalism. He was the son of James Mill, friend of Jeremy Bentham and the promoter, with the latter, of a group known under the term "philosophical radicalism", adherent of utilitarian moral philosophy and the principles of political liberalism. This movement pursued the transformation of English political and legal institutions. J. S. Mill's main contributions belong to the fields of ethics, political philosophy, logic end economic theory. Among his works are *A System of Logic Ratiocinative and Inductive* (1843), *Principles of Political Economy* (1848), *Considerations of Representative Government* (1861) and *Utilitarianism* (1863).[1] *Autobiography*, published posthumously on the year of his death, is worth reading as it provides useful information on the education he received, its value and limitations, and on the nature and evolution of his ideas. He believed that society can only achieve a satisfactory state when the most capable men exercise the highest authority. Civilisation is defined by the presence of two characteristics: the existence of a responsible government and the emergence of scientific knowledge. Freedom is a prerequisite for progress, and equality, when taken to the extreme, collides with justice and may damage freedom and respect for intellectual and moral excellence, a necessary condition for social progress and wellbeing.

I. Sánchez Cámara (✉)
Rey Juan Carlos University, Madrid, Spain
e-mail: ignacio.sanchez@urjc.es

[1]Mill (1974).

A. Masferrer (ed.), *Criminal Law and Morality in the Age of Consent*, Ius Gentium: Comparative Perspectives on Law and Justice 84,
https://doi.org/10.1007/978-3-030-64163-4_6

1 Utilitarism and Representative Government

Although he always remained loyal to Bentham's utilitarianism, this agreement was eventually reduced to the acceptance of the principle of utility as a moral criterion: the greatest happiness of the greatest number is the criterion for determining what is morally right or wrong. Mill stopped believing in the possibility of determining utility scientifically or objectively, and rejected the claim that pleasures (and therefore, goods) were homogeneous and therefore commensurable, since some were, in themselves, superior to others. He distinguished between the utility of the action and of the norm that regulates it; and this consideration was decisive for him. He also introduced into his ethics elements from other doctrines, such as Stoicism and Christianism. One could in fact consider his work a revision of Bentham's utilitarian ethics, more valuable to politics and law than to actual morals.

The basic principle of utilitarianism is that nothing other than happiness is desirable as an end. In order to prove this, Mill argues that:

> The only proof capable of being given that an object is visible, is that people actually see it. The only proof that a sound is audible, is that people hear; and so of other sources of our experience. In like manner, I apprehend, the sole evidence it is possible to produce that anything is desirable, is that people do actually desire it.[2]

But if this were so, it would entail moral ruin, as good would be identified with the desire of the majority and have nothing to do with the conviction or loyalty to principles. In the moral sense, desire would not be what people actually desire, but rather what ought to be desired, what is worthy of being desired.[3] This consideration would change if addressed from a legal-political perspective.[4]

Mill defends individualism and seems to pay greater attention to the individual than to society. However, this must be qualified, as the defence of individuality is based on the increased social benefits it promotes.

Mill defends democracy (the representative government) although he believes that it only becomes possible when people achieve a certain level of civilisation. Despotism is, for him, legitimate among barbarian people groups, who cannot but be subjected to tyranny. His theory has no universal validity. In fact, it's only valid in situations where society becomes more important than the State.[5] Distinction must be drawn between the progress of societies towards civilisation and their progress once they have become civilised.[6]

---

[2]Mill (1974), *Utilitarianism*, cap. IV, X, 234.

[3]Moore (1959), 66.

[4]Rodríguez Paniagua (1993), vol. II, 400.

[5]Magid (1987), 784 ff.

[6]"The problem of the subsequent stages of progress is to prevent the individual from being oppressed by the mass of humanity, increasingly powerful and confident. Progress towards civilisation demands restraining individual liberty; progress in civilisation demands liberating the individual from these restrictions" (*ibidem*, p. 801 ss.).

The main objectives of the State are to maintain order and the attainment of progress in society. Citizens' qualities are crucial to achieve these aims. Good government promotes the virtue and intelligence of people. The only rival of the representative government is benevolent despotism, although free peoples have prospered more than those living under despotism, whether paternalist or not. Mill advocates a capable, competent democracy. He considers the concept of democracy that reduces it to the government of the majority to be mistaken. For Mill, the pure idea of democracy is the government of the whole people by the whole people, equally represented, where representatives take into account everyone's opinions and not only those of their voters. Without individual representation, universal suffrage would lead to the tyranny of the majority. He considers it necessary to ensure that the opinions of educated people are not drowned by the votes of the less educated. Otherwise, he accepts and defends all the new and great political and social causes of his time, such as women's suffrage; his stance regarding economics could well be described as socialist.

2 The Criterion of Harm

The issues he addresses, and the solutions he provides, are still relevant today.[7] This doesn't mean they are not without flaws and inconsistencies. Berlin argues that he has an outdated conception of psychology as well as a lack of logical coherence. Mill's defence of individual liberty will probably be his contribution that stands the test of time. His essay *On Liberty*,[8] published in 1859, is perhaps the most eloquent and vibrant argument in favour of individual freedom ever written. Mills declares in *Autobiography* that this work was undertaken jointly with his wife, Harriet Taylor, and that, except perhaps for his book on logic, it was likely to survive longer than anything else he had written:

> (...) because the conjunction of her mind with mine has rendered it a kind of philosophic text-book of a single truth, which the changes progressively taking place in modern society tend to bring out into ever stronger relief: the importance, to man and society of a large variety in types of character, and of giving full freedom to human nature to expand itself in innumerable and conflicting directions.[9]

The doctrine defended here is individualism. As Mill himself recognises, its originality is limited. He also admits that the main thesis of the book owes a lot to the ideas of Wilhelm von Humboldt, especially to those included in his essay on the limits of State power; not to mention Tocqueville's influence regarding the tyranny of the majority or the consequences of the spread of democracy and social equality. Nevertheless, it remains difficult to find a work which defends the value of individual liberty with such energy and passion, both for the development of human capacities

---

[7]Ryan (1974), 1 ff.
[8]Mill (1974).
[9]Mill (1924).

and the wellbeing and progress of society. What is distinctive and peculiar to man is his ability to choose. Mill's greatest concern is the necessity to spread individual liberty and, especially, freedom of expression. And he includes tolerance and respect for others' opinions and beliefs as vital ingredients of this liberty. Therefore, it may be argued that liberty is more valuable as a means than as an actual end. Mill undertakes an energetic defence in favour of variety, diversity, personal vigour, individual genius; against uniformity, massification, mediocrity and vulgarity.

The objective of the book is indicated by the author at the beginning: "The subject of this Essay is not the so-called Liberty of the Will, (…) but Civil, or Social Liberty: the nature and limits of the power which can be legitimately exercised by society over the individual".[10]

His aim is to warn of the necessity to limit the power of democracies. Believing that it's unnecessary to protect the nation from its own will is a serious mistake which may involve dire consequences:

> The 'people' who exercise the power, are not always the same people with those over whom it is exercised, and the 'self-government' spoken of, is not the government of each by himself, but of each by all the rest.[11]

This need to limit power is not mitigated by the government of the majority, or those who represent it. Nor by the fact that governors are held responsible before the community. Society must be on guard against the "tyranny of the majority" as one of the evils it may face. Mill's idea is that society in general, or the majority of society, can in fact exercise a type of tyranny that is more formidable that many types of political oppression. Tyranny of the majority may apparently seem benevolent and lack the power to oppress or enslave the body, but it may potentially exercise oppression on the soul and conscience, penetrating into the details of life and incarcerating the spirit. In short, Mills defends liberal democracy, committed to the limitation and dissemination of power, rather than radical democracy, which rejects the necessity to limit the power exercised on behalf of the people.

According to Tocqueville, democracies tend to concentrate all their social force and authority in the legislative body. This gives way to the "despotism of the majority". This concentration of power, as well as hindering the successful running of affairs, introduces the "despotism of the majority".[12]

The necessary guarantee against this despotism of the majority is freedom of political association. Therefore, Tocqueville believes this right to be as inalienable as that of individual liberty. The rule of the majority is not accidental to democracy but rather a part of its natural tendencies. In democracy, nothing prevails over the majority and, therefore, its power becomes compelling. Moral rule of the majority is based on the theory of equality applied to the intelligence.[13]

---

[10]Mill (2001), 6. Among other works on the author, the following is recommended: Ten (1980); Scarre (2007).

[11]Mill (2001), 8.

[12]Tocqueville (2012), 249.

[13]"The moral dominion of the majority is based in part on the idea that there is more enlightenment and wisdom in many men combined than in one man alone, more in the number than in the choice

However, the main objective of Mill's essay is not to only to limit the political power of the majority but also, on the whole, to restrict the intervention of society in the lives of its members. His aim, therefore, is broader and more general than the mere limitation of the power of the State. Thus, the book's main thesis is the defence of a criterion or principle aimed at limiting the legitimate intervention of society in the lives of its members.

> The object of this Essay is to assert one very simple principle, as entitled to govern absolutely the dealings of society with the individual in the way of compulsion and control, whether the means used be physical force in the form of legal penalties, or the moral coercion of public opinion. That principle is, that the sole end for which mankind are warranted, individually or collectively, in interfering with the liberty of action of any of their number, is self-protection. That the only purpose for which power can be rightfully exercised over any member of a civilised community, against his will, is to prevent harm to others. His own good, either physical or moral, is not a sufficient warrant. He cannot rightfully be compelled to do or forbear because it will be better for him to do so, because it will make him happier, because, in the opinions of others, to do so would be wise, or even right. These are good reasons for remonstrating with him, or reasoning with him, or persuading him, or entreating him, but not for compelling him, or visiting him with any evil in case he do otherwise. To justify that, the conduct from which it is desired to deter him must be calculated to produce evil to someone else. The only part of the conduct of any one, for which he is amenable to society, is that which concerns others. In the part which merely concerns himself, his independence is, of right, absolute. Over himself, over his own body and mind, the individual is sovereign.[14]

This criterion establishes the suppression of paternalism and the basis for the harm principle: individual conduct can only be constrained by society when it affects others, harms or damages them in some way. Although this criterion is, in principle, clear, its application to regulate people's behaviour entails certain problems. It isn't easy to discern between what affects others and what doesn't and, following Mill's criterion, it isn't difficult to justify many interferences which may otherwise be unacceptable. The objective of the author is, however, very restrictive. What affects someone must be understood as whatever has an immediate and close effect, rather than a remote and indirect one. The burden of proof rests with society, who must justify the necessity for intervention, and not with the individual.[15] It is, therefore, not a matter of following a moral criterion to distinguish between right and wrong, nor of pretending—falsely—that everything that doesn't affect others is morally acceptable. Mill doesn't deny the existence of man's duties to oneself; he simply rejects the idea that they are a social obligation, unless the circumstances involved affect or harm others, in which case they become duties to others. The criterion is, therefore, legal and social, but not moral, despite an unfortunate statement which seemingly fails to distinguish between law and morality:

---

of legislators. It is the theory of equality applied to minds. This doctrine attacks the pride of man in its last refuge. Consequently the minority admits it with difficulty and gets used to it only with time. Like all powers, and perhaps more than any other, the power of the majority thus needs to last in order to seem legitimate. When it is beginning to be established, it makes itself obeyed by force; only after living under its laws for a long time do you begin to respect it" Tocqueville (2012), 404 ff.

[14] Mill (2001), 13.

[15] Magid (1987), 751.

> Whenever, in short, there is a definite damage, or a definite risk of damage, either to an individual or to the public, the case is taken out of the province of liberty, and placed in that of morality or law.[16]

For Mill, social and political liberty comprise freedom of thought and conscience, the freedom to determine one's aims in life and establish goals following one's own personal criteria, and freedom of association. A society is not free, whatever its form of government—therefore including democracy—unless these three freedoms are fully and entirely guaranteed. And guaranteeing these freedoms is not only beneficial for individuals, but also for mankind, which will always gain from allowing people to live however they want. Nevertheless, the dominant tendency in democratic societies is to strengthen society and diminish the power of the individual.

Freedom of press is vital to guarantee other freedoms and to eliminate the possibility of a tyrannical government. No government can legitimately supervise opinions. Not even when supported by the majority. Oppression is just as harmful, if not more, when it's exercised in agreement with public opinion than when public opinion is against it. Freedom of press is not only a guarantee against the abuse of power, it's also one of the fundamental pillars of civilisation.

3 Artistocratic Liberalism and the Benefits of Freedom

Another noteworthy feature of the essay is the acceptance of an aristocratic concept (in the spiritual sense, i.e. intellectual and moral) of society. In this regard, Mill may be considered a representative of aristocratic liberalism. Man, as a being, is capable of rectifying and can rise from error to truth. It is true that, in each sphere of reality, only a few, a minority, are right. Most are, in fact, wrong. The opinion of the majority is not a criterion for scientific, moral, religious or aesthetic truth. This constitutes a further and powerful reason in defence of individual liberty and against the oppression of the majority.

> It is not too much to require that what the wisest of mankind, those who are best entitled to trust their own judgment, find necessary to warrant their relying on it, should be submitted to by that miscellaneous collection of a few wise and many foolish individuals, called the public.[17]

Even those who cannot appreciate their own freedom can benefit from the fact that others use it without obstacle. Only in an atmosphere of freedom can ideas and opinions arise that stand apart from the vulgar criteria of the majority, enabling humanity to abandon error and improve itself intellectually and morally. These few people are the salt of the earth, as they introduce new things that didn't exist before and give life to those already existent. Men of genius are necessarily a small minority. Genius is a plant which only breeds in the fertile grounds of freedom. These men

[16] Mill (2001), 75.
[17] Mill (2001), 22.

are necessarily the least equipped to adapt to the criteria and principles established by the crowds of common people. Only by enabling men to live their own way and stand apart from the criteria of the majority is it possible to favour the appearance and development of great men. Their originality feeds off their disconformity towards the average man. All good things are the result of originality, and only freedom can prevent the obstruction of its sources. It is necessary to fight against the general tendency that turns mediocrity into the supreme power among men. Public opinion governs the world and merely amounts to collective mediocrity. And now, at this point in time (yours as well as ours) it takes shape based on the criteria of men at the same level. The government of the mediocre cannot but be a mediocre government. All noble things arise from individuals, but only from a few of them. Therefore, it is urgent to enable these exemplary men to act differently from the masses, even if their behaviour is eccentric.

> That so few now dare to be eccentric marks the chief danger of the time.[18]

Only liberty can be the breeding ground of this charitable eccentricity. In order to promote this, the long arm of the law must be prevented from acting against the best men and noble doctrines. In this context, Mill mentions Socrates, Christ and Marcus Aurelius. Freedom of thought is not only necessary to produce such great men, but also to enable average men to reach their full potential. Great thinkers may exist in an atmosphere of mental enslavement, but what cannot exist under this condition is an intellectually active people.

In sum, Mill puts forward four motives in favour of the benefits that freedom of thought and expression provide to the intellectual wellbeing of humanity: an opinion, reduced to silence, can be true; even when it's an error, it can contain a grain of truth; even when the commonly admitted opinion is true, without criticism it will be admitted by many as a prejudice and lacking in real basis; and, finally, an opinion that is thus admitted is at risk of weakening and losing its vital effect on character and conduct. As can be observed, Mill's argument is based on an intellectual stance that relies on the value and supremacy of ideas.

None of this implies that freedom of expression is absolute or unlimited; nor that it's impossible for speech to become an accessory to crime and must, therefore, be restricted and even punished. However, this only happens when freedom of expression incites criminal or harmful actions. What seems to be excluded from any kind of limitation is the issue of opinions, criticism or evaluations. Opinion is never considered a crime; speech sometimes is. But individual liberty can only be legitimately limited when it becomes harmful to others. Mill's objective is to promote individuality and the free development of personality as far as possible. And conformity implies the greatest danger, the loss in individuals of any idea and/or feeling that comes from themselves. Anything that destroys individuality is despotism. There cannot be a liberal government without a liberal society. And there is no liberal society without the existence of free men.

---

[18] Mill (2001), 62 ff.

In Chap. 5, Mill establishes the two maxims that provide the entire basis for the essay's doctrine. The first is that "the individual is not accountable to society for his actions, in so far as these concern the interests of no person but himself".[19] The second is that "for such actions as are prejudicial to the interests of others, the individual is accountable, and may be subjected either to social or to legal punishment, if society is of opinion that the one or the other is requisite for its protection".[20] But there are other considerations in favour of liberalism and regarding the need to limit the power of the State and the intervention of government. First of all, it must abstain from interfering whenever it's possible that individuals' own actions may provide better results; secondly, it is not a means for citizens' education, to strengthen their mental faculties, judgement and initiative; and finally, an unnecessary increase of power represents a serious problem. Both individuals and society profit from this reasonable limitation. Furthermore, an increase of State power constitutes, in itself, a serious wrong. To avoid this, it must be curbed, and the effective dispersal of power must be promoted as far as possible.[21] Government must not be given the power to manage education either. It should be accountable for the existence of a good education for all children, but this should never be left in its hands to provide or direct. Failing to do so would mean opening the doors to despotism over the spirits and, therefore, to all the evils this essay warns us against, ending with the following words:

> The worth of a State, in the long run, is the worth of the individuals composing it; and a State which postpones the interests of their mental expansion and elevation to a little more of administrative skill, or of that semblance of it which practice gives, in the details of business; a State which dwarfs its men, in order that they may be more docile instruments in its hands even for beneficial purposes—will find that with small men no great thing can really be accomplished; and that the perfection of machinery to which it has sacrificed everything will in the end avail it nothing, for want of the vital power which, in order that the machine might work more smoothly, it has preferred to banish.[22]

The ruling regime of public opinion, unless individuality is safeguarded, can drive Europe to become another China. Its superiority, the reason for its excellence, which has enabled it to develop the most progressive sector of humanity, has resided in its "remarkable diversity of character and culture", i.e. in freedom and the variety of situations. The massification and homogenisation of situations (as Tocqueville mentioned) represent therefore the main threat against European civilisation. Perhaps this is the primary achievement of this essay which, on the other hand, is not lacking in defects. Some of its arguments are simplistic and include certain incoherencies. The criteria to restrict the power of society—and of the State—over individuals is very problematic, since in practical terms it's impossible to separate the part of man's behaviour that refers to others from the part that refers to oneself. The essay is more valuable as an expression of a tendency than as a strict criterion to limit

[19] Mill (2001), 86.
[20] Mill (2001), 86.
[21] Mill (2001), 104.
[22] Mill (2001), 106.

the intervention of society. However, it must be admitted that Mill "has as much right as any other moralist to vagueness in a subject that does not allow ulterior precision".[23] On the other hand, it can be asserted that freedom of expression—the right to freedom of opinion and expression, evaluation and criticism—is, for Mill, absolute. The reasons he provides to justify his defence of liberty are also problematic. He maintains that liberty favours the appearance of men of high moral character. He believes that "the intellectual changes are the most conspicuous agents in history" and that mankind's speculative faculties are the main and determining factor for social progress.[24] This shows a remarkable, and perhaps unjustified, optimism, which is confirmed and increases when considering that his position presupposes that when there is freedom to defend all opinions and ideas regarding life's goals, the best will prevail over the worst. It should not be forgotten that if the most excellent opinions always belong to a minority, the most despicable, in principle, must do also. Mill seems to presuppose that when total freedom is allowed, both for goodness, truth and beauty, and for evil, falsity and ugliness, the former will prevail over the latter. Otherwise, it could not be argued that liberty favours the intellectual and moral development of society. In sum, Mill's theses manifest the inherent flaws of progressive ideologies. The current degradation of culture, in the hands of the mass media, especially the audio-visual sector, and of the new technologies, adds even more difficulties to Mill's optimism. How his defence of liberalism can be compatible with his justification of socialism is also not clear.[25] But perhaps his greatest weakness lies in the basis of his position. Mill not only talks as if the progress of the human being were an absolute and essential goal, he also understands that this progress depends on intellectual development, which can only be achieved by the most remarkable of individuals.[26] Mill believes that intellectual changes are the most conspicuous agents in history.

> This optimism regarding the role of ideas and, therefore, of intellectuals in history, which at the same time presupposes and ethical optimism regarding the efficiency of ideas, ideals, in human behaviour, is also accompanied by a further optimism regarding the good results, never absolute or definitive, but always progressive, attributed to the intellectual activity in search for truth.[27]

Hence, the greatest value of the essay resides in its warning, following the tenets of Tocqueville, against the dangers involved for the survival of liberty and civilisation in the imposition of public opinion, and against the wrongs caused by the diminishment of mankind and uniformity; in sum, the dangers of the "tyranny—not exclusively political or parliamentary, but rather, on the whole, social—of the majority". In no case does this strange position entail the government of an intellectual elite. Mill always defended democracy—liberal democracy, not the radical kind which identifies

[23]Plamenatz (1966), 130.

[24]Mill (1974) *A System of Logic Ratiocinative and Inductive*, VI, XI, 3 y VI, X, 7, VIII, 935 and 927.

[25]Regarding the relationship between Mill and socialism, see Negro Pavón (1975).

[26]Rodríguez Paniagua (1993), 412.

[27]Rodríguez Paniagua (1993), 413.

moral truth with the criteria of the majority, or which rejects the need to limit the power of the majority, since the people could never damage themselves or legislate against their own interests, thereby opening the way to State interventionism or even to democratic totalitarianism—and the value of what constitutes one of mankind's most precious goods: the freedom to choose. If only for its energetic and vibrant defence of freedom of expression, despite its defects and incoherencies, Mill's *On Liberty* rightfully belongs to the collection of books which have contributed to forge Europe's spirit.

His position regarding freedom of expression and certain legal problems involved is particularly relevant. Of course, this includes freedom of religion and worship. In this regard, his characterisation of Christian morality seems highly partial and, ultimately, mistaken.[28]

The problem of intellectual authority and the potential imposition of a "political religion" is also worth discussing.

Tzvetan Todorov states in *In the Defence of the Enlightenment* that, during the French Revolution, Condorcet warned of a new danger for individual autonomy. The danger consisted in the fact that those who held temporal power would aspire to establish a new cult whose main objective would be the State itself, its institutions or representatives.

> The very same people who strove to free men from the shackles of religion risked becoming the servants of a no less oppressive cult. When ruling powers dictate to people what they should think, then we are dealing with 'a kind of political religion' that is hardly preferable to the one it replaced. To Condorcet 'Robespierre is a priest and never will be anything else'. This is the first known occurrence of the expression 'political religion', a concept very different to Rousseau's 'civil religion', which simply involved recognizing the principles of communal life.[29]

There is a new "plenitude of power", and temporal power also imposes the beliefs that it finds suitable.[30]

The world described by Condorcet anticipates totalitarism. He tries to defend the "freedom of Moderns", in Constant's sense, from the new "political religion".[31]

---

[28]Mill (2001), 46–49. He states, among other things, that it's a reaction against paganism, that its ideal is more negative than positive, that it feels horror towards sensuality, that it's a passive doctrine and that its only expressly recognised value is obedience.

[29]Todorov (2009), 65.

[30]"By its control of education, it transformed instruction—theoretically be liberating—into an instrument of greater subjugation; it presented its political decisions as immutable dogmas or, what's worse, as scientific truths. By its control over the news, it could make sure that 'the citizens never learn anything that is not appropriate to confirm them in opinions their masters have wished to inspire in them' (Condorcet). Manipulated in this way, people think they're acting freely, when they are actually executing the programme conceived by the ruling power" (*Ibidem*, p. 65 s.).

[31]"Condorcet unfolds before the reader's eyes a doomsday scenario. Imagine, he says, that 'a troop of audacious hypocrites' manages to get control of the central power in a country and to create relays throughout its regions. It could lay its hands on the main sources of information and consequently be believed by 'a people whose ignorance makes them pray to a phantom of fear'. Alternating seduction and threat, it 'will exercise under the mask of liberty' a tyranny that is in no way less efficient that those that preceded it".

Jacobin terror was already a political religion, but Cordorcet's worst fears were to be fulfilled with communism, Nazism and fascism:

> this new type of fusion between temporal power and spiritual power, precisely because of its totalitarian grip, eliminates more radically than ever before the individual freedom that secularism ensures.[32]

In 1742 Hume wrote in his essay "The Sceptic", included in his *Essays, Moral and Political*, that:

> Though all humans should for ever conclude, that the sun moves, and the earth remains at rest, the sun stirs not an inch from his place for all these reasonings; and such conclusions are eternally false and erroneous.[33]

Truth does not depend on universal suffrage.

Condorcet, in his *Mémoires*, defended religious tolerance and, more specifically, the right of Protestant teachers to teach in the same conditions as their Catholic counterparts. The religious beliefs of the teacher are irrelevant, since the subject taught doesn't depend on faith, but rather on science. "It is as respectable to try to entrust an ecclesiastical dignity to men of irreproachable orthodoxy as it would be ridiculous to worry about the orthodoxy of a physics or anatomy professor".

But then a boundary clearly separates two types of subjects in teaching. On one hand, religions, opinions and values; on the other, objects of knowledge, whose ultimate aim is not goodness, but rather the truth.

"On the whole, all power, whatever its nature, whatever hands it's in, however it has been granted, is by nature an enemy of the Enlightenment". "Truth is as much an enemy of power as those who execute it" (Condorcet).

Good government worries more about the wellbeing of citizens than about its own success.

> Good government is not opposed to the increase and propagation of knowledge. But its role ends there. In no case must it insist on contributing to the progression of truth, since truth is not a matter of will. Public power must not show its options and try to pass them off as truths.
>
> Its duty is to arm the full force of truth against error, which is always a public evil. But it does not have the right to decide where truth or error is to be found (Condorcet).

"Such fullness of power would even be worse that earlier forms, since the areas covered by the new political religion is conflated with man's entire worldly existence. Traditional religion sought to control the individual's conscience, either by exercising temporal power directly, or by delegating the task of constraint to the latter. Political religion, on the other hand, could directly oversee and govern everything. As a result, the freedom that Condorcet advocated was not only freedom of conscience; as Benjamin Constant, an attentive reader of Cordorcet's *Mémoires*, noted fifteen years later, it was all of the freedom of the Moderns. Indeed, the Ancients did not conceive of freedom in these terms; they did not imagine that the individual needed to be defended against his own representative. The territory of the new religion exceeds by far that of the old and consequently the territory that the citizen has to defend is that much greater" Todorov (2009), 66 ff.

[32]Todorov (2009), 67.

[33]Hume (1742), 218.

> It is not up to the people to pronounce what is true or false; it is not up to parliament to deliberate over the meaning of historical facts; it is not up to the government to decide what is taught in school. The collective will or the sovereignty of the people comes up against a limit here, which is that of truth, over which it has no influence. At the same time, this independence of truth protects individual autonomy, since individuals can claim vis-à-vis the ruling power that they truth on their side. Truth is above laws. Reciprocally, a country's laws do not follow from an establish truth: they are the expression of public will, which is always subject to variation. The search for truth is not a matter of public deliberation, and vice versa.[34]

According to Condorcet,

> To know the truth in order to make the social order conform to it, that is the sole source of public happiness.[35]

Condorcet's idea of political religion has been developed by Eric Voegelin.[36] He considers totalitarianisms to be political pseudoreligions and to be linked to the sacralisation of closed communities.

The world is going through a serious crisis, a breakdown process arising from secularization of the spirit. Only a religious renewal can provide a cure. National Socialism is to a back to the darkest Middle Ages, but a satanic power endowed with a great force of attraction.[37]

---

[34]Todorov (2009), 77 ff.

[35]Condorcet (1849), 203.

[36]Voegelin (1984).

[37]At the end of his prologue to *The Political Religions*, he writes: "When considering National Socialism from a politic standpoint, one should be able to proceed on the assumption that there is evil in the world and, moreover, that evil is not a deficient mode of being, a negative element, but also a real substance and force that is effective in the world. Resistance against a satanical substance that is not only morally but also religiously evil can only be derived from an equally strong, religiously good force. One cannot fight a satanical force with morality and humanity alone".

"Nonetheless, this difficulty cannot be remedied by resolve alone. There is no distinguished philosopher or thinker in the Western world today who, firstly, is not aware—and has not also expressed this sentiment—that the world is experiencing a serious crisis, is undergoing a process of withering, which has its origins in the secularization of the soul and in the ensuing severance of a consequently purely secular soul from its roots in religiousness, and, secondly, does not know that recovery can only be achieved through religious renewal, be it within the framework of the historical churches, be it outside this framework. Such renewal, to a large extent, can only be initiated by great religious personalities, but everyone can be ready and willing to do his share in paving the way for resistance to rise up against the evil".

"It is precisely in this respect that the politicizing intellectuals fail completely. It is dreadful to hear time and time again that National Socialism is a return to barbarians, to the Dark Ages, to times before any new progress towards humanitarianism was made, without these speakers even suspecting that precisely the secularization of life that accompanied the doctrine of humanitarianism is the soil in which such an anti-Christian religious movement as National Socialism was ever able to prosper. For these secularized minds the question is a taboo, and they are suspicious of bringing it up seriously and radically—perhaps they would also consider this barbarism and a relapse into the Dark Ages".

"Thus, I believe that discussing the basic religious issues of our times as well as describing the phenomenon of evil that is to be combated is more important that participating in that ethical defensive struggle. If my representation gives rise to the impression that it is too 'objective' and

All government interference in education entails the risk of establishing a political religion. Mills delimits this function of government and writes on the subject as follows:

Mill delimits this function by considering that the task of the Government is to ensure the exercise of the right to education for all citizens, and not to determine the material content of education. An universal education imposed by the State will mean the destruction of freedom.[38]

'advertises' for National Socialism, then that to me seems a sign that my representation is good—for the Luciferian aspects are not simply morally negative or atrocious but are a force and a very attractive force at that. Moreover, my representation would not be good if it gave rise to the impression that we are concerned with merely a moral inferior, dumb, barbaric, contemptible matter. That I don't consider the force of evil to be a force of good will be clearly evident to all readers of this treatise who are open to religious questions" Voegelin (1984), 22 ff.

[38]"Consider, for example, the case of education. Is it not almost a self-evident axiom, that the State should require and compel the education, up to a certain standard, of every human being who is born its citizen? Yet who is there that is not afraid to recognise and assert this truth? Hardly anyone indeed will deny that it is one of the most sacred duties of the parents (or, as law and usage now stand, the father), after summoning a human being into the world, to give to that being an education fitting him to perform his part well in life towards others and towards himself. But while this is unanimously declared to be the father's duty, scarcely anybody, in this country, will bear to hear of obliging him to perform it. Instead of his being required to make any exertion or sacrifice for securing education to his child, it is left to his choice to accept it or not when it is provided gratis! It still remains unrecognised, that to bring a child into existence without a fair prospect of being able, not only to provide food for its body, but instruction and training for its mind, is a moral crime, both against the unfortunate offspring and against society; and that if the parent does not fulfil this obligation, the State ought to see it fulfilled, at the charge, as far as possible, of the parent. Were the duty of enforcing universal education once admitted there would be an end to the difficulties about what the State should teach, and how it should teach, which now convert the subject into a mere battlefield for sects and parties, causing the time and labour which should have been spent in educating to be wasted in quarrelling about education. If the government would make up its mind to require for every child a good education, it might save itself the trouble of providing one. It might leave to parents to obtain the education where and how they pleased, and content itself with helping to pay the school fees of the poorer classes of children, and defraying the entire school expenses of those who have no one else to pay for them. The objections which are urged with reason against State education do not apply to the enforcement of education by the State, but to the State's taking upon itself to direct that education; which is a totally different thing. That the whole or any large part of the education of the people should be in State hands, I go as far as anyone in deprecating. All that has been said of the importance of individuality of character, and diversity in opinions and modes of conduct, involves, as of the same unspeakable importance, diversity of education. A general State education is a mere contrivance for moulding people to be exactly like one another: and as the mould in which it casts them is that which pleases the predominant power in the government,

> All attempts by the State to bias the conclusions of its citizens on disputed subjects are evil.[39]

Hobbes had written against this thesis:

> The monarch or the sovereign assembly only have immediate authority from God to teach and instruct the people; and no man but the sovereign receives his power Dei gratia simply; that is to say, from the favour of none but God.[40]

Only when the power to instruct is concentrated in the hands of the ruler does he hold absolute power. Granting the ruler the power to decide the contents of education opens the doors to absolutism and totalitarianism.

The key lies in determining the holder of spiritual power. With the expression "spiritual power" I refer to the situation of those who exercise influence on other, with their consent and adherence, not through force, especially regarding the goals and ends in life. Those who influence the formation of others' consciences, who supply the models or patterns for their lives, have spiritual power. Spiritual power is influence, exemplariness, intellectual and moral direction. In this regard, there is no comparable power.

4 Spiritual Power

At the end of his essay *Mission of the University,* Ortega y Gasset addresses the problem of spiritual power. After presenting the missions entrusted to the university and affirming that the institution is different but inseparable from science, he argues that it should also be something else, open to current affairs, in the middle of them, submerged in them. Public life needs the intervention of the university as such. It is worth quoting extensively:

> On this point there is much I should like to say. But to be brief, let me simply allude to the fact that in the simple life of society today there is no other 'spiritual power' than the press. The corporate life, which is the real life of history, needs always to be directed, whether we

whether this be a monarch, a priesthood, an aristocracy, or the majority of the existing generation; in proportion as it is efficient and successful, it establishes a despotism over the mind, leading by natural tendency to one over the body. An education established and controlled by the State should only exist, if it exists at all, as one among many competing experiments, carried on for the purpose of example and stimulus, to keep the others up to a certain standard of excellence".

"Unless, indeed, when society in general is in so backward a State that it could not or would not provide for itself any proper institutions of education unless the government undertook the task: then, indeed, the government may, as the less of two great evils, take upon itself the business of schools and universities, as it may that of joint stock companies, when private enterprise, in a shape fitted for undertaking great works of industry, does not exist in the country. But in general, if the country contains a sufficient number of persons qualified to provide education under government auspices, the same persons would be able and willing to give an equally good education on the voluntary principle, under the assurance of remuneration afforded by a law rendering education compulsory, combined with State aid to those unable to defray the expense" Mill (2001), 96–98.

[39] Mill (2001), 99.

[40] Hobbes (1839), 228.

like the idea or not. Of itself it has no form, no eyes to see with, no guiding sense of direction. No then, in our times, the ancient 'spiritual powers' have disappeared: the Church because it has abandoned the present (whereas the life of the people is ever a decidedly current affair); and the State because with the triumph of democracy it has given up governing the life of the people, to be governed instead by their opinion. In this situation the public life has devolved into the hands of the only spiritual force which necessarily concerns itself with current affairs—the press.

I should not wish to throw too many stones at the journalists; among other motives, there is the consideration that I may be nothing more than a journalist myself. But it is futile to shut our eyes to the obvious fact that spiritual realities differ in worth. They compose a hierarchy of values, and in this hierarchy, journalism occupies an inferior place. It has come to pass that today no pressure and no authority make themselves felt in the public consciousness, save on the very low spiritual plane adopted by the emanations of the press. So low a plane it is that not infrequently the press falls quite short of being a spiritual power, and is rather the opposite force. By the default of other powers, the responsibility for nourishing and guiding the public soul has fallen to the journalist, who not only is one of the least cultured types in contemporary society but who moreover—for reason I may hope to prove to have been merely transitory—admits into his profession the frustrated pseudo-intellectuals, full of resentment and hatred towards what is truly spiritual. Furthermore, the journalist's profession leads him to understand by the reality of the times that which creates a passing sensation, regardless of what it is, without any heed for perspective or architecture. Real life is, certainly, purely of the present; but the journalist deforms this truism when he reduces the present to the momentary, and the momentary to the sensational. The result is that, in the public consciousness today, the image of the world appears exactly upside down. The space devoted to people and affairs in the press is inversely proportional to their substantial and enduring importance; what stands out in the columns of the newspapers and magazines is what will be a 'success' and bring notoriety. Were the periodicals to be freed from motives that are often unspeakable; were the dailies kept chastely aloof from any influence of money on their opinions—the press would still, of itself, forsake its proper mission and paint the world inside out. Not a little of the grotesque and general upset of our age—for Europe has been going along for some time now with her head on the ground and her plebeian feet waving in the air— is the result of this unchallenged sway of the press as sole 'spiritual power'.

It is a question of life and death for Europe to put this ridiculous situation to rights. *And if this is to be done, the university must interfere, as the university*, in current affairs, treating the great themes of the day, from its own point of view—cultural, professional or scientific. Thus, it will not be an institution exclusively for students, a retreat *ad usum Delphini*. In the thick of life's urgencies and its passions, the university must assert itself as a major 'spiritual power', higher than the press, standing for serenity in the midst of frenzy, for seriousness and the grasp of intellect in the face of unashamed stupidity. Then, the university once again, will come to be what it was in its grand hour: an uplifting principle in the history of the western world.[41]

The previous paragraphs define what Ortega understands as spiritual power, who is currently in charge of it and the evils derived from its exercise. Also evident is his open invitation extended to the university to fulfil this function, while remaining faithful to its essence.

I believe there are currently huge difficulties that stand against the university becoming a spiritual power. These difficulties are similar to those endured by the State, since the State has also become dependent on public opinion, in a constant search for its support rather than its criticism and rectification.

---

[41] Ortega y Gasset (2005), 567 ff.

In any case, it is clear that one mustn't confuse spiritual power with political control or power.

5 Consequences of the Application of Mill's Criterion

We will now try to apply Mill's ideas to the analysis of certain current legal problems.

Mill provides good grounds to reject the legitimacy of crimes of opinion. The problem here, like in other cases which will be dealt with later, resides in determining the limits of the concept of harm. The concept of what affects only the agent and what affects also others is clearly imprecise and unsatisfactory, since unless we are talking about an isolated and lonely being, it's very difficult for the conduct of one person not to affect others. They key lies in the concept of harm understood in its strict and direct sense. The annoyance, discomfort, dissatisfaction or indignation provoked by the behaviour or opinion of others is not sufficient reason for legitimate forbidding. It's not enough if their conduct offends or irritates; it's necessary for it to cause objective or direct damage. Otherwise, there would be no defence of freedom of expression, as all public statements affect others and, therefore, can annoy or anger them.

Isaiah Berlin suggests that this assumption of Mill's depends on the acceptance of the thesis that human knowledge is incomplete and fallible.[42] On the other hand, I don't believe that Mill accepts ethical relativism or that it's the only feasible argument in favour of freedom of expression. It is possible to defend the freedom of expression of what the majority, or the minority, or men of wisdom, or the government consider to be wrong. This is the core of tolerance. We don't defend liberty because truth doesn't exist, but because no one has the right to impose it by force.

Scientific theories or theses can be true or false, but they are never criminal. In this respect, I don't think that the expression of any statement should be prohibited, however much it infringes upon historical evidence or may offend a few or many people, or the majority. Thus, for example, denial of Nazi or communist crimes, racism, the defence of totalitarianisms, the view of homosexuality as a disorder,

[42]"His argument is plausible only on the assumption which, whether he knew it or not, Mill all too obviously made, that human knowledge was in principle never complete, and always fallible; that there was no single, universally visible, truth; that each man, each nation, each civilization might take its own road towards its own goal, not necessarily harmonious with those of others; that men are altered, and the truths in which they believe are altered, by new experiences and their own actions—what he calls 'experiments in living'; that consequently the conviction, common to Aristotelians and a good many Christian scholastics and atheistical materialists alike, that there exists a basic knowable human nature, one and the same, at all times, in all places, in all men—a static, unchanging substance underneath the altering appearances, with permanent needs, dictated by a single, discoverable goal, or pattern of goals, the same for all mankind—is mistaken; and so, too, is the notion that is bound up with it, of a single true doctrine carrying salvation to all men everywhere, contained in natural law, or the revelation of a sacred book, or the insight of a man of genius, or the natural wisdom of ordinary men, or the calculations made by an elite of utilitarian scientists set up to govern mankind" Berlin (1991), 144 ff.

the defence of the Popular Front republican government or Francoism, asserting the superiority of women over men or vice versa, etcetera, must be allowed, however offensive or annoying they may be to others. Neither experts nor the government, however democratic it may be, can silence any opinion.

This, however, doesn't mean that speech is not potentially criminal, although never when used to express judgements, opinions, criticism or evaluations. The limit can be found in the dividing line between opinion and insult, slander or the incitement to commit an offence. Mill himself established the distinction:

> No one pretends that actions should be as free as opinions. On the contrary, even opinions lose their immunity, when the circumstances in which they are expressed are such as to constitute their expression a positive instigation to some mischievous act.[43]

A professor of economics may, legitimately, express his thesis that the famine suffered by a country is due to the artificial increase in the prices of wheat, caused by businessmen. But that same thesis, on the other hand, expressed by an impassioned speaker before a hungry audience and in front of the house of a wheat trader, urging the people to obtain revenge, is incitement and must be banned.

> The liberty of the individual must be thus far limited; he must not make himself a nuisance to other people.[44]

The regulation of hate crimes under the current Spanish Criminal Code doesn't follow Mill's approach and, in my opinion, doesn't follow legal reasoning. In Spain, opinion becomes a crime when someone can prove that it represents an incitement to hatred or discrimination. Chapter IV of title XII of book II is titled: "On the Felonies Committed when Exercising the Fundamental Rights and Public Liberties Guaranteed by the Constitution". Perhaps it would have been better to refer to "abuse", as it doesn't seem reasonable that exercising fundamental rights and public liberties could ever be considered a felony. Article 510.1 establishes prison sentences from one to four years and a fine from six to twelve months for:

> a) Those who publicly promote, provoke or incite, whether direct or indirectly, hate, hostility, discrimination or violence against a group, a part of it or against any specific individual because of his/her membership to it, due to racist, anti-Semitic reasons or any other related to ideology, religion or belief, family situation, belonging to an ethnic group or race, nation origin, sex, sexual orientation or identity, gender, illness or disability.
>
> b) Those who produce, elaborate, own with the objective of distributing, provide access to third parties, distribute, disseminate or sell writings or any other type of material or supports that due to their contents are suitable to promote, provoke or incite, whether direct or indirectly, hate, hostility, discrimination or violence against a group, a part of it or against any specific individual because of his/her membership to it, due to racist, anti-Semitic reasons or any other related to ideology, religion or belief, family situation, belonging to an ethnic group or race, nation origin, sex, sexual orientation or identity, gender, illness or disability.

Perhaps the most problematic or misleading aspect of the article is the inclusion of the adverb "indirectly", as it opens the door to the violation of freedom of expression.

---

[43]Berlin (1991), 52.

[44]Berlin (1991), 52.

The article doesn't only punish the direct incitement to hate, hostility, discrimination or violence, but also any opinion which, indirectly, may provoke these. It is well known that criminal legislation cannot include concepts that may be interpreted extensively or arbitrarily. How can one determine, guaranteeing and observing the principle of legality, what may or may not incite hate?

The article implies, on the other hand, the destruction of books, materials or articles that contain expressions classified as criminal offences, i.e. book burning. Let's take for example the affirmation that polygamy is immoral, is it or is it not an incitement to hatred of Mormons? The opinion that eating pork is immoral, is it or is it not an incitement to hatred of ham eaters? Arguing that homosexuality is a disorder that needs medical or psychological treatment, does it incite hatred of homosexuals? The defence of Marxist theses, does it incite hatred of capitalists? Are we not perhaps the witnesses of a witch-hunt promoted by the apostles of political correction? Paraphrasing Aristotle, it could be said that one should befriend public opinion, or even propaganda, but even so more the truth.

I doubt that Mill's work provides grounds for the existence of a *right to do wrong*, a right to what is wrong or crooked, i.e. what is immoral.[45] Perhaps the first author to defend the existence of this right to do what is wrong or immoral has been Jeremy Waldron.[46] For him, the morality of rights has the fundamental objective of protecting personal autonomy. The right to do wrong or moral wrong would be a true *claim right*, and not only the possibility to choose between various courses of action. He doesn't consider it to be a mere liberty, but a true right. This is perhaps excessive. One thing is what is licit, the scope of my conduct where I cannot be forced or bothered by others, and another thing is possessing a genuine subjective right. Kant maintains that having a right is having the capacity to constrain or force others, and not merely a realm of liberty that must be permitted or tolerated. In this respect, it may be licit to do something society or its majority considers immoral, although there cannot be, strictly speaking, a right to do moral wrong. Immoral action may be legally recognised and allowed, but not accepted as a subjective right.

"But, in the legal world, there is a big difference between having a right to something and acting legally".

"Human aspirations don't automatically become rights; that is, man cannot demand in legal terms everything he hopes to achieve, even though he has power in his hands (backed by the State) to condition the conduct of others...".

> Without a just title there is no subjective right. This implies that the existence of the right demands reasons. Which is not absurd, since granting a right means putting in the hands of its holder a power that allows him/her to control the conduct of others, determine what they can and cannot do, and doing so with State backing.[47]

---

[45]Ollero (2005), 63–77.

[46]Waldron (1981), 21–39.

[47]Albert (2016), 209 ff.

Waldron's thesis has been defended by Ori J. Herstein.[48] The right to do something immoral seems to be based on the ethical neutrality of the State, a thesis which is not only incorrect but which, in my opinion, Mill doesn't support.

The defence of terrorism is another relevant issue. Is it a criminal offence or does it fall within the scope of freedom of expression? We don't know what Mill would have thought, since, in his day, terrorism didn't exist, but we can speculate. The limit, certainly not fully precise, is to be found between opinion and the incitement to crime or mockery of the victims. Defending political violence, however repugnant many people may find it, is legitimate. Marx, for example, did so. Incitement to commit a particular act of political violence, on the other hand, isn't. Offending or mocking the victims isn't either. It is evident that theory or opinion can influence the facts, and that ideas carry consequences, but it's possible to establish a distinction between the statement of a thesis and the incitement to commit a crime, between criticism and slander or injury.

A further case worthy of discussion is blasphemy. I don't think it falls within the scope of freedom of expression, but it's outside the scope of opinion or criticism and entering the realm of offence. Of course, criticising religion in general or specific religious conviction, such as atheism, must be permitted, but offending or insulting any belief mustn't. Yet again, the boundary is to be found in the criterion of harm.

In no case is Mill's defence of liberty without limits. He considers that the laws that in many countries of the continent ban marriage, unless the parties can prove that they have the means to support a family, are not censurable as violations of liberty.

> Such laws are interferences of the State to prohibit a mischievous act—an act injurious to others, which ought to be a subject of reprobation, and social stigma, even when it is not deemed expedient to add legal punishment. Yet the current ideas of liberty, which bend so easily to real infringements of the freedom of the individual in things which concern only himself, would repel the attempt to put any restraint upon his inclinations when the consequence of their indulgence is a life or lives of wretchedness and depravity to the offspring, with manifold evils to those sufficiently within reach to be in any way affected by their actions.[49]

Mill considers that it cannot be right or acceptable for a person to sell him/herself as a slave. So personal autonomy is again limited. By selling him/herself, he/she destroys the reason which is the justification of allowing him/her to dispose of him/herself. "The principle of freedom cannot require that he should be free not to be free. It is not freedom to be allowed to alienate his freedom".[50]

Other issues are addressed regarding the sale of poisons, drunkenness and idleness. In no case does he take the stance of a relativist or favour over tolerance. Although he condemns these activities, as well as polygamy, with severe criticism, he does seem

[48] Herstein (2012), 343–365.

[49] Mill (2001), 100.

[50] Mill (2001), 94.

to be tolerant.[51] He believes gambling and prostitution should be tolerated, although not procuring nor the existence of gambling houses.[52]

Although again it's a matter of speculation, it's unsure whether he would place euthanasia or surrogacy within the scope of individual liberty. In principle, they may go under the defence of personal autonomy. In the case of euthanasia, the dying person gives his/her consent or would have given his/her consent, and in the case of surrogacy, the parts would have freely come to an agreement. Whether these conducts are moral or not, they would fall within the scope of the protection of liberty. But, similar to other cases that Mill dealt with, concluding in the lawfulness of prohibition, it could be supposed that he would oppose them, arguing the potential surrender of liberty in the case of surrogacy, and the principle of harm in both cases. Martin Albert argues with reason against accepting surrogacy following the principle of autonomy of the will.[53]

Indeed, it is possible to disagree with Mill in something very relevant. He considers that this defence of liberty, despite its alleged individualism, is based on the fact that it represents a benefit for society. For my part, I would be willing to defend it, even if it were only for its contribution to the defence of freedom and the dignity of people. As we mentioned before, no government is entitled to legally impose any scientific, moral, religious, aesthetic or historical truth. The objective of politics and government is justice, not truth. Would a genuine parliamentary debate be possible if one of the positions were condemned as illegal? I refer, naturally, to a thesis, not to a breach of law or of the constitution.

The main argument in defence of liberty is not, in my opinion, that it's a necessary condition for the discovery of truth. Truth may arise in liberty, but so may error.

> It may well be that without full freedom of discussion the truth cannot emerge. But this may be only a necessary, not sufficient, condition of its discovery; the truth may, for all of our efforts, remain at the bottom of the well, and in the meantime the worse cause may win, and do enormous damage to mankind.[54]

It is possible to agree with Mill's thesis without sharing his utilitarian basis. Mill seems to confirm Ortega y Gasset's thesis that the 20th Century has been a collectivist century, since during this time even individual liberty has been defended due to the collective benefits it would yield.

Berlin thinks that "what Mill seems really to be asking for is diversity of opinion for its own sake".[55] I don't think that what Mill requires is pure diversity of opinions for its own sake. And, if this were the case, I wouldn't share his view. Diversity is not an end, but rather an almost necessary consequence. My main difference with Mill in this respect would be that he, despite his intentional distance from strict utilitarian

---

[51]Mill (2001), 84 ff.

[52]Mill (2001), 89 ff.

[53]"In the case of surrogacy, both the children and the surrogate mothers are submitted to many antilegal privations. The alleged "autonomy of the will" must, even for those who recognise it as such, take second place when human dignity is at stake" Albert (2017), 195.

[54]Berlin (1991), 144.

[55]Berlin (1991), 146.

consequentialism, is too dependent on the beneficial consequences of freedom of expression; while for me it is a fundamental principle which, additionally, can have beneficial consequences. Perhaps our agreement resides in his belief that what makes man human is his capacity to choose between right and wrong.

> At the centre of Mill's thoughts and feelings lies, not his utilitarianism, nor the concern about enlightenment, nor about dividing the public from the private domain—for [Mill] himself at times concedes that the State may invade the private domain in order to promote education, hygiene or social security or justice—but his passionate belief that men are made human by their capacity for choice—choice of evil or good equally. Fallibility, or the right to err as a corollary of the capacity for self-improvement; distrust of symmetry and finality as enemies of freedom—these are the principles which Mill never abandons.[56]

Mill, in accordance with these assumptions, defends liberty of the press as one of the fundamental pillars of civilisation and "as one of the securities against corrupt or tyrannical government".[57] He assumes that it's no longer necessary to argue in its favour. Government cannot impose opinions, even when people fully identify with it.

> But I deny the right of the people to exercise such coercion, either by themselves or by their government. The power itself is illegitimate. The best government has no more title to it than the worst. It is as noxious, or more noxious, when exerted in accordance with public opinion, than when in opposition to it. If all mankind minus one were of one opinion, and only one person were of the contrary opinion, mankind would be no more justified in silencing that one person, than he, if he had the power, would be justified in silencing mankind.[58]

However, Tocqueville adopts a cautious attitude towards it, lacking in love and enthusiasm. He appreciates it more for the evils it avoids than for the certainty of the benefits it produces.

> I admit that to freedom of the press I do not bring that complete and instantaneous love that is given to things supremely good by their nature. [I do not see freedom of the press in the same way that I consider *patriotism* or *virtue,* for example.][b] I love it much more from consideration of the evils it prevents than for the good things that it does.[59]

Freedom of press is consubstantial to democracy. Without freedom of press there is no political freedom or democracy. Censorship is not only dangerous but absurd in a country where the dogma of popular sovereignty rules. It's absurd to grant people the right to govern society and withdraw their right to hold opinions and express them freely. He states that "the press is the chiefest democratic instrument of freedom".

The press is as necessary for liberty as it is inconvenient for order.

> In America, as in France, the press is an extraordinary power, a strange mixture of good and evil; liberty cannot live without it and order can hardly be maintained with it.[60]

[56]Berlin (1991), 148.

[57]Mill (2001), 18.

[58]Mill (2001), 18.

[59]Tocqueville (2012), I, 289 ff.

[60]Tocqueville (2012), I, 293.

Possibly, despite its flaws, Mill has written the most brilliant defence of individual liberty and, in particular, of liberty of expression. There is no lack of difficulties to define the illegitimate existence of damage to others or to society as a whole, but it seems clear that, for Mill, the expression of opinions, judgements, evaluations or theories is absolutely free, unlike the expression of insults, slander, injuries or the incitement to commit crimes. It is also clear that a government cannot legitimately impose ideas, evaluations or opinions on its citizens.

Mill's beliefs are uncomfortable for those who expect to impose their personal convictions on others through political power or the control of education and freedom of expression, as well as for those who expect to raise personal autonomy as an absolute value that can never harm or damage others. Perhaps the most contemporary sense of Mill's political philosophy resides in its warning, following the tenets of Tocqueville, against the dangers involved for the survival of liberty and civilisation in the imposition of the social tyranny of the majority and, therefore, in his radical opposition to the criteria of the majority becoming the criterion for truth, goodness and beauty.

Perhaps, and despite the discrepancies expressed, we should conclude with Isaiah Berlin's words:

> The critics of Mill have, on the whole, exceeded the number of his defenders. Nevertheless, the inner citadel—the central thesis—has stood the test. It may need elaboration or qualification, but it is still the dearest, most candid, persuasive, and moving exposition of the point of view of those who desire an open and tolerant society.[61]

References

Albert M (2016) Privacidad y derecho a morir. In: Santos JA, Albert M, Hermida C (eds) Bioética y nuevos derechos. Comares, Granada, pp 209 ff

Albert M (2017) La explotación reproductiva de mujeres y el mito de la subrogación altruista: una mirada global al fenómeno de la gestación por sustitución, *Cuadernos de Bioética*, XXVIII, 2ª, pp 177–197

Berlin I (1991) John Stuart Mill and the ends of life. In: Mill JS (ed) On liberty, in focus. Edited by John Gray and G. W. Smith, York University, London, New York, p 144 ff

Condorcet N (1849) Vie de Turgot. In: Oeuvres, vol V

Herstein OJ (2012) Defending the right to do wrong. Law Philos 31:343–365

Hobbes T (1839) Leviathan. In: The English works of Thomas Hobbes. London, John Bohn

Hume D (1742) A dissertation on the passions: Of the dignity or meanness of human nature: the epicurean. The Stoic; the platonist; the sceptic, In: Essays moral and political, A. Kincaid, Edinburgh

Magid HM (1987), John Stuart Mill (1806–1873). In: Strauss L, Cropsey J (compilers) History of political philosophy. The University of Chicago Press, Chicago, Illinois, pp 784 ff

Mill JS (1924) Autobiography. Columbia University Press, New York

Mill JS (1974) Collected works of John Stuart Mill. Toronto University Press, Routledge and Kegan Paul, London

---

[61] Berlin (1991), 156.

Mill JS (2001) On liberty. Batoche Books, Kitchener, Ontario
Moore GE (1959) Principia ethica. Cambridge University Press, Cambridge
Negro Pavón D (1975) Liberalismo y socialismo. La encrucijada intelectual de Stuart Mill, Instituto de Estudios Políticos-CEC, Madrid
Ollero A (2005) El derecho a lo torcido. In: Puig V (ed) El fraude del buenismo. FAES, Madrid, pp 63–77
Ortega y Gasset J (2005) Misión de la Universidad, Obras Completas, IV, Taurus, Madrid, pp 567 ff
Plamenatz J (1966) The English utilitarians. B. Blackwell, Oxford
Rodríguez Paniagua JM (1993) Historia del pensamiento jurídico, Servicio de Publicaciones de la Facultad de Derecho, vol II, Universidad Complutense, Madrid
Ryan A (1974) J. S. Mill, Routledge and Kegan Paul, London-Boston
Scarre G (2007) Mill's "On liberty." Continuum, London
Ten CL (1980) Mill on liberty. Oxford University Press, Oxford
Tocqueville A de (2012) Democracy in America, Edited by Nolla E. Translated from the French by Schleifer JT, Liberty Fund, Indianapolis
Todorov T (2009) In defence of the enlightenment, translated from the French by Gila Walker. Atlantic Books, London
Voegelin E (1984) The political religions and science, politics and gnosticism: two essays. In: The Eric Voegelin reader. Politics, history, consciousness. University of Missouri, Press, Columbia
Waldron J (1981) A right to do wrong. Ethics 92(1):21–39

Criminal Law and Morality: Philosophical and Criminal Law Perspectives

The Fundamentals of Ethics

Francisco Carpintero Benítez

Abstract The foundations of morals is a complex topic. Today there is deso. The cause is rooted in theological discussions from the Late Middle Ages and onward. That discussion is centred in the opposition between Thomists and nominalists. Aquinas and his followers thought that practical norms were founded in teleological principles. Nominalists thought that norms were imperative: the key was the will of God, not the reason of the precept. At last, the winner was the nominalist way, and the idea of moral diffused in our culture was a system of imperatives. This legacy makes difficult to speak today about reason in ethics.

1 Introduction

Undertaking research into the relationship between law and morals involves wading through a wide range of previous knowledge because it has been one of the most controversial subjects during the nineteenth and twentieth centuries.[1] As it is not possible to establish a doctrinal history on this matter, not even throughout the Contemporary Era, it would be more appropriate to limit research to a historical allusion to the process which has created the prevailing view of the fundamentals of ethics, namely, the reasons why morality obligates.

Since we are on the subject of fundamentals, a distinction should first be made between ethics and morals. Morals are a set of rules which prohibit lying or stealing, while ethics consist of theoretical studies—normally within the sphere of universities—into the foundations, scope and limits of moral rules. Generally speaking,

F. Carpintero Benítez (✉)
University of Cádiz, Campus La Asunción, Facultad de Derecho, Jerez de la Frontera, Cádiz, Spain
e-mail: francisco.carpintero@uca.es

[1]The reader will excuse a tone as egocentric in the quotes. It happens that the fundamental subjects of the reflection about Law have been assumed by the Author of these lines and what he has considered interesting in other studies, that has been assumed in those of his works which are quoted.

A. Masferrer (ed.), *Criminal Law and Morality in the Age of Consent*, Ius Gentium: Comparative Perspectives on Law and Justice 84,
https://doi.org/10.1007/978-3-030-64163-4_7

morals are composed of automatically compulsory rules, which explains why nobody questions why we should not steal. In contrast, ethics are not binding as they are formed from abstract explanations of the rules of morality.

Nowadays, ethics is used to refer to what we have always called morals, but this is a simple switching of terms since in daily life those who use "ethics" do so in the same way that "morals" was used before. The reason behind this switch is the idea that expressing morals implies dogmatism or inquisitorial attitudes. Thus, as opposed to the old restrictive definition of morals, which was very demanding and inflexible, ethics today places us before a more agreeable way of life that is more in accordance with the vein of tolerance in democratic practices. Nevertheless, with this disassociation between morals and ethics we find ourselves confronted by a kind of philosophical doublespeak: ethicists, as and when it suits them, use dogmatism and the immutability of the rules of ethics in the same way as moralists in former times did when they put the demands of morals into practice. All of which appears to indicate that there has been little progress in theoretical research into the principles which should govern our behaviour.

It would seem that the most pressing question we should be addressing are the reasons why morals have come to be considered so contemptible, that is, the negative aspects which are associated with this term.

2 Two Philosophies, Two Schools of Thought

Here in the twenty-first century we are the rightful heirs to philosophical interpretations which were developed centuries ago. This is a rather odd fact given that our knowledge of physics is moving forward at such a pace—the progress in computing in the last 20 years is an example par excellence—, yet what we know about ourselves, what we are and could be, dates back to ancient time.

This inheritance from other times is both positive and negative. Positive because the questions which have remained unanswered for so long underline a substantial continuity regarding the main human problems, and it is thanks to this that modern researchers have much of the work already done. The negative side to this continuity emerges in the reflections on humankind, especially when some philosophies are deeply rooted in Universities and generate ways of thinking which discriminate against other discourses in fields such as philosophy or anthropology, bringing in its wake cultural impoverishment. "Positivism" does not replace speculations with facts, but rather one theory for another.

I have just mentioned controlling categories, which can be validly used in anthropological discourse. These categories, or notions, are expressed through words which could be called concepts, ideas, at times postulates and in other ways. But whatever the case, they are words which claim for themselves exclusivity and legitimacy in philosophical discourse, to the degree that those who do not use them are *ipso facto* disqualified.[2] The leading school of thought at any given moment attempts to impose its categories, those expressed in its own jargon, and control through language is the aim of all philosophies. If anybody has any doubts on this matter, they only have to look to Locke or Hume, who were very familiar with the scholastic philosophy in which they had been educated; Hobbes was likewise familiar with this philosophy and used it unconsciously. Once installed in the scholastic language, this internationally intelligible philosophical language was used to destroy itself. This is nothing more than naivety, but it is enough to take a look at the success of David Hume to understand that there was, and is a great interest in discrediting the previous philosophy. Ollero rightly speaks of "double language philosophies",[3] and Massini about "schizophrenia", in reference to these interests.[4]

The previous philosophy which needed to be destroyed, is what we generically call Scholasticism. This is a school of thought that cannot be described (or alluded to) as a whole as if forming a single unit, because it was made up of several mutually incompatible theories, all of which were applicable during the late Middle Ages and a good part of the Early modern period.[5] Taking this idea a step further, it would not be inaccurate to state that there were two coexisting major schools of thought which were at odds with each other.

One was Nominalism, headed by John Duns Scotus, which lasted until the end of the seventeenth century (although its medieval founders were not expressly alluded to). It was during this period that the aforementioned philosophers received their training, and inspired by this philosophy which essentially provided them with the categories or notions that would allow them to reject metaphysics. This does not mean that they were expressed followers of Duns Scotus or Gabriel Biel, whose works they

---

[2]For further reading on this, see my study, Carpintero (2012a) per totum. For more general studies, see: Carpintero (2010/1), 20–58; Carpintero (2012b), 11–52; Carpintero (2012c), 315–352. These articles are available at www.franciscocarpintero.com.

[3]Carlos Massini notes this paradox of the relativists who, nevertheless, do affirm human rights. It is the paradoxical attitude of those who state that rights are indemonstrable, etc., yet they take for granted that they are "desirable". See Massini (1994), 137. On page 104 he points out that that according to these relativists we would have to understand that rights could only be defended accidentally.

Andrés Ollero calls this attitude "Double language culture". See Ollero (2007), 240. He adds that, "to be positivist and rigorous at the same time is easy when you are willing to accept that ethical demands (both moral and legal) are not open to any rational foundation; something so at odds with the daily reality of Law, so as to assume that judges cannot give any 'judgement'". Ollero (2007), 318. He refers to R. L. Vigo, who writes, "It seems quite evident that legal positivism moves around more comfortably in the academic world than among legal practitioners and legal practice". See Vigo (2003), 200.

[4]Massini writes that "stating (i) the demands of justice can be truly known, while at the same time (ii) the Law is totally independent from these demands, inevitably leads to a kind of intellectual schizophrenia. There would accordingly be a strict duty to obey a commandment which is objectively recognized—with pretensions of truth—as grave and evidently iniquitous. The reality is the human intellect intrinsically demands unity a need for coherence, which makes it unattainable to attempt to maintain two statements which strictly imply an unsurmountable contradiction." Massini (2004), 67.

[5]Vid. mis estudios Carpintero (2008) per totum. Más completo Carpintero (2013) per totum.

had likely not read or whose names were perhaps no more than an echo from the past. They had Molina and Suárez who effectively took their place. And even if they had been familiar with them, they could not cite them, because a progressive seventeenth century author citing a medieval or sixteenth century Spanish scholar would have been discredited immediately.

The other philosophical trend was Aristotelianism, whose major exponent was Thomas Aquinas.[6] Aristotelianism was not well-known in scholarly circles, and the explanations given by Thomas Aquinas were a kind of benchmark in Middle Age and Modern cultures. Curiously enough, many philosophers and theologians afterwards often quoted him, and some went as far as to state they wanted to develop his ideas. But the only philosophers who did know Aristotle were Philopunus, Simplicius and particularly Alexander of Aphrodisias, essentially required reading to understand the moral philosophy of Thomas Aquinas. This is true to the degree that it is advisable to read the works of these authors both before and after reading Aquinas: they pave the way to understanding him and, after, they provide an overview for a better appreciation of Aquinas' extensive and complex writings. With the passing of time there were publications by Spanish authors, mainly during the sixteenth century, but they each followed Aquinas in different ways.[7] But, let us leave the topic at this: from the thirteenth to the seventeenth centuries the Schools of Philosophy saw themselves split, often antagonistic towards each other and faced with the two ethical and theological philosophies to which we give the common name of Scholasticism.[8]

This split has been fundamental force behind the general development of ethical doctrines, not so much due to split itself as to having often attributed the characteristics of one school of thought to the other. Indeed, over time, each has been disfigured with nuances and theses which originated from the other school, to the degree that universities finally managed to achieve a mediocre *mixtum compositum*. Readers, however, should not find this strange. For example, many history philosophy reference books consider Fichte, Schelling and Hegel as making up a single progressive line. But Hegel did not even remotely adopt the idealism proposed by Fichte, nor trivialise his explanations according to the level established by Schelling. Yet, they are presented as chain of "equally" idealist philosophers. If our appreciation of the nineteenth century is so poor, then the lack of knowledge of this particularly complex movement, known as Scholastic thinking that lasted for centuries, should come as no surprise.

---

[6] Carpintero (2002), 11–60; Carpintero (2003a, b), 13–117. On a topic which has raised a good deal of debate see, Carpintero (2000), 470–530. Available at franciscocarpintero.com.

[7] See my study Carpintero (2019) per totum.

[8] For an overview see my study Carpintero (2014), 63–128.

2.1 Aristotelianism

Thomas Aquinas is a primary consideration when speaking of Aristotelianism. He reworked the writings of his Master and eventually provided a synthesis which goes beyond the works of Aristotle.[9] He sets out the sources of morals and justice (justice is a part of morality) very extensively in *Summa Theologiae* I–II, q. 94 art. 2, in which he explains that order of natural law precepts follow the order of natural tendencies in human beings. The first, which is common to all living beings, is self-preservation. The second comprises the group of instincts we have in common with animals, such as the union between males and females. The third comprises the requirements for humankind's rational condition, such as living in society and thirst for knowledge. It should be noted that Aquinas classified knowledge as a human right as far back as the thirteenth century.

The foundations of Aquinas' ethics lie very much at ground level and, in a manner of speaking, have an earthy flavour. He attempts to explain facts. Aquinas does not trace his way back to a mysterious Noumenon world, be it metaphysical realities (as did Gabriel Vazquez de Belmonte and later Luis de Molina) or rules assumed to be promulgated by God (as did the nominals and later Francisco Suárez). His Aristotelian way of thinking leads him to examine the real human being, the being who is shaped (the soul) as a man, and in whom he finds tendencies common to other living beings as well as those which are specifically human: humans depend on their own constitution (or way of being) and their rights are the result of their way of being. Aquinas did not look for coherent doctrinal constructions but rather the explanation of facts.

I would now like to turn to this third group composed of essentially rational tendencies. He states that humans know (in a very rudimentary manner) what is right and what is wrong by the participation of human reason in God's reason, and this *participatio* is sometimes called natural law.[10] This was the moment of *ratio participata*. It is for this reason that everybody knows the obligation of the *pacta sunt servanda* principle, among many others. Unfortunately, there have been several authors who have held on to this "participative" moment and who define the meaning of natural law solely by this *participatio*, whereas Thomas rejects the usual term (*lumen*) to highlight the poor quality of this participation. At this moment of *participatio* human reason acts passively, since it limits itself to knowing what comes from a higher level. However, these first principles soon abandon us and then human

[9]For a summary of the Aquinas text see the following publications by me. Carpintero (2004) per totum Carpintero (2003a, b), 35–288. These can be found at franciscocarpintero.com. Carpintero (2008) per totum Carpintero (2013). Carpintero (2017) both of them per totum.

[10]He synthesises his doctrine on this by stating that "Quia vero forma est principium actionis, necesse est quod omne illud quod ex abundanti participatione influxus superioris agenti acquirit actionem ejus, habeat duas actiones: unam, scilicet, secundum propriam formam; aliam, vero, secundum formam participatam a superiori agente: sicut cultellus ignitus secundum propriam formam incidit; inquantum vero est ignitus, urit. Sic igitur et supremorum intelligentiarum unaquaeque, quae divina dicitur, habet duplicem actionem: una quidem inquantum participat abundantem bonitatem divinam; alia autem secundum propriam naturam". Aquinas (1972) § 386.

reason is left to work alone, combining principles and the consequences of applying them. This second step is called *ratio essentialiter*,[11] meaning, it is the time of the "rational essence" or reason working according to its own rules.[12]

This *ratio essentialiter* has to figure out what is best for humans in accordance with human purposes. Aristotelian Anthropology, and especially Aquinas anthropology, are the basis for an ethics of purposes or ends. Aquinas explains on several occasions that God does not move the world through orders or commandments, but rather by establishing purposes.[13] This idea based on ethics places humans in a very dynamic place, as they must not only obey but also discover, sometimes guided by the values that come from the participation in God's reason, and sometimes by this *'ratio essentialiter'* that calculates principles in their purest form and the consequences of applying them. If humans could completely understand what things are (what reality is), they would immediately know their place and purpose in the world. However, this is not the case, because he states that we only know what things are through some of their effects.[14] Although Aquinas maintains that a metaphysical knowledge is possible, this knowledge does not fully explain everything that exists: the search for (theoretical) truth is a path which lies before humans.

The *'ratio essentialiter'* further unfurls when we have to calculate for a given case what one person owes another. Everyone must reach a "middle ground", a so-called "happy medium" (not too much, not too little), and for this St. Thomas proposes what he calls the *medium rei* criteria.[15] We will better understand this criterion by comparing it with the criteria used by morals, known as *medium rationis*. The half-way point of morals depends on the—personal or individual—possibilities of each person. For example, what for Flacus would be eating too much for Fortis is sufficient. In contrast, the half-way point in terms of law, *medium rei*, is established differently, because law is not as personalised as morals. For example, a sale requires that somebody provides a good and that another provides money in exchange; both things must be balanced. The "happy medium" aimed for is the sales contract, not the perfection or realization of the parties involved.

---

[11]There are many Thomistic texts which expound the difference between the knowledge of the first principles, which is a task belonging to synderesis, and the conclusions reached by man when reasoning, by the application of those *prima principia*. A wide explanation, contrasting conscience with free will, see. Aquinas (1570) L. II, Dist. 39, q. 1, art. 2.

Since one is the *ratio participata*, and another one the results which are reached by reason when it works *essentially*. The dimension of reason that St. Thomas calls "ratio essentialiter" must work "secundum naturam rerum, de similibus ad similia" so that man goes after real human goods, that is to say, without moving away from what he already is. Thomas's golden rule in these matters is what we could enunciate as the treatment *subiectam materiam*, that implies we can ask for or demand no more than what belongs to the matter we are studying. See in particular Aquinas (1964) § 135, where he writes that "In singularibus subiectam materiam, prout scilicet proprium est illi doctrina, quae circa illam materiam versatur".

[12]My study (1998), 11–38.

[13]See in particular, Aquinas (1961) § 2724–2725; or Aquinas *Suma teológica*, I, q. 105, art. 4.

[14]See my study (2009), 95–120.

[15]See Aquinas (1978) II-II, q. 58, todo el art. 10.

Law has two types of criteria: one of them consists of making natural tendencies a reality, and the other of making each "thing" a reality. Since a sale requires that money be paid and the object of sale be given in exchange, the laws are fulfilled and the buyer and seller do what falls to them. I once again return to the observation made earlier: legal norms are not a question of obeying existing metaphysical noumena or laws. What justice is comes from what there is and already exists.

However, this way of introducing the foundations of ethics was doomed to failure because humans have always desired ideals, regardless of whether this perfect world had a metaphysical reality or if it was an accident. The great change, losing sight of things, was made by Spanish Scholastics who concluded the Second Scholastic, namely Gabriel Vazquez de Belmonte, Luis de Molina[16] and Francisco Suárez.[17] In their intellectual exquisiteness they could not accept the dependence on the rules based on events.

Ethics, by being composed of efforts to try and reach "the truth" through persistent inquiry into its purpose, is not normative. In other words, it is not composed of commandments and orders dictated to us by God. God governs the world through purposes, which is why he does not tell us "do this!" (*Fac hoc*!), but rather "this is for you to do" (*Hoc est tibi faciendum*).[18] Clearly sin is not so much disobeying God but rather deviating from the purpose (*deviatio a fine*), and if someone should be contemptuous of the purpose it is considered an aversion to the purpose (*aversio a fine*), which is a serious sin.[19] Since sinners do not usually reject the purpose, but are only people attracted by some illusion of good, Thomas of Aquinas does not call them evil, *pravi* or *mali*, but foolish or silly, *stulti*[20]; they are people who do not know how to find the fullness of their humanity. So, Aquinas sees God not so much as a legislator but the purpose of all that exists.

Aquinas' proposal implies that humankind is not governed passively, but rather that in the moment of *ratio essentialiter*, people also actively intervene in governing

---

[16]It might seem that Molina, being a scholastic, was left behind in the race of typically modern liberties. But Alfred Dufour points out that "Dans cette perspective rénovatrice du Droit naturel, ouvert tant à l'historicité qu'à l'spécificité du droit en un monde changeant, les premiers jalons d'une doctrine de l'autonomie de l'ordre moral par rapport à la volonté divine seront posées de manière significative par le grand apologète de la liberté humaine, célèbre dans l'histoire de la théologie par son doctrine de la Grâce fustigée par Pascal, mains dont l'oeuvre juridique présente en fait un intérêt autrement capital pour l'histoire de la science du Droit: Luis de Molina". Dufour (1972), 54–55.

[17]Suárez could not speak of the *ex objecto* criterion, but leaves his axiomatic moral doctrine set in Stone, which leads to the same results as Vázquez de Belmonte.

[18]"Sed ratio potest aliquid intimare dupliciter. Uno modo absolute; quae quidem intimatio exprimitur per verbum indicativi modi: sicut si aliquis alicui dicat: *Hoc est tibi faciendum*. Aliquando autem ratio intimat aliquid alicui movendum ipsum ad hoc. Et talis intimatio exprimitur per verbum imperativi modi: puta, cum alicui dicitur: *Fac hoc* ... Ratio movet imperando, sit ei ex virtute voluntatis. Unde reliquitur, quod imperare sit actus rationis, praesupponitur actus voluntatis, in cujus virtute ratio movet per imperium ad exercitium actus ... radix voluntatis est voluntas, sicut subjectum; sed sicut causa est ratio". Aquinas (1978) I-II, q. 17, art. 1.

[19]My study (2011), 562–588.

[20]See my study (2009), 95–120.

their life, since they create the rules and laws that have to govern, and in an attempt to designate this he uses the passive and active verb forms "to be governed" (*gubernari*) and govern (*gubernare*): humans are not only governed but also govern. Their existence is creative because the positive laws we humans create—natural law and Eternal Law—finally converge towards a common goal.[21] It is clear that Aquinas contemplates an unfinished being (perhaps always unfinished) who has to learn from those things which are similar to them in order to discover the rules of their life: *de similibus ad similia*. So, if humans have eyes, it is because there are colours to see; if they have ears it is because there are sounds to be heard, and so on. They live in an environment which is "theirs" and from which they come.[22]

In these acts to rule our own life, human reasoning—now understood as *ratio essentialiter*—starts with the first self-evident principles and performs an intelligent task in which one has to choose the principles to be applied in each act. Well, for Thomas Aquinas, principles do not have a specific place on a scale of importance, but rather move up or down according to the demands of each problem. The first problem is we humans: he explains that what is appropriate for one person (because it is proportionate and in their interests), is bad for another because is it not.[23] A platonic way of thinking would see principles as always applicable, without giving further thought. However, we can see that this direct application is not possible in Aquinas' ethical terms. If the chain of deductions from principles to consequences is broken, how are we to understand the "life" of principles? Aquinas explains that we have two intellects: one which speculates on principles, and another which looks for the best solution at any given moment. These reflections are discussed *Prima secundae* in *Summa Theologiae*, when dealing with laws.

There are people who are shocked when they read this because they understand natural law in terms of a chain of deductions which goes from the first principles of practical reason to more specific conclusions. This axiomatic method was the one developed by nominalists, albeit lacking in clarity, and it was adopted by Scholastics beginning with Francisco Suárez. This shock comes from the current way of thinking, set out by Suárez, which attempts to understand St. Thomas according to the ways of proceeding in recent centuries and understands that everything is either absolute or necessary (metaphysically), and all law is relative to each person and at any given time. None of these solutions is appropriate. To understand St. Thomas' proposals we need to set aside current prejudices and delve into the heart of the science of

[21] This is a thesis which is fully developed by Michel Bastit (1990) per totum.

[22] I refer to my study (2009).

[23] Aquinas' dealt extensively with this. It occasionally notes that reasonings that deal with principles are different from the reasonings that deal with conclusions. See Aquinas (1961) § 475. At other moments it explains that there is no necessary connection between principles and conclusions. Aquinas (1978) I, q. 82, art. 2. In stronger terms it explains that there have to be two distinct intellects: one which deals with conclusions and the other that deals with principles. Aquinas (1961) § 1247. There is a generally pervading attitudes which concludes that there exists no need between principles and their outcomes in "ea quae sunt ad finem". See, Aquinas (1992) q. 22, art. 6.

law characterised by *Jus Commune*, of which St. Thomas was its major proponent.[24] Furthermore, in his works we can find more than forty specific rules which he bases directly on natural law.[25]

Humankind finds itself before purposes which mark their lifestyle. Aquino's is not an ethical doctrine which depends on specific orders or commandments, but rather rests on an existence which is natural and supernatural at the same time. He repeatedly rejects the theory that assumes a double purpose in human life, natural and supernatural—a doctrine known as *In puris naturalibus*,[26] because he tries to point "the person as a whole" towards God. For this reason, along with sin, but as a distinct reality from it, he denounces the existence of *miseria*, and explains that although there are behaviours that are not sinful, they are even worse because they show great misery.[27]

2.2 *Nominalism*

The nominalist tradition dates back to the Early Middle Ages, although the theory proposed by its members has never really been clear. If we begin with John Duns Scotus, we can see that his work is above all a direct attack on Aquinas' way of thinking. In his commentary on *Sentences* one often has to fish around for his thesis bit by bit. His opposition to St. Thomas is clearly evident if we consult *Summa Theologiae* edited by Jerónimo de Montefortino in Rome in 1728, where he explains Scotus' thesis by strictly following the order of the subjects set out in Aquinas' *Summa Theologiae.*[28]

Duns opposed Aquinas, above all, regarding the teleological view of humankind and the world. For Aquinas, humans are to some degree incomplete or in the making, progressing both in terms of their history as well as their surroundings. We know that sometimes the point of departure is the *ratio participata* that shows them fundamental principles of their own moral acts, and sometimes makes them use their reasoning

---

[24]Regarding the doctrines about the *jus naturale* in Common Law, and the "derogations" which Natural Law has undergone, see my study (1981), 33–100. Another study which should not be overlooked is Bonuci (1906) per totum, whose solitary efforts were not surpassed for many decades. A more recent, and comprehensive study is by Weigand (1967) per totum.

[25]Georgette of St. Hilaire sets out approximately forty precepts that Aquinas bases directly on Natural Law. See St. Hilaire (1962) per totum.

[26]Thomas Aquinas, especially in his comprehensive works written during his youth, repeatedly rejected this doctrine. As one example, see Aquinas (1570) L. II, Dist. 34, q. 1, a. 3.

[27]This not been dealt with much in the literature. For example, *Super Sent.*, lib. 4 d. 49 q. 1 a. 3 states that "Ergo se habet ad opposita. Beatitudini autem opponitur miseria. Ergo si potest aliquis appetere beatitudinem, potest etiam appetere miseriam." However, generally speaking the word misery refers to those cases in which the lack of freedom and willingness to do good caused by vices. This term is also used to refer to extreme poverty, which results in the duty to give alms.

[28]Full title: *Johannis Duns Scoti Doctoris Subtilis Summa Theologica. Ex universis operibus ejus concinnata, juxta ordinem et dispositionem S. Thomae Aquinatis per Fratrem Hieronymum de Montefortino.*

to figure out which principles need to be chosen in accordance with the demands made by specific problems: as pointed out in Ecclesiastes, one is the time to laugh and another the time to cry.

For Scotus, these points of departure were too bold. Above all, he was a mystic and saw humans as directly dependent on God. His view of humans is not that of Aquinas: they are not perpetually developing but rather a *potentia* equipped with their five senses, memory, reason and will. This being is already perfect, as narrated in the Book of Genesis. Humans, in the same way as God, are "trapped" by what God is and by the love of God. That means that neither God nor humans can refuse the requirements of God's love, although this thesis must be qualified.

These scholastics divided the Decalogue into two parts: the First and Second Tablets. The First Tablet deals with duties to God, and includes the first three Commandments in the Decalogue. According to Scotus this is also derogable and binding for God, because God cannot contradict what God is.[29] The remaining seven commandments are only binding if they "are in consonance with" the law of Love. For example, polygamy is not allowed because this is disrespectful to women and not in consonance with the requirements of Love, which was the same explanation proposed by Aquinas.[30]

But, apart from Love, the other precepts of not stealing, lying or committing adultery lack "entity". From a metaphysical point of view, they do not exist because they are not "substances", but rather contents found in our minds which appear as binding. What kind of existence or reality do they have? According to him, those realities are *modal*. From among the ten ways of being established by Aristotle, the modal is the weakest and is used to describe what we know exists in some way but which we know is not "necessary".

Ratio debiti is questioned, that is, the reason why these rational contents create the obligation to be obeyed. Modal realities alone do not require obedience, rather only because these contents we contingently have in our reasoning have been ordered and provided by God, in such a way that should God so wish he could have commanded us to lie, rob etc. To maintain *ratio debiti* he needs to explain that our reasoning is divided into two parts or dimensions. One is the *lex indicans* (a divine indication) through which we know that to lie is morally bad. The other is *lex imperans seu*

---

[29] Man, according to Scotus, was placed so high, with so much superiority over what surrounds him, that he is a being who ask questions, but they are questions that cannot be answered from within his environment: He only has God as a speaker. An attitude well-suited to a mystic like Scotus. As might be expected, the notion of Natural Law disappears in his hands, because the very idea of Natural Law implied that human beings are recognised in their natural tendencies and, now, in the Franciscan thinking which he proposes, Nature is rather the enemy of humans. He only recognises one law of God towards us, which is composed of three kinds of precepts: the "nota ex terminis": the tenet of non-contradiction, those belonging to the law of God's Love, and those behaviours which "are consonant" with the law of love.

[30] "Allegat Gratianus: "Omnia quaecumque vultis ut faciant vobis hominibus, et vos facite illis", Matthei 7. Idem dicendum de una vel pluribus uxoribus habendis. Etsi enim non necessario sequatur ex notis lumine naturae". Scotus (1728) I-II, q. 94, art. 1.

praecipiens, by which God commands obedience according to what *lex indicans* shows us.[31]

The God portrayed by Duns Scotus is somewhat whimsical, because he indicates and tells us what must we do, but does not tell us what he arbitrarily wants us to do in accordance with his capricious and arbitrary will. Duns heads down a dangerous path: for him committing adultery, stealing or killing are not bad behaviours "in themselves", but rather they are only morally reprehensible because God has so ordained, without us being able to contribute any kind of 'rational' argument as to why these things should be prohibited. The prohibition of stealing and killing—stripped of their metaphysical basis—appears to us as without foundation.

William of Ockham took this presentation of the free will of God to the extreme, because he understood that the commandments of the First Tablet depend on the arbitrary will of God. He had to establish this doctrine in order to contradict those who opposed the claims of fourteenth-century Franciscans by attacking all metaphysical needs. However, this topic is quite extensive and best left aside here—it has been debated at length in the aforementioned cited sources.

As regards the positive laws which we humans create, their *ratio debiti* lies—according to Scotus—in the consensus of citizens; a consensus he assumes is included in the "existence of the community".[32] Natural law depends on God's will and positive law depends on the will of humans. Humans must obey because they have the potential to obey, *potential obedientialis*.[33]

If the final basis of morality is posed in this way, all believers have the right to ask themselves why they have to obey what God commands in the Second Tablet of the Decalogue. We must remember that, according to Scotus, there are two sources of morality and law: the demands of the law of love of God, and that which is indicated by the *lex indicans*, and prescribed by the *lex imperans*. In reality, this topic is not particularly important because in a Christian era, all behaviours presented in the second tablet are also opposed to the law of Love. But he left various ways of thinking for posterity which proved questionable. One, is that the natural law is a *lex descendens* from God to humans. The other is that most moral rules are without any

[31]Scotus writes that "Lex ergo naturae vel inditum lumen intellectus non est proprie lex, quia etsi indicat quae oportet facere, non tamen imperat … Accedit, quod leges aliquae generalis de operabilibus dictantes, praefixae sunt a voluntate divina, et non ab intellectu, ut praecedit actum voluntatis divinae, quia in illis legibus non invenitur necesitas ex terminis". I–II, q. 90, art. 1 de la *Suma Theológie Johannis Duns Scotus… Tomus tertius. Ex universis operibus ejus concinnata, juxta ordinem et dispositionem S. Thomae Aquinatis per Fratrem Hieronimus de Montefortino*, mentioned earlier.

[32]In reference to *usucapio*, he writes: "Istud etiam apparet probabile per hoc, quod si quilibet posse suum dominium transferre in alium, tota communitas posset cujuslibet de communitate transferre dominium in quamlibet (quia in facto communitatis suppono inclusi consensu, cujuslibet) ergo illa communitas habens justum consensum, quasi jam oblatum, in hoc quidem quilibet consentit in leges justas condendas a communitati vel principe, potest per legem justam cujuslibet dominium transferre in quemlibet". Ockham (1626) L. IV, distinctio XV, q. 2, 10.

[33]"Et potentia obedientialis … pertinet ad dependentiam causati ad causam". Scoto (1530) L. III, q. 1, art. 4.

entity: they are only "modes", and in the end we must obey laws because we have a "potential to obey".

There is a third topic which needs to be mentioned, namely the rigidity which natural law acquires over natural law. For Thomas Aquinas, humans are active and are as much governed as they govern their own lives. Aquinas can be classed as a "metaphysician" because he understands that the principles set down in the Second Tablet are "justified" (without delving further into the matter here). This implies that the commandment not to kill responds to a "substance", as according to him, to kill is "in itself" a wicked act. But he is a "flexible" metaphysician because he does not establish a chain of deductions which run from the law of God to humans: faced with a problem, each human has to study it, look for the principle which is best suited to the ends and, once chosen, to find the best answer to the problem posed. In this, humans have to be virtuous, that is, guided by the virtue of prudence, which guides all other virtues: *auriga virtutum.* As is obvious, in the end the choice of principles has to be guided by the end purpose.

But prudence is not valued by the nominalists. For them, humans are *subditus*, a being subject to either the law of Love or to those rational contents (both accidental and contingent, whose nature is simply modal) whose reasoning is shown to them through *lex indicans.* This last law "obligates" because the "potential to obey" lies within humans. According to Aquinas' theory, when a person takes on a task (in this case the task of life), there is leeway for them to govern themselves. But for nominalists, humans can only look to God's commandments, a question which is exacerbated when they consider these orders as simple "modes" in our reasoning which do not respond to an already existing reality. Faced with this problem, nominalists began an escape route forward, and to make up for this lack of entity in these "modal entities" they accentuated both the precision in their knowledge as well as their utter immutability. The rigidity in the doctrine of Natural Law did not come from Thomas Aquinas, but from the immutability that nominalists gave to the contingent contents of our reasoning. Later on, at the end of the sixteenth century, Luis de Molina transformed these rules into metaphysical truths and Francisco Suárez (though a nominalist), stressed the immutability of what is ordered by God in such strong terms—because God does not contradict himself – that he actually achieved a noumenon similar to Molina's.[34]

Let us contrast again the immutability of ethic contents with St. Thomas' way of thinking. For him, we hardly know things, and what we know of them is learned through their effects: his metaphysical ethics are limited in scope, although sometimes can arrive at incontrovertible results. Nominalists did not have any metaphysics they could lay claim to: when faced with a lie, they could not simply maintain that to lie is in itself bad, but rather that lying goes against God's will. We know this through *lex imperans*, which God has placed in our reasoning, and *lex indicans* is absolutely immutable because God cannot be contradicted.

---

[34] See my book (2013), previously cited.

And what if we dispense with God? They maintained that the moral contents of reason would still be the same even if God did not exist.[35] A sin against reason would be a rational sin, in the same way that good things are good and bad things are bad, even if "God did not exist": *Etiamsi Deus non daretur*.[36] The origins of secularisation started amongst Catholics not Protestants. Hugo Grotius, in 1625, established a similar doctrine and likewise maintained this independence of morals as regards God. This idea is generally attributed to him, and in it an example of the secularisation of modern ethics and law which is typical of the modern period.

The less entity they granted to moral mandates, the more they emphasized their clarity in knowing them and their immutability when applying them. The doctrine of immutability in the natural law did not originate from Thomist ranks but from the nominalists. It was not a metaphysical but rather a nominalist creation; neither was it Protestant but rather Catholic.

2.3 *The Second Spanish Scholastic*

When the scholastic tradition seemed to have run its course, Francisco de Vitoria started to explain Aquinas' *Summa Theologica* at the University of Salamanca in the early sixteenth century. This period was especially rich in prompting a renewal of philosophy and moral theology because it was a converging of the Aquinas tradition and the nominalist inheritance, which had been comprehensively recorded in the fifteenth century by Jean Gerson, Konrad Summenhart and Gabriel Biel. Gerson's contributions were decisive, and well-known among Spaniards, in the same way that they showed they were familiar with Scotus, Summenhart and Biel.

[35]Jean Gerson wrote: "Nulla trangressio legis naturalis, ut naturalis est vel humana, est de facto peccatum mortale ... quia lex naturalis est humana, ut tales sunt, non possunt attingere ad cognitionem aeternitatis in poena vel praemio; non ergo seruntur ad finem supernaturalem". *Liber de vita spirituali*, Lectio IV, Corollarium Primum, columna 38. He took this way of thinking from Scotus, who wrote that, "Quare non intellecto voluntatis imperio adstringentis alios ad servadum legem, quaecumque representarentur contra judicium rationis, esse reputanda mala, non moralia, vel theologica, sed mala naturae et philosophiae ... Homo faciens contrarium, contra naturam, comitti malum, sed non esse talem malum reputandum demeritorium aut offensa Dei". *Johannis Duns Scoti Doctoris Subtilis Summa Theologica. Ex universis operibus ejus concinnata, juxta ordinem et dispositionem S. Thomae Aquinatis per Fratrem Hieronymum de Montefortino*, I-II, q. 91, art. 2.

[36]Gabriel Biel, who lived during the last fifteenth century, wrote: "*Nam per si impossibile Deus non esset, qui est ratio divina: aut ratio illa divina esset errans, ad huc si qui sageret contra recta rationem angelicam, vel humanam, velalia maliquam, si qua esset, peccaret. Peccatum est voluntaria carentia conformitatis ad rationem rectam debiti voluntati*". Biel (1574) L. II, Dist. 28, quaestiounica, p. 165-E.

This thought was used by Scoto, who wrote ''Quare non intellecto voluntatis imperio ad stringentis alios ad servadum legem, quae cum que representarentur contra judicium rationis, esse reputanda mala, non moralia, vel theologica, sed mala naturae et philosophiae...Homo faciens contrarium, contra naturam, comittimalum, sed non esse talem malum reputandum demeritorium autoffensa Dei'. Scotus (1728) I-II, q. 91, art. 2.

In the wake of Vitoria, culture underwent renewal at the hand of Domingo de Soto (perhaps the most lucid of these scholastics) and secondary figures emerged such as Aragón, Salón, Oviedo, Hurtado, Cardillo, Zumel, etc. This century ended with three particularly important Jesuits who were theologians and philosophers: Gabriel Vázquez de Belmonte, Luis de Molina and Francisco Suárez. The seventeenth century also saw some leading exponents in the form of Leonardo Lessius and Juan de Lugo. In the eighteenth century, the persistence of Suárez's ideas survived in Ignatius Schwarz, and in Anselm Desing (in a style with more nuances of Aquinas).[37] Secondary authors are too numerous to list here.

What was to be done in the face of these converging and excluding attitudes? According to Belda, scholastics dealt with new problems by adapting scholastic philosophy.[38] However, they moved within a confusing environment. The prestige of St. Thomas Aquinas was such that even the then statutes of the Society of Jesus required its members to follow his philosophy and theology. But this "prestige" was quite unique, because those scholastics were not very familiar with Aquinas' thinking[39]: generally speaking they only cited *Summa Theologiae*, as we can see in the *Tratado de las leyes* or *Defensio Fidei* by Francisco Suárez, and all of them were aware of Gerson, Konrad and Biel along with Aquinas. To a lesser degree Scotus is cited directly, while Ockham is hardly mentioned. The only author I know who really understood St. Thomas was Conrad Koellin[40]; the fact that his name is not even mentioned in any history of philosophy books or ethical-legal thinking, gives food for thought. St. Thomas' work constitutes a kind of band aid in the scholarly culture running from the thirteenth to the seventeenth centuries, and it was never entirely understood.

The problem now posed was the entity or *perseitas* of ethics. Time and once again the question with platonic undertones prevailed: Are things good because God so wants, or does God want them because they are good? Thomas Aquinas had designed a hilltop with two slopes: one was principles and the other consequences; the hilltop summit being the ultimate human goal. The sixteenth century has been one of the most conflictive in our history because Reformists imposed a change which meant going back to a simple Christianity, regardless of philosophical speculations. What is good or bad was known as that set out in the Book of Revelation, while there was an overabundance of books about moral theology. St. Thomas Aquinas' theory, which was full of distinctions, *rationes* and reflections on humankind's ultimate goal, was simply too complicated.

The task of making moral theology easier fell to Gabriel Vázquez de Belmonte, who openly rebelled against Aquinas' doctrine and, in the face of the doctrine of

[37]This period has not been sufficiently studied by historians of legal thinking. See, Cabrera (2001) per totum.

[38]Juan Belda-Plans (2000) per totum.

[39]The complete title is *Johannis Duns Scoti Doctoris Subtilis Summa Theologica. Ex universis operibus ejus concinnata, juxta ordinem et dispositionem S. Thomae Aquinatis per Fratrem Hieronymum*de Montefortino.

[40]Koellin (1589).

purposes or ends, established the exclusivity of the theory known *ex objecto*.[41] The *ex objecto* criterion states that all things good are good in themselves, just as are the bad. Good and bad are ultimate categories that cannot be deduced from other considerations. Vázquez thought that Tomas, by establishing the ethics of ends, accepted that the ends justify the means, and he proposed taking into account the importance of behaviour "in itself". "Committing adultery will always be bad and helping people in great need will always be good".

Some years later (around 1595), Luis de Molina began to publish his *De justitia et jure*, a work in which he also flaunts the most extreme metaphysics. For Molina what is now considered reasonable and fair, will always be fair "in itself". He appears to lean heavily on Gabriel Biel, according to whom the modal being that constitutes law and morality is unchangeable, even if they deny the existence of God. Therefore, all actions which are against this rational order are considered to be a sin because they are "against reason". Molina almost states the same idea, but with the difference: where Scotus, Gerson, Konrad and Biel had placed a simply modal being, he creates a metaphysical order composed of unchangeable moral essences. In this way, sinners sin against the essence of things, not just against mental contents. In the same vein as Gabriel Vázquez, he also claims that *lex imperans* is not necessary; it is sin enough for someone to rebel against reality or what exists.

Francisco Suárez, from the hands of Scotus and Gerson, reacted against those who supported these metaphysical theories. He affirmed the modal being subject to *lex imperans*, which is a dimension of natural law placed in our reasoning by God. But his colleagues, Gabriel Vázquez and Luis de Molina, made things difficult, because everyone wants to believe that all that they do is good and what others do is always evil: metaphysics suited this way of feeling and thinking and feeling better than any other philosophical doctrine. Suárez faced the task of confirming the very same, but dispensing with metaphysics.

From the point of view of the fundamentals of ethics, Suárez is quite syncretic and not very original. The path he found had already been mentioned: God has contingently instilled in us a rational law composed of *lex indicans* and *lex imperans*. Natural law must be obeyed only because it is imposed by God imperatively: *Quia praeceptum est.* But he was successful where others failed, because—it is a question of nuances—Gerson or Biel left behind them the idea that natural law is composed of contingent contents. Suárez stated that natural law is unchangeable so enthusiastically that in the wake of his writings, it was clear to all that this law was absolutely eternal and unchangeable.

Suárez created a state of confusion. If we distinguish between understanding and realising (*verstehen* and *erklären* in German), everybody can see that moral order depends on the will of God, but in principle nobody can understand that God makes demands of us simply because it is his will. We need to talk in terms of confusion because the moderate authors of Modernity accepted Suárez' theory as

[41] A doctrine which could be summarized in one of his sentences "Conclussio est, voluntas discordans a ratione, sive recta, sive errante, semper est mala". Vázquez de Belmonte (1611) q. 19, art. 6, Disp. 58, p. 415.

something different, because they saw him as a metaphysic who maintained the order of the immutable being. Suárez was syncretic and lacking in originality in his theory concerning legislation and law, but he explained in an organised and keen manner what could be found scattered across many other philosophical and theological treatises.

There is one remaining topic of interest which would be appropriate to address at this point. When we study Thomas Aquinas, it can be seen that he addresses "all mankind" in order to establish ethical rules. It is for this reason, that "The order of the principles of natural law follows the order of the natural tendencies of humankind", and it is necessary to address the demands of that which is being done in order to know what is the right balance in each case – the example of the sale. He called this final criterion *medium rei*. But now all of this has disappeared, because Molina and Suárez have intellectualised ethical theory, which they tend to see above all as either noumenic order (Molina), or simply intellectual (Suárez). Objects regulated by ethics no longer have a voice and their role is simply passive: they are those "things" simply governed by reason. Suárez graphically explained that they constitute "simple" objects governed by rationality,[42] as they only constitute *materia contracta* through reasoning.

3 Implications for Posterity

Post Suárez it no longer made sense to distinguish between the notions of law and natural law—it is one and the same reality with God and basks in his eternity. This took place in a time of decline in scholastic studies, increasingly trivialised until the nineteenth century. The vigour of Aquinas, Scotus, Gerson or Suárez had been lost, and the centres of learning offered notes of a very low quality that they claimed represented scholastic thinking; several generations of seminarists studied in these institutions. With the "enshrining" of natural law it was not surprising when Luigi Taparelli d'Azeglio (possibly the most lucid of the nineteenth century scholastics) stated that the purpose of human life was to make moral order happen: a possibility that Thomas Aquinas had considered, and had dismissed.

On the edge of this popularisation, law was understood as a mandatory law, in such a way that the science of the law made no sense: the work of the moralist and jurist was to know laws cognitively and apply them to existing problems, as the seamstress applies the pattern to the fabric that she must cut. Causing the burden of all that is

[42]"Quia lex naturalis non reguletur per convenientiam ad naturam sensitivam; sed ad rationalem. Sensitivam autem respicit solum ut contractam, et speciali modo perfectam per differentiam rationalem; ergo illa convenientia generica impertinens est ad distinguendam legem naturalem". Suárez (1967) L. II, cap. 17, § 6. He follows Duns Scotus Vid. Scotus (1728) I-II, q. 94, art. 3. This causes Bastit to reflect that: "La loi concernera d'abord l'homme et son action morale détaché du cosmos. Si l'on a dû ainsi détacher la loi proprement dite des inclinations naturelles, c'est que celles-ci n'ont plus du tout pour Suarez le même sens que pour Saint Thomas, elles sont des états de fait dont ne peut dire qu'ils sont obligatoires». Bastit (1990), 313.

normative to fall on the rules, law and justice changed from being studies on the needs of humans to become studies about the rules themselves, expounded by Hans Kelsen in the twentieth century in an exemplary manner. According to Aquinas, the rules of natural law depended on the natural needs or tendencies of humans and on what each thing requires for itself, *medium rei*. Suárez in particular cuts the ties between rules, human tendencies and what things are, and causes justice to depend on laws from a higher will, in such a way that the rules become law. It was the universe of Must-be, the purely normative, a reason which constantly turns on its own axis without finding support in what mankind is and what things are. When this view came together, to a large degree it created a new "academic" subject: legal logic, which delighted some analytical philosophers in the twentieth century.

Once again, we can see the problem behind all this, namely why each human has to follow what is established by natural law. Once ethical doctrine has been stripped of its source of sustenance and its rules emancipated from the reasons why they exist, the ethical question is reduced to ingenious topics toying between Be and Must-Be. From here we have Hume's complaint, called the *naturalist fallacy*: How can we go from Be and Must-Be, or from "is" to "ought"?

With the increasing trivialisation of scholastic studies, Taparelli wrote "God commands, so man must obey". They did not resort to "potential to obey" which, in this frame of thought, no longer made sense. But anyone can ask themselves why they have to obey laws. For the nineteenth century authors God is Almighty, and humans cannot question these divine principles. The more atheism advanced, the more these ecclesiastics shut themselves up in their own explanations about the reality and the immutability of natural laws. There is the suspicion of what we can consider a kind of "sporting spirit": those who wish to get closer to God must obey a set of rules, in the same way that a football player who scores a goal has done so by following a set of regulations.

The problem is too complex and it is better to be satisfied with making note of some of its aspects. What is in the end true is that Scholastics from the last few centuries have left us a poor theoretical legacy. For this reason, we must take up the path which was left interrupted in the fourteenth century, when John Duns Scotus replaced complexity with apparent clarity which casts out all outright explanations.

References

Aquinas T (1992) Quaestiones disputatae. Studio Domenicano, Bologna
Aquinas T (1961) Liber de Veritate Catholicae Fidei contra errores infidelium seu Summa contra Gentiles. Marietti, Torino-Roma
Aquinas T (1972) Librorum de causis Expositio. Marietti, Torino, p 1972
Aquinas T (1964) In decem libros Ethicorum Aristotelis ad Nicomachum Expositio Marietti, Torino-Roma
Aquinas T (1570) In IV Sententiarum (In Primum et Secundum Sententiarum) Tomus Sextus, Opera Omnia. Roma
Aquinas T (1978) Summa Theologiae. BAC, Madrid

Bastit M (1990) Naissance de la loi moderne. La pensée de la loi de Saint Thomas à Suárez, PUF, París
Belda-Plans J (2000) La Escuela de Salamanca y la renovación de la teología en el siglo XVI. Biblioteca de Autores Cristianos (BAC), Madrid
Biel G (1574) Commentarii doctissimi in IIII Sententiarum libros. Brixiae.
Bonuci A (1906) La derogabilità del diritto naturale nella scolastica. Vicenzo Bartelli, Perugia
Cabrera L (2001) Modernidad y Neoescolástica: Anselmo Desing. Servicio de Publicaciones de la Universidad de Cádiz, Cádiz
Carpintero F (1981) El derecho natural laico de la Edad Media. Persona Y Derecho 8:33–100
Carpintero F (1998) Persona humana y prudencia jurídica. Ars Juris 18:
Carpintero F (2000a) La mutabilidad de la ley natural en Tomás de Aquino. Rivista Internazionale Di Filosofia Del Diritto 67:470–530
Carpintero F (2002b) Tomás de Aquino ante la ley natural. Dikaiosyne 8:11–60
Carpintero F (2003) Los principios de la justicia en Tomás de Aquino. Ars Juris 29:13–117
Carpintero F (2003) El desarrollo de la facultad individual en la Escolástica. In: Carpintero F/Megías J J/Rodríguez M/De Mora, E El derecho subjetivo en su historia. Servicio de Publicaciones de la Universidad de Cádiz, Cádiz, 35–288
Carpintero F (2004) Justicia y ley natural: Tomás de Aquino, y los otros escolásticos. Servicio de Publicaciones de la Facultad de Derecho Universidad Complutense, Madrid
Carpintero F (2008) La ley natural. Historia de un concepto controvertido Encuentro, Madrid
Carpintero F (2009) La adaequatio hermeneutica en Tomás de Aquino. Philosophica 35:95–120
Carpintero F (2011) El carácter no imperativo del derecho en Tomás de Aquino. In: Estudios Jurídicos en Homenaje al Prof. Alejandro Guzmán Brito. Edizioni dell'Orso, Alessandria
Carpintero F (2013) La ley natural. Historia de una realidad inacabada, UNAM, México
Carpintero F (2010/1) Métodos científicos y método del derecho: una historia superada. Persona y Derecho 62:20–58
Carpintero F (2012a) La crisis del Estado en la Edad Posmoderna. Thomson Aranzadi, Cizur Menor
Carpintero F (2012b) ¿Pueden las teorías sobre la justicia sustituir a la doctrina de la ley natural? Persona Y Derecho 66(67):315–352
Carpintero F (2012c) Crisis de la ciencia, crisis del escepticismo ético. Dikaion: 11–52.
Carpintero F (2014) Desarrollo histórico de la idea de ley natural (Edad Moderna). In: Contreras F J (ed) El sentido de la libertad. Stella Maris, Barcelona 2014
Carpintero F (2017) Sobre la ley natural. Una historia controvertida, Ideas y Libros Ediciones, Madrid
Carpintero F (2019) La crisis del derecho en los escolásticos españoles del siglo XVI. Sindéresis, Madrid
Dufour A (1972) Le mariage dans l'école allemande du droit naturel moderne au XVIII siècle. PUF, Paris
Duns Scotus J (1530) Super Tertio Sententiarum. Lyon.
Duns Scotus J (1728) Johannis Duns Scoti Doctoris Subtilis Summa Theologica. Ex universis operibus ejus concinnata, juxta ordinem et dispositionem S. Thomae Aquinatis per Fratrem Hieronymum de Montefortino. Roma.
Koellin K (1589) Commentaria in Primam Secundae St. Thomas Aquinatis, Venetiis.
Massini CI (1994) Los derechos humanos en el pensamiento actual. Abeledo-Perrot, Buenos Aires
Massini CI (2004) Constructivismo ético y justicia procedimental en John Rawls. Unam, México
Ockham W (1626) In Primum, Secundum, Tertium et Quartum Sententiarum quaestiones subtilissimae. Antwerpiae.
Ollero A (2007) Derechos humanos. Entre la moral y el derecho, UNAM, México DF
St Hilaire G. (1962) Precepts of Natural Law in the text of Sto.Thomas. Unpublished doctoral thesis, Saint Louis University, USA
Suárez F (1967) Tractatus de legibus ac Deo legislatore. Instituto de Estudios Políticos, Madrid
Vázquez de Belmonte G (1611) Commentariorum ac Disputationum in Primam Secundae Sancti Thomae. Ingolstadt.

Vigo RL (2003) El jusnaturalismo actual. De M. Villey a J. Finnis, Fontaneda, México
Weigand R (1967) Die Naturrechtslehre der Legisten und Dekretisten von Irnerius bis Accursius und von Gratian bis Johannes Teutonicus. M. Hueber, München

What is Perfectionism?

Francisco J. Contreras

Abstract The mainstream tradition of Western moral and political philosophy was perfectionist, that is, it believed law and government could and should contribute to the moral improvement of people. This article examines the perfectionist arguments of Aristotle, Saint Augustin and Aquinas, as well as John S. Mill's "harm principle", a classical reference for anti-perfectionists. It also reconstructs the controversy between Patrick Devlin and H.L.A. Hart on the matter of "morals laws". Finally, it proposes Rawls's work as a paradigm of contemporary anti-perfectionism, and Joseph Raz's "perfectionist liberalism" and Robert P. George's considerations on "moral ecology" as instances of a perfectionism that lives up to the needs and constraints of our time.

Perfectionism is the tenet whereby the state and the law may legitimately contribute to "making men good", that is, help them to choose what is morally right, to practise virtue, and thus to attain the good life. *A contrario*, antiperfectionism would be the philosophical approach which, as stated by Joseph Raz, "rejects the idea that the state has a right to impose a conception of the good on its inhabitants". The government, in the antiperfectionist view, "should be blind to the truth or falsity of moral ideals, or of conceptions of the good"; "governments must be neutral regarding different people's conceptions of the good".[1]

The antiperfectionist state may certainly use coercion to prevent people from damaging or taking the life, freedom or property of their fellow citizens. But murder, robbery or agression are not punished *qua* inmoral conduct, but in so far as they are

F. J. Contreras (✉)
Universidad de Sevilla, Sevilla, Spain
e-mail: fjcontreraspelaez@gmail.com

[1]Raz (1986), 108. Likewise: "The anti-perfecionist principle claims that implementation and promotion of ideals of the good life, though worthy in themselves, are not a legitimate matter for governmental action […]. Such a doctrine is a doctrine of restraint […]. Beyond that there is the deep-felt conviction that it is not within the rights of any person to use the machinery of state in order to force his conception of the good life on other persons" Raz (1986) 110–111.

A. Masferrer (ed.), *Criminal Law and Morality in the Age of Consent*, Ius Gentium: Comparative Perspectives on Law and Justice 84,
https://doi.org/10.1007/978-3-030-64163-4_8

incompatible with other citizens' rights. We find a typically antiperfectionist inspiration, for example, in John S. Mill's famous "harm principle": "The only purpose for which power can be rightfully exercised over any member of a civilized community, against his will, is to prevent harm to others. His own good, either physical or moral, is not a sufficient warrant. He cannot rightfully be compelled to do or forbear something because it will be better for him to do so, because it will make him happier, because, in the opinion of others, to do so would be wise, or even right... The only part of the conduct of anyone, for which he is amenable to society, is that which concerns others. In the part which merely concerns himself, his independence is, of right, absolute. Over himself, over his own body and mind, the individual is sovereign".[2]

1 Perfectionism in Aristotle, Saint Augustin and Aquinas

To be sure, the default position in most cultures and societies of the past had always been perfectionism. The "central tradition" (Robert P. George) of Western thought conceived politics and law as "the continuation of ethics by other means": laws enforce virtuous conduct on those stubborn individuals who do not lend an ear to sermons, reasoning or parental advice. Aristotle, for example, displays a perfectionist understanding of law and state when he asserts in his*Nicomachean Ethics* that: "legislators punish and take vengeance on those who do wicked acts [...], while they honour those who do noble acts, as though they meant to encourage the latter and deter the former".[3] And, in his *Politics*, Aristotle maintains that "a state [...] does not exist for the sake of alliance and security from injustice, nor yet for the sake of exchange and mutual intercourse"; such governmental functions—the only ones an antiperfectionist would be ready to admit—are, in Aristotle's view, "necessary but not sufficient" for the existence of a proper state. Because "a state exists for the sake of a good life, and not for the sake of life only [...], whence it may be further inferred that virtue must be the care of a state properly so called".[4] The Aristotelian polis is a pedagogic-moralist body politic: "legislators make citizen good by forming habits in them, and this is the wish of every legislator".[5]

Aristotle did not endorse Socratic ethical intelectualism, namely, the notion that the will wills necessarily whatever the intellect identifies as good (thus, an intellectual error lies always at the root of immoral conduct). Socrates thought one can convince an immoral person by intellectual argument, proving to her that she failed to grasp the real good, and this demonstration will suffice to lead her to right behavior. But Aristotle knows that man does not consist in reason only, and that passions make him desire things the intelligence knows to be evil; moral life, hence, involves a constant struggle of right reason against passions: "The incontinent, knowing that what he

[2] Mill (2006).

[3] Aristotle (2009), III, 5, 1113b, p. lwwvi.

[4] Aristotle (1999), *Politics*, III, 9. p. 63.

[5] Aristotle (2009), *Nicomachean Ethics*, II, 1, 1103b, p. lvi.

does is bad, does it as a result of passion, while the continent man, knowing that his appetites are bad, refuses on account of his rational principle to follow them".[6] Moral education based on argument will fail when applied to incontinent men prisoners of their passions, for these need a more pressing pedagogy, provided by laws: "He who lives as passion directs will not hear argument that dissuades him, nor understand it if he does; and how can we persuade one in such a state to change his ways? And in general passion seems to yield not to argument but to force [...]. For this reason, their nurture and education should be fixed by law, for they will not be painful when they have become customary. But it is surely not enough that when they are young they should get the right nurture and attention; since they must, even when they are grown up, practise and be habituated to them, we shall need laws for this as well, and generally speaking to cover the whole of life; for most people obey necessity rather than argument, and punishments rather than the sense of what is noble. This is why some think that legislators ought to stimulate men to virtue [...]".[7]

To be sure, this public-legal moral education is to be complemented by parental education, the latter presenting the advantage of being able to take into account individual peculiarities. The Aristotelian state is not a totalitarian Leviathan claiming to replace families; family education proceeds on a case by case basis: "Individual education has an advantage over communal, as individual medical treatment has; for while in general rest and abstinence from food are good for a man in a fever, for a particular man they may not be; and a boxer presumably does not prescribe the same style of fighting to all his pupils. It would seem, then, that the detail is worked out with more precision if the oversight is on an individual basis [...]".[8]

Medieval Christian thought possessed also a deep perfectionist quality. In *The City of God*, Saint Augustin provided, with stunning foresight, a prescient outline of present antiperfectionist positions (associating antiperfectionism with paganism): "The worshippers [...] of those gods [...] are unconcerned about the utter corruption of their country. "So long as [...] it enjoys material prosperity [they say], and the glory of victorious war, or, better, the security of peace, why should we worry? [...] It is all right [...] if the people applaud those who supply them with pleasures rather than those who offer salutary advice; [...] if kings are interested not in the morality but in the docility of their subjects [...] [Pagans think that]. The laws should punish offences against another's property, not offences against a man's personal character. No one should be brought to trial except for an offence against another's property, house or person; but anyone should be free to do as he likes about his own, or with his own, or with others, if they consent [*Nullus ducatur ad iudicem, nisi qui alienae rei domui saluti uel cuiquam inuito fuerit inportunus aut noxius; ceterum de suis uel cum suis uel cum quibusque uolentibus faciat quisqu e quod libet*]".[9]

Saint Thomas Aquinas endorsed Aristotelian perfectionism as well: parental education and personal conscience suffice to induce the virtuous to right behavior;

---

[6]*Nicomachean Ethics*, VII, 1, 1145b, cit., p. cxxxviii.

[7]*Nicomachean Ethics*, X, 9, 1179b-1180a, cit., p. ccvii.

[8]*Nicomachean Ethics*, X, 9, 1180b, cit., p. ccviii.

[9]Saint Augustin, *De civitate Dei*, II, 20 [quoted by George (1993), 36].

but there are men who are enslaved by their passions and vices, especially when young: such men require legal pedagogy and coercion: "Man has a natural aptitude for virtue; but the perfection of virtue must be acquired by man by means of some kind of training [...]. And as to those young people who are inclined to acts of virtue, by their good natural disposition, or by custom, or rather by the gift of God, paternal training suffices, which is by admonitions. But since some are found to be depraved, and prone to vice, and not easily amenable to words, it was necessary for such to be restrained from evil by force and fear, in order that, at least, they might desist from evil-doing, and leave others in peace, and that they themselves, by being habituated in this way, might be brought to do willingly what hitherto they did from fear, and thus become virtuous. Now this kind of training, which compels through fear of punishment, is the discipline of laws".[10]

Nevertheless, in other texts of Aquinas' dawns the awareness that not all moral duties are legally coercible, and not all vices can deterred by the law: "Now human law is framed for a number of human beings, the majority of whom are not perfect in virtue. Wherefore human laws do not forbid all vices, from which the virtuous abstain, but only the more grievous vices, from which it is possible for the majority to abstain; and chiefly those that are to the hurt of others, without the prohibition of which human society could not be maintained: thus human law prohibits murder, theft and such like".[11]

Ancient and medieval perfectionism indulged in excesses that modern conscience could hardly endorse (as conceded, for example, by a contemporary perfectionist like Robert P. George). While Aristotle seems to assign a primary pedagogic role to law and state, current perfectionists tend to define law's role as only subsidiary and complementary in regard to that played by families and other agents of civil society. Additionally, both Aquinas and Saint Augustin are prepared to resort to state coercion not only in strictly moral matters, but also in those of religious belief: not that they warrant the coercive enforcement of faith (which is impossible in and of itself), but they do approve of coercive repression of heresy.[12] But what Aquinas concedes with regard to faith (namely, that faith is not genuine except if embraced voluntarily) applies to virtue as well: virtue can only consist in the free choice of morally upright behavior.[13]

---

[10] Saint Thomas Aquinas, *Summa theologica*, 1–2, q. 95, a. 1.

[11] *Summa theologica*, 1–2, q. 96, a. 2.

[12] "Turning to Aquinas, the fundamental and (to the modern reader) obvious problem with his view is that it assumes the propriety of legislating not only morals, but also faith [...], thus proposing a radical establishment of religion that is utterly inconsistent with a due regard for religious liberty" George (1993), 41.

[13] "There are many important goods that people ought to realize in their lives whose realization is only possible if people freely choose to do "the right thing" [...]. One cannot participate in these goods otherwise than by acts of choice, that is, internal acts of the will [...]. As internal acts, they are beyond legal compulsion" George (1993), 43.

2 The Hart-Devlin Debate

From the seventeenth century onwards, this perfectionist Aristotelian-Thomist "central tradition" was gradually displaced by liberalism. At first, (classical) liberalism developed within a theistic natural law framework; but, starting from John Stuart Mill, a new radical liberalism will emerge, which conceives individual freedom as an absolute, a value for its own sake, only to be limited on the grounds of the need to respect the freedom, property and life of fellow citizens.

A significant milestone in that evolution was the debate on "morals laws" held by Herbert L.A. Hart and Patrick Devlin. In 1957, the Commitee on Homosexual Offences and Prostitution of the British parliament, headed by Sir John Wolfenden, issued a famous report calling for decriminalization of consented homosexual relationship among adults. But, beyond this particular recommendation, the report went on to establish a general theory of antiperfectionism: "Unless a deliberate attempt is made by society, acting through the agency of the law, to equate the sphere of crime with that of sin, there must remain a realm of private morality and immorality which is, in brief and crude terms, not the law's business".[14]

Patrick Devlin was a High Court judge of liberal persuasion and, thus, initially leaning favourably to the ideas conveyed by the Wolfenden Report. However, study and reflection, he confessed,[15] finally led him to divert from the Wolfenden Report and enunciate such disagreement publicly in his 1959 Maccabean Lecture in Jurisprudence. Devlin grasped the fact that English penal law had always attempted to serve moral principles that embraced more than mere guarantee of life and property. For example, consent of the victim is not accepted as an exempting circumstance in crimes like homicide. And there were in English law at the time penal precepts punishing "conducts freely agreed upon among adults" that did not apparently damage the rights of others, such as voluntary euthanasia, assisted suicide, suicide pacts, duels, abortion, incest... To Devin's mind, it was obvious that penal law does not only protect individual freedom and property, but society's interest as well, the latter sometimes overriding the former: "There is only one explanation of what has hitherto been accepted as the basis of the criminal law, and that is that there are certain standards of behaviour or moral principles which society requires to be observed; and the breach of them is an offence not merely against the person who is injured but against society as a whole".[16] "I think it is clear that the criminal law as we know it is

---

[14]Wolfenden Report, § 62 [quoted by Devlin (1989), 3]. However, the Report assigned penal law wider functions than mere protection of life, freedom and property: "Its function, as we see it, is to preserve public order and decency, to protect the citizen from what is offensive or injurious, and to provide sufficient safeguards against exploitation and corruption of others [...]" (Wolfenden Report, § 13).

[15]"The statement which [...] I completely approved, that there was a realm of private morality which was not the law's business, and the distinction between crime and sin [...]. But study destroyed instead of confirming the simple faith in which I had begun my task" (Patrick Devlin, "Preface", in *The Enforcement of Morals*, cit., p. vii).

[16]Devlin (1989), 6.

based upon moral principle. In a number of crimes its function is simply to enforce a moral principle and nothing else".[17]

By legally enforcing the respect of certain moral principles "as such" (i.e., not because their violation involves plain infringement of the rights of specific citizens), society, Devlin argues, is defending its own cohesion and survival: "What makes a society of any sort is community of ideas, not only political ideas but also ideas about the way its members should behave and govern their lives; these latter ideas are its morals. Every society has a moral structure as well as a political one".[18] For example, the identity and cohesion of Western societies relies on a moral code of Christian origin, which includes institutions like monogamous marriage[19] and a variety of rules of sexual morality. The state may and must protect both legally: "Society may use the law to preserve morality in the same way as it uses it to safeguard anything that is essential to its existence".[20]

The aspect of the Wolfenden Report Devlin is most critical of is its attempt to put forward an abstract principle whereby "morality as such" is not the law's concern. Devlin is ready to admit that, depending on circumstance, prudential considerations might advise not to enforce major moral obligations legally: for instance, even if adultery is an immoral act that erodes the moral code of society on marriage and the family, its criminalization might not be convenient in this moment for reasons of practical applicability, and the same could be said of fornication.[21] Devlin does not forget either that "the law is concerned with the minimum and not with the maximum [...]. We all recognize the gap between the moral law and the law of the land".[22] Nor that "as far as possible, privacy should be respected".[23]

Therefore, in Devlin's view, the precise scope of moral imperatives the compliance of which can be legally enforced will depend on various circumstances, and will require prudent weighing of, on the one hand, the need to defend the moral code of society and, on the other hand, the respect owed to the private realm, the degree of

---

[17]Devlin (1989), 7.

[18]Devlin (1989), 9.

[19]"Whether a man should be allowed to take more than one wife is something about which every society has to make up its mind one way or the other. In England we believe in the Christian idea of marriage and therefore adopt monogamy as a moral principle. Consequently the Christian institution of marriage has become the basis of family life and so part of the structure of our society. It is there not because it is Christian. It has got there because it is Christian, but it remains there because it is built into the house in which we live and could not be removed without bringing it down [...]. Marriage is part of the structure of our society and it is also the basis of a moral code which condemns fornication and adultery. The institution of marriage would be gravely threatened if individual judgments were permitted about the morality of adultery; on these points there must be a public morality" Devlin (1989), 9–10.

[20]Devlin (1989), 11.

[21]"Adultery [...] seems to me to be just as harmful to the social fabric as homosexuality or bigamy. The only ground for putting it outside the criminal law is that a law which made it a crime would be too difficult to enforce [...]. All that the law can do with fornication is to act against its worst manifestations [...]" Devlin (1989), 22.

[22]Devlin (1989), 19.

[23]Devlin (1989), 18.

social tolerance concerning specific immoralities, and the likelihood of counterproductive effects of an overreaching moral-legal regulation. But on no account can the question be settled by a simplistic theoretical principle—"private conduct harmless to third parties is not the law's business"—as that stated by the Wolfenden Report.[24] For the truth is that the law exists, not just for the protection of privacy, but "for the protection of society" as well, and consequently "the law must protect also the institutions and the community of ideas, political and moral, without which people cannot live together".[25]

H.L.A. Hart replied to Devlin in essays subsequently collected in the volume*Law, Liberty and Morality*. Hart challenges Devlin's core claim, namely, that private immoralities erode the commonly accepted moral code and thus endanger the sustainability of society. Hart argues, conversely, that private moral dissent may represent an instance of "critical morality" which will, over time, end up superseding the morality commonly accepted nowadays (which Hart, following nineteenth century utilitarians, names "positive morality"). Devlin errs, Hart contends, in asserting a monolithic, fixed moral code, and in regarding moral rigidity as essential for the survival of society: "He [Devlin] appears to move from the acceptable proposition that *some* shared morality is essential to the existence of any society to the unacceptable proposition that a society is identical with its morality as that is at any given moment of its history, so that a change in its morality is tantamount to the destruction of a society".[26] Changes in the moral code of a society do not mean its extinction, but simply its evolution and adaptation to new circumstances.

Hart derides particularly the relevance attributed by Devlin to sexual morality and its necessary legal protection. He likens it to emperor Justinian's belief that "homosexuality causes earthquakes".[27] He suggests that, even if the repeal of sexual morals laws did produce a social change in the direction of wider permisiveness, such an evolution would not be disfunctional.[28]

---

[24]"It is not possible to set theoretical limits to the power of the State to legislate against immorality. It is not possible [...] to define inflexibly areas of morality into which the law is in no circumstances to be allowed to enter [...]. The suppression of vice is as much the law's business as the suppression of subversive activities [...] [The limits of legal intervention in the private realm are to be settled] not by the formulation of hard and fast rules, but by a judgement in each case taking into account the sort of [prudential] factors I have been mentioning. The line that divides the criminal law from the moral is not determinable by the application of any clear-cut principle. It is like a line that divides land and sea, a coastline of irregularities and indentations [...]. The boundary between the criminal law and the moral law is fixed by balancing in the case of each particular crime the pros and cons of legal enforcement [...]" Devlin (1989), 12–14 y 21–22.

[25]Devlin (1989), 22.

[26]Hart (1978), 51.

[27]"No evidence is produced to show that deviation from accepted sexual morality, even by adults in private, is something which, like treason, threatens the existence of society. No reputable historian has maintained this [...]. As a proposition of fact it is entitled to no more respect than the Emperor Justinian's statement that homosexuality was the cause of earthquakes" Hart (1978), 50.

[28]"No doubt it is true that if deviations from conventional sexual morality are tolerated by the law and come to be known, the conventional morality might change in a permissive direction [...].

With half a century hindsight, we can hold HartEnglish edition by W.Dand other liberals of the 50 s and 60 s who ridiculed "reactionaries" like Devlin—accountable for subsequent harmful developments. No, the loosening of sexual morality criteria did not result in the dissolution of society. But in 2018 Europe, the fertility rate has dropped 30% below the level of population replenishment; almost half the children are born out of wedlock, in de facto couples shown to be statistically more conflictual and less child-protective than married couples; less and less children are raised by both their mother and father until they come of age. And the consequences of this child helplessness are blatant: educational failure, substance and alcohol consumption among youths, teen pregnancies, emotional disorders in children, increasing sexual violence among youths....[29] All these rates have shot up significantly in Western society since the 60 s.[30] This has been the cost of the "liberations" applauded by Hart and others.

Yet, Devlin's position is not immune to criticism, not only from the libertarian perspective, but also from the Aristotelian-Thomist-perfectionist "central tradition". Because, as Robert P. George rightly pointed out,[31] Devlin turned out to be a communitarian *avant la lettre*: he valued public morality **just** as an ingredient of communitarian identity and cohesion. Because the moral codes professed by societies along history are multiple and reciprocally contradictory, consistent communitarianism seems to imply ethical relativism: it avoids judgment on the truth or falsity of the moral beliefs shared by different societies, and it only values their contribution to social cohesion, understood as a good for its own sake. For example, the Aztecs' belief in human sacrifice as a moral good constituted, indisputably, an identitarian-cohesive

---

But even if the conventional morality did so change, the society in question would not have been destroyed or "subverted" Hart (1978), 52.

[29]"A closer look at the facts of the past thirty years reveals a marked weakening of families and other subsidiary communities [...]. These societies may still "exist", it might be argued, but only in a weakened condition. Unless they somehow manage to attain a measure of moral agreement around which a reintegration can take place, they are doomed to a continued erosion of social bonds, and ultimately [...] to collapse" George (1989), 64.

[30]"Dies gilt als ein erstrebenswerter Fortschritt an Freiheit, so als wäre die subjektive Freiheit des Individuums, alles tun zu dürfen, was ihm Spass und Lust bereitet, ein Königsweg zum Glück. Aber ist das so? Schauen wir nüchtern auf den Zustand unserer Gesellschaft, auf die zerbrochenen Familien, auf die alleinerziehenden Mütter und Väter und ihre Kinder, auf die Jugendlichen mit tiefen seelischen Wunden, auf die Millionen Pornographiesüchtigen, auf die Millionen sexuell missbrauchter Kinder, auf die Millionen abgetriebener Kinder und auf unseren eigenen Lebensweg, fragen wir Lehrer, Ärzte, Psychiater, Therapeuten, Sozialarbeiter, Jugendämter, so scheint sich das Glück von dieser Art von Freiheit erschrocken abzuwenden. Wir beschwören die Jugend als Garant des Glücks, aber wir schaffen eine Gesellschaft, in der es immer weniger lachende Kinder gibt und immer mehr traurige Alte" Kuby (2013), 17.

[31]"The public interest served by morals laws, according to the tradition, consists in the maintenance of a cultural context conducive to *genuine* virtue and inhospitable to *genuine* vice [...]. Under a non-relativist (and non-utilitarian) conception of the public interest, [...] social cohesion is not always or unconditionally desirable. The integration of human beings around shared principles of *injustice* or other forms of wickedness is an *undesirable* integration" George (1993), 79. "He [Devlin] would not ask of the alleged vice, "Is it truly wicked?" but, rather, "Is it widely considered to be truly wicked?" George (1993), 6.

element in Mexican society. However, Aquinas—or the thinkers of the Spanish School of Natural Law, like Francisco de Vitoria[32] or Juan Ginés de Sepúlveda—regarded such belief and the practices associated to it as abhorrent, because they violated primary principles of natural law. The Spanish conquerors in the sixteenth century acted as consistent Aristotelian-Thomist perfectionists when they destroyed the "cohesion" of pre-Columbine societies grounded on moral error. The moral principles of those peoples, however "cohesive" they could be, were to be replaced, since they were false.

3 Liberals Versus Communitarians

In subsequent decades, the debate between perfectionists and antiperfectionists has tended to overlap—as was the case between Hart and Devlin already—with that opposing communitarians to liberals. If we assume Rawls is the archetypical exponent of the liberal camp—his socio-economic interventionism notwithstanding[33]—it may be interesting to note that, both in *A Theory of Justice* and *Political Liberalism*, Rawls proposes a metaphysically neutral state that suspends judgment in matters of values and the good life. In *A Theory of Justice*, the people who, cloaked in the "veil of ignorance", choose the principles of justice, do not only ignore their respective sex, profession, race, etc., but also their respective understanding of the good: "[T]he persons in the original position [...] know that they have (or may have) certain moral and religious interests and other cultural ends [...]. Moreover, they are assumed to be committed to different conceptions of the good [...]. The parties do not share a conception of the good by reference to which the fruition of their powers or even the satisfaction of their desires can be evaluated. They do not have an agreed criterion of perfection [...]. Thus it seems that the only understanding that the persons in the original position can reach is that everyone should have the greatest equal liberty consistent with a similar liberty for others. They cannot risk their freedom by

---

[32]"Otro título [para la conquista] puede existir, fundado en la tiranía de los señores de los bárbaros o en el carácter inhumano de leyes que entre ellos imperen en daño de los inocentes, como son las que ordenan sacrificios de hombres inocentes o permiten la matanza de hombres exentos de culpa para comer sus carnes. Afirmo que, aun sin necesidad de la autorización del Pontífice, pueden los españoles prohibir a los bárbaros todas estas nefandas costumbres y ritos, pues les está permitido defender a los inocentes de una muerte injusta" Vitoria (1975), 101.

[33]Actually, as rightly remarked by Roger Scruton, Rawls's theory of justice is closer to socialism than to classical liberalism. Rawls assumes socialism's basic premise, namely, the priority given to the distribution of goods, overlooking the fact that they are produced and possessed by someone prior to their distribution: "Rawls, summarizing his celebrated "difference principle", writes that "all social primary goods—liberty and opportunity, income and wealth, and the bases of self-respect—are to be distributed equally unless an unequal distribution of any or all of these goods is to the advantage of the least favoured" (*A Theory of Justice*). Ask the question "Distributed by whom?" and you will search his book in vain for an answer. The state is omnipresent, all-possessing, all-powerful in organizing and distributing the social product, but never mentioned by name" Scruton (2015), 45.

authorizing a standard of value to define what is to be maximized by a teleological principle of justice".[34]

In *Political Liberalism*, Rawls developed his ideal of "worldview neutrality" further. His starting point is the inability of human reason to reach indisputable conclusions about the most important questions in human life: Who are we?, How did it all begin?, How should I live?... There are various "comprehensive" views of life and the universe[35]; in a free society, not everybody will choose the same: there will be atheists, agnostics, believers of different religions, etc. And each of these worldviews is linked to a different conception of the good and the meaning of life. Rawls calls this metaphysical poliphony "the fact of reasonable pluralism": metaphysical dissent is, in his view, a structural, permanent feature of open societies.[36] But plural societies need laws, rules, a constitutional framework. An "overlapping consensus" among the various understandings of the world and the good coexisting in free society needs to be found. The key to such compromise is the "worldview neutrality" of the rules: they should appear as acceptable to people who profess diverse metaphysical and moral beliefs.

Rawlsian principles of justice, therefore, provide each individual with a pack of "primary social goods": "rights, freedoms and opportunities, as well as income and wealth". These primary social goods constitute a sort of life equipment which each individual will employ for the pursuit of ends that are valuable according to his own conception of the good. The state should only guarantee the **means**; on no account should it enforce or even encourage the pursuit of speficic **ends**.

Now then, the claimed "worldview neutrality" of Rawls's theory of justice was questioned from the start by various critics. Thomas Nagel, for example, argued that beneath its supposed neutrality there actually underlay the option for an individualistic-libertarian notion of the good: the good life would be simply "the life lived according to one's wishes, provided the freedom of others is respected": "The [rawlsian] original position seems to presuppose not just a neutral theory of the good, but a liberal, individualistic conception according to which the best that can be wished for someone is the unimpeded pursuit of his own path, provided it does not interfere with the rights of others".[37]

The crux of the matter lies probably in the Rawlsian premise of the "inevitable worldview pluralism in open societies". His claim would appear to be very close to non-cognitivist relativism: the question of the good—what ends are worth pursuing for their own sake?—would be rationally intractable; hence, in a free society, a wide

---

[34]Rawls (1971), 327–328.

[35]See Rawls (1993), 54 ff.

[36]"The diversity of reasonable comprehensive religious, philosophical, and moral doctrines found in modern democratic societies is not a mere historical condition that may soon pass away; it is a permanent feature of the public culture of democracy. Under the political and social conditions secured by the basic rights and liberties of free institutions, a diversity of conflicting and irreconcilable—and what's more, reasonable—comprehensive doctrines will come about and persist if such diversity does not already obtain" Rawls (1993), 36.

[37]Nagel (1973), 82: 220.

range of notions of the good will flourish, and the state should remain neutral on their behalf.[38]

Now then, a large segment of mankind regard their conception of the good not merely as "a metaphysical option" among many others, but precisely as the only well grounded conception, the one that fits the true nature of things. They believe it is possible to demonstrate the truth of their conception of the good. Rawls's theory of justice makes no sense for all such objectivists.

Communitarian criticism of Rawlsian antiperfectionism has focused primarily on the conception of the person apparently presupposed by Rawls's theory of justice, as well as on its wrong interpretation of the relationship between individual and community.

Rawls considers the identity of the person to be fixed "before" she belonged to a particular community, and before she possessed a specific understanding of the good and the ends of life. Rawls actually asserts that "the self is prior to the ends that are affirmed by it".[39] Rawls constructs a theory aimed at the preservation of the individual's ability to choose (and, perhaps, subsequently revise) his own conception of the good: the bond between the self and its ends seems to be, therefore, of a volitional nature. However—communitarian critics (like Michael Sandel) will argue—people do not usually understand their relationship with the conception of the good they profess in **volitional**, but in **cognitive** terms: they do not consider to have chosen a conception of the good out of a wide range of available options, but to have learned or discovered the only true conception.[40] And they experience this rational bond with certain ends or values as constitutive of their identity: they are the very persons they are precisely because they possess that specific conception of the good. They were not "themselves" previously (and then bought a notion of the world and of the good in the "worldview supermarket", as the Rawlsian theory seems to imply). It's the other way round: they discovered or learned what (they consider to be) the truth, and that knowledge of the truth made them the persons they are. Ahmed does not consider to have chosen Islam: Ahmed knows he is a Muslim, he believes Islam is the truth, and feels that, were he not a Muslim, he would not be Ahmed.

And Rawls, like other antiperfectionists, misconceives as well, in the communitarians' view, the relationship between the individual and his community. Individuals do not develop or choose their conception of the good in a void, out of

---

[38]"[D]oes their emphasis on the individual's choosing her own way of life mean that liberals must believe that such choices are arbitrary expressions of preference, that value is in the eye of the beholder, that moral judgements are completely subjective? [...] The reasons why one might take liberalism and moral subjectivism or scepticism to go together are reasonably straightforward. If no way of living is better than any other, if people's choices are simply expressions of preference, with no rational grounds available to justify claims about their value, like choices between flavours of ice cream, then it would seem crazy for the state to do anything other than let people make their own choices" Mulhall and Swift (1994), 21–22.

[39]Rawls (1971), 560.

[40]"On such a picture, establishing one's own ends is not a matter of choosing from a menu of available possibilities, but one of discovering what one's ends are or ought to be; and then my fundamental preference, in morality as well as in politics, would surely be for the conditions of self-knowledge rather than the conditions of choice" Mulhall and Swift (1994), 50.

nothing, but, rather, they learn or endorse a conception of the good preexisting in their cultural environment. Charles Taylor, for example, put forward a "social thesis" which emphasized the cultural dependence of the individual with regard to a communitarian framework.[41] The pre-social self of antiperfectionist liberalism does not exist in real life; but, if he did exist, he would not be capable of recognizing any value or give his life any meaning whatsoever: "complete freedom would be a void in which nothing would be worth doing, nothing would deserve to count for anything".[42] Real freedom can only be "framed liberty": framed by a social-cultural framework "which sets goals for us, which thus imparts a shape to rationality and provides an inspiration for creativity".[43] These ideas bear some resemblance to those expounded by Alasdair Macintyre in *After Virtue*: we could not orient ourselves morally, did we not possess a communitarian environment made of "practices", "traditions" and social roles assigning us duties: "[T]o be a man is to fill a set of roles each of which has its own point or purposes: member of a family, citizen, soldier, philosopher, servant of God [...]. It is only when man is thought of as an individual prior to and apart from all roles that "man" ceases to be a functional concept".[44]

4 Joseph Raz's Perfectionist Liberalism

Communitarianism would appear to be logically akin to perfectionism.[45] However, communitarian criticism of liberal antiperfectionism indulges sometimes in the symmetrical mistake of idealizing whatever sort of social-cultural framework (a problem we already spotted in Devlin's thought) and insufficient concern for individual freedom.[46]

---

[41]See Kymlicka (2002), 221–228.

[42]Taylor (1979), 157.

[43]Taylor (1979), 157.

[44]Macintyre (1981), 56.

[45]For the reasons explained here by Will Kymlicka: "A communitarian state can and should encourage people to adopt conceptions of the good that conform to the community's way of life, while discouraging conceptions of the good that conflict with it. A communitarian state is, therefore, a perfectionist state, since it involves a public ranking of the value of different ways of life" Kymlicka (2002), 220.

[46]"Es posible que en el Occidente postmoderno el florecimiento humano esté amenazado por el ultraindividualismo y la atomización. Pero en buena parte del **mundo no occidental** el peligro viene aún del lado de la **pertenencia tribal** opresiva. La comunidad impone al individuo una visión del mundo y una forma de vida inescapables: creencias, costumbres, adscripción religiosa, profesional y familiar no electiva (pensemos en los matrimonios forzados, en la persecución de los conversos al cristianismo en países musulmanes, en costumbres bárbaras como la mutilación genital femenina, etc.). Los comunitaristas idealizan los vínculos comunitarios sin las debidas distinciones y matices. En el conflicto entre la libertad individual y esas imposiciones tribal-culturales, los derechos humanos están del lado del individuo" Contreras (2014), 303.

Of all thinkers of recent decades, it is probably Joseph Raz who has most clearly rejected the exclusionary disjunctive between antiperfectionist liberalism and antiliberal communitarianism. Raz favours a middle way: perfectionist liberalism.

We have already seen how an antiperfectionist state only seeks to guarantee social conditions in which each citizen enjoys the widest freedom for the pursuit of his own ends compatible with the freedom of other citizens; the antiperfectionist political ideal seems thus to be the maximization of "wish satisfaction". The state is not entitled to judge the legitimacy of such wishes, so long as they don't interfere with the freedom of others. But Raz highlights the "reason-dependent character of goals and desires": "the desire is not itself a reason; it is merely an endorsement of a reason independent of it".[47] Scilicet, our desires are not wanton: we desire what we desire for reasons which can be true or false. I wish to purchase drug A because I think it can cure my bronchitis. If the reason underlying my desire turned out to be wrong—if the drug that heals bronchitis is not A but B—I would desire something else.[48] Therefore "wish satisfaction as such"—i.e., regardless of the validity of the reasons that render such wishes rational—does not appear to be a reasonable political ideal.[49] If law and state can help people avoid living according to "false desires" grounded on wrong reasons, the possibility of such assistance should not be ruled out a priori: "One does not help people to lead the lives they want to have by satisfying their false desires. People do not wish to have a life based on falsehood".[50]

Taking one more step, Raz questions the intrinsic value of autonomy (understood as "the free choice of goals and relations as an essential ingredient of individual well-being"). Is the behavior of someone who chooses autonomously to do an evil thing more morally valuable than that of someone who does the same evil thing non-autonomously (out of coercion or deceit)? Our intuition indicates the opposite.[51] Thus, autonomy, in Raz's view, is not unconditionally valuable: "Autonomy

[47]Raz (1986), 141.

[48]"Agents do not wish their desires satisfied if their belief in the existence of a reason for their desires is unfounded" Raz (1986), 143. "To be sure, we want to reach our goals [...]. But we are not stuck with our goals just because we have them [...]. We can deliberate on their merits, and if they are found wanting we can modify them [...]. Whatever we want for a reason we want to the extent that it serves that reason [...]. The person has the goal on condition that his reason is a valid, valuable one" Raz (1986), 300–301.

[49]"People do not want their false desires satisfied [...]. Hence want-satisfaction *qua* want-satisfaction is not intrinsically valuable [...]. The picture I have in mind is that of live and let live. Peoples's lives [so the picture goes] are their own affairs. They may be moral or immoral, admirable or demeaning, and so on, but even when immoral they are none of the state's business except those whose lives they are. All that politics is concerned with is providing people with the means to pursue their own lives, i.e., with helping them satisfy their wants and realize their goals [...]. Attractive though this simplified picture is, it is riddled with ambiguities and difficulties [...]" Raz (1986), 143.

[50]Raz (1986), 144.

[51]"Indeed autonomously choosing the bad makes one's life worse than a comparable non-autonomous life is" Raz (1986), 412. "Has autonomy any value qua autonomy when it is abused? Is the autonomous wrongdoer a morally better person than the non-autonomous wrongdoer? Our intuitions rebel against such a view" Raz (1986), 380.

is valuable only if exercised in pursuit of the good [...]. The autonomy principle is a perfectionist principle. Autonomous life is valuable only if it is spent in the pursuit of acceptable and valuable projects and relationships".[52]

Therefore, autonomy requires both negative (not being subjected to the will of someone else) and positive conditions (availability of a variety of valuable options).[53] Enlarging the range of valuable options to choose from amounts to reinforcing autonomy and filling it with meaning. The labels "positive freedom" and "positive conditions of freedom" are commonly employed to allude to the possession of a minimum of well-being and need coverage (if I am hungry or illiterate, if I lack housing, "I am not really free").

Raz does not question the necessity of such material conditions, but he is alluding to something else: the availability of morally valuable options: "A person is autonomous only if he has a variety of acceptable options available to him to choose from, and his life became as it is through his choice of some of these options".[54]

And such valuable options consist sometimes in "collective goods" that can only be produced socially. Radical liberalism—initiated by John S. Mill—overestimates the existential creativity of the individual, his ability to create vital options out of nothing: "The completely autonomous person is an impossibility. The ideal of the perfect existentialist with no fixed biological and social nature who creates himself as he goes along is an incoherent dream".[55] It is very unlikely for an individual to invent a valuable lifestyle or practice. For example, art is a social phenomenon: it requires art schools, an esthetic tradition, learning of techniques and styles, an artistic education enabling the individual to appreciate beauty... The "artistic lifestyle" requires a social framework.[56] And the same is true of other valuable ways of life—or valuable aspects of life—mentioned by Raz, like family bonds, or national belonging: "Personal friendships, marital relations, one's loyalty and sense of pride in one's workplace or one's country, are among the most valuable and rewarding aspects of many people's lives. Such relations are culturally determined forms of human interaction and it is through learning their value that one acquires a sense [...] of the possibilities of one's life".[57]

To designate such valuable life patterns, Raz employs the term "social forms", rather than "practices" or "conventions". "Social forms" consist in conducts or lifestyles which are socially shaped or regulated, even if they allow for a certain degree of internal flexibility. Social forms, according to Raz, do not just comprise conducts, but also "shared beliefs, folklore, high culture, collectively shared metaphors and

[52]Raz (1986), 381 and 417.

[53]"The conditions of autonomy are complex and consist of three distinct components: appropriate mental abilities, an adequate range of options, and independence" Raz (1986), 372. Cf. Raz (1986), 408.

[54]J Raz (1986), 204. "If having an autonomous life is an ultimate value, then having a sufficient range of acceptable options is of intrinsic value [...]" Raz (1986), 205.

[55]Raz (1986), 155.

[56]Vid. Raz (1986), 201.

[57]Raz (1986), 216,

imagination, and so on".[58] By participating in such social forms, individuals "will be pursuing their own goals, enhancing their own well-being, and also serving their communities, and generally living in a morally worthy way".[59]

Raz's "social forms" might include, for example, professions,[60] artistic and recreational activities endowed with a communitarian dimension (singing by yourself in the shower is not a social form; belonging to a choir is),[61] as well as institutions like marriage. All these fill the individual's life with meaning: they assign the individual long-term aims ("comprehensive goals"), creating "new ways of succeeding and new ways of failing".[62] To be a doctor, to be an artist, to be a husband and father… are possibilities of accomplishment that would not exist, would they not be sustained by social forms. Social forms provide "second order goals", namely, "goals about what kind of goals people should have"[63]: prospects and commitments which, while demanding sacrifice,[64] also endow life with unity of purpose and teleological coherence. The life of the individual thus acquires a consistency which it would lack if it consisted in sheeer improvisation and whim.[65]

---

[58]Raz (1986), 311.

[59]Raz (1986), 319.

[60]But Raz is thinking of professions endowed with a certain institutional-corporative structure: "Some comprehensive goals require social institutions for their very possibility. One cannot pursue a legal career except in a society governed by law, one cannot practise medicine except in a society in which such a practice is recognized [...]. It takes more than medical knowledge or curing powers to [be a medical doctor]. A doctor participates in a complex social form, involving general recognition of a medical practice, its social organization, its status in society, its conventions about which matters are addressed to doctors and which not [...]" Raz (1986), 311.

[61]"Activities which do not appear to acquire their character from social forms in fact do so. Bird watching seems to be what any sighted person in the vicinity of birds can do. And so he can, except that that would not make him into a bird watcher. He can be that only in a society where this [...] is recognized as a leisure activity, and which furthermore shares certain attitudes to natural life generally" Raz (1986), 311.

[62]"Having embraced certain goals and commitments we create new ways of succeeding and new ways of failing. In embracing goals and commitments, in coming to care about one thing or another, one progressively gives shape to one's life, determines what would count as a successful life and what would be a failure" Raz (1986), 387.

[63]Raz (1986), 294.

[64]"They are normally goals others can help him reach, by providing the right environment, the right conditions. But they cannot reach them for him" Raz (1986), 306.

[65]"Our notion of a successful life is of a life well spent, of a life of achievement, of handicaps overcome, talents widely used, of good judgment in the conduct of one's affairs, of warm and trusting relations with family and friends, stormy and enthusiastic involvement with other people [...] and so on" Raz (1986), 306. Compare to Charles Murray: "Once you start to think through the kinds of accomplishments that do lead people to reach old age satisfied with who they have been and what they have done, you will find that the accomplishments have three things in common. First, the source of satisfaction involves something important [...]. Second, the source of satisfaction has involved effort, probably over an extended period of time. The cliché "Nothing worth having comes easily" is true. Third, some level of personal responsibility for the outcome is essential [...]. You have to be able to say, "If it hadn't been for me, this good thing wouldn't have come about as it did". There aren't many activities in life that satisfy the three requirements [...]. Having been a

Some social forms, like monasticism, imply a thoroughly regulated lifestyle. Most of them, however, permit a certain internal flexibility and reversibility: "They allow for variations [...] and some of the conventions governing their form delineate the [...] circumstances and reasons which are legitimate occasions for changing one's mind and abandoning the pursuit, without any whiff or failure in the air".[66]

Raz underlines, however, that internal flexibility is limited.[67] And he suggests that some bedrock social forms like marriage are in jeopardy of extinction precisely because their threshold of internal flexilibity or redefinability has been overstepped. He is referring, specifically, to innovations such as "communal families", "open marriages" and "homosexual families": "It is too early to have a clear view of the consequences of these developments. But one thing can be said with certainty. They will not be confined to adding new options to the familiar heterosexual monogamous family. They will change the character of that family. If these changes take root in our culture then the familiar marriage relations will disappear".[68]

This erosion of some social forms raises the question of the state's responsibility in their preservation. Some basic social forms—typically, marriage, the example Raz recurrently invokes—have historically been strengthened and promoted by legal regulation.[69] The institutionalization of some social forms has facilitated their acceptance and generalization: "Monogamy [...] cannot be practised by an individual. It requires a culture which recognizes it, and which supports it through the public's attitude and through its formal institutions".[70]

Now, if the state provides institutional support to social forms which constitute pathways of moralization and flourishing for individuals, it would seem to follow that

---

good parent qualifies. Being part of a good marriage qualifies. Having done your job well qualifies. Having been a faithful adherent of one of the great religions qualifies. Having been a good neighbor and good friend to those whose lives intersected with yours qualifies" (Murray (2012), 258.

[66] Raz (1986), 384.

[67] "It remains the case that every pursuit has its form, according to which certain modes of behaviour are disloyal to it, incompatible with dedication to it" Raz (1986), 384.

[68] Raz (1986), 393. Raz seems to diagonse a general tendency to internal corrosion of many social forms due to an excessive "voluntarization" of its features. Every social form implies a balance between the rigidity of its objective structure and a margin of individual appreciation and interpretation. This balance is breaking owing to oversubjectivization (for example, "each couple has a right to understand marriage as it sees fit and practise it accordingly"). A threshold of recognizability is overstepped, that beyond which "a Ball is no longer a Ball" (Jane Austen's *Pride and Prejudice*: "I should like Balls infinitely better if they were carried on in a different manner", said Caroline Bingley, "it would surely be much more rational if conversation instead of dancing made the order of the day"; "Much more rational, I dare say", replied her brother, "but it would not be near so much like a Ball"). The absolutization of individual autonomy would involve the withering away of social forms: "It would be a mistake to think that those who believe, as I do, in the value of personal autonomy necessarily desire the extension of personal choice in all relationships and pursuits. They may consistently with their belief in personal autonomy wish to see an end to this process, or even its reversal" Raz (1986), 394.

[69] "It is clear that, in giving legal recognition and public status to a particular form of sexual union and not to others, contemporary states encourage their citizens to live one sort of life rather than another" Mulhall and Swift (1994), 254.

[70] Raz (1986), 162.

antiperfectionists are wrong. Wherever there have been institutions like marriage—that is to say, virtually everywhere—there has been as well a perfectionist involvement of the state in mores and morals. The legal regulation of social forms "facilitates their use by members of the community who wish to do so" and helps transmit "belief in their value".[71] The withering away of such regulation—or a deviated regulation that would denature the social form concerned—would threaten the survival of valuable institutions like marriage: "Antiperfectionism [...] would undermine the chances of survival of many cherished aspects of our culture".[72]

Therefore, the state, to Raz's mind, should encourage its citizens to practise morally valuable ways of life.[73] Such acknowledgement means the overcoming of the antiperfectionist tenet of state neutrality with regard to conceptions of the good, that is, the claim that "implementation and promotion of ideals of the good life [...] are not a legitimate matter for governmental action".[74]

Antiperfectionism rests on two premises: (1) autonomy is inherently valuable, and (2) we cannot trust the state for the promotion of the good life (because there is no such thing as a "true" conception of the good, or because, even if there is, we cannot expect the state will be able to identify it and promote it).[75] We have already explained that, for Raz, autonomy is not unconditionally valuable. And he does not believe the identification of "the good" to be more unlikely than that of "the right" (namely, that of behavior compatible with the freedom of others).[76] Now then, we all agree that the state is competent to determine and enforce compliance with "the

---

[71] "Perfectionist political action may be taken in support of social institutions which enjoy unanimous support in the community, in order to give them formal recognition, bring legal and administrative arrangements into line with them, facilitate their use by members of the community who wish to do so, and encourage the transmission of belief in their value to future generations" Raz (1986), 161.

[72] Raz (1986), 162.

[73] The weakest point in Raz's argument is, probably, the excessive vagueness of the category of "social forms". Mulhall and Swift have a point when they criticise this: "It is true that some valuable social forms may derive part of their significance from the very fact that they are endorsed or recognized by the state. It is arguable that part of what makes marriage the institution that it is in our culture is precisely the fact that it is the form of sexual union that enjoys official state support and encouragement [...]. [But] Even if it were the case that opera, for example, would not survive without state subsidy, and even if opera is one of the most valuable and cherished social forms currently available to people, it would be hard to argue that a society without opera fails to provide its members with an adequate range of valuable options from which to choose" Mulhall and Swift (1994), 276–277.

[74] "The anti-perfectionist principle claims that implementation and promotion of ideals of the good life [...] are not a legitimate matter for governmental action" (Raz, op.cit., p. 110).

[75] "Even if there is no reason in principle why judgements about the art of life are more likely to be wrong than judgements about people's rights and duties, might we not think that governments are not to be trusted to get them right?" Mulhall and Swift (1994), p. 258.

[76] "There is, for someone espousing [...] [antiperfectionist] liberalism, a distinction between two kinds of moral judgement: judgements about the good life, which are subjective and should be kept out of politics, and judgements about the rights and duties that people have and that should govern their relations with one another, which are objective and are properly protected and enforced by the coercive apparatus of the liberal state. Raz is deeply suspicious of the idea that these two types of judgement are different [...]. [In his opinion] we should be no more sceptical with regard to

right" (the rights and duties of citizens): "The question is: is there reason to think that one is more likely to be wrong about the character of the good life than about the sort of moral considerations which all agree should influence political action, such as the right to life, to free expression, or free religious worship? I know of no such arguments".[77]

Therefore, just like the state ensures "the right" (the rights of citizens), nothing precludes it from contributing to the realization of "the good" as well.[78] The state can contribute to the preservation of a social environment where morally valuable options abound, and where morally repugnant options do not proliferate. The state should encourage virtue and disencourage vice.[79]

In so doing, the state does not destroy the autonomy of citizens, but, on the contrary, it guarantees the conditions required by valuable autonomy[80]: "Autonomous life is valuable only if it is spent in the pursuit of acceptable and valuable projects and relationships. The autonomy principle permits and even requires governments to create morally valuable opportunities, and to eliminate repugnant ones".[81]

Now then, if the goal is to ensure the conditions of valuable autonomy, the means employed should not imply the suppression of autonomy, that is, they should not be coercive. Genuine virtue must be chosen voluntarily. It is intrinsically impossible to "compel someone to be virtuous"—coercive adoption of virtuous behavior would lack moral value—but it is possible to promote social conditions favouring the free choice of virtue.[82] Raz commends the use of encouragement and disencouragement, rather than that of coercion and prohibition: "Perfectionist goals need not be pursued by the use of coercion. A government which subsidizes certain activities, rewards their pursuit, and advertises their availability encourages those activities without using coercion".[83] The state can convey pegadogical-moral messages by subsidizing—or, conversely, by taxing more or less intensively—certain activities, by burocratically facilitating certain initiatives, by awarding honors and distinctions

judgements that concern the art of life than with regard to those that concern, for example, the rights of others" Mulhall and Swift (1994), 257.

[77]Raz (1986), 160.

[78]"Since autonomy is valuable only if it is directed at the good, it supplies no reason to provide, nor any reason to protect, worthless let alone bad options" Raz (1986), 411.

[79]"Governments should promote the moral quality of the life of those whose lives and actions they can affect" Raz (1986), 415.

[80]"The conditions of autonomy [...] include the existence of a public culture which maintains and encourages the cultivation of certain tastes and the undertaking of certain pursuits" Raz (1986), 421–422.

[81]Raz (1986), 417.

[82]"Given that people should lead autonomous lives, the state cannot force them to be moral. All it can do is to provide the conditions of autonomy [...]. Seen in this light, the harm principle allows perfectionist policies so long as they do not require resort to coercion" Raz (1986), 420.

[83]Raz (1986), 417. "The perfectionism advocated here [...] [upholds] measures which encourage the adoption of valuable ends and discourage the pursuit of base ones [...]. The perfectionist policies must be compatible with respect for autonomy" Raz (1986), 423.

to those who excell in virtuous pursuits[84]... This priority given to incentivation—rather than coercion—constitutes, in Raz's view, the distintive feature of liberal perfectionism,[85] as opposed to forms of perfectionism which are less respectful of individual freedom: "[My proposals] differ from many collectivist doctrines in that they do not lead to strong centralist government [...]. The role of government is extensive and important, but confined to maintaining framework conditions conducive to pluralism and autonomy".[86]

Another liberal aspect of Raz's perfectionism is its compatibility with (some degree of) moral pluralism. What the state must promote is not a specific way of life—one and only one[87]—but a social atmosphere in which various morally valuable options thrive. There are many valuable lifestyles (but not all lifestyles are): "Perfectionism is compatible with moral pluralism, which allows that there are many morally valuable forms of life which are incompatible with each other".[88] "Value-pluralism means that there will be a multiplicity of valuable options to choose from, and favourable conditions of choice".[89] Vicious ways of life should be disencouraged.

Finally, Raz, like Lord Devlin, concedes that perfectionist liberalism is an abstract doctrine the implementation of which will greatly depend on factual circumstances such as the moral reliability of the government in place (what if the government errs in its understanding of the good?),[90] the likelihood of social reluctance to legal pedagogy, etc.: "The pursuit of full-blooded perfectionist policies [...] is likely, in many countries if not in all, to backfire by arousing popular resistence leading to civil strife. In such circumstances, compromise is the order of the day. There is no abstract doctrine which can delineate what the terms of the compromise should be. All one

[84]"Not all perfectionist action is a coercive imposition of a style of life. Much of it could be encouraging, and facilitating action of the desired kind, or discouraging undesired modes of behaviour. Conferring honours on creative and performing artists, giving grants or loans to people who start community centres, taxing one kind of leisure activity, e.g., hunting, more heavily than others [...]" Raz (1986), 161.

[85]Critics of Raz argue that fiscal encouragement, for example, is coercive too, as explained by Mulhall and Swift: "If you do not cut your hair, we will send you to prison" would seem to be a paradigm of a coercive threat. What is the difference, the antiperfectionist might ask, between this [...] and the statement "If you do not stop hunting, the state will tax you heavily"? [...] Clearly, the penalty for non-compliance is greater in the first case than in the second, but it is not obvious that it is a difference of quantity rather than of quality [...]" (Mulhall and Swift 1994), 262.

[86]Raz (1986), 427.

[87]"There is no single pattern anyone can identify as *the* proper model of a human life, not because there is no such thing as good and bad, but because there are many goods" George (1993), 39.

[88]Raz (1986), 161. "Such a [perfectionist] morality presupposes competitive pluralism. That is, it presupposes that people should have available to them many forms and styles of life incorporating incompatible virtues [...]. [My doctrine] does not protect nor does it require any individual option. It merely requires the availability of an adequate range of options" Raz (1986), 425.

[89]Raz (1986), 412.

[90]"But the general effect of the risk of failure cannot lead to anti-perfectionism. It leads to general caution" Raz (1986), 160.

can say is that it will confine perfectionist measures to matters which command a large measure of social consensus [...]".[91]

5 Robert P. George and the Role of Government in the Maintenance of Moral Ecology

Will Kymlicka, referring to Rawls, raised an objection to perfectionism (whether that of a communitarian like Taylor or Macintyre, or that of a liberal like Raz) which merits consideration. It is not true, Kymlicka argues, that all antiperfectionists are relativists: many of them are ethical cognitivists and, therefore, are persuaded that there are objectively good ways of life and others which are not, and that freedom is valuable only if exercised in the pursuit of the former. They differ from perfectionists, however, in the conviction that the state be an agent properly qualified for encouraging the choice of the good. In their view, "free competition"—with no state interference—between the various lifestyles should be allowed, and the most valuable options will eventually win: "Good ways of life will in fact sustain themselves in the cultural marketplace without state assistance, because in conditions of freedom, people are able to recognize the worth of good ways of life, and will support them".[92]

Two counterarguments can be raised. First, total governmental neutrality is impossible: as long as there is taxation, for example, a choice will have to be made as to which activities should be taxed; as long as there is a family law, you will have to choose which kind of family unit (monogamous or polygamous?, heterosexual or homosexual as well?, dissoluble or indissoluble, and which requirements for divorce?) is to be institutionalized and promoted, etc. Robert P. George has proposed numerous examples of legal encouragement/disencouragment of certain conducts and attitudes: laws of the 60 s, for example, delegitimized racist conduct in the USA[93]; nowadays, "LGTB rights" laws are regulating more and more coercively attitudes regarding homosexuality; public health campaigns incentivate sport practice, disencourage tobacco use or "unprotected sex", etc. And the changes in family

[91] Raz (1986), 429.

[92] Kymlicka (2002), 247. "Freedom of speech and association allows each group to pursue and advertise its way of life, and those ways of life that are unworthy will have difficulty attracting adherents. Since individuals are free to choose between competing conceptions of the good life, liberal neutrality creates a marketplace of ideas, as it were [...]" Kymlicka (2002), 248.

[93] "It is an evident fact that laws regularly, and often profoundly, affect notions in society about what is morally acceptable, forbidden and required [...]. For example, American society is very different today from what it was thirty-five years ago [that is, in 1957] because many people's moral views and attitudes toward race have changed dramatically. Any account of this transformation that failed to note the significance of both the decision of the Supreme Court of the United States in *Brown v. Topeka Board of Education* in 1954 and the Federal Civil Rights Act of 1964 in shaping American perceptions of the morality of, say, forced segregation or interracial marriage would seem naïve" George (1993), 2–3.

law—for example, the introduction of no fault divorce or gay marriage—definitely have an impact on the mores and moral beliefs.

Second, "fair competition among lifestyles" is of itself impossible, since the competition is unbalanced: non-virtuous ways of life play the game, as it were, with the advantage of appearing superficially attractive and powerfully tempting. Vice is more seductive than virtue. The hedonistic-permissive lifestyle will always have the most chances to win, if it is to "compete freely" with the virtuous, austere, temperate ways. Virtue only gets some chance of winning if it is "favoured by the referee". Virtue cannot beat vice in a fair game.

Robert P. George concedes that laws cannot "make men moral" directly: "Laws can compel outward behavior, not internal acts of the will; therefore, they cannot compel people to realize moral goods".[94] He also grants that the primary responsibility for the moral education of people pertains, not to the government, but to families, churches, cultural associations and other entities of civil society.

Nevertheless, we should not gloss over a point stressed by Raz as well: families, churches, etc. could prove insufficient[95]: they might turn out to be incapable of transmitting values in a cultural environment where incitement to vice is pervasive. It is a fact well known by parents who fail in the moral education of teenagers who are constantly exposed to a popular culture disseminating the much more alluring message of "enjoy yourself, you only live once", etc..[96] The state is more powerful than those entities, and it could be reasonable to assign it a subsidiary role in moral pedagogy. George goes further than Raz: the responsibility of the state in the preservation of a healthy "moral ecology" may include the resort to prohibitions—not merely disencouragement—of certain morally toxic activities, like prostitution or the production and dissemination of pornographic material: "People become morally bad by yielding to vice; and they can be protected from the corrupting influence of powerfully seductive vices by laws that prohibit them [...] and prevent them from flourishing in the community [...]. [S]uch laws can protect people from strong temptations and inducements to vice. To the extent that morals laws help to preserve the quality of the moral environment, they protect people from moral harm [...]. A good moral ecology benefits people by encouraging and supporting their efforts to be good; a bad moral ecology harms people by offering them opportunities and

[94]George (1993), 44.

[95]Not least because families are increasingly volatile and churches become, at least in Europe, more and more desserted. Kymlicka argues that liberals must trust civil society (families, associations, etc.) as "perfecting agent": "The dispute should perhaps be seen as a choice, not between perfectionism and neutrality, but between social perfectionism and state perfectionism" Kymlicka (2002), 248. However, sociologists have ascertained a clear decline, not only of families and churches, but also of civic associations, neighbourhood activities, etc. Robert Putnam diagnosed this phenomenon, focusing on American society: Putnam (2000).

[96]"Even people who themselves stand fast in the face of powerful temptations may find their best efforts to instill in their children a sense of decency and moral integrity thwarted by a moral environment filled with activities and images or representations which, in the unfashionable but accurate phrase of the common law, "tend to corrupt and deprave" George (1993), 45–46.

inducements to things that are wicked. A physical environment marred by pollution jeopardizes people's physical health; a social environment abounding in vice threatens their moral well-being and integrity".[97]

Thus, from Aristotle and Saint Augustin all the way to Joseph Raz and Robert P. George, an important tradition of thinking has upheld a claim which, however "bigot" it may sound in present times, is actually quite obvious: that law and state inevitably have a profound influence on a society's mores; and that, therefore, it is vital that such influence should be as healthy and positive as possible.[98]

References

Aristotle (1999) Politics. English edition: B Jowett Batoche books. Kitchener

Aristotle (2009) Nicomachean ethics. English edition: Ross WD, Brown L. Oxford University Press

Contreras FJ (2014) Los derechos humanos como versión moderna de la ley natural (III). In: Contreras FJ (ed) El sentido de la libertad: Historia y vigencia de la idea de ley natural. Stella Maris, Barcelona

Devlin P (1989) Morals and the criminal law. In: Devlin P (ed) The enforcement of morals. Oxford University Press, Oxford

George RP (1993) Making men moral: civil liberties and public morality. Clarendon Press, Oxford

Hart HLA (1978) Law, liberty and morality [1963]. Oxford University Press, Oxford

Kuby G (2013) Die globale sexuelle Revolution: Zerstörung der Freiheit im Namen der Freiheit. Fe, Regensburg

Kymlicka W (2002) Contemporary political philosophy: an introduction, 2nd edn. Oxford University Press, Oxford

Macintyre A (1981) After virtue. Duckworth, London

Mill JS (2006) On liberty [1859]. Penguin Classics, Cambridge

Mulhall S, Swift A (1994) Liberals and communitarians. Blackwell, Oxford

Murray C (2012) Coming apart: the state of white America, 1960–2010. Random House, London

Nagel T (1973) Rawls on Justice. Philosop Rev 82:220

Putnam RD (2000) Bowling alone: the collapse and revival of American community. Simon & Schuster, New York

Rawls J (1971) A theory of justice. Harvard University Press, Cambridge (Mass.)

Rawls J (1993) Political Liberalism. Columbia University Press, New York

Raz J (1986) The morality of freedom. Clarendon Press, Oxford

Scruton R (2015) How to be a conservative. Bloomsbury, London-New York

Taylor C (1979) Hegel and modern society. Cambridge University Press, Cambridge

de Vitoria F (1975) Relecciones sobre los indios y el Derecho de guerra [1538-39]. Espasa-Calpe, Madrid

[97] George (1993), 44–45.

[98] To acknowledge this is not tantamount to regarding "morals laws" as a magic cure-all: "It is a mistake to suppose that laws by themselves are sufficient to establish and maintain a healthy moral ecology. It is equally a mistake to suppose, however, that laws have nothing to contribute to that goal [...]. Laws can powerfully reinforce, or fail to reinforce, the teachings of parents and families, teachers and schools, religious leaders and communities, and other persons and institutions who have the leading roles in the moral formation of each new generation" George (1993), 46.

Build and Restore Good Human Relationships. Overcoming the Retributive Paradigm as a Key Issue for the Theory of Justice

Luciano Eusebi

Abstract The paper assumes as a central ethical necessity of our time the farewell to a model of justice based on mutual behaviours correspondence: according to which it's just that the negative judgment towards the other is followed by the action against him, that is to say in order to overwhelming him. This, in fact, has led to theorize the logic of conflict as natural in human affairs: for which every duality implies an opposition. Now, however, this logic entails the risk of total destruction. The aim of the paper is, therefore, to highlight how different sectors of human relationships (between people, parties or States) remain largely marked out by a retributive model of justice. It's proposed a vision of justice intended as building and restoring the good in the face of evil, which can give rise to good life conditions and relationships between all involved subjects.

1 Duality as a Conflict?

The human condition is composed of plural situations and not of solitary unisubsistent realities, skilled to avoid the experience of the border.[1] This is an existential datum, so that it would represent a forcing to regard it as something of pathological nature: considering, in this way, mandatory to elide it, in the most different contexts and at any cost. On better grounds, that datum assumes an anthropological value, in which should rather be found a reading key, or if you want a chance, so that everyone's life—«both as an individual and in the social groups where human personality is

[1] It's well known, in this sense, the Hannah Arendt's phrase: «Not Man but men inhabit this planet. Plurality is the law of the earth» (Arendt 1978, 19).

Translation from Italian by Rosa Palavera, Ph.D. at the Catholic University of the Sacred Heart of Milan.

L. Eusebi (✉)
Catholic University of the Sacred Heart of Milan, Milan, Italy
e-mail: luciano.eusebi@unicatt.it

A. Masferrer (ed.), *Criminal Law and Morality in the Age of Consent*, Ius Gentium: Comparative Perspectives on Law and Justice 84,
https://doi.org/10.1007/978-3-030-64163-4_9

expressed» (in that terms states the Article 2 of the Italian Constitution)—could achieve self-fulfilment in a complete way. It is no coincidence, moreover, that almost nothing in the human environment can be built in solitude. As it cannot be considered a coincidence that life has manifested itself, over time, through the complementary duality of masculine and feminine, to whose relationship has been reconnected, along the centuries, even the reproduction of the human family.

Yet, one of the most culturally rooted ideas in our culture is that every plural situation, every *duality* implies—potentially, if not necessarily—a conflict. So much so that, for instance, Hegel's own intuition, under which each individual reality must be read in relational—*dialectical*—terms in respect to realities it historically interacts with (and, therefore, in its overcoming through accessing together, by this way, a more authentic and fuller form of expression), has turned out to be perceived not as a need for mediation, dialogue or integration among these realities, but as the inevitability of competition, that is to say rivalry or struggle, among them: with the result of the *prevailing* of one—that is, of his victory—and the detriment of the other (but always aware of a subsequent contraposition and, therefore, of further wounds, which hardly heal).

Thus, the awareness about the ubiquity of the *border*—which is the place where each personal or social human story sees its cultural paths, interests, and projects approaching and almost overlapping to those of the *other*[2]—has been, for the most part, transformed into the construction of *confines*, sheltered by which periods of truce can only disguise a permanent hostility.

In this scenario, becomes clear the fundamental ethical question of every era: what does the existential reality of others—individuals, entire people or any of the aforementioned «social formations» (political, economic, religious …)—represent for each of us or for human aggregations in which we recognise ourselves? The answer choice is a radical one. Does the presence of the *other* constitute an *obstacle* to our own realization, because his existence does not allow the unlimited expansion of the desire for access to goods or the purpose of conforming the social arrangements to unilaterally defined and unquestionable rules (so that the interest for the *other* will depend only on his functionality with respect to the pursuit of such objectives)? Or, does only the search for the good that can *bond* and be so, therefore, also *for the other*—beyond the sphere of the *do ut des*—open to a non-ephemeral existential realization and to conditions of mutual security (although the relationship with the *other* could be, without a doubt, difficult)?

Today, the question assumes unprecedented impellence profiles. Since forever, truly, the rather widespread option for the first alternative has meant suffering and death, for the unsuccessful ones but also for not so few of the enlisted among the ranks of the winners. Tragedies in large part left hidden in the sphere of a solitary and incommunicable pain, which from the outside, even when a narration is attempted, can only be evoked in a blurry way: history—it cannot be otherwise—reflects the point of view of survivors, who (especially if they didn't gain any profit from that) must anyway try to give meaning to the hostile acts that saw them involved. And

[2]Hence the expression of an ancient yearning: «*He grants peace to your borders*» (*Psalm* 147:14).

yet there is a new and epoch-making fact: since 1945, the prospect of conflict as an ordinary dynamic of human relationships had been able to lead as a result, in its extreme manifestation, that after a war clash *there are no more survivors*, nor, therefore, winners. Since that time, in fact, we have been having weapons for the total destruction of humanity. Nor do the major world powers seem able to ensure reliable control over the availability of access to such death instruments.

Indeed, the orientation which merely coined criteria of malleable acceptability for the recourse to a war consequently considered to be *just*, but did not challenge the underlying relational model, reveals itself, today, as dramatically obsolete, as, unfortunately, still vital.[3] If, after 1989, someone had imagined the end of history (as *a fil rouge* of armed oppositions), and this following the facts icastically highlighted by the fall of the Berlin Wall,[4] it has been inescapable to ascertain, immediately afterwards, the reaffirmation in great style of political and military strategies of competition and domination, favoured precisely by the loosening of deterrence related to reciprocal antagonism (which today, not by chance, risks to be re-proposed) between the two main holders of the war arsenals.

Therefore today, as never before, the fundamental moral question on how to conceive the relationship with the *other* pertains not only to the relational criteria between individuals or social groups, but to the very possibility of a future for humanity.

2 Justice Does not Consist in Behaviour Correspondence

What has just been said about the extent to which war justifying criteria, in the course of history, much beyond the perimeter of legitimate self-defence (non-artificial) contexts, have been constructed—as much as in criminal systems it was considered *just* and fair to conceive the answer to crime in terms of a *malum pro malo*, so that modern preventive theories (apart from the hopeful, laborious work in progress of *restorative justice*) have not abandoned at all the scheme of *prevention through retribution*—induces to reflect, however, about the existing connections between the moral problem, as so far identified, and the law.

The conflictual pattern, according to which the profiles of negativity recognized in the action of the other demand to be addressed acting, reciprocally, *against* the other, that is, for his disadvantage (and thus pursuing his defeat, submission, economic ruin, social expulsion, suffering, etc.), has found a decisive support for its success, in fact, precisely in the theory of law. Given that the archetype of justice, in accordance with the Western judicial model spread throughout the world, is commonly identified through the image of the scales, which, far more than an expression of impartiality and evaluating balance, refers—since ancient Greece—to the idea of correspondence (according to a secularized interpretation, we could say, of the *psychostasis* known

[3]Eusebi(2010), 109 ff.

[4]Fukuyama (1992).

by Egyptian and Persian culture): one must respond to the *positive* with the *positive*, but the *negative* must follow the *negative.*

As a matter of fact, however, the encounter with the negative constitutes the ordinariness, and not the exception, in the human story: at least, since everyone must admit some negative aspects regarding the choices of his own life. So, if the criterion of acting towards the *other* is given by the correspondence with respect to the positive or negative judgment given to him, there may always be an argument, or rather an *alibi*, which justifies acting negatively towards the *other*, being a single individual or a collective subject. This allows to well understand how that justice model acts as a *multiplier* of the negative in human relationships: all the more considering the frequency with which, today like yesterday, the *other* is negatively judged, not on the basis of an fair assessment of the ethics of his conduct, but, *tout court*, in relation to the contrast of his actions, if not of his own existence, with respect to the interests of the judging one.

The law has certainly enforced important profiles of the protection of the person in the context of conflictual relations, destined, in the absence of rules, to the pre-eminence of the logic of force. And this has happened, in modern times but not only, attributing recognition to human rights considered to be at least tendentially inviolable, which fulfilment has been pursued, with more or less conviction or success, through both domestic laws, and (to a lower extent) relevant norms in supranational relationships.

However, legal systems have not perceived that the although commendable endeavour of contrasting force (the law is born to support claims of *weak* ones, because the force is well able to autonomously defend itself) still remained referenced—assuming in fact, against it, mere mediating intentions—to a background juridical theory broadly fostered by the concept of correspondence. As vividly shown by the history of criminal law, which remained anchored (with still marginal exceptions) to *retributive* criteria for the determination of sanctions to be imposed at the end of the trial, but introduced rules that would like to *humanize* the subsequent execution, orienting it, at least according to the statements of principle, to the social reintegration of the condemned and allowing, in the course of it, forms of partial modification of the contents of the sentence.

The law—which, like every other sector of human action, responds to a moral examination referring to the specific area of its competence (without prejudice, therefore, for the circumstance that not every moral claim can require legal coverage)—acted as a spokesman, in other words, for instances of moralization of human relationships. But it has avoided a critical evaluation of the morality of that relational model, represented by the image of the scales, which, in the common sense, embodies the very idea of lawfulness: largely assuming it as a given premise and crediting it as unquestionable from an ethical point of view.

Thus, it may have happened that the *upright* idea that human beings should symmetrically behave towards each other according to the mutual recognition of their equal dignity has been transformed into the idea that the actual or alleged transgressions of this precept seek reaction in terms of correspondence. So, the golden rule, «*whatever you wish that others would do to you, do also to them*» (expressed in *Matthew* 7:12 in its active form, rather than as a negative command), has turned into a very different rule, according to which *whatever [you think] men have done to you, it is right that you do to them too*. Except for the attribution to the law of the duty to mitigate, in the aforementioned sense, the most bitter outcomes of a similar (not abjured) operating scheme: which happens, for instance, in determining punishments as a temporal *quantum* of detention instead of applying the law of retaliation; and, in this way, safeguarding the criminal law from a too evident perception of its continuity with the paradigm of revenge.

The fundamental problem of law is not the eventuality of its transgression, but that evil can take possession of norms. And the fact that this has happened in a sensational manner with regard, for instance, to the European dictatorships of the twentieth century does not exempt from the duty to read, even in contexts in which the law has represented and continues to represent an irreplaceable tool for human promotion and for social progress, the persistent and contradictory link between the notion of juridicity and the scheme of acting in a specular way to the positive or negative appreciation attributed to a given individual or to a given collective subject.

Therefore, it is not a matter of devaluing the role of law as an instrument—precious and without alternatives—aimed at making possible a peaceful and, for each one, profitable coexistence: nor to neglect that, with all its limitations, the juridical norm is configured as the only unifying point of reference in social aggregations ever more diversified on the ethnic and cultural level. Rather, it is a question of freeing the theory of law from what still holds it bound to a vision of human relations founded on the delimited obligation to act according (also) to the good of the *other* only if that *other* has acted in advantage of his interlocutor. By accepting, in this sense, that the abyssal depths of cruelty that have characterized the genocides of the last century do not constitute the indecipherable, self-standing explosions of absolute evil, but the extreme outcome of that ancient woodworm of our culture that admits to acting to the detriment, until their annihilation, of the human realities to which a negative judgment has been ascribed.[5]

That such a vision represents a dangerous ballast, needing an *ab imis* rethinking, for the configuration of social or international relationships emerges, moreover, where considering the gap so often detectable between the attitude of individuals who come to find themselves (sometimes despite themselves) as counterparts and the *modus operandi*, which dominates them, of the aggregations or institutions in which they are involved.

It is quite unusual, generally speaking, that wars have been undertaken *by popular acclaim* and that the individual members of a people at war (including individual soldiers) harbour feelings of hate towards each of the *enemies* (so much so that in many military events those feelings had to be artfully fomented). And this is true even for the individual rulers who led their countries to war, with regard to the opposing rulers. But it also concerns the executioner who carried out a death sentence, and that in the past, not by chance, was used to ask (and often obtained) the pardon of the condemned one. Likewise, it can be true for the judge who, without any

[5]Bauman (1989).

subjective intent to cause harm, applies a merely payback sanction. And, indeed, it can sometimes be observed regarding the victims of a crime, to which the routine proposal of the classic legal model of reaction to the illicit act does not seem to offer, often, neither compensation, nor pacification.

If this, however, is true, then it must be recognized that there is a fundamental question of method—which challenges the theory of law—about the criteria with which we believe to face, beyond any (although meritorious) compromise, the difficulties encountered in human relationships. Not surrendering, thus, in the future, to the deemed ineludibility of conflictual logics that end up justifying to act in detriment of the *other* where the interaction with the same seems problematic and that, on this path, induce to remove, in conforming to them, the very perception of a *personal* (co)responsibility: acting this way merely because the *science of politics* or the *criminal law*—as emblematic disciplines, albeit not exclusive, of the manifestation of similar dynamics—take for granted that it should be so. Therefore, every overlapping of interests, every wrongdoing and, in general, every *duality* risks to imply the activation of hostile relations.

3 The Retaliation of Evil Does not Reactivate the Good

The list of the areas in which can be found the logic of conflicting action towards another subject reputed, in various ways, as a bearer of negativity is undoubtedly very extensive: so that the scales paradigm, also by virtue of its legal accreditation, can well rise to represent one of the most established and transversal behavioural constants in the different branches of human activity.

It must remain quite clear, however, that submitting such a paradigm to criticism does not at all mean endorsing inertia towards what manifests itself as evil. An obvious clarification, but a necessary one, because it captures a rather insidious aspect of the rooting of that paradigm in our culture: it is so acquired that simply questioning it is understood as a renunciation of the task assumedly assigned to it, that is, to prevent the supremacy of evil.

Therefore, it is not a matter of leaving the field open to evil (firmly taken the many cases in which the ascription to others of the negative is arbitrary, but also the fact that the line between light and shadow in human relationships is not traceable according to a Manichean approach). It is rather a matter of acknowledging that acting against the *other*, even if found guilty, neither erases the already done evil nor activates—even when it succeeds in ending unfair behaviours—different relational styles, oriented towards the good. This attitude, hence, does not express, through the reaction to evil, what is to be considered good, but adds evil to evil: relying on force and crediting, in this way, the assumption that the match between good and evil (*rectius*, between what will be considered good and what will be considered evil) constitutes only a matter of prevalence among belligerents; but, equally, fomenting the ancient and perverse illusion by which from the *doubling of evil*, in terms of retaliation, would spring, almost by magic, the good.

On the other hand, in order to corroborate such an acting criterion at the ethical level, the very notion of self-defence has been not infrequently expanded in an undue way, up to the point of making it an usable concept with respect to any hostile initiative towards others intended to the (supposed) protection of oneself, of a given group or of the whole society: for which, identified an enemy, every act aimed at eradicating him would be legitimate. Instead, as well known, self-defence concerns only the proportionate contrast of a *present* and not otherwise preventable aggression: that is to say, the contrast of the evil in the moment in which it is put in place against someone. Therefore, this notion certainly cannot support the idea that the prevention of the evil practicable in the future should be granted, and pursued, neutralizing or assaulting all those who are considered as possible architects of that evil (it follows, for instance, that the penalistic concept of *social defence*, even with all the ambiguities connected to its positivistic roots, has nothing in common with the concept of self-defence, nor can respond to related application criteria).

The goal of doing justice will necessarily be, then, to reactivate the good in front of the evil, in a (ubiquitous) sense that, although it may require, also when laborious, a path of reappropriation of self-direction towards the good by those who have committed the evil, does not end in the ruin of the latter and in indifference to his destiny. But acting according to justice also requires knowing how to resist the fascination of evil, especially when it appears to impose itself as a model of conduct, to the point of making hard to recognize evil as such (so that when evil seizes even the law, imposing to *do the evil*, the lantern of good ends up being left to the personal testimony of loyalty to it, despite possible costs).

Consequently, justice firstly requires to identify the evil, both in principle and in its specific and concrete manifestations. Only by making truth about evil, in fact, it can be curbed and, when committed, *overcome* (face to the committed evil, only *reconstruction* is possible). On this basis, justice is called to break, rather than to perpetuate, the insatiable chain of retaliation: with this, letting emerge, among other things, that evil does not become such because its fulfilment exposes the author himself to receive evil (while, if this does not happen, the action that we qualify *evil* would represents, for him, the good), but as it is evil *in itself*.

Obviously, it is not always easy to agree, even on the legal level, on what is evil. Although the sphere of indubitable evil is much more extensive than some theorizations would let believe. And yet, recognizing the effort of discernment, in some cases, with regard to good and evil is something far different from denying that there is an evil to recognize: because in the latter case the criterion of action will be expressed exclusively by force, that is, the ability to grant that a given behaviour, whatever it is, will be followed by the infliction of an evil.

Justice, in other words, is called to make clear that it is not the contingent eventuality of a retaliation that makes evil the evil and, therefore, that the latter represents—not only with respect to the one who has been the victim, but for the author of the evil too—a missed realization of the human, as implying openness to relationships and possibility of trust in the other's attitudes of *proximity*. So that acting according to justice brings the idea of a *liberation*, for everyone, from evil (as stated in article

3, second paragraph, of the Italian Constitution, it's a matter of «removing—*erga omnes*—the obstacles that prevent the full development of the human person»).

Hence the connection, paradoxically *natural*, between justice and forgiveness. In the sense that justice is possible only when one renounces the logic of reacting to evil by re-proposing its own contents (even if trying to legitimize them by virtue of the retaliation paradigm); and when, at the same time, one remains engaged in pursuing the result that the author of negative conducts assumes attitudes of responsibility in relation to them and returns to choose as his own an existential option in conformity to the good. Elements, these, which precisely identify the concept of forgiveness: which, equally, has nothing to do with inertia, and least of all with indifference, towards evil.

4 Multidisciplinary Contexts in Which the Retributive Paradigm is Manifested

Yet, as mentioned, conceiving the right action in terms of correspondence with the negative judgment of the *other* pervades a wide range of relationships between people. It is not just a matter of war and punishment: even ideas confrontation, in which is most evident the human condition, namely the capacity for thought and mutual listening, has often been transformed, for instance, in the identification of the one expressing different points of view as an enemy. Indeed, the need to have an enemy to give oneself an identity seems to frequently emerge. So that aggregation into groups becomes functional, in many cases, to create conflicts: in order to simplify the approach to complex problems and to avoid the challenge of putting oneself in question, or of renouncing the logic of own exclusive interest protection.

Building justice, therefore, also means abandoning, starting from the educational approach, the conviction that one's own realization depends on affirming oneself to the detriment of *others*, perceived as adversaries or competitors. But, if this is the case, asserting an identity must be completely disconnected from the perspective of imposing oneself in a conflict. Or, even better, the notion of *identity* itself should be overcome, because the only identity we have good reasons to speak of is, in fact, the human identity and, beyond it, there are always and uniquely people in search: which, no doubt, are called to live in a coherent way the paths of the good their respective itineraries have allowed them to perceive, but considering these paths as a heritage to offer, reciprocally, to the reflection of those who have beaten other paths, and not as the premise of an inescapable hostility.

The problem also arises regarding the way of understanding, today, the typical institutions of a democracy, which is the best model produced by humanity to make the comparison of opinions compatible with a profitable and peaceful organisation of social life. Objective which, however, risks to remain completely frustrated if the political debate is reduced to the reciprocal systematic denigration between the parties involved, that is to a tactic that pursues, in any way, the electoral success, raised as a goal in itself. All this facilitated by the tendencies to devalue the instruments of representative democracy, in favour of strategies seeking direct consent of the citizen through problems simplifications, which appeal to the emotional dimension, always willing to identify enemies to fight against and little inclined to demand wide scope projects. So that the very role of citizens risks being reduced to the cyclical investiture of leaderships (whose selection criteria often slip away), which proceed, in internal relations as in foreign ones, according to a domino effect of moves and countermoves responding to unilateral priorities, but without the ability, on occasion, to oppose the strongest interests. And without the courage to disrupt the "already seen", operating according to criteria of justice *for all*.

Likewise, it is a matter of managing economic relations, refusing to assume that the good of markets efficiency must consider and accept the cost of someone's succumbence: concretely, today, avoiding to consider unquestionable dynamics in which the ever-increasing profit of privileged classes, holders of economic (and not only economic) power, corresponds to the impoverishment of the other classes involved in the various fields of work activities (with related difficulties in the constitution and decent maintenance of families) and the misery—both in rich and in less developed countries—of those who remain marginalized. Trends, which history should have taught to be very dangerous even for the stability of democratic institutions (and which prove to be all the more illogical when one considers that the economic system has been proved capable of granting in the last decades, worldwide, a clear statistical improvement of both life expectancy and levels of emancipation from absolute poverty).

Again: it is only the departure from perspectives of qualifying the *other* as a negative reality, because taking charge of him would require personal or material commitment, which can act as an antidote, regarding bioethical themes, to the recurrent temptation of indifference towards the condition of existential weakness, due to illness, to the (early or advanced) phase of the life path or even simply to the scarce availability of personal economic resources.

On the other hand, the general mentality of affirming oneself through contraposition has largely become part of private relationships too: maybe more than in the past. So that, often, the attempt of a mediation intervenes only to rearrange debris of a fracture already produced, when perhaps many pains could be avoided if only the relationship with the *other* was *ab imis* liberated from the logic, sometimes even hidden to one's own conscience, of domination, of pitiless stigmatization or, in any case, of unwillingness to listen.

And that the conflict is part of the ordinary process of relationships can be also inferred from less delicate contexts: if it is true, for instance, that the vocabulary of the chronicles pertaining to sports competitions often uses, and to a large extent, terminology borrowed, by analogy, from the stereotype of war. Which, however, brings to much more concerned evaluations when considering how electronic games (that is, virtually conducted *in video* under the shield of only fictitious relationships) give vent to explicit violence, making the win coinciding with the annihilation of the *other* or similar outcomes: according to patterns that lead to internalization—especially in the psychologically frailest subjects and much more, obviously, in the pre-adolescents too frequently left alone—behavioural styles of violent self-assertion. Concerns that become more extended with regard to the way in which apparently harmless mass media products, proposed above all to the youngest ones (from fantastic sagas to cartoons), continue to spread unreal stereotypes of antinomy without nuances between the *good* and the *evil*, the *honest* one and the *bad* one, the *friend* and the *foe*, which foment the perception of the *other* as an enemy, on the basis of an inexorable judgment towards him; as well as, subsequently, the propensity to rancour and revenge.

But the impact force achieved during history by the image of justice conceived as compensation of the negative with the negative manifests itself in another extremely singular way, among many possible examples, even on the theological ground: having, so to speak, *taken possession* of the very core of the Christian faith, with all the evident consequences in terms of weakening of the cultural contribution ascribable to it. That image, indeed, has allowed to read the salvation, that Christianity bases on the death and resurrection of Jesus, as an effect of the suffering endured by Jesus himself on the cross: suffering that would have compensated, since no man but the *Son of God* could have done so, the condition of sin of the humankind, expressed by the sin of Adam, and in this way he would have reconstituted the wounded alliance of humanity with God (according to a reading, really simplified, generally referred to Saint Anselm's doctrine of *vicarious satisfaction*). But if this were the case—apart from the generosity of God, who takes upon himself, through the *Son*, the burden necessary for reconciliation—the criterion of saving action would remain the human justice classical one: to restore justice, evil must, however, be compensated with a corresponding evil.

Nothing, on closer inspection, could be more distant from what the Christian faith means to announce, despite centuries of preaching that have lingered in the described scheme. The salvation does not rely on the evil suffered by Jesus on the cross (there is no salvific gibbet): on the contrary, through the resurrection is revealed as salvific the option for good in front of evil—religiously, the testimony of *love*, in which the very being of God manifests himself—embraced by Jesus and in which his own justice is summarized (in continuity with the notion of divine salvific justice, the *tzedakah*, as it emerges in the Old Testament tradition).[6] Therefore, what can most profoundly comply—if one will, in very secular terms—with the Christian faith is the challenge, proposed to the conscience of every human being, according to which, perhaps, the only reality with a breadth wider than the extreme negative of the death is the adhesion, even when it may humanly entail a cost, to the logic of love, which is the logic of God.[7]

---

[6]Wiesnet (1980).

[7]Eusebi (2014).

5 The Role of *Restorative Justice* as a Prototype of a Cultural Reversal.

It is evident, then, that the path towards a different justice is configured as a reversal of a cultural route that invests multiple sectors of human relationships, requiring for each of them specific competences in terms of theoretical and practical elaboration. The penal system represents, moreover, the context in which the classical retributive modality of interpreting justice is manifested in the most evident way: as if it were the visible emerging part, in common perception, of a much more massive and insidious iceberg. And this is why, in the last decades, the development, throughout the world, of the hypothesis—still minoritarian, but now consolidated both as a disciplinary area in the academic setting, and through some practical implementations—of the reparative justice (i.e. *restorative justice*)[8] as an alternative tool for the management of the consequences of a crime, since it is an issue characterized by high social sensitivity, can act as a paradigm for a new approach to the overall theme of acting according to justice.

In brief, reparative justice (the term is widespread among non-Anglophones, but speaking about *restorative* justice would be more precise) expresses a very simple concept: it is a matter of responding to the crime with a project, rather than with a retaliation. An *inclusive* project: namely, able to assume meaning with respect to all the parties involved in the illicit act, that is to say *also* for its author and, therefore, his relationship with the victim and the social community. Hence overcoming the *negative for negative* scheme, ie. a sanctioning response that borrows its contents from the contents of the crime and is thought as a (presumed) good for the society resulting from a damage (*damnatio*) for the recipient: thus, according to that scheme, any effects of *recovery* of the sentenced person are, not very reasonably, sought only through forms of management or remodulation after the retributive sanction imposed at the end of the trial, which are, otherwise, difficult to be understood for public opinion because the realization of justice (and, *a fortiori*, of the preventive intentions considered relevant for society) is traced back exactly to the application of that kind of punishment.

Reparative justice, on the other hand, does not expect hypothetical outcomes useful for society, in terms of deterrence or warning, *future* and *extrinsic* with respect to the corresponding sanction traditionally applied with the conviction, but wants that the very response to the crime, already in the moment of its determination (and not only with regard to a separate executive phase), is conceived as a *fact* having *hic et nunc* a preventive value, as a concrete form of treatment of the relational fracture represented by the committed crime.

This, in the firm belief that the maintenance of general prevention does not depend on contingent mechanistic deterrence factors, but on the effectiveness of a continuous appeal to personal choices of adhesion to normative precepts with criminal relevance, an appeal that is required to manifest itself through the sanctionary apparatus too.

---

[8]Braithwaite (1989); Zehr (2014), Mannozzi and Lodigiani (2017), Mazzucato (2011).

For this reasons, acting after the fracture represented by the crime in interpersonal and social relationships in order to re-establish, as soon as possible, with regard to the offense concretely put in place, a responsible relational context—made of critical reworking, by the author, about his own anti-juridical conduct (also involving, where appropriate, the offended party), of reparative personal commitment, of resetting of his own path of life according to legality—is not important only for the social recovery of someone who has infringed the law or as a reason for an although laborious pacification, based on the recognition of the endured injustice, with regard to the victim, but also as a fundamental element of reconfirmation, in the social feeling, of the validity of the aforementioned precepts, suitable to generate discredit or doubt about the delinquent lifestyles among the affiliated to the criminal organizations. Not withholding that the paths intended to actively take distance from criminality, consisting in *doing* something, rather than merely suffering something, can be demanding and, sometimes, not without risks. As well as not neglecting, at the same time, that only through projectual responses to crime dynamics of two-way commitment between criminal agent and society can be established, allowing the society itself to return to the first the needed opportunities expendable in the civil context, of which many of the aforementioned agents have been deprived in the previous course of their lives.

Therefore, it is a matter of promoting autonomous choices complying with legality, considering personal autonomy (*freedom*) above all as a *chance* that can still be spent, even by those who have made a mistake, for the future. Whereas, instead, the retributive vision considers freedom in a merely retrospective sense: *you have freely chosen to commit evil (since your capacity to act consciously and voluntarily has not been excluded), so you deserve the sanction.* This neglects how, although recognizing the individual capacity for freedom, the range of the factors that have influenced certain life choices is knowable, but the use of freedom is not ponderable: that is, it's not ponderable what an individual, through his actions, has expressed *as fully own.* If, however, doing evil can be understood as the failure of freedom (it is really free the one who can find the resources in himself to do what his conscience indicates to him as good, even if it may imply a cost), then it is not such a matter of punishing the freedom expressed in the crime, but of creating the conditions for the abandonment—and it is, on closer inspection, a challenge that accompanies every man throughout entire life—of conditions of lack of freedom.

The indication offered by the Italian Constitution, according to which punishments «shall aim at re-educating the convicted» (Article 27, third paragraph), does not constitute, then, a mere indication of (though fundamental) humanitarian character, but a strategic choice: the really effective prevention is the one that aims to *motivate*, considering the recipient of the incriminating norms as an interlocutor from which the legal system aspires to obtain an independent choice of respect for the criminal law. Therefore, if the task of criminal law is to contribute in detaching citizens from committing crimes, this is achieved in the most credible way through what can be defined as the perspective of a *reintegrating* general prevention.

Obviously, all this does not exclude that reacting to the crime implies contrasting criminal intentions of prevarication. On the contrary, restorative justice privileges precisely the prompt intervention on the concrete practice of a criminal activity, in order to reduce its effects and to avoid its reiteration. Firmly reasserting the need for a strict intervention on the illegally achieved economic profits, as the factual observation that, facing a critical danger of major crimes reiteration or persisting links between the criminal agent and the organized crime, the recourse to the deprivation of personal freedom is hardly substitutable. Provided, nevertheless, that even such a recourse remains planned as part of a program which pursues, not only in theoretical terms, the *resocialization* of the condemned person: therefore, without excluding this objective, a priori, for anyone.[9]

Contrasting crime, however, does not imply at all acting in terms of retributive mutuality: something that, on the other hand, does not even grant certainty of sanctioning limits, since the type and extent of the sanction considered to be in conformity with the criminal offense still constitute a social convention, open to any kind of emotionality.[10] The real guarantee for the crime perpetrator against the public punitive power is rather given by the basic choice of the penal system to actually aim to achieve, within the possibly shortest time frame, the social recovery of the one who has committed crime, as also by the fact that the paths destined to do so move from a serious consideration of his life situation: according to legal principles and intervention tools set by the legislator in relation to the characteristics of the culpable fact.

Thus, even with regard to criminal themes, it is a matter of taking action according to positive projects in relation to negative facts, moving from a concrete management of the crime and its consequences in order to resew personal and social relationships, more or less profoundly wounded by the transgression of the law. Reconsidering, in this way, the very notion of *proportionality* of the punishment, on which often, in criminal matters, the jurisprudence of the European courts relies too: no longer as a quantitative correspondence between a *malum passionis* and a *malum actionis*, but as *congruity* of the sanctioning answer, also in light of similar situations, to the goal of *reintegrating* prevention.

Nor should it be overlooked that such an orientation of the sanctioning system does not only act, as has been said, in terms of general prevention, strengthening the consensus around the validity of the penal precepts, but also in terms more properly referable to the *primary* prevention. As it questions the behavioural pattern at the origin of the criminal act itself, that is the model according to which the human and existential reality of the *other* can become irrelevant compared to the pursuit of one's own objectives: if this is not considered possible for the perpetrator, it cannot even be possible for any other member of the social community.

The forms and levels of concretization of reparative justice can be different, although all of them have in common the aim of re-establishing a responsible dialogue between the legal system and the perpetrator of the crime. And it is just as well to

---

[9]Consequently, this perspective is antithetical to the theses of those who have theorized some years ago, with regard to the alleged perpetrators of terrorism-related or strongly antisocial offenses, the so-called *enemy criminal law*, implying a reduced application of the rule of law and the exclusion of the condemned one from the context of civil coexistence: on the subject, e.g., see Cancio Meliá and Gómez-Martín Díez (2006).

[10]Hegel (1996) § 218, 379.

accept such a gradualness, in order to ensure that this type of justice can realistically influence the existing criminal systems, rather than be configured as a pure ideal model completely antithetical to them, and in fact an unincisive one. So, it ranges from the relevance of repairing or restoring conducts, to prescriptive sanctions and, in particular, to any paths monitored by the social service or of therapeutic-rehabilitative nature, to work of public utility, to the re-socializing configuration of custodial sanctions effectively applied according to the canon of the *extrema ratio*, to forms of probation (e.g., the italian *messa alla prova*) that can be activated with the consent of the interested party, if adult, already in the trial phase, up to the most proper and most pregnant mode of restorative justice, which is given by *penal mediation*: through which the re-elaboration of the committed fact and the reconstitution of a responsible relational attitude by the offender (also through the autonomous proposal of a specific reparative commitment) take place in direct dialogue with the victim or with a representative of the offended legal values, so that a mutual recognition can be established between parties as subjects bound by bonds of solidarity.

This represents, in short, the objective of acting in agree to justice. According to what is made clear, once again, by the Italian Constitution, which in the first paragraph of article 3 declares that the social dignity of each person does not depend on a judgment on his «personal and social conditions», thus allowing emersion to the idea that it depends, instead, only on his own existence in life as a human being: so that, as it follows, the behaviour complying with justice in relation with each *other* should not be related to such a judgment, but must always correspond, even in the most difficult situations, to such a dignity.

References

Arendt H (1978) The life of the mind, vol. I. In: Thinking. Secker & Warburg, London.

Bauman Z (1989) Modernity and the holocaust. Basil Blackwell, Oxford

Braithwaite J (1989) Crime, shame and reintegration. Cambridge University Press

Cancio Meliá M, Gómez-Martín Díez C (eds) (2006) Derecho penal del enemigo. El discurso penal de la exclusión. Edisofer, Madrid, Buenos Aire,– Montevideo

Eusebi L (2010) Visioni della giustizia e giustificazioni della guerra. In Bresciani C, Eusebi L (eds) Ha ancora senso parlare di guerra giusta? Le recenti elaborazione della teologia morale. Dehoniane, Bologna.

Eusebi L (2014) La Chiesa e il problema della pena. Sulla risposta al negativo come sfida giuridica e teologica, La Scuola, Brescia

Fukuyama F (1992) The end of history and the last man. Free Press, New York

GWF Hegel (1821) Grundlinien der Philosophie des Rechts oder Naturrecht und Staatswissenschaft im Grundrisse. Nicolaische Buchhandlung, Berlin. Italian edition: Hegel GWF (1996) Lineamenti di filosofia del diritto (trans: Cicero V). Rusconi, Milano

Mannozzi G, Lodigiani GA (2017) La giustizia riparativa. Formanti, parole e metodi. Giappichelli, Torino

Mazzucato C (2011) Giustizia esemplare. Interlocuzione con il precetto penale e spunti di politica criminale, in Va.Aa., Studi in onore di Mario Romano. Jovene, Napoli I:407–434

Wiesnet E (1980) Die verratene Versöhnung. Zum Verhältnis von Christentum und Strafe. Patmos Verlag, Düsseldorf. Italian edition: Wiesnet E (1987) Pena e retribuzione: la riconciliazione tradita. Sul rapporto fra cristianesimo e pena (transl. Eusebi L). Giuffrè, Milano.

Zehr H (2014) The little book of restorative justice. A bestselling book by one of the founders of the movement. Good Books, New York

Paternalism and Moral Limits of Criminal Law

Luigi Cornacchia

Abstract This paper compares the paternalistic program of protecting the person from self-regarding harm or directly from moral evil for the sake of own moral integrity with some criticism about the libertarian foundation of anti-paternalism, as unable to protect the person in weakness: in particular, the spill-over effects of the 'individual-oriented' Harm Principle mediated by the *Volenti* maxim; the inadequacy of simple 'procedural' guarantees, such as the validity of consent, in order to protect human being in weakness; the question of the social acceptance of some behaviours and the problem of 'miscalculation' or 'misalignment'; the lack of capacity of the abstract concept of individual freedom to enable the social cohesion and coexistence, which are conditions of freedom too. The aim of the chapter is to reveal the current risk of transition from the respect for patient autonomy to a new paternalism, namely of the best interests indeed, that enshrines the quality of life as the main technocratic 'gold' standard, established by experts, and to highlight the moral limits of criminal law in order to offer solutions.

1 Introduction

More than sixty years after the famous Wolfenden it seems common heritage of most of the west countries of liberal tradition, that the state is not allowed to criminalize a behaviour only because of its immorality.

The debate on paternalism has often intersected such an issue, for the interference of a state or an individual with another human being, against their will, has been grounded on the idea of protecting the person from self-regarding harm (which can be intended as physical, psychic, but moral too), or directly from moral evil for the sake of his own moral integrity.

L. Cornacchia (✉)
Dipartimento di Giurisprudenza, Università degli Studi di Bergamo, Bergamo, Italia
e-mail: luigi.cornacchia@unibg.it

A. Masferrer (ed.), *Criminal Law and Morality in the Age of Consent*, Ius Gentium: Comparative Perspectives on Law and Justice 84,
https://doi.org/10.1007/978-3-030-64163-4_10

Indeed, a peculiar form of paternalism is the so called 'Moralistic legal paternalism',[1] that endorses the legitimacy of restrictions designed to protect [... an actor ...] from "moral harm."[2] The Kantian version assumes that every reasonable human being has duties to himself, which prohibit self-endangering behaviour.[3] And in the frame of the debate about punishment the account of Herbert Morris is particular, in that it emphasizes a potential and actual peculiar wrongdoer's *moral* good as a principal justification for punishment, namely the capacity to appreciate the nature of the evil involved for others and for oneself, in one's doing wrong, to feel empathy with the victim, comprehension of evil caused and remorse.[4]

Furthermore, the principle of protection of the person in weakness has clearly moral grounds, in particular it is based on the moral duty of solidarity.[5] Thus the connection of criminal law and morality has to be compared with the moral limits of criminal law as a tool to protect the person from harm to self. But the Wolfenden Report stated that "It is not... the function of the law to intervene in the private life of citizens, or to seek to enforce any particular pattern of behaviour".

My focus in this paper is to deal with some criticism about the libertarian foundation of anti-paternalism, as unable to protect the person in weakness, and to highlight some (positive and negative) current developments, which make it necessary to review issues of the debate on paternalism.

2 Main Arguments Against Paternalism: Autonomy as Core Value, Principle of no Interference, Relationship State/Citizens

The debate on paternalism has significantly decreased in the last decades, because the principle of respect for autonomy has prevailed.

Outlining the basic lines of such approach, criminal paternalism should be rejected because it's inconsistent with the most important theories of punishment and in fact is never necessary or sufficient to justify punitive intervention, because from both perspective of utility-maximization and desert is hard to legitimize punishment for harm to self (teleological aspect, or justification of punishment on the ground of own

---

[1]"...(where paternalism and moralism overlap via the dubious notion of "moral harm"): It is always a good reason in support of proposed prohibition that it is necessary to prevent *moral harm* (as opposed to physical, psychological, or economic harm) to the actor himself. Moral harm is "harm to one's character", "becoming a worse person", as opposed to harm to one's body, psyche or purse": Feinberg (1988), XX.

[2]Feinberg (1988), 16. See Dworkin (2005), 305 ff. About the two kinds of paternalism (material and moral) see Tincani (2015), 56 ff.

[3]See Maatsch (2001), 210 ff.

[4]Morris (1981), 263 ff.

[5]See Ronco (2019), 131 ff.

aim)[6]; because criminal law doesn't care about harm to self, but rather only about harm to others (aspect of the moral limits of criminal law); because the state is not allowed to a substitution of individual choices for its own, that would be an insult to the autonomy of the person (in the frame of a non-despotic relationship between state and citizens).

Three main issues typical of the liberal tradition undermine the legitimacy of the use of coercive means to compel citizens to act in their own best interests against their will. First, the principle of no interference of the state in the choices of citizens, as that are self-regarding harms: the fully voluntary choice or consent of a mature, rational and informed person concerning his own interests doesn't admit an interference of others, and certainly not a coercive intervention of the state for the person's own good. It is never legitimate for the state to impose pain, privation, or a loss of liberty on its citizens as a means of preventing them from engaging in conduct that can be predicted to bring them pain, privation, or a loss of liberty: the main reason is, that the state is not allowed to substitute its own conception of good to the free elections of the citizens, and even less to practice force to induce it. Paternalistic practises invade the space of free choices: thus it's forbidden for the state to choose, instead of the individual, what is his own good.

Second, and symmetrically, because every human being has a fundamental right to voluntarily dispose of his own life whatever the effect in terms of benefits or harms to self, paternalistic practises insult the autonomy of the person. Worth mentioning is Mill's political metaphor of autonomy as 'independence', 'legitimate rule', dominion and "sovereignty over himself", that is the ground of an absolute right to choose for himself.[7]

The third argument concerns the relationship between the state and the citizens, which is based on mutual recognition and not on domination/submission (or as a father regards his children, "…as a permanent guardian of those interests in loco parentis").[8]

3 Paternalism and Criminal Law

In the specific field of criminal law, anti-paternalism is grounded on the "Harm to Others" Principle: in the famous claim of John Stuart Mill, "the only purpose for

[6]See Hurd (2018), 280 ff.

[7]Such terms are clearly legalistic and non-utilitarian according to the opinion of Feinberg (1971), 108 with reference in footnote 5.

[8]Feinberg (1971), 105 ("a preposterous doctrine", that legitimates to treat adults as children); see also Hartmut Kreß (2017), 409, who interprets "Paternalism" as an older equivalent to "Patriarchalism"; and Birnbacher (2010), 11. "Arguably, the state lacks an appropriate (or special) relation to its citizens to be eligible to treat them paternalistically": Husak (2015), 84.

which power may be rightfully exercised over any member of a civilized community, against his will, is to prevent harm to others".[9]

According to Joel Feinbergh's account, the "Harm to others" principle mediated by the *Volenti* maxim, only the prevention of harm[10] justifies coercion.[11] Every person has a moral right to voluntarily dispose of his own life and goods whatever the damaging effects for himself: just the right to free choice ('*de jure autonomy*'), which is of value in itself.[12] Even more so, what a person consents to is not "harm". The "Harm Principle" protects the personal autonomy of the individual from the choices of other people or of the state.[13]

The first big consequence is that consent to harm is not to count as harm (consent as opposite of Harm Principle).[14]

The second aspect worthy of consideration is that the fully voluntary consent of a mature and rational human being concerning matters that affect only his own interests has a real *performative power*[15]: it means, a valid consent makes the act not simply something neutral, but rather something *worthy*.[16] Consequently, there is a duty not to interfere with other's life-plans.

4 Soft Paternalism

According the strong version of paternalism, the state is legitimate in protecting a person, against his will, from harm to self, or from the harmful consequences of his fully voluntary choices. But such intervention is an insult to autonomy: the state has a right to prevent self-regarding harmful conduct "*when and only when* that conduct is

---

[9]Mill (1859), 223 f. About the "Harm-Principle" see Feinberg (1984), 3 ff and 31 ff; in the Italian debate Donini (2008), 1546; Simester, von Hirsch (2010), 35 ff; Romano (2008), 896 ff; Forti (2006), 283 ff; Forti (2008), 43 ff; Francolini (2008a), 1; Francolini (2008b), 276; Tincani (2009), 57 ff, 60 ff; Cadoppi (2008), 83 ff; Cadoppi (2011), 223 ff; Cornacchia (2011), 239 ff; Micheletti (2011), 275 ff; Tordini Cagli (2011), 313 ff; Fiandaca (2010), 207 ff; Pulitanò (2011), 489 ff; Risicato (2011), 525 ff; Maniaci (2012).

[10]Extended to offence (such as laws against public nudity, prohibitions on public masturbation, restrictions on noise pollution, sex-segregated restrooms, visible junk collection prohibitions, and so forth): Feinberg (1985), 16 ff, 97 ff and passim.

[11]Coercive intervention such as compulsory vaccinations focus on prevention of harm to others (the spread of the disease).

[12]Feinberg (1971), 120; (1986a, b), 65.

[13]Feinberg (1984), 115 ff; (1986a, b), 11.

[14]Feinberg (1986a, b), 9 ff, 100. "The mercy-killer…, who kills the paralyzed B at B's request, is only acting as the instrument of B's will, by which B in effect kills himself" (ibidem, 177). See also von Hirsch and Neumann (2010), 81; Jakobs (1998), 14 ff, 16 (the request of mercy-killing is nothing but a way of organising own suicide based on the division of labour, with consequent imputation to the requester).

[15]"Transactional process" by Simester and von Hirsch (2011), 174 f.

[16]Critical remarks, in the context of legal moralism, have been formulated by Hurd (1996), 121 ff.

substantially nonvoluntary, or when temporary intervention is necessary to establish whether it is voluntary or not".[17]

Because it's necessary to be sure that a person genuinely consented, a temporary intervention may be appropriate in order to give him or her an adequate opportunity for reflection and reconsideration and to help implement his or her real choice: for this purpose waiting periods are needed. It's also permissible that the state intervenes to protect a person from his own ignorance or from other circumstances that render the deliberation defective.[18]

The aim of soft or weak paternalism is to protect an individual from nonvoluntary choice: therefore, such kind of intervention is legitimate because it is oriented to the safeguards of the autonomy and therefore in compliance with the harm principle.[19]

On liberal grounds, such approach is based on '*welfare-promoting*', without compromising the freedom to choose.[20] In order to achieve welfare and prevent bad consequences of own choices, the libertarians suggest models of 'situational engineering', which affect the operating preconditions of the choices (i.e., duty to install safety belts in cars; prohibition to sell pharmaceuticals without medical prescription): "it is legitimate for choice architects to try to influence people's behaviour in order to make their lives longer, healthier, and better".[21]

Furthermore, the harm principle mediated by the *Volenti* maxim in the liberal view would be sufficient to ensure the protection of persons against the choices of other people.

5 Tutelary Paternalism: The Asymmetry of Human Relationships

Such approach, developed with a complex net of distinctions, arguments and counterbalances in order to guarantee fully voluntary choices of competent, free and informed individuals, or, with the words of Joel Feinbergh, "the standard of voluntariness",[22] emphasizes the main role of autonomy in the definition of what is moral worth.

The legacy of liberal anti-paternalism is the definitive unacceptability of so called 'despotic paternalism': it occurs, when the state imposes its own idea of good to

[17]Feinberg (1986a, b), 12 f. On the famous distinction between hard and soft paternalism see *ibidem*, 98 f; (1971), 113. Concerning the sentence 242/2019 of the Italian "Corte Costituzionale" on the crime of "Suicide Aid" (Art. 580 codice penale) see Fornasari (2020), 1 ff., who argues that it would be an example of soft paternalism, compared to the sentence of the German Bundesverfassungsgericht, BVerfGE 26.2.2020.

[18]Cadoppi (2008), 114 ff; Feinberg (1986a, b), 113 ff; Simester and von Hirsch (2011), 172 f., 179, 186. See Mill (1859), 117.

[19]Feinberg (1986a, b), pp. 12 ss.

[20]Sunstein and Thaler (2003b), 175 ff; Sunstein and Thaler (2003a), 1159 ff.

[21]Thaler, Sunstein (2008), 5.

[22]Feinbergh (1971), 114.

a person, regardless or against his or her willingness, and pretends to use forcible means to induce citizens to substitute the state's conception of their good for their own. Different is the issue of tutelary paternalism (not coincident with weak or soft paternalism).[23] This last model recognises duties, based on solidarity, to place care about the protection of the person in weakness and avoid self-damage for a person, who lacks basic competence[24]: such protection is not guaranteed by the simple validity of consent, but needs to deal with the fundamental issues of the debate about paternalism and with the particular social welfare policies adopted by the state.

And indeed, the Wolfenden Report stated that "the law's function is ...to protect the citizen from what is offensive or injurious, and to provide sufficient safeguards against exploitation... of others, particularly those who are especially vulnerable because they are young, weak in body or mind, inexperienced, or in a state of special physical, official or economic dependence".[25]

So among the aims of tutelary paternalism we can mention the protection of weak people from their self-prejudicial or dangerous choices, in the case of cognitive and volitional deficiencies, or lack of information; and furthermore, the protection of weak people from other's unexpressed insidious choices—paternalism means to avoid that one person exploits the weakness, or foolishness, or old age, or recklessness of another; and, more controversial, the protection of the dignity of the person.[26]

About the notion of dignity, it is honest to recognise that this has become a very easily manipulable concept, so that it is difficult to deal with the multitude of its meaning. The objective, ontological significance brings out the sanctity and inviolability of human nature because of its dignity. The same occurs with the Kantian concept of humanity, which nobody is allowed to alienate: to exploit another human being is inherently immoral, and such argument is clearly rather moralist than paternalist.[27] Furthermore, today the individual model of dignity has become widespread, as defined by the unquestionable choices of the person: a concept, which coincides exactly with the liberal version of autonomy.

Often the two issues of human dignity and autonomy have been addressed as different, sometimes opposed. But if we intend paternalism in the meaning, of all duties of taking care of vulnerable human being, we can discover easily, alternative to the dominant understanding of autonomy and paternalism as opposites, that the principle of respect for autonomy and the principle of care, which form the basis of paternalism, are related.[28]

---

[23]Spena (2014), 1215.

[24]Garzón Valdés (1988), 165 f.

[25]Wolfenden Report, Para. 13.

[26]See Masferrer (2016), 221 ff; (2017), 494 ff.

[27]Feinberg (1971), 118: The Author underlines that "Kant was an uncompromising foe of legal paternalism".

[28]As shown in Emmanuel Lévinas's interpretation of paternity, that refers to a particular form of interpersonal relationships in which ethics of care demand of us the willingness to assume (paternalistic) responsibility for the other: paternalistic measures that really aim for the welfare of

The acknowledgement of human dignity as something inviolable and inalienable justifies rules that prohibit the enforcement of an employment contract when its terms (i.e. working time, salary) are too unfavourable for the employee; explains the ban on acts which constitute flagrant infringements of personal dignity (such as slavery and '*dwarf throwing*'); and open the debate about other critical case (hard sadomasochistic practices; gladiatorial combat).

6 A Neutral State in Moral Issues? The Duff's Relational Account

The Harm-Principle forbids the public authority to impose an incontrovertible value of moral good and requires the state to remain neutral on moral issues: it is not only a matter of limits of criminal law—as *extrema ratio*, rather the cornerstone of liberal political view, grounded in the refusal of state interference in the moral choices of citizens. Public neutrality in ethics as a guarantee of individual freedom.

Remarkable and paradoxical too is the claim to ground *in moral terms* the mentioned limits (not for nothing, *moral* limits): to prohibit self-harming acts, or to punish others for providing the means by which someone makes self-injuring choices is *morally wrong*.

The liberal approach is grounded on following axiological principle: all moral views are relative (moral relativism); nobody is entitled to impose his moral view on anyone else and, *a fortiori*, least of all the state with his power of coercion; also, laws forbidding activities that don't harm others are *immoral law*.[29]

It's clear, however, that the last propositions express moral judgements. As explained by Robert George, there are also two alternatives: if the propositions are relative, then they are not binding and everyone could share or not such statements; if the propositions are not relative,[30] they are inconsistent with the premises of the liberal approach.

Although liberalism aims to be a purely political doctrine, it can't ignore typically moral arguments. Furthermore, the principle of autonomy seems unable, without a moral foundation, to justify the preference given to some moral views of social

---

the other do not lose sight of the autonomy of the other, but, by the opposite, do preserve it (Lévinas (1982), 92 ff; (2011), 85 ff). See Aurenque (2015), 272 ff, who considers Lévinas's interpretation of paternity with its underlying ethical asymmetries consistent with the traditional understanding of the doctor-patient relationship. See also Husak (2003), 387 ff: paternalistic interferences are reasonable when they promote the conditions of personal autonomy.

[29]George (1999), 302. Joel Feinberg compares that form of ethical relativism to a "*red herring across the trail*" (Feinberg (1988), 305 ff).

[30]Joel Feinberg seems to confirm such interpretation in the "Conclusion" of "*Harmless Wrongdoing*" (as a sort of "testament" of "*The Moral Limits*"): "*My conclusion is that if there is a personal sovereignty anywhere, then it exists everywhere, in traditional societies as well as in modern pluralistic ones. Liberalism has long been associated with tolerance and caution, but about this point it must be brave enough to be dogmatic*" (Feinberg (1988), 338).

relationships with regard to individual choices: for example, in the cases of usury,[31] or protection of the worker's rights, sadomasochistic practices, gladiatorial combat,[32] whereby "the 'human spirit' of liberalism seems to be in conflict with its 'letter'".[33]

In the case of these activities or state of affairs it's really hard to find solutions consistent with a pure liberal theory based on the 'Autonomy Principle' and the "Harm to others" mediated by the *Volenti* maxim. Then the critical remarks of Antony Duff hit the mark. We can't expect, according to Duff, to constrain coercive interference to prevent self-harming actions and to find reasons to criminalise only with consent as the opposite of the Harm Principle (*volenti non fit iniuria*), or performative items, which rule out wrongfulness or make the conduct a matter of private morality which is, "in brief and crude terms, not the law's business".[34]

In the account of Duff, the pure fact of autonomy is not crucial: the key factor is "the moral significance of the object of consent, the meaning of the actions in their context, so we have to check if the behaviours "pursue ends, and express values, which we should respect",[35] it means, values of mutual respect and concern by which our collective life as a polity is supposedly structured.[36]

Consistently Duff considers worthy of moral respect the activities of the members of a sadomasochistic group, engaged in mutual violence, because it is oriented towards morally legitimate ends and, when understood in their particular context, it is informed by values of love and respect.[37]

On the other hand, in the example of gladiatorial combat Duff argues that, despite the consent of all gladiators, the mutual dehumanisation constitutes serious violation of the most basic values, of mutual concern and respect, by which the polity is supposed to be structured.[38]

In the frame of the relationship between person and polity is to look for the correct definition of the moral limits of criminal law and justification of coercive paternalism too.

---

[31]Feinberg argued that usury when freely consensual ought not to be a crime (contrary to dueling and slavery, because of insolvable problems of verifying voluntariness): Feinberg (1986a, b), 263 ff; (1988), 166.

[32]Feinberg (1988), 128 ff argues that, first, in this case it would be difficult to determine genuine willingness of gladiators, because "The higher the risk of harm involved, the stricter must be the standards, one would think, for voluntariness" (129); second, if thousand of spectators will pay to experience pleasure at the sight of maiming and killing, they are clearly dangerous, and it could lead to an increase in violent crimes (but, we can reply, the same could be argued about pornography and the consequent risk of rape); third, "when the moral dispositions that are corrupted include concern about the suffering of others, then the interest of others become vulnerable, and the corrupting activity can no longer be thought to be exclusively self-regarding" (132).

[33]George (1999), 308.

[34]Wolfenden Report, para 61.

[35]Duff (2009), 133. The question is, off course, if we can consider permanent harms (e.g. mutilations) worthy and lawful.

[36]Duff (2009), 132.

[37]Duff (2009), 131.

[38]Duff (2009), 133. See Kleinig (2017), 19 ff ("...only in cases in which those self-chosen ends will result in serious and ongoing dehumanization should the law intervene", 35).

7 The Moral Limits of Libertarian Criminal Law

We can summarize the criticism to the libertarian model in four cornerstones.

First, the spill-over effects of the 'individual-oriented' Harm Principle: the criminalisation of harm-threatening as well as harm-causing acts make it hard to constrain the expansion of criminal law.[39]

If we recognize a pure right to die, it involves, that we can forbid someone to rescue a person, who has suicidal intentions, either the caregiver or the physician, who try to prevent suicidal behaviour, or even have them charged with assault: but if the rescued person kills the rescuer in order to free himself, it could be considered as self-defence. And more, in such perspective, it's hard to tolerate an interference in order to inspect the reasonable motivation of choice (and not only in the situation of deteriorating terminal patients who are experiencing intense physical pain) in the typical frame of soft paternalism.

Second, the welfare-oriented nature of liberal anti-paternalism admits only 'procedural' constraints to individual freedom: a deliberation requires time, information, rational faculties, in order to warrant a reasonable choice.[40] But the simple validity of consent isn't enough to guarantee the protection of the human being in weakness. The debate today is no more about a comparison between paternalism and anti-paternalism—only the second is legitimate—but rather about the importance of a true protection of the vulnerable person in the decisions of legislator.[41]

Third, the combination of harm and autonomy is not adequate to facilitate the social acceptance of behaviour such as self-doping or drug-addiction. And the exclusion of intervention to prevent some self-damaging decisions that, although voluntary, are made without considering their bad consequences and as a result are not aligned with their longer-term interests and goals (i.e. refusal of the use of a seat belt, with the risk of grave injuries as a consequence), because the mentioned combination is not always reasonable: the problem of 'miscalculation' or 'misalignment' has nothing to do with lack of capacity to understand the implications of such decisions, but rather with the limits of a soft paternalism.[42]

Fourth, the abstract concept of individual freedom is not sufficient to enable the social cohesion and coexistence, which are conditions of freedom too: for the sake of them we need furthermore some levels of solidarity, warranted by institutions, legal duties to protect, etc.

---

[39] See Duff (2009), 124 ff, 135.

[40] Maniaci (2012), 147 ff.

[41] See Masferrer (2017), 537 ff (claiming that such protection of the dignity of vulnerable human beings is difficult to achieve in the frame of a voluntarist concept of law, as grounded on utilitarianism and positivism). About the ambiguity of the claimed so called "right to die" Eusebi (2020), 502 ff.; (2018), 434 ff.

[42] Simester and von Hirsch (2011), 184 f: the argument is grounded on the 'living-standard-approach' (concept suggested by Sen (1987), 20).

8 Changing Lens Concerning Relations Among Legal Paternalism and Legal Moralism

Surely we have to recognise as an indisputable worth of liberalism (but maybe earlier, of Christianity) the distinction between the legal order and morality: especially it is to stress that the legal enforcement of morals is something inconsistent because it leads, absurdly, to some immoral consequences, such as the coercion of free will instead of the call to a responsible choice, the repression of free thinking and pluralism, the coercive imposition of moral values, which are no more broadly accepted etc.

Maybe the affirmation that arguments about immorality have no place in decisions about criminalisation, because of the distinction between the legal order and the moral wrong could sound apodictic (distinction doesn't mean separation, and law without moral basis is no more than imposition) and even simplistic (there is no clear boundary between moral and legal statements but the positive nature of the last, and both are functional to the cohesion of society). And perhaps some liberal postulates sound too naïve.

But there is general agreement about some counter-arguments against the enforcement of morals as aims of law, and especially of criminal law, which make it hard to accept. The "ontological" version of legal moralism, which claims to discover and defend "true values" independently of their actual acceptance in a given society, needs a legitimate authority, which can establish the contents of such morality, and indeed has to demonstrate its beneficial output for society (or to restrain only the moral rules, that are so, for example in the sense of the harm principle). A "conventional", non-cognitive interpretation, that appoints on the broad acceptance of some rules in society independently of their "truth" and focuses on the gluing function of such morals, has to show its validity but recognize its gradual obsolescence too.[43]

Some of such values concern the—moral or physical or psychic—welfare of the person and the respect for his dignity from self-perpetrated harms: in other words, some aspects of paternalism seem to have, originally, a background in common with moralism, although the main aim of the former is not to prevent immorality, but rather to protect persons from self-harming or self-endangering acts.

The ground for rejecting legal paternalism, at least in its strong version, as a justification for criminal law is the respect for the—"sanctity" of—individual autonomy: such a main principle of the liberal concept assumes a moral connotation.

The real problem, and the persistent challenge of paternalism, however, remains how to protect vulnerable human beings from exploitation, but especially from the insidious pressure of the surroundings, which can easily lay the blame on those who are weak, old, ill or disabled because of their vulnerability (for the cost, not purely economic, involved in their conditions). And this last is clearly a *moral* problem.

---

[43] See Hörnle (2014), 177.

9 Paternalism in Transition: Toward New Challenges

Arguments about moral wrongfulness have been rejected for their moral foundation, but later some issues have been discussed from a different perspective. Main concepts have revealed their own ambiguous meaning and have been manipulated in order to legitimate peculiar ideological statements. The most emblematic is the concept of dignity, which has been denounced as "the name given to whatever principles give you the answer that you think is right".[44]

However, more recent developments in health care have led to new issues regarding paternalism in the field of public health measures. The objective value of dignity is replaced by other so-called objective standards, such as the "best interests" in decision-making on behalf of very sick children[45]: whereby a new kind of *hard* paternalism—namely of the judges[46]—dictates coercively a decision in the name of the "best interests" of the child—despite the different interpretation of such interests by the parents, considered wholly irrelevant—in contempt of the principle of respect for autonomy.

It marks the transition from the respect for patient autonomy to a new paternalism, namely of the best interests indeed, that enshrines the quality of life as the main technocratic 'gold' standard, established by experts (physicians, scientists): and the interpretation about the best interests of an human being, who lacks the capacity to make a choice in relation to future arrangements for himself (neither to oppose to the decisions of others), is final because of the supposed expertise underlying the decision. Furthermore, it's remarkable to observe another transformation of the point of view concerning some typical situations: some issues, formerly matters of debate between moralists and libertarians, recently urge a rethink in the frame of the debate on paternalism.

For example, the consideration of prostitution, or pornography—increasingly massive and often hard to distinguish from straight-up slavery[47]—have changed from the idea of censuring some immoral behaviours—because sexual immorality disintegrates society—[48] to the discovery, or rediscovery of the vulnerability of the subjects

---

[44]A short history of the concept of dignity in Foster (2011), 24.

[45]Expressly qualified as "Gold Standard" by the Supreme Court in *Evans v Alder Hay Hospital* (https://www.supremecourt.uk/cases/docs/alfie-evans-reasons-200318.pdf, para 14 and 16. Accessed 29 Sep 2020).

[46]"The judge must decide what is in the child's best interests" (so The Court of Appeal in Wyatt v Portsmouth NHS Trust: [2005] EWCA Civ 1181, [85]).

[47]This is about people, who are perfectly competent, mentally fit, informed, but often forced by living conditions and exploited as slaves from others.

[48]Thus Lord Devlin's statement seems meaningful that "the prostitute exploits the lust of her customers and the customer the moral weakness of the prostitute" (Devlin (1959), 14).

and the real lack of freedom of their choices[49]: some forms of paternalistic intervention are needed in order to protect such persons, although not decisions of criminalisation (except for pimps or abuser in general), but rather welfare-policies, aid networks in order to guarantee real chances of getting out, or simple prohibitions.[50]

Something similar occurred in the debate on euthanasia, which has moved from the rejection of the legitimacy of suicide as a violation of duty to self or as an infringement of the sanctity of human life to the need for protection of vulnerable persons from the "duty to choose", or against the possible pressure or even exploitation of others (in a broad sense too, including the surroundings): in front of such risks the mystic of 'free choice' seems powerless and indeterminate. The role of criminal law is also gradually conceived and deployed in the name of protecting our 'vulnerable autonomy'.[51]

At the same time criminal law seems not to be always the right and appropriate tool to achieve the protection of the person in weakness, and of course is illogical and even inconsistent with the fundamental principle to punish precisely those in order to protect them.[52] It is correct to affirm that the Harm-Principle (in common-law systems) and the doctrine of 'legal goods' (in civil-law systems) have been developed as undeniable limits of criminal law, that prevent the penalisation of only immoral or self-harming behaviours.

The only assignment of criminal law is to prevent abuse: it means, for example incrimination of pimps, brothel-keeper or the householder who permits habitual prostitution; but it concerns the insidious conditioning by others in the self-harming "free" choices of individuals too.

The suggestion to offer "nudges", paternalistic interventions which take the form of incentive, that "*are most likely to help and least likely to inflict harm*",[53] rather than coercive threats of penalties, is oriented to look for tools to prevent vulnerable persons in such contexts, without burdening them.

Such a metamorphosis of the role of legal enforcement of ethics brings out the simplistic feature of liberal criminal theory.

References

Albertson Fineman M (2008) The vulnerable subject: anchoring equality in the human condition. Yale JL & Feminism 20(1):1–23

---

[49] About the issue of vulnerability of sex workers, Fineman (2008), 1 ff; Munro and Scoular (2013), 30 ff.

[50] By contrast, the gradual ban of smoking is halfway between offence or even harm to others (caused by passive smoking), paternalism (struggle against nicotine-addiction) and pure moralism (hysterical witch hunt).

[51] Munro and Scoular (2013), 43 and 49; see Ramsay (2008).

[52] Simester and von Hirsch (2011), 172.

[53] See Thaler, Sunstein (2008), 74 ff; Conly (2012), 18 ff, 30 ff, 39 ff; Dworkin (2013), 25 ff; Blumenthal and Barby (2013), 184 ff., 190 ff.; Blumenthal (2013), 200 ff; Kelly (2013), 226 ff, 294; White (2013), 43 ff; Sunstein (2014); Alemanno (2015); John (2018).

Alemanno A, Sibony A-L (2015) Nudge and the law: A European perspective. Hart Publishing, Oxford
Aurenque D (2015) Selecting embryos with disabilities? A different approach to defend a "soft" paternalism in reproductive medicine. In: Schramme T (ed) New perspectives on paternalism and health care. Springer, Heidelberg, pp 265–276
Birnbacher D (2010) Paternalismus im Strafrecht – ethisch vertretbar? In: von Hirsch A, Neumann U, Seelmann K (eds) Paternalismus im Strafrecht: Die Kriminalisierung von selbstschädigendem Verhalten. Nomos, Baden-Baden, pp 11–26
Blumenthal JA, Barby JS (2013) Choice architecture: a mechanism for improving decisions while preserving liberty? In: Coons C, Weber M (eds) Paternalism: theory and practice. Cambridge University Press, Cambridge, pp 178–196
Blumenthal JA (2013) A psychological defense of paternalism. In: Coons C, Weber M (eds) Paternalism: theory and practice. Cambridge University Press, Cambridge, pp 197–215
Cadoppi A (2011) Paternalismo e diritto penale: cenni introduttivi. Criminalia 6:223–237
Cadoppi A (2008) Liberalismo, paternalismo e diritto penale. In: Fiandaca G, Francolini G (eds) Sulla legittimazione del diritto penale. Culture europeo-continentale e anglo-americana a confronto, Giappichelli, Torino, pp 83–124
Conly S (2012) Against autonomy: justifying coercive paternalism. Cambridge University Press, Cambridge
Cornacchia L (2011) Placing care. Spunti in tema di paternalismo legale. Criminalia 6:239–274
Devlin P (1959) The enforcement of morals: Maccabean lecture in jurisprudence of the British Academy 1959. Oxford University Press, Oxford
Donini M (2008) 'Danno' e 'offesa' nella c.d. tutela penale dei sentimenti. Note su morale e sicurezza come beni giuridici, a margine della categoria dell''offense' di Joel Feinberg. RIDPP 51 (4): 1546–1593
Duff RA (2009) Answering for crime: responsibility and liability in the criminal law. Hart Publishing, Oxford and Portland
Dworkin G (2005) Moral paternalism. Law & Phil 24:305–319
Dworkin G (2013) Defining paternalism. In: Coons C, Weber M (eds) Paternalism: theory and practice. Cambridge University Press, Cambridge, pp 25–38
Eusebi L (2018) Decisioni sui trattamenti sanitari o «diritto di morire»? I problemi interpretativi che investono la legge n. 219/2017 e la lettura del suo testo nell'ordinanza di rimessione alla Corte costituzionale dell'art. 580 c.p. RIML 2:415–438
Eusebi L (2020) Diritto a vivere, suicidio, euthanasia. Corti Supreme E Salute 2:501–510
Feinberg J (1971) Legal Paternalism. Canadian J Philos 1:105–124
Feinberg J (1984) The moral limits of the criminal law: volume one: Harm to others. Oxford University Press, New York, Oxford
Feinberg J (1985) The moral limits of the criminal law: volume two: offense to others. Oxford University Press, New York, Oxford
Feinberg J (1986a) The moral limits of the criminal law: volume three: harm to self. Oxford University Press, New York, Oxford
Feinberg J (1986b) The moral limits of the criminal law: volume four: harmless wrongdoing. Oxford University Press, New York, Oxford
Fiandaca G (2010) Punire la semplice immoralità? Un vecchio interrogativo che tende a riproporsi. In: Cadoppi A (ed) Laicità, valori e diritto penale. Giuffrè, Milano, pp 207–232
Fornasari G (2020) Paternalismo *hard*, paternalismo *soft* e antipaternalismo nella disciplina penale dell'aiuto al suicidio. Corte Costituzionale e *Bundesverfassungsgericht* a confronto. Sistema Penale. https://sistemapenale.it/pdf_contenuti/1591598222_fornasari-2020a-confronto-corte-costituzionale-italiana-tedesca-aiuto-suicidio-autodeterminazione.pdf. Accessed 29 Sept 2020
Forti G (2006) Per una discussione sui limiti morali del diritto penale, tra visioni «liberali» e paternalismi giuridici. In: Dolcini E, Paliero CE (eds) Studi in onore di Giorgio Marinucci. Giuffrè, Milano, pp 283–342

Forti G (2008) Principio del danno e legittimazione personalistica della tutela penale. In: Fiandaca G, Francolini G (eds) Sulla legittimazione del diritto penale. Culture europeo-continentale e anglo-americana a confronto, Giappichelli, Torino, pp 43–82
Foster C (2011) Human Dignity in bioethics and law. Hart Publishing, Oxford and Portland
Francolini G (2008b) L'Harm Principle del diritto angloamericano nella concezione di Joel Feinberg. RIDPP 51(1):276–308
Francolini G (2008a) Il dibattito angloamericano sulla legittimazione del diritto penale: la parabola del principio del danno tra visione liberale e posizione conservatrice. In: Fiandaca G, Francolini G (eds) Sulla legittimazione del diritto penale. Culture europeo-continentale e anglo-americana a confronto, Giappichelli, Torino, pp 1–27
Garzón Valdés E (1988) ¿Es éticamente justificable el paternalismo jurídico? Doxa 5: 155–173
George RP (1999) Moralistic liberalism and legal moralism. In: George RP (ed) Defense of natural law. Oxford University Press, Oxford New York, pp 300–314
Hurd HM (1996) The moral magic of Consent. Legal Theory 2:121–146
Hurd HM (2018) Paternalism and the criminal law. In: Grill K, Hanna J (eds) The Routledge handbook of the philosophy of paternalism. Routledge, New York, pp 277–293
Husak D (2015) Paternalism and consent. In: Schramme T (ed) New perspectives on paternalism and health care. Springer, Heidelberg, pp 67–86
Husak D (2003) Legal paternalism. In: LaFollette H (ed) The Oxford handbook of practical ethics. Oxford University Press, Oxford, pp 387–412
Hörnle T (2014) "Rights of others" in criminalisation theory. In: Simester AP, Du Bois-Pedain A, Neumann U (eds) Liberal criminal theory: essays for Andreas von Hirsch. Hart Publishing, Portland, pp 169–185
Jakobs G (1998) Tötung auf Verlangen: Euthanasie und Strafrechtsystem. Beck Verlag, München, Verlag der Bayerischen Akademie der Wissenschaften, C.H
John, 2018.John P (2018) How far to nudge? Assessing behavioural public policy. Edward Elgar Publishing, Cheltenham, UK, Northampton, MA
Kelly J (2013) Libertarian paternalism, utilitarianism, and justice. In: Coons C, Weber M (eds) Paternalism: theory and practice. Cambridge University Press, Cambridge, pp 216–230
Kleinig J (2017) Paternalism and human dignity. Crim L & Phil 11(1):19–36
Kreß H (2017) Paternalismus. In: Hilgendorf E, Joerden JC (eds) Handbuch Rechtsphilosophie. Stuttgart, J.B, Metzler, pp 409–413
Lévinas E (1982) Éthique et infini. Dialogues avec Philippe Nemo, Librairie Arthème Fayard et Radio-France, Paris
Lévinas E (2011) Le temps et l'autre. Press Universitaires de France, Paris
Maatsch A (2001) Selbstverfügung als intrapersonaler Rechtspflichtverstoβ: Zum Strafunrecht einverständlicher Sterbehilfe. Duncker & Humblot, Berlin
Maniaci G (2012) Contro il paternalismo giuridico. Giappichelli, Torino
Masferrer A (2017) Una historia retrospectiva de la dignidad humana. De la Constitución española al Descubrimiento de América. GLOSSAE. Europ J Legal History 14:494–546
Masferrer A (2016) Taking human dignity more humanely: a historical contribution to the ethical foundations of the constitutional democracy. In: Masferrer A, García-Sánchez E (eds) Human dignity of the vulnerable in the age of rights: interdisciplinary perspectives. Springer, Dordrecht-Heidelberg-London-New York, pp 221–256
Micheletti D (2011) Il paternalismo penale giudiziario e le insidie della Bad Samaritan Jurisprudence. Criminalia 6:275–312
Mill JS (1859) On Liberty. John W. Parker and Son, West Strand, London. In: Robson JM (ed) The collected works of john Stuart Mill: volume XVIII - Essays on politics and society part I (on liberty). University of Toronto Press, Routledge & Kegan Paul, p 1977
Morris H (1981) A paternalistic theory of punishment. Am Philos Q 18(4):263–271
Munro VE, Jane S (2013) Harm, vulnerability and citizenship: constitutional concerns in the criminalization of contemporary sex work. In: Duff RA, Farmer L, Renzo M, Tadros V (eds) The constitution of criminal law. Oxford University Press, Oxford, pp 30–52

Pulitanò D (2011) Paternalismo penale. Studi in onore di Mario Romano I. Jovene, Napoli, pp 489–524
Ramsay P (2008) The theory of vulnerable autonomy and the legitimacy of the civil preventative order, LSE Law, Society & Economy Working Paper Series 1/2008. https://ssrn.com/abstract=1091782. Accessed 29 Sept 2020
Risicato L (2011) Verso un diritto penale illiberale? La crisi di senso dell'intervento penale tra derive securitarie e paternalistiche. Studi in onore di Mario Romano I. Jovene, Napoli, pp 525–574
Romano M (2008) Danno a sé stessi, paternalismo legale e limiti del diritto penale. RIDPP 51(3):984–1003
Ronco M (2019) Impegno solidale per la vita. In: Ronco M (ed) Il "diritto di essere uccisi: verso la morte del diritto? Giappichelli, Torino, pp 129–326
Sen A (1987) The Standard of Living. In: Hawthorn G (ed) Tanner lectures in human values. Cambridge University Press, Cambridge, pp 1–38
Simester AP, von Hirsch A (2011) Crimes, harms and wrongs. On the principles of criminalization. Hart Publishing, Oxford and Portland, Oregon
Spena A (2014) Esiste il paternalismo penale? Un contributo al dibattito sui principi di criminalizzazione. RIDPP 57(3):1209–1248
Sunstein CR, Thaler RH (2003a) Libertarian paternalism is not an oxymoron. U Chi L Rev 70:1159–1202
Sunstein CR, Thaler RH (2003b) Libertarian paternalism. Am Econ Rev 93:175–179
Sunstein CR (2014) Why nudge? The politics of libertarian paternalism. Yale University Press, New Haven & London
Thaler RH, Sunstein CR (2008) Nudge: improving decisions about health, wealth, and happiness. Yale University Press, New Haven & London
Tincani P (2009) Harm Principle. Il principio del danno. In: Sciacca F (ed) L'individuo nella crisi dei diritti. Genova, Il nuovo melangolo, pp 55–80
Tincani P (2015) Principio del danno e omosessualità. Diritto e questioni pubbliche, 53–71
Tordini Cagli, 2011.Tordini Cagli S (2011) "Il paternalismo legislativo". Criminalia 6: 313–337
von Hirsch A, Neumann U (2010) "Indirekter Paternalismus" im Strafrecht – am Beispiel derTötung auf Verlangen Sollte selbstbeschädigendes Verhalten kriminalisiert werden? In: von Hirsch A, Neumann U, Seelmann K (eds) Paternalismus im Strafrecht: Die Kriminalisierung von selbstschädigendem Verhalten. Nomos, Baden-Baden, pp 71–98
White MD (2013) The manipulation of choice: ethics and libertarian paternalism. Palgrave Macmillan, New York
Wolfenden J, Adair J, Cohen MG, Curran D, Demant VA, Diplock K, Linstead H, The 12th Marquess of Lothian (Kerr, Walter PF), Lovibond K, Mishcon V, Rees G, Scott RFV, Lady Stopford, Wells WT, Whitby J (1957) Report of the Committee on Homosexual Offences and Prostitution, Her Majesty's Stationery Office, London

Human Dignity and Legally Protected Goods in Criminal Law

Pedro Talavera

Abstract Criminal law protects certain basic goods because they are directly or indirectly connected with the dignity of the person. However, in cases such as euthanasia, prostitution or surrogacy motherhood, the appeal to the dignity of the person is used, in the opposite sense, as the basis for decriminalization. In these cases, dignity is identified with the autonomy of the person and their capacity to dispose of all their goods, even if they are essential. This work argues that there is an ontological core of dignity (requirement of absolute respect) that is subtracted from autonomy and that is protected by the concept of 'moral integrity'. It prevents certain conducts from being decriminalized regardless of changes in social morality or whether it includes the consent of those who perform them. So, prostitution or surrogate motherhood, since always constitute an attack on the moral integrity of the person, regardless of their consent, in no case must be decriminalized.

1 Introduction

The exercise of *ius puniendi* by the modern state has always required compelling reasons to justify or legitimise the ensuing restriction of liberties and rights, but nowadays classifying certain conducts under criminal law has become a political question of the first order. On the one hand, this is because Law has definitively taken on its promotional function and its role to guarantee freedoms, while tending to play down its clearly repressive facet.[1] On the other hand, this is due to the increasing plurality in western societies which host a wide range of moral and ideological beliefs. Within this open and plural setting nurtured by a substrate of "lay anthropocentrism", attempts to restrict freedom through punitive state intervention stir up

P. Talavera (✉)
Department of Philosophy of Law, School of Law, University of Valencia, Valencia, Spain
e-mail: ptalaver@uv.es

[1]Bobbio (1991), 34–39.

A. Masferrer (ed.), *Criminal Law and Morality in the Age of Consent*, Ius Gentium: Comparative Perspectives on Law and Justice 84,
https://doi.org/10.1007/978-3-030-64163-4_11

major reservations and, consequently, they require an even more solid justification and rational foundations.[2]

In order to adapt to this context in which freedom and moral pluralism have primacy, criminal law dogma has, in recent decades, developed the category of 'legally protected good' as a criterion to legitimise punitive intervention by the State. The concept of 'legal good' fulfils three roles: it systematises, allowing for the classification of offences according to the goods protected; it interprets the categories of criminal offences which protect the legal good; and, above all, it guarantees placing limits on criminalising conducts – or put another way, the undue use of *ius puniendi.*[3]

Although this continues to be one of the most debated topics from the perspective of criminal law doctrine,[4] most definitions put forward for the concept of a legal good could well find a common ground in the classic definition by Von Liszt: "a vital interest for the development of individuals in a given society, which comes to be recognised by law."[5] Here we have three fundamental considerations for this concept: a) it affects 'vital interests' – namely, an individual's fundamental goods which pre-exist in the legal system; b) the fundamental nature of these goods must be housed within a socio-cultural context; c) it is its fundamental (constitutional) nature which requires protection under the law, or put another way, Criminal Law protects these goods due to their fundamental nature and not vice versa.[6]

The category of legal good has been established as a general criterion for legitimising democratic criminal law by means of the 'principle of harm',[7] which only requires criminalising those conducts that harm fundamental goods.[8] By means of this principle, criminal law is granted the exclusive tutelage of basic goods, thus establishing an explicit relationship between the category of protected legal good and constitutionally protected goods.[9] So, the essence or fundamental nature of certain goods is what justifies their protection under criminal law, and this is granted by the constitution. But what finally determines the fundamental (constitutional) nature of a good is its relationship with the individual's dignity, as expressly set out in the majority of European constitutions.[10]

---

[2]Peces-Barba (1995), 56.

[3]Ferrajoli (1995), 59–65.

[4]The extensive doctrinal debate on the classification of legal good, which is generally accepted, falls outside the scope of this article. Suffice it to point out the following: In Spain, Muñoz-Conde and García (2007), 59–61. In Germany, Roxin (1997), 55–73. In Italy, Donini (2010). The category of legal good has been critically challenged by Jakobs for whom the end purpose of criminal law is not the protection of goods, but rather the safeguard of the regulations in effect. See: Jakobs (1995) y Jakobs (2003), 41–56.

[5]Re-translated from the Spanish translation in Von Liszt (1999), 6.

[6]Roxin (1997), 54.

[7]Ferrajoli (2012), 100–114. Concerning how the harm principle has been interpreted in Spain, see: García-Pablos (2006), 538–545.

[8]Amelung (2007), 233–239. Hormazábal (1991), 8, 13, 30–33.

[9]Guardiola (2003), 192–199. García-Pablos (2006), 548–557.

[10]The following serve as important illustrative examples. The *Basic Law of the Federal Republic of Germany* (art. 1): "(1) Dignity of man shall be inviolable. To respect and protect it shall be the

It is clear that the final point of reference of legal goods protected by criminal law is found in the notion of the dignity of the person, hence the reason why this concept should be a fundamental consideration both for establishing criminal offences from a theoretical perspective as well as for regulating them through legislation and effectively applying them via jurisprudence.[11] Some of these fundamental goods (life, integrity, intimacy, freedom, etc.) are commonly called 'highly personal' because they constitute the most intimate core of dignity as an indispensable prerequisite so that any individual can properly develop their personal and social life. Other types of goods (heritage, environment, public administration, etc.) do not have such a direct bearing on the core of dignity, but they are also protected by criminal law in that they have a bearing on the personal and social development of the individual. As a consequence, criminal law protects those goods which directly or indirectly make inherent demands on the dignity of the individual.[12]

Criminalising conducts linked to the protection of goods not directly associated with the intimate core of dignity, which above all affect social coexistence, often awakens a wide-ranging consensus among citizens. This happens in cases of, for example, crimes related to corruption, fraud or against property, crimes against the environment, etc. However, when criminal classification affects conducts related to the protection of 'highly personal' goods such as life, physical integrity, sexual freedom, etc. – directly linked to the core of dignity –, this generates intense debates on the primacy of the individual's will as opposed to the supposed indisposability of these goods because of their fundamental nature. This happens in cases such as euthanasia or prostitution.

There are, indeed, conducts such as homicide, torture, slavery etc., in the face of which the dignity of a person directly and explicitly constitutes a criterion for intervention under criminal law to protect basic goods such as life, integrity or freedom against the agression of third parties. But when individual willingly consents to undergoing these very same conducts, then many appeal to the notion of dignity in precisely the opposite sense, that is, as a premise to call for the decriminalisation of these conducts. In this scenario, the dignity of the person is identified with their autonomy: their capacity to legitimately decide over themselves without hindrance (*volenti non fit injuria*). Dignity is no longer the basis for protecting fundamental goods and then becomes the basis for protecting the subject's will. Thus, euthanasia

---

duty of all state authority. (2) The German people therefore acknowledge inviolable and inalienable human rights as the basis of every human community, of peace and of justice in the world. (3) The following basic rights shall be binding as directly valid law on legislation, administration and judiciary". The *Spanish Consitution* (art. 10.1): "The dignity of the person, their inviolable rights which are inherent to them, the free development of personality, respect for the law and the rights of others are the basis of political order and social peace". The *Portuguese Constitution* (art. 1): "Portugal is a sovereign Republic, based on the dignity of the individual person and the people's will, pledged to the construction of a free, just and solidary society". The *Italian Constitution* (art. 3): "All citizens shall have the same social dignity and shall be equal before the law"; etc. Vid. Oheling (2011), 135–178.

[11]Ferrajoli (1995), 459–467.

[12]Ferrajoli (1995), 323–331. Some authors claim there is a progressive spread of the notion of legal good: Donini (2002), 132.

is no longer conceived in terms of homicide or aiding suicide, but rather the discretionary disposal of life; prostitution as the discretional exercise of sexuality; surrogate motherhood, the discretional use of procreative capacity; experimenting with human embryos as discretional donations of biological material for science, etc. We thus have the concept of dignity being identified with the principle of the free development of personality in absolute terms, understood as the 'unrestricted' capability of self-determination, which implies conceiving of a person's basic goods as absolutely discretional.

The concept of the dignity of a person embraces a wide area of autonomy and self-determination issues but, as we shall see, it does not justify a person's absolute access to their essential goods. Along with a parallel line of reasoning the concept of dignity is not alien to the majority of notions of good and bad or justice and injustice held by society nowadays, which not only determine to a large degree the criminalisation of certain conducts, but decriminalisation as well (adultery or homosexuality are illustrative examples).[13] However, if we accept that the contents of criminal law are governed by the essential or fundamental nature of the goods it protects, then social values cannot be the only consideration which determines them. What grants the fundamental nature of a good and justifies its protection under criminal law is its connection to the dignity of the individual.[14]

Although many criminal laws are a response to socio-cultural conditions, within them there has always been an irreducible basic core which enjoys a kind of 'objective assessment' which protects certain fundamental goods beyond the realms of religious, historical, cultural or social values. In other words, there are conducts whose classification under criminal law should be enforceable in any event, even if society does not de facto view them negatively. And it is this point which constitutes the main aim of this article: to clarify the concept of human dignity and the existence of an irrevocable and inalienable core of goods inherent in dignity that must be protected by law over and above social views of certain conducts and the wide-ranging sphere covered by the notion of autonomy of the individual. The pages that follow justify why conducts such as prostitution or surrogate motherhood effectively harm this irreducible core of dignity and for this reason must be penalised by law.

2 The Philosophical Debate Over the Concept of the Dignity of a Person

Philosophical reflections on the notion of human dignity have a long history linked to humanist thought, nevertheless a precise definition remains elusive and it continues

[13]Silva (2003), 143–163.

[14]By way of example, in Spain there is a very high percentage of people who support applying the death penalty to paedophiles or terrorists, however it does not seem reasonable that such a point of view should be translated into a law, overriding the fundamental nature of life as a fundamental good.

to generate controversy. Perhaps the only consensus we can find nowadays is to state that dignity is the basis of human rights.[15]

Dignity was not assigned an actual value as a legal principle until the mid-twentieth century.[16] It did not feature in the emblematic declarations of rights by the United States of America or France at the end of the eighteenth century, nor in subsequent texts. It was the upheavals resulting from the two world wars, along with the atrocities committed in the colonial wars, which brought about including dignity in the Charter of the United Nations (1945) and the Universal Declaration of Human Rights (UDHR) in 1948.[17] So, it was in this manner that dignity became the cornerstone of human rights and the basis for constructing an unquestionable and universal core of public morality, over and above ideologies and cultural traditions.[18]

The preamble of the UDHR makes mention of dignity on two occasions. In the first paragraph: "recognition of the inherent dignity and of the equal and inalienable rights of all members of the human family is the foundation of freedom, justice and peace in the world." Then again in the fifth paragraph, in which the United Nations reiterate their faith in "fundamental human rights, in the dignity and worth of the human person." But it is in Article 1 where we find firmly set out that, "All humans are born free and equal in dignity and rights…" This reference proves decisive since, for the first time, the notion of "dignity" takes on a real regulatory value by being included in the enacting terms of an international document with a universal scope.[19]

From this point on it is almost impossible to find any international document concerning human rights which does not refer to, invoke or apply, the concept of human dignity.[20] And in these documents dignity is contemplated, more or less

[15]Masferrer (2017), 493–545. Aparisi (2013), 201–205.

[16]Häberle (2008), 177–182. Masferrer (2018), 1–55.

[17]Bobbio (1991), 35–61. Masferrer (2016), 221–256.

[18]Gros-Espiell (2003), 204–205.

[19]Gros-Espiell (2003), 206. Glendon (2012), 253- 262.

[20]For example, the *Declaration on the Elimination of All Forms of Racial Discrimination*, proclaimed by the General Assembly of the United Nations on November 20 1963, which states in the Preamble: "Considering that the Charter of the United Nations is based on the principles of the dignity and equality of all human beings…"; and article 1, which states that: "Discrimination between human beings on the ground of race, colour or ethnic origin is an offence to human dignity…". Along similar lines, the *International Covenent on Economic, Social and Cultural Rights*, which came into effect on January 3 1976, and states in its Preamble: "Recognizing that these rights derive from the inherent dignity of the human person…". The *International Covenent on Civil and Political Rights* expresses itself in similar terms, stating that, "these rights derive from the inherent dignity of the human person". In turn, the *World Conference on Human Rights* (Vienna, June 1993) once again picks up these ideas in the Preamble: "Recognizing and affirming that all human rights derive from the dignity and worth inherent in the human person (…)"; it echoes the Preamble to the United Nations Charter, particularly in reaffirming faith in the fundamental rights of man, dignity and the value of human beings. The first paragraph reads that "Human rights and fundamental freedoms are the birthright of all human beings; their protection and promotion is the first responsibility of Governments". This humanist vein has also appeared in international declarations on bioethical issues, enshrining human dignity as the basis of principles and regulations that should govern any actions concerning human beings, their organs or genome. The Council of Europe Convention for the protection of Human Rights and Dignity of the Human Being with Regard to

explicitly, as an inherent attribute to all human beings and as the cornerstone of Law.[21] However, an ideal common understanding of dignity in the contemporary world has arisen at the cost of a vague and ambiguous term. In fact, international documents have carefully avoided defining or clarifying it in an attempt to circumvent the age-old antagonisms between natural law and legal positivism, as well as the stumbling blocks of cultural and moral pluralism in Western societies. This has led to the present situation in which the idea of human dignity is so open that some have qualified it as vacuous notion, which can be resorted to justify all manner of ideological or political proposals.[22] It has even led to various doctrinal spheres calling for the need to move beyond this notion and progress towards others less vulnerable to manipulation.[23]

In short, we can see a 'practical convergence' in accepting dignity as a foundation of human rights, as reflected in the international documents, but equally noteworthy is a 'theoretical divergence' concerning its meaning.[24] This theoretical divergence emerges from two important lines of thinking: those who maintain an ontological notion of dignity, founded in human nature, and those who maintain an exclusively phenomenological notion of the same, founded in the principle of individual autonomy.[25]

2.1 *The Ontological Notion of Dignity*

The Declarations of human rights mentioned earlier confer an ontological dimension to dignity, as they see it as a quality which is intrinsic to, and inherent in, all human beings.[26] And it is for this reason that dignity appears imbued with a certain axiomatic and self-evident nature that hardly requires demonstrating.[27] From this ontological perspective, human dignity refers to a value which all human beings have within them,

the Application of Biology and Medicine (Convention on Human Rights and Biomedicine) came into effect on December 1 1999. Statements have been made along similar lines in declarations approved by UNESCO on this issue: the Universal Declaration on the Human Genome and Human Rights, adopted at the 29th General Conference on November 11 1997 and ratified by the United Nations General Assembly December 9 1998. Also, the International Declaration on Human Genetic Data (2003) and the Universal Declaration on Bioethics and Human Rights (2005), both UNESCO initiatives. See: Ballesteros (2004).

[21] Dignity appears to have taken the place traditionally occupied by natural law, understood as the ontological origin and basis for law. See: Aparisi (2013), 204.

[22] González (1986), 19–20. Melendo/Millán-Puelles (1996).

[23] Macklin (2003), 1419. Hoerster (1992), 91–96.

[24] Palazzani (2007), 383–384.

[25] Spaemann (1988), 16.

[26] Along these lines the most relevant authors include: Kant (1995), 94–99.; Arendt (1992). Spaemann (1988), 13–19. González (1986). Pavía and Revet (1999). Ballesteros (2001), 179–203. Andorno (1996). Choza (1995). González (1996).

[27] Marin (1998), 143–147.

beyond their existential circumstances and which merits unquestioned respect.[28] Along this line of thought, the words of Kant prove paradigmatic when he defined the concept as: "that which has a price can be substituted for something which is equivalent; in contrast, that which is beyond price, and therefore has no equivalent, that has dignity."[29] So, an ontological difference is established between people and things and between subjects and objects. This radical difference is what allows us to identify those actions which, in any event, are injurious or detrimental to a person, namely, those which reduce a person to the category of thing, because by objectifying them (treating them as a thing) violate their dignity.

This conception of dignity implies acknowledging a quality of excellence in a human being that not only makes them superior to other living beings but also ranks them in the order of beings. A human being as an individual not only belongs to a higher species, but also develops her/his existence in a substantially different dimension. Thus, dignity indicates a particular and unique 'way of being' which confers upon the subject the possibility to be something more than an individual of a species: it allows them to develop a personal existence.[30] The term 'person', tied to the concept of dignity, was devised precisely to highlight that a human being cannot be enclosed in the notion of 'individual of a species'. In this term there is a unique fullness and perfection in absolute terms which go the limits of the species and make them a unique and irrepeatable subject.[31] Accordingly, the ontological concept of dignity could be defined in terms of "the perfection or intensity of the being who corresponds to human nature and that falls within the person insofar as it is the existential realisation of human nature."[32]

Particularly after Kant, dignity refers to an idea of a person as an 'end in itself', deserving unconditional respect which prevents s/he from being treated as a mere instrument. The words contained in *Groundwork for the Metaphysics of Morals* are more than well-known: "rational beings, by contrast, are called persons, because their nature already marks them out as ends in themselves, i.e., as something that may not be used merely as means, hence to that extent limits all arbitrary choice (and is an object of respect). These are not merely subjective ends whose existence as effect of our action has a worth for us; but rather objective ends, i.e., things whose existence in itself is an end, and specifically an end such that no other end can be set in place of it, to which it should do service merely as means...".[33]

To claim the ontological nature of dignity means not to endow it with a subjective basis (a person is not an end "for her/himself or for others"), but rather an objective

---

[28] Spaemann (1989), 45–59.

[29] Kant (2002), 69.

[30] Spaemann (2000).

[31] Aparisi (2013), 205–206.

[32] Original citation, "la perfección o intensidad del ser que corresponde a la naturaleza humana y que se predica de la persona, en cuanto que es la realización existencial de la naturaleza humana." Hervada (1991), 361–362.

[33] Kant (2002), 65.

basis (a person is an end in itself).[34] In other words, the basis of dignity does not lie in autonomy or in social covenant, but rather in the absolute value of all human beings.[35] Indeed, no person merits unconditional respect because they consider themselves to be meritworthy, or because society or political power has awarded them this value. Ontological dignity is above any individual will or social consensus, as it considers human beings themselves to be meritworthy, that is in the absolute and unconditional sense. Consequently, neither legal regulations nor the subject's very own will can harm or destroy the basic goods which make up the most intimate core of the dignity of a person.[36] Establishing the autonomy of the individual or social consensus as a basis of dignity is not only insufficient, but also dangerous. The autonomy of the individual, in effect, could decide to destroy basic goods (such as their own life, health or freedom) or alienate them (selling organs or children). Meanwhile, social consensus is subject to change and can vary substantially, across time or from one society to another, when it comes to determining the requirements of dignity or even those who merit dignity and those who do not. We have already seen this with Nazism and nowadays with human embryos, deformed foetuses, those who are terminally ill or in a vegetative state.

2.2 *Non-ontological Notions of Dignity*

The most important line of thinking which rejects the ontological dimension of dignity is known as 'personism', which identifies dignity with the individual's exercise of autonomy.[37] The characteristic feature of 'personism' is the distinction it

[34]Spaemann (1988), 20.

[35]Spaemann explains the difference between the subjective and objective meaning of dignity in the following terms: The fact that something is for itself its own and final end and cannot be turned into a mere medium for a totally alien end by another, hardly needs to be demonstrated. The mouse is also a final end for itself, whereas this is not the case for the cat…If man is only a value for himself and not an "aim in itself", then the perfect crime would be valid for this case: if someone who considers his own life to be something of value is eliminated, then for this man one cannot talk in terms of a "loss of value". The valuable nature of this life depends on this someone for whom such a loss does have a value. And the same can be said for the annihilation of mankind because of an atomic explosion. If all value is relative to the subject who assigns the value, the total annihilation of all the subjects who assign value cannot be considered a crime…Only the value of the man "in itself" – not only for other men – makes his life sacred and confers this ontological dimension on to the concept of dignity, without which one cannot even think about what this concept tries to express." Vid. Spaemann (1988), 20–21.

[36]Spaemann claims that: "From this perspective, which I would call anti-ontological (that which considers the individual as end in itself for itself), one cannot draw any conclusive argument against the silent murderer and without pain of the man who lacks a family. If this man is only a value for himself (like a value relative to the very subject who gives value) and not an "end in itself", then the perfect crime would be valid for this case. Vid. Spaemann (1988), 20. Masferrer (2016), 235–240. Masferrer/García-Sánchez (2016), 1–25.

[37]Concerning the meaning of this expression and current reductive notions of human dignity: Ballesteros (2001), 182–185.

makes between the concept of human being and person. The idea of 'human being' would refer to the purely biological dimension that designates members of the *homo sapiens* species. The notion of 'person', on the other hand, refers to a 'biographical' dimension, designating the individual in terms of self-conscious and free, that is, a rational, autonomous and independent subject. These are the characteristics which grant the individual dignity and, consequently, merit recognition and respect and guarantee her/his status as titleholders of basic human rights. Dignity is conceived here from a phenomenological perspective, as an attribute linked to the effective exercise of rationality (self-awareness) and self-determination (freedom of choice). Dignity is identified, all said and done, with autonomy, which means rejecting it as a quality inherent to all human beings.[38] 'Personism' thus ends up denying the unity of human species by stating that not all human beings have dignity and, therefore not all are owed absolute and unconditional respect.[39]

In effect, 'personism' denies the status of person to individuals of the *homo sapiens* species who lack the ability to reason or who are not autonomous (which would be the case for embryos, foetuses, new-born babies, anencephalic, those with serious deficiencies or those in a state of coma). This means to deprive them of dignity and reduce them to the status of a mere biological organism. Along this line of thought the postures adopted by Parfit, Singer and Engelhardt are illustrative.[40] Parfit states the following: "Most of us do not distinguish persons from human beings. But some of us, following Locke, make a distinction… If we draw this distinction, we may think that, while it is bad to kill a human being, it is worse to kill a person. We may even think that only the killing of persons is wrong."[41] Along similar lines, Singer states that: "Not all members of the *homo sapiens* species are people, neither are all people members of the *homo sapiens* species…newly-born babies are not born with an awareness of themselves, nor are they able to understand that they exist in time. They are not persons."[42]

'Personism' adopts Cartesian dualist postulates: the distinction between *res extensa* and *res cogitans*. All that exists belongs to the material world – can be

[38] Ballesteros (2001), 180.

[39] 'Personism' has a decidedly excluding dimension as it weakens protection under law precisely for those who are most vulnerable: those who lack autonomy. An illustrative example is the ruling by the Spanish Constitutional Court 53/1985, April 11, endorsing the partial decriminalisation of abortion. The judgment does not recognise the dignity of the *nasciturus*, only the woman, precisely because only she has, in fact, an autonomous and rational life. The *nasciturus* has the condition of human being, however s/he is not attributed the condition of 'person' and the correlating rights which derive from this condition. The Spanish Constitution Court made a similar ruling, 116/1999, along similar lines by denying all protection under law to human embryos conceived in vitro, ruling out that they could be subjects with rights. Vid. Aparisi (2013), 211.

[40] Among the most representative: Singer (2016). Singer (2002). Singer (1994). Engelhardt (1995). Parfit (1984). Peces-Barba (2002), 21–39. González-Amuchastegui (2004), 417–430.

[41] Parfit (1984), 322.

[42] For Singer: "There is no reason why a chimpancee should be killed rather than anencephalic children…I'm not going to defend the position that all life has the same value without taking into account its quality and characteristics…And from the point of view of revised ethics…the right to life is not an exclusive right of the *homo sapiens* species". Vid. Singer (1994), 182, 199, 202, 206.

reduced to being seen as an object – except the human mind, which is what determines the condition of the subject. So, the human being owns a body – understood in terms of pure material –, and a mind – the source of thinking and rationality –, which is where her/his identity as a subject resides.[43] By contrast, from the perspective of empiricism, that which is natural is identified with that which is material, with objects, what is external to the body, something which is purely inert, devoid of any teleology and, therefore, can be used for any ends. The subject, defined as a thinking and autonomous thing, acquires its identity in so far that it is something 'distinct' from nature.[44] Accordingly, the human being does not conceive of itself as a natural being, but rather as 'something different'. It becomes aware of itself in that it is a *res cogitans*; it is exclusively freedom and rationality, as opposed to nature which is only raw material.[45]

It was Locke who, influenced by this Cartesian division, first made the distinction between the *persona*, as a subject capable of conscious and free life – biographical life –, and the simple *human being*, as an individual of the species, a purely biological being of irrelevant value.[46] Neither Descartes nor Locke drew ethical consequences from their anthropological thinking, however, the neolockeans of the twentieth century, such as Engelhardt, did. They claim that the foundation of dignity lies in autonomy and it is this which constitutes the person and grants them ownership of rights, reducing human beings to a purely biological entity bereft of any value. In effect, Engelhardt only considered an adult, conscious and autonomous as worthy of dignity, as dignity only dwells in those who are moral agents, that is, able to freely develop their personality. Accordingly, he denies dignity and rights to those individuals who are not self-aware, even though they may belong to the *homo sapiens* species. Working from this basis, he classifies human beings according to their proximity to an ideal of autarky. Embryos and human foetuses are considered to be inferior (less valuable) than higher mammals (gorillas, orangutans, large cetaceans…) as they lack cognitive capacity: they would only have the right, like any other living being, not to suffer unnecessarily. Anencephalic individuals or those in a continual vegetative state are equated with the dead: their status would depend on the interests which someone endowed with autonomy has over them.[47]

The 'personist dualism' has also contributed to developing a utilitarian conception of dignity which nowadays, to a large degree, is buttressed by the notion of 'quality

[43]"I know that I exist and that nothing else belongs to my nature or essence except that I am a thinking thing; from this it follows that my essence consists solely in my being a thinking thing, even though there may be a body that is very closely joined to me." "Sixth Meditation: The existence of material things, and the real distinction between mind and body". In Descartes R (2017), 29. See also, Ballesteros (2001), 180.

[44]Ballesteros (1989), 22.

[45]González (1997), 215–217.

[46]Locke (2004), 32–35.

[47]Engelhardt (1995), 358–361. Along similar lines, Dworkin (2011), contends that nothing that does not have interests can have a right and nothing that does not have consciousness can have an interest. Accordingly, since foetuses (at least in the early stages of the pregnancy) do not have a conscience, they cannot have interests nor rights.

of life'. This is an imprecise and vague concept, advocated from the sphere of public health and which has been cast into the arena of public debates over important issues such as abortion – to avoid birth defects –, or euthanasia – arguing that suffering (lack of all physical well-being) renders the individual's life as having no sense or value.[48] Here a link is established between dignity and wellbeing (the capacity to experience pleasure). It is Peter Singer who, reinterpreting the traditional utilitaritarian principle, has put forward a new basis for contemporary ethics: good has to be identified with well-being and bad with suffering; that is, all that provides pleasure (which should be encouraged) should be considered as good, and as bad, all that brings about suffering (which should be minimised or eliminated). It follows that, all those actions which lead to maximising wellbeing and minimising suffering in the highest number of people possible should be considered legitimate. From this line of argument, the fundamental requirement of the dignity of a person is nothing other than avoiding suffering and maximising wellbeing. However, Singer goes even further contending that the capacity to experience pleasure and pain is the criterion to determine those who should be considered 'persons'. And this criterion does not allow for establishing differences between human beings and superior primates.[49]

Working from the premise that a 'suffering' life, a life without wellbeing, lacks dignity and, therefore, does not deserve to be lived, 'quality of life' become the parameter to assess the dignity of a human life and to justify an extraordinarily relevant legal outcome: a life without wellbeing is a life which 'does not have dignity' and should not be afforded protection under law and can be legitimately eliminated.[50] To state that there are human lives 'unworthy of dignity' which no longer deserve to be

---

[48] Aparisi (2013), 213–215.

[49] Singer backs Ryder in what has come to be known as "speciesism" (attempted narcissism of the human species that considers itself to be superior to the rest) and rejects the distinction between human beings and animals, postulating the existence of a "moral community" between humans and superior animals, which justifies the requirement of "human rights for animals". Singer has become one of the principal promotors of the Great Ape Project. For Singer, as for those among the ranks of sociobiology, there is a genetic similarity between humans and the great apes (gorillas, orangutans, chimpanzees and bonobos) in addition to a major coincidence between the experiences of pleasure, pain and awareness, which would justify not making distinctions regarding recognising and guaranteeing rights. At the same time, he rejects the status of person for those incapable of experiencing pleasure or pain: human embryos, those who are terminally ill or in a state of coma, etc. Vid. Singer (1995), 58–79.

[50] In Spain, linking dignity and quality of life has been defended by: Peces-Barba (1999), 15–26.

lived is the argument wielded to justify abortion induced for eugenic reasons, eliminating foetuses or new-born babies with Down syndrome or other malformations,[51] and euthanasia for the terminally ill or physically or mentally disabled.[52]

In effect, we find ourselves faced with another way of affirming the link between dignity and autonomy. The body is seen as something which is purely material, at the discretional disposal of the individual, which can be subjected to standards of biological quality. Put another way, the body only has value to the degree that is able to satisfy the demands of the autonomous subject's life, and when this material support displays limitations or imperfections which prevent the subject from clearly exercising her/his autonomy, then it can be disposed of.

In the final analysis, 'personist dualism', is at the heart of a voluntarist (contractualist) notion of the Law, in which the autonomy of the subject prevails (ability to decide) over the protection of basic goods, which are no longer considered to be inalienable. With this, the classic aphorism *volenti non fit injuria* becomes the quintessential ethical and legal criterion. This has transcendental consequences for the human body since, thus reduced to a purely material object, it becomes something which can be disposed of, manipulated and even marketed unconditionally at the discretion of the subject's will.

3 Autonomy and Dignity of the Person

The 'personist dualism' is founded on a profound anthropological error: a human being cannot only be a *res cogitans*, pure rationality and autonomy in a vacuum, relegating the body to something which is purely material, available and disposable. Rationality and autonomy are not entelechies but rather attributes of human nature which take on an original form in each individual human, who not only 'has' but also

---

[51] Along these lines, any action which leads to interrupting the life of embryos and those foetuses that, on the basis of pre-birth diagnosis, are going to suffer from health disorders, could be performed considering that, in the future, their faculties would be impaired, their family would have to maintain them, and this would mean a high financial cost for society. Likewise, one would have to bear in mind that "the general wellbeing is not only adversely effectuated by having to….be responsible for defective individuals, but also because, if they are allowed to reproduce, one acts against the principle of natural selection and, therefore impairs what could be understood as biological or genetic wellbeing." Vid. Gracia (1984), 67.

[52] Also, worth noting is the increasing number of cases admitted to court concerning wrongful birth and wrongful life.We can trace the origins of this tendency back to the US. In the case Gleitman v. Cosgrove (1967) indemnity for wrongful birth and wrongful life was denied in the case of a child allegedly affected by various malformations resulting from rubella contracted by the mother during pregnancy, who had been told that it would not affect the foetus. The New Jersey Court rejected the claim on the basis of public order arguments and the impossibility of identifying damages given the sacred nature of life. However, this criterion later changed. In 1975, in the case Jacobs v. Theimer, the claim for indemnity was accepted for wrongful birth concerning the birth of a child with congenital defects, due to the fact that the mother caught rubella during the first month of pregnancy, and the doctor failed to make the correct diagnosis. There have been many more cases based on this acknowledgment. Vid. Aparisi (2013), 214.

'is' a body. Therefore, human beings do not acquire dignity when they demonstrate their ability to exercise autonomy, but rather the opposite: all human beings are worthy because dignity is the characteristic attribute of human nature endowed with rationality and freedom.[53]

Dignity is effectively an attribute of a person and this includes the body dimension. Historically, the protection under law of the life and physically integrity of any human being has been founded on the premise that there is a person with dignity and rights within all living human bodies; and, accordingly, the condemnation of any ideology that has promoted eugenics. To contend that there are lives not worthy of dignity, which lack value and can be eliminated because they do not correspond to an ideal of autonomy, would mean finishing with the universalist concept of humanity, justifying discrimination between human beings and, consequently, finishing with the very idea of dignity.[54] A conception of dignity that would not guarantee the universal recognition of all human beings in terms of absolute and unconditional respect, and instead establish classes or degrees of humanity, is a contradiction in terms.[55]

Strictly speaking, it is without doubt that both the UDHR as well as the other international covenants mentioned earlier, have enshrined an ontological notion of dignity to a greater or lesser degree of explicitness. Recognising it as inherent to "all members of the human family" (Preamble to the UDHR), is the way to spotlight that dignity is an attribute of all individuals who belong to the *homo sapiens* species, without the need for any other additional requirements (stage of intra or extrauterine development, intellectual capabilities, physical attributes, degree of moral autonomy or degree of present/future wellbeing).[56] In the final analysis, human dignity only makes sense as a concept and as a legal principle if it is stated as a universal attribute, inherent to the human condition.[57] Attempts to invoke it as a criterion for discriminating between human beings (simple biological life subjects) and persons (subjects with an autonomous biographical life) rather than a criterion which makes people equal, is totally incongruent with the concept itself.[58]

---

[53] Aparisi (2013), 212. Ballesteros (2001), 185.

[54] Ballesteros (2001), 187.

[55] Ballesteros (2001), 188.

[56] Suffice that a living being possesses a human genome to be considered a member of the human family, but this does not mean reducing the person to a genome. Vid. Ballesteros (2001), 183–185. It is unequivocally expressed in the *Universal Declaration on the Human Genome and Human Rights* cited earlier, by stressing that the dignity of individuals is independent of their genetic characteristics. Along the same lines, article 2, section a) maintains that: "Everyone has a right to respect for their dignity and for their rights regardless of their genetic characteristics". And point b) states: "That dignity makes it imperative not to reduce individuals to their genetic characteristics and to respect their uniqueness and diversity." Also, along the same lines, the Preamble of the *Convention on Human Rights and Biomedicine* by the Council of Europe sets out: "the need to respect the human being both as an individual and as a member of the human species," acknowledging the importance of guaranteeing their dignity. Furthermore, the first article expressly refers to protecting the dignity of all human beings.

[57] Spaemann (1988), 25. González (1997), 54–55.

[58] To claim the universal nature of human dignity is the basis of essential equality among members of the human species and, therefore, requires an identical respect for all human beings and equal

Putting forward an ontological conception of dignity means conferring upon it an inalienable nature; that is, to consider it irrevocable and indisposable. No human being can reject or relinquish dignity because it is inherent to the human condition, and no human being can stop being a human being or renounce being one. For this reason, nobody can renounce or rid themselves of the essential goods inherent in dignity. The transcendence and operability of dignity as a legal principle lies precisely in that the Law must protect these essential goods against whomever may attempt to destroy or damage them, including the very same subject. It therefore follows that that nobody can sell their freedom by signing a contract of slavery, or sell an eye or a kidney. This is the role of the fundamental rights: to be instruments that guarantee and protect those basic goods which are inherent requirements to a person's dignity. When it comes to guaranteeing these, the obligation essentially falls to the public administrations; but when it comes to protecting them and not damaging them, the obligation affects everyone, and this includes the very same subject who owns these rights. Here lies the notion of 'inalienability', in that these basic goods are outside the autonomy of the subject and, for this reason, must be protected including against her/his own will, if a wilful act were to lead to their possible injury.[59]

Clearly, not all basic goods are absolutely indisposable (outside the discretion of the individual), since many are the expression of the subject's autonomy and, logically, it is the will of the subject which determines them. Intimacy, for example, forms part of the sphere of the subject's autonomy, therefore it must be the subject's will that defines its limits. If someone freely decides to publish a personal diary or private correspondence, this is perfectly coherent with dignity since it pertains to the author's sphere of autonomy. The same is the case for other basic goods protected by fundamental rights, such as freedom of speech – which includes the option to remain silent, or religious freedom – which includes the option not to follow any religion, etc.[60]

Autonomy, constitutes a fundamental dimension of a person's dignity, but it cannot be exclusively identified with it, since dignity is something more than autonomy. Hence, there are certain essential goods, such as life or physical and moral integrity, which do not attempt to guarantee or protect autonomy, but rather something prior and much more radical: the very human condition of the subject, without which her/his autonomy would have no meaning...[61] In effect, life or physical integrity can never

---

recognition of their rights. In other words, the operability of the principle of dignity lies in establishing it as a guarantee of equality, non-discrimination and non-exclusion of any human being. Robles G (1995), 47.

[59]Talavera (2006), 208–212.

[60]Talavera (2006), 218–223.

[61]Along these lines the Human Rights Committee made the following ruling September 26 2003, in the case of Wackenheim v. France (nº. 854/1999) by which Mr. Wackenheim, a dwarf who was a resident of a French village, claimed his right to freely perform his job, which consisted of allowing himself to be thrown against a padded wall (dwarf tossing) in certain venues of nocturnal entertainment amidst of all manner of degrading comments, arguing that he was exercising the legitimate use of his autonomy. Among other arguments, the Committee interpreted "dwarf tossing" as an action that was contrary to human dignity and this decision should prevail over Mr. Wackenheim's

be disposable since, under no circumstances would it be licit to deprive someone of their life or subject them to some kind of torture, whatever the subject's motivations or regardless of their consent. To do so would be an attack on the very foundations of the human condition, and that is the ultimate meaning of dignity: to state that what is specifically human for everyone. The same can be said of any kind of mutilation of the body or act of euthanasia: these conducts mean the irreversible destruction of basic goods (life and physical integrity) which constitute this irreducible and irrevocable core of dignity.[62] This limitation also applies to acts of extreme risk to one's life without the corresponding professional qualifications (bull fighters, fire fighters, etc.). Something like this would happen, for example, with a radical attempt to exercise one's freedom, by attempting to make free use of their freedom in order to sell themselves as a slave.[63]

4 Dignity and Free Development of Personality

The claim that dignity is something more than autonomy has been reinforced by references in international covenants and modern constitutions to the concept of 'free development of personality'. This notion has its origin in the UDHR, which envisages it under two parallel formulations. Article 26.2 describes it as basic to education: "Education shall be directed to the *full* development of the human personality and to the strengthening of respect for human rights and fundamental freedoms (italics mine). Article 29.1 describes it as a foundation of solidarity: "Everyone has duties to the community in which alone the *free* and *full* development of his personality is possible." (italics mine).

From here on the concept can be found in European constitutions, always linked to human dignity.[64] In the Spanish Constitution, article 10.1 links the dignity of a person

---

will to allow himself to be subjected to such humiliations in return for money. "Dwarf tossing", as a circus act, had been condemned in various countries and had disappeared from all types of public entertainment.

[62]Here lies the criminal basis of euthanasia and other forms of assisted suicide in force practically all over the world. In Spain they are set out in art. 143 of the *Criminal Code.*

[63]Talavera (2006), 214–217.

[64]The *Basic Law of the Federal Republic of Germany, May 23* 1949, the basis of modern European constitutionalism, established the free development of personality within the context of human dignity as a basic premise. Article 2.1 points out that: "Everyone shall have the right to the free development of his personality, insofar as he does not infringe the rights of others or offend against the constitutional order or the moral code". Although its link to human dignity is not explicit, it is nevertheless clear since article 1.1 establishes that, "The dignity of man shall be inviolable. To respect and protect it shall be the duty of all state authority." The *Constitution of the Italian Republic*, 1947, also refers to this in the second paragraph of article 3, when it states that "It is the duty of the Republic to remove those obstacles of an economic or social nature which constrain the freedom and equality of citizens, thereby impeding the full development of the human person and the effective participation of all workers in the political, economic and social organisation of the country." Here the role of law is enshrined as regards the full development of personality. The

to inherent inalienable rights and the free development of personality, understood in terms of the "basis of political order and peace in society."[65]

Linking the free development of personality with dignity has made possible to devise 'dignity' as a static, global all-encompassing concept, which refers to the human condition and the absolute respect it is due. On the other hand, the 'free development of personality' constitutes a dynamic concept understood as the capacity of every individual to clearly lay out and develop a life project (an original way of being) throughout their existence. Here autonomy is stressed as an indispensable requirement so that an individual can develop as a complete person.[66] Dignity, thus, affects the ontological condition (having rights), while autonomy affects the existential or phenomenological dimensions (exercise of rights). Therefore, the free development personality is nothing other than the exercise of autonomy of the subject, which enjoys a wide-ranging freedom of action by virtue of which the individual can develop their own life project under the protection of the Law, restricted only by the limitations the Law itself imposes not to harm the life project of others and to safeguard the basic demands of dignity, upon which it is ultimately based.[67]

Moving beyond the ins and outs of free development of personality as a source of theoretical debate, it in no way proposes a different legal consequence depending on the formula applied. The free development of personality cannot state the absolute sovereignty of the subject's will nor presuppose an arbitrary and unlimited exercise of freedom in any sense. The constitutional State certainly does not advocate an ideal model of a person (each citizen defines their own), but there is a framework of

---

Constitution of the Republic of Portugal, 1976, in article 26 stipulates that: "1. Everyone shall possess the right to a personal identity, to the development of their personality, to civil capacity, to citizenship, to a good name and reputation, to their likeness, to speak out, to protect the privacy of their personal and family life, and to legal protection against any form of discrimination."; "3. The law shall guarantee the personal dignity and genetic identity of the human person, particularly in the creation, development and use of technologies and in scientific experimentation." Here a direct link is established between personal dignity and the development of personality.

[65] The connection between the principle of human dignity in article 10.1 of the Spanish Constitution and the free development of personality, has been pointed out by Latorre (1995), 81. The author notes that human dignity is inextricably linked to the right to the free development of personality, of which it is not only the basis but required consequence.

[66] Some authors have stoked a theoretical debate about the different meanings of the concept, according to whether expressed as 'full' or 'free' development of personality, claiming that the legal consequences are different for each individual context. To speak of 'full development of personality' would mean to contend the implicit existence of an ideal model of a person which should be the aim of all citizens "correctly" using their natural potential. The development of personality would not be free but rather directed towards a predetermined end. In contrast, to speak of 'free development of personality' would mean accepting there is no ideal model of a person, but rather that everyone can freely define and decide on it without any hindrance by authority over their will. According to this notion, the will of the individual is the governing factor. No other can decide how to focus her/his personal development. There are no previous ends which determine or condition exercising their freedom. It is their will which in itself constitutes the supreme end aside from any moral or social context. Vid. Santana (2014), 104–107.

[67] Robles (1995), 45–48.

fundamental goods and rights that make up the limits of autonomy of the subject.[68] This basic framework is what prevents someone from trying to, for example, self-define themselves as a paedophile stating that they find sexual relations with children to be very enriching. The free development of personality cannot be divorced from the inherent requirements of human dignity, since it constitutes its specification in those spheres governed by autonomy but in no way constitutes a principle which is autonomous and independent from that upon which is based. This is a "general freedom of action which corresponds to the individual in as much as s/he has the obligation to shape their own moral personality, but this is not a blank cheque to underwrite and allow whatever action they take. It is quite the opposite; it is crossed cheque which can only be cashed in to invest in the full development of the person."[69]

In summary, in order to establish a comprehensive concept of person one has to consider, on the one hand, factors characteristic of their ontology, closely linked to the concept of dignity universally shared by all human beings (rationality, morality, equality); and, on the other hand, factors which emerge from exercising their freedom (autonomy and self-determination). The binomial 'dignity-autonomy' relates dignity of the person with those areas of freedom recognised as rights (freedom of speech, of conscience, intimacy, etc.) that mark out the subject's private sphere excluded from all external intervention (*negative freedom*[70]). But this binomial can only find meaning and a basis in the binomial 'dignity-ontology' which enshrines the universal and inalienable dimension of dignity, inherent to all members of the human species.

5 Criminal Law Protection of Dignity: Moral Integrity

The dignity of the person, as a legal principle, today constitutes the most important criterion for limiting the extent to which legislation can intervene.[71] No public administration regulation or measure can contradict the requirements of dignity of the person.[72] This is a principle of material justice over and above all positive Law,

---

[68]Espinar (1995), 65. Robles (1995), 48.

[69]Robles (1995), 50. Along similar lines, J. Espinar, after reminding us that those which he considers social conceptions of freedom identify the basis of the same in the "possibility to fully carry out the ideal of person and not merely that of the individual", claims that freedom "can only be used to develop some very specific types of personality: those which are in accordance with models accepted by the nation's legal system, as and how they are set out constitutionally". Vid. Espinar (1995), 65–77.

[70]Ferrajoli (2008), 42–59.

[71]Alonso (2007), 4.

[72]The constitutional text which likely has had more repercussions within Europe when it comes to establishing dignity as the basis for legal systems, considering its safeguard as the ultimate goal of all Law, has been the *Basic Law of the Federal Republic of Germany*, de 1949, with its famous first article: "1. Dignity of man shall be inviolable. To respect and protect it shall be the duty of all state authority. 2. The German people therefore acknowledges inviolable and inalienable human rights as the basis of every. 3. The following basic rights shall be binding as directly valid law on legislation, administration and judiciary." This text has had a direct influence on all the current

but particularly over Criminal law, to the degree of constituting an a priori, an immanent limit to punishment through legislation, which would prevent any regulation or measure being qualified as a Law that violates any of its requirements.[73]

As already explained, the dignity of the person is linked, without exception, to human rights recognised in international charters and covenants,[74] and those attributed with inalienability and imprescriptibility.[75] However, it must be stressed that dignity is not, in the true sense, a human right, but rather it constitutes the very foundation of human rights, in that it is a guarantee of the goods required by the ontological structure of the human being (by their nature) in order to satisfy their adequate development as an individual being.[76]

Recognising that dignity is not a fundamental right but rather the foundation of rights, along with its value and material principle of justice,[77] makes it something which cannot be reduced to the category of a legal good protected by Criminal law.[78] Indeed, it is not possible to establish a criminal classification (a kind of 'crime' against dignity) which could specify an action that would include all that could harm or violate human dignity. Hence, it is the concrete manifestations of dignity which are protected by criminal law: life, physical or moral integrity, freedom, intimacy, honour, etc.[79] In other words, dignity is not protected directly or in any immediate sense by criminal law since it is not a legal good or a specific fundamental right. Instead, it is the underlying feature of all criminal Law, behind all kinds of criminal classifications which protect basic legal goods. This is where we find the protection of dignity.[80]

European consitutions and, although it has not been especially developed in legal doctrine, it has defined dignity as premise and limit on *ius puniendi* used by the Estado.

[73]Cerezo Mir (2004), 193.

[74]Peces-Barba (1993), 194. Dignity as "core content" of fundamental rights is underlined by Romeo Casabona while at the same time acknowledging the informative and interpretive function dignity over the aforementioned rights. See also Romeo (1994), 67–75.

[75]Talavera (2006), 212–216.

[76]Robles (1995), 48.

[77]Distinguishing between rules and principles is still an on-going debate. Nevertheless, we could say that principles respond to the demands of justice, equity or – generally speaking – ethical demands. They do not typify specific behaviours, but instead provide objective reasons to act in a given direction. On the other hand, as opposed to rules, they are not identified by their origin, but rather by their content and argumentative force. Vid. Dworkin (1980), 85–86 and Esser (1961). Nevertheless, there are authors who consider principles to be a special class of rule. For Laporta, a principle is a normative standpoint of a very general or abstract nature, but that, leaving this generality and abstraction, it does not have a structure which is different from a specific norm". Vid. Laporta (1985), 5. Along similar lines: Prieto (1998), 25–27. Atienza and Ruiz-Manero (1991), 21–32.

[78]Gracia (1996), 581–593.

[79]Montano (1997), 418.

[80]Gracia states the following: "Human dignity is not any kind of legal good…human dignity is a totalising attribute, a synthesis of the totality of specific physical and spiritual dimensions of the human person …all human goods of a highly personal nature (life, physical integrity, personal health, freedom, honour,, etc.) lead finally to the dignity of a person. But the dignity of a person cannot

But, what is fundamental lies in stressing – corroborated by its ontological nature – that a person's dignity is something more than just the sum of fundamental rights which emanate from them. Put another way, dignity is something more than the sum of basic goods that guarantee the exercise of autonomy by the subject and the free development of their personality. Dignity is the basis of the requirement of absolute and unquestionable respect to all people by virtue of the acknowledgment of their humanity. It is the acknowledgment of humanity in each human being. Accordingly, the protection of dignity under law does not end with the specific protection under law of life, physical integrity, freedom, honour, intimacy and other basic goods.[81] In effect, the goods and rights under the protection of Criminal law basically affect the expressions of freedom and autonomy of the subject, and it is precisely because of this that they cannot exhaust all the requirements of recognition and respect required by the dignity of the person. So, what does this mean, and what are the consequences?

It means that dignity can be harmed by the violation of a right, but a right can also be violated without directly harming the dignity of the person. For example, to reveal the contents of a private conversation can affect the right to intimacy, but this does not necessarily harm the person's dignity if it refers to matters of sport or artistic taste, etc.[82] On the other hand, since the dignity of a person is something more than their rights, it is also possible to conceive of evident injuries to dignity which do not directly affect any fundamental right: this is what happens, for example, in cases of bullying: nobody has the right to require that others socialise with them, but isolating a boy or girl at school means denying acknowledging and respecting them as a person, which clearly means harming their dignity.

Accordingly, beyond the specific legal protection of goods and fundamental rights, there is within a person something that could be called an 'ontological remnant of humanity', which can be attacked or harmed without necessarily harming a specific fundamental right (life, freedom, intimacy, honour, etc.).[83] There are actions which are not classifiable as an attack on a fundamental right but which can harm or undermine dignity because they involve exploiting, objectifying, debasing, degrading or humiliating the person. Examples of this would be hazing or initiation ceremonies that can take place on university campuses, or to force someone under arrest to strip or adopt a particular body posture, etc.

Stating that there is this 'remnant of humanity' does not mean admitting there are conducts that can harm dignity with impunity because, by not directly violating a fundamental right, they are not covered by criminal law. To avoid this from happening,

---

be a legal good from which one can deduce the specific unjust contents of a given punishable act." Vid. Gracia (1996), 583–584. Arguing along similar lines Díez-Ripollés points out that the notion of personal dignity "is not particularly adequate to characterise a legal good". Vid. Díez-Ripollés (1999), 242. Díez-Ripollés (2004a), 178. Díez-Ripollés (2004b), 242.

[81] Alonso (2007), 8.

[82] Romeo Casabona believes that human dignity can be harmed through a violation of one of the basic rights, but that not all such injuries necessarily involve harming dignity. From which one derives that dignity is something which is behind and informs rights, but is 'something' which is distinct from these rights. Vid. Romeo C (1994), 68.

[83] Alonso (2007), 5–6.

some authors have pointed out that this 'remnant of humanity', which refers to the ontological core of dignity (requirement of absolute respect), is covered and protected by the concept of 'moral integrity' which usually complements that of 'physical integrity, as contemplated in article 15 of the Spanish Constitution. Through the concept of moral integrity one would be 'consecrating' that there is this ontological core of dignity and, as a consequence, protection under criminal law of the stronghold of humanity not expressly included in the criminal laws which protect fundamental rights.[84] In Spain the codification of offences 'against moral integrity' is paradigmatic, particularly in art. 173.1 del Criminal Code,[85] in which effectively actions are contemplated which affect the very essence of dignity, its ontological nature: actions in which the very human condition of the victim is humiliated, degraded, debased, denied her/his condition as a person and treated as a thing.[86]

Can this 'remnant of humanity' inherent to a person's dignity really be identified with the notion of moral integrity and be considered to be protected by this under criminal law?[87] To my view, the notion of moral integrity constitutes positivation of this final remnant of dignity of the person; in other words, the embodiment of dignity as a legal principle in all which is not expressly taken into consideration in the sphere of fundamental rights.[88] And the protection of moral integrity under criminal law means codifying those conducts which are a direct attack on this last outpost of dignity, against what is enclosed within the most intimately human in everyone and which means, de facto, to objectify them, deny them humanity and the absolute respect the human condition deserves.[89] Moral integrity thus establishes an essential nucleus, an absolutely inviolable sphere of the person which protects them

[84]The judgement by the Spanish Supreme Court, 957/2007, of November 28, pointed out that: "Moral integrity is defined as a conceptual category in itself, as a human life value which is independent from the right to life, physical integrity, freedom in its various forms, or honour.".

[85]Art. 173.1 Spanish Criminal Code: "Whoever inflicts harm through degrading treatment upon another person, seriously undermining their moral integrity, will be punished with a prison sentence between six months and two years.".

[86]For example, the crime of sexual aggression constitutes an attack against the sexual freedom of women, which includes the violation of their dignity (the woman is being used as a thing or object). In the case of an offence against moral integrity, what is being attacked is exclusively the most intimate dimension of dignity, without any connection to any other good or right.

[87]Pérez (2005), 142–171; especially, p. 161. In her understanding, the line between dignity and moral integrity, if it does exist, is a very fine one, but there is no need to establish an equivalence between dignity and moral integrity.

[88]The introduction to the Spanish Penal Code of 1995, Título VII del Libro segundo, *De las torturas y otros delitos contra la integridad moral*, sparked off a still-running debate in the Spanish legal doctrine concerning the concept of moral integrity and how it related to identity, autonomy and independence with regard to dignity. Much has been published on this subject; see the following as representative examples: Díaz (1997), 54–60. Rodríguez (2000), 157–169. Barquín (2001), 50–56. García (2002), 1241–1257. Pérez (2005), 133–139. De la Mata/Pérez (2005), 26–32. For further information on the various doctrinal positions see Alonso (2013), 287–338.

[89]Muñoz (1999), 24.

from humiliating, degrading or debasing treatment which does not correspond to their condition as a human being.[90]

In this sense, moral integrity is not a response to a subjective criterion, feeling or awareness of the actual value or consideration which a person may have of themselves. It is not the person who can determine the value of their humanity since humanity is an 'objective' reality manifest in everyone and which must be safeguarded, even against their own will. Hence, moral integrity, insofar as protecting this final stronghold of humanity must be 'inalienable' (irrevocable and indisposable); in other words, independent from the will of a person, from their feelings or their perception of themselves and must be above any moral or religious notion.[91]

In short, moral integrity means the irrevocable requirement of all persons, inherent to their humanity, to be treated as such and not degraded, debased or objectified; a requirement which constitutes a fundamental legal good that merits protection under criminal law. And this protection under criminal law, insofar as it is linked to the most intimate core of dignity, prevents certain conducts from being decriminalised or set aside from protection under criminal law, regardless of changes in social morality or whether it includes the consent of those who perform them.

In effect, 'moral integrity' is not linked to any given religious notion or a response to 'dominant social morals' at any given moment in time, but instead it is linked to that which objectively forms an irrevocable part of human dignity. Therefore, this is not moralising Criminal law, but instead protecting the most intimate essence of the person's humanity, which takes form in its irrevocable requirement to be treated always, in accordance with dignity which is inherent to them as a person and not as a thing. In this sense, as already stated, it is not the will of the person which subjectively determines their dignity, but instead it is dignity, as an objective value, which constitutes, always and in all cases, them as a person. Hence, moral integrity, as regards the 'stronghold of humanity' is not a discretionally disposable good. For this reason, conducts such as sadomasochism (humiliating another person) can never be qualified as legitimate because they always constitute an attack on the moral integrity of the person, regardless of their consent. And the same can be said for prostitution (in which a person is exploited as a mere object of sexual pleasure) or surrogate motherhood (in which it is simply the woman's reproductive capacity which is purchased).

---

[90]The judgment by the Audiencia Provincial [Regional Court] of Guipúzcoa, May 25, 2000, is illustrative. It condemned five youths who were friends. They had driven in two cars to a mountain called Jaizkibel, where they forced a sixth friend who was travelling with them to strip off and then they spray painted his entire body pink, cut his hair and then left him there. The court decided to sentence them according to 173.1 of the Spanish Criminal Code, for having caused the victim feelings of fear, anguish and inferiority, susceptible to humiliation and damage to his physical or moral resistance. It refers to the judgments by the ECHR in the cases of 'Soering' July 7 1989 and 'Tomasi v. France' August 7 1992, where said requirements were presented to consider as to whether there had been a degrading treatment.

[91]Talavera (2006), 224. Alonso (2007), 8.

6 Dignity, Moral Integrity and Prostitution

The social and legal question of prostitution obviously goes beyond the sphere of criminal law, however the peculiarities of prostitution-related offences, from the point of view of a protected legal good, has been given scant attention by legal dogma.[92] After the 1990s, sex offences abandoned the paternalistic paradigm of the protection of honesty and were defined as attacks against sexual freedom, bringing with it a wide-reaching liberalisation of the practice of prostitution, implicitly considered as a legitimate sphere of autonomy of the person in relation to their sexuality.[93] As a consequence the conduct which was prosecuted was that of the third party who profits from the prostitution of another, either in the form of exploitation, trafficking in human beings or corruption of minors,[94] or with the consent of the person who prostitutes themselves.[95]

However, to consider prostitution as the supreme exercise of freedom is difficult to equate with the concept of dignity of the person, in its irrevocable stronghold of 'moral integrity', which must be protected by the Law, even against the own person's will. The secularisation of criminal laws on sexual offences has been based on disassociating sexuality from social moral codes, establishing sexual freedom as a protectable legal good to the detriment of honesty. But in this process what has been lost sight of is the unique nature of prostitution from the perspective of dignity and moral integrity. In effect, it is without question that exercising sexuality is an expression of a person's legitimate freedom and autonomy, but prostitution is not freely exercising one's sexuality, but rather it is determined by a financial component at its core (sex for a price). Accordingly, to frame prostitution within the sphere of sexual freedom

---

[92]Concerning how crimes related to prostitution in Spain have been dealt with over time, Alonso (2007), 9–16.

[93]It was expressed in such terms by the most distinguished criminal lawyers: prostitution as a degrading way to express sexuality, means a certain degree of deterioration of 'sexual freedom', but not the absence of this, rather quite the opposite: the broader exercise, deformed if you like, of this freedom ..., to the extent which this freedom is limited, the crimes of coercion and keeping in prostitution are comprehensible..., but when this is not the case and prostitution is exercised without any kind coercion... it is difficult to conceive in terms of an attack against the freedom of anybody." Vid. Muñoz-Conde (1996), 180.

[94]The benevolence of the Spanish penal code of 1995 towards prostituting others brought in its wake an unprecedented growth in in this business in Spain. This, alongside the EU requirements to pursue trafficking in human beings and the sexual explotación of children led to the reform of the Spanish Law Code in 1999 regarding sex offences. The title of *Título VIII* was modified, and renamed as "crimes against sexual freedom and indemnity". In el chapter V, whose title was changed to "concerning crimes relating to prostitution and the corruption of minors", the crime of the corruption of minors and disabled (art. 187 CP) was reintroduced, and in the chapter concerning prostitution trafficking in human beings was reintroduced concerning sexual exploitation, requiring there be violence, intimidation, deception or abuse of superiority or necessity or vulnerability of the victim (art. 188 CP).

[95]As a consequence of the reform of the Spanish Penal Code 2003, in article 188.1 a final paragraph was added in which the conduct of those who profit by exploiting the prostitution of another person is incriminating, even with their consent. Concerning the current law on prostitution-related crimes and discussion on the concept of prostitution, see: Rey/Mata/Serrano (1994), 76–85.

means to contend that sexuality can become available merchandise and that trading in sex can be comparable to any other free exchange of goods, governed exclusively by the principle of freedom of choice. Working from this basis, what has to be guaranteed is that in this line of business, as in any other, there is no lack of consent.[96] We have here a very serious factual and conceptual error concerning this question.

From a factual point of view, prostitution can hardly be considered as the legitimate exercise of sexual freedom. Even if between consenting adults, it invariably goes hand-in-hand with exploitation, trafficking, marginalisation and poverty, in a such way that the assumed free will in the overwhelming majority of cases turns out to be clearly influenced or tainted to the point of echoing the offence under criminal law which punishes the conduct of third parties who profit from it. But the fact is that even allowing for, or assuming, the exercise of prostitution were really 'free' (or perceived or experienced as free), from the conceptual point of view, an expression of sexual freedom cannot be equated with 'providing sex services' for a given price, even if this has been freely agreed. With the price as a mediating element, we are not talking about the legitimate exercise of autonomy by the person in the sphere of sexuality, but rather something radically distinct: we are looking at an alleged exercise of 'contractual freedom' whose legitimacy depends on whether the object of this contract (sex in exchange for a price) respects the person's dignity and, in particular, this irreducible nucleus of humanity we call 'moral integrity'. What is offered here as the object of the contract for sex services is the very person themself, since the sexual dimension of the person cannot be unhinged from the actual person. Accordingly, all people are reduced to the status of a piece of merchandise, a thing or an instrument through which a third party obtains sexual pleasure. And, as regards dignity, what criminal justice precisely attempts to prevent is reducing a person (as an end in itself) to a thing (a usable means for a given end).

Therefore, the unique criminal category of prostitution does not lie in circumstances of violence, trafficking, exploitation, corruption of minors, etc., in which case this would be an attack on sexual freedom or indemnity, since it is the third parties who exercise violence over others forcing their will. The criminal uniqueness of prostitution lies in its very own nature, in the very conduct of the person who prostitutes themselves, in that delivering sex services in exchange for a price means,

[96]Defence of the regulations-based model, defended by certain feminist positions, works from the premise that prostitution is not an undignified and degrading activity and that to invoke dignity is to refer to a "puritanical feminism dating back to the moral reforms at the end of the nineteenth century", and argue that the State should intervene to regulate prostitution whenever it is voluntary. This model rules out State intervention under criminal law whenever there is the consent of the person prostituting themself and proposes limiting state intervention to the incrimination of the conduct of third parties who violate sexual freedom. This model, which apparently is respectful towards the freedom of the person prostituting themself, fails to take into account that this supposed freedom, in the vast majority of cases, is clouded by poverty, marginalisation, status as a foreigner etc., not to mention more deep-rooted historical-cultural reasons. By accepting the fact that prostitution is, in the end, free and propose it should be governed by labour and health regulations, etc., overlooks the essential core of this reality, namely reducing a person to the status of merchandise and, with it, contributing – maybe involuntarily – to the perpetuation of this attack on their dignity. Vid. Maqueda (2009), 163–171.

per se, reducing the 'person' to a 'thing', no longer an end and instead a mere 'instrument': the actual person is, degraded and debased by being reduced to an object in a contract. And this means a direct attack on their moral integrity.

The reform of article 188.1 of the Spanish Penal Code in 2003, including a final subsection which categorises the conduct of those who profit from exploiting the prostitution of another person, even with their consent, means that 'sexual exploitation' takes place always when prostitution benefits a third party, regardless of the victim's own will. With this, one is arguing it is incompatible to 'be employed by others' in sexual matters; that is, nobody can hire another person to manage and organise their sex trade with third parties. However, this assumption acknowledges that exercising one's sexuality cannot be reduced to the category of 'service' or 'hire': something with which the person can trade freely. Otherwise, there would be no objection to being commercially exploited by third parties. Put another way, there could be companies whose profit-making activities could consist of offering 'sex services'.

It is precisely here where the contradiction lies: why does the sexual freedom of the person justify being self-employed as a sex worker but not employed by others (i.e. delegate their business to another)? The answer, to my mind, lies in the fact that the good being protected here is not sexual freedom but rather moral integrity. That is, reducing prostitution to a sex service, that can be managed in terms of a business by third parties (applying criteria of efficiency and financial profit), unavoidably assumes that the person is reduced to an object in financial trafficking and this directly violates their dignity. Only in this way can it be understood that having their consent becomes irrelevant when it is a third party who benefits financially, because we are faced with a clear situation of financial exploitation of the actual person (the whole person is involved in sexuality) and this conduct goes beyond the sphere of legitimate autonomy and the free development of personality.[97] Thus, to be exploited (like being enslaved or tortured) are conducts that always represent an attack on a person's moral integrity, regardless of consent, because they violate the irreducible core of humanity, irrevocable and indisposable, which must be protected by law, including against the will the person themself.[98]

In summary, although nowadays this view is often written off as being reactionary, in my view, a coherent notion of dignity requires considering the legal good protected in sex crimes, rather than sexual freedom, is the person's moral integrity that, as an irrevocable assumption of their humanity, should also be extended to include prostitution. Abolishing prostitution today indeed poses very similar questions today to those put forward for the abolition of slavery at the time. Precisely because of this, it is essential to fight for this cause.[99]

---

[97] As maintained by some authors, pornography and child prostitution, as crimes, imply that a person is reduced to the condition of a mere object, limiting and undermining other individual legal goods which are distinct from sexual freedom (Musacchio/De la Cuesta/Aguado (2006), 55–57.

[98] Rey/Mata/Serrano (1994), 71. Dignity… "is a good *extra commercium* and it is inalienable".

[99] Maqueda (2009), 271.

Protecting moral integrity in relation to prostitution is to speak of the requirement inherent to all people not to be treated as a thing (not to be used or exploited, nor humiliated, debased or degraded), whether by third parties or by oneself. So, we are not dealing with protecting a given 'conservative' sexual morality nor adopting a paternalistic legal position.[100] Rather, this is understanding that moral integrity is one of the most authentic legal goods of the Constitutional State, which although vulnerable to attacks by other actions, is under a very direct attack by prostitution-related crimes.[101]

7 Dignity, Moral Integrity and Surrogate Motherhood

Surrogate motherhood is a practice which, despite being prohibited in almost all the countries in the world,[102] is increasingly gaining social legitimacy bolstered by an idea of dignity which takes for granted the two basic assumptions which have been cited throughout this article: dualism –which considers the body in terms of something which is purely material at the discretionary disposal of the person –, and autonomy – understood in terms of unrestrained capacity to decide one's own life project.[103]

Leaving aside other considerations, to gestate a baby for someone else in return for monetary remuneration collides head on with two of the most universally accepted principles in Law in the civilised world: the principle that the human body, whose dignity is inviolable,[104] must be excluded from all manner of sale of assets (it cannot be turned into an object for trade) and the principle *mater semper certa est* (the mother is who gives birth). It is acknowledged in this manner in the Spanish Law 14/2006, concerning Assisted Human Reproduction Techniques (AHRT), possibly the most advanced in the world: it declares null and void any gestational surrogacy contract in favour of a third party (art. 10.1) and reiterates that only birth determines natural filiation as regards the mother (art. 10.2). In addition, this law attempts to prevent contracts becoming a way to legitimise the sale and purchase of new-born

[100] Rey/Mata/Serrano (1994), 72.

[101] Alonso (2007), 17–18.

[102] Of the current 28 EU member states, it is only recognised in Greece, Portugal and the United Kingdom – in the case of the latter the transfer of paternity is, in addition, required after the birth. It is expressly prohibited in eight countries (Germany, Austria, Bulgaria, Spain, France, Italy, Malta and Switzerland), while in the remaining countries there is no law on this matter. For their part, Ukraine and Russia, Belorussia, Georgia and Armenia, authorise it. In The US, legal authorisation rests with the individual states – the majority prohibit it. The state most open to this practice is California, which has turned it into a simple business transaction, with agencies and specialised clinics. As regards developing countries, the practice is quite widespread in India, Nepal, Thailand and Cambodia.

[103] Talavera (2017), 197–231.

[104] Aparisi (2017), 167–168.

babies,[105] and, as a result, another way to exploit the women who are most vulnerable by taking advantage of their situation of need or poverty – particularly in those countries where they are still subject to abuse and discrimination for a whole range of cultural or social reasons.[106] Nevertheless, in spite of all of this, the majority view in society nowadays is that surrogate motherhood can constitute a legitimate reproductive alternative, provided it is duly regulated to protect the interests of the various parties.

The case of surrogate motherhood offers a number of parallels with the above analysis concerning prostitution. Indeed, there are two serious conceptual mistakes which have already been pointed out: firstly, there is an attempt to define pregnancy as a simple biological function at the woman's discretionary disposal; secondly, an attempt to reduce this function to the category of 'service' which is open to be commercialised; that is, offered in exchange for a financial remuneration. Working from this premise, this would be a legitimate expression of freedom of choice that would establish the price and conditions of providing the service to third parties in the context of a contract: namely, gestating a baby. Viewed thus, what would take place is a legitimate legal business, in which the will of the parties involved must be respected and in which it is only necessary to guarantee that there is no lack of consent, as is that case in any other contract.

Notwithstanding, is it possible to separate the body-biological dimension in pregnancy from the rest of the person? The answer, as in the case of prostitution, can only be negative. Human gestation is a process which involves the entire person. It is not something which can be depersonalised and objectified as a mere bodily function torn from the person: it is the person, not the uterus that gestates. This is not a simple capacity such as memory, nor it is a simply skill such as skating or drawing. Gestation obviously involves the biological dimension, but it also includes psychological and emotional aspects as well. To attempt to argue that gestation is reduced to simply developing a foetus in the uterus and that the pregnant women can voluntarily decide to be on the side-lines from this process is in contradiction with the most elementary anthropological facts of maternity. As pointed out in psychological studies concerning the "attachment",[107] the mother–child relationship during

---

[105]The parallel has been pointed out, with some accuracy, between renting an uterus and buying or selling a child, prohibited by the Protocol relating to the buying/selling of children and child prostitution (May 25, 2000) of the United Nations Convention on the Right of the Child 1989, when there is no genetic link between the principals and the gestated baby, resulting the genetic child from the gestating mother. It is acknowledged in the ECHR Grand Chamber judgment in the case of *Paradiso Campanelli v. Italy* (Albert (2017), 179–180).

[106]López (2017), 169–172.

[107]The 'attachment' theory, begun by John Bowlby (1998) and outlined and developed by Mary Answorth (1989), 709–716; states that the main affective bond and the most lasting of all, is that established between the mother and the baby during pregnancy and breast feeding. This bond is the basis upon which all bonds are developed that a human will establish with other people throughout their life. The studies by both authors (and those who have followed them) indicate that this bond begins with the interactions during pregnancy, continues with breast feeding and is definitively forged during the period between 3 and 36 months after birth. When this bond between mother and baby is stable and lasting, it has a decisive influence on the child's self-esteem and her/his ability to

pregnancy is a determining factor in the future of both, and explains why a significant number of women who are commissioned as surrogate mothers experience a high degree of frustration and suffering when they hand over the babies that they have been carrying, and who, in a number of cases, require specific therapy to overcome this trauma.[108]

Accordingly, if pregnancy involves the whole of the person, to turn it into something which is available on the market means to exploit the person themself, reducing their reproductive potential of that of a 'service' that can be the object of a contract. To claim this not only contradicts the most basic anthropological and psychological premises, but also directly attacks one's dignity: the person is reduced to the condition of a thing, exploited as merchandise and becomes the object of a contract. Furthermore, it is not just a woman's reproductive capacity which is involved here; there is a third person– the baby – whose dignity is violated also since s/he becomes a piece of merchandise seen in terms of the end product of a service, subject to periodic quality control checks, and even subject to rejection at any time should s/he not fulfil the conditions set out in the contracts by the principals. This is underlined by the Spanish Supreme Court: "…the commodification which assumes that the filiation of a minor could be determined in favour of whoever has commissioned this, by means of a contract for her/his gestation, violates the dignity of the minor by converting them into the object of commercial trafficking."[109]

The consent of women in this conduct, as can be clearly seen, becomes irrelevant since the irrevocable and indisposable nature of dignity, both hers and the baby's, in this irreducible core of humanity that moral integrity represents, requires the Law to protect her including against her own will. It is precisely for this reason that it is necessary to advocate the universal prohibition of this practice to exclude the human body from all manner of commercial transactions, and an inherent and irrevocable requirement of the dignity of a person, acknowledged by all international agreements on this matter.[110]

At his point I would like to pose a final question on this matter: can altruism modulate or qualify in some way the absolute indisposability of the human body to be used as merchandise? Put another way, is it only financial gain that would be the

establish healthy relationships throughout her/his life. On the other hand, the abrupt break of this bond (physical or emotional separation from the mother) or fragility (absence of affection or care) can cause the child to develop an affective disorder or asocial personality, and states of anxiety and frustration in the mother. Vid. Delgado and Oliva (2004), 65–81.

[108] Wilkinson (2003), 180.

[109] Spanish Supreme Court judgement, February 6, 2014, FJ. 7, nº 8.

[110] The Spanish Supreme Court ruling of February 6, 2014, points this out in the following terms: "Other legal goods can concur with those with which it is necessary to put under consideration. Such are the respect for dignity and moral integrity of the pregnant woman, to avoid the exploitation of this state of need in which young women can find themselves in a state of poverty, and to prevent the commercialization of gestation and filiation. This concerns principles safeguarded by the constitutional texts of our country, those surrounding and the international agreements on human rights, and other sectors referring to infancy and family relations such as the Convention relating to the Protection of Children and Cooperation in Respect of Intercountry Adoption, The Hague 29 May, 1993" (FJ. 5, nº 7).

obstacle to making the body available for a third party in order to gestate a baby for them? The answer is quite simple. Financial gain is not the determining factor in surrogate motherhood, but rather the violation of dignity and moral integrity of the person which means reducing their procreative capacity to a mere service or for hire to a third party. That is, the notion of the body as something which is merely instrumental, that can place its functions (particularly that of reproduction) at the disposal of the market.

References

Albert M (2017) La explotación reproductiva de mujeres y el mito de la subrogación altruista: una mirada global al fenómeno de la gestación por sustitución. Cuadernos de Bioética XXVIII-2: 179–192
Alonso M (2007) ¿Protección penal de la dignidad? A propósito de los delitos relativos a la prostitución y a la trata de personas para la explotación sexual. Revista Penal 19:4–18
Alonso M (2013) Derecho Penal y dignidad humana: De la no intervención contraria a la dignidad a los delitos contra la dignidad. Libro homenaje al profesor Luis Rodríguez Ramos. Tirant lo Blanch, Valencia, pp 287–338
Amelung K (2007) El concepto «bien jurídico» en la teoría de la protección penal de bienes jurídicos. In Hefendehl R (coord.) La teoría del bien jurídico. ¿Fundamento de legitimación del derecho penal o juego de abalorios dogmático? Marcial Pons, Barcelona, pp 233–257
Andorno R (1996) La distinction juridique entre les personnes et les choses à l'épreuve des procréations artificielles. LGDJ, París
Aparisi A (2013) El principio de la dignidad humana como fundamento de un bioderecho global. Cuadernos de Bioética XXIV-2: 201–223
Aparisi A (2017) Maternidad Subrogada y Dignidad de la Mujer. Cuadernos de Bioética XXVIII-2: 161–178
Arendt H (1992) La condición humana (transl. Gil R). Paidós, Barcelona
Atienza M, Ruiz-Manero J (1991) Sobre principios y reglas. Doxa 10: 21-32
Ballesteros J (1989) Postmodernidad: Decadencia o Resistencia. Tecnos, Madrid
Ballesteros J. (2001) Exigencias de la dignidad humana en biojurídica. In: Tomás G (coord.) Manual de Bioética. Ariel, Barcelona, pp 179–203
Barquín J (2001) Delitos contra la integridad moral. Bosch, Barcelona
Bobbio N (1991) El tiempo de los derechos. Sistema, Madrid
Choza J (1995) El descubrimiento de la dignidad humana. In: Arechederra JJ (ed.) Bioética, psiquiatría y Derechos Humanos, I.M. & C., Madrid
Cerezo Mir J (2004) Curso de Derecho Penal Español. 6ª edn. I. Tecnos, Madrid
Delgado AO, Oliva A (2004) Estado actual de la teoría del apego. Revista De Psiquiatría Y Psicología Del Niño Y Del Adolescente 41:65–81
De la Mata/Pérez (2005) El concepto de trato degradante en el delito contra la integridad moral del art. 173.1 del Código Penal. Revista Penal 15: 26-32
Díaz MP (1997) El bien jurídico protegido en los nuevos delitos de tortura y atentado contra la integridad moral. Estudios Penales y Criminológicos XX: 54–60
Díez-Ripollés L (1999) El objeto de protección del nuevo Derecho Penal sexual. Estudios De Derecho Judicial 21:235–249
Díez-Ripollés L (2004a) Comentarios al Código Penal. Parte Especial. I, Tirant lo Blanch, Valencia
Díez-Ripollés L (2004b) Comentarios al Código Penal. Parte Especial, II, Tirant lo Blanch, Valencia
Donini M (2010) El derecho penal frente a los desafíos de la modernidad. Estudios de derecho penal, Ara Editores, Lima

Donini M (2002) Prospettive europee del principio di offensività. In: AA.VV., Verso un codice penale modello per l'Europa. Offensività e colpevolezza. Cedam, Padova
Descartes R (2017) Meditations on First Philosophy in which are demonstrated the existence of God and the distinction between the human soul and body (trans. Bennett J) on-line edition
Dworkin R (2011) Life´s dominion: an argument about abortion, euthanasia and individual freedom. Random House, New York
Dworkin R (1980) ¿Es el Derecho un sistema de normas? In: Dworkin R (ed) La Filosofía del Derecho. FCE, México, pp 72–89
Engelhardt T (1995) The foundations of bioethics. Harper Perennial Modern Classics, New York
Espinar J (1995) Consideraciones en torno al libre desarrollo de la personalidad desde un planteamiento social. In García San Miguel L (coord.) El libre desarrollo de la personalidad. Universidad de Alcalá, Madrid, pp 59–71
Esser J (1961) Principio y norma en la elaboración jurisprudencial del Derecho privado. Bosch, Barcelona
Ferrajoli L (1995) Derecho y razón: teoría del garantismo penal. Trotta, Madrid
Ferrajoli L (2012) El principio de lesividad como garantía penal. Nuevo Foro Penal 8:100–114
García M (2002) La protección penal de la integridad moral en la Ciencia del Derecho Penal ante el nuevo siglo. Libro Homenaje al Profesor Doctor D. José Cerezo Mir. Tecnos, Madrid, pp 1241–1257
García-Pablos A (2006) Introducción al derecho penal. 4ª edn. Editorial Universitaria Ramón Areces, Madrid
Glendon MA (2012) La soportable levedad de la dignidad. Persona Y Derecho 67–2:250–262
Gonzalez AM (1996) Naturaleza y dignidad. Eunsa, Pamplona
González AM (1997) Naturaleza y dignidad personal desde el pensamiento de Robert Spaemann. VVAA El primado de la persona en la moral contemporánea. Eunsa, Pamplona, pp 209–229
González J (1986) La dignidad de la persona. Cívitas, Madrid
González-Amuchastegui J (2004) Autonomía, dignidad y ciudadanía. Una teoría de los derechos humanos, Tirant lo Blanch, Valencia
Gracia D (1984) Ética de la calidad de vida. Fundación Santa María, Madrid
Gracia L (1996) El delito y la falta de malos tratos en el Código Penal español de 1995. Actualidad Penal, Juny 13:581–593
Gros-Espiell H (2003) La dignidad humana en los instrumentos internacionales sobre Derechos Humanos. Anuario Derechos Humanos (Nueva Época) IV: 195–209
Guardiola J (2003) La realización arbitraria del propio derecho. Tirant lo Blanch, Valencia
Häberle P (2008) La dignidad del hombre como fundamento de la comunidad estatal. In Fernández-Segado, F (coord.) Dignidad de la persona, derechos fundamentales, justicia constitucional y otros estudios de Derecho público. Dykinson, Madrid, pp 172–189
Hervada J (1991) Los derechos inherentes a la dignidad de la persona humana. Humana Iura 1:351–369
Hoerster N (1992) Acerca del significado del principio de la dignidad humana. In: AA.VV. En defensa del positivismo jurídico. Gedisa, Barcelona, pp 89–98
Hormazábal H (1991) Bien jurídico y Estado social y democrático de Derecho. El objeto protegido por la norma penal. PPU, Barcelona, pp 8–41
Jakobs G (1995) Derecho penal, parte general. Fundamentos y teoría de la imputación, 2ª edn. Marcial Pons, Madrid
Jakobs G (2003) ¿Qué protege el Derecho penal: bienes jurídicos o vigencia de las normas? in Montealegre E (coord.) El funcionalismo en Derecho penal. Homenaje al profesor Günther Jakobs. I. Universidad Externado de Colombia, Bogotá, pp 41–78
Kant I (1995) Fundamentación de la metafísica de las costumbres, 11a edn. Espasa-Calpe, Madrid
Kant I (2002) Groundwork for the metaphysics of morals. Yale University Press, Edit and trans. Wood AW
Laporta F (1985) El principio de igualdad: introducción a su análisis. Sistema 67:5–19

Latorre A (1995) El desarrollo de la personalidad en la jurisprudencia del Tribunal Constitucional. In: García San Miguel L (coord.) El libre desarrollo de la personalidad. Universidad de Alcalá, Madrid, p 76–89
Locke J (2004) An essay concerning human understanding. Penguin, New York (Book I, Introduction)
López J (2017) Dimensión económica de la maternidad subrogada (habitaciones en alquiler). Cuadernos de Bioética XXVIII-2: 201–217
Macklin R (2003) Dignity is a useless concept. BMJ 327:1415–1421
Maqueda ML (2009) Prostitución, feminismos y derecho penal. Granada, Comares
Muñoz A (1999) Los delitos contra la integridad moral. Tirant lo Blanch, Valencia
Muñoz-Conde F (1996) Derecho Penal. Parte Especial. 11ª edn. Tirant lo Blanch, Valencia
Marin ML (1998) La Declaración Universal de Derechos Humanos de 10 de diciembre de 1948: ¿Nuevo Derecho Natural de la Humanidad? In Balado M, Regueiro JM (dir.) La Declaración Universal de los Derechos Humanos en su 50 aniversario Bosch, Barcelona, pp 131–149
Muñoz-Conde F, García M (2007) Derecho penal. Parte general. 7ª edn. Tirant lo Blanch, Valencia
Masferrer A (2017) Una historia retrospectiva de la dignidad humana. De la Constitución española (1978) al Descubrimiento de América (1492). GLOSSAE. European Journal of Legal History 14: 493–545 (https://www.glossae.eu/wp-content/uploads/2017/12/Masferrer-Historia-retrospectiva-DH-GLOSSAE-22.pdf)
Masferrer A (2018) La dignidad humana en el Constitucionalismo moderno. Análisis retrospectivo de su evolución: del actual México a la Nueva España. 1916 Rumbo a la Constitución de 1917. Instituto de Investigaciones Jurídicas–UNAM, México
Masferrer A (2016) Taking human dignity more humanely: a historical contribution to the ethical foundations of the constitutional democracy. In: Masferrer A, García-Sánchez E (eds) Human dignity of the vulnerable in the age of rights: interdisciplinary perspectives. Springer, Dordrecht-Heidelberg-London-New York, pp 221–256
Melendo T, Millán-Puelles L (1996) Dignidad: ¿una palabra vacía? Eunsa, Pamplona
Montano PJ (1997) La Dignidad humana como bien jurídico tutelado por el Derecho penal. Actualidad Penal, May 11, p 418
Musacchio/De la Cuesta/Aguado (2006) El concepto de prostitución en la normativa penal contra la explotación sexual de menores en Italia y España. La Ley Penal 24:46–58
Oheling A (2011) El concepto constitucional de dignidad de la persona: Forma de comprensión y modelos predominantes de recepción en la Europa continental. Revista Española De Derecho Constitucional 91:135–178
Palazzani L (2007) Bioética y Derechos Humanos. In Ballesteros J, Fernández E (coord.) Biotecnología y posthumanismo. Thomson-Aranzadi, Navarra, pp 371–394
Parfit D (1984) Reasons and persons. Clarendon Press, Oxford
Pavía ML, Revet T (1999) La dignité de la personne humanine. Economica, París
Peces-Barba G (1993) Derecho y derechos fundamentales CEC, Madrid
Peces-Barba G (1995) Ética, poder y Derecho. CEC, Madrid
Peces-Barba G (1999) La eutanasia desde la filosofía del derecho. In Ansuátegui FJ (coord.) Problemas de la euthanasia. Dykinson, Madrid, pp 15–26
Peces-Barba G (2002) La dignidad de la persona desde la filosofía del Derecho. Dykinson, Madrid
Pérez AI (2005) El delito contra la integridad moral del artículo 173.1 del vigente Código Penal. Aproximación a los elementos que lo definen. UPV/EHU, Bilbao
Prieto L (1998) Ley, principios, derechos. Dykinson, Madrid
Rey/Mata/Serrano (1994) Prostitución y Derecho. Thomson-Aranzadi, Madrid
Robles G (1995) El libre desarrollo de la personalidad (Artículo 10.1 de la CE). In García San Miguel L (coord.) El libre desarrollo de la personalidad. Universidad de Alcalá, Madrid
Rodríguez MJ (2000) Torturas y otros delitos contra la integridad moral cometidos por funcionarios públicos. Granada, Comares
Romeo C (1994) El Derecho y la Bioética ante los límites de la vida humana. Centro de Estudios Ramón Areces, Madrid

Roxin C (1997) Derecho Penal, parte general. Civitas, Madrid
Santana E (2014) Las claves interpretativas del libre desarrollo de la personalidad. CEFD 29:99–115
Silva JM (2003) Valoraciones sociales y Derecho penal. Persona Y Derecho 46:143–163
Singer P (1994) Ethics. Oxford University Press
Singer P (1995) Rethinking life and death: The collapse of our traditional ethics. Saint Martin's Press, New York
Singer P (2002) Animal liberation: a new ethics for our treatment of animals (1975). Harper Perennial Modern Classics, New York
Singer P (2016) Ethics in the real world: 82 brief essays on things that matter. Princeton University Press
Spaemann R (1988) Sobre el concepto de dignidad humana. Persona Y Derecho 19:11–24
Spaemann R (1989) Lo natural y lo racional: Ensayos de antropología. Rialp, Madrid
Spaemann R (2000) Personas. Acerca de la distinción entre algo y alguien, Eunsa, Pamplona
Talavera, P (2006) ¿Derechos inalienables e indisponibles? In: Megías JJ (coord.) Derechos Humanos. Thomson-Aranzadi, Pamplona, pp 201–221
Talavera P (2017) Maternidad subrogada: ficción jurídica contra verdad biológica. Revista de Derecho y Genoma humano/Law and the Human Genome Review. Genetics, Biotechnology and Advanced Medicine 46:197–231
Von Liszt F (1999) Tratado de Derecho penal. II. 4ª edn. Reus, Madrid
Wilkinson S (2003) The exploitation argument against commercial surrogacy. Bioethics 17–2:171–183

From Eunomia to Paideia: The Educating Nature of Law

Vicente Bellver

Abstract Education and Law are two of the institutions which most directly influence the configuration of the individual and of society. Furthermore, there is a close relationship between them in that each determines the development of the other. From their very beginnings, political and legal philosophy have asked what is Law, what is education and what should the relationship between them be. This chapter deals with the relationship between Law and education from this philosophical-practical perspective. It begins by illustrating the notable similarities between both and then goes on to address two questions: (1) whether Law should educate citizens in moral virtues; and (2) if the education of citizens should concern itself with reinforcing obedience to laws. As regards the first, I shall discuss Aristotelian thinking, while for the second Rousseau's.

Law and education are intimately linked. Reflections on how *eunomia* and *paideia* are related date as far back as classical philosophy and, without wishing to oversimplify, this relationship can be seen from three perspectives: technical-legal, sociological-functional and philosophical-moral.

(1) *Technical-legal*. Law essentially governs formal education.[1] Public policies in matters of education take form within an extensive regulatory system whose final objective is to effectively acknowledge the right to education. Laws relating to education regulate the structure of the education system, the role of parents, criteria for selecting teachers, education methodology, contents and skills to be taught that are the object of education. Taken as a whole, these regulations are housed under the umbrella term Education Law.

Education, in turn, exercises a major influence on people as citizens, because it conveys a particular conception of politics and Law. Sometimes this education takes

V. Bellver (✉)
Department of Legal and Political Philosphy, Universitat de València, Valencia, España
e-mail: vicente.bellver@uv.es

[1]When referring to education, we commonly distinguish between formal, non formal and informal education; La Belle (1982), 159–175.

A. Masferrer (ed.), *Criminal Law and Morality in the Age of Consent*, Ius Gentium: Comparative Perspectives on Law and Justice 84,
https://doi.org/10.1007/978-3-030-64163-4_12

the form of a subject or curricular field which is given the name of Democracy and Human Rights Education or Citizenship Education.

The education of the future judiciary is of transcendental importance in this context, especially for those who become judges. It is they who will interpret and apply Law in accordance with preconceptions concerning human life, society, justice and whatever Law they have; and these very same people tend to be heavily influenced by the education they receive in the Schools of Law.[2] The name given to this training is Legal Education and the Schools of Law, the bodies mainly responsible for this, attempt to train their students according to pre-agreed conceptions and values of Law.

Formal education is shaped by what Law establishes; but Law, in turn, is heavily influenced by formal education and, in particular, what is taught in Schools of Law.

(2) *Sociological-functional.* Law fulfils a transcendental educational role. One can compare the educational influence of legal regulations to that of the influence of the education system itself, which is more often than not greater. Regulations are not usually followed out of fear of sanctions, but rather because we acknowledge they express an inherent moral authority, that is, we presume that they are legitimate. When this is not the case, a citizen obeys the laws out of fear or simply ceases to obey by rebelling against them to one degree or another.

Whatever a citizen's reaction to Law may be, it always exercises a decisive influence over people because it offers them a guideline from which to act, not act or even rebel, and because it can cause them to follow or reject narratives and values implicit in any Law.

This educational function of Law, however, cannot be disassociated from the regulatory function which education fulfils. The degree to which citizens adhere to laws depends a great deal on the education they have received regarding what is good and just. The influence of education on Law can become so notable that it can trigger changes in the laws. The sociology of Law studies both the educational role of Law as well as the regulatory role of education.

(3) *Philosophical-practical.* The technical-legal approach looks at the relationship between Law and education as a phenomenon subject to regulation, while the sociological-functional perspective sees it in terms of a social fact. However, neither approach addresses the question of what the correct relationship between education and Law should be, which is what is posed by the philosophical-practical perspective. Should Law educate citizens as regards morals, or not?[3] What position should

---

[2]An illustrative example of this is Charles Sutherland, who was a US Supreme Court judge between 1922 and 1938: "For teachers in American law schools, Sutherland is of further significance since he was in large measure the logical product of his formal education. His teachers not only supplied him with the ingredients of the political philosophy which governed his general outlook; they supplied him with specific answers to specific problems. In this, they were certainly exceptional" Pachal (1946), 334.

[3]Law is always built on a base of moral values, which it transmits to citizens via laws and regulations. Some authors claim that Law should transmit just values, while others argue that the existence of Law does not depend on fulfilling this obligation: "The tendency to identify law and justice is the tendency to justify a given social order. It is a political, not a scientific tendency. In view of this

education adopt in relation to Law? Should education always stress that we should abide by the law, take a neutral and purely informative stance or adopt a critical approach to laws, which could even lead to defying them? When the relationship between Law and education is studied from this perspective, we assess how suitable the answers are.

Education and Law are two of the institutions which most directly influence the configuration of the individual and of society. Furthermore, there is a close relationship between them in that each determines the development of the other. From their very beginnings, political and legal philosophy have asked what is Law, what is education and what should the relationship between them be. Even before Plato, pre-Socratic philosophers and tragic poets[4] pondered the manner in which both should be related, and this concern with finding the right relationship between Law and education is a vein which runs through to present times. The very Universal Declaration of Human Rights (1948) recognises the relationship between Law and education when it sets out the aim of education: "Education shall be directed to the full development of the human personality and to the strengthening of respect for human rights and fundamental freedoms." (art. 26.2). This article can be seen in terms of establishing a virtuous circle between education, developing human personality and human rights. The aim of education is the full development of human personality, which is only possible from a position which respects and promotes human rights; and to promote human rights requires paying special attention to the right to education.

This chapter deals with the relationship between Law and education from this philosophical-practical perspective. It begins by illustrating the notable similarities between both and then goes on to address two questions: (1) whether Law should educate citizens in moral virtues; and (2) if the education of citizens should concern itself with reinforcing obedience to laws. As regards the first, I shall discuss Aristotelian thinking, while for the second Rousseau's. Both writers offer interesting, yet incomplete, proposals on these questions, so I shall attempt to compensate by recourse to two emblematic texts in the political and legal history of the world: one ancient text, Pericles' funeral oration, and the other contemporary, the Universal Declaration of Human Rights.

Werner Jaeger, one of the twentieth century authors who most studied the relationship between Law and education states that, "the structure of every society is based on the written or unwritten laws which bind it and its members. Therefore, all education in any human community (be it a family, a social class, a profession, or some wider complex such as a race or a state) is the direct expression of its active awareness of a *standard*."[5] (Jaeger 1967). Although Jaeger speaks of laws, he does not refer exclusively to those which are peculiar to Law but rather a combination of legal and, in particular, moral laws which are at the basis of the former. According to this German philologist, education both receives and transmits these laws from

---

tendency, the effort to deal with law and justice as two different problems falls under the suspicion of repudiating altogether the requirement that positive law should be just" Kelsen (2005), 5.

[4]Jaeger (1947).

[5]Jaeger (1967), xiv.

one generation to the next. But since these dynamics are not simply passive and the transmission is not purely mechanical: education not only prolongs validity of these laws across time, but also changes their contents. So, we find ourselves before a situation in which education transmits a moral regulatory core upon which Law is constructed in each society, yet education has the power to transform the contents of these moral and legal rules. This intimate relationship between Law and education is found in every society. At this point, I wonder if this relationship entertains a value judgment, that is, if there are some modes of this relationship which are more correct than others. In order to address this question, I shall begin by illustrating this very close relationship.

1 Similarities Between Law and Education

Law and education are fundamental institutions of any society, with their own distinctive features; nevertheless, there are also noteworthy similarities, from which it would follow that all Law is educating and all education regulatory. The following paragraphs illustrate the main similarities between Law and education.

(1) *Law and education aspire to bringing out the best in humans as regards their individual and social facets, and resort to legislation and rules in order to achieve this*. It might seem that the main purpose of Law is to limit individual freedom, while the purpose of education is to contribute to developing individual freedom. Law is external to the individual, formally requiring them to abide by the laws under threat of sanctions, but is not concerned with the degree to which individuals believe in or agree with them. In contrast, education focuses on the individual as a whole and provides them with the abilities to reach full personal development. This distinct mode of operation is illustrated by the different way in which society perceives the authorities responsible for Law and education. Even if both are respected by the citizens, those charged with enforcing the law (judges and police) have a tendency to generate fear, while education authorities tend to be held in esteem. If we turn to the terms used in Ancient Rome, Law is founded on *potestas*, while education is based on the *auctoritas* of the teachers which is recognised by students and society.

The truth is that Law and education are more closely related than they may at first appear. Law justifies the limitations it imposes on individual freedom, precisely in order to guarantee the freedom of everyone. The first requirement for an individual to develop is being able to enjoy conditions under which they can act freely, which are achieved when the individual enjoys freedom from want and freedom from fear, to quote the phrases coined by Roosevelt in his Four Freedoms Speech de 1941.[6] It is

[6]This speech has been qualified as the most important State of the Union speech in the history of the United States; Fischer (2014). In this speech, President Franklin D. Roosevelt defined the four freedoms upon which the world should be built in the following words: "In the future days, which we seek to make secure, we look forward to a world founded upon four essential human freedoms. The first is freedom of speech and expression—everywhere in the world. The second is freedom of every person to worship God in his own way—everywhere in the world. The third is freedom

the extent to which a person is free from fear and need, where we find the conditions to develop their projects for a dignified life: through the freedom of worship and freedom of speech. Law is the instrument by which we free ourselves of fear and need, and it does so through the two main categories of human rights: civil and political rights; and economic, social and cultural rights.

To be able to enjoy freedom of worship and freedom of speech, education is essential: without it, a person cannot achieve the right conditions in order to forge a conception of the world which would guide their thinking and individual and social actions. For this reason, education is part of these social rights.

Like Law, education also limits individual freedom. Education is a right, but it is also an obligation: it requires students to go to school during the years classified as compulsory education, and to subject themselves to the disciplinary regulations laid out by the schools. This prescriptive nature of education goes even further because, as stated in article 26 of the Universal Declaration of Human Rights, education aspires to strengthening respect for human rights (synthesised in the aforementioned four freedoms); and to achieve this objective it is necessary, albeit insufficient, a certain degree of regulation in education.

In summary, Law creates an adequate social framework in which the individual can develop, while education provides the individual with the capacity, competences, abilities and attitudes which allow them to achieve full development. So, to reach their respective goals, both Law and education need to resort to legislation and rules.

(2) *Law and education are built on the balance between formal legality and social legitimation.* In contemporary societies, Law is the outcome of highly formalised procedures, yet so is education, at least formal education. But at the same time, both Law and education require a wide legitimating consensus from society.[7] When this is not given, the position of Law and education is weakened with the ensuing resistance to legislation and lack of consideration towards the education system.

(3) *Law and education consist of narratives.* Nowadays, both Law and education require complex structures to function. Without parliaments, courts, police or prisons, there is no Law. Likewise, without schools and universities, regulations governing education and qualified teachers, there is no education. These organisational structures are required conditions, but alone they are not sufficient. Law[8] and education[9] consist of narratives, which provide the lives of individuals and societies with meaning and sense, and which evolve over time.

---

from want, which, translated into world terms, means economic understandings which will secure to every nation a healthy peacetime life for its inhabitants—everywhere in the world. The fourth is freedom from fear, which, translated into world terms, means a world-wide reduction of armaments to such a point and in such a thorough fashion that no nation will be in a position to commit an act of physical aggression against any neighbour—anywhere in the world. That is no vision of a distant millennium. It is a definite basis for a kind of world attainable in our own time and generation"; Roosevelt (1941), 20–21.

[7]Díaz (1978).

[8]Ost (2004), 8–9; Dworkin (1982), 179–200; West (1985), 145–211; Talavera (2006), 7–58.

[9]Meirieu (2015).

The studies which come under the general umbrella term "Law and literature" are organised into two parts: Law "as" literature and Law "in" literature. The former deals with how the nature of Law is built on a narrative foundation; the latter studies the influence of literary works on shaping Law. To my way of thinking, a relationship can be established between Law "as" literature and the educating aspect of Law, and between Law "in" literature with education's regulatory or prescriptive nature.

(4) *The alliance and the contract are equally important in Law and in education.* It is commonly believed that Law is the sphere of contracts and the exercise of free will. On the other hand, education is considered as a paradigm of alliance in which educators and students join in the pursuit of a common goal.[10] While both statements are true, they are only so up to a point.

Firstly, Law is based on an ethical–political alliance. The final basis of the legitimacy of Law is outside the system of rules which have been passed and approved by the state.[11] In more specific terms, the legal regulations of democratic states are legitimised nowadays by their ability to guarantee human rights, which come before any condition set out in any contract. Education plays a fundamental role when it comes to shaping this ethical–political alliance.

Secondly, education is an alliance which can only reach its common goal when it recognises flexible margins within which parents can exercise free will, as those finally responsible for the education of their children. When the education alliance is not open to free social initiatives it heads towards a path of social manipulation or the imposition of an ideology, which is contrary to education. In conclusion, Law is a contract built on an alliance and education is an alliance which is expressed through a contract.

When one considers the relationship between Law and education, we usually end up with two essential, but insufficient, viewpoints: education is seen from the perspective of Law as a human right and Law is seen from the perspective of education as the contents which make up the curriculum either directly (as in Schools of Law), or indirectly (as in primary and secondary education). This perspective is insufficient.

Law, as noted earlier, exercises an educational function of the first order. For Marx, Law is nothing more than the will of the ruling class raised to the level of legitimate law,[12] while for others, the opposite is the case, that is, it protects those without power from those who do.[13] Whether it deludes the people by making them believe that it represents legitimate mandates, or it really is the means by which to protect those unable to defend themselves, Law aspires to educate the citizens in their obligation to abide by laws and persuade them of its legitimacy. Law achieves its aim to the degree that it educates citizens about the values upon which it is based, but for citizens to spontaneously abide by laws, and by conviction, it is not enough

[10] Sacks (1996/1997), 11–20; Cortina (2001), 15.

[11] Ballesteros (1984), 91.

[12] "[Y]our jurisprudence is but the will of your class made into a law for all, a will, whose essential character and direction are determined by the economic conditions of existence of your class"; Marx and Engels (1908), 32.

[13] Cfr. Ballesteros (1973–1974), 159–165.

that they are formally valid. It is only when citizens perceive laws as legitimate that they are likely to spontaneously observe them.

But it is precisely here where the crucial role played by education lies. Its leading role can serve to reinforce adhering to Law, much more effectively even than the formal system of sanctions. But education can also dampen the backing of society towards (some of the) laws and pave the way to changes in the legal system.

(5) *Law and education justify their existence by the goals they pursue, which subjects them to a dual evaluation: internal and external.* Every legal system endows itself with a justification which is, in turn, the basis upon which it is built and its aim. However, this internal justification can never be the final word. It needs an ulterior justification which goes beyond (or closer to) the legal system itself. Accordingly, we can find that a legal system which ensures the pursuit of justice on the basis of certain provisions, comes to be qualified as an arbitrary or repressive system from bodies alien to this system. It has been the subject of much debate whether this "second justification" should be part of Law or whether it is a meta-legal and ideological judgment. This debate has been to some degree overtaken by Neo-constitutionalism.[14] For more than half a century, Constitution, as the supreme rule in democratic states, has fulfilled this function of a "second justification". The legal system is not only subjected to a judgement of legality (first justification), but also a judgement of constitutionality (second justification).

Something analogous happens with education. All education policies (within which I include pedagogical proposals) are built upon an internal justification. But this justification, which acts as a keystone of the education system, likewise is not the final word in the education system either, as it is always subject to a second evaluation. Any education system will claim that its goal is the human flourishing of individuals so that they can integrate into society; however, judgments can also be made from outside the education system which either confirm or refute this. Consequently, one could well arrive to the conclusion that what appears to be an education system is, in fact, a structure of domination and the perpetuation of social inequality.[15] Is this second judgment part of education, or does it constitute an external evaluation of an ideological nature? Unlike what we find with Law, in the case of education there is no state Constitution which acts as a referent to which we can resort to make judgements. But, we can count upon a wide consensus of opinion forged from reflecting on the goals of education, which are synthesised in article 26 of the Universal Declaration of Human Rights, all the international laws which have developed this precept[16] and in the very comprehensive reflections on education by UNESCO, for the most part contained in three important reports: "Learning to be the world of education today and tomorrow" (Faure Report, 1972)[17]; "Learning: the treasure within" (Delors Report

[14]Pozzolo (2001).

[15]Freire (1970).

[16]Bellver (2019).

[17]Faure et al. (1972).

1996)[18]; and “Rethinking education. Towards a global common good?” (UNESCO Report 2015).[19]

It is interesting to point out that there is often a common base rationale for both of Law and education. When a society is built on a conception of Law dominated by the protection of the interests of the individual owner, the education model will generally be aimed at promoting competitive individuals and future income generators, with a somewhat tenuous civic commitment.[20] In contrast, a conception of Law aimed at social justice and fortifying democracy will promote an education model that is heavily committed to social inclusion and promoting political participation.[21] When this common base is not sufficiently robust, it is at the mercy of continual political changes, which at the same time generates legal instability and uncertainty in education.[22]

(6) *Law and education are undergoing an accelerated process of expansion and formalization, which touches all spheres of an individual's life.* People's lives are always subject to laws. In the past people were subject to socialisation by their parents, family and the community to which they belonged, which exercised a powerful educational influence. Informal education and social uses dictated a major part of an individual's thinking and actions. The regulatory systems of these societies, which were homogenous in terms of moral values, were not the result of a citizen's agreement but rather that of a community culture heavily influenced by the dominant religion.

The advent of modernity, which questions religion as a basis for society, appeared to emancipate people from the heteronormative yoke. Thus, free from the moral tradition, individuals could freely decide about their lives and contribute to deciding over the laws which governed their social life. So that the principle of exercising free will could be effective, it was essential to eliminate the tradition which prescribed a way of behaving not necessarily decided by the individual.[23]

This interpretation of the transition from pre-modernity to modernity does not take into account two phenomena which have to be included to avoid a totally distorted view of the past and present. First, traditional societies were not founded on a religious base imposed from without, but instead collectively accepted and continually reworked by each new generation. For this reason, it is inaccurate to speak of an imposed religious-moral yoke, and more accurate to speak of a freely assumed tradition under continual revision.[24]

---

[18]International Commission on Education for the Twenty-first Century (1996), Elfert (2015), 88–100.

[19]UNESCO (2015).

[20]Nussbaum (2016).

[21]Hess (2006).

[22]Marcos and Pérez Marcos (2018), 190–191.

[23]Bellamy (2016).

[24]Chesterton (1919).

Second, education and Law in the contemporary world share the goal of promoting and guaranteeing freedom, but they are in fact fostering a state of self-alienation.[25] The main innovations in the field of primary and secondary education in the last twenty years have had three objectives: improving the mastery of English for whom it is not their first language; improving knowledge of economics and, above all, understanding society in economic terms; and incorporating digital technology as a privileged instrument for teaching and social relations.[26] These three elements empower the new generations to effectively and acritically uphold the capitalism which dominates the world at this moment. Law, for its own part, has become an insatiable Hydra which encompasses even the most intimate spaces of human relations. Legal rules have completely substituted the principle of trust in human relations, consequently, civil society loses its autonomy and is reduced to a parasite of public powers. To top it off, the regulatory tangle which governs citizens' lives is sanctioned by a wide range of powers which operate on behalf of the citizens in name only.[27]

Law and education, converted into highly protocolised institutions, are more present than ever in all spheres of our lives. Do Law and education, thus configured, contribute to freedom and personal development in complex societies or, rather, do they convert the individual, imperceptibly but effectively, into the machinery of the capitalist system?[28]

The morality upon which the most developed societies are based at present is hedonist individualism.[29] This morality consecrates all desires that do not directly harm another individual and which can be financed, or recognised as a right. This morality is thus converted into the principal mainstay to perpetuate capitalism, which can only be maintained through the sustained growth of solvent demands by the individual.[30] Education and Law have created a dense weft which channels all individual initiatives towards the aim of satisfying all desires, to the extent that this has produced two devastating effects on society. First, individuals tend to see themselves as merely generating income, and insofar as they can effectively do this, they can develop their "project for a good life", which consists of an unlimited capacity to satisfy desires. The second outcome is that social practices based on a tradition are eliminated, which deprives people of any source of meaning or collective project not channelled through the protocolised forms of Law and education.

---

[25] Han (2017).

[26] Postman (1996).

[27] Capella (1997).

[28] Graeber (2015).

[29] "The cultural, if not moral, justification of capitalism has become hedonism, the idea of pleasure as a way of life"; Bell (1976).

[30] Ballesteros (2012), 250–267.

2 On the Educational Nature of the Law: Aristotle

Having studied the close relationship between Law and education, the question I am now going to address is how Law should exercise its inexorable educating role. Although the ancient Greeks believed that Law played a fundamental role as an educator of the citizens, it was Plato, and in particular Aristotle, who justified this role. In the *Nicomachean Ethics*, Aristotle dedicates chapter 9 of Book 10 to this question, which concerns some brief reflections that have had an enormous impact on the history of thinking. However, it is in his *Politics* where he most clearly states the importance of laws in education: "No one will doubt that the legislator should direct his attention above all to the education of youth; because the neglect of education does harm to the constitution."[31]

In the present day, little attention is given to the educating function of Law, despite the fact that never has Law governed to such a detailed degree so many aspects of citizens' lives as right now. As a consequence of this exhaustive regulation to which we citizens throughout the world are subject, the mere fulfilment of these current laws at all times has turned into a process of standardising thinking and nature of citizens, as effective as it is imperceptible to the eyes of the majority. It is appropriate to reflect on how Law should fulfil this function so that the result is beneficial to the individual and to society. I shall begin by reference to Aristotle.

In order to really understand Aristotle's proposal concerning the educating role of Law, we need to consider the context in which it is formulated. Book 10 revolves around two central questions in its conception of ethics: pleasure and happiness. Aristotle considers pleasure an essential part of the good life to which humans aspire, but he distinguishes between reasonable pleasures, which contribute to happiness, and those which separate us from happiness because they make it difficult for us to live in accordance with virtue.

Aristotle considers happiness to be the "objective of all that is human"—the goal which all humans aspire to –, and it consists of a desirable action for its own ends alone. This is the virtuous action: "to do what is honest and good". Aristotle links happiness with virtue, that is, with the habit of choosing the good. But he does not stop here: "If happiness is activity in accordance with virtue, it is reasonable that it should be in accordance with the highest virtue; and this will be that of the best thing in us."[32] And what is the best thing in humans? Their mind, which is participating in the divine that is within them. Consequently, for humans, "the life according to reason is best and pleasantest… This life therefore is also the happiest."[33] The life of the gods is the happiest because it is entirely contemplative. The life of humans will be happy to the degree to which it resembles a divine activity. Other living beings will not be able to participate in happiness because they do not participate in any way in contemplation.

---

[31] Aristotle (1999), 1337 a.

[32] Aristotle (1997), book 10, Chapter 7.

[33] Ibídem.

It may seem that Aristotle incurs two contradictions when it comes to outlining his conception of happiness. The first consists of simultaneously stating that happiness consists of contemplation, because it is the activity of the gods, and at the same time that happiness is most befitting of man. Is contemplation proper to the gods or humans? The second contradiction appears when he maintains that happiness is simultaneously the action in accordance with virtue and contemplation. Does happiness lie in the action or in contemplation? Both questions have been analysed in great depth, however this is not the place to delve further into these. Nevertheless, I hold that these apparent contradictions can be resolved, and allow a more precise interpretation of Aristotle's thinking, if they are identified as two paradoxes that could be formulated in the following terms: it is most befitting for humans to participate in the divine, and contemplation is the action which generates the most happiness.

One of the distinctive features of Aristotle's thinking is his unwavering attention to the real world. It follows that when speaking of happiness in terms of contemplation, he is quick to remind us that "but, being a man, one will also need external prosperity; for our nature is not self-sufficient for the purpose of contemplation, but our body also must be healthy and must have food and other attention."[34] Therefore, what is essential to attain happiness are the goods that guarantee our external wellbeing. Without the minimum goods necessary one cannot practice virtue.[35] But it is enough that these goods are sufficient to do what we ought ("for one can with but moderate possessions do what one ought"[36]). To strive for more than is necessary does not contribute to attaining the good life.[37]

This proposal could be seen as the precursor to the modern Social State governed by the rule of law. On the one hand, the basic needs of citizens have to be covered so that they could opt for the contemplative life, while on the other hand, it is only necessary for these to be moderate. Present day Social States manage, to one degree or another, to satisfy these needs, but they find it impossible to provide moderate goods and services. In a sustained (and non-sustainable) model of economic growth, the luxuries of the present tend to turn into the needs of the future, and in this context of perpetual striving for a wellbeing which can never be fully satisfied, the goal of the contemplative life remains indefinitely postponed.

Aristotle does not settle for ending his work on ethics with only a theory concerning the happiness of humans; he understands that it is necessary to go further asking by what means it can be achieved: "with regard to virtue, then, it is not enough to know, but we must try to have and use it."[38] And it is in the last chapter of the *Nicomachean Ethics* where he refers to the role that laws play in achieving a moral life.

---

[34] Ibídem, book 10, chapter 8.

[35] Ballesteros (1986), 26.

[36] Aristotle (1997), Book 10, Chapter 8.

[37] "The origin of this disposition in men is that they are intent upon living only, and not upon living well"; Aristotle (1999), Book 1, Part IX.

[38] Aristotle (1997), Book 10, Chapter 9.

Although earlier Aristotle states that life pursuant to knowledge is the most befitting for humans and that which makes them happiest, he acknowledges that most people cannot rule their passions through reasoning, but rather only when faced with the force of law: "For these do not by nature obey the sense of shame, but only fear, and do not abstain from bad acts because of their baseness but through fear of punishment."[39] The law thus becomes a main player in the moral education of citizens.

"But it is difficult to get from youth up a right training for virtue if one has not been brought up under right laws; for to live temperately and hardily is not pleasant to most people, especially when they are young. For this reason, their nurture and occupations should be fixed by law; for they will not be painful when they have become customary. But it is surely not enough that when they are young they should get the right nurture and attention; since they must, even when they are grown up, practice and be habituated to them, we shall need laws for this as well, and generally speaking to cover the whole of life; for most people obey necessity rather than argument, and punishments rather than the sense of what is noble."[40]

Aristotle here demonstrates his observational and practical spirit. When obligations are required by law, the young do not usually consider them burdensome and become accustomed to abiding by them. And in order to facilitate maintaining this habit throughout their lives, it is necessary for laws to also continue obliging them to do so beyond adolescence.

The virtuous life, which leads to happiness, requires an education that parents cannot exclusively ensure; they need the backing of law:

> If (as we have said) the man who is to be good must be well trained and habituated, and go on to spend his time in worthy occupations and neither willingly nor unwillingly do bad actions, and if this can be brought about if men live in accordance with a sort of reason and right order, provided this has force, -if this be so, the paternal command indeed has not the required force or compulsive power (nor in general has the command of one man, unless he be a king or something similar), but the law has compulsive power, while it is at the same time a rule proceeding from a sort of practical wisdom and reason. And while people hate men who oppose their impulses, even if they oppose them rightly, the law in its ordaining of what is good is not burdensome.[41]

Aristotle admits that the majority of cities have not dictated laws aimed at the moral education of their citizens. In these cases, it will have to be the citizens themselves who guide their children and friends towards virtue:

> In the Spartan state alone, or almost alone, the legislator seems to have paid attention to questions of nurture and occupations; in most states such matters have been neglected, and each man lives as he pleases, Cyclops-fashion, 'to his own wife and children dealing law'. Now it is best that there should be a public and proper care for such matters; but if they are neglected by the community it would seem right for each man to help his children and friends towards virtue, and that they should have the power, or at least the will, to do this.[42]

---

[39] Ibídem.

[40] Ibídem.

[41] Ibídem.

[42] Ibídem.

Regardless of whether the city fulfils, or not, its obligation to legislate over education, Aristotle shows himself, in principle, to be in favour of the primacy of private education over public education:

"For as in cities laws and prevailing types of character have force, so in households do the injunctions and the habits of the father, and these have even more because of the tie of blood and the benefits he confers; for the children start with a natural affection and disposition to obey. Further, private education has an advantage over public, as private medical treatment has; for while in general rest and abstinence from food are good for a man in a fever, for a particular man they may not be; and a boxer presumably does not prescribe the same style of fighting to all his pupils. It would seem, then, that the detail is worked out with more precision if the control is private; for each person is more likely to get what suits his case."[43]

In this *Politics*, however, he maintains an apparently contrary position:

> No one will doubt that the legislator should direct his attention above all to the education of youth (…). It is manifest that education should be one and the same for all, and that it should be public and not private (…). Education should be regulated by law and should be an affair of state.[44]

Once again, we find ourselves faced with an apparent contradiction in Aristotle's thinking. In fact, these are two complementary proposals aimed at creating the ideal conditions to develop a moral life and harmony among citizens.[45] Both parents and legislators have the mission to provide moral education for the citizens. For parents, it is their responsibility while their children are dependent on them, while the legislator helps in this task by means of promulgating laws which will not only serve in this period but also in the other stages of citizens' lives. These laws contribute to creating conditions which are favourable to the moral development of the individual.[46]

The following points attempt to synthesise Aristotle's position concerning the educating function of Law:

1. The majority of people do not manage to control passion through reasoning and they need the law, which is imposed by force, in order to create the habit of virtue.
2. These laws play a primordial role during their youth, but also fulfil a valuable educating function throughout the lives of all the citizens.
3. Aristotle insists at all times that the laws that should educate citizens have to be wise and righteous: the law that has to regulate and educate the citizens is not the will of the legislator alone, but rather a righteous law.
4. The citizens tend to assume that the law is righteous and for this reason they abide by it without resentment.

---

[43] Ibídem.

[44] Aristotle (1999), Book 8, Part I and II.

[45] Marcos and Pérez Marcos (2018), 168.

[46] Aristotle deals with education mainly in two of his works: la *Politics* and *Nicomachean Ethics*. In the former he focuses on civic education and instruction, while in the latter he is exclusively concerned with the role of laws in the moral education of the individual. If one bears in mind that each work deals with distinct topics, the criticism by Robert George loses force; George (1993), 28.

5. The parents are the main actors responsible for educating the young, as it is they who can offer a comprehensive education tailored to the needs of each person.
6. The authority of the parents (and, generally, of the educators) requires the backing of law in order to be effective.
7. When the State does not legislate concerning the education of the citizens, or does not do so righteously, it is the citizens themselves who should fulfil this obligation.

In my opinion, this conception of the educating nature of Law, which is known as the central tradition of western thinking concerning politics and morals,[47] and which has been fiercely fought against since Modernity, continues to be appropriate to manage contemporary societies. However, it is necessary to point out the following aspects to prevent this tradition from falling into abuses: the law does not make citizens morally better, as this task falls to each individual when they freely judge and act; the law plays a subsidiary role to the main role played by parents in moral education; the educating role of the law is limited to "forbid the grosser forms of vice, but certainly cannot prescribe the finer points of virtue;"[48] that in contemporary societies, which are morally pluralistic, it is essential to recognise the existence of a shared moral base without which the law cannot fulfil its function of educating the citizens; and the law fulfils its educating role in a particularly valuable manner when it recognises the right to conscientious objection.

3 On Education Aimed at Obeying the Law

In the previous section I have dealt with the educating role of Law. More specifically, I have presented Aristotle's proposal about how Law should contribute to forging the moral character of citizens. He was the first to do so and to my thinking this proposal continues to be of great value today, even though it has come under fierce criticism. In this section I shall concern myself with the role that education can play to reinforce abiding by the law and the political commitment of the citizens. I do so following Rousseau and his proposal for a civil religion, which appears to have exercised a significant influence over the political life of many countries since then.

Before Rousseau other authors had reflected on the importance of religion in political stability; two notable examples being Machiavelli and Hobbes, who were not that far removed in time from Rousseau himself.[49] But unlike them, who were more inclined to politicise religion—in particular, Christianity—to achieve the political cohesion of the people, Rousseau maintains that none of the existing religions

[47]The main sources of this tradition can be found in the writings of Aristotle and Saint Thomas Aquinas; George (1993), 5.

[48]Ibídem, 47.

[49]Beiner (1993), 617–638.

adequately serves this aim and proceeds to create a kind of political religion,[50] to which he gave the name "civil religion".

For Aristotle the reasoning of most citizens alone could not develop their moral life, while Rousseau considers that most citizens, through reasoning alone, cannot come to appreciate and endorse laws. This distinction between the proposals of both thinkers is very important. Aristotle is concerned with the moral development of the citizens and defends the position that law can help to achieve this objective. In contrast, Rousseau wonders about how citizens subject themselves to political power and finds that religion is the most effective instrument. One deals with the contribution of the city to personal development and the other the measures so that citizens voluntarily subjects themselves to power.

Rousseau concerns himself with this question in the final chapter of *The Social Contract*.[51] But in chapter VII of book II he already announces his vision of the function of religion.

"Then since legislators are unable to employ either force or reasoning, they must have recourse to the authority of another order, which will lead without violence, and persuade without convincing.

This state of things has always forced the fathers of the nations to have recourse to the intervention of heaven, and to give honour to the gods, for their own wisdom, so that the people, submitting to the laws of the state as they submit to the laws of nature, and recognizing the same power in the creation of man and in the formation of the city, obey freely, and bear the yoke of public welfare with docility."[52]

Rousseau claims that "men had at first no kings but the gods, and no government but a theocratic one."[53] He does not share the belief in the theocratic basis of a government, but understands that religion is essential in order to found and sustain the State, going on to distinguish three categories of religion along the passage of time: the religion of man, the religion of the citizen and the religion of the priest. Since he does not consider any of these to be adequate to guarantee the backing of the citizens of the State, he ends up proposing his civil religion.

First, he considers the religion of man, which he identifies with evangelical Christianity. This religion, purely spiritual in nature, only concerns itself with heavenly matters: "But this religion, having not special relation with the political body, leaves to the laws the force which they have in themselves, without adding to them; and thereby, one of the great bonds of social life remains without effect."[54]

Second, he turns to the religion of the citizen. Its reach is not universal, but rather restricted to the territory of a nation. As opposed to the religion of men, the religion of the citizen is not purely spiritual, since it requires a commitment to local laws from the citizens. It integrates divine worship with the love of laws and teaches the

---

[50] Linz (2004), 107–125.

[51] Rousseau (1893).

[52] Ibídem, 63.

[53] Ibídem, 202.

[54] Ibídem, 212.

citizens, "that to serve the state is to serve its tutelary god."[55] This religion proves most convenient for sustaining the State as its believers, at the same time, most scrupulously abide by the laws. The problem is that it makes those who live by this religion intolerant and bloodthirsty, by transmitting the conviction that all those who do not recognise their gods can be killed. The potential aggressiveness of these peoples places them in a situation of permanent insecurity.

But the most pernicious of these three types of religion is the religion of the priest, which Rousseau identifies with the Roman Christianity because, "it gives to man two legislations, two chiefs and two countries; it submits him to contradictory duties, and prevents him from being devout and at the same time a citizen."[56] He considers that it is not necessary to dwell on demonstrating the dangers of this religious form. When the individual is placed between two conflicting loyalties, the city of God and the city of men, he is faced with a contradiction within himself and social cohesion breaks down. A religion of this kind is totally lacking,[57] and furthermore is a danger to society.

After this review of the religions of the world, Rousseau concludes by offering his civil religion. This is nothing more than a strong feeling of sociability which leads citizens to love and fulfil their political and legal obligations:

> now it is important to the state that each citizen have a religion which will make him love his duties; but the dogmas of that religion are of no interest to the state nor to its members, except as these dogmas pertain to morals and to the duties which he would professes it is bound to fulfil towards others.[58]

Civil religion radically separates beliefs, which affect the spiritual world of each believer, and one's obligations to others. Concerning beliefs, civil religion establishes complete tolerance. Each person may hold with whichever they wish, providing they do not attempt to project them on to their social life. To do so would encroach on the competences of the Sovereign since only he is entitled to regulate the obligations of the citizens.

To be coherent with this proposal, Rousseau sets forth the following civil religion dogmas:

> The existence of a powerful, intelligent, benevolent, prescient, and provident Divinity, the life to come, the happiness of the just, the punishment of the wicked, the sacredness of the social contract and the law: these are the positive dogmas. As to the negative dogmas I limit them to one, intolerance; it enters into the religions we have excluded.[59]

---

[55]Ibídem, 211.

[56]Ibídem, 211.

[57]August Comte, an author who shares Rousseau's aversion to Roman Catholicism, maintains quite the opposite view on this point. For him, only after the separation between political and spiritual power, mainly carried out by Catholicism, could human morals begin to take on a systematic nature, establishing truly general rules for the totality of our personal, domestic and social existence; Comte (2017).

[58]Rousseau (1893), 217–218.

[59]Ibídem, 219.

As can be seen, the only positive dogmas consecrated by this religion are those which make the citizens believe that if they do not fulfil the social contract and its laws, they will be eternally punished by God. But if they do, they achieve happiness in the next life.

Civil religion consecrates tolerance towards every religious belief as long as it only concerns itself with the afterlife. At the same time, it imposes unconditional adherence to the social contract and its laws, with exile or capital punishment for those who do not:

> Without being able to oblige any one to believe them (the dogmas of civil religion) he (the sovereign) can banish him not as impious, but as unsocial, as incapable of loving law and justice sincerely, and of immolating, at need, his life to his duty. If any one, having publicly acknowledged these dogmas, conducts himself as if he did not acknowledge them, he should be punished with death; he has committed the greatest of crimes, he has lied before the law.[60]

Under the auspices of religious tolerance Rousseau establishes a regime of civil intolerance which condemns, in this life, those who do not adhere completely to the civil religion.[61]

The feeling of sociability which civil religion promotes among citizens is incompatible with the free exercise of reason. The dogmas of civil religion must be, "simple, few in number, announced with precision, without explanation or commentary."[62] The important thing about these dogmas is not that they are true, or even that they invite one to reflect on them or employ reasoning; what is important is that they incite unanimous fervour towards the Sovereign and their laws. As Nussbaum points out, "Civic love, then, is incompatible with active critical thought about the political order, and with a sense of the separateness of the individual from the group. The test for sincerity is unanimity."[63]

Rousseau reduces religion to an instrument of social cohesion. Civil religion is the only religious form which effectively and pacifically achieves this by simultaneously taking on two roles: proclaiming, "the sacredness of the social contract and the law" and prohibiting religious intolerance. The other religions fall short in providing guarantees in this regard. The religion of the citizen guarantees the first, but not the second, because it instigates violence against non-believers in their faith. The religion of man likely promotes religious tolerance, but in no way "the sacredness of the social contract and the law," because it is a religion which dissuades citizens from any interest in matters of this world. Finally, the religion of priests is the worst of the three options because it does not guarantee adherence to the law nor religious tolerance.

---

[60]Ibídem. It is noteworthy that the sentence set out by Rousseau for those who stop endorsing the civil religion had already been proposed in almost identical terms by Thomas Aquinas, someone whom Rousseau would consider as representing thc religion of the priest: "On the other hand, there are unbelievers who at some time have accepted the faith, and professed it, such as heretics and all apostates: such should be submitted even to bodily compulsion, that they may fulfil what they have promised, and hold what they, at one time, received"; Aquinas, II-II, q. 10, a. 8.

[61]A proposal to resolve this contradiction in Walker (2018), 206–229.

[62]Rousseau (1893), 219.

[63]Nussbaum (2013), 45.

The religion of the priest distinguishes between civil laws and moral obligations, and judges the former in the light of the latter. For this religion, law is not legitimated on the basis of its origin (the general will),[64] but on its content (the justice of its mandates). Consequently, the religion of the priest requires one to obey the laws which are just, but disobey those which are not. According to Rousseau, this religion confounds the citizens by presenting them with two authorities to obey; it dissolves social cohesion because it invites citizens to subject the laws approved by the general will to criticism; and it allows priests to usurp civil power, because they are raised to the level of ultimate authority which determines whether the laws are just or not, or whether they should be obeyed or not.

Rousseau's civil religion poses three serious problems. The first has just been mentioned: it places the foundations of social cohesion and political life in a sphere as unstable as emotions. But it goes beyond this: it punishes those who, when exercising reason, express any doubts regarding unconditional adherence to these emotions. When religion consecrates certain emotions and places them at the service of politics, it becomes an extraordinarily effective force, but with potentially devasting effects for those who raise a critical voice.

Secondly, and following on, it makes any form of dissent impossible. Who dares to question the general will is considered a danger for society for putting their own interests above the general. S/he will be obliged to obey the law (to be free, in Rousseau's terms[65]) and, if they show themselves to be uncompromising, they will have to be eliminated.[66] If, as Rousseau proposes, the political community is the only valid body in its own right and the value of the citizen depends on the belonging to this community, it follows that whoever opposes the general will should be eliminated. If, on the other hand, we understand that the political community is not above people and their rights, then it would be intolerable to apply the sentence of exile or death to dissidents.

Thirdly, it reduces religion to an instrument of politics and a collection of subjective beliefs[67] without any projection in social life. But religion can also be understood as the relationship between humans and divinities, which endow all aspects of someone's existence with meaning, from the most intimate to that which related to their life in society. Understood in this way, the free exercise of religion becomes a human right. Furthermore, religious points of view about the diverse aspects of social life, with their criticisms and proposals, can enrich political life. However, the right conditions are necessary so that religions can play this role in society: the faithful must be able to translate their arguments into a common language, stripped of "religious rhetoric" which would make it unintelligible to non-believers. Secular reasoning, in turn, must assume that it does not have the monopoly on truth and that politics has an inherent religious content.[68]

---

[64]Rousseau (1893), 55.

[65]ibídem, 26.

[66]Ibidem, 219.

[67]Rousseau (1921).

[68]Habermas (2011), 25.

Despite the importance which Rousseau bestows upon civil religion, he neglects to develop some essential considerations: are there ministers of this religion who are given the responsibility to promote it and oversee that it is adhered to? Who sits in judgment when this religion disobeyed, civil tribunals or others created specifically for this purpose? Is it possible to scrutinise the conscience of those of whom we have doubts about their civil religiosity, or can we only punish people for their irreligious acts and not their thoughts? It hardly needs to be spelled out that the answers to these questions lead us to confirm the totalitarian nature of Rousseau's civil religion.

Although putting faith in civil religion seems to subject the freedom of the citizens to the cohesion of the State, Rousseau acknowledges that there are other recourses which also contribute to enhancing love of the homeland and that do not entail forgoing reason and personal freedom. The problem is that he only mentions them in passing and fails to develop them. The first appears in a chapter prior to the one on civil religion in *The Social Contract*. Here, Rousseau claims that the best way to guarantee that citizens abide by the laws is through custom and public opinion, which he comes to qualify as authentic fundamental laws of a political community. Rousseau distinguishes three types of law: political or fundamental laws, which are those which govern the political community; civil laws; and criminal laws. However, he then goes on to mention a fourth category of laws, upon which the other three rest: laws which are not written down anywhere and often overlooked by politicians. These are customs and public opinion, which foster love of the homeland, and adherence to civic obligations and are the authentic foundations of the political community:

> To these three kinds of law may be added a fourth, the most important of all, which is graven neither upon marble nor brass, but in the hearts of the citizens. It makes the true constitution of the state; it gathers new strength every day; when other laws grow older and pass away, it animates or replaces them; it keeps a people in sympathy with the spirit of its establishments, and insensibly substitutes force of habit for authority. I speak of manners, custom, and above all public opinion; a law ignored to our politicians, but upon it depends the success of all the others.[69]

Another element which contributes to upholding the political community is mentioned in book V of *Emile, or Education*. Rousseau criticises Plato for overlooking:

> all the tenderest of our natural feelings, which he (Plato) sacrificed to an artificial sentiment which can only exist by their aid. Will the bonds of convention hold firm without some foundation in nature? Can devotion to the state exist apart from the love of those near and dear to us? Can patriotism thrive except in the soil of that miniature fatherland, the home? Is it not the good son, the good husband, the good father, who makes the good citizen?.[70]

As can be seen, Rousseau recognises that, in addition to civil religion there are other recourses which are crucial to give weight to the political community: the customs of each nation; and the affective bonds forged in the home projected outwards into the political sphere. Those three elements, far from being incompatible, turn out

---

[69]Rousseau (1893), 82–83.

[70]Rousseau (1921), 326.

to be complementary. The affective bonds among those closely related can generate an appreciation of the political community. The genuine *pietas*, or spontaneous love towards close friends or relatives, does not have to generate exclusion towards others; it can also be the basis for love of the political community and, in general, for all human beings. *Pietas* can lead to *humanitas*. This shift from *pietas* to *humanitas* constitutes an authentic *paideia.*

Aristotle attributes Law with the functions of educating the citizens, with the objective of providing them with the right circumstances so that they can develop worthy moral lives. This stance has been criticised as much by those who think that we cannot know what is morally correct, as by those for whom regulating aspects of moral life is an intrusion. Despite being mainly overlooked nowadays, I believe that Aristotle's proposal continues to be valuable to facilitate the moral life of citizens, something which is quite distinct from imposing specific moral conceptions under the force of Law. The Law should separate citizens from the most vulgar vices, as Robert George states following Aristotle's reasoning, but it should also foster civic virtues that guarantee political coherence for the people. Rousseau understands that educating the people in an effective civil religion is the preferred instrument to get citizens to identify with their political community and subject themselves to its law. The problem with his proposal is that in order to achieve the stability of the State it reduces religious life to a personal practice which is socially irrelevant, while at the same time it demands unconditional adherence to a civil religion based on collective emotion.

4 An Ancient Proposal to End with

Sometimes, a good example from the past teaches us a better lesson than an elaborate theory from the present. Pericles' *Funeral Oration* was read out in 431 BC before the tombs of the first Athenians killed in the wars between Athens and Esparta and in which Athens finally fell. In order to pay tribute to those who had fallen in battle, Pericles evokes the Athenian spirit of democracy. It does not illustrate so much what Athens was at that time in its history as what it believed and wanted. To my way of thinking, this short text constitutes the best guide to Law correctly fulfilling its educating role and so that education persuades citizens to abide by the laws.

Pericles, after mentioning the foundations upon which the political life of Athens is built, states:

> "Taking everything together then, I declare that our city is an education to Greece, and I declare that in my opinion each single one of our citizens, in all the manifold aspects of life, is able to show himself the rightful lord and owner of his own person, and do this, moreover, with exceptional grace and exceptional versatility."[71]

He puts forward the Athenian democracy as a model for civic education for the rest of the Greek peoples, but he says something more: that each Athenian citizen is

[71] Tucydides (1972), 143–51.

a model of self-sufficiency. The robustness of Athenian democracy lies, therefore, in the value of each of its citizens.[72] We find here a fundamental contrast to Aristotle, and particularly to Rousseau, for whom the cohesion of the group is above the value of the individual.

So, what are the foundations of political life in Athens according to Pericles?

"Let me say that our system of government does not copy the institutions of our neighbours. It is more the case of our being a model to others than of our imitating anyone else. Our constitution is called a democracy because power is in the hands not of a minority but of the whole people. When it is a question of settling private disputes, everyone is equal before the law; when it is a question of putting one person before another in positions of public responsibility, what counts is not membership of a particular class, but the actual ability which the man possesses. No one, so long as he has it in him to be of service to the state, is kept in political obscurity because of poverty. And, just as our political life is free and open, so is our day-to-day life in our relations with each other. We do not get into a state with our next-door neighbour if he enjoys himself in his own way, nor do we give him the kind of black looks which, though they do no real harm, still do hurt people's feelings. We are free and tolerant in our private lives; but in public affairs we keep to the law. This is because it commands our deep respect. We give our obedience to those whom we put in positions of authority, and we obey the laws themselves, especially those which are for the protection of the oppressed, and those unwritten laws which it is an acknowledged shame to break.

And here is another point. When our work is over, we are in a position to enjoy all kinds of recreation for our spirits. There are various kinds of contests and sacrifices regularly throughout the year; in our own homes we find a beauty and a good taste which delight us every day and which drive away our cares."[73]

In general terms, this quote underlines the following foundations of political life: democracy as a political regime; social recognition of the citizen based on their individual merit and not their social class; tolerance with respect to the private relations of everyone; scrupulous fulfilment of the law, above all when it legislates in favour of those who suffer injustices; respect for the unwritten laws which, nevertheless, make those who do not obey them feel ashamed; and a civil religion that does not consist of uncritically subjecting oneself to political power but rather to enjoying the culture and annual feast day celebrations, as well as the material goods which distract from their worries.

The citizens of Athens love art and beauty, cultivate wisdom and appreciate wellbeing, but do so in moderation. They concern themselves as much with personal as with public matters, and they decide over that which affects everyone after public debate.[74] Pericles' discourse concludes by insisting on the fact that the greatness of

[72]Wallace (1996), 105–119.

[73]Tucydides (1972), 143–51.

[74]"Our love of what is beautiful does not lead to extravagance; our love of the things of the mind does not make us soft. We regard wealth as something to be properly used, rather than as something to boast about. As for poverty, no one need be ashamed to admit it: the real shame is in not taking

the city is in its men, who are able to give their lives for the common good, and in doing so receive immortal praise and a most glorious tomb in the heart of their fellow citizens.[75]

The democracy described by Pericles in his *Funeral Oration* is not that which was really experienced in Athens, but it was the democracy they yearned for. This ideal of life in common has been maintained as a model for many nations. The Gettysburg Address can be understood as an abridged modern version of this funeral oration.[76] As already pointed out, this ideal can be synthesised as follows:

- The political life of a nation is based on the freedom and equality of all people.
- Each person has the right to have their private life respected, and the right to participate in public life.
- Every human being must obey the laws sanctioned by the authorities, above all those which protect the most vulnerable; and also the unwritten laws which cause those who fail to abide by them to feel moral shame.
- People have the right to certain material wellbeing, to enjoy and participate in an enriching cultural life, and to share symbols that give meaning to their life in common.
- In order to safeguard these ideals, it is worth giving one's life and those who do so deserve immemorial honour. The testimony of these people and memory of them from generation to generation is a principle agent of political stability.
- The shared exercise of public reason is an imperative condition so that citizens are truly free and adopt measures towards the common good.

When the law has these foundations it encourages the civic education of the people without incurring either undue limitations of individual freedom, or paternalism which hinder the moral development of the citizens. These pre-political bases generate a kind of civil religion which appeals to the emotions without cancelling out

---

practical measures to escape from it. Here each individual is interested not only in his own affairs but in the affairs of the state as well: even those who are mostly occupied with their own business are extremely well-informed on general politics—this is a peculiarity of ours: we do not say that a man who takes no interest in politics is a man who minds his own business; we say that he has no business here at all. We Athenians, in our own persons, take our decisions on policy or submit them to proper discussions: for we do not think that there is an incompatibility between words and deeds; the worst thing is to rush into action before the consequences have been properly debated. And this is another point where we differ from other people. We are capable at the same time of taking risks and of estimating them beforehand. Others are brave out of ignorance; and, when they stop to think, they begin to fear"; Ibídem.

[75]"What I would prefer is that you should fix your eyes every day on the greatness of Athens as she really is, and should fall in love with her. When you realize her greatness, then reflect that what made her great was men with a spirit of adventure, men who knew their duty, men who were ashamed to fall below a certain standard. If they ever failed in an enterprise, they made up their minds that at any rate the city should not find their courage lacking to her, and they gave to her the best contribution that they could. They gave her their lives, to her and to all of us, and for their own selves they won praises that never grow old, the most splendid of sepulchers—not the sepulcher in which their bodies are laid, but where their glory remains eternal in men's minds, always there on the right occasion to stir others to speech or to action"; Ibídem.

[76]Wills (1992), 41.

the exercise of reason, and promotes subjecting the citizen to the law without having to renounce criticism. Aristotle understood that law had to fulfil an educating function, but failed to outline to what extent in order to avoid abuses. Rousseau understood that political society rests on pre-political bases, but his proposal for civil religion almost inevitably leads to an authoritarian regime.[77] In Pericles' *Funeral Oration* one can find the limits so that law is able to correctly fulfil its educating role, and the religious pre-political bases which involve citizens in constructing a life in common.

References

Aquinas ST (1947) Summa Theologica. Benzinger Brothers, New York
Aristotle (1997) Nicomachean ethics. Batoche Books, Kitchener
Aristotle (1999) Politics. Batoche Books, Kitchener
Ballesteros J (1974) El Derecho como no discriminación y no violencia. Anuario De Filosofía Del Derecho 17:159–165
Ballesteros J (1984) Sobre el sentido del Derecho. Tecnos, Madrid
Ballesteros J (1986) Postmodernidad: decadencia o resistencia. Tecnos, Madrid
Ballesteros J (2012) Escuela neoclásica, valores y derechos. CEFD 26:250–267. https://doi.org/10.7203/CEFD.26.1996
Beiner R (1993) Machiavelli, Hobbes, and Rousseau on civil religion. Rev Polit 55(4):617–638. https://doi.org/10.1017/S0034670500018027
Bell D (1976) The cultural contradictions of capitalism. Basic Books, New York
Bellamy FX (2016) Les déshérités ou l'urgence de transmettre. Paris, J'ai lu
Bellver C (2019) Educar en Derechos Humanos: orientaciones del Derecho internacional e implementación en la educación superior. Revista de Educación y Derecho 20. https://doi.org/10.1344/REYD2019.20.30022
Capella JR (1997) Fruta prohibida. Una aproximación histórico-teorética al estudio del derecho y del estado, Trotta, Madrid
Chesterton GK (1919) Heretics. John Lane Co., New York
Comte A (2017) Discurso sobre el espíritu positivo. Alianza, Madrid
Cortina A (2001) Alianza y contrato. Política, ética y religión. Trotta, Madrid
Díaz E (1978) Legalidad-legitimidad en el socialismo democrático. Taurus, Madrid
Dworkin R (1982) Law as interpretation. Critical Inquiry 9(1):179–200
Elfert M (2015) UNESCO, the Faure Report, the Delors Report, and the Political Utopia of Lifelong Learning. Euro J Educ 50(1):88–100. https://doi.org/10.1111/ejed.12104
Faure E et al (1972) Learning to be the world of education today and tomorrow. UNESCO, Paris. https://unesdoc.unesco.org/images/0000/000018/001801e.pdf. Accessed 4 Jan 2019
Fisher J (2014) The best state of the Union of All Time. The Washington Post, January 28. https://www.washingtonpost.com/news/the-fix/wp/2014/01/28/the-best-state-of-the-union-of-all-time/?utm_term=.b24ef483982a. Accessed 6 Jan 2019
Freire P (1970) Pedagogía del oprimido. Siglo XXI Editores, Madrid
George RP (1993) Making men moral. Civil liberties and public morality, Oxford University Press, Oxford
Graeber D (2015) The Utopia of Rules: On Technology. Stupidity and the Secret Joys of Bureaucracy, Melville House, New York

[77] Nussbaum (2013), 5.

Habermas J (2011) The political: the rational meaning of a questionable inheritance of political theology. In: Mendieta E, Van Antwerpen J (eds) The power of religion in the public sphere. Columbia University Press, New York
Han BC (2017) Psychopolitics: neoliberalism and new technologies of power. Verso Futures, New York
Hess DE (2006) Controversy in the classroom: the democratic power of discussion. Routledge, New York
Jaeger W (1947) Praise of law: the origin of legal philosophy and the Greeks. Oxford University Press, New York
Jaeger W (1967) Paideia: the ideals of Greek culture, vol 1, Archaic Greece, The Mind of Athens. Oxford University Press, Oxford
Kelsen H (2005) General theory of law & state. Routledge, New York
International Commission on Education for the Twenty-first Century (1996) Learning: the treasure within. UNESCO, Paris. https://unesdoc.unesco.org/images/0010/001095/109590eo.pdf. Accessed 8 Feb 2019
La Belle ThB (1982) Formal, nonformal and informal education: A holistic perspective on lifelong learning. Int Rev Educ 28:159–175. https://doi.org/10.1007/BF00598444
Linz JJ (2004) The religious use of politics and/or the political use of religion: Ersatz ideology versus Ersatz Religion. In: Maier H (ed) Concepts for the comparison of dictatorships. Routledge, London, pp 107–125
Marcos A, Pérez Marcos M (2018) Meditación de la naturaleza humana. BAC, Madrid, 2018
Marx K, Engels F (1908) Communist Manifesto. New York Labor News Co., New York
Meirieu P (2015) Frankenstein Pédagogue. ESF Editeur, Montrouge
Nussbaum MC (2013) Political Emotions: why Love Matters for Justice. Harvard University Press, Cambridge
Nussbaum MC (2016) Not for profit: why democracy needs the humanities. Princeton University Press, Princeton
Ost F (2004) Raconter la loi. Aux sources de l'imaginaire juridique, Odile Jacob, Paris
Pachal JF (1946) The education of a Justice. J Legal Educ 1(3):333–360
Postman N (1996) The end of education: redefining the value of school. Vintage Books, London
Pozzolo S (2001) Neocostituzionalismo e positivismo giuridico. Giappichelli, Torino
Roosevelt FD (1941) Message to the Congress. https://fdrlibrary.org/documents/356632/390886/readingcopy.pdf/42234a77-8127-4015-95af-bcf831db311d. Accessed 24 Jan 2019
Rousseau JJ (1893) The social contract. G. P. Putnam's sons, New York
Rousseau JJ (1921) Emile, or education. New York, E.P, Dutton
Sacks J (1996–1997) Rebuilding civil society: a biblical perspective. Responsive Community 7 (1):11–20
Talavera P (2006) Derecho y literatura. Granada, Comares
Tucydides (1972) History of the Peloponnesian War. Penguin, London
UNESCO (2015) Rethinking education. Towards a global common good? UNESCO, Paris. https://unesdoc.unesco.org/images/0023/002325/232555e.pdf Accessed 24 Jan 2019
Walker DH (2018) The Tolerant Pessimist: Jean-Jacques Rousseau on Civil Religion and Religious Toleration. Oxford J Law Religion 7(2):206–229. https://doi.org/10.1093/ojlr/rwy035
Wallace RW (1996) Law and the concept of citizens' rights in democratic athens. In: Ober J and Hedrick C (eds) Demokratia—a conversation on democracies, ancient and modern. Princeton University Press, Princeton
West R (1985) Jurisprudence as Narrative: an Aestetic analysis of modern legal theory. New York University Law J 60(2):145–211
Wills G (1992) Lincoln at Gettysburg: The Words that Remade America. Simon & Schuster, New York

Criminal Law and Morality: Controversial Issues

From Crime to Right

Marta Albert

Abstract The purpose of this chapter is to analyze the complex transition in the legal consideration of certain types of conduct from being considered a crime to being recognized as a right. From the perspective of the philosophy of law, both the assumptions of this transition and its theoretical consequences will be discussed in order to shed light on this paradoxical phenomenon and its conceptual consequences.

1 Introduction. Real Issues

This study aims to analyze the process by which a conduct considered criminal may become a right, that is, a claim legally enforceable. A priori it seems that we would be dealing with a "laboratory" case because we usually tend to think that a crime cannot become a subjective right. This would mean that the same action could move from social censure not to tolerance but to protection, defense and promotion by the State.

Despite the strangeness of this process, we have not only witnessed this phenomenon in the Spanish legal system in the past (it happened, as we will see, with the voluntary termination of pregnancy), but it is very likely that there will be a similar evolution in the legal status of a conduct, if the decriminalization of euthanasia is finally approved.[1] In this case, moreover, the shift from crime (very tempered liability for homicide) to right (to die) will be carried out in an imminent manner: the same legal text would decriminalize the conduct and elevate it, always in certain cases, to the category of right.

It should be noted that the way from crime to law is through the partial decriminalization of certain conducts. This is not the only stage of the journey, but it is the

M. Albert (✉)
Rey Juan Carlos University, Madrid, Spain
e-mail: marta.albert@urjc.es

[1] Vid., Proposición de Ley Orgánica de Regulación de la Eutanasia, presented by Grupo Parlamentario Socialista (Iniciativa 122/00239). 21 may 2018.

A. Masferrer (ed.), *Criminal Law and Morality in the Age of Consent*, Ius Gentium: Comparative Perspectives on Law and Justice 84,
https://doi.org/10.1007/978-3-030-64163-4_13

initial stage. As just pointed out, the first example in the Spanish legal system has been the partial decriminalization of abortion (a measure that, sooner or later, the vast majority of European countries have adopted, so we are not referring here to an exclusively national phenomenon).

In this case, the punishable conduct did not become a right in the same draft legislation of its decriminalization (at least, not in an explicit way). The decriminalization took place in 1985, but at that time the question of termination of pregnancy as a legally enforceable conduct was not openly raised. Years later, Organic Law 2/2010, on Sexual and Reproductive Health and Voluntary Termination of Pregnancy, used somewhat ambiguous expressions, such as the "right to decide freely whether and when to have children" cited in Article 3 of the Explanatory Memoradum of the Law.[2]

Article 3 also refers to fundamental rights in the field of sexual and reproductive health, which are the classic fundamental rights of freedom, dignity and personal autonomy.[3] Article 12 states that the Law "guarantees access to voluntary termination of pregnancy under the conditions set out herein". Finally, Article 18 refers to a "right to the voluntary termination of pregnancy" by restricting public health services from adopting the necessary measures to guarantee it. Article 19 includes a provision similar to the previous.

Despite the Legislator's "timidity", and since the turn of the new millennium, there is no room for doubt in Spain on the existence of a right to abortion. The social perception of the legality of the conduct was mainly inclined to consider it, even before the adoption of the law, as a woman's right, partly due to the general situation of factual non-compliance with the assumptions established in the reform of the penal code.[4] Fifteen years had passed since its decriminalization.

The case of the partial decriminalization of euthanasia, at least in the form in which the issue has recently been raised in Parliament, is significantly different, because of the immediate shift from prohibited conduct to subjective right. This draft, which in its first final provision, amends article 143.4 of the Penal Code, considering the type described therein "not punishable", conceives the "help to die" as a right from the Explanatory Memorandum. Thus, the law aims "to regulate the right of individuals to request and receive assistance to die under the circumstances envisaged in the law, the procedure to be followed and the guarantees to be observed" (Article 1 of the

[2]As it follows: "La presente ley reconoce el derecho a la maternidad libremente decidida que implica, entre otras cosas, que las mujeres puedan tomar la decisión inicial sobre su embarazo, y que esa decisión, consciente y responsable, sea respetada. El legislador ha considerado necesario, de acuerdo con las indicaciones de las personas expertas y el análisis del derecho comparado, dejar un plazo de 14 semanas en el que se garantiza a las mujeres la posibilidad de tomar una decisión libre e informada sobre la interrupción del embarazo, sin la interferencia de terceros" (Explanatory Memorandum). Ley 2/2010, 3 de marzo, de Salud Sexual y Reproductiva e Interrupción Voluntaria del Embarazo.

[3]It is worth mentioning that nor dignity neither free development of personality are fundamental rights in Spanish legal system. Article 10 talk about both of them as "foundation of political order and social peace" and are absolutely crucial principles in Spanish Law. Cfr. Albert Márquez (2015).

[4]"Lo cierto es que años de experiencia condujeron a la despenalización de facto, sobre todo por la vía del fraude de ley en el supuesto de la salud psíquica de la madre", Sánchez Cámara (2012), 27.

Draft law). In the Explanatory Memorandum the legislator is even clearer: "In short, this law introduces into our legal system a new individual right such as euthanasia". As in the voluntary termination of pregnancy, the new right is linked to fundamental rights that do exist such as life, and above all, freedom, dignity and personal privacy.

Decriminalizing, as its name suggests, means that a conduct is no longer punishable, in other words, it is no longer considered by a legal system subject to sanction. Does this make it a right? Is conversion into positive law the inevitable fate of all decriminalized conduct? Why do we think that something that is no longer punishable can become immediately enforceable? Do we have a right to something simply because it is no longer a crime?

In the following pages we will try to address these issues by delving deeper into the ideas underlying these approaches as a supposition. First, I will refer to partial decriminalization as a legal technique, and to the effects of circumventing the sanction of certain punishable conducts, carried out under a certain modality (normally, non-imputation per se) through the mechanism of legal *standardization*. Second, I will deal with the notion of subjective right, with particular emphasis on the theses that affirm the existence of a right "to do wrong". The study of both phenomena will allow us to understand the shift from crime to law. Then, I will examine the consequent conceptual issues, and will conclude with some ideas that may help, in my view, in a new way of tackling this problem.

2 Decriminalization and Legal Asset Protection

From a legal standpoint, human conduct can be considered from the perspective of three basic categories, which is important to bear in mind from the very outset of these considerations.

All conduct can be legally categorized as *prohibited* (the commission of the criminal action will be accompanied by a criminal penalty); as *lawful*, that is, because it is not expressly prohibited, it can be performed without violating the legal system, but does not enjoy special legal protection or, finally, as a *right*. In the latter case, the desired conduct may not only be carried out, but, in these cases, citizens (right holders) may demand the effective realization of their claim against third parties and, ultimately, against the State, regardless of the will of the third parties involved, who will be under an obligation in any case. And precisely being holder of a duty will entitle them, or not, depending on the circumstances, to exercise their right to conscientious objection, which indicates that even the possibility of objecting does not mean that there is no duty, but quite the opposite).

Law is an essentially dynamic reality that not only tolerates but also requires a certain circulation of conducts across these three basic categories. That means it is within the historical nature of the Law that the same action can be considered as a crime at any given time and then being considered non punishable (for instance, prostitution or same-sex sexual relations). The opposite can also occur, that is, the law responds by criminalizing previously unpunished or barely punished conducts (for example crimes related to "male" violence or new "hate" crimes as defined in the reform of the Spanish penal code of 2015).

Conducts are typified and offences are repealed, and this simply reveals the fact that criminal law reflects the axiological choices of societies that are alive and evolving in their morals, and in the perception of the legal assets that must be protected especially in each historical moment.[5]

We are used to witness how law criminalizes new conducts as a result of the valuation of new assets as legal, or makes certain facts legally irrelevant as belonging to the private sphere and therefore cease to be considered criminal, such as adultery.

But, in the latter case, the act itself remains as reprehensible as when it was considered a crime (although now irrelevant to the law)… However, this continuity in the censure makes no sense when the criminal conduct becomes legally enforceable. How does the shift from crime to law occur?

Let us begin with the shift from the forbidden to the lawful. A certain conduct is no longer established as a criminal offence. It is often referred to as "decriminalization", although the use this terminology is not unanimous. Some criminal lawyers, such as Ruiz Vadillo, prefer to use the term "non-criminalization" to refer to "any legislative process or decision by virtue of which a conduct is extracted from the Penal Code or from a penal law, thus eliminating, definitively, the possibility of associating a sanction with it. In short, It is the opposite of typification or criminalization". The word "decriminalization" is then reserved to mean "a qualitative and quantitative reduction of the sanction. For example, replacing a custodial sentence with a disenfranchisement, or a prison sentence with one of arrest. In these cases we are in the presence of a de-escalation in the punitive system. It could be said, in some regards and with certain reservations, that it is also decriminalized when alternative sanctions are established. For example, an imprisonment is replaced by a penalty of arrest or a fine. The reverse system would lead to the strengthening of criminal sanctions".[6]

But fact is, it seems that in order to designate the elimination of criminalization, most of the doctrine and also the Legislator tend to use the term "decriminalization" more frequently, and in this sense we also use it, as the "decision of the authority tending to remove certain conduct from the criminal catalogue of criminal laws in the States".[7] This is how the Spanish legal dictionary defines the decriminalization: "the approval of a law that repeals the criminalization of a certain conduct".[8]

All of the above refers unreservedly to the decriminalization of what we might call "complete", that is to say, to cases in which the standardized conduct becomes lawful. However, in legal practice, decriminalization may be complete or partial, depending on whether all or only some of the types of conduct in question are decriminalized.

---

[5]Criminal Law does not protect social morality, but concrete legal goods. Vid., Roxin (2016), 433–448.

[6]Ruiz Vadillo (1999), 100.

[7]Medina Jara (1996), 331.

[8]Consejo General del Poder Judicial-Real Academia de la Lengua Española, Muñoz Machado, Manuel (ed) http://dej.rae.es/#/entry-id/E100820

Thus, for example, the Spanish decriminalization of abortion in 1985 only decriminalizes certain cases in which the criminal conduct (the voluntary termination of pregnancy) can be carried out from that moment onwards, that is, in "therapeutic" (existence of a serious risk to the woman's health), eugenic cases, when malformations in the fetus were detected or "ethical", when the pregnancy was the result of a crime against the woman's sexual freedom.[9]

The Legislator may also decide, however, to repeal it regardless the forms or modalities of its perpetration (as when adultery was repealed), without setting any assumptions in which the conduct continues to be a crime.

This distinction appears to be purely technical, but contains a few conceptual difficulties, particularly regarding "partial" decriminalization. What is intended, and what objective is pursued when a conduct is partially decriminalized? It seems clear that the criminal law protection of the legal asset is not a matter of dispute, otherwise the criminalization would be completely repealed. The aim is to establish certain exceptions to the punishment of criminal conduct, when it occurs under certain circumstances (thus, in the above example, the voluntary termination of pregnancy is considered an offence *except* if it is committed under the decriminalized indications). The same might be said of euthanasia: when it is decriminalized, homicide obviously does not stop being a crime, it is decriminalized when committed in certain situations.[10]

---

[9]Under Article 417 bis of the Organic Law n. 9/1985, an abortion can be legally performed by or under the direction of a physician in an approved public or private health centre or establishment, provided that the woman gives her express consent to the procedure and one of the following conditions is met: (a) the abortion is necessary to avert a serious risk to the physical or mental health of the pregnant woman, in accordance with an opinion expressed prior to the abortion by a physician, other than the one performing the abortion or under whose direction the abortion is to be performed, and who holds an appropriate specialist qualification; (b) the pregnancy is the result of rape, provided that the rape has been reported to the police and the abortion is performed within the first 12 weeks of pregnancy; or (c) the foetus, if carried to term, will suffer from severe physical or mental defects, provided that the abortion is performed within the first 22 weeks of pregnancy and the medical opinion, communicated prior to the abortion, is expressed by two specialists of an approved public or private health centre or establishment, neither of whom is the physician by whom or under whom the abortion is to be performed.

[10]Article 143.4, of Proposition of Law for Decriminalization of Euthanasia describes them as it follows: "No será punible la conducta del médico o médica que con actos necesarios y directos causare o cooperare a la muerte de una persona, cuando esta sufra una enfermedad grave e incurable o discapacidad grave crónica, en los términos establecidos en la ley.

Se entiende por enfermedad grave e incurable aquella que por su naturaleza origina sufrimientos físicos o psíquicos, constantes e insoportables, sin posibilidad de alivio que el o la paciente considere tolerable, con un pronóstico de vida limitado, en un contexto de fragilidad progresiva.

Se entiende por discap acidad grave crónica la situación en la que se produce en la persona afectada una invalidez de manera generalizada dc valerse por sí misma, sin que existan posibilidades fundadas de curación y, en cambio, sí existe seguridad o gran probabilidad de que tal incapacidad vaya a persistir durante el resto de la existencia de esa persona. Se entienden por limitaciones aquellas que incidan fundamentalmente sobre su autonomía física y actividades de la vida diaria, así como sobre su capacidad de expresión y relación, originando por su naturaleza sufrimientos físicos o psíquicos constantes e intolerables, sin posibilidad de alivio que el o la paciente considere tolerable. En ocasiones pudiere suponer la dependencia absoluta de apoyo tecnológico".

This objective (criminalization is maintained but exceptions to the penalty are provided for) can be achieved in two different ways. Partial decriminalization of conduct is one of them, but not the unique. It logically requires the intervention of the legislator. As the Constitutional Court pointed out: "the legislator, who must always bear in mind the reasonable enforceability of conduct and the proportionality of the penalty in the event of non-compliance, can also forego the criminal sanction of a conduct that could objectively represent an *unbearable burden*, notwithstanding that, if applicable, the duty of protection from the State still exists with regard to the legal asset in other areas".[11]

What is the other possibility that allows the protection of the legal asset by excluding the sanction for its violation on those cases when respecting it "would represent an unbearable burden"? In principle, the very dynamics of the application of the law in the courts. If decriminalization is based on its general character (by the generalized establishment of exceptions to the prohibition), the other possibility leaves the leading role to judicial activity, which, through the use of exempting, aggravating or determining circumstances, appreciates, case by case, the existence of exceptions to the establishment of the sanction generically foreseen.

If the point is to maintain the protection of the legal asset that the generic prohibition allows, but renouncing the criminal sanction when the conduct signifies an "unbearable burden" that is a little less than heroic for the one who would carry it out, it is really necessary to question the legislator's need to come into the play, since it is unlawful to demand liability to non-imputable people.

As Ollero points out, the most extreme conflict, in this sense, is expressed in the assessment of the exoneration of the state of need. If it is not a matter of altering the legal asset, does the legislator have to necessarily intervene? Could not the determination of legal liability be left to the judicial activity of applying the law itself, which already provides for the possibility that persons for whom a cause of exemption from criminal responsibility comes into play may not be punished?

That issue is extremely relevant because the intervention of the legislator causes certain effects that are absent in the judicial solution, and have to do with the vigor with which the legal asset continues to be defended beyond the partial decriminalization of certain conducts aimed at its protection.

In the words of Andrés Ollero, by partially decriminalizing (in the strict sense) certain conducts within the criminal code, the legislator assumes "the negative social cost that its "pedagogical" dimension will inevitably entail".[12] The "negative social cost" has to do with the (literal) standardization of the exception, because what was considered exceptionally not punishable becomes a normalized action. The exceptions, "with the help of the rule pattern"[13] become a normative conduct, with the consequent weakening of the prohibition reflected in the general legal definition of the conduct as criminal. And, the next step, as we will see below, is the confusion between the explicit permission and the subjective right.

---

[11]STC 53/1985, 11 of April. Legal Ground 9. Our emphasys.

[12]Ollero Tassara (2006a, b), 94.

[13]Ibid.

It is true that when the task of excluding the sanction in certain cases (those which represent, in the words of the Constitutional Court, an "unbearable burden") is entrusted to judicial activity, it is obvious that this weakening of the protection of the legal asset does not occur. The disadvantage is that the exemption from liability does not happen automatically in exceptional cases, but rather a legal process must take place in which the judge assesses that the necessary circumstances to exclude or minimize the sanction do indeed exist, with the consequent cost to citizens who have committed the criminal conduct under special circumstances that would exempt them (or not, as the judge may not consider it) from criminal liability.

Concerning the use of normative decriminalization, the costs of legal procedure (obviously, not only economic), disappear and also the uncertainty on the very exemption from criminal liability due to the absence of a repeal, which corresponds in principle (except the presumption of innocence) to the individuals who commit such a crime. In return, as we have just shown, the protection of the legal asset is weakened by the inevitably pedagogical effect of the standardization of the exemption from the sanction in certain cases.

Bearing in mind this transcendent effect of the partial decriminalization of conduct, is it legally relevant social morality that determines the "removal" from the criminal code of certain definitions, or is it the decriminalization of conduct that causes it to be considered as normal or even mandatory?

The reference to the classic debate on the relationship between law and social morality is, in this case, practically unavoidable. It is obvious that, by referring to the abovementioned categories, a decriminalized conduct ceases to be a criminal offence and becomes lawful, but decriminalization in itself cannot imply the conceptualization of conduct as a subjective right.

However, in legal practice, decriminalized conducts start to be considered by public opinion as subjective rights, despite the controversy. For example, in the case of the voluntary termination of pregnancy, it did not take too many years since the decriminalization of 1985 for the conduct in question to be considered by women as an enforceable healthcare provision.

The recent bill, which aims at decriminalizing euthanasia, already appeals in the Explanatory Memorandum to the existence of a social demand for the existence of a right to die. The law would bring the right into line with social reality.

It is not surprising that, precisely in relation to the abortion, Ollero wonders "to what extent what is presented as a mere exceptional decriminalization of certain conducts does not end up conferring on them in practice the character of a right, or even a fundamental right. Proof of this would be that decriminalization -although it does not allegedly legalize conduct or confer rights- confers on third parties (doctors) specific duties; and of such a scope that it would force them to take refuge in the exceptional (conscientious objection) if they want to refuse to carry out an exceptionally decriminalized conduct, which -in practice- is normally presented to them as mandatory".[14] The answer to the question is clear in the case of euthanasia. As

[14]Ollero Tassara (1998), 279.

previously mentioned, the current draft not only amends Article 143(4) of the Penal Code, but creates a new right: the right to euthanasia or to "be helped to die".

Decriminalization therefore has, at the very least, a clear normalizing effect on conduct that is no longer typical. The issue that arises is whether, in certain cases, the legislator does not set himself a more ambitious objective: to alter the social perception of a certain action, which remains part of the penal code, but also begins to be considered as an enforceable conduct, as a result of a change in the dominant social values under the pedagogical effect of the penal code.

3 Right to Do Wrong: Individual Autonomy and State Neutrality

In this way, it is essential to understand correctly what a subjective right is. In theory, as we have indicated, conduct that ceases to be a criminal offence does not therefore become a right. It becomes lawful, but not enforceable. However, things are far from clear. In practice we have already seen that by normalizing the exceptions to legal asset protection, decriminalization feeds the idea that it must be mandatory (it is in the norm). Let us ask ourselves what happens in the theoretical sphere, what conceptions of subjective right allow us to consider a merely decriminalized conduct as enforceable.

Let us now turn our attention on two essential ideas that pervade certain theories of subjective right, if not dominant, that are at least widespread in contemporary academic debate.

The first step is to decouple the existence of a right from the existence of reasons for the conduct to be protected by law, and the consequent link between the right and individual autonomy from decision-making capacity. The second focuses on the *liberty rights* category: on the one hand, this category suggests that an explicit permission to engage in lawful conduct brings us into the realm of what is required by expressly speaking of *rights*; on the other hand, even if it is merely semantic, it increases the confusion between freedoms and rights, and in some ways it paves the way between something lawful (still expressly lawful) and something enforceable.

Particular attention should be paid to the academic debate on the existence of a *right to do wrong*.

Waldron was the first to defend the existence of a "moral"[15] right to do the wrong thing. According to him, "it is necessary to insist that wrong actions as well as right actions and indifferent actions can be the subject of moral rights. So the clusters of actions that we find subsumed under our general rights are likely to include, in the circumstances that face us, actions that would be stupid, cowardly, tasteless,

---

[15]The paradoxical expression "moral right" is referred to the rights whose binding force is based upon its own nature.

inconsiderate, destructive, wasteful, deceitful, and just plain wrong, as well as actions that are wise, courageous, cultured, compassionate, creative, honest, and good".[16]

For Waldron, in my view, the morality of rights is fundamentally aimed at protecting personal choices, that is to say, personal autonomy.[17] However, the morality of what is right or wrong, is to direct these choices.

In this way, under the affirmation that a person has the right to perform a certain action, the range of options within which the action in particular is located "represents an important area of decision for the person".[18] According to Waldron, there are some types of choices and key areas of decision-making that are particularly important for both individual integrity and one's identity.[19] Obviously, all possible types of decision are not equal and do not deserve the same legal protection. But, apart from this "material" consideration, the right to do wrong would in any case be a genuine claim right and not merely a factual possibility among different courses of action.[20]

For Waldron, the right to do wrong cannot be a mere freedom. He considers it as a genuine right. To be free means to have explicit permission to perform a certain conduct. However, this permission does not extend to the possibility of forcing others to cooperate in the attainment or effective fulfilment of the claim by the person in possession of a freedom. It does extend to the power to prevent third parties interference in our action if they wish to prevent us from doing so.

On the other hand, when a claim right is exercised, other people may be forced to contribute to the carrying out of the conduct in question, and certainly none of them will be authorized in any way to prevent the satisfaction of the claim.

In his opinion, the existence of a moral right to the realization of something immoral implies that the right to do wrong is conceived as a claim right. As we pointed out earlier, the ultimate foundation lies on the value of autonomy as a legitimizing element of conduct.[21] Herstein argues an identical thesis: "while a right to do wrong must correspond to some duty in others, it need not necessarily correspond to the 'negative' duty of non-interference. Conceptually, a right may also correlate to 'positive' duties to facilitate, enable, and realize what one has a right to".[22] It is

---

[16]Waldron (1981), 37.

[17]"I have spoken as if the morality of rights and the morality of rightness and wrongness -the morality that gives rise to statements like 1 and the morality that gives rise to statements like 2- were distinct. And so they are, for they have distinct functions: the former has the **function of protecting choices** and the latter the function of guiding them", Ibid., 37; Our emphasis. A similar thesis can be found in Herstein (2012), 344.

[18]"That is why the claim that someone has the right to perform one particular action does not stand alone: the claim is understood in the light of the more general proposition that the range of options in which that action is located represents an important area of choice for that person", Ibid., 35.

[19]There are certain types of choice, certain key areas of decision making, which have a special importance for individual integrity and self-constitution, Ibid., 34.

[20]On the difference between liberty rights and claim rights, vid., Hohfeld (1919); Finnis (2011), 199 ff.

[21]Williamson (2012), 1.

[22]Herstein (2012), 344.

clear that: "In Hohfeldian terms the presumed moral right to do moral wrong is best conceived of as a claim-right".[23]

Logically, this conception of the morality of rights separates them from the reasons under which they are exercised, that is, from the whole discourse on the reasons that justified the action. Reasons become completely irrelevant when it comes to conceptualizing and evaluating the exercise of a right. For Waldron, the right to carry out a particular action does not give a reason to perform it. This right confers only *the power to decide* within the scope of the action. It does not imply that there are any operating reasons to carry it out.[24]

The dissociation between the attribution of rights and the reasons for exercising them or not, leads us to a thesis which Waldron does not stop at, but which, in my view, cannot be decoupled from his conception of rights: it is the supposed ethical neutrality of the State.

As Waldron notes, when the legislator recognizes a right, it is not informing, in any sense, about the goodness or moral perversity of the action that is especially protected by the legal system. It is simply recognizing that, in this particular area, the power of decision must devolve upon the individual, and not the State, which as a result, is limited to playing a neutral role, guaranteeing the possibility to choose.

For this reason, anyone who seeks to oppose the recognition of a subjective right on material grounds contrary to its consideration as legally worthy to be protected by law, would be mistakenly arguing, on the basis of a wrong assumption. From this perspective, it does not mean that the law considers "good" or "better" conducts which should be legally protected, but rather that there are areas of human life in which the State should abstain and leave the power of decision in the hands of the individual. However, this requirement demands intervention by the supposedly neutral State in order to recognize the citizens' ability to carry out their decisions, especially when it does not consist of an omissive conduct.

For example, referring to the voluntary termination of pregnancy, it could be said that when this claim becomes a right, the only thing the State makes explicit is its conviction to leave women to freely decide whether and when to have children. Those who do not want to abort have enough to do without it so, because they will be free of any kind of pressure, and those who want to do that will have public support services to carry out their decision.

In short, the ultimate foundation of the existence of the right "to do wrong" lies in personal autonomy and in the conviction that the right must serve, above all other purposes, the strengthening of such autonomy and its development throughout the life of individuals. In the background, the idea of the existence of a right to "moral independence" remains, as put forward by Dworkin, among others".[25]

---

[23]Ibid., 345.

[24]"That is why the fact that an individual has the right to perform some particular action does not in itself provide a reason for his performing that action. For the claim that he has the right to perform it refers us to the wider area of decision, in which the action is located and in which alternatives are available, and asserts only that his decision making in this area is to be protected. To protect decision making is not to provide a reason for the making of any particular decision", Ibid., 35.

[25]See Dworkin (1981), 177–212. For an interesting critique of Dworkin, vid., George (1993).

4 From Crime to Right: A not-so-Long Road

The shift from criminally reprehensible conduct to another worthy of protection, which is something seemingly paradoxical, can be better understood if we look at it in the light of the ideas underlying the above headings. First, we believe that the defense of the legal asset will not suffer because of the exemption of punitive sanction in certain cases. Nevertheless, the pedagogical effect of the rule inevitably leads to fractures in the protection of legal good. And, since certain conducts are legally authorized, they end up generating genuine duties on third parties, which in my view, allows us to speak of the existence of a right benefiting the other part of the legal relationship.

In the new *right to do wrong* scheme, the emphasis stops to reside in the nature of the conduct that becomes enforceable. What matters most is whether people are able to make decisions in the area to which the right belongs.

As we will see below, if we decriminalize what would correspond to states of necessity, the commission of the crime becomes a legalized action and, from there, in practice, a right. We have seen how Waldron conceives the right to do wrong as a claim right. We could speak of the existence of a freedom, at most, insofar as people act under a coverage rule that give them an express permission to act and, to this extent, the ability or power to prevent others from interfering in the realization of the claim. But the step from having the power to prevent others from interfering with our freedom, to having the power to force others to act positively for the effective guarantee of the claim, is sometimes a very subtle one.

In this regard, the ruling of the European Court of Human Rights in *Hass v. Switzerland* case is very enlightening. In its decision the Court addresses the issue of the existence of a "right to decide by what means and at what point his or her life will end" under Article 8, from the point of view of whether there is "a *positive obligation on the State to* take the necessary measures to permit a dignified suicide" (par. 51 and 53). The Court rightly focuses on whether or not there is an obligation on the State or on third parties when it comes to analyzing the existence or not of a subjective right. Such a right could not be proclaimed if the consequent duties were unlawful. It is as unlawful as the duty to kill, even with the consent of the victim.

The thesis of Mr. Hass's counsel had sought to demonstrate that in order for his client to properly exercise (without interference) his right to private life, the State should have intervened by authorizing him (or forcing the judges) to make it possible in this case prescribing the lethal substance that would allow him to commit suicide, thus giving him the power to decide, within the scope of his right to privacy, where and when to die.

However, the Court refuted the existence of such a decision-making capacity based on its inherent consequences, as we mentioned earlier. These consequences are also considered in the light of an overall view of the legal system, of its construction as Rule of Law, of the meaning of respect for human life in this context, and of the duties arising for third parties.

As we can see, in order to avoid the non-legitimate shift from freedoms to authentic rights, it is necessary to overcome an atomistic vision of the right to be exercised in the specific case. Otherwise, the path from the forbidden to the enforceable becomes, in effect, shorter than expected.

5 Unintelligibility of Right and Other Issues

As seen above, decriminalization as a normalization of the exception and right as legal protection to do even the "wrong", may help to bridge the gap between crime and right. Also, they explain to us this apparently paradoxical process whereby a crime becomes an enforceable conduct.

It is now necessary to determine whether this perception raises any issues from the point of view of law. In my view, the understanding of the shift from crime to right poses two major conceptual drawbacks (which are obviously reflected in practice sooner or later).

The first is the progressive and practically unstoppable weakening of the criminal definitions. It is partially decriminalized when the conduct performed under a certain modality is carried out by means of legalization (not totally but largely free of charge, since there is no decriminalized assumption that is not reduced to an exemption from liability). *Generally*, it introduces obvious risks for the protection of the legal asset intended to be defended, and not only in such cases affected by decriminalization.

The inconsistency of the will to maintain the protection of the legal asset and to legally decriminalize related cases of violation, invites us to consider whether there will not be a social engineering project in the background, that begins with the decriminalization. In this case, it would be extremely striking in the context of a conception of rights that is justified in the duty of the State to maintain an ethically neutral position. We will leave this issue merely stated to focus on the second.

The second disadvantage is that the way of understanding rights underlying this conception ends up making them a basically unintelligible category.

Both Waldron and Herstein seem to have proved the logical consistency of the thesis of the existence of moral rights to do something immoral, and, in my opinion, they have not failed in their attempt. Personally, I agree with Robert P. George's criticism, when he points out that, in any case, the existence of a duty of State non-interference, guaranteed by law, does not necessarily imply the existence of a right to do wrong. There are other reasons that justify the State non-intervention, mainly those of prudence, which, in certain cases, may exist to justify the no ban on something morally wrong. What is not justified is that the right to do the wrong thing is the logical correlate of the State's duty of non-intervention.[26]

My discourse now aims to demonstrate a conceptual impossibility more widely understood than the debate between Waldron and George reflects.

---

[26]George (1993), 118–122.

In what sense do I say that this conception of rights makes them unintelligible? First of all, I would like to say that it is practically impossible to distinguish between what is required and what is lawful, and therefore to understand what having a right means. If we are entitled to everything that is not expressly prohibited, or to what has been expressly permitted,[27] then almost everything could become a right, which obviously implies not only a devaluation of the category, but the impossibility of identifying it adequately by separating it from other legal categories such as the lawful.

The difference between exercising a right and acting within the scope of the "agere licere" must be kept alive and as clear as possible. The Spanish Constitutional Court itself has made this clear in its rulings on the forced feeding of GRAPO prisoners on hunger strike. Concerning the right to life, the Court recalls that there is a difference between the possibility of a factual provision on one's own life and the existence of a right to die. The latter would imply the capacity to commit third parties and, ultimately, the State, in guaranteeing the effective fulfilment of the service. It states that: "the right to life [has] a positive protection content that prevents it from being configured as a right of freedom which includes the right to one's own death. This does not prevent us, however, acknowledging that life being a good, which is part of the sphere of individuals' freedom, they may in fact decide on their own death. But this provision constitutes a manifestation of the "agere licere", inasmuch as the deprivation of one's own life or the acceptance of one's own death is an act that the law does not prohibit in any way, a subjective right that involves the possibility of mobilizing the support of public authority to overcome resistance to the will to die, nor, much less, a subjective right of a fundamental nature in which that possibility is extended even against the resistance of the legislator, which cannot reduce its essential content".[28]

We are therefore not entitled to everything that is not prohibited. The absence of prohibition implies the factual possibility to act, but not the legal backing in the form of granting rights. Nor does this support exist when the absence of a ban has been explicitly expressed, for example, during a decriminalization process. Unlike the mere absence of a prohibition, decriminalization makes the possibility of carrying out the conduct in question visible as something that is not punishable by law. But even that explicit permission does not make it a right. At best, we would be talking of freedom, in the language of the Anglo-Saxon debate, but not of legally enforceable conduct.

Second, the unintelligibility of the category of right itself is because moral rights are based on the autonomy of the will and not on the reason or reasonableness of the claim. If the existence of rights relies on personal self-determination, when the existence of a good for individuals who give an account of their rights is explicitly discarded, these rights are based on something as incomprehensible as the will to inspire a personal life project that can be constructed in a completely arbitrary manner.

---

[27] Decriminalization works as an express permission and I think that when Ollero refers to a right to do what is not forbidden he is really talking about a right to do what is expressly permitted.

[28] STC 120/1990, de 27 de junio (HH1).

Rights become, not immoral, but simply opaque to anyone who seeks to grasp them rationally, by linking themselves to the will and disassociating themselves from reasons.

Devaluation and poor intelligibility of rights, thus conceived, can be expressed by denouncing the crisis of an element that has traditionally been considered essential in the configuration of subjective right: I am referring to the just title that legitimizes its exercise. By title in the strict sense we mean any "legal document or act which serves as a legal basis for the exercise of a right".[29] In this context, appealing for the need to base every right on a just title means to appeal for reasons that account for the existence of something as important as a subjective right, and, above all, for the existence of the duty of third parties, who must contribute, whether or not they wish to do so, to the effective realization of the conduct in question. For there to be a right, as Ollero points out in his criticism of Waldron, there must be a "just title as the ground of every right", which justifies the existence of a duty of third parties and ultimately of public authorities.[30]

Moreover, by making the individuals and their autonomous decision-making capacity the main center of the discourse on rights, proclaiming the ethical neutrality of the State, something essential is being forgotten: the State is the only one that *always* decides. The idea that it is the need to endow individuals with the capacity to decide on certain spheres of their life withholds that this approach, in itself, is already a decision, and a decision that they have not taken, that has been completely usurped in the name of their own freedom and the guarantee of their rights.

6 Ideas to Understand Crime and Right in Another Way

The existence of the aforementioned issues forces us, in a way, to try to formulate an alternative. We shall confine ourselves here to five ideas, which in my view, could rescue the intelligibility of the notion of right and contribute to a better relationship of its understanding with crime and, in particular, with the crime without sanction.

We have to start, in the way we should, with the foundations. The first idea that we should not banish at all, but we should relocate into the legal world is that of individual autonomy. The *logos* of law do not consist in the development of one's own autonomy without damages to third parties, but in the act of giving people their right, what they objectively deserve, in the context of a relationship with others and with the community outside of which the whole notion of law becomes confused.[31]

From this approach, in order to avoid the detrimental effects of the shift from crime to right would, we need:

First. To undertake a thorough review of the opportunity and necessity of using the partial decriminalization technique. As we have seen so far, "decriminalization

[29] http://dej.rae.es/#/entry-id/E259430.

[30] Ollero Tassara (2006a, b), 68.

[31] Cfr. Cotta (2017), 97–98.

is often only a euphemism, camouflaging the contradiction until the conflicts to be avoided are triggered".[32]

In the case of abortion, the majority of the criminal doctrine considers that the cases decriminalized in article 417 bis of the Penal Code correspond to states of necessity understood as a basis of justification, or at least as a manifestation of the principle of interests balancing.[33]

In fact, the Constitutional Court itself, in its ruling 53/1985, legitimizes the use of indications by referring to the impossibility of obliging an individual to engage in "heroic" conduct through the law. That is to say, it clearly addresses the issue as a conflict of interest between the pregnant woman and the intrauterine life (which, as is well known, constitutes the legal asset that explains the existence of the criminal definition of abortion).

Second. It should even be added that denial of the correspondence between the indications of article 417bis and the state of necessity, or at least the thesis that the indications represent much more than states of necessity, in connection with other grounds for justification, has its origin in an interpretation of decriminalization based on the perception of the existence of a right linked to women's autonomy. Thus, according to Ropero, "the indications do not show a collision between the life of the fetus and the diffuse interests of women, but rather that these interests are, as the Constitutional Court recognizes, fundamental rights protected in our Constitution: especially, the rights to freedom, to the free development of the personality, dignity and privacy".[34]

Apart from the interpretation that can be made of the literal nature of Judgment 53/1985, (which refers to such rights,[35] although it establishes that in any case can they be absolute, but that they must be considered in such a way that their exercise does not entail the disappearance of the legal right protected by Article 15 and which embodies a "core value of the constitutional order"[36]) it should be said that if Ropero's thesis is correct, then it is not only a matter of making abortive conduct legal, but, in so far as it would constitute an expression of the exercise of fundamental rights, it should be understood as an enforceable conduct that does not correspond to decriminalization, but rather to the recognition of the voluntary termination of pregnancy as a right (recognition that is neither peaceful nor much less explicit, even

---

[32]Sartea (2015), 192.

[33]It doesn't mean the recognition of an occlusive effect of specific norm (Article 417 bis Spanish Criminal Law) on general norm (Article 20.5 Spanish Criminal Law). Vid., Ropero Carrasco (2004), 347 ff.

[34]Ibid., p. 352.

[35]Legal Ground 8.

[36]On Legal Ground 9: "Se trata de graves conflictos de características singulares, que no pueden contemplarse tan sólo desde la perspectiva de los derechos de la mujer o desde la protección de la vida del nasciturus. Ni ésta puede prevalecer incondicionalmente frente a aquéllos, ni los derechos de la mujer pueden tener primacía absoluta sobre la vida del nasciturus, dado que dicha prevalencia supone la desaparición, en todo caso, de un bien no sólo constitucionalmente protegido, sino que encarna un valor central del ordenamiento constitucional".

after the adoption of Organic Law 2/2010 of March 3, on Sexual and Reproductive Health and Voluntary Termination of Pregnancy[37]).

If the indications basically correspond to states of necessity and are legitimized insofar as they decriminalize the "unbearable" cases and are not called upon to respond to the generality of the cases in which pregnancies occur,[38] then it would be necessary to assess whether it would not be preferable to leave it to the judicial application of the law itself to determine the cases in which such "unique or exceptional situations" exempt from criminal liability exist (as long as we want to maintain the protection of the legal asset).

Third. Is essential to clearly distinguish between conducts merely permitted (whether explicit or implicit) and conducts that can be legally required. Just because something is *legal* means that it is not prohibited and that the legal system considers the conduct to be expressly lawful. Legality is one thing, however, and enforceability something else. The key, in my view, is the extent to which the realization of such conduct gives us the legitimacy to force third parties and, ultimately, the State.

It is no coincidence that Kelsen himself considers subjective right as the "legal power to enforce the fulfilment of an existing duty".[39]

When that obligation is foreseen and recognized as valid, then and only then can we safely affirm the existence of a right. There are no rights without duties, as Ollero recalled.[40] The European Court of Human Rights itself, in the Hass case mentioned above, is quite explicit in this respect.[41]

Fourth. The exercise of subjective rights should not be understood in isolation, but rather within the specific framework of a legal relationship and, more generically, within a unit represented by the legal system which makes their effectiveness possible.

In order to discuss about the existence of a right, it is important to determine whether the individual is able to decide on the matter or whether this right can be structured within a reasonable legal relationship.[42] It is necessary to be able to indicate, for the specific case, the subjects of the relationship (the holder of the right and the person on whom the correlative duty falls), the object of the relationship (an asset, a conduct, the provision of a service, etc.), the delimitation of its content (which faculties recognize its holder, including the capacity to demand the fulfillment of the

[37]Vid., Albert Márquez (2013), 87–109.

[38]As Spanish Constitutional Court has shown, on legal ground 9 of sentence 53/1985: "Las leyes humanas contienen patrones de conducta en los que, en general, encajan los casos normales, pero existen situaciones singulares o excepcionales en las que castigar penalmente el incumplimiento de la Ley resultaría totalmente inadecuado; el legislador no puede emplear la máxima constricción -la sanción penal- para imponer en estos casos la conducta que normalmente sería exigible, pero que no lo es en ciertos supuestos concretos".

[39]Kelsen (1991), 324.

[40]Ollero Tassara (2006a, b), 122.

[41]What did not prevent the Court from considering that the decision to die falls into the scope of Article 8 of the European Convention of Human Rights. See Gross v. Switzerland (may 2013). That decision was annulled by judgment of the Court of September 2014, Vid., Albert Márquez (2014), 1027–1045.

[42]Sánchez González (2010), 314. Among these "new rights", the right to abortion.

correlative duty), and, finally, the legal guarantees of its enforceability (that is to say, that there exists active procedural legitimization to make the right effective).

Above all, the relational structure of law requires that the holder of a right should be able to brandish a just title that legitimizes his privileged position within the framework of the legal relationship, since this is not indifferent to others, but implies the existence of duties that fall on them.

The panorama which emerges, and has its origin in the commented theories and other that are equally operative, has rightly been described as a scenario where "we now find not individuals objectively understood in their own relational structure, but the arbitrary will of each individual; therefore, the legal rules must be limited to protecting them in their determinations and strengthening their claims with the support of the norms and institutions".[43] On the other hand, if we place at the center of the system not an individual, but a network of rights and duties that characterizes the relational nature of the human condition, the panorama changes. Before recognizing a right, it will be necessary to consider whether the reasons used to justify its exercise are sufficiently powerful to justify the correlative obligation in third parties. As Finnis has rightly pointed out, the law is essentially an "adjustment" of social relations (rather than the recognition of spheres of power to the citizen as such). The primary explanation of law is related to "aright" rather than "rights".[44]

Finally, let us bear in mind that, once the exercise of a right is linked to the existence of a title that justifies it (based on the common good), the abuse of right may come into play as a limit to do "wrong". From my point of view, Waldron is partly right in his assertion that a right can be exercised with an immoral intimate motivation, but it cannot be exercised with an unlawful motivation. When this assumption is made, the very dynamics of law is prepared to react and prevent the right to do an unfair thing (right to do wrong, not in the immoral sense, but in the sense of unfair and, therefore, unlawful).

To this end, it is essential, as previously mentioned, to consider subjective right into the legal system considered as a whole, with its inherent principles, demands, choices…

Concerning the abuse of right, it is necessary to recall here the content of article 7 of the Spanish civil code: «*1. Rights must be exercised in accordance with the requirements of good faith. 2. The law does not support abuse of rights or antisocial exercise thereof. Any act or omission which, as a result of the author's intention, its purpose or the circumstances in which it is performed manifestly exceeds the normal limits to exercise a right, with damage to a third party, shall give rise to the corresponding compensation and the adoption of judicial or administrative measures preventing persistence in such abuse*» .[45] Also relevant, in my view, is Article 6.7, which regulates the institution of fraud against the law: "*Acts performed pursuant*

---

[43]Sartea (2015),193.

[44]Finnis (2011), 206.

[45]Also Article 17 of the European Convention of Human Rights, as follows: Nothing in this Convention may be interpreted as implying for any State, group or person any right to engage in any activity or perform any act aimed at the destruction of any of the rights and freedoms set forth herein or at their limitation to a greater extent than is provided for in the Convention". A material conception of

to the text of a legal rule, which pursue a result forbidden by the legal system or contrary thereto shall be considered to be in fraud of the law and shall not prevent the due application of the rule which they purported to avoid".

In general terms, it would be fair to say that a right is exercised abusively when it is performed contrary to good faith or to the *purpose* for it is recognized and guaranteed.[46] On the other hand, fraud against the law occurs when there are "apparently lawful conducts, because they are carried out under the protection of a certain law in force, but which produce a contrary or prohibited result due to another rule considered fundamental in the regulation of the same matter"[47] or, in general, by the legal system. In this case, the purpose of the legal order betrays the right holder's conduct and not the very purpose of the right holder. In fact, the Explanatory Memorandum of the 1974 reform of the Spanish Civil Code justified the precept as follows: "*the idea of considering the legal system as a whole is predominant; it is therefore considered fraudulent to submit to a rule carried out with the purpose of obtaining a result that is prohibited or contrary to the legal system as a whole*".

Concerning the fraud against the law, even the Spanish Supreme Court, in its judgment of 21 December 2000, emphasizes that the action is characterized by a violation of the "*ethical content of the precepts in which they are protected*", whether or not one is aware of circumventing the law. Even if the word "ethical" is used, it is clear that this content is legally relevant, or more simply lawful, since its violation rightly implies action in the case of fraud against the law.

The same idea of abuse of right already shows us a teleological element in the legal phenomenon and an essential unity within the legal system. It is therefore impossible to interpret every subjective right considered in itself. It can be understood only within a legal fabric that has its own dynamisms and interconnections, and in which "the functioning of such a system depends essentially on the submission of each rule and principle to other principles and rules that justify it and give it a sense".[48]

Referring to the reasons for exercising a right, this matter is not irrelevant to the legal theory. It is true that not all reasons are relevant to law, but the fact remains that law has its own reasons (its own logos) and that no right can be configured in order to ignore it. When *rights* are understood outside the *Law*, we run the risk of Law stop functioning in the long term as a limit to power, against which it represents the force of reason.

---

fundamental rights can be found here. This conception can only be understood in close relationship with european history, in particular with a relativistic conception of human rights which led to the dismantling of democracy. Vid., Sánchez Martínez (2009), 832.

[46]Castillo Blanco (2008), 15. Our emphasys.

[47]Wolter Kruger, Guía Jurídica Derecho Civil, voice *Fraude de Ley*, available on line: http://guiasjuridicas.wolterskluwer.es.

[48]Sartea (2015), 196.

References

Albert Márquez M (2013) ¿Tenemos derecho a abortar? De la despenalización a la exigibilidad jurídica: el proceso de reforma legal del aborto en España. In: Revista de Derechos humanos de la universidad de Piura (4) 87–109

Albert Márquez M (2014) Derecho a morir y abuso de derecho. La inadmisibilidad del caso Gross v. Suiza Comentario a la Sentencia de la Gran Sala del Tribunal Europeo de Derechos Humanos de 30 de septiembre de 2014. Medicina e Morale. (6)1027–1045

Albert Márquez M (2015) Privacidad y derecho a morir. In: Santos JA, Albert M, Hermida, C. Bioética y Nuevos Derechos. Comares. Granada

Castillo Blanco F (2008) La interpretación y aplicación del ordenamiento jurídico. Especial referencia al abuso de Derecho. Instituto Nacional de Administración Pública. Madrid

Cotta S (2017) Perché il Diritto?. La Scuola, Brescia

Dworkin R (1981) Is there a right to pornography? Oxford J Legal Stud (1.2):177–212

Finnis J (2011) Natural law and natural rights. Clarendon Press, Oxford

George RP (1993) Making men moral. Oxford University Press, Oxford

Herstein OJ (2012) Defending the right to do wrong. Law Philos 31:343–365. https://doi.org/10.1007/s10982-011-9126-x

Hohfeld WN (1919) Fundamental legal conceptions. Yale University Press, New Heaven

Kelsen H (1991) General theory of norms. Clarendom Press, Oxford

Medina Jara R (1996) Despenalización o reforma penal. Algunos rasgos en la Ley 19450. Revista de Derecho de la Universidad Católica de Valparaiso (XVII) 331–337

Ollero Tassara A (1998) Todos tienen derecho a la vida. ¿Hacia un concepto constitucional de persona? In: Massini CI and Serna P (eds) El derecho a la vida. Eunsa. Pamplona

Ollero Tassara A (2006a) El derecho a lo torcido. In: Puig V (ed) El fraude del buenismo. FAES, Madrid

Ollero Tassara A (2006b) Bioderecho. Entre la vida y la muerte. Thompson Aranzadi, Cizur Menor

Ropero Carrasco J (2004) Las “disfunciones” establecidas por el sistema de indicaciones en la protección de la vida y de la salud en el periodo prenatal. Una interpretación sistemática de los delitos de aborto y de lesiones al feto a partir de la provocación de la situación de conflicto. Revista de Derecho Penal y Criminología 2:331–400

Roxin C (2016) ¿Es la protección de bienes jurídicos una finalidad del Derecho penal? In: Hefendehl R, Von Hirsch A, Wohlers W (eds) La Teoría del Bien Jurídico, ¿Fundamento de legitimación del Derecho penal o juego de abalorios dogmático? Marcial Pons. Madrid, Barcelona, Buenos Aires, Sao Paulo

Ruiz Vadillo E (1999) Descriminalización y despenalización. Reforma penal y descriminalización. Eguzkilore 13:97–104

Sánchez Cámara I (2012) De delito a derecho. El declive de la protección jurídica de la vida. Cuadernos de Bioética (XXIII) 25–36

Sánchez González S (2010) ¿Todavía más derechos?, ¿De qué derechos hablamos? Teoría y Realidad Constitucional 25:1

Sánchez Martínez O (2009) El abuso de derecho: Del Código Civil al Convenio Europeo de Derechos Humanos. In: VVAA. Estudios de Derecho español y europeo: Libro conmemorativo de los primeros veinticinco años de la Universidad de Cantabria. Universidad de Cantabria. Santander

Sartea C (2015) Aventuras y desventuras del derecho a la privacy. In: Santos JA, Albert M, Hermida C. Bioética y Nuevos Derechos. Comares. Granada. 2015

Waldron J (1981) A right to do wrong. Ethics 92(1):21–39

Williamson J (2012) Against the right to do wrong https://www.academia.edu/3678472/Against_the_right_to_do_wrong?auto=download

The Role of the Criminal Law in Regulating Pornography

Gerard V. Bradley

Abstract Over the last decades, especially with the arrival and persisting rise of the internet's influence on culture and communication, the prevalence of pornography has seen a massive increase. Corresponding cultural shifts have taken place, gradually bringing pornography into the mainstream and even moving towards its normalization. It is not unconnected that prosecutions for the production or distribution of pornography involving adult actors are rare. But such a culture awash in pornography does not come out unscathed; there is growing evidence of pornography's profound detrimental effects on individuals, groups, and the culture at large. The law always has an important culture-shaping role to play, and thus society's goal should be for public actors who shape the law to contribute to morally stigmatizing pornography. Although this effort would likely span decades and, even if successful, not eradicate pornography completely, it would nevertheless instill in the broader culture a sense that pornography is morally wrong and should be avoided. In Part I of this paper, I shall consider the genesis of today's dominant cultural narrative in the United States *about* pornography. This narrative is the story that pornography is good for many people and no worse than harmless entertainment for all those who like it. Successfully stigmatizing pornography must explode this master narrative. In Part II, I explore how digitalized porn envelops even the unwilling in a pornified culture; I will identify some of the leading social harms of contemporary pornographic traffic. Part III responds to a paternalistic objection against pornography criminalization. Finally, in Part IV, I offer several specific legal proposals, including recommended prosecutions, as part of an overall cultural offensive to stigmatize pornography.

Criminal prosecution in the United States for producing or distributing pornography featuring adult actors has gone the way of the eight-track tape and the videocassette. All are now museum pieces. The most recent figures available for the total number

---

G. V. Bradley (✉)
Professor of Law, Notre Dame Law School, 3156 Eck Hall of Law, Notre Dame, IN 46556, USA
e-mail: Gerard.V.Bradley.16@nd.edu

A. Masferrer (ed.), *Criminal Law and Morality in the Age of Consent*, Ius Gentium: Comparative Perspectives on Law and Justice 84,
https://doi.org/10.1007/978-3-030-64163-4_14

of federal prosecutions (cases initiated by the United States, as opposed to those initiated by one of the fifty states or a political subdivision thereof) are from the Obama Administration from 2009 to 2017: none. Prosecutions at the state and local level do occur, but they are very rare.

These numbers crown a decades-long retreat from the use of criminal law as a means for the social control of pornography. An authoritative United States government study in 1986 (popularly called the "Meese Commission," after the Attorney General who sponsored it) already observed that criminal prosecutions were rare, and sentences where convictions were obtained were exceedingly light. What the Commission described as "striking under-enforcement" of state laws against obscenity[1] (the relevant legal term for pornography) has obviously accelerated in the decades since.

During these decades pornography became ubiquitous. All sorts of metrics verify the point: one-quarter of all search engine requests relate to pornography[2]; pornography sites attract more traffic monthly than Amazon, Netflix, and Twitter combined[3]; a 2017 survey by a University of Texas research team found that 43 percent of men intentionally accessed pornography within the previous week.[4] But perhaps any reader who has ever connected to the Internet is already nodding his (or her) head in agreement: Americans (and probably most Europeans, too) are awash in pornography.

The concurrence of these two developments suggests that reinvigorating criminal prosecutions for commercialized pornography (leaving aside, then, simple possession of material for one's private use[5]) might stem the flood of pornographic materials. But evaluating that proposal depends critically upon considering another aspect of

---

[1]Final Report of the Attorney General's Commission on Pornography (1986), p. 225 (hereafter "Meese Report")

[2]Paasonen (2011), pp. 424–45.

[3]Molloy (2014).

[4]Regnerus (2017), p. 114. This is compared to just nine percent of women who accessed intentionally in the previous week, indicating one of the many ways in which pornography use, as well as content, is strikingly gendered. In other words, pornography is largely produced for men's pleasure by showing women in sexual poses and performing sexual acts.

[5]The United States Supreme Court established an effective immunity from prosecution for *in-home* use of pornography in 1969, in the case of *Stanley v. Georgia*, 394 U.S. 557 (1969). In that case, police officers executing a search warrant for gambling paraphernalia instead found what the Court, speaking through Justice Marshall, coyly described as "three reels of eight-millimeter film". In truth and as the opinions in the lower court made unmistakably clear, these were three hard-core stag films. The Court reversed Stanley's state-court conviction for "knowing possession" of "obscene matter". The *Stanley* Court seemed to base its decision upon its own moral judgment that pornography was *good* at least for some people. The Justices observed that human well-being had cognitive, religious, and emotional aspects. Then the Court asserted an intimate connection between this account of flourishing and the materials seized, as if the stag films truly enriched Mr. Stanley's life. The Court then cut diagonally across this terrain, and advanced an argument against state paternalism: Georgia was "trying to control the moral content of a person's thoughts". The Court pivoted next to consider the case as one about, not human well-being and pornography, but about the limits of the state's coercive jurisdiction, either with regard specifically to criminal law or to home searches, or both.

today's inundation, one that is both cause and effect of the numerical frequency of pornography, namely, pornography's cultural *mainstreaming,* and perhaps even its *normalization.* This is the very widespread acceptance of an increasingly bizarre pornographic *oeuvre*[6] as indelible cultural wallpaper. It is acceptance, or learning to live with pornography as a fact of life. For some it is more. Brian McNair's *Porno? Chic!* explores "the process whereby the once heavily stigmatized and marginalized cultural form we call pornography has become not only more plentiful, and more visible, but also fashionable".[7]

Now the challenge of pornography and the question about prosecutions come into plain view: What is (can be? should be?) the role of criminal prosecution in tackling a phenomenon with which many millions of people are involved, and which now enjoys considerable social approval or, at the very least, is so honeycombed into ordinary lives that the forces of inertia and of human rationalization make it appear to be a permanent civic fixture? How can criminal law and its enforcement productively contribute to ameliorating what is now a widespread *cultural* problem?

The answer is that what has become a cultural force must be stymied by cultural counter-force. Effective social control of obscenity in a free, porn-saturated society calls for a creative, synergistic partnership among many opinion-shapers, educators, pastors, and other culture-forming actors to *morally stigmatize* pornography as degrading and harmful. Public authority has an indispensable role to play in this partnership, for law powerfully shapes culture and thus shapes *us*—our actions, our attitudes, and our conception of right and wrong.

There is no realistic prospect of measurably impacting the production, distribution, or consumption of pornography solely through the criminal law; the Internet and public acceptance of pornography conspire to ensure that much. There is no practical way for law enforcement to effectively interdict the supply chain for pornography, which often originates overseas or in the privacy of bedrooms, and finds its way invisibly into so many persons' hand-held devices. One might as well try to catch all the flies in a garbage dump as attempt to prosecute even a fraction of those accessing pornography on their computers.

My opinion is that, as a matter of principle, justice does not require the immunity so unstably defended by the *Stanley* Court. But the result in *Stanley* is quite possibly right. At least, a disciplined, persuasive argument could have been mounted in favor of the result reached there. This argument would be rooted mainly in the limits of the political common good, the value of home privacy, and a subtle use of a morally justified anti-paternalism. In brief: although using pornography even in one's home is morally degrading, it stands near the outer limit of political society's jurisdiction, on the assumption that a person engaged in solitary masturbation at home could not justly be punished by the state for doing so because his vicious action is truly *private.* Mr. Stanley, however, connected his act to a stream of commerce in degrading material by acquiring the stag-reels in some sort of transaction. For this reason, his possession of them even at home implicated the public interest in suppressing an immoral traffic. But one could reasonably conclude (here relying upon additional premises omitted from this synopsis) that it would do more harm to the overall common good to authorize police officers to invade a man's home in order to enforce anti-obscenity laws, than it would to simply *tolerate* conduct such as that of Mr. Stanley.

[6]For a brief description of "gonzo" pornography, see Dines (2010), pp. 59–78.

[7]McNair (2013), p. 3.

The state's *coercive* jurisdiction—its criminal laws and their enforcement—can and should play a modest but strategically essential part within that wider role for public authority. Prosecution of some pornography traffickers is certainly appropriate. But the objective of any pornography prosecution strategy must be to efficiently contribute to stigmatizing it as an industry that hurts people and pollutes our common culture. The proper measure of criminal law enforcement is that which is needed in a given cultural context to generate and sustain that stigma.

That stigma would produce many benefits. It will steer many people away from pornography; establish an authoritative benchmark for consequent adverse legal, social, and commercial policies about pornography; embolden moral criticism of those who continue to be involved in pornography; and make even many of them at least morally ambivalent about their actions. The end product would look much like the present cultural situation of, say, cigarette smoking, using racist language, flouting recycling norms, or committing adultery: some people do it, but far fewer than would in the absence of prevailing social norms against it, and everyone understands that doing any of these things is undesirable, embarrassing, regrettable. These things are never something to boast about or recommend to children for imitation.

Creating the needed stigma will be no easy task. Fifty-four scholars concluded in a path-breaking study called *The Social Costs of Pornography* that "today's internet pornography is qualitatively and quantitatively different from any that has come before". According to these eminent scholars, "Society has only begun to grapple with these new problems".[8] The disintegration over the last half-century or so of a public morality that judged pornography to be shameful, corrupting, and "dirty" has opened the sluicegates. Pornography is meant, of course, to arouse; that is what makes it pornography.[9] Its appeal has always been to arouse. But its appeal has also always been in its transgressive quality. Brian McNair, who maintains that pornography makes the world a better place, argues that it always "works in the same way, no matter by whom and for whom it is made, representing desires and activities which are in some sense *taboo*" (emphasis added).[10] Few cultural taboos now inhibit the sex one may enjoy on a consensual basis. In cyberspace (with the important exception of pornography depicting children), there is none. As the common spaces where public morals used to intersect with pornography have been superseded by the smartphone and the cloud, the content of pornography is no longer in (one might cautiously say) a healthy dialectic with the respectable. The perennial interplay between respectable and underground, between mainstream and marginal, between conventional and avant-garde, which used to shape pornography, is gone.

The effects of this devolution include an online bacchanalia that would make a libertine blush. Paasonen cites Mark Dery who "argues that online pornographers aim to grab users 'by their eyeballs' by showing them images amazing in their

[8]Stoner and Hughes (2010), p. 8.

[9]A common working definition of pornography, employed very widely throughout the research literature and which suffices for present purposes, would be: "sexually explicit visual material (photos, videos, etc.) that is intended to arouse".

[10]Lecture on "Sex and the Cinema" (copy in author's possession).

novelty, eccentricity or extremity in order to mark themselves apart from what is already familiar".[11] Paasonen continues that "online porn has meant unprecedented visibility of sexual subcultures, diverse sexual preferences, niches, and tastes".[12] She notes that "European scholars in particular have discussed this proliferation under the term *netporn*, denoting 'alternative body type tolerance and amorphous queer sexuality, interesting art works and writerly blogosphere, visions of grotesque sex and warpunk activism'".[13]

We shall say no more about the troubling menu of options available to the pornography-seeker. In Part I of this paper, I shall consider instead the genesis of today's dominant cultural narrative in the United States *about* pornography. This narrative is the story that pornography is good for many people and no worse than harmless entertainment for all those who like it. According to the narrative, those who do not like pornography should (a) simply avoid it, and (b) refrain from adversely judging those who like it because there is no good basis for an objective moral judgment that pornography is harmful. What pleases one's palette may offend another's sensibilities; it is all a matter of taste. The social and legal norm to be applied in such circumstances is of the private order: arrange things so that the willing have ready access to pornography, and the unwilling do not have to put up with unwanted encounters with it.

The necessary next stage of any argument in favor of stigmatizing pornography as harmful is to explode this master narrative. Whatever might have been the sense of a "private-order" approach to pornography decades ago, when it merely concerned centerfolds and zoning red-light districts, there is no sense now. In Part II of this essay, we shall explore how digitalized pornography envelops even the unwilling in a pornified culture, a social condition which has revealed itself to be corrosive not only of traditional sexual morality, but also of more contemporary anchor values of sexual progressivism like the autonomous control of one's sexual identity and equality in male-female sexual relationships. In other words, in this Part we shall identify some of the leading social harms of contemporary pornographic traffic.

Part III takes up one longstanding philosophical objection to criminalizing trafficking in pornography: that it is unjustly *paternalistic* for the state to "punish" anyone for engaging in putatively immoral conduct which harms no one else. This objection depends upon a descriptive substratum about the strictly self-regarding nature of pornography consumption, a story which is falsified by the description included in Part II. My argument in Part III builds upon that data and finishes off a philosophical refutation of the paternalism objection. In this Part, I take up the particular question which heads this entire chapter: the role of criminal law enforcement in the social control of pornography. At least in America, prevailing cultural attitudes towards law and morality, especially the perceived effects of legal permissions concerning sexual acts, require maintenance of criminal prohibitions against pornography even if they are rarely or never enforced.

---

[11] Paasonen (2011), p. 428 (citing Dery (2007), p. 135).

[12] *Id.*, p. 427.

[13] *Id.* (citing Jacobs et al. (2007), p. 2).

In Part IV, I offer several specific legal proposals, including recommended prosecutions, as part of an overall cultural offensive to stigmatize pornography.

I

The master narrative about pornography today originated in the sexual revolution of the 1960s. By 1970 in America, elite opinion-makers and progressive legal reformers, along with a substantial and growing body of ordinary people, proffered a benign estimation of pornography: it supplied some welcome measure of frank sexual education, and beyond that, it was no worse than harmless amusement for a lot of people.[14]

In constitutional law, however, and even though it had become in American culture an instantiation of justice and respect for human rights, the Supreme Court continued to hold that something called "obscenity" *lacked* First Amendment protections accorded to other speech. But the three-part test for identifying such "obscenity" promulgated by the Court in the 1973 *Miller* case[15] did not say or imply that there was anything *wrong* with "obscenity". The test did not call for, much less require, that any "obscene" act or work be prosecuted or legally discouraged in any way. Nowhere did the Justices in their own voices squarely advocate any such adverse legal action. Several members of the Court consistently called in dissent for the complete decriminalization of "obscenity".

The *Miller* Court simply clarified a *concept*—"obscenity"—that the Framers bequeathed to their descendants as an exception to First Amendment protection of "speech". But what the First Amendment does not protect is not perforce evil or harmful. It is just unprotected, by dint of a historical fact about the Founders' thinking. It is likely that, if the legacy of the American constitutional tradition was not that "obscenity"—understood by the Court to denote "hard-core pornography"—lacked First Amendment protection, the Supreme Court would not itself have created such an exception.

At the heart of the Court's curious moral reticence about pornography's harmfulness was an implicit meta-ethical commitment: neither public authorities nor popular majorities (nor anyone else, for that matter) can reasonably say that pornography is *objectively* detrimental to anyone. It is all a matter of taste and preference, finally to

[14]What came to be generally called the "President's Commission on Obscenity and Pornography" was created by Congress on October 3, 1967, to address a "matter of national concern". Its findings and opinions were published in 1970 as *The Report of the Commission on Obscenity and Pornography*. That publication is remarkable for its extraordinarily benign view of pornography and for the liberality of its legal recommendations. For example, the commission found no "causal relationship" between use of pornography and specified harms, including downstream anti-social acts. *Report* (1970), pp. 1, 27. More startlingly, the Commission made the same finding for child users. "[E]xposure to explicit sexual materials in adolescence is widespread and occurs in a group of peers of the same sex or in a group involving several members of each sex. The experience seems to be more a social than a sexual one". *Id.*, p. 21. The Commission members were convinced by experts—namely, "[a] large majority of sex educators and counselors"—"that most adolescents are interested in explicit sexual materials … [out of a] natural curiosity about sex. They also feel that if adolescents had access to … appropriate sex education, their interest in pornography would be reduced". *Id.*, p. 29.

[15]*Miller v. California*, 413 U.S. 15 (1973).

be arbitrated where such matters could only be settled—in the mind of the individual consumer. This determination that pornography was itself ethically indifferent led those who opposed its proliferation to conclude that campaigns to regulate it would have to be founded on contingent, associated facts about pornography, grounds which skirt free of any adverse moral judgment of pornography.

When it comes to legal regulation of pornography as such,[16] what do we see in the American constitutional and legal corpus?

The bases for regulation offered by the Court (and by the vast bulk of other legal professionals and opinion writers) for exposing obscenity to legal regulation include moral ballast. But the moral concerns pertain to contingent, ancillary problems. These bases include *indecency*, or the offense taken by passersby, which is a fact about the viewer and not a moral judgment of any kind about the matter. In fact, public decency laws protect the sensibilities mainly against *public* display of acts that should be performed in private. Restricted "indecent" acts include urinating in public, excessive public displays of affection (even by married couples), nude sunbathing, and loud parties. None of these acts is in itself immoral. Some are positively good. None is pornographic in any familiar sense of that term. Thus, *feelings* of revulsion or disgust are essential to grasping what "indecency" connotes. Because "indecent" acts performed in private cannot give offense, they cannot—so long as done privately—be regulated to promote public decency.

The second line of justification is, perhaps, a corollary of the first. The moral touchstone of regulation here is *consent*; more precisely, it is the fair and equal (as far as possible) protection of everyone's choices and tastes as they bear upon sensitive and, especially, erotic materials. In canonical form, this basis of regulation could be summarized as: "The state has constitutional power to protect unwilling adults and minors from pornography". Or, as a reworking of the first entangling strand: "People should be protected—within limits—against the *uninvited* intrusion of (and consequent disgust at) erotic imagery". So, an "adult emporium" may not be closed by the police for the public menace to morals that it truly is. But they may and should see to it that its pleasures are limited to those, and only those, adults who go for that sort of thing. The law may and should require that advertising be discrete, that signage be bland, and that entrances be clearly marked, so that anyone who chooses to enter knows what to expect.

Lastly, there are some assertedly harmful *secondary effects* of pornography. These might be the alleged fact that a strip club or pornographic bookstore, for example, attracts and festers such anti-social behaviors as prostitution, sexual assault, drug use, and other criminal activity. Nothing in these legitimate concerns implies or even suggests that obscenity is in itself morally harmful to anyone.

---

[16]Of course, many legal regulations of pornography have nothing to do with pornography. Pornography is regulated, sometimes intensively, under various non-moral descriptions for diverse non-moral reasons. A pornographic *book* is subject to copyright and commercial laws. A porno-movie *theater* must conform to fire safety and construction codes. Internet and satellite television pornography is very largely unregulated—just as everything else traveling those media is. For that matter, in Nevada (and in some foreign countries) bordellos are regulated for sanitary and commercial purposes, but not for moral reasons.

This curious moral reticence is most extraordinary in the case of child pornography. Possession of child pornography, even in one's own home, is frequently prosecuted in America. The penalties upon conviction are severe. This contraband material depicts *real* children in sexual poses. What adverse moral judgment lies at the heart of this severe regime? The courts' authoritative rationale has nothing to do with the moral depravity of sexual desire for children. It has nothing to do with sexual morality at all. The proffered rationale (in the Supreme Court's authoritative expression of it) concerns child labor.[17] These harsh laws are based upon the hope to destroy a market for the exploitative use of children in producing the material.

The reason proffered by the Court (in words from the later child porn case, *Osborne v. Ohio*[18]) is to protect the "victims of child pornography". These "victims" are not children in general, who are put at greater risk of being viewed as objects of sexual desire and satisfaction by the trade in child porn. Nor do the "victims" include the sometimes hapless and invariably corrupted consumers (usually adults) of child pornography. The Court's "victims" are exclusively the children who appear in the pornographic matter. The stated reason for the Court's affirmation of sweeping authority to prosecute child pornography is the "hope[] to destroy a market for the exploitative use of children" in the *production* of child pornography.[19] No negative moral judgment of adults' sexual gaze, desire for, and fantasizing of children—as young as you like—is implied or presupposed or even entailed by these prosecutions and the laws which they vindicate.

This rationale was confirmed by seven members of the Court in *United States v. Williams*,[20] decided in 2008: "Child pornography harms and debases the most defenseless of our citizens".[21] That case made explicit a certain implication of *Osborne*: only material "depicting *actual* children engaged in sexually explicit conduct" counts as "child pornography". *Only* that material—and neither sexually explicit material with adult actors who look like children, nor material which relies upon life-like "virtual" children—involves the exploitation of society's "defenseless". This implication (now made explicit) implies, in turn, that the state's authority to combat "child pornography" has nothing to do with sexual perversion or lust or age-inappropriate attractions or even with the possible stimulation of sexual predators to act. The proffered rationale would apply equally to a ban on the possession of snuff movies, which have nothing to do with sexual immorality.[22]

---

[17] *New York v. Ferber*, 458 U.S. 747 (1982).

[18] *Osborne v. Ohio*, 495 U.S. 103 (1990).

[19] *Id.* at 109.

[20] *United States v. Williams*, 553 U.S. 285 (2008).

[21] *Id.* at 307.

[22] Recall (note 4, *supra*) that under the Supreme Court's holding in *Stanley v. Georgia*, the Constitution is held to forbid prosecution of anyone for the possession of obscene materials in the privacy of one's own home. This immunity does not extend to possession of child pornography, per the Court's holding in *Osborne v. Ohio* (1990).

Nonetheless, the United States Supreme Court in 1973 rejected the proposition that the only constitutionally permissible basis for public interference with the distribution and exhibition of pornography was the distinction between the willing and the unwilling and children, who were deemed to be incapable of determining themselves to be either.

The Court in both *Miller* and its companion case, *Slaton*,[23] clearly wanted to say that pornography somehow affected *all* of us. And the Court did say it: legitimate state interests included the "quality of life and total community environment". The Court at one juncture came very close to expressing the heart of the matter, in terms which could be transported to today with little loss of cogency: "The sum of experience, including the last two decades, affords an ample basis for legislatures to conclude that a sensitive, key relationship of human existence, central to family life, community welfare, and the development of human personality, can be debased and distorted by crass commercial exploitation of sex".[24] But this promising line was not developed further by the Court in 1973, or at any time thereafter. It was never integrated into a whole-orbed account of pornography's harms.

The Court was unfortunately very tentative about these harms. The Justices even conceded that "there is no conclusive proof of a connection between anti-social behavior and obscene material". The Constitution did not prohibit a state, however, from acting on what the Court called "unprovable assumptions" about the connection.[25] The Court adduced several examples of legislation founded upon such "unprovable assumptions," including (a) "imponderable aesthetic assumptions" presupposed by environmental regulations to preserve national parks; and (b) the "unprovable assumption that a complete education requires the reading of certain books".[26] This whole accounting of constitutionally cognizable reasons for public regulation of pornography could be whittled down to: seeing to more family-friendly streets and storefronts, and rumors of crimes.

The Court identified public *interests* with public *spaces*. "In particular, we hold that there are legitimate state interests in stemming the tide of commercialized obscenity". The relevant sphere of interest was "local commerce and ... all places of public accommodation". Those "interests" were said to be "the quality of life and the total community environment, the tone of commerce, in the great city centers, and

---

[23] *Paris Adult Theatre I v. Slaton*, 413 U.S. 49 (1973).

[24] *Id.* at 63.

[25] One pungent articulation of where this left traditionalists who could not, or would not, think themselves out of the impoverished vocabulary and conceptual apparatus on offer was Attorney General John Mitchell's reason for rejecting the Commission Report: "Pornography should be banned even if it is not harmful". *New York Times* (1970), p. 31.

[26] A prosaic expression of this gap between pornography and anti-social sexual conduct, especially including sex crimes, was that by the manager of the Ritz adult movie theater in northern Times Square. He was arrested forty-one times for showing "obscene" movies between 1968 and 1973. Then he was quoted to the following effect: "You go to see a comedy, you don't come out as a comedian; you go to see an opera, you don't come out as a musician; you go to a pornographic movie, you don't come out a rapist".

possibly the public safety itself"—all on the view that there is an "arguable correlation between obscene material and crime".[27] The Court described as "one problem of large proportion, aptly described by Professor Bickel as 'the tone of the society, the mode or ... the style and quality of life'". As one of America's greatest constitutional scholars wrote, in words adopted by the Supreme Court in 1973: "Even supposing that each of us can, if he wishes, effectively avert the eye and stop the ear (which in truth we cannot), what is commonly heard and done intrudes upon us all, want it or not".[28] Bickel located the sphere of regulation in the "market" and "public places".[29]

By 1982, the Supreme Court completely abandoned even this inchoate effort to speak of pornography's cultural pollution. In the child pornography case of *New York v. Ferber*, the Court declared that the *Miller* standard, "like its predecessors, was an accommodation between the State's interests in protecting the 'sensibilities of unwilling recipients' from exposure to pornographic material and the dangers of censorship inherent in unabashedly content-based laws".[30] And so the constitutional matter stands today: laws seeking to control obscenity are limited in their ambition to limiting feelings of revulsion which some people report when they encounter pornography. For reasons not stated, the *Ferber* Court distanced itself from even this retreat, by placing this ambition in unexplained scare quotes.

II

The Meese Commission in 1986 was keenly aware that its subject matter was rapidly changing due to technological progress. The *Final Report* briefly commented on what was then a novelty: "personal home computers". There were few of them. Some sexually oriented services were available on them, which the Commission dutifully catalogued. These six services accounted for made for a combination bulletin board and home shopper (swinging couples, sex toys, videos, and the like). No pornographic video images whatsoever could be downloaded. The Commission presciently stated that in the sixteen years since the last national investigation of pornography, "the world has seen enormous technological changes that have affected the transmission of sounds, words, and images".[31] American society had been affected by innovations such as cable television, satellite communication, video tape recording, the computer, and competition in the telecommunications industry. "It would be surprising to discover that these technological developments have had no effect on the production, distribution, and availability of pornography, and we have not been surprised".[32]

The digital revolution and the Internet have so dramatically changed the contours of our social interaction, diffused and multiplied the formative influences upon us, and shifted our expectations for what life has to offer—all this, mind you, in less than

[27] *Slaton*, 413 U.S. at 59.

[28] Here the Court cited A. Bickel (1971), pp. 25–26.

[29] The Court consistently spoke of regulations of the commons throughout the opinion: "the public street," a "bar or a 'live' theater stage," "Times Square".

[30] *Ferber*, 458 U.S. at 756.

[31] Meese Report (1986), p. 225.

[32] *Id.*, pp. 225–26.

a generation—that life in our political community has been dramatically remapped. Some old challenges to our common life have evaporated into the ether; some new ones have materialized. We are thus required to devise new ways of fostering the common good, to develop and establish fresh laws and social norms which are faithful to abiding principles, but which nonetheless get the job done. The new pornography is indeed everywhere. Its seekers no longer need to traipse across town to a dirtier and slightly menacing neighborhood to see it. Porn no longer comes in plain brown wrappers. The postman no longer casts a disapproving glance. There is no Vice Squad. If we should judge that the effects of this amazing development adversely impact the common good of society, the challenge of devising policies and practices both effective and respectful of privacy would be daunting indeed.

The central challenge to any regimen of criminal law enforcement against pornography today is plain enough. It is the private quality of almost all consumption (on smartphones and laptops), and the *invisibility* of its transmission through (over, beyond) streets and storefronts and other common areas. We face the paradox of having largely achieved the goals in view for several decades: public spaces have mostly been scrubbed of "XXX" billboards, "massage parlors," and "adult emporiums," so much so that few people walking down even New York City's 42nd Street are bombarded with unwanted salacious proposals anymore. (I know what I am talking about: not only did I grow up in New York City in the sixties and seventies, I also was a Manhattan prosecutor in the eighties.)

Yet we are immersed in pornography. It has commandeered our culture. No one until recently could have imagined that pornography could have been so much *privatized* and, at the same time, so much insinuated into our common life. The master narrative inherited from the 1970s provides almost no resources, then, for constructing a social control strategy today.

According to the inherited master narrative (here explored in Part I), opponents of pornography were aspiring censors who adhered to an old-fashioned sexual morality and who intolerantly wanted everyone to conform to their moral code. So far stated, this rendering is entirely false. But censorship is not the issue. Besides, these opponents almost uniformly understand themselves to hold the moral truth about sex, a cluster of anthropological and metaphysical insights and moral norms which were either *true* (in which case nothing was *theirs*, *mine*, or *yours*) or *false* (in which case the cluster should be rejected outright for that reason). Besides, the underlying importance of the position had nothing to do with conformity, but rather with freedom, namely, the freedom to enter into and sustain valuable relationships and to avoid exploitation (as victim as well as perpetrator) in them.

This anti-pornography position is finally grounded in a realistic prospectus for a genuinely free self-constitution, as well as truer reciprocity and equality in sexual relationships. Today's digital-fueled, pornified culture is a peculiarly potent threat to precisely these important realities. John Finnis articulated the bases for this position well in his masterpiece *Natural Law and Natural Rights*:

> Now if it is the case that sexuality is a powerful force which only with some difficulty, and always precariously, can be integrated with other aspects of human personality and well-being—so that it enhances rather than destroys friendship and the care of children, for

> example; and if it is further the case that human sexual psychology has a bias toward regarding other persons as bodily objects of desire and potential sexual release and gratification, and as mere items in an erotically flavoured classification (e.g. 'women'), rather than as full persons with personal and individual sensitivities, restraints, and life-plans, then there is reason for fostering a milieu in which children can be brought up (and parents assisted rather that hindered in bringing them up) so that they are relatively free from inward subjection to an egoistic, impulsive, or depersonalized sexuality.[33]

Now, it is a postulate and not a truth about pornography today that the women who, for example, submit to penetration by several men simultaneously, and who wince and groan in pain throughout the ordeal, are really enjoying it. The reason for this "consent" hypothesis is that even the most dedicated pornography consumers do not want to think of themselves as masturbating witnesses to rape and sexual abuse. Nonetheless, a significant number of those who appear in pornography today are trafficked women (and others), who are more or less forced into performing.

Besides this pool of semi-professional performers, there are now countless amateur producers, directors, and participants in online pornography. Many are teens. "Sexting"—the sending of arousing and often nude selfies to significant others—is a kind of amateur pornography. Occasionally, the amateur is literally forced to perform, perhaps by male acquaintances who threaten to disclose other embarrassing information or photos of the woman if she does not cooperate. But one common reason for these ad hoc productions is felt social pressure. And, once the images are transmitted, the "sexting" teen loses all power of consent over their circulation to the entire world.

It is easy to see that what might well be described as the ambient "pornified" culture plays a causal role in this sad syndrome, for digitalization makes it *possible.* As Jonathan Coopersmith wrote in 2006, "[T]his technology can be seen as liberating and empowering, allowing individuals to actively create their own pornography, not just passively consume the work of someone else".[34] Yes, but there are serious collateral risks and foreseeable side-effects, too.

Let's turn now to the consumer side, recognizing that our understanding of "consumer" is complicated by the standing opportunity of a viewer to produce and distribute pornography as well. The notion of "consumer" is also destabilized by digitalization's effacement of the fission that allows pornography to emerge into human experience as a distinct subject matter, namely, the divide between representation and reality. (The etymological roots of the word "pornography" involve a combination of harlot or prostitute, and writing). At some risk of gilding the tawdry, our whole tradition of thinking about pornography supposes the interposition of a presenter—an artist—between the viewer and the imaginings depicted in the art. Pornography is that art. It supposes that the sexual behavior depicted is not real. It is the construct of an artistic vision. The prevailing morality, if not criminal law, would prohibit actually engaging in the sexual behavior depicted. But now the "consumer" does not so much contemplate another's art as he engages in something more like real sex, albeit mediated by modern technology.

---

[33]Finnis (2011), p. 217. Much of the remainder of this Part tracks portions of my article entitled "Prolegomenon on Pornography" (2018).

[34]Coopersmith (2006), p. 11.

Modern technology also enables the scientific study of how technological sex affects us, and the prospects for genuine consent to consuming pornography. In his 2007 book *The Brain That Changes Itself*, Norman Doidge explored at length the concept of *neuroplasticity* as it pertains to online pornography. Doidge noted the established finding that the brain continually reshapes and rewires itself as a result of certain regularly repeated actions. In a later essay, Doidge wrote that "the plastic influence of pornography on adults can also be profound, and those who use it have no sense of the extent to which their brains are reshaped by it".[35] He concluded that "pornography delivered by high-speed Internet connections satisfies every one of the conditions for neuroplastic change".[36]

This phenomenon so far considered raises questions about just *what* it is that any online pornography viewer is—and is not—making an informed choice to do: Does anyone going online agree to be mutated in the process? Another effect in many cases is how much of a *choice* it really is. Neuroplasticity raises the lively prospect of a compulsion, if not an addiction, to internet pornography.[37] The American Psychiatric Association recognizes that *behaviors* (as well as substances) can be addictive. Now that the authors of the standard reference (*The Diagnostic and Statistical Manual*, or *DSM*) have identified Internet Gaming Disorder as a "condition for further study," the predicates for identifying an "Internet Pornography Disorder" as a subset of behavioral addictions are in place.[38]

It is surely not the case that most, or even very many, regular users of pornography are addicted to it, or even under significant compulsion. But a non-negligible percentage is at serious risk of becoming addicted. *Ex ante* no user knows what his particular risk factors are. Most will not give it a thought. Internet pornography providers are not likely candidates to fill in the information gap with adequate warnings and recommendations. Managing this risk devolves into a social responsibility in some important sense.

The stakes have been raised by a recent seismic shift in the way that our culture valorizes sexual satisfaction and sexual "identity". This remarkable development both explains and reflects "pornotopia". At first glance, this cultural shift might seem to justify "pornotopia," as if the importance of individual sexual autonomy calls for easy access to pornography's unlimited menu of possibilities. In fact, the leading justification on offer from those who try to justify "pornotopia" is its transgressive

---

[35] Doidge (2010), p. 30.

[36] *Id.*, p. 29. If something like this notion of plasticity and the social mortgage of our sexual taste and appetites is not true, then we would have a very difficult time explaining how (by everyone's account) the content of online pornography has careened into hardcore scenarios and fetishistic minutiae in the space of just a few years. Indeed, if human sexuality were more fixed and hard-wired, then pornography might be a more or less constant feature of social life, but the quantity and quality of it would scarcely change. But no one at all has denied that pornography has *exploded.*

[37] See Love et al. (2015), pp. 389–433.

[38] *Id.* The description of Gaming Disorder tracks the accounts provided by Doidge and others. The APA declared that Internet pornography was not "analogous" to Gaming Disorder, a decision which was described by reviewers as "inconsistent with existing and emerging scientific evidence".

wallop, which breaks down, they allege, any remainders of traditional sexual morality and all other norms about who one should, or should not, be, sexually speaking.

But many careful observers, including some who share the same ideals about sexual individuality and autonomy as those who defend pornography, worry that pornography has precisely the opposite effect. They argue that "pornotopia" breeds a master narrative sexual script. In this script, the male is dominant, the female is submissive, and their sexual congress is entirely for the male's edification.[39]

British writer Sean Thomas described in the London *Spectator* his porn-induced descent into the depths of himself beyond his awareness:

> My interest in spanking got me speculating: what other kinks was I harbouring? What other secret and rewarding corners lurked in my sexuality that I would now be able to investigate in the privacy of my flat? Plenty, as it turned out. Over the following months I discovered a serious penchant for, *inter alia*, lesbian gynaecology, interracial hardcore, and images of Japanese girls taking off their hotpants. I was also into netball players with no knickers, drunk Russian girls exposing themselves, and convoluted scenarios where submissive Danish actresses were intimately shaved by their dominant female partners in the shower. *The Net had, in other words, revealed to me that I had an unquantifiable variety of sexual fantasies and quirks, and that the process of satisfying these desires online only led to more interest* (emphasis added).[40]

Is Sean Thomas's sexuality *his*? He did not consciously choose it and would not have discovered it but for the whimsy of his internet surfing. The quotient of true choice in internet explorations is diminished, too, because the viewer does not initiate each successive encounter. Pornography sites commonly use pop-ups and force-forward viewers to new pages, even if the viewer is seeking to leave.

Sean Thomas's recollection is an apt (if most colorfully related) example of the basic ideal which apologists for "pornotopia" say it promotes: excavation of a deeply subjective, individuated sexuality like none other's, a true picture of the real *me* (or you), deep down beneath social norms and stereotypes. But Thomas's experience and the research of Norman Doidge raise a significant question about the authenticity of any such discoveries. One does not have to be a Freudian to suspect that what pornography pulls to the surface is not some atavistic, real *me* (or you), but rather a jumble of imprints and combinations which one's environment and life with others have put there.

The etiology of sexual "identity" aside, it is apparent that Sean Thomas and the ideal which he awkwardly personifies lead to an extraordinary solipsism, which—according to an exploding body of clinical and statistical evidence—greatly impedes sexually reconnecting with real people, including one's spouse. "Results showed the more pornography a man watches, the more likely he was to use it during sex, request particular pornographic sex acts of his partner, deliberately conjure images of pornography during sex to maintain arousal, and have concerns over his own sexual performance and body image".[41]

---

[39]Gail Dines's *Pornland* is the leading presentation of the sexual-scripts critique of pornography.

[40]Thomas (2003), pp. 2–3.

[41]Sun et al. (2014), p. 983.

The gendered adjectives and pronouns in almost all this research is no accident. Nor is it a politically incorrect convention. For the social scientific evidence about frequency of masturbation and pornography use,[42] the number of sexual partners,[43] as well as more qualitative research into the nature of male and female sex drive and their preferred place of sex within the overall pattern of the relationship,[44] all confirm that nature, and not just nurture or socialization, explains the differences between men and women that almost anyone who has dated has observed from the get-go. (That the paraphilias listed in the *Diagnostic and Statistical Manual*, which is in effect the psychiatrist's desk book, are, with the partial exception of sadomasochism, almost entirely male phenomena, is further evidence.) The prevailing free market in pornography enlarges and aggravates this natural gap between the sexes. Plainly put: Turn a population loose to access pornography, and women evince no more than moderate, intermittent interest. A culture saturated with pornography drives men and women apart.

The sex-differential which is turbo-charged by pornography is irrelevant to same-sex relationships. It is not disruptive of transient, more sex-focused heterosexual relationships, for they are fleeting and the parties to them are geared to walk away if the net sexual satisfaction dips below zero. The impact is obviously felt by heterosexual couples who are trying to make their relationship stick. The evidence of this stress upon married couples is especially alarming, leading to family turmoil and, often, breakdown.[45] The woman "cuckolded" by online pornography, and her children, suffer from that pornography they themselves never invited into their lives. Even in relationships which endure the stress introduced into it by the man's pornography use, the achievement of a genuine mutuality, reciprocity, and equality across the whole of the life together is adversely impacted.

More alarmingly, seventy percent of America's *children* report viewing online pornography.[46] The average age of first exposure to adult material is eleven.[47] For *them* what happens on the screen has consequences off of it. "Research also shows that increased pornography exposure is associated with earlier and/or quicker onset of sexual activity, more permissive attitudes toward casual sex, and a higher likelihood of engaging in risky sexual behaviors such as anal sex, sex with multiple partners, and using drugs or alcohol during sex".[48]

Juvenile access to online pornography is almost by definition unsupervised; if adults were nearby, one would expect (at least reasonably hope) that the juvenile's access would be terminated. For that reason, and because the internet is so much

[42]"[A]lthough overall pornography and masturbation self-reports are notably lower for women than for men, the effect of pornography on masturbation seems comparable for women and men". Regnerus (2017), p. 140.

[43]See, e.g., Brown and Sinclair (1999).

[44]Regnerus (2017), pp. 22–23.

[45]See statistics and related references in Richard Krueger et al. (2013), pp. 68–69.

[46]*Id.*

[47]*Id.*

[48]Sun et al. (2014), p. 984.

like an open-access, toll-free highway, there are many forms of serious and often criminal collateral damage inflicted upon those—children and teens—who are by law incapable of effective consent: cyber-bullying, sexual harassment, online solicitation, sexting, and "revenge porn".

Our society's increasing emphasis upon autonomous sexual identity and experience has penetrated youth culture. Many grown-ups and even some institutions actively promote acceptance of what a child says about his or her sexual "identity" as *prima facie* authentic, and therefore deserving of adult respect. (The societal debate about transgender children is one example.) When combined with adolescents' natural curiosity about all things sexual and with the allure of misbehaving online with ones' peers, easy access to digitalized pornography makes for a perfect storm of childhood trauma. All the scientific evidence shows that children's brains are most especially malleable and subject to formation by intense experiences epitomized by sexual excitement. Even if, for a very few, this aspect of "pornotopia" realizes the hazy dream of the 1970 President's Commission that children be sexually educated by "harmless" pornography, no one should mistake the effects for products of anything like genuine consent.

Of course, the truth is rather that, unless adults are willing to make dramatic changes to their own moral and legal rules about pornography, if for no other reason than for the sake of our children, we are playing what amounts to game of Russian roulette with the formation and education of our children when it comes to one of the most precious parts of their lives. This concern for the formative influences upon children does not arise solely from a concern for their proper continence and chastity during their adolescent and teen years. Even someone committed to a more modern sexual ethic and to the sexual agency of young people should be greatly concerned to maintain cultural "taboos" upon the pornification of children.[49]

Nearly everyone agrees with this proposition when it comes to the participation of children *in* pornography; in any event, such participation is strictly illegal and possessing even one image of child pornography is a serious felony in America. There is at least lip-service agreement nearly across the board that pornography involving adult actors is not for children, either. But the magnitude of the risks to healthy psycho-sexual development of young people is too-often downplayed, frequently as a rationalization for adult access so effortless that it is a statistical certainty that many children will end up exploring what turned on Sean Thomas.

III

What is the appropriate role of the criminal law in government's proper care for a culture which is afflicted with pornography?

Answering this question, even as briefly as I attempt to do here, requires meeting head-on the objection that any serious proposal for criminal-law control of pornography inescapably involves unjust state paternalism. At the heart of this

[49] Angela McRobbie notes the "encroachment by commercial forces on the role and authority of the various institutions which have, in the past, presided over the lives and conduct of young women and girls". Furthermore, "commercial values now occupy a critical place in the formation of the categories of youthful femininity". McRobbie (2008), p. 532.

anti-paternalist objection is a very high valuation of each mature individual's *self-constitution* by and through his or her free choices. This valuation is sound. Part II of this chapter rebuts much of the anti-paternalism charge, however, for it shows how (among other evils) a pornified culture compromises persons' realistic opportunities to freely constitute themselves and their sexual relationships.

Valuing highly the *autonomous life*—well defined by Joseph Raz as a life which "to a considerable extent [is one's] own creation"[50]—does not mean that we should value social isolation. It does not mean that we should welcome the prospect that anyone could constitute himself without engaging in a dialectic with the surrounding culture. Such an austere path to adult maturity is empirically unavailable; we are all to some significant extent the creatures of our environment, even though it is invariably true that each of us retains the power to shape oneself by what we choose to do. Living the autonomous life does not mean being left alone by everyone else. On the contrary, and as Raz asserts, there is an autonomy-based duty to "help in creating the inner capacities required for the conduct of an autonomous life".[51] Government efforts to control pornography can and should aim to help persons, especially those who are young and immature, to shape themselves up into the sorts of individuals who *can* constitute themselves.

Thus, the initial statement of the refutation of the paternalism objection: the objection is rooted fundamentally in a surpassing commitment to persons' self-constitution. So too is—or should be—government attempts to establish social control of pornography!

One brute fact of social existence is that who we are and who we can be depend mightily upon the culture in which we live. The reason is simple: many opportunities for human flourishing realistically depend upon social forms. Raz notably rejects as "simplistic" the presuppositions of a reflexive anti-paternalism, which "disregards the dependence of people's tastes and values on social forms, on conventions and practices which are the result of human action (though usually not of action designed to achieve these results)".[52] The family is perhaps the prototype of these socially, and legally, maintained social forms.

Cultural forms often require the help of law in order to be sustained through time and to remain effectively accessible to people. (Some forms always do.) The proper duties of public authority, therefore, include the morally guided selection of *which* forms of life to sustain, for the sake of persons' genuine well-being. Rejecting state paternalism is not the same thing, then, as rejecting state *perfectionism*. Anti-paternalism is not same thing as "neutrality" about what is morally good, a position central to the liberalism of (most notably) John Rawls. Anti-paternalistic perfectionism embraces the crucial importance of persons taking ownership of their own lives, precisely by constituting their own characters. There is a steep social mortgage upon our choices, insofar as ambient culture shapes the options available to us at any

[50] Raz (1986), p. 408.
[51] *Id.*
[52] *Id.*, p. 426.

given time and, moreover, shapes our understanding of what is choice-worthy, good, satisfying—and what is not.

The civil law as a whole plays an important, but secondary, role in making this inescapably common force, which powerfully shapes our lives and our choices, a wholesome one. Law shapes culture, and culture shapes possibilities for choice because so many opportunities for human flourishing (especially in relationships) realistically depend upon *social* forms, and thus upon a cultural and often legal commitment to maintain those forms and effective access to them. Raz, for example, rejects as the "simplistic" presuppositions of a reflexive anti-paternalism, which "disregards the dependence of people's tastes and values on social forms, on conventions and practices which are the result of human action (though usually not of action designed to achieve these results".[53]

The civil law does not shape us only by setting up green lights and red lights. It does so sometimes by simply prohibiting some acts and requiring others. The law also shapes us by creating incentives and disincentives. Permitted acts can be discouraged by taxes and burdensome regulations. Others can be encouraged and even subsidized. But the law can and does shape us more powerfully, yet more subtly, by shaping the *culture* in which we live. Civil law today powerfully shapes the social understandings, practices, and meanings of the good life that constitute our *culture.* Raz reminds us that "perfectionist goals need not be pursued by the use of coercion. A government which subsidizes certain activities, rewards their pursuit, and advertises their availability encourages those activities without using coercion".[54]

Even when the government's actions against pornography include criminal law enforcement, it need not involve straightforward moral paternalism. The heart of the anti-paternalist position is rejection of government *coercion* just for the sake of improving the character of the persons coerced. This norm rests upon the sound insight that a person who abstains from using pornography for fear of external sanction and not because it is the right thing to do, has not constituted himself rightly for the right reasons. So far considered, his character lacks a relevant perfection. A criminal law enforced against someone for simple possession of pornography could therefore run afoul of this anti-paternalism norm *if it were enforced solely for the sake of that person's virtue.*

But such a prosecution need not have that aim. If it has the *effect* of breaking someone's pornography habit, that benefit would be a welcome *side-effect* of laws justified on other grounds, namely, the maintenance of a morally wholesome public realm. For someone who frees himself from pornography for any reason or cause is better off for it.[55]

---

[53] *Id.*, p. 426.

[54] *Id.*, p. 417.

[55] Even those people in a given society who disregard the criminal law (including those prohibiting pornography) are still shaped to some degree by their presence as overriding norms in that society, either by dint of a guilty conscience or by being made aware that one (so far considered) is in a certain anti-social posture. At a minimum, their disregard of criminal law tactically affects their actions, as they seek more or less carefully to avoid detection and prosecution.

An effective criminal-law strategy to control pornography in any event should tolerate private possession of it for personal use. Criminal law enforcement should be limited to prosecutions for producing and distributing pornography, in a way roughly analogous to most law enforcement strategies for controlling the use of narcotic and other addictive drugs. In the case of narcotic drugs, possession for personal use is technically criminal. But simple possession is very rarely the basis of criminal penalties. According to most such strategies in use today, it is not to be prosecuted save where it is joined to other offenses in a larger criminal episode. (For example, someone arrested for theft might be incidentally searched after arrest and found to possess heroin; often the drug charge is prosecuted to leverage a plea of guilty to the theft charge.)

Common law enforcement approaches to prostitution often make the same set of distinctions. Even where prostitution itself remains a crime, it is infrequently prosecuted. Scarce resources are instead expended upon prosecutions of pimps and others who would profit from others who sell their bodies for sex. In each case—drugs, prostitution, and pornography—moral opprobrium still affects the simple action, if only because it remains technically a crime. But law enforcement concerned to reduce the incidence of the simple action focuses elsewhere up the supply chain.

Here is a second refutation of the anti-paternalist objection: prosecutions should as a rule be limited to those who would profit by exploiting others' appetites for pornography, and in that way *harm* them.

A third refutation pertains to the uniquely powerful *educative* effects of the criminal law in the United States today. Early in this century, Francis George described how the law "has peculiar and unique cultural functions in American society":

> The many components of our culture are largely united by law, not by blood, not by race, not by religion, not even by language, but by law. It's the one principal cultural component we all have in common … [L]aw is more important in teaching or instructing us than it is in directing us … [O]ne must therefore ask how it is that law functions as a cultural carrier in [this country], and what does that mean for cultural institutions that are universal [i.e., objective, natural] but that are qualified by law: marriage, family [and others].[56]

George's insight suggests what the Supreme Court the same year confirmed: what is (or is not) a crime in America, regardless of whether it is ever prosecuted, has immense cultural effects. The reason is that the criminal law is a powerful moral teacher. According to the United States Supreme Court in *Lawrence v. Texas*[57] in 2003, the existence of never-enforced laws criminalizing sexual acts between persons of the same sex adversely "stigmatized" homosexuals. This "stigma" led straightaway to their negative treatment in society.

The precise issue in *Lawrence* was the constitutionality of a Texas criminal law against sodomy, an offense there statutorily defined without reference to sex—that is, to gender. A man and a woman as well as two persons of the same-sex could then have been criminally liable under Texas law. The law nonetheless seems to have been very rarely enforced. In the event leading to the case, police officers pursuing a false

[56]George (2003), p. 135.

[57]*Lawrence v. Texas*, 539 U.S. 558 (2003).

tip about possible gun violence in Lawrence's apartment interrupted a sodomitical act, and made the arrests.

The *Lawrence* Court was not motivated to overturn the Texas law by the prospect that the unusual prosecution there commenced would be repeated. The Justices in the majority worried instead about the wider legal and cultural effects of the *existence* of the sodomy statute. They were keenly concerned to reverse what they called the "state-sponsored condemnation of these men for engaging in intimate acts of their choosing".[58] Moreover, "[t]he stigma [the Court's term of choice] this criminal statute imposes, moreover, is not trivial".[59] This "stigma" began (if you will) with an insult to "the dignity of the persons charged".[60] Furthermore, "the Texas criminal conviction carries with it the other collateral consequences always following a conviction, such as notations on job application forms, to mention but one example".[61]
The Court added:

> Equality of treatment and the due process right to demand respect for conduct protected by the substantive guarantee of liberty are linked in important respects, and a decision on the latter point advances both interests. If protected conduct is made criminal and the law which does so remains unexamined for its substantive validity, its stigma might remain even if it were not enforceable as drawn for equal protection reasons. When homosexual conduct is made criminal by the law of the State, that declaration in and of itself is an invitation to subject homosexual persons to discrimination both in the public and in the private spheres.[62]

It is disputable whether keeping criminal sanctions always perpetuates a stigma upon the prohibited conduct. It is almost certain that repealing an existing criminal penalty would lead, in America ca. 2018 at least, to social acceptance and eventually even to approval of the decriminalized conduct. My judgment is that, even if very rarely enforced, the repeal of criminal laws (where they exist) against simple possession of pornography ought to be retained. Adding *de jure* decriminalization of pornography to that prevailing de facto norm would very likely communicate an endorsement of pornography.

IV

The central aim of a coherent anti-pornography legal strategy today should be, not to ameliorate a "stigma" (as in *Lawrence*), but instead to *cultivate and sustain* one against pornography. Increasing recognition across the world of pornography's diffuse but significant harms have promoted several new approaches to reviving criminal law enforcement against it. These initiatives are an encouraging sign.

Three of these initiatives are:

1. Defining and proscribing "pornography" as a form of discrimination against women. This idea seems to have taken flight with the 1980s work of two feminist

---

[58] *Id.* at 576.

[59] *Id.* at 575.

[60] *Id.*

[61] *Id.* at 576. Most importantly, the *Lawrence* Court's repeal of criminal laws against sodomy was a necessary step on the Court's way to elevating same-sex sexual relationships to the status of civil marriage in 2015. *Obergefell v. Hodges*, 576 U.S. 644 (2015).

[62] *Lawrence v. Texas*, 539 U.S. at 575.

legal theorists, Andrea Dworkin and Catherine MacKinnon. Their work (among that of others) promoted the adoption of an anti-pornography ordinance in Indianapolis, Indiana, which was held to be constitutionally invalid by the Seventh Circuit Court of Appeals in 1985,[63] a holding later summarily affirmed by the Supreme Court.[64] That ordinance defined "pornography" as "the graphic sexually explicit subordination of women, whether in pictures or in words," that also includes one or more of several specified aggravating features, like presentation of the myth that women enjoy being raped or as enjoying physical abuse. It was invalidated on free speech grounds.

2. Proscribing "extreme pornography". This was the focal point of a 2008 British enactment prohibiting even private possession of "explicit and realistic" images of extraordinarily offensive images, including (for example) bestiality and necrophilia.[65]
3. Limiting the reach of obscenity proscriptions by application of this criterion: "principles integral to a free and democratic society". This language (or its cognate) is found in several extant constitutional charters. One explanation of it is the Canadian Supreme Court's holding in *R. v. Butler* (1992),[66] which determined that only a certain sort of moral corruption associated with the diffusion of obscenity could constitutionally be interdicted by public authority, namely, that which has certain detrimental effects upon "a free and democratic" polity.

Pursuit of any one of these three initiatives by public authorities would be better (and maybe much better) than doing nothing about pornography. But none of the three is particularly appealing, and for much the same reason. The first identifies one wrongful feature of pornography, namely, its relentless misogyny. Even assuming that one could defend the move from there to brand pornography as "sex discrimination," this first approach still is too limited: it holds that only *some* pornography is problematical for a *particular* reason.

So, too, are the second and third proposals insufficient. Each picks out a perhaps tiny fraction of the ambient pornographic product for criminalization, and only then for a specific reason—either its "extrem[ity] (evidently, its extraordinarily disgusting quality or, in some instances, its dangerousness), or its politically subversive tendencies. In all three cases, the pertinent harm is not actually pornography or its peculiar effects upon healthy psycho-sexual development: the harm which animates the prosecutorial initiative is non-sexual.

No doubt scarce law enforcement resources should be expended strategically upon prosecutions which will deliver the greatest return for the investment. Priorities should indeed be established. While these three proposals may not imply it, they very strongly suggest that much (most?) pornography is fine. It is just that a subset of it happens to offend some particular extrinsic value.

---

[63] *American Booksellers Ass'n v. Hudnut*, 771 F.2d 323 (7th Cir. 1985).

[64] *Hudnut v. American Booksellers Ass'n*, 475 U.S. 1001 (1986).

[65] See Section 63 of the United Kingdom's Criminal Justice and Immigration Act 2008.

[66] *R. v. Butler*, 1 S.C.R. 452 (1992).

Among the prosecutions which *should* be initiated in order to *stigmatize* pornography just as such are some prosecutorial efforts directed towards major traffickers of medium-grade pornographic fare, on the view that these would communicate effectively that it is *pornography* which is the problem. Even a few annual prosecutions in a given jurisdiction would serve well to affix the moral stigma which criminal conviction conveys. Limiting prosecutions to large-scale traffickers might deter other like-minded individuals. The occasional proceeding against a major distributor, whose profit margins and predatory trading upon other people's weakness of character make him particularly odious, would be a welcome reminder of the *social* evils of pornography.

In addition, criminal law enforcement should be intensified against those who recklessly expose children to pornography. The particularly callous disregard for the child's well-being, as well as for his or her parents' rightful authority to educate their children, shown by such malefactors makes them proper targets for prosecution. Also opportune would be vigorous enforcement of anti-human-trafficking laws against those who use force or other illicit incentives to keep women (mostly women, as a matter of fact) laboring in various sectors of the sex-trades. Some existing prostitution laws could even be enforced against pornography producers who characteristically pay people to have sex, albeit usually with other actors and not (usually) with the producer himself.

These and other criminal-law enforcement initiatives should be nested within an overall legal strategy to stigmatize pornography. The non-criminal initiatives could well include government personnel and employment policies that establish that employees' knowing use of government equipment or of any equipment to view pornography during work hours constitutes grounds for dismissal. These proposals could also include well-crafted legislation requiring any institution receiving government funds to enact and enforce stringent policies governing the unauthorized use of computers for viewing pornography. All such usage would have to be forbidden as a condition of government funding. Lastly, government actors—from the President on down to the local school board—should seize all appropriate opportunities to teach, by word and deed, that pornography is *not* a harmless pastime. It is instead a cultural plague that we should seek to eradicate once and for all.

References

American Booksellers Ass'n v. Hudnut, 771 F.2d 323 (7th Cir. 1985)

Bickel A (1971) On pornography: II. The Public Interest p 25–26

Brown N, Sinclair R (1999) Estimating number of lifetime sexual partners: men and women do it differently. J Sex Res 36(3):292–297

Coopersmith J (2006) Does your mother know what you really do? The changing nature and image of computer-based pornography. Hist Technol 22:1–25

Dery M (2007) Paradise lust: pornotopia meets the culture wars. In: Jacobs K, Janssen M, Pasquinelli M (eds) C'lick me: a netporn studies reader. Institute of Network Cultures, Amsterdam

Dines G (2010) Pornland: how porn has hijacked our sexuality. Beacon, Boston

Doidge N (2010) Acquiring tastes and loves: what neuroplasticity teaches us about sexual attraction and love. In: Stoner J, Hughes D (eds) The social costs of pornography: a collection of papers. Princeton, Witherspoon, pp 29–30
Finnis J (2011) Natural law and natural rights, 2nd edn. Oxford, New York
George F (2003) Law and culture in the United States. Am J Juris 48(1):131–147
Hudnut v. American Booksellers Ass'n, 475 U.S. 1001 (1986)
Jacobs K, Janssen M, Pasquinelli M (eds) (2007) C'lick me: a netporn studies reader. Institute of Network Cultures, Amsterdam
Krueger et al (2013) The impact of internet pornography use and cybersexual behavior on child custody and visitation. J Child Custody 10(1):68–98
Lawrence v. Texas, 539 U.S. 558 (2003)
Love T et al (2015) Neuroscience of internet pornography addiction: a review and update. Behav Sci 5:388–433
McNair B (2013) Porno? Chic!. Routledge, Abingdon
McRobbie A (2008) Young women and consumer culture. Cultural Studies 22(5):531–550
Miller v. California, 413 U.S. 15 (1973)
Molloy A (2014) Porn studies journal publishes its first issue. Independent. http://www.independentco.uk/news/uk/home-news/pornstudies-joumal-publishes-its-first-issue-9209885.html. Accessed 23 Sept 2020
New York v. Ferber, 458 U.S. 747 (1982)
Obergefell v. Hodges, 576 U.S. 644 (2015)
Osborne v. Ohio, 495 U.S. 103 (1990)
Paasonen S (2011) Online pornography: ubiquitous and effaced. In: Consalvo M, Ess C (eds) Blackwell handbook of internet studies. Blackwell, Oxford, pp 424–439
Paris Adult Theatre I v. Slaton, 413 U.S. 49 (1973)
Butler RV (1992) 1 S.C.R. 452
Raz J (1986) The morality of freedom. Oxford, New York
Regnerus M (2017) Cheap sex: the transformation of men, marriage, and monogamy. Oxford, New York
Stanley v. Georgia, 394 U.S. 557 (1969)
Stoner J, Hughes D (eds) (2010) The social costs of pornography: a collection of papers. Princeton, Witherspoon
Sun C et al (2014) Pornography and the male sexual script: an analysis of consumption and sexual relations. Arch Sex Behav 45:983–994
Thomas S (2003) Self abuse. The spectator. https://www.spectator.co.uk/article/self-abuse. Accessed 23 Sept 2020
United Kingdom (2008) Criminal Justice and Immigration Act 2008. Section 63
United States v. Williams, 553 U.S. 285 (2008)

Dignity at the End of Life and Decriminalization of Euthanasia

Jorge Nicolás Lafferriere

Abstract This article will analyze the notion of euthanasia and the proposal to decriminalize it, presenting three views on dignity that underlie the euthanasia debate. To start with, I will consider the vision that highlights autonomy as the main meaning of dignity. I will identify its inconsistencies and the problems that such a perspective presents in connection with unconscious individuals, and I will discuss whether a right to die exists. Secondly, I will look into utilitarian arguments in favor of legalizing euthanasia in those cases where the quality of life is not dignified. This will entail addressing the slippery slope argument. Finally, I will examine the position that sustains dignity as a value, inherent in the person, that implies the respect for the inviolability of human life, and I will present the distinctions that need to be made when making decisions at the end of life.

1 Introduction

Powerful technologies, medical procedures, and drugs have extended human life.[1] This increase in life expectancy has had enormous benefits. But new legal issues arise concerning dignity at the end of life. Guaranteeing the dignity of the dying person is a widely recognized demand for justice. However, depending on the underlying conception of dignity, there will be very different answers that will not always respond to all the demands for justice.

In some cases, medical procedures, drugs, or biotechnologies applied to people with terminal illnesses imply little or no expectation of improvement, and the problem arises as to whether it is morally permissible to reject such therapies. In other cases,

J. N. Lafferriere (✉)
Law School, Pontificia Universidad Católica Argentina, Buenos Aires, Argentina
e-mail: nicolas_lafferriere@uca.edu.ar

[1]Global life expectancy at birth in 2015 was 71.4 years, and global average life expectancy increased by 5 years between 2000 and 2015, the fastest increase since the 1960s. Global Health Observatory (2016).

A. Masferrer (ed.), *Criminal Law and Morality in the Age of Consent*, Ius Gentium: Comparative Perspectives on Law and Justice 84,
https://doi.org/10.1007/978-3-030-64163-4_15

end-of-life suffering leads people to consider the possibility of deliberately ending their lives, either by taking their own lives or by asking someone else to do so. Other people would allow euthanasia for the most diverse reasons: from mental disorders to social conditions, or even fatigue.

The question then arises as to whether it is just to take the life of another person at their request or assist them in committing suicide.[2] Thus, although there have always been proposals to decriminalize or legalize euthanasia under certain circumstances, the issue now takes on new dimensions due to the emergence of drugs, procedures, and biotechnologies that extend human life.

The aim of this article[3] is to consider the arguments that are used in favor of decriminalizing or legalizing euthanasia as an exception to the law of murder.

The proposals in favor of legalizing euthanasia are linked to three views on dignity: dignity as autonomy, dignity from a utilitarian perspective of quality of life, and dignity as excellence in being (Sect. 2). In Sect. 3, I will analyze the view that maintains that there is a right to cause one's own death, either through euthanasia or assisted suicide, as a legitimate expression of personal autonomy. I will consider the inconsistencies of this conception of dignity and analyze the limits that it presents in relation to cases of unconscious people. Ultimately, the connection between dignity, autonomy and euthanasia involves answering the question whether there is a "right to die". In Sect. 4, I will consider the utilitarian arguments of those who contend that, when a deterioration in the quality of life makes life unworthy, it would be legitimate to take the life of the person in a terminal state. In this section, I will approach the so-called slippery slope argument. Finally, I will study the view that posits human dignity as a value, inherent in the person, in connection with human nature and its consequences in relation to the inviolability of life (Sect. 5). This will also mean making distinctions in relation to making end-of-life decisions, excluding as unjust the action that deliberately takes the life of the patient but admitting as legitimate the renunciation of disproportionate treatments that do not provide prospects for improvement in the face of imminent death.

2 Three Competing Views on Dignity at the End of Life

Underlying the debate over euthanasia, I find three competing views on dignity at the end of life. A recent Draft of a General Comment on Article 6 of the International Covenant on Civil and Political Rights[4] that is under discussion in the United Nations

---

[2]Euthanasia is understood as the act of the physician who complies with a request from a patient to end their life. If the physician helps a patient to end their own life, this is known as assisted suicide. Although there are differences between euthanasia and assisted suicide, in this paper we will deal with them as having the same moral meaning of deliberately putting an end to someone's life.

[3]I would like to thank Mariela Santoro for helping me with the translation of this article.

[4]Article 6.1 of the International Covenant on Civil and Political Rights states: "Article 6. 1. Every human being has the inherent right to life. This right shall be protected by law. No one shall be arbitrarily deprived of his life".

Human Rights Committee gives a very good example of these underlying visions. The Draft proposes the following text in relation to end-of-life issues:

> 10. [While acknowledging the central importance to human dignity of personal autonomy, the Committee considers that States parties should recognize that individuals planning or attempting to commit suicide may be doing so because they are undergoing a momentary crisis which may affect their ability to make irreversible decisions, such as to terminate their life. Therefore,] States should take adequate measures, without violating their other Covenant obligations, to prevent suicides, especially among individuals in particularly vulnerable situations. At the same time, States parties [may allow] [should not prevent] medical professionals to provide medical treatment or the medical means in order to facilitate the termination of life of [catastrophically] afflicted adults, such as the mortally wounded or terminally ill, who experience severe physical or mental pain and suffering and wish to die with dignity. In such cases, States parties must ensure the existence of robust legal and institutional safeguards to verify that medical professionals are complying with the free, informed, explicit and, unambiguous decision of their patients, with a view to protecting patients from pressure and abuse.[5]

This Draft attaches central importance to personal autonomy for human dignity. Hence, as an expression of this autonomy, the Draft advocates that physicians be allowed to apply euthanasia under certain circumstances. It also makes distinctions among individuals planning to commit suicide, expressing a stronger concern for those who are in vulnerable situations. There is an ambivalence surrounding suicide that reveals the limitations of the view that would connect dignity with autonomy.

The Draft also contains elements belonging to the utilitarian view, which connects dignity with quality of life. In fact, the text refers to the possibility of applying euthanasia in cases of catastrophically afflicted adults, such as the mortally wounded or terminally ill, who experience severe physical or mental pain and suffering. Thus, the Draft is making appraisals of life conditions, explaining that in such cases those individuals should be allowed to "die with dignity". Here what is underlying is the utilitarian logic that considers that under certain circumstances a life that fails to satisfy certain quality criteria is not dignified.

Finally, in the Draft there is also a connection between dignity and the inviolability of human life. Above all, it should be noted that this Draft is a general comment on Article 6, which deals with the right to life. In addition, the text mentions the duty of the States to prevent suicides, which implies a certain respect for the inviolability of life even against the will of the individuals themselves. Moreover, it highlights that individuals considering suicide may be undergoing a crisis that places them in a vulnerable situation, acknowledging the inherent value of life even in such cases. The importance of preventing situations of euthanasia under pressure or abuse also reveals that the question regarding the quality of life and autonomy are restricted by the inviolability of human life.

In this sense, throughout this article I will maintain that, if the debate over euthanasia adopts as a starting point the principle of autonomy as the only element of

---

[5]Human Rights Committee, "General Comment No. 36 on Article 6 of the International Covenant on Civil and Political Rights, on the right to life", Revised draft prepared by the Rapporteur, http://www.ohchr.org/Documents/HRBodies/CCPR/GCArticle6/GCArticle6_EN.pdf (bracketed matter in the original).

dignity, the arguments appear weak and insufficient to correctly place the debate on legal tracks which respond to fundamental questions brought out by biotechnologies applied to the end of life. If our starting point is the principle of autonomy, there are no consistent answers to the demands for justice. Nevertheless, I believe that if a view is adopted to link dignity with quality of life notions, based on a utilitarian criterion, we cannot either offer a coherent and robust answer to the various issues underlying end-of-life decision making. Instead, I believe that starting from the ontological dignity as an individual's intrinsic value, which includes inviolability of life as well as freedom for personal realization, we will be able to make significant distinctions that will allow us to respond to the problems that arise at the end of life, especially when terminally ill.

3 Autonomy and Euthanasia as a Right to Put an End to One's Life

Discussion about the legal admissibility of euthanasia is at present rooted in arguments that seek to legitimate such conduct within the framework of personal autonomy.

According to Diego Gracia, there are three stages in the history of euthanasia: (a) ritualized euthanasia, (b) medicalized euthanasia, and (c) autonomized euthanasia.[6] Unlike former times in which euthanasia was motivated by social, political, medical, and eugenic concerns,[7] today, as Gracia explains it, the question is whether it is ethically possible to give a positive answer to an individual who wishes to die and asks for help in doing so.[8]

On this view, taking one's life is a legitimate part of the exercise of personal autonomy. Therefore, as we have seen in the Draft mentioned in Sect. 2, in general the discussion about euthanasia focuses on persons who are terminally ill or experiencing severe suffering. In this sense, in the following paragraphs, I will study the question of autonomy and euthanasia in individuals who are terminally ill or suffering beyond endurance, making a distinction between conscious and unconscious individuals. The case of unconscious persons introduces serious difficulties for the view in favor of legitimizing euthanasia on the grounds of autonomy, even when there are attempts to construct alternative or forced criteria for autonomy. In Sect. 3.3, I will address what happens when the notion of autonomy is stretched to its ultimate consequences as implying a right to die or legitimacy in the decision to take one's life under any circumstances, and I will try to provide critical answers to these arguments since I

[6]Gracia (1996), 67–91. See also Vivanco Martínez (2014), 44–64.

[7]It is remarkable how, after the systematic elimination of persons through euthanasia in Nazi Germany, even with the collaboration of physicians, the movement for euthanasia soon recovers certain social legitimacy and is expanded, mainly after the 1960s. See Santos (2017), 781–82.

[8]Gracia (1996), 84.

understand that if euthanasia is legalized a person is deprived from an indefeasible good, with serious social consequences.

3.1 Autonomy of Persons in a Conscious and Terminal State or with Unbearable Suffering

Euthanasia challenges the principle of respect for life that considers any conduct oriented to taking the life of another person or assisting them in their suicide to be unjust. The case for euthanasia has been made gradually and progressively, mainly after some very dramatic cases where the end-of-life decisions were at stake due to the expansion of biotechnologies. In other words, rather than invoke the right of any person to take their own life under any circumstances, it is alleged that such a right is a prerogative of persons who are terminally ill or severely suffering at the end of their lives.

The debate over euthanasia arose in cases related to terminally ill persons receiving vital assistance from medical procedures, drugs, or biotechnological support. The decision to remove vital support mechanisms as a consequence of the right of self-determination over one's body, even when there is a risk of death, meant the first step towards the normalization of euthanasia.

For example, Dworkin says that in a society marked by ethical individualism, one master idea is accepted: autonomy. And autonomy implies the right to make personality-defining or life-defining decisions for oneself.[9] He observes that, in the United States, the Supreme Court in *Cruzan v. Director, Missouri Department of Health*[10] has constitutionally accepted that the State has no power to forbid a physician from terminating life support even when death soon and inevitably follows.

As Gorsuch says, those who propose a right to assisted suicide "typically emphasize the dire medical condition of a particular patient, the unpleasantness of the hospital settings, and the compassion of individual physicians".[11] In Sect. 5.2, I will address the problem with attempting to draw a distinction between euthanasia and renunciation of overzealous treatment. This problem was at the onset of the proposals in favor of legalizing euthanasia as an expression of personal autonomy. To anticipate, there is a decisive difference between conduct oriented to causing death, whether by action or omission, and the rejection of disproportionate treatments against the prospects for improvement when death soon and inevitably follows. Here I will present the reasons why I consider that the argument favoring euthanasia for persons who are terminally ill or suffering beyond endurance is unjust.

A first objection to this claimed right to put an end to one's life in cases of terminal illnesses or extremely severe suffering questions where to draw the dividing line. In his debate with Dworkin, Finnis asks about the right to die: "Where is the

---

[9] Solum et al. (1997), 1490.

[10] 497 U.S. 261 (1990).

[11] Gorsuch (2000), 695.

proposition specifying who has the right, to what acts, by which persons? Is it the right of terminally ill patients? (And what is terminal illness?) Or only those who are suffering? (And what sort and degree of suffering?)".[12] Dworkin considers that the line should be drawn so that only those who will die within a period of six months are eligible.[13] But the line is arbitrary, and no one can explain why we allow euthanasia in certain cases and not in others.

Another argument against euthanasia for the terminally ill says that if the law of murder were amended to legalize euthanasia, the ethics of doctors, nurses, and hospital administrators would change very rapidly, mainly because of the law of torts.[14] "Killing with intent becomes a routine management option".[15] Murphy talks about an obligation to kill that seems implicit in the rights language used by euthanasia and assisted suicide activists.[16] He asks what would happen if the drugs did not cause death as expected, and he thinks that there will be an obligation of attending physicians to take steps to ensure that the patient is "thoroughly killed".[17]

Along the same lines, the physician-patient relationship is denaturalized and affected by doubt and distrust, since a sensible patient might be afraid to express all their feelings and fears where this could be perceived as a request to die. Such fear will make a patient lonelier and more isolated, even from their family if their relatives have had an active role in the decisions involving unconscious patients.

Palliative care physicians are one of the specialties that are more deeply affected by the legalization of euthanasia, because they want to accompany patients through all the symptoms and stages of their disease, and euthanasia or assisted suicide betrays that purpose.[18] Even pharmacists are involved in euthanasia, as happened in Belgium, where in November 2005 parliament decriminalized the act of dispensing a lethal prescription.[19]

When we face extreme situations, such as a terminal illness or severe suffering, a powerful argument against euthanasia is that there is an actual risk that the decision may not be authentically autonomous, but rather guided by the pressure of guilt, depression, poor care, or economic worries.[20] These pressures may be explicit, implicit or even imposed by context, since the patient may think that her o his relatives expect her or him to decide on the application of euthanasia himself.[21]

An excessive individualism underlies such arguments justifying euthanasia, which conceive of a patient alone, existentially isolated and detached from their family and social bonds, providing a kind of atmosphere which is consistent with the play of

---

[12]Finnis (1998), 1130.
[13]Solum et al. (1997), 1500.
[14]Finnis (1998), 1133.
[15]Finnis (1998), 1133.
[16]Murphy (2017), 369–70.
[17]Murphy (2017), 372.
[18]Murphy (2017).
[19]Saad (2017), 198–99.
[20]Finnis (1998).
[21]Finnis (1998).

interests alien to the patients themselves, or at least with their invisibilization in the discussion. This in fact damages the dignity of all parties involved and leads to a consequence: the isolation of the patient, who is alone in their autonomy. But it is possible to see other relational options in the subsidiary and joint interaction among the individual, their family, intermediary institutions, and the State.

In sum, the arguments linked to the legalization of euthanasia on grounds of autonomy for persons who are terminally ill or undergoing severe suffering have deficiencies and fail to provide convincing reasons to justify its legalization.

3.2 *Autonomy and Euthanasia of Unconscious or Terminally Ill Persons*

The argument that proposes the legalization of euthanasia based on personal autonomy finds a limitation that is difficult to overcome in connection with cases of unconscious persons. In principle, euthanasia could not be applied to these persons since it would not be the result of an autonomous decision and, in general, there are opinion is uniform in considering that "involuntary" euthanasia is severely unjust and inadmissible. Paradoxically, it was thanks to highly publicized cases of persons in minimally conscious states that stronger pressure was exerted to make progress in legalizing a dignified death, and even euthanasia.

Once again, what is relevant here is the distinction between euthanasia and overzealous treatment, which will be analyzed in Sect. 5. In this section, I will exclusively refer to those arguments contending that it would be legitimate, as an expression of the patient's autonomy, to apply euthanasia even to unconscious persons.

Extolling personal autonomy has resulted in looking for criteria and procedures to anticipate or reconstruct a patient's will so as to determine whether to apply euthanasia. Thus, even in cases of unconscious persons who are terminally ill, it has been proposed to end their lives as a logical consequence deriving from the principle of autonomy.

A first argument to justify euthanasia in unconscious persons consists in resorting to anticipated directives, that is to say, written documents in which the person previously stated the medical decisions that the patient would wish to make in the event they become unconscious at the end of their lives.

The problem with these anticipated directives is that it proves impossible to foresee all the health circumstances and conditions that will surround the decision. In other words, when the time comes to apply such a directive, there may be unforeseen factors that materially change the judgment made in advance.

A second way to justify euthanasia in unconscious persons as an expression of autonomy consists in trying to reconstruct the patient's will (*substituted judgement*), or in the surrogate's constructing a preferential criterion (*constructive preference*), taking into account both the substitution as well as the best interest criteria,[22] or in the surrogate's giving testimony about the actual will of the patient.

Theoretically speaking, decisions may be made on behalf of an unconscious or incompetent patient by a physician[23] or a surrogate, generally someone appointed by the patient himself or by a family member, based on an order of preference that may be established by law or otherwise.[24] Others suggest a decision jointly made by the physician and the patient's family members.[25]

This proposal of euthanasia by decision of a surrogate has received sharp criticism. Among the negative remarks, it has been argued that testimony as to the patient's will may be based on a comment either casually or thoughtlessly made. The will may have been changeable, or may have been expressed in an emotional setting conditioning the patient's judgement, or may have been made without the information required for adequate discernment and consent. Cantor highlights that the courts in some states like Missouri and New York have ruled that in order for the surrogate's decision to be admitted, "clear and convincing" evidence should be left by the patient to demonstrate that the patient would have wanted such an action under the given circumstances.[26]

From the physician-patient relationship perspective, testimony as to a person's will does not constitute informed consent properly speaking, since giving information becomes irrelevant because the surrogate's role limits to give testimony.

A fundamental problem with the participation of relatives in a decision on euthanasia is the presence of potential financial incentives, differing religious or moral beliefs, or family conflicts.[27] It is interesting to note that although Article 12 of the UN Convention on the Rights of Persons with Disabilities refers to the wishes and preferences of the person in question, it also introduces the "conflict of interests" and "undue influence" criteria as restrictions on action by persons who help express the will of a person with disabilities.

From the logic of autonomous will, some authors wonder whether the order of priority fixed by law is the one that the incapacitated individual would have chosen.[28] In addition, there might be a conflict between the cultural perspectives of the patient and the surrogate. Similarly, the surrogate may simply be wrong as regards the patient's wishes, or project her own's preferences onto the patient.

All in all, it becomes untenable to maintain that in such cases the decisions made regarding terminal illnesses may be considered to be autonomous. This autonomy is a reconstructed or a fictitious autonomy.

---

[22]Cantor (2001), 193.

[23]See Krupp (1998), 99–128 (demonstrating the ethical problems inherent in decisionmaking by surrogates or doctors, pointing to economic incentives and paternalism as potential issues).

[24]In *In re Quinlan*, 355 A.2d 647 (NJ 1976), the Supreme Court of New Jersey held that if Karen Ann Quinlan had been in a conscious state, she would have had the right to resist vital life support measures and that, given her incapacity, her right had to be exercised by a "guardian" or surrogate like her father. See Cantor (2001).

[25]Cai et al. (2015), 131–41.

[26]Cantor (2001), 190.

[27]Krupp (1998).

[28]Kohn and Blumenthal (2008), 979–1018.

3.3 *Is There a Right to Die?*

The autonomy criterion is only consistent if we accept that a right to die may be advanced by any person at any time. But can that be justified?

When ending his debate with Finnis, Dworkin acknowledges: "it all comes down to this question of individual freedom… there must also be a respect for the dignity of having control over your own life".[29] To Harris, preventing a person from making by themselves one of the most important decisions in their lives—as euthanasia undoubtedly is—is a form of tyranny.[30] Dworkin emphasizes how important it is for individuals to be able to control the timing and the manner in which they die.[31]

Several authors have responded very properly to this argument of making autonomous will so absolute a notion as to legitimize an act causing one's own death, either on one's own or with the assistance of someone else.

Arguing that there is a right to die puts at stake the view of life as a basic human good, which will be discussed in depth in Sect. 5. In any case, I may say now that I understand it to be an indefeasible good and that, as explained by Massini Correas, the expression 'right to die' or 'right to death' "is self-contradictory, since one cannot have the right to the frustration of a human good, and especially for the perpetration of a human evil par excellence: the annihilation of life".[32]

Some others justify this right alleging that suicide is not a crime. Andorno reasons that "it is true that, generally, if someone wishes to commit suicide, they can do it. But it does not follow that there is a 'right' to die, that is to say, a right that may require of the State a support for such desire, let alone demanding other persons to take their lives. Death does not constitute a 'good that is owed' in terms of justice".[33] In addition, the State is not unconcerned about suicide, but it opts not to punish the perpetrator of suicide or attempted suicide since society believes that this act is generally carried out in circumstances that vitiate free will and, besides, a completed suicide is not amenable to typical punishments.[34] As regards the purported right to die, there is no foundation for such a right, that is to say, the objective human good rationally justifying the existence of such a right; and, more importantly, it threatens a basic human good—a person's life.[35]

Allegedly, the autonomy to take one's own life would be the realization of the principle that requires informed consent for any action affecting an individual's physical integrity. Keown refutes this argument, explaining that "the legal requirement of consent to medical treatment provides a shield against unwanted touching, not a sword to demand interventions. It does not follow from the fact that physicians may not treat patients without their consent that they can terminate them with their

[29] Solum et al. (1997), 1505.

[30] Harris (2004), 47.

[31] Dworkin (1994), 273.

[32] Massini Correas (2003), 404.

[33] Andorno (2012), 166.

[34] Serrano (2006), 237.

[35] Massini Correas (2003), 404–5.

consent. Moreover, the killing of patients has never been regarded by the law as a medical treatment but as a serious crime (and by the medical profession as a whole as inconsistent with the physician's role as healer)".[36]

There are several rules "restricting" the autonomous will that are consistent with safeguarding life as a fundamental legal good. Let us just think about the rider's obligation to wear a helmet or the duty to fasten a seatbelt when driving an automobile. More important is the abolition of slavery, a practice which implies a radical form of disposing of your own life.[37] Nor is a person allowed to dispose of their organs when it amounts to committing suicide, and this does not constitute a violation of their autonomy.

The autonomy principle is insufficient grounds by itself to justify euthanasia because "it does not provide any reason to act; no one just acts to realize their autonomy, but to perform valuable conducts with freedom".[38] Although Mill is usually quoted as providing grounds for the legalization of euthanasia, one must recall that to Mill there is no freedom not to be free, and allowing individuals to alienate their autonomous will betrays their own autonomy.[39]

Gorsuch says that "there are autonomy interests on both sides of the assisted suicide issue: the interest of those persons who wish to control the timing of their deaths and the interest of those vulnerable individuals whose lives may be taken without their consent due to acts of mistake or abuse".[40] As the slippery slope argument demonstrates, if only those that have an "autonomous will" are granted legal protection, the most vulnerable are neglected.[41]

In sum, autonomy fails to justify euthanasia. Certainly, such explanations also require answers to the arguments about the quality of life of terminally ill patients, presenting a substantive development concerning the inviolability of human life.

4 The Utilitarian Perspective in the End-of-Life Issues

4.1 *Euthanasia and Dignity as Quality of Life*

Along with the argument of autonomous will, another school of thought seeks to justify euthanasia from a utilitarian perspective. According to this view, dignity would require that a person be allowed to take their life because the life they lead

[36] Keown (2014), 1–41.

[37] Ollero wisely addresses this argument surrounding euthanasia and the unrenounceable nature of freedom as well as the right to life. Ollero Tassara (2006), 205.

[38] Quintana (2011), 637.

[39] Faulconer (2016), 322. Quotation of the passage from the book by Mill *On Liberty*: "The principle of freedom cannot require that he should be free not to be free. It is not freedom, to be allowed to alienate his freedom".

[40] Gorsuch (2000), 660.

[41] Masferrer (2016), 251.

while terminally ill or with severe suffering is no longer compatible with dignity and indeed amounts to an undignified condition.

One of the problems surrounding the application of the utilitarian logic at the end of life is how to calculate quality of life or determine what constitutes an undignified living condition. In reality, it is very difficult to weigh the state of being alive, against pain, economic problems, or other circumstances. Human life could never be weighed in the same way as other goods or ills.[42] "Weighing the liberty interest of the person seeking death against the right of persons to avoid being killed as a result of abuse or mistake is literally impossible due to the incommensurability of the goods being weighed".[43]

Within this utilitarian calculus, a widespread idea of "quality of life" is involved that ends up considering any illness or suffering condition to be "undignified". Zambrano emphasizes that "physical and emotional suffering does not only deprive life of any sense, but many times it is transformed in order to serve your fellows more intensively, and, above all, that your fellow finds in the suffering life a reason to live".[44] Quintana adds that the concept of "quality of life" associated with euthanasia has discriminatory implications.[45] Along the same lines, Gormally explains that asserting that a patient lacks a life worthy of being lived is a justification incompatible with the acknowledgment of the patient's inalienable dignity and value.[46]

Pilar Zambrano gives a good explanation for the anthropological background underlying this issue: "If what is valued by Law is not human life in itself, but life as desired and wished by its own holder, the conclusion is evident: once the capability of valuing and loving yourself is lost, what is also lost is one's own condition to be valuable and desirable or susceptible to be beloved".[47]

The utilitarian criterion, in connection with dignity, entails classifying lives as worthy or unworthy of being lived. Unless doctors are permitted to kill anyone and everyone who makes a 'stable and competent' request for death, they are going to have to proceed on a classification of lives as 'worth living' or 'not worth living'.[48] "Legalization would require society's active participation in making comparative moral judgements about the value of different kinds of human lives. Unless we adopt the neutralist's position that assisted suicide should be open to all rational adults, an individual's request to die would not be honored without social ratification. Society would have to regulate which lives are worth living and which ones are not".[49]

In a study on factors of influence at the time of death in relation to the perception of dignity, Chochinov and his team confirmed that the most mentioned items regarding the potential loss of dignity were "not being supported by the community," "feeling

---

42 Andorno (1997), 973–79.
43 Gorsuch (2000), 679.
44 Zambrano (2005a).
45 Quintana (2011), 638.
46 Gormally (2004), 171.
47 Zambrano (2005b), 265.
48 Finnis (1998), 1144.
49 Gorsuch (2000), 690.

unworthy or useless," "incapable of managing vital body functions", "not feeling that a long-lasting or significant contribution was made," "not having control over one's life," "feeling like a burden to others," and "not being treated with respect and understanding".[50] These findings cast a different light on the idea that any terminal situation implies an undignified condition, and they serve to draw attention to the significance of the relational dimension of a person, assistance to the patient and, above all, palliative care, which help overcome pain in almost every case, being an ethically acceptable alternative in view of the demands for legalizing euthanasia.

Finally, although it is impossible to develop this topic thoroughly in this Article, we should consider the underlying issue when the utilitarian calculation is further applied to other goods at stake, such as public health or hospital expenditure. These factors are never explicitly included in the debate, but they undoubtedly influence, and greatly, the issues surrounding end-of-life decisions. Finnis considers that the healthcare financial interests could push for the legalization of euthanasia, and those interests could influence physician's decisions at the bedside.[51] Gorsuch says that "given the laws of economics, the increasing availability of assisted suicide (a cheaper solution) might serve as a deterrent to the development and dissemination of (more expensive) palliative and hospice options".[52]

Another complex problem that implies a conflict of interest is the connection between euthanasia and organ procurement. The need to have more organs available could lead to loosening the relevant controls and facilitating the application of euthanasia if the patient was an organ donor. In Belgium, organ donation after euthanasia is permissible under the law and there is an ongoing debate as to whether this situation might create situations of exploitation and coercion.[53]

4.2 *The Slippery Slope Argument*

In general, legalization of euthanasia is initially introduced in exceptional cases, linked to patients facing imminent death. Nevertheless, experience has shown that then the dividing line drawn (for example, severely and terminally ill patients with a six-month life expectancy) becomes blurred and euthanasia is applied to other cases involving less terminally ill and less severe patients. This criticism of the legalization of euthanasia is known as the slippery slope argument,[54] and there are four significant bases of the argument. First, from the most severe and dramatic cases of terminally ill persons, euthanasia started to be applied to other persons with curable illnesses or undergoing merely temporary situations. Second, and relatedly, the number of euthanasia cases has increased. Third, euthanasia is applied not only to conscious

[50]Chochinov et al. (2006), 666–72.

[51]Finnis (1998), 1139.

[52]Gorsuch (2007), 332.

[53]Saad (2017), 201–3.

[54]Schauer (1985), 363 argues that it was Kamisar (1958). See also Kamisar (1991).

persons, but also to persons who are unconscious or incapable of giving their consent, such as children. Fourth, controls over the application of euthanasia are problematic due to the ambiguity inherent in diagnosis and the clinical situations involved.

The slippery slope argument is linked to the practical experience of the countries that have legalized euthanasia. In the Netherlands, the legalization of euthanasia began with a series of court cases in 1973. In 1984 there was a significant milestone with a Supreme Court ruling in the *Alkmaar case*, in which a physician was prosecuted for giving a fatal dose of curare to a 95-year-old woman who had begged to die. The doctor was acquitted and that year the Royal Dutch Medical Association issued an influential statement on euthanasia. From that moment, euthanasia has been practiced legally in the Netherlands. In 1994, in the *Chabot case*, the Supreme Court ruled in favor of the assisted suicide of a mental patient.[55] In 2002, the Termination of Life on Request and Assisted Suicide (Review Procedures) Act was passed and euthanasia was legalized in those cases where the physician fulfils the due care criteria set out in Article 2 of the Act. To act with due care the physician must: be satisfied that the patient's request is voluntary and well-considered; be satisfied that the patient's suffering is unbearable, with no prospect for improvement; have informed the patient about their situation and prognosis; have come to the conclusion, together with the patient, that there is no reasonable alternative in the patient's situation; have consulted at least one other independent physician, who must see the patient and give a written opinion on whether the due care criteria set out above have been fulfilled; have exercised due medical care and attention in terminating the patient's life or assisting in the patient's suicide.[56]

Under this Act, in 2016 there were 5856 cases of euthanasia (96.14%), 216 of assisted suicide (3.54%), and 19 of a combination of the two (0.31%). Among the disorders invoked to apply the Act in those 6091 cases were: cancer (4137), neurological disorders (411), cardiovascular disease (315), pulmonary disorders (214), multiple geriatric syndromes (244), dementia (141), psychiatric disorders (60), combination of disorders (465), and other conditions (104).[57]

The list shows that euthanasia has not been confined merely to terminally ill patients. Applying euthanasia and assisted suicide (EAS) to psychiatric disorders has proven troublesome. In a study published in 2016 on these patients in the Netherlands, the conclusion was that "persons receiving EAS for psychiatric disorders in the Netherlands are mostly women and of diverse ages, with complex and chronic psychiatric, medical, and psychosocial histories. The granting of their EAS requests appears to involve considerable physician judgment, usually involving multiple physicians who do not always agree (sometimes without independent psychiatric input), but

[55] Gevers (1996), 326–33.

[56] Regional Euthanasia Review Committees (2017).

[57] Regional Euthanasia Review Committees (2017).

the euthanasia review committees generally defer to the judgments of the physicians performing the EAS".[58]

The increase in the number of euthanasia cases is significant in the Netherlands. In 2002 there were 1882 cases; in 2007, 2120; in 2012, 4188; and in 2016, 6091, accounting for the 4% of the total number of deaths (148,973).[59]

Another situation that demonstrates the slippery slope is the application of euthanasia to children and unconscious people, which I have already analyzed in part in the previous paragraphs. In the Netherlands, under the Termination of Life on Request and Assisted Suicide (Review Procedures) Act it was illegal to apply euthanasia to children under the age of 12, but a Protocol was created at the University Medical Center Groningen, in consultation with the Groningen district attorney in September 2004 giving guidelines for applying euthanasia to severely ill newborns. The Groningen Protocol has been ratified by the Dutch National Association of Pediatricians and those physicians acting under this Protocol will not be prosecuted.[60]

Applying euthanasia to children and unconscious people is a consequence of a utilitarian calculation,[61] and euthanasia would be justified if pain exceeds pleasure. Keown explains that

> once the principle of the inviolability of life is abandoned by endorsing voluntary euthanasia in some circumstances, the bright line grounded in the intrinsic and ineliminable dignity of each patient is usurped by an arbitrary line dependent on subjective judgments about which patients would be 'better off dead' and that, in particular, the endorsement of voluntary euthanasia logically entails the endorsement of non-voluntary euthanasia, that is, the killing of incompetent patients.[62]

Another aspect of the slippery slope argument is whether the State can effectively control the practice of euthanasia once it has been legalized. Nancy Cruzan, Terri Schiavo, Eluana Englaro, Vincent Lambert, and others were the subjects of very disputed end-of-life cases in which it was hard to make a "best" decision. Those cases attracted great public attention and gave rise to large debates in the public sphere. The circumstances of their illnesses and their situations were highly scrutinized, and every single aspect of the decisions was thoroughly analyzed. Those difficult and unique cases also generated proposals to change the regulatory framework in various states and countries so as to legalize euthanasia. But those were extraordinary cases, while the laws that decriminalize euthanasia apply to everyday situations in medical facilities where there are different scenarios and no such in-depth analysis would be done.

The problem of controlling euthanasia is inherent in the ambiguity of the underlying diagnosis that must be made. The "Annual Report 2016" of the Regional

[58] Kim et al. (2016), 362–68. See also George (2007), 1–33 (presenting evidence of a risk that the decisions of some women for assisted death are rooted in oppressive influences inimical to genuine autonomy).

[59] Ferrer (2017).

[60] Vivanco Martínez (2014), 74–75.

[61] Farrell (1985), 118.

[62] Keown (2014), 22.

Euthanasia Review Committees (RTE) in the Netherlands acknowledges this ambiguity when it asks: "When is euthanasia an option for people with a psychiatric disorder or people with (advanced) dementia? When can it be said that a person regards their life as completed? And when does the suffering of a patient with multiple geriatric syndromes have a medical dimension?"[63]

In 1958, Kamisar warned that legalizing euthanasia carried too great a risk of abuse and mistake to warrant a change in the existing law, remarking that "under any euthanasia program the consequences of mistake, of course, are always fatal".[64] For instance, since 1990 in the Netherlands there has been a continual controversy over the application of euthanasia to persons who do not meet the law's requirements. The "Annual Report 2016" found that in ten cases the due care criteria set out in the Act had not been complied with (0.16% of the total number of notifications).[65] In 2018 criminal investigations have been launched into four cases of euthanasia in the Netherlands.[66] Although these cases represent a low proportion of the total number of euthanasia decisions, they indicate a problem that has not been completely resolved. As Gorsuch says,

> The alternative to an absolute rule against private intentional killing, moreover, is troubling territory. Once some intentional killings become acceptable, society becomes enmeshed in making moral decisions about which ones are deemed permissible. In the assisted suicide and euthanasia context, unless we unleash the full-throttle neutralist and harm principle right open to all adults, society is forced into a debate over the relative value of different kinds of human life. Judging whose lives may and may not be taken in turn depends upon assessments of quality of life—whether one is young and fit or old and sick. Different human lives are thus left with different moral and legal statuses based on their perceived 'quality of life'.[67]

5 The Right to Life and Justice at the End-of-Life

5.1 Euthanasia and the Inviolability of Life

In the two previous sections, I analyzed the arguments proposing the legalization of euthanasia on the grounds of autonomous will and of utilitarian considerations of quality of life. In this section, my aim is to analyze dignity as a value, inherent in the person, that implies the respect for the inviolability of human life. This conception will allow us to analyze the demand for justice in end-of-life decisions.

Any human being, by virtue of his or her humanity alone and irrespective of acknowledgement by the positive legal system, has the fundamental right to life (Article 3, Universal Declaration of Human Rights). The right to life is a pre-requisite for other rights and assumes respect for the inviolability of the physical integrity of

---

63Regional Euthanasia Review Committees (2017).

64Kamisar (1958), 73.

65Regional Euthanasia Review Committees (2017).

66Boffey (2018).

67Gorsuch (2000), 701–2.

each human being. As John Finnis says, life is one of the "basic goods" which make up the fundamental human rights.[68]

The right to life has a double expression: it has a positive sense, which translates into promoting human life; and a negative sense, whose mandate is reflected in the prohibition on killing. In both cases, the underlying principle is the respect for the physical life of every human being. As Gorsuch says, "the intentional taking of human life by private persons is always wrong".[69]

Shepherd considers that there is a default position in favor of continued life in the structure of the law concerning end-of-life decisions.[70] I think that this default position expresses the basic principle of medical care: the protection of life.[71]

The inherent dignity of every human being cannot be conditioned on whether one has autonomous will or not or whether one's life satisfies certain criteria of quality. In fact, in complex end-of-life challenges, instead of letting the individual decide alone we are called to confirm bonds and solidarity, taking charge of the other's needs and accompanying them even through the most painful and difficult moments. As Finnis says, "a just society cannot be maintained, and people cannot be treated with the equal concern and respect to which they are all entitled, unless we hold fast to the truth… that none of us is entitled to act on the opinion that the life of another is not worth living".[72]

If dignity is inherent in personhood and is an intrinsic attribute of any human being, then we may strongly argue that it cannot be subject to the swings of autonomous will; euthanasia, therefore, is rendered inadmissible.[73]

5.2 *The Distinction Between Euthanasia and Refusal of Overzealous Treatment*

The connection between dignity and the inviolability of life does not mean that appropriate distinctions need not be made in order to avoid situations where new medical or biotechnological procedures may lead to protracted agony without genuine improvement. This issue is known as overzealous treatment. Logically, such a refusal or withdrawal or treatment raises questions of coherence in light of the principle of respect for inviolability of human life. In these cases, I maintain that it is legitimate to renounce such treatments.

The conditions[74] for such a renunciation to be legitimate are as follows:

---

[68]Finnis (2000), 117–21.

[69]Gorsuch (2000), 606.

[70]Shepherd (2014), 1693–1748.

[71]Padrón (2015), 173.

[72]Finnis (1998), 1145.

[73]As regards the debate on dignity and the person, see Herrera (2012); Hoyos Castañeda (2005).

[74]Basso (1993), 444.

(a) disproportionate medical treatment or intervention, in relation to the prospects for improvement, assessed on a case by case basis, according to the prevailing circumstances of time and place, and also considering the individuals involved;[75]
(b) imminent and unavoidable death;
(c) maintenance of habitual treatment necessary for the patient in these kind of cases, including—in principle—food and hydration.

In this case, the right to life is not affected by permitting the subject's death, since what occurs is simply the acceptance of death, which is an unavoidable aspect of human life. These distinctions are important as far as principles are concerned, although it is clear that their actual application is linked to prudence in any specific case.

A complex aspect in this matter has been the relationship between refusal of overzealous treatment and euthanasia by omission. Some authors contend that euthanasia can only be committed through actions, while any renunciation of a medical treatment is uniformly acceptable. This logic fails to address euthanasia by omission, which is a form of causing death as a consequence of not providing the required treatment. My opinion is that euthanasia may be committed by action or by omission, and, in turn, both cases should be distinguished from renunciation of overzealous treatment. The debate has been mainly focused on the problem surrounding the withdrawal of food and water.[76]

The object of the action and the pursued purpose need to be taken into account for a fair consideration of conduct. What is at stake is a person's life. Similarly, the subtleness of intent should be considered, which enables drawing a distinction between a patient who orders their death to be inflicted and the one who only renounces treatments which prove out of proportion to the prospects for improvement in the face of unavoidable and imminent death As explained by Finnis, there is a difference between refraining from choosing to harm a fundamental human good, and accepting damage to human goods as undesired secondary effects.[77]

In sum, it is important to emphasize once again that euthanasia always consists in causing death, and such causation may be realized by action or by omission. By contrast, in refusing disproportionate procedures there is an essential difference which lies in the absence of causing death. Euthanasia "by omission" should not be confused with the refusal of disproportionate or extraordinary measures in those cases where death is soon to occur and there are no prospects for improvement.[78]

[75] Sambrizzi (2005), 208.

[76] McGee (2005), 357–85; Keown (2005), 393–402.

[77] Finnis (2004), 57.

[78] Basso (1993), 462.

6 Conclusion

Throughout this article, I have sought to analyze the views proposing the decriminalization or legalization of euthanasia, mainly based on the different views on human dignity at the end of life. I took as a starting point the assertion that taking a human person's life is an unjust act.

Firstly, regarding the view proposing that autonomy is the core element of human dignity and that this entails the need to decriminalize euthanasia and assisted suicide, I highlighted the inconsistency in affirming that certain persons with terminal illnesses or severe suffering are authorized to decide to put an end to their own life, apart from the ambiguity present in the dividing lines that are proposed. Moreover, those patients, may suffer different pressures that condition their freedom. On the other hand, euthanasia by request profoundly alters the physician-patient relationship in including the possibility of killing as another available option. Regarding the right to death, it entails the frustration of a basic human good, which is human life. And, as Finnis has remarked, the ultimate horizon is the common welfare conducive to the flourishing of all the members of a community.[79]

Regarding the theories proposing the legalization of euthanasia on the grounds of a utilitarian vision of quality of life, I have noted that this view leads to a distinction between lives that are worth living and lives that are not worth living. Such a distinction will necessarily be made by physicians and by society, which can only lead to new forms of oppression of an individual's dignity. The slippery slope argument reinforces this conclusion, since in those jurisdictions that legalized euthanasia for very exceptional and terminal cases, there has been an increase in the frequency with which euthanasia is carried out and the practice has increasingly been extended to situations that are becoming less final and severe.

Finally, I maintain that depriving a person of human life should be legally blameworthy at all times, even in those cases which have been identified as euthanasia. In this sense, I have demonstrated that the connection between dignity and inviolability of life offers a safe criterion for weighing euthanasia, while allowing us to make appropriate and fair distinctions between euthanasia and the rejection of overzealous treatment. What is involved is a certain proportionality between therapeutic measures and the patient's health.[80] In this sense, those who practice medicine must be stronger in demanding endorsement of the principle of inviolability of life.[81]

Ultimately, what is at stake is the question of admissibility of conduct that deprives certain persons of life as a basic good in certain circumstances. In an age in which the biotechnological applications tend to consider that life is a mere biological material available, it is imperative to affirm the demands for justice deriving from the dignity of the human person, especially when the most vulnerable individuals are involved. While it is legitimate to reject biotechnologies in situations of overzealous treatment,

---

[79] Finnis (1987), 456.

[80] Arias de Ronchietto (1996), 15–48.

[81] Gómez Lobo (2008), 780.

it is unjust to put an end to human life deliberately, either by action or omission, using the excuse of a claimed autonomy or a lack of quality of life.

Legalizing euthanasia betrays the meaning of dignity. Instead of expressing the high value of human life, to die with dignity is understood as getting rid of your life because of its low value.[82] As Finnis says, "persons keep their radical dignity until death",[83] and it is our duty to accompany them until the end of their life, recognizing their inherent dignity with solidarity and compassion.

References

Andorno R (2012) Bioética y dignidad de la persona, 2nd edn. Tecnos, Madrid

Andorno R (1997) El debate ético-jurídico en torno al ensañamiento terapéutico y la eutanasia. El Derecho 171:973–979

Arias de Ronchietto CE (1996) Consideración bioético-jurídica actual sobre el morir humano. Morir ¿Un derecho? Rev la Univ Mendoza 15:15–48

Basso D (1993) Nacer y morir con dignidad, 3rd edn. Depalma, Buenos Aires

Boffey D (2018) Dutch prosecutors to investigate euthanasia cases after sharp rise. Guard

Cai X, Robinson J, Muehlschlegel S, White DB, Holloway RG, Sheth KN, Fraenkel L, Hwang DY (2015) Patient preferences and surrogate decision making in neuroscience intensive care units. Neurocrit Care 23:131–141. https://doi.org/10.1007/s12028-015-0149-2

Cantor NL (2001) Twenty-five years after Quinlan: a review of the jurisprudence of death and dying. J Law Med Ethics 29:182–194

Chochinov HM, Krisjanson LJ, Hack TF, Hassard T, McClement S, Harlos M (2006) Dignity in the terminally ill: revisited. J Palliat Med 9:666–672. https://doi.org/10.1089/jpm.2006.9.666

Dworkin R (1994) El dominio de la vida. Una discusión acerca del aborto, la eutanasia y la libertad individual. Editorial Ariel, Barcelona

Farrell MD (1985) La ética del aborto y la eutanasia. Abeledo-Perrot, Buenos Aires

Faulconer AW (2016) Rebranding death. BYU J Public Law 31:313–332

Ferrer I (2017) Holanda, donde bien morir es cotidiano. El País

Finnis J (1998) Euthanasia, morality, and law. Loyola Los Angel Law Rev 31:1123–1145

Finnis J (1987) Legal enforcement of "duties to oneself": Kant v. Neo-Kantians. Columbia Law Rev 87:433–456. https://doi.org/10.2307/1122666

Finnis J (2000) Ley natural y derechos naturales. Abeledo-Perrot, Buenos Aires

Finnis J (2004) Un argumento filosófico contra la eutanasia. In: Keown J (ed) La eutanasia examinada. Perspectivas éticas, clínicas y legales. Fondo de Cultura Económica, México, pp 49–63

George K (2007) A woman's choice? The gendered risks of voluntary euthanasia and physician-assisted suicide. Med Law Rev 15:1–33. https://doi.org/10.1093/medlaw/fwl017

Gevers S (1996) Euthanasia: law and practice in The Netherlands. Br Med Bull 52:326–333. https://doi.org/10.1093/oxfordjournals.bmb.a011547

Global Health Observatory (2016) Life expectancy. In: World heal. Organ. http://www.who.int/gho/mortality_burden_disease/life_tables/situation_trends_text/en/. Accessed 2 Apr 2018

Gómez Lobo A (2008) Bienes humanos y eutanasia, frente a frente. Humanitas (Monterey N L) 13:772–789

[82]Hartling (2006), 189–99.

[83]Finnis (1998), 1143.

Gormally L (2004) Walton, Davies, Boyd y la legalización de la eutanasia. In: Keown J (ed) La eutanasia examinada. Perspectivas éticas, clínicas y legales. Fondo de Cultura Económica, México, pp 169–200
Gorsuch NM (2000) The right to assisted suicide and euthanasia. Harv J Law Public Policy 23:599–710
Gorsuch NM (2007) A reply to Raymond Tallis on the legalization of assisted suicide and euthanasia. J Leg Med 28:327–332
Gracia D (1996) Historia de la eutanasia. In: Urraca S (ed) Eutanasia hoy. Un debate abierto. Editorial Noesis, Madrid, pp 67–91
Harris J (2004) La eutanasia y el valor de la vida. In: Keown J (ed) La eutanasia examinada. Perspectivas éticas, clínicas y legales. Fondo de Cultura Económica, México, pp 29–47
Hartling OJ (2006) Euthanasia—the illusion of autonomy. Med Law 25:189–199. https://doi.org/10.1177/0952695114551655
Herrera DA (2012) La persona y el fundamento de los derechos humanos. EDUCA, Buenos Aires
Hoyos Castañeda IM (2005) De la dignidad y de los derechos humanos, 1st edn. Universidad de la Sabana, Bogotá
Kamisar Y (1958) Some non-religious views against proposed mercy-killing legislation. Minn Law Rev 42:969–1042
Kamisar Y (1991) When is there a constitutional "right to die"? When is there no constitutional "right to live". Georg Law Rev 25:1203–1242. https://doi.org/10.1525/sp.2007.54.1.23
Keown J (2005) A futile defence of bland: a reply to Andrew McGee. Med Law Rev 13:393–402. https://doi.org/10.1093/medlaw/fwi032
Keown J (2014) A right to voluntary euthanasia? Confusion in Canada in Carter. Notre Dame J Law Ethics Public Policy 28:1–41
Kim SYH, De Vries RG, Peteet JR (2016) Euthanasia and assisted suicide of patients with psychiatric disorders in the Netherlands 2011 to 2014. JAMA Psychiatry 73:362–368. https://doi.org/10.1001/jamapsychiatry.2015.2887
Kohn NA, Blumenthal JA (2008) Designating health care decisionmakers for patients without advance directives: a psychological critique. Georg Law Rev 42:979–1018
Krupp AN (1998) Health care surrogate statutes: ethics pitfalls threaten the interests of incompetent patients. West VA Law Rev 101:99–128
Masferrer A (2016) Taking human dignity more humanely. a historical contribution to the ethical foundations of constitutional democracy. In: Masferrer A, García-Sánchez E (eds) Human dignity of the vulnerable in the age of rights. Springer International Publishing, Cham, pp 221–256
Massini Correas CI (2003) La eutanasia activa voluntaria: ¿existe un derecho a morir? Riv Internazionale di Filos del Dirit 80:3790410
McGee A (2005) Finding a way through the ethical and legal maze: withdrawal of medical treatment and euthanasia. Med Law Rev 13:357–385. https://doi.org/10.1093/medlaw/fwi023
Murphy S (2017) Legalization of assisted suicide and euthanasia: foundational issues and implications. BYU J Public Law 31:333–394
Ollero Tassara A (2006) Bioderecho. Entre la vida y la muerte, Eitorial Aranzadi, Navarra
Padrón HJ (2015) ¿Por qué sostener una vida digna hasta morir? In: Andruet AS (ed) Directivas anticipadas en Argentina (Muerte digna). Derecho, bioética y ética. Advocatus, Córdoba, pp 155–173
Quintana EM (2011) El fin de la vida humana y sus prolegómenos: consideraciones ética-jurídicas. In: Conte-Grand J (ed) Estudios de Derecho Civil con motivo del Bicentenario. EDUCA, Buenos Aires, pp 615–641
Regional Euthanasia Review Committees (2017) Annual report 2016. The Hague
Regional Euthanasia Review Committees Due care criteria. https://english.euthanasiecommissie.nl/due-care-criteria. Accessed 2 Apr 2018
Saad TC (2017) Euthanasia in Belgium: Legal, historical and political review. Issues Law Med 32:183–204
Sambrizzi EA (2005) Derecho y Eutanasia. La Ley, Buenos Aires

Santos JA (2017) Eutanasia y suicidio asistido en el debate contemporáneo: selección y análisis. Anu Derecho Eclesiástico del Estado XXXIII:779–804
Schauer F (1985) Slippery slopes. Harvard Law Rew 99:361–383. https://doi.org/10.2307/1341127
Serrano JM (2006) Sentencias constitucionales sobre la muerte digna. Pers Derecho 229–256
Shepherd L (2014) The end of end-of-life law. North Carol Law Rev 92:1693–1748
Solum L, Dworkin R, Finnis J (1997) The fifth annual fritz B. burns lecture: euthanasia, morality, and the law. Loyola Los Angel Law Rev 30:1455–1505
Vivanco Martínez A (2014) Disposición sobre la vida humana y principios constitucionales: análisis del caso chileno. Ediciones Universidad Santo Tomás, Santiago
Zambrano P (2005a) Elementos para un debate racional en torno a la legalización de la eutanasia. La Ley
Zambrano P (2005b) Sobre la moralidad y la juridicidad de la suspensión de tratamientos médicos vitales. La Ley B:265

GPSR Compliance
The European Union's (EU) General Product Safety Regulation (GPSR) is a set of rules that requires consumer products to be safe and our obligations to ensure this.

If you have any concerns about our products, you can contact us on

ProductSafety@springernature.com

In case Publisher is established outside the EU, the EU authorized representative is:

Springer Nature Customer Service Center GmbH
Europaplatz 3
69115 Heidelberg, Germany

www.ingramcontent.com/pod-product-compliance
Ingram Content Group UK Ltd.
Pitfield, Milton Keynes, MK11 3LW, UK
UKHW020234290926
15470UKWH00002B/527
9783030641627